❧ Mary Queen of Scots

She had everything—dazzling beauty, brilliant wit, captivating charm, unflinching courage. Born to reign, she was every inch a queen as she made her imperious moves on the chessboard of power. But she could not rule her own impulsive heart, and she scandalized her people with her passions, was betrayed by the brutal and powerful man she loved, and was lured into the deadly spider's web woven by her envious and unforgiving cousin, Elizabeth of England. Here is the unforgettable story of Mary Queen of Scots, who lost a throne for love, and gained immortal triumph in her ultimate hour of tragedy.

"Compassionate, illuminating, rich in human interest!"
—*The New York Times*

(Please turn page)

**"A BEAUTIFUL QUEEN IN A VIO-
LENT AND TREACHEROUS AGE . . .
A COLORFUL, GLITTERING, ENJOY-
ABLE, VERY RARE BIOGRAPHY!"**
—Houston Post

"Lady Antonia Fraser, one of Scotland's
most talented aristocrats, has obviously
steeped herself in her subject. Here is a
book notable for the high level of its prose
and a narrative quality that will leave few
readers unmoved."
—San Francisco Chronicle

"A glamorous figure . . . intrigues, plots and
conspiracies . . . murder, rape, romance and
terror. . . . The author has done a splendid
job!" *—Bridgeport Post*

"A first-rate job . . . beautifully written."
—New York Review of Books

MARY QUEEN of SCOTS

by ANTONIA FRASER

A DELL BOOK

Published by
DELL PUBLISHING CO., INC.
750 Third Avenue
New York, New York 10017

Dell ® TM 681510, Dell Publishing Co., Inc.
Reprinted by arrangement with
Delacorte Press
New York, New York
Printed in the U.S.A.
First Dell printing—March 1971
Second Dell printing—April 1971
Third Dell printing—April 1971
Fourth Dell printing—May 1971
Fifth Dell printing—May 1971
Sixth Dell printing—May 1971

To Hugh, with Love and Thanks

Contents

'*A King is history's slave.*
History, that is the unconscious general swarm-life
of mankind, uses every moment of the life of kings,
as a tool for its own purposes.'

TOLSTOY

The English

showing the position of Mary Queen of Scots and

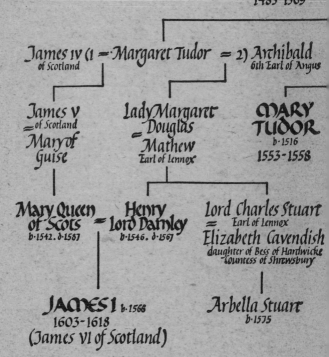

HENRY VII
1485-1509

James IV (1 = Margaret Tudor = 2) Archibald
of Scotland   6th Earl of Angus

James V
= of Scotland
Mary of
Guise

Lady Margaret
= Douglas
Mathew
Earl of Lennox

**MARY
TUDOR**
b·1516
1553-1558

Mary Queen
of Scots
b·1542. d·1587
= Henry
Lord Darnley
b·1546. d·1567

Lord Charles Stuart
Earl of Lennox
=
Elizabeth Cavendish
daughter of Bess of Hardwicke
Countess of Shrewsbury

JAMES I b·1566
1603-1618
(James VI of Scotland)

Arbella Stuart
b·1575

succession

Lord Darnley, in relation to the English throne

Elizabeth of York

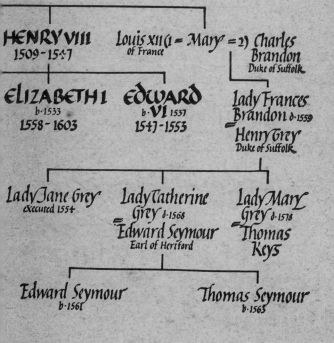

HENRY VIII 1509–1547	**Louis XII** (1 = **Mary** = 2) **Charles** of France **Brandon** Duke of Suffolk	
ELIZABETH I b·1533 1558–1603	**EDWARD** b·VI 1537 1547–1553	**Lady Frances** **Brandon** d·1559 **Henry Grey** Duke of Suffolk
Lady Jane Grey executed 1554	**Lady Catherine** **Grey** d·1568 = **Edward Seymour** Earl of Hertford	**Lady Mary** **Grey** d·1578 = **Thomas** **Keys**
Edward Seymour b·1561	**Thomas Seymour** b·1563	

The Scottish

Royal Stewarts, Lennox Stewarts, Hamiltons, showing

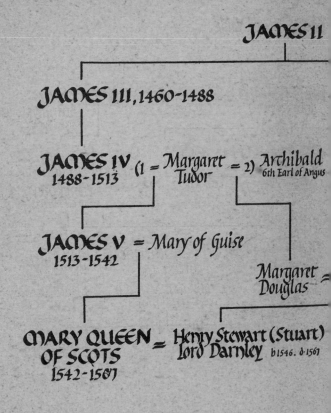

JAMES II

JAMES III, 1460-1488

JAMES IV (1 = Margaret = 2) Archibald
1488-1513   Tudor   6th Earl of Angus

JAMES V = Mary of Guise
1513-1542

Margaret
Douglas =

MARY QUEEN = Henry Stewart (Stuart)
OF SCOTS   Lord Darnley b 1546. d 1567
1542-1567

succession

their relation to the throne in the sixteenth Century

1437-1460

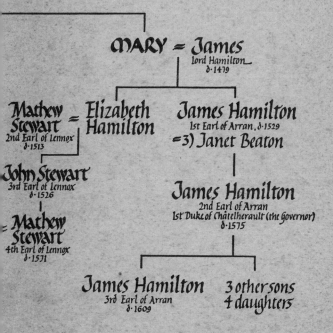

MARY = James
Lord Hamilton
d·1479

Mathew Stewart
2nd Earl of Lennox
d·1513
= Elizabeth Hamilton

James Hamilton
1st Earl of Arran, d·1529
=3) Janet Beaton

John Stewart
3rd Earl of Lennox
d·1526

= Mathew Stewart
4th Earl of Lennox
d·1571

James Hamilton
2nd Earl of Arran
1st Duke of Châtelherault (the Governor)
d·1575

James Hamilton
3rd Earl of Arran
d·1609

3 other sons
4 daughters

Author's Note

I had two principal aims when I began to write this biography. First, being possessed since childhood by a passion for the subject of Mary Queen of Scots, I wished to test for myself the truth or falsehood of the many legends which surround her name. In order to tear away these cobwebs—or in certain cases reverently replace them—I delved into as many published and unpublished sources as I could discover, taking as my starting-point Mary's own letters and the calendars of state papers (although of course there may well be some sources of which I was unhappily ignorant). Secondly, for the sake of the general reader, I hoped to set Mary anew in the context of the age in which she lived. In the course of my own inquiries I was surprised to discover that despite the enormous quantity of research on the sixteenth century published during the last fifty years, radically changing our attitudes to certain of its aspects, no general life of Mary has yet appeared, taking it all into account. There have been detailed treatments of certain episodes in her life—notably that of the Kirk o'Field murder and the Casket Letters, and later the Babington Plot—and Stefan Zweig's fascinating psychological interpretation, written in the thirties. But the last full-length biography, giving documentation, was that of T. F. Henderson in 1905. So in the end my two aims converged, and I found myself with the single objective of showing, with as much accuracy as is possible in the light of modern research, what Mary Queen of Scots must have been like as a person.

In the interests of clarity, I have not entered into the various complications of dating in the sixteenth century, i.e. I have ignored the fact that the calendar year was held to start on 25 March during this period, and have used the modern style of dates starting on 1 January throughout. I have also ignored the ten days' difference between English and European dates in the period of the Babington Plot, due to the fact that the adjustment to the Gregorian calendar was not made in England until the eighteenth century; and, in order to avoid confusion, have given the dates of letters coming from abroad as if they originated in England.

With regard to Scots words and spelling, and documents both in Scots and French—notably Queen Mary's own letters, which were nearly always written in French—I have translated, adapted to modern spelling, and in certain cases, paraphrased the text, as it seemed to me necessary to make the meaning clear to the general reader today.

It will be found that sums of money relevant to Scotland are given in pounds Scots and those concerning England in pounds sterling—the pound Scots being worth roughly one-quarter of the pound sterling in this period.

The task of writing such a book—covering ground well-trodden by scholars of the present, as of previous generations—would not have been possible without the benefit of their works, which are listed in the bibliography, and whose assistance I gratefully acknowledge. I was also fortunate enough to be able to draw upon the advice of a number of people, whose suggestions concerning the lines of research to pursue were a major contribution to my book (although the conclusions drawn are of course all my own). In the first place I should like to thank Sir James Fergusson of Kilkerran, Keeper of the Records of Scotland, for valuable advice over reading-matter as well as guidance in researches within the Register House itself; Sir Iain Moncrieffe of that Ilk on whose encyclopaedic knowledge of Scottish history I frequently drew; Archbishop David Mathew for advice and encouragement at an early stage; and Father Francis Edwards S.J., Archivist of the English Society of Jesus, for advice and help in researches within the Farm Street Library, including the opportunity to use the notes of the late Fr J.H. Pollen.

I would also like to acknowledge most gratefully the help of the following: Mr Andrews, Clerk of the Works, Westminster Abbey; the Duke of Argyll; Sir Charles Barratt, Town Clerk of Coventry; Mr and Mrs Godfrey Bostock of Tixall, Stafford; Dr C. Burns of the Vatican Archives, Rome; Fr Philip Caraman S.J.; Miss Margaret Crum, Deputy Keeper of Western MSS, Bodleian Library, Oxford;

Mr Stanley Cursiter; Fr Martin D'Arcy S.J.; Dr Chalmers Davidson; Professor A.A.M. Duncan of Glasgow University; the Duke and Duchess of Hamilton and Brandon; Mr R. E. Hutcheson, Keeper of the Scottish National Portrait Gallery, for advice on the authenticity of Scottish portraits of the period; Mr and Mrs W. J. Keswick of Glenkiln, Dumfriesshire; Mr A. H. King of the Music Room, British Museum and Miss Marion Linton of the Music Room, National Library of Scotland for help over Riccio's music; Mr King, Northamptonshire County Archivist; Mr Eric Linklater; Dr Ida Macalpine and Dr Richard Hunter for additional help on the subject of porphyria, beyond their B.M.A. publication; Mr John MacQueen of the University of Edinburgh, for advice on the literature of the period, and for showing me his paper on Alexander Scott in advance of publication; Dr William Marshall of Peterborough; the Earl of Mar and Kellie; Mr James Michie for his translation of George Buchanan's poem on page 207; Miss Elizabeth Millar of Jedburgh; Mr J. W. Moore, of Stone; the Duke of Norfolk and his archivist Mr Francis Steer; the Earl of Oxford and Asquith; Mr Peter Quennell; Sir Patrick Reilly, then British Ambassador in Paris, and Mr C. S. de Winton, British Council representative in France, for assistance in the course of French researches; Mr Jasper Ridley (whose own life of Knox was unfortunately published after this book went to press), for suggestions and criticism at the manuscript stage; the Marquess of Salisbury for permission to research at Hatfield House and reproduce certain documents in the illustrations, and also his librarian, Miss Clare Talbot for special assistance over the Casket Letters; Mr F. B. Stitt, Staffordshire County Archivist; Dr Roy Strong, Director of the National Portrait Gallery, for generous help over the complicated subject of the iconography of Mary Queen of Scots; M. Marcel Thomas, Conservateur en Chef of the Cabinet des Manuscrits, Bibliothèque Nationale, Paris; Mr Hugh Tait of the Department of British and Mediaeval Antiquities, British Museum; Mr F. A. Warner, of the British Embassy, Brussels; Mr Neville Williams, Assistant Keeper at the Public Record Office; the late Mr F. Wismark of Madame Tussaud's; Mr T. S. Wragg, librarian to the Duke of Devonshire at Chatsworth; Canon A. de Zulueta.

I am grateful to G. Bell & Sons Ltd for permission to

quote passages from *Queen Mary's Book* edited by Mrs P. Stewart-Mackenzie Arbuthnot.

Lastly I should like to thank the Librarian and staff of the London Library; the staff of the Reading Room of the British Museum; my aunt Lady Pansy Lamb who kindly read the proofs; and my mother Elizabeth Longford, who made vital critical suggestions at the manuscript stage, and without whose admirable example I should never have attempted to write the book at all.

September 1968   ANTONIA FRASER
52 Campden Hill Square, London W8
Eilean Aigas, Beauly, Inverness-shire

MARY
QUEEN
of
SCOTS

PART ONE
The Young Queen

1 *All Men Lamented*

'All men lamented that the realm was left without a male to succeed.'

JOHN KNOX

The winter of 1542 was marked by tempestuous weather throughout the British Isles: in the north, on the borders of Scotland and England, there were heavy snow-falls in December and frost so savage that by January the ships were frozen into the harbour at Newcastle. These stark conditions found a bleak parallel in the political climate which then prevailed between the two countries. Scotland as a nation groaned under the humiliation of a recent defeat at English hands at the battle of Solway Moss. As a result of the battle, the Scottish nobility which had barely recovered from the defeat of Flodden a generation before, were stricken yet again by the deaths of their leaders in their prime; of those who survived, many prominent members were prisoners in English hands, while the rest met the experience of defeat by quarrelling among themselves, showing their strongest loyalty to the principle of self-aggrandizement, rather than to the troubled monarchy. The Scottish national Church, although still officially Catholic for the next seventeen years, was already torn between those who wished to reform its manifold abuses from within, and those who wished to follow England's example, by breaking away root and branch from the tree of Rome. The king of this divided country, James v, having led his people to defeat, lay dying with his face to the wall, the victim in this as much of his own passionate nature, as of the circumstances which had conspired against him. When James died on 14 December 1542, the most stalwart prince might have shrunk from the Herculean task of succeeding him. But his actual successor was a weakly female child born only six days before, his daughter Mary, the new queen of Scotland.

James v, the last adult male king of Scotland for nearly

fifty years, has been treated kindly by contemporary historians, who look back to his reign with nostalgia across
the turbulence of that of his daughter. He has been credited with the qualities of King Arthur, whereas on balance
his character seems to have been more like that of Sir
Lancelot. Since his physical description, 'of midway
stature',[1] bluish grey eyes, sandy hair, weak mouth and
chin, does not justify the general reputation he enjoyed
among his contemporaries for good looks, he clearly possessed an animal magnetism, impossible for another century to understand through pictures. This, and his health,
seems to have been his chief physical legacy to his daughter, since in all other respects, starting with her height and
athletic carriage, the features and build of Mary Queen of
Scots are far easier to trace among her physically magnificent Guise uncles, than in her Stewart forbears. Ronsard
described him as having 'le regard vigoureux': James certainly possessed the cyclical high spirits and gaiety of the
Stewarts—another quality which he handed on to his
daughter—and the ability to fire the imagination of his
subjects, an attribute generally described in monarchs as
possessing the common touch. Unfortunately there is no
doubt as to the reverse side of this golden coin: the evidence of the debauchery of James v is unanimous. 'Most
vicious we shall call him,' wrote Knox with relish,[2] relating
how he spared neither man's wife nor maiden, no more
after his marriage than he did before.

James inherited a kingdom bankrupted by his mother
Margaret Tudor and her second husband, the earl of Angus; unfortunately his various efforts to search about him
for new sources of income brought further troubles in
their train. Even his prolonged search for a wealthy foreign bride set his feet firmly on the path of a foreign
policy which proved in the final analysis to be disastrous.
In view of the predatory attitude of his uncle, Henry VIII,
towards Scotland, James determined upon the traditional
Scottish alliance with the French king, in order to bolster himself with French aid against any possible English
claims of suzerainty. Rightly or wrongly, James viewed
Henry's offer of his daughter Mary Tudor as a bride, as a
further effort on the part of his uncle to envelop Scotland
in his bear's hug. At one point James even dangled after
the young Catherine de Medicis, niece of the Pope, lured
by the thought of her magnificent inheritance.[3] The results

of such a union, between Mary Stuart's father and the
woman who was later to be her mother-in-law, provide an
interesting avenue of historical speculation; in fact the
match was doubly vetoed, by the Pope's reluctance to see
his niece set off for the far land of Scotland, and by
Henry VIII's anger at the idea of such a powerful match
for his nephew. James's mother had been the elder of the
two daughters of Henry VII; later this share of Tudor blood
was to play a vital part in shaping the life story of
James's daughter Mary; the deaths of two out of the three
surviving children of Henry VIII meant that by the time
Mary was sixteen she was next in line to the English throne
after her cousin Queen Elizabeth. But in the 1530s, at the
time of James V's marriage projects, these coming events
had not yet cast their shadow. It was Henry VIII, in the fulness of his manhood, and with two children to his credit
already branching out of the Tudor family tree, who
seemed blessed with heirs. His nephew James on the other
hand singularly lacked them.

The position of the Stewart monarchs in the fifteenth
and sixteenth centuries was peculiarly perilous in dynastic
terms, for a number of reasons. In the first place chance
had resulted in a total of seven royal minorities—there
had been no adult succession since the fourteenth century
—which had an inevitable effect of weakening the power
of the crown and increasing that of the nobility. Secondly,
the Stewarts had a special reason for needing to separate
themselves from the nobility, and raise themselves above
it into a cohesive royal family, by the nature of their
origins. These were neither obscure nor royal. On the contrary the Stewarts were no more than *primus inter pares*
among the body of the Scottish nobles. They had formerly
been stewards, as their name denotes, first of all to the
ruling family of Brittany, and later more splendidly, great
stewards to the kings of Scotland. It was Walter, sixth
great steward, who by marrying Marjorie Bruce, daughter
of Robert I, fathered Robert II, king of the Scots, and thus
founded the Stewart royal line.

The ramifications and interconnections of the Stewart
family were henceforward focused on the throne. The
many intermarriages, common to all Scottish noble families of this period, meant that by the 1540s there were
descended from younger sons or daughters of the kings a
number of rival Stewart families[4]—the Lennox Stewarts,

who later came to use the French spelling of Stuart and
thus handed it officially on to the royal line through the
marriage of Mary to Henry Stuart, Lord Darnley;* the
Atholl Stewarts, the Stewarts of Traquair, the Stewarts of
Blantyre, and the Stewarts of Ochiltree. Even those dignitaries whose name was not actually Stewart often stood in
close relationship to the crown through marriage or descent; throughout her reign Mary correctly addressed as
'cousin' the earls of Arran, Huntly and Argyll, heads
respectively of the families of Hamilton, Gordon and
Campbell. Kinship as a concept was all-important in Scotland of the period: unfortunately kinship to the monarchy
was universally held to strengthen the position of the family concerned, rather than add to the resources of the
monarchy. Compared to the Stewarts, how fortunate then
—or how prudent—were their Tudor cousins in England.
By the reign of Queen Elizabeth, her Tudor forbears had
seen to it long ago that the crown was not surrounded by
a host of ambitious relatives, by a policy of steady elimination directed towards possible rivals. The many Scottish
minorities meant that the Stewart kings had never ruled
for long enough to follow this same course.

Determined to cut his way free from this prickly dynastic hedge, on 1 January 1537 James finally brought about
his marriage to Madeleine, daughter of the French King
Fràncis I. Her dowry—100,000 *livres* on the marriage day,
and annual rents on a sum of 125,000 *livres*—was obviously desirable, and so was the support of her father; but
the Maytime beauty and fragility of this *princesse loin-
taine* seems to have played on a genuine chord of romance
in the nature of the Scottish king. Her hand had already
been refused him by her father on the grounds of her
physical delicacy, and James had actually set out for
France to marry Marie, daughter of the duke of Vendôme.

* According to modern practice, Mary Queen of Scots was born
a Stewart (as her father had been) and became a Stuart only
through her marriage to her cousin Lord Darnley. But as the Anglo-
French spelling of her name—Stuart—was adopted on her behalf
during her upbringing in France, and always employed by her in
the many devices and anagrams of her own name, it has been used
to indicate her throughout this book. James VI and I was quite properly Stuart, rather than Stewart, taking the surname of his father
Darnley. But of course too much importance should not be attached
to the spelling of names in an age when many people spelt their own
names in a variety of different ways on different occasions.

The sight of Madeleine prompted him to pursue his original aim with pertinacity, and at length success. Alas! her father's premonitions concerning the effect of the Scottish climate on a girl brought up in the soft air of the Loire valley proved all too correct. The sixteen-year-old queen, who arrived in Scotland in May, was dead by July; the mourning veils which were thus for the first time introduced into Scotland, remained the only permanent memorials of a summer's marriage.[5]

The woman on whom King James's matrimonial negotiations were now focused, through his envoy Cardinal Beaton, was like himself recently widowed. Mary of Guise was the eldest daughter of the large and flourishing family of Claude, duke of Guise, and his wife Antoinette of Bourbon. She had been married at the age of nineteen to Francis of Orleans, duke of Longueville, and was left a widow at the age of twenty-two, by his premature death in June 1537, a month before James himself was left a widower. Unlike James, she had one small son, Francis, the new duke of Longueville, and gave birth to another son shortly after her husband's death, who died. In appearance, she was a tall well-built girl, not exactly beautiful, but of the healthy type calculated to appeal to sixteenth-century monarchs in search of heirs. Mary of Guise also possessed remarkable inner qualities of prudence and tolerance, as well as the courage and intelligence which might fairly have been expected of a Guise. However, none of these characteristics was greatly tested by her staid and happy married life with her first husband, spent placidly at his various castles at Châteaudun on the Loire, and at Amiens and Rouen. According to Brantôme, she also had her ration of Gallic gaiety, and loved to gamble and play cards. At all events she was quite happy at this stage in her life to form part of the great Guise family network, a domestic triangle at the apex of which stood the formidable Duchess Antoinette.

James had possibly met Mary of Guise in France at the time of his first marriage, which she attended: but he tendered for her hand for strictly conventional reasons; she would be provided with a dowry by Francis I, was clearly capable of child-bearing, and strengthened once again the important French alliance. So matrimonially suitable did she seem indeed in the terms of the time, that in the autumn of the same year, Henry VIII also offered for her hand, after the death of Jane Seymour. He referred approvingly to her fine stature, at which Mary of Guise is said to have wittily replied that although her figure was big, her neck was small. Certainly Francis had no particular wish to increase the pretensions of the Guises still further by placing one of them on the English throne. The marriage contract with James was thus prepared in January 1538, and the marriage performed by proxy, with Lord Maxwell acting the part of the bridegroom, on 18 May in the cathedral of Notre Dame in Paris.

Accompanied by a navy of ships under Lord Maxwell, and 2,000 lords and barons whom her new husband had sent from Scotland to fetch her away, Queen Mary landed at Crail in Fife on 10 June 1538, just over a year since the landing of Queen Madeleine.[6] She was formally received by the king at St Andrews a few days later with pageants and plays performed in her honour, and a great deal of generally blithe rejoicing, before being remarried the next morning in the cathedral of St Andrews. Immediately afterwards she was received into the king's palace with trumpets and still more pageants, in all the celebrations a prominent part being played by Sir David Lyndsay of the Mount, later to become famous for his denunciation of the state of the Scottish Church, *The Satire of the Three Estates*. The next day the royal couple were conveyed on a tour of churches, colleges and universities within the town by the provost and burgesses.

These arrangements, like the steps of a formal dance, convey little of the feelings of the people concerned: but clearly Queen Mary, a woman of innate tact, was at pains to please her husband by praising his country. Fife, for example, she admired extravagantly, and confided to James that although she had been warned in France that she would find Scotland a barbarous country, destitute of comforts, ever since her arrival she had found the exact reverse, for she had never seen so many fair personages of men and women and also young babes and children, as she saw that day. Delighted with this graceful and diplomatic speech, King James swore to show her even better sights as she passed through Scotland. After forty days had been spent at St Andrews in merriment, games, jousting, archery, hunting, hawking, dancing and minstrel playing, the court then passed on to further celebrations in other towns, culminating in the queen's reception at Edin-

burgh, which she entered in triumph on St Margaret's
Day.[7]

Despite this elaborate pageantry, despite the queen's gracious compliments to her adopted country, the marriage
of James and Mary does not seem to have been a particularly happy one in its early stages. It was rumoured in
England that James had a mistress at Tantallon and 'set
not much store by the queen'.[8] The letters exchanged between Mary of Guise and her mother, Duchess Antoinette,
give a picture of secret homesickness, the mother both advising her daughter on her role in Scotland, and trying to
reassure her with an abundance of family news about affairs in France.[9] Nearly every letter contains some reference to the little boy Francis whom the queen had been
obliged to leave behind. The melancholy of a mother who
had to abandon a three-year-old child for a state marriage
in a far-off country may be imagined; sadly, Mary of
Guise, a woman of undoubtedly maternal nature, was deprived of the upbringing of both her surviving children,
Francis and Mary Stuart, after the first years of infancy.
Francis was clearly a delicate child: Duchess Antoinette's
letters abound with details of his diseases. Later he learns
to say his Paternoster, has his hair cut like his uncles, has
supper with his grandfather the duke of Guise in the garden and picks strawberries, and relates how his Uncle Aumale hid in his room while his aunt put him to bed. As
the little duke grows up, far from his mother, he sends
her a string to show his height, and by 1547, after the
battle of Pinkie Cleugh, writes to her to say he is practising tilting to come to her rescue. The next year, on the
same theme, he is keeping up with the French king out
hunting to prove himself a man able to come to the help
of his mother.[10]

A mother's homesickness was not Queen Mary's only
problem. There was trouble with King Francis over the
payment of her dowry to the Scottish king, for Francis,
in arranging for her dowry, used the money already given
to her on her first marriage, to the annoyance of both
Duchess Antoinette and her daughter, who feared that
the little duke's rights would be thus prejudiced. There
was a further problem ingenuously exposed by Francis
of Longueville, when he sent his love to Papa (James v)
and hoped that he would soon give a little brother to the
queen.[11] By the end of 1539 no royal heir had appeared,

although the marriage of James and Mary was eighteen
months old; a proposal of the duke of Guise to voyage to
Scotland in January 1540, to see how his daughter was
faring, indicated that Queen Mary's parents were genuinely
concerned as to her situation.

The birth of James, prince of Scotland, the longed-for
heir, in May 1540 put an end for the time being to this
particular problem. The news was received with ecstasy
by Duchess Antoinette, who bombarded her daughter alternately with questions and advice. By December of the
same year, the queen was again with child, the royal marriage thus considered satisfactory in both countries. In the
meantime Mary of Guise took a number of steps to introduce the amenities of French life into Scotland. The
material objects she sought from France ranged from pear
trees and plums to wild boars for hunting; the personages
included masons, miners from Lorraine to mine the 'golden
strand' of Crawford Muir, where substantial amounts of
gold were discovered in the sixteenth century, an armourer,
tailors, and—typically of an expatriate—French doctors
and apothecaries. From Antwerp one Eustating de Coquiel
wrote to the queen that he was sending his servant with
merchandise and certain luxuries ('*gentillesses*')—of
which she was to have first choice.[12] Obviously *gentillesses* to the French way of thinking, were not in abundance in Scotland, and Mary of Guise turned her practical
mind to remedying the deficiency.

A double tragedy now struck both king and queen in
the area in which they were most vulnerable. In April
1541 at Falkland the queen gave birth to a second son,
Robert, duke of Albany, who died two days later, and
within a few days the little prince of Scotland was himself dead at Holyrood. Thus King James was once more
left without a direct heir; Queen Mary's feelings may be
imagined to have been equally desperate, but according to
Pitscottie she still managed to behave admirably: '. . . telling the king that they were young enough to expect to
have many more children'.[13] Her mother did not fail to
write immediately from France, devoutly hoping that the
king had not taken it too badly, expressing her daughter's
own opinion that they were both young and might have
many more children, and finally ascribing the death of
Prince James to overfeeding, or at least a change of
nurses.[14] Contemporary opinion in Scotland advanced a

more dramatic explanation for the tragic deaths of the two princes. Although there were the usual rumours of poison, common to all unexpected deaths of the period, the most general explanation was that the sins of King James v were being visited upon his children. It was said that Sir James Hamilton of Fynart, the king's former master of the works, whom he had had executed in dubious circumstances, appeared to him in a dream as he lay asleep, and warned him that he would shortly lose both his arms, and finally his head. According to Knox, Sir James Hamilton himself struck off both the king's arms in the vision with his sword, crying: 'Take that while thou receive a final payment for all thy impiety.'[15]

Although the precarious nature of infant life in the sixteenth century is a more probable explanation for the double tragedy than either poison or divine vengeance, at the same time the deaths of the young princes did mark the point at which the fortunes of King James seemed to take a final downward turn. There was no sign of another heir. While James's domestic policy had the natural effect of alienating those of his nobles who felt the corrective side of it, especially the powerful family of Douglas, headed by the earl of Angus, his refusal to join Henry VIII in plundering the Catholic Church did not endear him to the menacing forces on the other side of the border. When Henry demanded a conference at York in September 1541, James was not allowed to attend on the grounds that his person was too precious since the deaths of his sons. His own clergy, fearful that Henry would sway James towards his predatory policy with regard to the Church, offered to finance a war if this should be necessary. Incensed at the Scottish king's failure to appear, Henry angrily asserted that the Scots had thus broken their words, and 'not satisfied their former promises'.

By the summer of 1542 the English forces were being mobilized in the north, with vicious instructions from their king for bringing the Scots to heel, should King James continue to ignore his uncle's request for a meeting in England. Queen Mary was once again expecting a child, but in his general statement claiming suzerainty over Scotland, King Henry particularly specified that this should not prevent her husband from coming to London by Christmas—there were to be no 'ifs and ands' from the king's wife, which King Henry thought would engender

great uncertainty over the whole situation, considering
'the common error of women in reckoning their time'.[16]
The check of the English forces by the earl of Home at
Haddonrig in August was only temporary. In the autumn,
as Queen Mary awaited the birth of another longed-for
heir, and Duchess Antoinette wrote constantly from France
advising her on her health (she is to eliminate her bad
colds by washing her hair once a month, having previously
cut it short, since greasy hair makes for colds; Duchess
Antoinette herself is careful to cut her hair every six
weeks)[17] the king of Scotland rallied his own army for
the final crisis of his reign. His difficulties in assembling
what was virtually a feudal host were in no way smoothed
by the fact that command was given to Cardinal Beaton,
who tried to invest the campaign with the character of a
holy war, on the grounds that England lay under the papal
interdict. Nor were the nobles any better pleased when another command was given to the king's favourite, Oliver
Sinclair.

On 24 November, the forces under Oliver Sinclair encountered the English deputy warden of the West March
near the River Esk at Solway Moss, and were driven back
in a disorderly rout, as a result of which 1,200 Scots
were captured, among them many of the leading nobles,
who were then taken to London for confrontation with
King Henry. Although Knox discerned the hand of God
in the discomfiture,[18] it was the great reluctance of the
Scots to pursue a long campaign away from their homes,
and the fact that as fighters they lacked not courage but
endurance, which had once more defeated their efforts.
The English increased in valiance as they fought, but the
Scots declined. As the Scots cast aside their weapons and
fled, many were drowned by the incoming tide, and others
still fell in the Moss, losing either horse or rider or both.
Some were so anxious to be saved by capture that they
surrendered themselves to women. An English eye-witness
wrote that night from Carlisle that anyone who wanted
prisoners had only to follow the retreating Scots, for they
were past making any sort of self-defence.[19]

The king of the stricken country, in a state of appalling
mental anguish, exacerbated by worry over the fate of
Oliver Sinclair, retired to Edinburgh, where he made an
inventory of all his treasure and jewels. From there he
went secretly to Hallyards, in Fife, the seat of Sir William

Kirkcaldy of Grange, the treasurer. When Kirkcaldy's wife tried to cheer him and persuade him to take the 'work of God' in good part, the king replied with conviction that his portion of the world was on the contrary short, and he would be dead in fifteen days. When his servants asked him where he wanted to spend his Christmas, he replied with a contemptuous smile: 'I cannot tell: choose ye the place. But this I can tell you, on Yule day, you will be masterless and the realm without a king.'

The working out of these gloomy prophecies took only a short time. James went to Linlithgow where he spent some days with Queen Mary, now in the last stage of her pregnancy. From there he went to Falkland, the beloved palace which he had built for himself in admiration of the French Renaissance, and which like an animal he now chose as his lair in which to die. Incapable of digesting the disasters of his hopes, his personal humiliation and the humiliation of his country, the king now underwent a complete nervous collapse. He lay on his bed, sometimes railing at the cruel fate which had led to his defeat, at other times silent and melancholy, meditating on the wastes of despair. He heard of the capture of Sinclair and cried out: 'Oh fled Oliver! Is Oliver tane [taken]? Oh fled Oliver!'[20] It seems to have been his last true pang of earthly emotion.

Into this sad sick-room came a messenger from Linlithgow who brought the news that the queen had been confined, and given birth to a daughter. The onlookers hoped that the king's sorrow might be somewhat alleviated by the fact that he now had an heir once more. But the king observed cynically: 'Adieu, fare well, it came with a lass, it will pass with a lass', thus alluding to the marriage of Marjorie Bruce and Walter Stewart, which had founded the Stewart dynasty.*[21] Six days later, on 14 December King James was dead at the age of thirty. In a letter to the king in 1540, Cardinal Pole reminded him how his uncle, Henry VIII, had once been a man of promise and goodness, and what he was now; the cardinal told King James that he dreaded to see him follow the same

---

* It has often been suggested that in the hour of his failure King James was at least successful as a prophet. But of course this prophecy was never actually fulfilled. The Stewart dynasty, far from ending with Mary, went on through her son James to extend its power still further, over the throne of England and of Ireland.

route.[22] It is likely that the cardinal was right in thus stressing King James's Tudor blood; if he had lived, his character too might have deepened in cruelty and sadism, to
have eradicated totally the fair impression of his youth.
He also seems to have included a mysterious, apparently
hysterical, streak in his nature: there is no need to regard
the contemporary suggestion of poison either by angry
prelates, or seditious heretics, to explain his nervous
breakdown after Solway Moss. Clearly a tendency to sudden physical collapse at moments of stress ran in the Stuart blood, a tendency which James handed on to his daughter, so that twenty-five years later, after Kirk o'Field, Scotland again witnessed the prostration of its monarch at the
critical moment in her fortunes.

The daughter and only surviving child of King James, who
now succeeded to the throne of Scotland, had been born
at the palace of Linlithgow, West Lothian, on the Feast
of the Immaculate Conception of the Virgin Mary, 8
December. She was baptized Mary, by tradition in the
church of St Michael, at the gates of the palace, although
one rumour stated that she had been named Elizabeth,
which if true would have led in later years to two rival
Queen Elizabeths on the thrones of England and Scotland.[23] A certain confusion surrounds the date of her birth,
as indeed it surrounds the date of her father's death, due
to the perilous political situation in Scotland at the time.
The date of James's death was finally established in the
seventeenth century by the discovery of the date engraved
on his coffin. The date of Mary Stuart's birth, although
given as the 8th by a concurrence of contemporary accounts, including Knox, is given as the 7th by her own
partisan Leslie, who had special access to official records.[24]
It has therefore been suggested that Mary was actually
born on the 7th and that the date was altered to the 8th
in order to coincide with the feast of the Virgin. Whatever
the truth of this, which can never be proved, Mary Stuart
herself always believed that she had been born on the
8th, heading a letter as late as 1584: 'December 8, the
forty second anniversary of my birth.'[25] It certainly seems
likely that she was born prematurely, the confinement of
Queen Mary being brought on by anxiety over her husband: on 12 December Lisle and Tunstall reported to England from Alnwick that 'the said Queen was delivered

before her time of a daughter, a very weak child, and not
likely to live as it is thought'. In a private letter to King
Henry on the same day, Lisle told him that the baby was
actually dead. For the first ten days of her life, all the
rumours spread about Mary Stuart were of an exceptionally frail baby, unlikely to survive, any more than her
brothers. On 17 December, Sir George Douglas, writing
from Berwick, still referred to 'a very weak child', and
although by 19 December Lisle was able to tell Henry
that 'the princess lately born is alive and good-looking',
rumours of her ill-health continued long enough for
Chapuys, the imperial ambassador in London to write to
the queen of Hungary on 23 December that both mother
and child were very ill and despaired of by their physicians.[26]

Perhaps with the English the wish was father to the
thought, since the death of the infant queen would have
increased the confusion of Scotland still further, to the
point of the possible extinction of their government. The
secret wishes of the Scots on the other hand are probably
expressed by the rumour of the time that the child was
actually a boy. The position of a country with a child
heiress at its head was widely regarded as disastrous in
the sixteenth century. As Knox put it, 'all men lamented
that the realm was left without a male to succeed.'[27] The
reason is not difficult to seek. In 1542, the successful reign
of Queen Elizabeth I lay very much in the future. The
birth of an heiress generally led to the swallowing up of
the country concerned, as happened in the case of Bur-
gundy, Spain, Bohemia and Hungary with Habsburgs, and
with England, in the time of Mary Tudor. To the disadvantages of Mary Stuart's situation at birth, herself frail
in health, the country divided and facing the prospect of
a long minority, was therefore added the disadvantage of
being of the weaker, and therefore the wrong sex.

The palace of Linlithgow, where Mary was born—in a
room in the north-west corner, overlooking the loch*—
and where she was destined to spend the first seven months
of her life, was a traditional lying-in place of queens.
James v himself had been born there. It was he who had

* Today the room where Mary Queen of Scots was born is roof-
less and the remaining structure of the palace of Linlithgow owes
much of its beauty to embellishments in the next century.

enriched it by many improvements and who had developed
it in a quadrangular form, from an earlier castle, in the
course of his munificent Scottish rebuilding schemes, and
it was certainly considered to be a splendid palace by the
standards of the time: Mary of Guise compared it approvingly to the castles of the Loire on her arrival, and Sir
David Lyndsay called it a 'palace of pleasance' worthy to
be put beside those of Portugal and France. Leslie wrote
warmly of its fine position, above the loch 'swimming full
of fine perch and other notable fishes', and even in the
next century, John Ray the naturalist called it 'a very good
house, as houses go in Scotland'.[28] However, in December
1542, above this serene place, and its youthful incumbent, hovered a series of political thunder clouds of a
highly ominous nature.

James v was buried with due pomp, says Leslie, with
lighted torches and the sound of mourning trumpets
(*buccinae querelae*); the nobles were in black, Cardinal
Beaton hung his head down, while the people were loud
in sorrow and lamentation. But with an outward delicacy
of feeling which probably sprang in fact from shrewd political calculation, it was now thought unseemly for the
English commander to pursue an attack against the kingdom of a dead man. Lisle reported as much to King
Henry: 'I have thought good to stay the stroke of your
sword until your majesty's pleasure be farther known to
me in that behalf' and he included in his forbearance 'the
young suckling', the late king's daughter.[29] Thus curiously
enough, the premature death of King James, which had
such dire results for Scotland in producing another long
minority, had the short-term effect of staying the avenging
hand of the English army after Solway Moss. As a result
the first year of his daughter Mary's existence, instead of
being threatened by English armies, was dominated by two
questions of important bearing on her subsequent history—
who was to govern the kingdom during her infancy, and
whom she was destined to marry.

Of these two issues, it was the first which demanded immediate settlement, for while the bridals of the queen
would only be a matter of speculation for many years to
come, if Scotland was to survive as an independent nation
the office of the governor had to be filled at once. Despite this urgency, a fierce controversy at once arose on
the subject, to add to the country's troubles. It arose out

of the clash of the hereditary claim of the earl of Arran, head of the house of Hamilton, to be sole governor, with the rival claim of Cardinal Beaton, which he based on a forged will supposed to have been made by the late king. This provided for four governors (Huntly, Moray, Argyll and Arran) with the cardinal himself to be the governor of the princess, and chief ruler of the Council. The prize was a rich one. The prestige and importance of the governor, or regent, was considered to be equivalent to that of the king himself; and the political powers were interwoven with the material rewards of office. It was tradition for the governor to take over the palaces, jewels and treasure of the late king during the minority of his successor; he was responsible for the administration of the crown revenues, for which he would be given a discharge signed at the end of his period of office.

As it happened, the man with the hereditary right to this important office at this critical juncture in Scottish history, James, 2nd earl of Arran and later 1st duke of Châtelherault, was singularly unfitted to hold it. Mary of Guise described him succinctly as the most inconstant man in the world: the most charitable verdict is that of a chaplain who called him 'a good soft God's man', presumably referring to the fact that for the past five years he had been a supporter of the reformed religion.[30] Yet this vacillating figure, by the very fact that he was the head of the house of Hamilton, was destined for the most prominent position among the Scottish nobles.

Arran's grandfather, James, 1st Lord Hamilton, had been married to Princess Mary Stewart, sister of James III.* If the child Queen Mary died, Arran could fairly claim the Scottish throne, as the next heir by blood. It was true that there was a complication: there was some doubt whether Arran's father had ever been properly divorced from his second wife and it was therefore conceivable that Arran, as fruit of the third marriage, was illegitimate: in which case, the Lennox Stewarts who descended perfectly correctly from Princess Mary and Lord Hamilton—but from the daughter not a son—were the true heirs to the throne. This in turn meant that the earl of Lennox, not the earl of Arran, had the hereditary claim

* See Genealogical Table in the front of the book for Scottish Royal succession

to be governor of Scotland, and second person in the realm. Despite this Lennox shadow across the Hamilton claim, a fact to be borne in mind when considering the perennially explosive relations between the two families during this period, the Hamiltons still managed to retain their position as heirs or next heirs to the Scottish throne for nearly a hundred years. Throughout much of the reign of Mary's father, her own reign, and that of James vi, until the birth of his quiverful of Stuart children in the 1590s, the Hamiltons were separated from the throne by only one life. Unfortunately the accidental importance of their position was in no way matched by the calibre of their blood. They possessed natural advantages other than their descent, in the shape of great estates, strategically placed close to the capital, and strong political connections in half a dozen counties. But at a time when most of the Scottish nobles made up in quickness and an eye to the main chance what they lacked in graces and civilization, the Hamiltons were strangely untypical of their kind: the Governor Arran was indecisive but his eldest son actually went mad and had to be confined. During the whole of this period, Hamilton blood was generally considered a convenient scapegoat on which to blame abnormalities of temper.[31]

There was nothing softened or indecisive about the character of David Beaton, cardinal-archbishop of St Andrews, the man who now opposed Arran's claim with the will of the late king, apparently made in his favour. The evidence that Beaton actually forged the will seems conclusive,[32] but in view of the weakness of Scotland at the time, it may be argued that Cardinal Beaton was at least making a bid to give his country some sort of strong government to combat England's rapacity. He was now a man of over fifty, having been made cardinal of San Stefano by Pope Paul iii five years previously, and succeeded his uncle as archbishop of St Andrews in 1539; he had considerable knowledge of Europe, having studied in Paris and acted on various diplomatic missions abroad. Certainly the cardinal's pro-French, Catholic policy, which had led to disaster at Solway Moss, did represent the only alternative to subjugation under the yoke of Henry viii. Knox has described the worldliness of the cardinal at length in his usual vivid phrases, referring to 'that kingdom of darkness, whereof within this realm he was the head' and

how he was 'more careful for the world than he was to
preach Christ . . . as he sought the world, it fled him not'.
Knox even goes so far as to hint at Cardinal Beaton's las-
civious relations with Mary of Guise—an accusation of
which the verdict of history has acquitted the queen, although undoubtedly the cardinal lived openly with at least
one woman, in a way which made nonsense of his vows of
celibacy.[33] Whatever the cardinal's moral deficiencies, he
was certainly not a man of straw; as a prelate without any
family that he might be bound to favour, he at least
showed some signs of identifying his personal policies with
those of Scotland, in contrast to the rest of the venal Scottish nobility.

Despite Cardinal Beaton's strength of purpose, the deciding factor in the contest for the governorship proved to
be the return of those Scottish nobles captured at Solway
Moss: after a sojourn in London, they were now despatched north again by Henry viii, like so many Trojan
horses, as emissaries of his policy; they included Cassillis,
Glencairn, Maxwell and Fleming, besides Angus and his
brother George Douglas, who were already in England in
exile. While in London they had been induced to sign a
series of articles which pledged them to help Henry bring
about the marriage of Mary and Prince Edward, and generally advance the cause of England in Scotland, in return
for which they were given suitable pensions of English
money. Ten of them had even gone further and promised
to help Henry himself to achieve dominion and government over Scotland, should the young queen die. The
signing of these articles seems to us by modern standards
unpatriotic to the point of treachery; it is only fair to
point out that they should be judged in the context of an
age, in which patriotism, as a modern concept, was only
just beginning to exist. Xenophobia there was, a primordial
dislike of the foreigner, at a period when bad communications made foreigners out of those who would seem
close neighbours today; but although this xenophobia was
starting to push out a few green shoots of patriotism from
time to time, it certainly cannot yet be too closely identified with it.

In January Arran was confirmed in his office of governor, and a few days after the return of the English faction among the nobles, Cardinal Beaton was arrested: it
seemed thus certain that the rulers of Scotland during

Queen Mary's minority were to be a protestant pro-English faction. Equally, the matrimonial future of the young queen seemed to lie in the direction of England. Only eleven days after Mary's birth, Lisle had expressed the general English wish concerning her future: 'I would she and her nurse were in my lord prince's house.'[34] Henry's son, Prince Edward, then aged five, seemed the ideal spouse to unite Scotland and England firmly forever under English suzerainty, and Henry furthermore intended to bring up the Scottish queen actually at the English court, in order to check any possible fluttering for liberty in the Scottish dove-cots. This marriage, which if Edward VI had lived, would have antedated the peaceful union of England and Scotland by half a century, would not necessarily have been such a terrible prospect for Scotland, had it not been for the savagely bullying attitude which Henry VIII persisted in adopting towards his neighbour. It must be recalled that at this date Mary's future husband the dauphin of France had not yet been born and his mother Catherine de Medicis, wife of the heir to the French throne, appeared to be barren, having been married ten years without producing any children at all. Thus there was no French prince in prospect whose merits could be weighed against those of Prince Edward.

If a match with a foreign prince was rejected altogether, then the other obvious matrimonial possibility before the queen's guardians was to wed her to the son of one of her own nobles: Arran, for example, took the line that his own son would make her the best bridegroom, because the marriage would keep the crown of Scotland within the control of its own people. In March Sir Ralph Sadler came to Scotland as Henry's envoy, charged with negotiating the marriage of Edward and Mary with the Scottish Parliament. He reported that the queen dowager was far from unfavourable to the project. Indeed at the time, the behaviour of the Scottish nobility may easily have encouraged Mary of Guise to believe that a royal match with her daughter, even with England, was the lesser of two evils. She certainly took the opportunity to display the baby proudly to Sadler, anxious no doubt to contradict the rumours at the time of her birth that the princess was frail and unlikely to live. She had her daughter brought into the room, now aged three and a half months, and with determined thoroughness had her unwrapped by her nurse out of all her clothes, until she was totally naked; thus there could be no suspicion afterwards of some deformity concealed under the swaddling clothes. Sir Ralph Sadler was duly impressed by the sight. He wrote back to King Henry: 'I assure your Majesty, it is as goodly a child as I have seen of her age, and as like to live, with the Grace of God.'[35] In the meantime, lest Arran suffer disappointment at the thought of this rich matrimonial prize being wrested from his own son, Henry deliberately wooed the earl with the prospect of a match between his son and Henry's daughter Princess Elizabeth.

On 1 July the Treaties of Greenwich were drawn up, providing for the marriage of Edward and Mary. These treaties respected Scotland's independence as a country and provided for the return of Mary as a childless widow if Edward died; the main point on which the Scots insisted and on which Henry disagreed was that the child should not actually leave Scotland until she was ten years old. Henry remained avuncularly anxious to oversee her upbringing personally at the English court—or perhaps he did not trust the Scots to implement their promises in ten years' time. But in any case the point was never put to the test, since already by the summer of 1543 the internal situation in Scotland had changed radically. Opinion, although Henry VIII might be ignorant of the fact, was no longer predominantly favourable to the Protestant and pro-English cause. It was true the advent of Arran as governor had led to the extension of the reformed doctrines and practices—especially the reading of the Bible and preaching in the vernacular. Knox commented cynically on the number of those who now flaunted their Bibles with the boast, not always true: 'This has lain under my bed-foot these ten years.'[36] Protestant sympathies formed the most natural bond between those Scots and those English who shared that inclination. But by the summer Cardinal Beaton had somehow eluded captivity—the English suspected that no great efforts had been made to hold him—and in Pitscottie's words, he began to rage as any lion loosed of his bond; in short he was once more in a position to galvanize Catholic pro-French opinion.[37] Two new arrivals on the Scottish scene—the governor's bastard half-brother John Hamilton, abbot of Paisley, and Mathew, earl of Lennox, himself—only helped to poison Arran's mind further against the English alliance. John

Hamilton pointed out that by abandoning the cause of
Rome, Arran put himself in a vulnerable position in which
his father's divorce might be questioned; Lennox, as head
of the rival Stewarts, represented a positive alternative
to Arran as governor. Under the circumstances Arran's
vacillating wits were no match for the machinations of the
cardinal. French subsidies began to enter Scotland, to
vie with the English ones, and the very day after the
Treaties of Greenwich had been signed, Sadler reported
to Henry that the French ships had been seen lying off the
coast of Scotland.

Henry reacted to this news predictably by demanding
that the queen be moved away from Linlithgow, which he
thought altogether too accessible to the French if they
landed. Arran replied smoothly to Sadler that the baby
was suffering from 'the breeding of teeth' and it might
be dangerous to move her at this precise moment. Sadler
noted that Arran was as much concerned for her well-being
as if she had been his own child. In point of fact, Linlithgow did no longer seem a suitable place in which to
guard their queen, although it was fear of abduction by
the English, rather than by the French, which now
prompted the Scots to move her. On 21 July Cardinal
Beaton assembled about 7,000 followers at Stirling and
marched down to Linlithgow, together with Huntly, Lennox, Argyll and Bothwell, with the avowed aim of putting
the child in charge of some reliable guardians at Stirling
Castle. There was as yet no conclusive evidence of a volte-
face on the part of the Scottish government. The Protestant
earl of Glencairn was deputed to make the new arrangements, and of the four lords thus chosen—Graham, Lindsay, Livingston and Erskine—Erskine was a natural choice,
since the Erskines enjoyed a hereditary right to guard the
person of the heir to the throne. (This same Lord Erskine had been one of the personal guardians of the young
King James v as well as guardian to Mary's dead brother
the prince of Scotland when his father visited the Isles in
1540.) Equally, since Stirling had formed part of Mary
of Guise's dowry, there was no particular reason why she
should not visit it at any time she wished, although additional care was taken to explain to Sadler that Linlithgow,
that splendid palace, was actually too small to lodge both
queens comfortably.

The new home of Mary, Stirling, had in the time of

Edward I's invasion, been considered the strongest castle
in Scotland. Even that optimistic maker of promises, Sir
George Douglas, thought it would be extraordinarily difficult to abduct Mary from Stirling in the autumn, and hand
her over to King Henry, although he characteristically offered to try, if supplied with enough gold. In spite of its
subsequent ornamentation, its commanding situation, sur-
veying both plain and mountain, looking towards the
Ochils on one side (where silver for the royal mint was
mined) and the Grampian and Trossachs on the other, the
castle was unaltered since the days of Edward I. Its attractions included the splendour of the great hall of James v,
which in 1618 John Taylor compared favourably to Westminster Hall,[38] and the palace, a jewel of the Scottish
Renaissance, today still showing King James's initials in
the carved panels over its windows. But in 1543 it was
the fortress aspect of the castle, high over the town of
Stirling, higher still over the plain, and standing at the
gateway of the impenetrable territory of the Highlands,
which commended it to the lords who there incarcerated
their queen for safety.

Henry VIII still felt secure enough in the terms of the
treaty he had just signed to imagine that he could put
Sadler in charge of the queen in her new abode, and he
actually laid it down that Mary of Guise was not to be
allowed to lodge in the castle with her baby, but should
be kept elsewhere in the town and allowed to visit her
from time to time, as the little queen's keepers should
think fit.[39] Such might be the distant relationship which
Henry in England considered suitable for a child and its
mother. But the time when Henry would have any say
in Scotland's affairs was rapidly passing. The king made a
series of frantic efforts to maintain his ascendancy over
Arran; he also tried to woo his former enemy Cardinal
Beaton, and tempt him to throw in his lot with the English, after lying aside his cardinal's hat and his religion;
but his arrest of some Scottish merchant ships sailing to
France, and the impounding of the merchants and their
goods, aroused popular indignation. Sadler warned him
that the temper of the country was turning against him.
After torments of indecision, Arran finally decided to
throw in his lot with Beaton and the pro-French party,
his mind probably made up in the end by the renewed
promise of the little queen's hand for his son. On 8 Sep-

tember, in the church of the Franciscans at Stirling, 'the
unhappy man', as Knox disgustedly termed him, did pen-
ance for his apostasy and received the Catholic sacrament
while Argyll and Patrick, earl of Bothwell, held the towel
over his head.[40]

The day after Arran's change of faith, on 9 September
1543, Mary Stuart was solemnly crowned in Stirling Castle
chapel at the age of nine months. It was an inauspicious
date, being the thirtieth anniversary of the battle of Flodden, and the coronation scarcely seems to have been an
occasion for universal rejoicing. Sir Ralph Sadler reported
back that Mary had been crowned 'with such solemnitie as
they do use in this country, which is not very costlie'.[41]
Certainly the Tudor use of ceremonial which Queen Elizabeth I was to put to such good effect in subjugating the
imagination of her subjects, was not understood in Scotland. Sixteen years later, Elizabeth's own coronation
was a magnificent display of pageantry, with the un-
crowned queen its centrepiece, sparkling with jewels, in
cloth of gold, revealed to an admiring populace in an open
litter. By contrast the coronation of the Stuart queen consisted of the hurried investiture of a tiny child, surrounded
by feudal nobility at least as powerful as the crown they
nominally served. At the ceremony, the earl of Arran bore
the crown, the earl of Lennox bore the sceptre, and the
earl of Argyll, also of royal descent from James I, bore
the sword. The pro-English party, including Angus, Gray,
Glencairn, Cassillis and Maxwell, stayed away altogether.

2 *England's Rough Wooing*

'I perceive that proverb to be very true
Unhappy is the age which has o'er young a King'

SIR DAVID LYNDSAY OF THE MOUNT

The defection of Arran marked the first turning-point in
the life of Mary Queen of Scots. It decided, among other
things, that Henry would no longer woo the Scots with
gifts, but attempt to constrain them by force. This was
indeed the course which he furiously advised his pension-
ers among the Scottish nobles to pursue, when he heard
the news of Arran's treachery. However, George Douglas
managed to put forward a number of objections to immediate action, while continuing to profess loyalty to Henry
and amazement at the turn events had taken in Scotland.
The world was full of falsehood, he exclaimed, he knew
not whom he might trust. Arran and Cardinal Beaton took
no immediate steps to break with England, but the knowledge that they had cut themselves free from close entangle-
ment with Protestant England encouraged both the papacy
and the French king to renew their support to Scotland.
The appearance of a papal legate, Marco Grimani, the patriarch of Aquileia, with a papal subsidy, and of French
envoys at the Scottish court, presaged the final change of
policy announced by the Scottish Parliament in December 1543. By the Treaty of 15 December, as Leslie put it,
the 'auld bands' between the Scots and the French 'so long
and religiously kept' since the days of King Robert the
Bruce, were now once more confirmed.[1]

A secondary effect of Arran's volte-face was the turning away of Lennox from the party of Scottish government. Lennox was unable to endure the fact that despite
his changes of allegiance, his rival Arran still retained his
position as governor of Scotland. The classical policy of
the Lennox Stewarts was to ally themselves with the enemies of the Hamiltons. Lennox now veered his eyes towards England, and offered himself as a bridegroom to

Lady Margaret Douglas, daughter of Margaret Tudor by
her second marriage to the earl of Angus, and niece of
Henry VIII. In time to come, this formidable lady was to
show herself a worthy combination of the intriguing talents of Douglas and Tudor. She was also, as the mother of
Henry Stuart, Lord Darnley, to play a significant part in
the history of her daughter-in-law, the queen of Scots. But
at the time of her marriage, in June 1544, her importance
was mainly dynastic: she brought Lennox within the
sphere of the English succession, and as Henry's nephew
by marriage, Lennox contracted a marriage treaty with
him, which put him henceforth firmly into the English
camp. Among other provisions, Lennox promised to do
all he could to hand over Mary Stuart to Henry, and
Henry in return swore to make Lennox governor of Scotland once he had subjugated the country, with Lennox's
help.

Thus by the time Mary Stuart was one year old, the
pieces on the traditional chess board which lay between
Scotland and England had been rearranged to form an altogether different pattern from that which was in evidence
when she first succeeded to the throne. In this realignment,
human frailty had played an important part—the pliable
character of the Governor Arran, steadfast in one thing
only—greed for his own family's advancement, the intemperate nature of Henry VIII's attitude towards Scotland, the mature cunning of the cardinal, able to play on
Arran's weakness, and lastly the remarkable character of
the Scottish nobles of the time, who saw no point in pursuing any policy out of principle, once it no longer suited
their purpose, even if they were being bribed to do so. In
twelve months the possibility of the peaceful annexation
of Scotland by England, through the marriage of Mary and
Edward, and the direction of Scottish affairs by King
Henry, had receded with amazing rapidity. With the renewal of the French alliance, and the birth of a son to
Catherine de Medicis and the future Henry II of France
in January 1544, the prospect of a very different education and marriage unfolded before the child queen.

Four and a half years were to elapse before the young
queen of Scots was finally despatched to the safety of
France. They were years in which the policy of Henry
VIII towards Scotland did little to correct the impression
he had already given, of a vindictive bully, once his will

was gainsaid. In May 1544 Henry's commander Hertford set out on the first stages of what has been aptly termed 'the Rough Wooing', in which Henry paradoxically attempted to win the loyalties of the Scots by a planned programme of devastation of Scottish territory. His instructions to Hertford strike a note of ruthlessness which chills the spirit,[2] and the English records make it clear that their armies were remarkably successful in carrying out this 'scorched earth' policy, until the point when they were checked by the fortress castle of Edinburgh, which withstood their siege. There was no pity in the English hearts: an eye-witness account of the campaign sent to the Lord Russell, the Lord Privy Seal, in London, exhibits a positively self-righteous spirit towards these fiery depredations —the English seem to have considered themselves taking part in a sort of holy war, as a result of the broken promises of the Scots. The burning of Edinburgh—which took two days—is vividly described, and in the course of it the abbey and palace of Holyrood were sacked.[3]

The English also broke up the pier at Leith Haven, captured the Scottish merchant ships and finally set off for home laden with booty, taking care on their way to devastate the castle of Lord Seton, including his gardens and orchards, said to be the fairest in Scotland, because he was held responsible for the release of the cardinal, the author of all this calamity. 'In these victories who is to be most lauded but God, by whose goodness the English hath had of a great season, notable victories,' exclaims Lord Russell's correspondent. Allowing for natural English exaggeration of their success, even if half the destruction he reported took place, the Scots may surely have supposed that God had temporarily deserted the side of David for that of Goliath. The next rough embrace on the part of the English took place in November 1544. Coming up from the borders, the English forces laid about them as before; in the course of their campaign, they devastated the ancient tombs of the Douglases at Melrose, one of the string of rich abbeys along the fertile valley of the Tweed, hives of life and industry, which made them enticing bait for predatory English soldiers. It was, however, not so much this insult to his ancestors, as the fact that the Scottish government had learnt to counter the English bribes with gifts of their own, which persuaded the venal Angus to lead the Scots to victory at Ancrum Moor in

February. But the effects of Ancrum Moor were not permanent: for in September 1545 Hertford himself led a second, equally destructive expedition to the south-east, at a time deliberately chosen in order to ravish and burn the newly-cut harvest.

In this atmosphere of violence, the safety of the young queen continued to be a matter of concern—Hertford reported that at the time of his forays in May 1544 she had been removed to Dunkeld for greater security. In the same summer the state-craft of her mother Mary of Guise made its first effects felt. She had impressed the patriarch of Aquileia with her prudent and cheerful disposition, in view of her continuously desperate situation in such a divided kingdom as poor Scotland. 'I say poor kingdom,' wrote the patriarch, 'because it is so divided and disturbed that if God does not show his hand and inspire these nobles to unite together, public and private ruin is clearly to be foreseen.'⁴ Hertford's spoliations of 1544 did nothing to heal such divisions. On the contrary, considerable dissatisfaction was now felt with the policy of the cardinal, which had plunged Scotland into such a state of physical misery. From the summer onwards, the weight of the queen dowager's counsels were also felt in the shifting scales of Scottish national policy. Many nobles were beginning to feel that she should share the regency with the weak Arran. From its first volume, the Register of the Acts of the Privy Council marks her presence—*Presentibus, Regina et Gubernator*. It is safe to assume that Queen Mary's secret wishes were by now steadily in favour of a French marriage—France, her own country, the country of her able family, and the country with enough resources to quell the English, on behalf of the Scots, if necessary. The climate of Scottish opinion was not yet ready for such a match: it needed further action on behalf of England, to point the lesson that a French alliance, however confining to their independence, was at least preferable to extinction at the hands of their neighbours. Mary of Guise had also two specific hazards to overcome—Arran's desire for the marriage of Mary and his own son, and the cardinal's steady opposition to the idea of a French marriage, as marked as had been his opposition to an English one, for the same nationalist reasons.

But Cardinal Beaton's days were numbered. Quite apart from its political confusion, religious life in Scotland was in a ferment. Not only had high office in the Church become a valuable part of royal patronage, but in a poor country such as Scotland, with a primitive economy, the Church still presented a picture of disproportionate wealth. In a report to Pope Paul IV in 1556 on the state of the Scottish Church, Cardinal Sermoneta wrote that 'almost one half of the revenue of the whole kingdom' was coming in to it; it has been calculated that the Church revenues on the eve of the Reformation must have been more than £300,000, whereas the royal lands only brought in £17,500.[5] Such riches had in all too many cases cut off the Scottish clergy totally from a sense of pastoral mission and many of them might well justify Knox's abusive term of 'a greedy pack'. It was felt that while monks and friars idled and were supported by the community, the true objects of social pity—'the blind, crooked, bed-ridden, widows, orphans and all other poor, so visited by the hand of God as may not work' in the words of one contemporary complaint—were being neglected. The majority of the parish churches in the country had been assigned or appropriated to bishoprics or monasteries, and other churches had no priest at all. The provincial council of 1549 enacted a significant amount of statutes denouncing concubinage among the priesthood, or the promotion and endowing of illegitimate children. Repeated enactments by provincial councils urging the clergy to preach to the people showed both that the problem was pressing and that it was not being cured.[6]

Against this background, it is easy to understand the success of any anti-clerical movement: by 1543, the flames of unrest were being fed by a continuous fuel of books, pamphlets and broad sides advocating the reformed religion. Many were spiritual in content; the others were mere lampoons. The same parallel exists in those people who were drawn to the new religion. Many were men of the most ascetic nature, who felt they could no longer stretch their wings under the tutelage of the corrupt Scottish Catholic Church; others were merely animated by a strong dislike of the Catholic clergy. In time past the Scottish nobles had often endowed the Church with land, in order that they might be prayed for in perpetuity: their reactions, once it was explained to them by the reformers that these prayers were not necessarily an assured passport to heaven were predictably angry; the nobility considered

that the land should be rightfully returned to them. In
March 1546 George Wishart, a leading Protestant preacher
of outstanding gentle character, in an age not over-en-
dowed with the pure in heart, was burned to death in the
forecourt of the castle of St Andrews. Cardinal Beaton
and his bishops watched from cushioned seats on the castle walls. Three months later, a band of Fife lairds, disguised as the masons whom the cardinal had commissioned
to re-fortify the castle, broke into St Andrews, and seized
the cardinal, as he was resting after a night spent with his
concubine Marion Ogilvy. After holding him at sword
point, and asking him to repent the shedding of Wishart's
blood, they did him to death. After death the cardinal's
savagely mutilated body was hung naked from the fore-
tower of the castle for the edification of the people.*
Later, the corpse was pickled in salt, and kept in a barrel
in the famous Bottle Dungeon of St Andrews for over a
year, while his assassins kept the castle in their thrall.

Knox related the death of the cardinal with all the relish
of an Old Testament prophet who knows that God is on
his side. It was indeed an almost Biblical end for this great
prince of the Church. But his murderers, whatever their
motives, did not receive the immediate help from Henry
VIII which they had anticipated, once they publicly announced their support of the English marriage. The murder of Beaton had the unexpected consequence of bringing the prospect of a French marriage for Mary closer.
Henry VIII lagged in sending aid to the 'Castilians' as they
were now termed. Arran dithered, unable to condone the
murder of a prelate since his half-brother John Hamilton was bishop-elect of Dunkeld, but unwilling to send for
French help, which might spoil the chances of his son's
royal marriage—moreover as this very son was being held
hostage in St Andrews, he had a special reason for not
wishing to press the Castilians too hard. He compromised
with a long but ineffective siege of the castle, which owing
to its spectacular position on the Fife coast, with the sea
washing round the very walls of the castle, was able to
hold out for the unbelievable period of fourteen months,
despite the most determined mining operations on the part
of the attackers, from the land side. There was, however,

---

* 'Ane callit Guthrie loosit done his ballops' poynt and pischit in
his mouth that all the pepill might sie'—*Pitscottie.*[7]

a long period of armistice in the course of the siege and
it was during this that Knox himself entered the castle,
and began his career as a preacher in the pulpit of the
parish of St Andrews: he confirms Pitscottie's account of
the impudent behaviour of those within the castle, who,
when the siege was not at its hottest would ride out and
harry the countryside 'using their body in lechery with
fair women'.[8] It took the arrival of a French expedition
off the coast to bring the siege to an end: the castle fell
on 30 July 1547, as a result of which the principal defenders were despatched to France as prisoners, and many
others of its inhabitants, including Knox, were sent to the
galleys.

The death of Francis I, and the accession of his son
Henry II to the throne of France in the spring of 1547
had made the climate of opinion in France newly favourable to notions of French aid for Scotland: Henry II was
anxious to conciliate his powerful Guise subjects, whose
sister and niece were evidently in such a dangerous situation there. The death of Henry VIII, on the other hand, in
January 1547, had no effect in reducing the savagery of
the English attitude towards Scotland. In late August of
that year, the former Hertford, now Protector Somerset,
mounted an expedition towards Scotland which was to
rival in ferocity anything the late king had commissioned.
Throughout the summer, the Register of the Scottish Privy
Council is full of enactments to do with the coming war:
to impress the country with a sense of the emergency facing them, the fiery cross was sent to every district, as a
result of which the divided Scots seem to have made some
sort of genuinely national effort: 36,000 people hastened
from all over the country towards Edinburgh. These also
included members of the clergy, who had a special reason
for wishing to fight off the heretical invader and provision
was made that if any kirkman died in battle, his next-of-
kin was to have his benefice. It was in this do-or-die spirit
that on 10 September the battle of Pinkie Cleugh was engaged.[9]

Under the command of Arran, the Scots drew up in a
strong position on Edmonstone Edge, behind the town
of Musselburgh. Their ranks and spears were thick as the
spikes of a hedgehog, as an English observer, William
Patten, put it; the clergy were there, marked out by their
shaven crowns, their black garments contrasting with the

white banner which they bore before them; among the
magnates Huntly was especially magnificent in gilt and
enamelled armour. Unfortunately there was nothing in
the situation now facing him to supply Arran with the
backbone which he had so singularly lacked throughout
his career. Certain of his leading nobles' names had been
discovered on a list of 'assured Scots', the contemptuous
English phrase for those on their payroll, within St Andrews' Castle. Not only was he doubtful of the loyalty of
his lieutenants, including the flamboyant Huntly recently
ransomed from England, but he had no greater confidence
in the discipline of his troops. When the Scots hurled
themselves upon their traditional foes, needlessly abandoning their strong position, Arran displayed none of the
qualities of leadership necessary to hold them back. The
result of the clash between these courageous but scarcely
disciplined troops, and Somerset's well-drilled army, was
another horrifying rout for the Scots.[10]

William Patten described scornfully how the Governor
Arran fled 'skant with honour', followed by Angus and the
other chiefs, whereupon the whole army turned and cast
down their weapons, preparatory to flight. Patten's details
of the English pursuit are revolting if vivid: some of the
Scots tried to elude capture by crouching in the river,
with their noses breathing through the roots of willow
trees. The dead had their wounds mainly in the head, because the horsemen could not reach lower with their
swords, although arms were sometimes sliced off, and
necks cut half asunder. Patten noted that the dead bodies
lying about gave the impression of a thick herd of cattle,
grazing in a newly replenished pasture. While admitting
the severity of the English reprisals, Patten takes the line
that the English were playing the role of a schoolmaster
chastising naughty children for their own good. But quite
apart from the pillaging of the countryside which followed,
the casualties suffered by the Scots at Pinkie Cleugh
decimated their finest fighting men yet again, only five
years after Solway Moss.

The unconscious cause of this holocaust, Mary Queen of
Scots, now aged four years and nine months, was removed
rapidly from the possible area of conflict, after the Scottish defeat. Stirling Castle was no longer considered safe
enough, as Somerset raged about the lowlands of Scotland,
like a beast of prey. The place of security chosen for her

repose was a romantic and secluded island, Inchmahone, off the north shore of the Lake of Menteith, a few hours' ride from Stirling. Here, amid pleasant trees and luxurious vegetation, had been built in the thirteenth century an exquisite island priory for the monks of the Augustinian order. This priory was still in existence, but as it had been given *in commendam* to members of the Erskine family ever since 1528, it had become practically speaking their hereditary possession. Robert Erskine, commendator from 1529 onwards, was actually killed at the battle of Pinkie, but his family connections with the monarchy made Inchmahone a natural choice for a retreat. Lord Erskine was still numbered among the queen's guardians and in 1545, together with Lord Livingston, had been exempted from military service such as armies or raids against England, to look after the queen's person.[11]

Inchmahone, seen from the shore low-lying on the horizon of the lake, with its religious buildings, its sedge, its views of mountains and water, makes an ideal focus for romance. It is therefore not surprising that a number of charming legends have grown up around Mary Stuart's visit to it. Queen Mary's Garden, Queen Mary's Bower and Queen Mary's Tree all honour the memory of the child, not yet five, who spent at the most three weeks on the island. Although there are records of letters being brought to the island on matters of state, after she had been committed to the safe keeping of the commendator, Leslie makes it clear that she was only sent to Inchmahone during the time the English were at Leith, i.e. between 11–18 September, and returned to Stirling as soon as the English left Scotland—the English re-crossed the Tweed on 29 September. So much for the legends which have grown up that Mary Stuart first learnt Latin and other languages there under the tutelage of a stern prior, as well as finding the time and strength to plant a garden and a number of trees. In the middle of the last century, Sir William Fraser suggested to the duke of Montrose, the then owner of the island, that he should restore the bower with new boxwood plants to please 'tourists from America', who would want a cutting from plants supposed to have been planted by Queen Mary herself.[12] The best hope for the authenticity of such a bower, which cannot in honesty be attributed to Mary Stuart's short infant stay on the island, would seem to be the fact that Mary often stayed at Stirling in later

years, and might then have paid some unrecorded visit to
the island, in the course of which the planting took place.
But the real romance of Inchmahone lies more in its genuine and touching association with Mary Stuart as a
child refugee from English oppression, rather than in any
specific historical relic.

After her return from Inchmahone Mary spent the winter once again at Stirling, before being transferred to
Dumbarton Castle on the west coast of Scotland, in February 1548. The victory of the English at Pinkie Cleugh
was making it increasingly clear to many of the Scots that
a French alliance, at the price of a French marriage for
their queen, was their best hope of extricating themselves
from the morass of defeat and disunity in which they now
found themselves. They could not even call all the country their own: ever since Pinkie, the English troops had
occupied Haddington, uncomfortably near Edinburgh,
from where they were able to exert a stranglehold on the
south-east of Scotland. A council was held in November
1547 at which the queen's removal to France was discussed, as well as the necessity of placing the Scottish
strongholds in the hands of the French. By the end of December, fifty French captains had arrived in Scotland,
and on 27 January a contract was signed between Arran
and Henry II by which Arran bound himself to assemble
the Scots Parliament, in order to give its consent to the
marriage of the queen with Henry's son, her deliverance to
France, and the handing over of the crucial fortresses. In
return Arran was to receive a French duchy.

By June 1548 the French were actually landed in Scotland, under the command of an experienced soldier, André
de Montalembert, Seigneur d'Essé. D'Essé was to show
admirable sang-froid as a general, the quality hitherto most
lacking in the Scottish command. When messengers came
to him crying: *'Monsieur, voici les ennemis qui viennent
à vous,'* he replied without a flicker of astonishment: *'Et
nous à eux'*.[13] He also brought with him an extremely well-
equipped body of 6,000 men, including German and Italian mercenaries, the latter probably engineers, as well as a
quantity of light horsemen under two French captains.
D'Essé's friend, Jean de Beaugué, who accompanied him,
and witnessed the campaign, formed the impression that
the Scots' troubles as fighters sprang not from their lack

of courage, nor from the fact that they were less *'belliqueux'*
than the English, but simply from the *'ligues'* and *'parti-
alités'* with which they were plagued. He concluded that
they had been chastened by God deliberately during their
recent misfortunes, to teach them the error of their ways,
going on to observe with irritating superiority, typical of
the French attitude to Scotland at this period, that luckily
for them things took a better turn immediately the French
came to their rescue.[14] Whether or not the Scots themselves shared this view of their predicament, their Parliament finally gave its assent to the marriage of Mary and
Francis in July 1548, on condition that the king of France
should defend Scotland as he did his own realm, and at
the same time respect Scotland's independence. On these
terms, the marriage was described as being 'very reasonable.'

In March of the same year, the cornerstone of the Scottish–French alliance nearly fell from its arch when Mary
became suddenly and dangerously ill. The disease, whatever its nature, was violent enough for there to be rumours that she was actually dead. Huntly told Somerset
that she had smallpox, but as Mary was to suffer a much
better attested attack of smallpox later in her childhood,
it seems to have been measles, the explanation given to La
Chapelle in Edinburgh, which was responsible for her collapse on this occasion.[15] The whole incident illustrates the
perils in the sixteenth century of founding foreign policy on
the lives of children. However, by the time the informa-
tive Frenchman de Beaugué saw Mary at Dumbarton, when
she was being prepared for her journey to France, he was
able to wax lyrical in her praises. Even allowing for Gallic
gallantry, the unanimity of all the early reports on Mary
as a child, both now and on her arrival in France, concerning her physical perfection and conspicuous health,
make it clear that she was an exceptionally attractive and
above all energetic little girl. De Beaugué called her one
of the most perfect creatures he had ever seen, and felt
that with such splendid beginnings anything could be expected of her. 'It is not possible to hope for more from a
Princess on this earth,' he wrote. Looking beneath the
natural hyperbole of a courtier faced with a queen, it is
obvious that observers confronted with the child Mary
Stuart for once did not have to work out guardedly en-

thusiastic phrases for some delicate and sickly prince: able
to be genuine in their appreciation, they were further
spurred on by poignant thoughts of her destiny.

In July the French galleys arrived at Dumbarton, on
the west coast of Scotland, King Henry having sent his
own royal galley for Mary's use, to demonstrate the honour
which he intended to pay to her in France. On 29 July
Mary embarked on her ship, after a tearful farewell to
her mother, and with her went the suite which was considered suitable for her new estate in France. Two of her
royal half-brothers—Robert and John Stewart—went with
her, demonstrating the closeness felt by the monarchy to
its own kin, and it seems virtually certain that her eldest
half-brother, James Stewart, later earl of Moray, went
for a short visit, although he was back in Scotland by November of the next year. Also included in Mary's suite
were her guardian, Lord Erskine, and her governess, Janet
Stewart, Lady Fleming, an illegitimate daughter of James
IV by the countess of Bothwell, and widow of the Lord
Fleming who had fallen at Pinkie. Her natural royal blood
once again was considered to fit her for a post in the
queen's immediate entourage. In France the nubile charms
of the volatile Lady Fleming—to the Venetian ambassador's admiring gaze 'a very pretty little woman'—were to
be the source of controversy; she showed her mettle even
at the outset of the journey, when she became thoroughly
discontented with the long delay between embarkment in
the Clyde at the end of July, and sailing on the desired
west wind on 7 August; growing bored with life on board
ship Lady Fleming demanded to be put ashore 'to repose
her'. The captain of the ship answered smartly that Lady
Fleming, so far from being able to go on land, could go
to France and like it, or drown on the way.[16]

Mary's departure to France also marks the first appearance in her story of those romantic concomitants of her
adventures, the four Maries. A train of noblemen's sons
and daughters, about Mary's age, were taken with her to
France, it having been long traditional for young men of
good family to be sent to France for a sort of chivalrous
education. The Maries, in Leslie's words, were considered
'special', not only because they all bore the queen's christian name, but because they came from four notably
honourable houses. Thus Mary Fleming, Mary Seton,
Mary Beaton and Mary Livingston are introduced into

Mary Stuart's history. In point of fact Maries, or maids,
had been known before in the train of a Scottish queen.
The word Marie has its etymological derivation in the
Icelandic word *maer*, the official designation given to a
virgin or maid; from there it had come to be used in Scots
especially for the maids-of-honour attendant on the queen.
Pitscottie describes how Queen Madeleine, the first wife
of James v, was called on by her father the king of France
to pass to his wardrobe and take his rolls of cloth of gold,
velvet and satins as he pleased, 'to clothe her and her
Maries'.[17]

All four little Maries were of noble birth, but Mary
Fleming was considered chief among them by reason of the
royal blood which flowed in her veins, through her mother
Lady Fleming. Mary Seton came from one of the grandest Scottish families, being the daughter of George, 6th
Lord Seton, by his second marriage to a French woman,
Marie Pieris, who had come to Scotland as one of Mary
of Guise's maids-of-honour. Mary Beaton was the daughter of Robert Beaton of Creich, and grand-daughter of Sir
John Beaton, the hereditary keeper of the royal palace
of Falkland; the Beatons of Creich were a younger branch
of that family whose senior line had given to Scotland
Cardinal David Beaton, and were to provide Queen Mary
with her faithful ambassador, Archbishop James Beaton;
Mary Beaton's mother like that of Mary Seton had been a
French lady-in-waiting. Mary Livingston was the daughter
of Mary's guardian, Lord Livingston, and thus also lay
within the magic inner circle of families who could expect
to attend on the queen. Mary Stuart's Maries were very
far from being four ciphers, who could be dismissed
by one generic name; of widely different characters, they
were to enjoy widely different adventures. Although their
public lives all began at the same point on a galley sailing
to France in 1548, they ended at points far from each
other, and in all but one case, far from the queen they
were appointed to serve.

Accompanied by her train of lords, and her miniature
train of children, Mary Stuart embarked for France. Her
mother's sorrow was extreme, as the Englishman Henry
Jones noted when he wrote to Somerset, on 9 August. 'The
Old Queen do lament the young Queen's departure, and
marvelleth she heareth nothing from her.'[18] Mary of
Guise's feelings can be readily understood. For the

second time in her life she had to endure the keen pain
of being parted from her child, to be brought up in a distant land, by other hands than hers. Furthermore, her
daughter's journey was believed to be hazardous, and there
was no certainty that she would arrive safely in France,
since it was thought that the English intended to intercept
the galleys. It is true that this danger proved in the end
to be illusory: the English, who must have known that
the Scottish queen would shortly be despatched to France,
once Parliament had given its assent to the marriage, made
no serious efforts at interception. But this was not appreciated at the time of Mary Stuart's departure, and elaborate
precautions were taken to send her on the longer western
route from Dumbarton, rather than the natural short
route from the east coast, in order to elude the English.
Mary of Guise had to suffer the natural pangs of a
mother's loss coupled with fears for her daughter's safety,
at the same time as the political situation in Scotland,
even with French aid, was scarcely such as to promote
peace of mind. The combination of anxieties called forth
all the resources of this stoical lady, who returned for a
short while to the pleasant palace of Falkland to ease
her sorrow.

For the alleviation of her unhappiness, the French commander sent by Henry II, the Seigneur de Brezé, wrote a
series of letters to Mary of Guise, for which we are indebted for an account of her daughter's behaviour on the
journey.[19] On 31 July de Brezé reports that Mary is 'as
cheerful as you have seen her for a long time'. Whether
out of diplomacy or genuine feeling, de Brezé announced
that in the ten days in which the queen and her retinue
remained at sea without sailing, it was only Mary who
did not fall sea-sick. On 3 August, de Brezé reports that
Mary is still in good health and has still not been sea-sick,
in spite of the storms, which makes him think she will do
well on the open sea. Finally, on 7 August, they departed,
although the weather was still far from settled, and de
Brezé wrote to the queen dowager that on two or three
occasions he even thought they would have to go back to
Dumbarton again. The route taken led them westwards,
right round the coast of the Isle of Man, Wales, the point
of Cornwall, and so to the English Channel and the coast
of France. The stormy weather chased them all the way,
and one night, when they were about ten leagues off the

Cornish point, the sea was so remarkably wild, and the
waves so high and vast, that the rudder of the ship was
smashed. Dismay was universal. According to de Brezé,
it was only due to divine intervention that they were able
to replace the rudder almost at once, and so proceed in
safety, in spite of the heavy seas which were running. In
all this drama, Mary Stuart alone seems to have remained
unmoved, unknowing of the dangers ahead, uncaring of
the dangers around her. In high spirits, untroubled by
the maladies which laid low her attendants, she was even
able to poke fun at them for their sea-sickness.

The company finally landed on the coast of France
on 13 August. The poet Joachim du Bellay mentions the
general relief of the French at reaching dry land in his
Epithalamion on the marriage of Mary and Francis ten
years later.

> *Estant au bout d'un voyage si long*
> *Sans craindre plus ny les vents ny l'orage*
> *Chacun joyeux saute au front du rivage*

he wrote, with a vividness which suggests some member
of the court had provided him with a personal description of the incident. On balance of probabilities it is to
Roscoff, a little fishing village near Brest which sits out
into the sea like a ship riding at anchor, that the honour
of receiving Mary's first footsteps on French soil must
be given.* But there is no contemporary evidence to support the story that this famous footstep was actually
traced on the rock on her arrival, nor the tradition that
the chapel of St Ninian, now standing to mark the spot,
was founded by Mary later in the year. As Mary did not
return to Brittany in 1548, the chapel's origins seem to lie
among the many pleasant cobwebs of fantasy which surround her story.[20]

According to John Knox, Mary Stuart had thus been sold

---

* It was Roscoff which Henry II named as the landing-place, when
he reported the news in a letter written from Turin. Since de Brezé
wrote to Mary of Guise from S. Pol de Leon on 15 August, the
royal party may have travelled on to the port by sea; W.M. Bryce
suggested that de Brezé decided to date his letter from the larger
town for the better information of the dowager.[21] At Roscoff, two
hundred years later, another Stuart landed, this time in flight—
Prince Charles Edward, after the battle of Culloden.

to the devil, and despatched to France 'to the end that in her youth she should drink of that liquor, that should remain with her all her lifetime, for a plague to this realm, and for her final destruction'.[22] In the eyes of Mary of Guise, whatever her personal unhappiness, her ewe-lamb had thus been snatched from danger in ever-changing and ever-perilous Scotland, and sent on her way to the glorious future which awaited her at the French court. Of Mary herself, nothing is known of her feelings beyond her high spirits on the journey itself. As she was five years and eight months at the time of her landing in France, it may be conjectured that Scotland, Scottish life and all it stood for, for better or for worse, must quickly have faded from her mind, in favour of new and vivid French impressions. Some memories there were which must have remained, and the visit of her mother to France two years later brought them back to the surface. But in general, her recollections were at the mercy of the tales told to her by her Scottish attendants in France, since stories, often repeated, soon achieve the status of memories in the minds of young children. Presumably Mary's remembrances of her native land became rapidly formalized. The next thirteen years of her life, from the age of six to nineteen, were to be spent in France. The development of her character is therefore predominantly a French creation. Up till now, vague events of violence, political intrigue and flight have swirled above her unconscious head. From the moment of her arrival in France, the career of Mary Stuart embarks on a more positive course.

3 The Most Perfect Child

'The little Queen of Scots is the most perfect child that I
have ever seen'

KING HENRY II OF FRANCE

From the moment of her arrival in France, and indeed
for the next twelve years, Mary Stuart was the focus of
excited happy interest. The eulogistic poems and formal
epithalamia which poured forth from the pens of French
poets such as du Bellay and Saint-Gelais on the occasion
of her marriage in 1558 were not more laudatory than
the enthusiastic descriptions which were now penned by
the entire French court as well as her Guise relations.
Henry II himself set the tone. When asked what prece-
dence Mary should be given, he ruled that *'ma fille, la
Royne d'Ecosse'* should walk before his daughters, the
princesses of France, first of all because the marriage with
the dauphin had already been decided on, and secondly
because she was herself a crowned queen of an independent country. 'And as such,' he wrote, 'I want her to be
honoured and served.'¹ In marked contrast to her childhood treatment in Scotland, where she was considered at
first a sickly child, unlikely to live, and later a pawn in
a dynastic game, even at five years old Mary was hailed
as a figure of romance in France, a brave little queen
who had been forced to flee the barbaric Scots, the cruel
English, for the safe arms of all-embracing France. The
stage was already set in French minds for the appearance
of a childish heroine; to their satisfaction, Mary Stuart
with her charm, her prettiness and the natural docility
of youth, was ideal material to be moulded into the playing of this golden role.*

* It is noticeable that the French love affair with Mary Stuart has
been gallantly continued by many French historians; this point of
view may be summed up by the words of the eminent chronicler of
her childhood, Baron de Ruble, who, writing in 1891, describes: *'les
belles années qu'elle passa en France, jusqu'à la date néfaste où elle*

The first stage of her two-month journey towards the French court took Mary merely to Morlaix, where she was received by the lord of Rohan, accompanied by the nobility of the country, and lodged in a Dominican convent. She was then taken to the church, where a *Te Deum* was sung in honour of her safe arrival, which appears to have had but a limited effect, since on her route past the town gate, the drawbridge broke, and fell into the river under the weight of horsemen. The Scottish lords in her suite, their natural suspicions of the foreigners unassuaged after a week in France, immediately started to shout 'Treachery! Treachery!', at which the lord of Rohan shouted out indignantly 'No Breton was ever a traitor!' However, for the few days Mary remained at Morlaix, to pacify the Scots all the gates of the town were taken off their hinges and the chains of the bridges were broken.[2]

From Morlaix, Mary's route lay overland to the Seine, and she then proceeded up the great river by boat towards the castle of Saint-Germain-en-Laye, where the royal children were then in residence. King Henry himself was absent from his family throughout the summer and autumn campaigning. A request for M. de Brezé to join him meant that Mary's companion during her sea voyage now handed her over in turn to the care of her grandmother, Duchess Antoinette of Guise, who, it was planned, should smooth over the next period of transition before she reached Saint-Germain. Although we learn from de Brezé's report to Mary of Guise, made many months later, that the whole journey was punctuated with tragedy—both guardians, Lords Erskine and Livingston, were severely ill, and one of the queen's train *'le petit Ceton'* (young Seton) died at Ancenis[3]—this decimation of Mary Stuart's suite seems to have passed comparatively unnoticed, since into her life now swept the formidable lady who was to exert one of the strongest influences on her childhood.

The kindly interference of Antoinette of Guise in her daughter Mary's Scottish affairs, at the time of her marriage to James v, has already been noticed. Alone of Mary Stuart's close relations, she was blessed with longevity, dying only in 1583, four years before her grand-

---

fut obligée d'échanger le sejour de son pays d'adoption, un riant climat, la cour galante, et polie des Valois, l'espérance d'un règne glorieux, contre l'Ecosse, un ciel brumeux et le commerce plein d'aigreur et de perfidie des laird presbyteriens'.

daughter's execution, at the age of eighty-nine, though perhaps she herself did not view her longevity as such a blessing, since in the course of her life she was fated to witness time's sickle cut such terrible swathes in her family, that she in fact outlived all of her twelve children except one. The daughter of Francis, count of Vendôme and Marie of Luxembourg, she was married to Claude, duke of Guise at the age of sixteen. The birth of twelve children, between 1515 and 1536, was not a particularly remarkable feat by the standards of the time, but the vigorous strain of the Guises appears to have resisted the inroads of infant mortality with unusual vitality and of the twelve, ten survived; the mother of this remarkable brood was, in herself, a remarkable woman. She exhibited considerable administrative talent, which she handed on to her daughter Mary of Guise—not only at domestic economy, a subject at which she was considered to excel, but in the running of the vast and increasing Guise dominions, surrounding their palace of Joinville. Unlike her sons, she seems to have had a genuine streak of austerity in her disposition, and the great life of the court, the magnificent but insubstantial rewards of human glory, seem to have plucked no chord of sympathy in her nature. Her family pride, on the other hand, was enormous, and her sense of her sons' destiny on a similar scale. Much later in her history, when Charles IX offered her a choice of rank as a princess of the blood, to which in spite of the pretension of the Guises, she was not strictly entitled, she replied loftily that no rank could be more honourable to her than that of her husband. Traditionally, she kept her coffin in the gallery which led the way to Mass, dressed herself in black and with a proper sense of her own end, reminiscent of Philip II of Spain, surrounded herself with objects necessary to her own funeral.[4]

Antoinette of Guise also possessed a vein of wry humour which doubtless enabled her to endure the many stresses to which a matriarch is subject, and maintain her health and courage intact. At Joinville, for example, her famous charity was dispensed with a certain amount of common sense. When a convent of nuns applied to her for funds for building, she is said to have remarked dryly: 'Edifiez vos moeurs, et j'édifierai vos murs.' Masculine frailty met with an equally practical approach: on one occasion Antoinette discovered that her husband was hav-

ing a liaison with a village-girl, and their trysting-place
was a certain little hut on the edge of the estate, called 'La
Viergeotte'. Without raising the subject of the girl with
the duke, Antoinette merely asked him to meet her also
at this particular hut; with some embarrassment, the
duke agreed, only to find that the hut had been transformed into a luxurious nest of pleasure, decorated in
palatial style, and now in his wife's opinion, worthy of
his ducal position. Subsequently Duke Claude built a little
castle on the spot, with the significantly interlaced initials,
A and C, and the motto: 'Toutes pur une: là, et non plus.'

Duchess Antoinette was in ecstasies at the appearance of
her granddaughter, and wrote immediately to Mary of
Guise in Scotland to express the measure of her approval;
she also assured her that she would see about the little
girl's wardrobe, which, coming from Scotland, Mary of
Guise obviously suspected might not be up to the elegant
standards of the French court. The duchess was, however,
a great deal less enthusiastic over Mary's Scottish train,
whom she described as thoroughly ill-looking and farouche,
and with the exception of the captivating Lady Fleming,
not even, in her opinion, properly washed. The duchess
clearly shared the general desire of the French, whether
on the part of the Guises or the court, to have the complete education of this child, and thoroughly expunge from
her all traces of her Scottish past, which it was felt would
ill equip her for her glorious future role as queen of
France. The possibility that she might also one day have
to act as queen regnant to her native land of Scotland
was felt to be definitely subordinate. No qualms were
therefore felt at the prospect of cutting the little Scottish
queen off immediately from her Scottish attendants.
Mary of Guise, however, with superior foresight,
had sent instructions that Lady Fleming was to continue as her governess, despite the claims of a French
woman, Mlle Curel. The duchess wrote back to say that
her daughter's wishes were being respected. Mary Stuart
also retained a Scotswoman, Jehane St Clare (or Jean
Sinclair) as her nurse; de la Brousse hinted to Mary of
Guise that the nurse was difficult to please, for which he
blamed her Scots blood ('You know that nation,' he wrote.
'I need say no more.'), but Jean Sinclair was presumably
merely grumbling at novelty, in the universal tradition
of her profession, when finding herself in a foreign land.[5]

Antoinette has left us a physical description of Mary as she appeared to French eyes on her first arrival, in a letter to her son written in October. She is described as 'very pretty indeed' as well as being extremely intelligent, and her grandmother hastens to prophesy that she will actually be a beauty when she grows up, especially as the little queen is also graceful and self-assured in her movements. With the help of this letter, which as it was not written to the child's mother seems candid enough, and the earliest picture of Mary Stuart, dating from July 1552, when she was 9½ years old, it is possible to form a definite impression of her childish, pre-adolescent appearance. This drawing, in the Musée Condé at Chantilly was done in response to a request from Catherine de Medicis for portraits of all her children, to include her future daughter-in-law, Mary; as the French queen was apparently weary of endless identical stylized profiles of her children, she asked that the picture should be done swiftly in crayon, to give some sort of genuinely child-like impression.[6] The charming oval of Mary's girlhood face is well captured: it is evident that her features were of the type inclined to be hawk-like in later life, which had a special attraction when still enveloped by the softness of youth. Her complexion was glowingly white, and the texture of the skin, as her grandmother noted, especially fine. The nose, which was to lengthen considerably as Mary grew older, was now still delightfully balanced in the contours of her face and Duchess Antoinette also commended her mouth and chin as being particularly well formed. The deep-set eyes of which her grandmother wrote, were prettily set like two almonds beneath her high forehead; and their bright golden-brown colour contrasted with the fair, almost ash-blonde, hair which Mary enjoyed as a young girl. All in all, it was not surprising that the French court and Mary's doting relations were alike well satisfied with what they saw.

Duchess Antoinette now set in train the second part of the journey to Saint-Germain, which she reported to her son on 9 October she was making by slow stages. The care of the Guises for their nursling was more than matched by the solicitude which King Henry himself was showing, by letter, from a distance.[7] So thoroughly were the cleaning operations of the castle of Saint-Germain taken in hand on his instructions, that the children of

France were still at the medieval fortress of Carrières when Mary arrived there on 16 October. Two months from her arrival on the soil of France, she was now propelled into the royal nursery. It is difficult to believe that any set of young princes in the history of Europe have been so fussed over, so lavished with care and attention, as the children of Henry II and Catherine de Medicis. The letters of their mother are replete with maternal anxieties of the sort most generally associated with mothers who have no nurses, rather than with a queen, who might be supposed to have at least the duties of the court to distract her. This devotion, this concentrated attention to the *minutiae* of a child's existence, was fully shared during her childhood, by Mary, who received in addition the extra care of her Guise relations: so concerned were they over her welfare that her uncle the cardinal, that great prince of the Church, appeared as worried over her toothache and her swollen face, as about matters of national policy. Her grandmother, dedicated to the cause of her moral welfare, and her uncle, bestowing on her in youth the tenderness of a father, combined with the king of France himself, and the governors of his children, to make Mary Stuart's upbringing one of rigorous supervision.

The solicitude bestowed in such rich measure on the royal nursery of France arose to some degree from the special circumstances of the children's birth. Catherine de Medicis, a woman who has gone down to history as a mother before all else, and to whom much has been forgiven on these grounds, was for many years denied by fate the very role she most craved. Married off to the dauphin, Henry of France, with nothing to commend her but her relationship to the Pope and her dowry, lacking birth in the strict aristocratic sense, and lacking beauty in even the most prejudiced eyes of her allies, her early years at the French court were made still more unbearable by the additional torture of sterility. By 1538 there were rumours that she was to be sent back to Italy, to make room for some more nubile bride for the dauphin, one who would at least have achieved the state of puberty, unlike the wretched Catherine. What potions, what prayers, what magic arts Catherine summoned to her aid in her struggles with her cruel destiny will never be fully known. By 1540, with the help, it was said, of pills of myrrh given her by the famous Jean Fernel, she finally reached the state of puberty; by April 1543 she was at last pregnant. Finally, in 1544, Francis of Valois was born. He was sickly from birth, it was true, a weakness generally attributed to the many remedies his mother had taken both before and during the pregnancy, but for all that he represented security —he was a child, and he was an heir. The royal children of France followed in quick and satisfying succession. Elisabeth, later to be third wife of Philip II of Spain, in April 1545; Claude, who married the duke of Lorraine, in 1547, the future Charles IX in 1550, the future Henry III in 1551, Francis, duke of Alençon, in 1554, and Marguerite, the bride of Henry of Navarre, in 1553. Three other children died at birth. The princes and princesses thus made up in numbers what they lacked in rude health: none of them was robust and together they gave Catherine ample material for concern, from the right clothes for little Henry in hot weather, to the correct amount of food which each child should consume to make it either thinner or fatter.

Tenderness towards the royal children was not the sole prerogative of their mother. The constable of France, Anne de Montmorency, was also deeply involved in their welfare —it was indeed to the constable that Queen Catherine broke the moving news of her first pregnancy, saying that she knew that he desired to see her with children just as much as she did.[8] Another powerful force in the royal nursery was that of Henry II's mistress, the legendary Diane de Poitiers. The enemies of Mary Stuart, in her later career, have sometimes suggested that she was debauched in early childhood by the corrupting influence of this woman, who although already aged forty-eight when Mary arrived in France, exerted and continued to exert till his death the most total fascination over her royal lover. Diane de Poitiers, as her letters show, was a woman who, quite apart from her attractive interest in the arts, took an enormous interest in every part of the kingdom's affairs. This was indeed a considerable part of her attraction for the king: she interpreted the role of mistress in the true Renaissance sense, rather than in the nineteenth-century style of a grand voluptuary. She herself had been married at the age of fifteen to a man much older than herself, Louis de Brezé, by whom she had two daughters, and with whom, as historians now agree, she led a blameless life. She has also now been acquitted of the accusation that she subsequently sacrificed her honour to Francis I, in order to save the life of her father, the Seigneur de Saint-Vallier; it was this smear which gave rise to the story that she acted as the mistress of two kings in her lifetime.[9] Diane should be judged as the mistress of Henry II only, a position which she undertook as though she felt it her duty to exploit her undoubted assets—the beauty which age could not dim, intelligence, energy, and abounding health to support it all, health over which she took great trouble.

Her flagrant adultery with the king may contrast paradoxically to our notions with the excellent upbringing which she gave to her own daughters—Françoise who married the duke of Boillon in 1547 and Louise who married Duke Francis of Guise's son in the same year— but to the age in which she lived, the paradox was not apparent. Equally, she exhibited, without any sense of impropriety, strong maternal instincts towards the king's own children, and even on occasion towards his wife—for stories were told that she actually hustled the king towards the royal marriage bed, so seriously did she take the role of mistress. Certainly, she took infinite trouble to make both the Dame and Seigneur d'Humières her allies; she recommended a nurse for the royal children, and actually trained her at Anet first, to make sure she would give satisfaction; she enquired ceaselessly over Mme Elisabeth's measles and other domestic matters; the subject of Charles d'Orleans's wet nurse, and her suitability or otherwise for her task, runs through a whole summer of letter-writing. As Mary Stuart arrives at Carrières, we find that it is Diane who passes on the king's request that Mary and Elisabeth should share a room, since it is the king's dearest wish that they should become friends; again, it is Diane who expresses Henry's desire that the Scottish suite should be sent away, and the situation is accepted as perfectly natural.[10]

The first crucial encounter for Mary at the French court was with her intended husband, the Dauphin Francis. It is to be presumed that if these two children, aged nearly six and nearly five respectively, had heartily disliked each other on sight, the Scottish–French marriage alliance would still have proceeded. Nevertheless, the French courtiers hung over the meeting of the two royal children like so many sentimental cupids: whatever the contrast between the bouncing and healthy little girl, and the timid, sickly boy a year her junior, whose health had already been the matter of much concern, owing to the abnormalities of his birth, the meeting was nevertheless pronounced to be a great success. At the wedding of Francis of Guise and Anne d'Esté in December 1548, they danced happily together, as Henry II hastened to report to Mary's mother, while the English ambassador looked on sardonically. A few weeks after the first meeting, Henry was writing to the duke of Guise that Francis and Mary already got on as well as if they had known each other all their lives. By the March of the year following, Constable de Montmorency, commenting on the love that the dauphin bore for his little bride, described him as feeling as much for her as though she were both his sweetheart *and* his wife —'sa mie et sa femme'—a touching commentary on the contemporary conventions of feeling.[11] On the principle of the sunflower and the sun, a frail child naturally rewards a more healthy specimen of the race with its admiration; a younger child hero-worships an older one; an unattractive child responds to a beautiful one by loving it. On all these counts, it was natural for Francis to love Mary Stuart, even if he had not been heavily encouraged to do so. As it is, the constant reiteration of tales of his somewhat pathetic passion for her, from many sources, make it certain that his adoration for her was indeed genuine, and not just the projection of courtly wishful thinking.

Since we have Brantôme's word that Mary Stuart could only speak Scots when she arrived in France—barbarous and ill-sounding, he called it—she had evidently picked up enough French in the past two months, with the facility of childhood, to communicate with a fellow-child. Later, she was to be described, also by Brantôme, as speaking French with perfect grace and elegance: although she did not lose her Scots, French became the language which Mary naturally wrote and spoke for the rest of her life.[12] Possibly it was the hope of bringing this about which had influenced Henry in his decision to send away the Scottish suite; even the four Maries were sent to the convent of the Dominican nuns at Poissy, where the Prior François de Vieuxpont was charged with their education, instead of being kept permanently at their mistress's side. It thus came about that the most intimate female friend of Mary Stuart's childhood and adolescence was Elisabeth of

France, younger by two and a quarter years, a friendship shared, to a lesser extent, by her younger sister Claude. With these two princesses, Mary Stuart had in common the elevating but separating gift of royal blood; the fact that Elisabeth also shared the same nurtured golden childhood made her the female human being of whom Mary Stuart felt herself afterwards to be most fond, and of whom she retained the most nostalgic memories in later life.

The portrait of Elisabeth by Clouet gives an attractive impression of her lively face, full but slanting eyes, dimpled chin and large faun-like ears: she has an air not so much of beauty as of enjoyment of life, as she looks coolly across her stiffly jewelled dress. In girlhood, she was a sweet-natured child, who loved to draw with Clouet, and also, according to Brantôme, was fond of poetry and music. Claude was also reported by Brantôme to be fond of learning, as had been her Aunt Marguerite, Henry's sister, who did not marry the duke of Savoy until 1559, and was thus still part of the royal family at this date. Henry's own daughter, Marguerite, the high-spirited heroine of many later adventures in French court life, was over twelve years younger than Mary Stuart, and only came into the royal nursery when the Scottish queen had already left it for the court; her exotic character can therefore have played no part in Mary Stuart's actual childhood. The three brothers of the dauphin, whose tender health caused their mother such agonizing concern, were also sufficiently younger than Mary to play no effective part in these early nursery years, which are thus dominated by Francis and Elisabeth.

As yet, Mary had not encountered the father of the young family into which she was now adopted. This meeting finally took place in November. The confrontation from both points of view was eminently satisfactory. Mary Stuart saw a man of thirty years, swarthy and melancholy of visage, seldom smiling, obsessed either with the troubles of his government, or with the physical exercise for which he had a mania; Henry II, as one Venetian ambassador observed, found conversation with women difficult; it was part of Diane de Poitiers's prolonged and successful hold over him that he enjoyed her somewhat masculine intelligence, where other women bored him. In children, however, he took a genuine and tender delight. Mary

Stuart was fortunate in that she charmed him as a child, and successfully converted later the appeal of childhood into the more alluring appeal of femininity. Of Mary, he wrote quite simply that she was the most perfect child he had ever seen. Soon the cardinal of Lorraine was writing happily off to the child's mother that the king had taken such a liking to her daughter that he spent much of his time chatting to her, sometimes by the hour together, and by the time Mary was eleven the cardinal was able to report proudly that she knew so well how to entertain the king with suitable subjects of conversation that she might have been a woman of twenty-five.[13]

The next ten years in the state of France were among the most ominous in her history—for they were the years in which the seeds of civil war were sown. As the realm floundered in inflation brought about by an endless series of foreign wars and rising prices due to the influx of silver from the New World, the lesser nobility turned away in vain from the crown, which could no longer support them financially, to the menacing circle of great nobles which surrounded the throne; now religious division also reared its head, to augment the nation's woes. But although Mary arrived in France at the very outset of this disastrous period it would be wrong to paint these years in her life as anything but a time of untroubled private happiness, in which all the dramas were domestic, and the griefs and pleasures only the inevitable ones of every childhood.

It is often said that a secure childhood makes the best foundation for a happy life. In marked contrast to her cousin Elizabeth Tudor, Mary Stuart enjoyed an exceptionally cosseted youth. It is left to the judgement of history to decide whether it did, in fact, adequately prepare her for the extreme stresses with which the course of her later life confronted her. What is certain is that the first six years of her life have a dream-like quality, in which she appears to have been cut off from the rough events of politics by a cocoon of servants and other satellites, whose only duty was to nurture the royal nurslings in as great a state of luxury as possible. Her life divided into two parts—at court with the princesses and with her Guise relations. The Guises were, however, fully aware of the value of maintaining their little half-royal cuckoo well and truly in the royal nest, and made no difficulties at the

prospect of having her brought up so much at court—as
Duchess Antoinette pointed out in January 1549, on hearing that Mary was sharing a room with Elisabeth, nothing
was better for her future prospects.[14]

At this time the establishment of the royal children
was by no means a fixed entity: it was essential that a
household of such dimensions should be moved every few
months in order that the castle which it had inhabited
might be literally spring-cleaned. Mary's life consisted
largely of a series of glamorous journeyings under their
aegis: for example, the royal accounts for the year 1551
show that in January all the children were at Saint-Germain until April, when they went to Fontainebleau. On
1 May they were back at Saint-Germain, on 4 October
they were at Mantes-sur-Seine, and on 24 November at
Bury in Touraine, to avoid an epidemic, staying on the
way at Diane de Poitiers's new palace at Anet. 1551
shows the same pattern of movement, with the children
beginning the year at Meudon, in April at the palace of
Blois, Mary herself at the court in June, then back to
Blois, with the dauphin going to Chambord. In January
1552, the king took them all again to Saint-Germain.[15]

Unconsciously, Mary began to form the impression that
these palaces of such splendour, such dimensions, were
the natural habitat of royalty. To one who still dimly remembered the infinitely smaller castles of Scotland, the
French palaces seemed like the grandiose dwellings of
another planet. Fontainebleau and James v's palace of
Falkland, in Fife, for example, both had their origin in
the traditional royal passion for the hunt, yet how different they were in scale. Although Fontainebleau was far
from completed in its ultimate estate when Mary Stuart
first arrived there, the magnificent structure laid down
by Francis I, the two wings joined by the lofty, painted
gallery of Primaticcio, cannot fail to have impressed her
with its sumptuous display of Italian opulence grafted on
to the French imagination. The completion and decoration
of the famous ballroom, under the direction of Philibert
de l'Orme continued throughout the reign of Henry II:
there the interlaced Hs and Cs still commemorate to questioning modern eyes, either the king and his wife, or the
king and his mistress, Diane the huntress, whose symbol
was the crescent moon. In the same way, the palace of
pleasure which Henry built over the vast fortress of Francis

I at Saint-Germain, safe on its strategic escarpment, was
in the course of construction during Mary's French life:
but the immensity and scale of the buildings were already
in existence. The *châteaux* of the Loire had in the main
already been endowed with their fabled beauty and dimensions in the previous reign: to Francis I is owed the staircase at Blois and its exquisite Renaissance wing, another
triumph of the Italian style in France. Chambord, with over
400 rooms, seems to foreshadow Versailles in the flourish
of its enormous scale, the most spectacular of all Francis's
creations, for which work went on steadily despite the
growing bankruptcy of the crown. The richness of its
decoration, the impressive white mass of its building,
the unforgettable north-west façade across the water, cannot fail to have left an indelible impression on the mind
of a child—that this was how monarchs lived.

It would seem that the favourite *château* of the royal
children, the place they regarded as the source of supreme
amusement, was in fact none of the actual royal dwellings,
but Anet, the home of Diane de Poitiers, which she had
built for herself as a sort of monument to the spirit of the
goddess Diana with Philibert de l'Orme as architect. Du
Bellay called it 'Dianet', playing on the name of the house
and its beautiful creator, and the dauphin wrote with
boyish enthusiasm of the pleasures of Anet—what a beautiful house; beautiful gardens! beautiful galleries! so many
other beauties! Indeed, he has never slept better than when
at Anet, in a huge bed, in the king's own chamber.[16] The
position of Anet on the river meant that some endless
journeyings of the court could be made conveniently
there by barge. Today, even what still exists of sixteenth-
century Anet dazzles the eye with the perfection of its detail, the exquisite gateway with its balustrade, the marble
dome with marble brought from Rome, the statues of Ger-
maine Pilon, the chastely elegant memorial chapel to
Diane's favourite colours of black and white. But under
the sway of Diane de Poitiers, Anet was as remarkable
for its reputation for *douceur de vivre,* as it was for the
novelty and beauty of its buildings.

These constant journeyings meant that each month
dawned with new pleasures for the children. Their daily
trappings were equally exotic. They were, for example, surrounded with pets—in 1551 there were four big dogs
and twenty-two little lap dogs, as well as falcons and pet

birds. Horses there were in abundance, Fontaine and Enghien being the dauphin's favourites, and Bravane and Madame la Réale the favourites of Mary Stuart; horses also frequently formed the subject for presents, since the dauphin, despite his frail physique, had the typical burning passion of the Valois for the chase. At one point the royal nursery was even sent two bears by the Marshal de Saint-André, although the cost of keeping them in food proved to be prohibitive, and in addition there were tiresome reparations to be made for the damage they did, as for example, at Blois, where the home of one Dame Pillonne suffered from their ferocious attentions. The children were shown wolves and boars, wild animals from Africa. There were also two-legged amusements—troops of travelling actors and Italian acrobats were stopped on their route by the royal governor to entertain his charges, by performing *farces et buffoneries';* a *maître de danse* was despatched from the court by the king; there were bills also for choirs of singers, and players of tabourins. There were bills for materials for the royal children to make the sweets of which they were particularly fond. 83 *livres,* spent on a ball for the marriage of one of the princesses' chambermaids, gives the impression that the slightest occasion for rejoicing was seized on by this pleasure-loving household.*[17]

The moves of the royal household, delightful as they may have been for the children, meant endless upheaval for their servants: they frequently entailed staying at meagre villages *en route,* where villagers were apt to be angry at the loss of their food to the grand strangers. Roads were difficult and the quantity of luggage involved was a constant problem, as were the beasts to carry the luggage, whom the stable men had somehow to find or commandeer. Consequently transport, wherever possible, was made by river, as at Anet. The mountain of luggage used by the children was in part accounted for by their wardrobes. It was thought right that Mary Stuart should

* One charming tradition concerning the childhood of Mary Queen of Scots is not founded on fact: there is a story that the word 'marmelade' originated when a chef in the royal kitchens stirred and stirred his oranges muttering over and over again the words: *'Marie est malade',* until the oranges turned into a delicious golden mixture. Unfortunately, the word marmelade was already in use in 1480, deriving from the Portuguese *marmelo* (a quince).[18]

be more richly attired than the princesses, to mark her future position as their brother's bride. Her accounts reveal both the abundance and the formality of a royal child's wardrobe: yards of shot red and yellow taffeta for dresses, dresses of gold damask, dresses of black edged with silver, canvas and buckram to stiffen the dresses, white Florentine serge stockings, a *vasquine* or type of farthingale to hold out the dresses, shot taffeta petticoats and orange taffeta petticoats lined with red serge. Her accessories are equally elaborate: there is mention of bonnets of silver thread and black silk, orange wool to be dyed scarlet for stockings, furs to trim her clothes. Shoes are plentiful—ten pairs of ordinary shoes in the accounts of 1551, three white, three purple, two black and two red and also white, yellow, red and black velvet shoes. There are bills for exquisite embroideries on the clothes— rose leaves of gold thread for caps, and a bill for the embroidery of a device on a favour of white taffeta which Mary gave to the dauphin. There are bills for leather gloves of dog-skin and deerskin. The accessories are in keeping with the rest: a black velvet purse to keep the combs of the queen of Scots in, a crystal mirror covered with velvet and silk ribbons, gold and silver paillettes to be sewn on to her clothes, endless chains, collars and gold belts, as well as three brass chests to hold her jewels, which included a chain of pearls and green enamel, a gold ring with a ruby in it, and jewelled buttons of many different colours and shapes.[19]

The attendants who surrounded Mary Stuart and the French princesses were on the same lavish scale: indeed much of the troubles of their peregrinations arose from the enormous quantities of servants who were thought necessary to maintain their estate. The royal household had already grown to alarming proportions before Mary Stuart's arrival, so that by the end of 1547 Henry was forbidding d'Humières to engage any more servants; but it swelled again on the Scottish queen's appearance. Chamberlains rose from four in 1550 to ten in 1558, and *maîtres d'hôtel* from four to seven. The stables were burdened with attendants to cope with the royal baggage, and the baggage of the household. There were five doctors, thirty-seven pages of honour to grow up alongside the dauphin (although these at least received no wages), porters, four masters of the wardrobe, two general con-

trollers, and twenty-eight *valets de chambre* at differing wages to carry the infant princes, feed them and
serve them. In order to attend to the babies the Dame
d'Humières had twenty-two ladies of various ranks under
her command. The number of apothecaries rose from one
to three, barbers from one to four, pantry aides from two
to six—although it may be noted that in all this panoply
of service, there was provision for only two laundresses
and one bearer of water, leading one to suppose that the
royal nurseries were more luxurious than they were hy-
gienic. The kitchen was especially well endowed with
roasters, soupmakers and the like, the numbers once again
perpetually on the increase. Indeed, when one considers
the vast amount of food consumed either by the children
or more probably by their attendants, one can see that in
the royal nursery of France, wages, attendants, children
and cost chased each other upwards in a spiral reminiscent
of the economy of a modern state. On one day alone, 8
June 1553, the household consumed over 250 loaves of
bread, eighteen pieces of beef, eight sheep, four calves,
twenty capons, 120 chickens and pigeons, three deer, six
geese and four hares.[20]

Despite all this concern for material well-being, the
need for more spiritual attainments was not neglected.
Education was taken seriously at the Renaissance court,
and Catherine de Medicis, herself nourished in the atmosphere of Italian learning, was a considerable patron of
the arts. In the past it was considered that Mary must have
been a child of considerable academic brilliance, since
Brantôme described her reciting a Latin speech of her
own composition before the king and entire court, before
she was twelve years old. Certainly she learnt Latin, but
the discovery of a book of her Latin themes in the last
century has corrected the impression somewhat and shows
that, with respect to Latin, Mary was more of an earnest
student than a prodigy.[21] These Latin themes now exist in
the shape of a bound book, with the original French
themes set by M. de Saint-Estienne or some other tutor
on the left-hand page, and the Latin on the right-hand
page. Some are in the form of letters to Princess Elisabeth,
occasionally jointly with her sister Claude. Two letters are
directed to the cardinal of Lorraine, one containing the
suitable, if somewhat priggish sentiment: 'Many people
in these days, *mon oncle*, fall into errors in the Holy

Scriptures, because they do not read them with a pure and clean heart.' Curiously enough, one of the letters is actually addressed to John Calvin: but there is no evidence that the letter with its solemn, childlike invocation: *'Christus filius Dei te avocet, Calvine'*, was ever actually despatched and it seems extremely improbable that it should have been more than a youthful exercise, the original inspiration for which remains obscure.* Many of the themes are occupied with the names of learned women and girls, as befits a princess of the Renaissance, and probably many of them were actually done in preparation for the famous Latin speech.

Mary Stuart as a child neither had nor was trained to have the brain of the calibre of, for example, an Elizabeth Tudor. She was, however, by nature bright and quick, with a pliant turn of mind which her governess praised, because it made her eager to learn. Her schoolmasters, chosen by Catherine, included Claude Millot and Antoine Fouquelin. In true Renaissance fashion, she was given all-round education; she learnt not only Latin, but Italian, Spanish and apparently some Greek;† she learnt to draw; she learnt to dance, an art at which she was universally agreed to excel both in childhood and in later life; she learnt to sing—the songs of Clément Marot were special favourites; she learnt to play the lute, for which Brantôme described her long white fingers as being ideally suited.[22] Graceful, athletic, she was above all anxious to please those around her.

Her letters to her mother, the earliest, preserved in the Register House at Edinburgh, dating from the age of seven, shows her as having a clear, legible hand, remarkably like the even, rounded hand-writing which she retained for the rest of her life (although with age the writing grew considerably larger). This early, polite little note—whose neatness probably bears witness to some sort of overseer—ends with the characteristic salutation of any seven-year-old child to its mother—M. de Brezé will give

* The editor of Mary's Latin themes, A. de Montaiglon, suggested that Mary might have heard the name of Calvin often mentioned since an edition of his Institutes was published in Paris in 1553. But there is no record of any such edition in France, either in French or Latin, before 1562. An edition of the Institutes was published in Geneva in 1554.

† Her Scottish library contained Greek books.

her all the rest of her news, thus saving her daughter a
longer letter.[23] Mary Stuart's letters to Mary of Guise
bear witness to the enormous interest which the mother
took in the smallest details of her daughter's upbringing,
despite the distance which separates them: the sphere in
which she appears to have exerted the strongest influence
of all is that of her daughter's religious education. Mary
of Guise laid it down that her daughter was to hear daily
Mass; she was given a French chaplain of her own,
Guillaume de Laon, as well as retaining her Scottish one,
the prior of Inchmahone, who stayed with her in France
out of devotion, and without wages. In all the travels of
the court, care was taken to transport the young queen's
own communion vessels, so that she could receive the
sacrament from them, without any risk of infection; her
accounts include payments for a coffer in which to carry
these vessels around.[24] The religious education of the royal
children was supervised among others by Pierre Danes,
professor of Greek and later bishop of Lavane, and Jacques
Amyot, abbot of Bellosaire and translator of Plutarch.

Happily, Duchess Antoinette was able to report to Mary
of Guise that her daughter was extremely devout. When the
duchess and the cardinal felt that it was time for the child
to make her first Holy Communion, Mary wrote to her
mother eagerly of her desire to do so. She was at her
grandmother's at Meudon for the feast of Easter, and requested the necessary permission, not only because her
grandmother and her uncle thought it right, but also because she herself fervently desired to 'receive God'. Mary
signed herself: 'Your very humble and obedient daughter,
Marie'.[25]

In 1550 Mary of Guise herself came to France to judge
the progress of her very humble and obedient daughter.
Her letters of 1549 show her to have become increasingly
depressed and lonely in Scotland, for which the internal
situation certainly gave her just cause; she longed to consult with her brothers on her best course of action, as well
as to see her daughter and son Francis again; furthermore,
there was the perennial vexed question of her French
dowry, whose emoluments were more than ever necessary,
as a result of her financial straits brought on by maintaining the French troops in Scotland. This visit represented
the central point of Mary's childhood; overjoyed at the

prospect, she wrote off ecstatically to her grandmother: 'Madame, I have been very glad to be able to send these present lines, for the purpose of telling you the joyful news I have received from the Queen my Mother, who has promised me by her letters dated April 23 that she will be here very soon to see you and me, which is to me the greatest happiness which I could wish for in this world, and indeed I am so overjoyed about it, that all I am thinking about now is to do my whole duty in all things and to study to be very good, in order to satisfy her desire to see me all that you and she hope for. . . .'[26] Evidently Mary had conceived a sort of hero-worship for her mother, a superior being, the female equivalent of her splendid uncles, an image of strength, reliability and comfort, whom she wished to do her best to impress.

Mary of Guise landed at Dieppe in September, and arrived at the court, which was then at Rouen, on 25 September. Her household had made detailed preparations for the journey to fashionable France—although the recent death of the dowager's father, Duke Claude of Guise, meant that her own clothes were all of black, and her ladies at brightest in grey velvet and taffeta.[27] Mary Stuart had had a dangerous attack of flux in early September, but she was apparently well enough to be present at the regal reception which Henry and Catherine gave to her mother in Normandy. Throughout all the next winter, the dowager queen of Scotland enjoyed the plentiful pageantry of the court ceremonies, and enjoyed also the company of her daughter. Nothing seems to have marred the love which existed between mother and daughter, when a year later Mary of Guise sailed back to Scotland again; having had what turned out to be the last sight of her daughter in her lifetime, she left behind such strongly growing roots of love in her daughter's heart that the young Mary had a virtual nervous breakdown with grief, at the news of her death in 1560, even though she had not actually seen her for nine years.

In other spheres than that of mother and daughter relations, the visit of Mary of Guise to France was considerably less successful. She herself marred it to a certain extent by her financial importunities towards the French king: anxious as she was to pave the way for her final assumption of the regency of Scotland as soon as possible, she was determined to secure as many honours and as

much French money as might be available for her Scottish
train, in order to bind them to her. Her personal finances
were also desperately in need of succour: her servants'
wages were in arrears, she was forced to borrow from her
friends such as the countess of Montrose and Elizabeth,
countess of Moray, who could ill afford it, and also to
lean on the Scottish merchants as a possible source of
aid.[28] The lawlessness of Scotland had increased mightily
in the last two years, and hatred of the new foreigner—
the French who were now attempting to administer this
apparently barbaric country, by their own lights—was succeeding ripely to the previous hatred of the English. In
May 1551 Sir John Mason reported from Tours that the
dowager of Scotland was making the whole court weary
of her, from the highest to the lowest by being such an
importunate beggar for herself and her chosen friends. 'The
King,' said Sir John, 'would fain be rid of her, and she,
as she pretendeth, would fain be gone.'[29]

Two untoward incidents also marred the atmosphere of
the visit. In the first place—although no hint of it reached
the young Mary's own ears—her daughter's safety did not
seem to Mary of Guise to be totally secure. At the end of
April 1551 a mysterious plot for poisoning the young
Scottish queen was discovered;[30] it was devised by an
archer of the guard named Robert Stuart, but a certain
mystery hangs over the whole conspiracy, and it has never
been made clear exactly why, or at whose instigation, the
murder was supposed to take place. The French ambassador in London reported to the Constable de Montmorency
in France that a Scot named Henderson had revealed to
him Stuart's fell design. The would-be assassin had suggested to Lord Warwick and Lord Paget that by com-
mitting such a crime he might render valuable service to
the English Council. Warwick, by his own account, expressed horror at the proposal, and sent Stuart to prison,
but finally let him be extradited to France. Stuart was
thus imprisoned in the castle of Angers, and finally
hanged, drawn and quartered, without the enigma of his
true inspiration or purpose ever being cleared up. It
seems an unlikely moment for the English government to
have sponsored any such plan: firstly, the English had
not yet given up all hope of the eventual marriage of
Mary Stuart and Edward VI, and when Lord Northampton came on a formal embassy to France in the summer of

THE MOST PERFECT CHILD 61

1551, to convey the Garter to Henry II, he once again applied for the Scottish queen's hand. Secondly, the English were not noticeably enraged by the refusal of the French to entertain the proposal—a refusal which they had certainly anticipated. Northampton took the denial calmly, and according to his instructions, merely applied formally for the hand of the Princess Elisabeth for the English king, in the place of that of Mary Stuart.[31]

The second untoward incident was the flagrant love affair which sprang up between Henry II and Mary's governess, Lady Fleming. The king's eye lighted on the pretty Scotswoman comparatively early in her stay at the French court, for de Brezé reported on the success she was having, and with perhaps a certain lack of taste, Henry himself took the trouble to write to Mary of Guise and tell her what an excellent job Lady Fleming was making of her task as her daughter's governess. Regarded as captivating by her admirers, Lady Fleming also appears to have had a strongly irritating streak, which involved her enjoying her success at the French court to the full, but making little effort to accommodate herself to French ways in a manner which would smooth the path of the Scottish queen's household. When the question of a doctor for Mary Stuart arose, a letter from Giovanni Ferreri to the bishop of Orkney puts forward the name of a certain Scotsman, William Bog—'so learned he will bear comparison with any Frenchman' and also particularly adept at 'diagnosing Scottish temperaments'.[32] The understanding of Scottish temperaments was felt to be particularly essential in this case, because not only was Mary's 'temperament' held, for medical purposes, to be Scottish, but also Lady Fleming would not otherwise be able to explain what was wrong with her mistress, as she was incapable of communicating with a French doctor.

Constable de Montmorency saw in Lady Fleming's charms, and their effect on the king, an excellent opportunity of spiting his established enemy, Diane de Poitiers. The liaison did not succeed in toppling the favourite: but it did result in the incautious Lady Fleming giving birth to a son, Henry, later known as the Bastard of Angôuleme, whose famous agility in later life at Scottish dances at the French court bore permanent witness to his hybrid heredity. According to Branôme's wittily malicious report, Lady Fleming scandalized the

court by exclaiming aloud in French, which she spoke
with a broad Scottish accent: 'I have done all that I can,
and God be thanked, I am pregnant by the King, for
which I count myself both honoured and happy.'[33] Her
happiness at her condition was short-lived: her indiscretion was punished by her being sent home to Scotland,
as a result of the combined wrath of Catherine and Diane,
to whom no interloper was tolerable, and Mary was given
a new governess in the shape of Mme de Parois.

The departure of Mary of Guise, first to London,
where the French fashions of her ladies impressed the
English court, and then to Scotland for a renewal of the
harsh struggle for stable government, marked the breaking of one more Scottish link in Mary Stuart's childhood.
Even Mary of Guise's last weeks in France were marked
by tragedy, for her son Francis of Longueville, who had
greeted the arrival of his half-sister in France with such
generous boyish enthusiasm, and declared her to be the
most charming sister in all the world, died suddenly in
September 1551, the victim of some swift, childish disease.
'I think, Madame, that Our Lord wills that I should be
one of His own,' wrote Mary of Guise sadly to her mother
on the subject, 'since he has visited me so often and so
heavily.'[34]

The substitution of Mme de Parois for the errant Lady
Fleming marked a further step in the obliteration of
Mary's Scottish personality. Mary still loved to dress herself
up in Scottish national dress. She even managed to charm
the French with the spectacle, although to their critical
gaze her attire seemed dreadfully outlandish, if not down-
right bizarre: however, as according to a French print
current at the time, 'Scottish dress' for a girl consisted
merely of a series of wild animals' skins draped about the
person,* perhaps the dismay of the sophisticated French
court is not too difficult to understand. At all events it
was the graceful deportment and queenly bearing which
Mary brought to her garb which was generally felt to
carry the day. But for all Mary's enthusiasm for her native
country or its customs Scottish clothes were by now for
her definitely a form of fancy dress. Patriotism, wilfulness

---

* Plaid of a sort was already known at this date, and Mary later
wore it in Scotland; but tartan, in the form we know it today, was
not, and nor was the kilt.

or the desire to please might lead her to don them: nothing could alter the fact with the passing of every year, the progress of Mary towards becoming a French woman —a child of the smooth land of France rather than of the rugged land of Scotland—became still more marked.

4 Betrothal

'How happy oughtest thou to esteem thyself, o kingdom
of Scotland, to be favoured fed and maintained like an
infant on the breast of the most magnanimous King of
France . . .'

ESTIENNE PERLIN, 1558

By the end of 1553, when she entered her twelfth year,
Mary Stuart's charmed childhood was drawing to a close, in
favour of a more troubled adolescence. As the princesses
of France grew older, Queen Catherine decided that they
should spend more time at court in order that she should
supervise their development personally. The question therefore arose whether Mary should not at this point be
awarded her own household since, with the departure of
the princesses, her domestic arrangements seemed on occasion almost threadbare. The main drawback to the establishment of such a household was that it would entail an
extra financial burden on the Estates of Scotland, who
were scarcely in the mood to find still further funds for
the maintenance of their young queen in France, while the
budget for the French troops in Scotland remained high.
The cardinal of Lorraine was obliged to write a series of
letters to his sister before the final permission was granted.
One of his arguments was the keen desire of Mary Stuart
herself to be thus set up since at present she felt herself
to be shabbily treated—the first hint of a rebellious character in this otherwise docile little paragon.[1] The pleadings of the cardinal prevailed. On 1 January 1554 Mary
Stuart entered into her new estate, and to celebrate the
occasion she invited her uncle to supper that evening.

The choice was significant. Up till now the Guises had
been content to let their nursling spend much of her time
in the royal household: but from now onwards it was important that her character should be formed in accordance
with their wishes, and that she should receive her early
lessons in statecraft from the people who stood to gain
so much from her future high position in France—the

Guises. On her mother's side, Mary formed part of one of the most fascinating family nexus in French history, and it is impossible to understand the extremes of hostility and popularity which the Guises aroused during this period without considering briefly their antecedents. The family of Guise only entered France at the beginning of the sixteenth century when the widow of a younger son of the duke of Lorraine (then an independent duchy) applied to the French king to become naturalized French, along with his family of twelve children. The eldest of this family was Claude of Guise, grandfather of Mary Stuart, who was not only a highly successful general himself, but was supported on the secular flank by his ambitious brother the Cardinal Jean of Lorraine. But with success inevitably came jealousy. The Guises were accused of being foreigners by their enemies—Lorrainers rather than true Frenchmen. The Guises riposted by claiming that the royal blood of Charlemagne flowed in their veins, which, they said, entitled them to the highest place at the French court. This in turn led their detractors to accuse them of aiming at the very throne of France.[2] In truth nothing as thin as the last *fainéant* drops of Charlemagne's blood flowed in the veins of the Guises: they possessed something infinitely more potent—a furious life force and an admirable feeling of blood brotherhood. It is possible that the manner in which they upheld each other may have tempted Mary Stuart later in Scotland to suppose that all relatives supported each other as the Guises had done— a theory which the behavior of the Stewarts sadly disproved. At all events, contemporary historians began to refer to the Guises as the Maccabees.

Mary's future was affected politically by the power of the next generation of Guises at the court of Henry II, principally the two eldest sons of Duke Claude's enormous family—Francis, second duke of Guise, and Charles who followed his uncle into the Church, and became first cardinal of Guise, later cardinal of Lorraine in his turn. During her childhood Mary also formed deep attachments to some of her Guise aunts and their children. For lack of any brothers and sisters she came to regard these young Guises as her own intimate family, especially once she was grown up, and back in Scotland, no longer in such close touch with the French royal family. Her gentle and cultivated aunt, Anne d'Esté, wife of Duke Francis, she

loved with an especial warmth. The attachment was reciprocated: Duchess Anne wrote rapturously to Mary of
Guise that her nine-year-old niece was 'the most beautiful
and prettiest little Queen that anyone could want',[3] and
she only hoped that her own daughter Catherine would
be allowed to serve her when she grew up. When Mary
was older, she used to dance with her aunt in front of the
court, a sight which Brantôme romantically compared to
the two suns of Pliny appearing together in the heavens
to astonish the world—Mary being all grace and slender-
ness, and Anne having the statelier, fuller figure and the
more apparent majesty of bearing. One effect of Mary's
friendship with her aunt was to throw her together with
her little Guise cousins, despite the disparity in their ages.
The future Duke Henry of Guise was eight years younger
than Mary, a handsome, blond, curly-haired little boy,
whom Marguerite de Valois, his contemporary, considered
arrogant and overbearing. Mary Stuart, however, from the
vantage point of superior age, described Henry and his
brothers more sentimentally as the best-looking little boys
in all the world.[4]

The three main centres of Guise family life were the
palace of Joinville in the north-east of France whose
gardens and parks were much beloved of Mary and her
cousins, the palace of Meudon, close to Paris, and the
Hôtel de Guise in Paris itself. Meudon was in the course
of construction under the direction of Primaticcio and his
pupils in the 1550s, at the cardinal's behest to include an
exquisite grotto: Mary boasted of its coming marvels in
a letter to her mother. The magnificent Hôtel de Guise occupied the site of four previous hotels: on the vast
quadrangular space, the duke and duchess of Guise built
a splendid new hotel, in which the chapel, decorated by
Niccolo del Abbate from drawings by Primaticcio, showed
them to be patrons of the arts, and the staircase, decorated
by their emblem of the Cross of Lorraine, signified their
conscious pride in their family. In each of these three
magnificent homes, Mary was welcomed as the young and
promising member of the Guise connection, from whom
much could be expected.

The influence of the Guise family was marked at the
very outset of the reign of Henry II: at his coronation,
the new king received his crown from the hands of

Charles of Guise, who was created cardinal five days later. At the royal tournament in celebration of the event, it was Francis of Guise who made a particularly brilliant appearance. The glamour of Duke Francis was indeed such that anti-Guisard historians like de l'Aubespine, the courtier, could not bring themselves to condemn him totally, but were inclined to ascribe his actions, of which they disapproved, to the ambitions of his brother Charles.[5] The spell which he cast over his contemporaries was, however, due not only to his pre-eminent generalship, but also to the fact that he was fortunate enough to be able to come to his country's rescue on two dramatic occasions. The history of Europe in the early part of the 1550s was dominated by the rivalry between the house of Austria, personified by the Emperor Charles V, who included Spain in his vast dominions, and the house of Valois under Henry II. When the Emperor Charles handed over Spain and the Netherlands to his son Philip in 1556, this struggle narrowed to a rivalry between Spain and France. In this rivalry both England and Scotland were involved as pawns —England was linked to the side of Spain by the marriage of the English queen, Mary Tudor, to the Spanish King Philip; Scotland was linked to France by the planned marriage of their queen, Mary Stuart, to Henry's son Francis. But at the beginning of 1552, by making an alliance with the federation of Protestant German princes, who applied for help against the emperor, which allowed him to occupy the key border fortress of Metz and Verdun, King Henry had brought to an end the uneasy peace which existed between France and the Empire. In reply, the emperor massed his troops with a view to regaining possession of Metz; and it was Francis of Guise who gallantly held the fortress during the prolonged siege which followed. In February the next year, the duke of Guise was solemnly thanked by the French Parliament for saving his country; he seemed indeed to justify the verdict of his brother, that he was 'the most valiant man in the whole of Christendom'.[6]

The character of the cardinal is both more complex and less outwardly attractive than that of his brother. He certainly possessed intelligence, erudition and statecraft, amply illustrated in his letters, but there was also another side to his character on which anti-Guisards loved to dwell:

he was accused of avarice, probably with truth (despite the fact that he died deeply in debt and did not show much skill in managing his own financial affairs or those of Mary) since he was in perpetual need of funds to keep up his army of couriers bringing him political news from every corner of Europe. His ecclesiastical career certainly provided an example of pluralism: however, as even in youth he showed sufficient precocity to present King Francis I with a thesis on morals and theology, perhaps his ecclesiastical advancement was not totally unjustified. His sermons aroused the general admiration of the French court; in Holy Week 1560 the Venetian ambassador reported that no one could think of anything else except these uplifting discourses, which were attracting huge audiences—although at the same time the cardinal's enemies were busy in the streets pinning up scurrilous placards against him.[7] In his career the cardinal of Guise summed up most completely of all his brothers the dichotomy in the Guise character: on the one hand lay their superb endowment of natural gifts, to grace the public life which they craved; on the other side of the balance lay their remarkable family ambition, which was capable, under certain circumstances, of vitiating all their services. The dichotomy is seen in the two contemporary explanations of the family emblem—the two-barred Cross of Lorraine. At the funeral oration of Duke Claude of Guise, it was pronounced that the cross meant that the Guises would die twice for Christ, once in France and once in the Holy Land. But at the time of the Holy League, under Duke Henry, it was cynically suggested the double cross meant that Christ had been crucified twice, once by the Jews, and once by the Leaguers.[8]

It is difficult to estimate the true nature of the cardinal of Lorraine's religion, since by modern standards his determined persecution of the French heretics arouses abhorrence, and by the political standards of the day they led not to peace but to the disastrous civil wars of the next ten years. The word tolerance has a mellifluous ring in modern ears. To us, tolerance of another's beliefs has become a touchstone of liberalism, and intolerance is considered, by many, to be the final crime in a civilized society; but in the sixteenth century tolerance was certainly not among the public virtues expected in a ruler. As Father Pollen

pointed out, what to us may seem like defence of the
weak, seemed to them more like allowing vice to flourish;
liberty of conscience was scarcely worthy of discussion, let
alone worth fighting for. Sufferers on both sides of religious issues certainly did not expect to find that their
ordeals had resulted in the spread of religious tolerance;
they merely bore witness to their faith. The question of
how far diversity of religion could be tolerated was indeed
largely a question of public order: the Guises believed
that French Catholicism was strong enough to eliminate
Calvinism altogether, whereas in the next decade, Catherine de Medicis was obliged to exhibit political tolerance
because she found that on the contrary neither religion
was strong enough to drive out the other. In neither case
can true conclusions be drawn about their private qualities
of mercy. It is an interesting fact that Mary Stuart, whose
religious views, as well as her views on statecraft, were
formed with such care by the cardinal during her adolescence, showed throughout her career a quite remarkable
clemency and lack of bigotry towards her subjects of a different religion, marking her off from almost all her contemporaries, except possibly her own mother. Every letter
to her mother bears some sort of witness to the detailed
supervision which her uncle was now giving to her upbringing: deeply impressionable as she was by nature,
Mary Stuart's admirable innate quality of mercy could
certainly have been tempered by the teachings of the cardinal, had he so wished. On the contrary, it was allowed to
flourish, and guide her actions as ruler of Scotland in her
later career, for better or for worse.

The cardinal's lessons in statecraft encouraged the
young queen to take an interest in Scottish affairs. In her
letters to her mother on the subject, she shows aptitude
and application, rather than any marked independence of
judgement, and at every juncture quotes, or refers back
to the opinion of one of her uncles. Scottish affairs were
also the more vivid to Mary Stuart now that her mother
had at last succeeded in ousting the ineffective Arran from
the official role of regent, and in April 1554 her appointment was ratified by the Estates of Scotland. At the end
of one letter on the subject of some presents she heard
were coming from the Duke Châtelherault (Arran had
been granted this French dukedom in 1549 and was now

known by his new title) Mary told her mother that she
had shown the missive to her uncle of Guise as she knew
this was what her mother would wish her to do. On another occasion, she paid tribute to the enormous care her
uncle and aunt of Guise had taken of her—and most of all
her uncle the cardinal. In 1555 specifically on the advice
of her uncle the cardinal she sent back blank letters to her
mother signed MARIE* for administrative purposes.[9]

Despite the agreeable tutelage of the cardinal, and her
modest advance into the realms of statecraft, Mary Stuart's
adolescence was marred by a tiresome domestic drama, the
more enervating because it occurred right in the heart of
her little household. Mme de Parois, the governess who
replaced Lady Fleming, proved to be admirably lacking
in the human frailty of her predecessor: but she had de-
fects of character of her own which were considerably less
beguiling. Money matters led to constant troubles. On
one occasion Mme de Parois was forced to write to Mary
of Guise and ask for more money to buy her mistress's
clothes; Mary Stuart positively had to have a dress of
cloth of gold for the approaching marriage of the Count
de Vaudermont since she had been so annoyed at lacking
a dress of cloth of silver for the marriage of the governor's
son. On another occasion Mme de Parois bemoaned the
fact that the princesses' dresses were now lined with cloth
of gold, which made them so dear to copy, and she explained that the Scottish queen was very anxious to have
embroidered ciphers on her dresses, also an expensive
luxury. Permission was sought for two new outfits a year,
for reasons of prestige, whatever the lack of finance at
home.[10]

There was another side of the story: some of Mary's
entourage took the line that there was quite enough money
to go round if only Mme de Parois had employed it more
economically. The controversy was at times bitter and at
times petty. In one letter, Mary of Guise's controller enquired angrily what had happened to some money which
the French king had given to Mary to spend at the fair at

* Throughout her life, Mary used the name in its French form in
her signature. A feature of this signature, seen already in her earliest letters, is the fact that all the letters, including the first M are
made to be of the same size. She may have modelled her signature
on that of her mother: the two signatures are not unalike.

Saint-Germain. Mme de Parois continued to grumble over
the general shortness of funds, although she pointed out
primly that she took care to keep her young mistress in
happy ignorance of the situation. The fact that Mary's
accounts for the year 1556–7 showed outgoings of 58,607
livres and incomings of only 58,000 *livres* showed that
wherever that fault lay, the financial situation was certainly
not a satisfactory one.[11]

But now the governess fell out with her mistress. In their
fractious disputes, which read like a domestic storm in a
tea-cup, the real irritant seems to have been Mme de
Parois's ill-health. When she finally surrendered the post
of governess it was due to advancing dropsy; no doubt
her declining health exacerbated her troubles with her
charge in her own mind, and equally made her difficult
to deal with. The trouble began with the distribution of the
Scottish queen's outworn clothing, which Mme de Parois
felt to be her own perquisite. Mary had other ideas. In a
furious letter to her mother she complained that she had
given some of the dresses to her Guise aunts, the abbesses
of Saint Pierre and Farmoustier to make vestments, and
others to her servants, all according to her mother's instructions. In April 1556 the cardinal himself intervened and
wrote to Mary of Guise that in his opinion Mme de
Parois was no longer suited to be her daughter's governess.
Nevertheless, in the May of the following year, Mme de
Parois still had not been dislodged; and Mary wrote again
to her mother complaining that Mme de Parois was now
making such bad blood between Mary, Duchess Antoinette
and Queen Catherine, that Mary was terrified that the
malicious governess would go further and stir up trouble
between mother and daughter.[12]

The dispute does reveal significantly the direction in
which Mary Stuart's character was developing. There is a
vein of near hysteria in some of her letters to her mother
on the subject: she was passionately upset at the notion
that the love of her mother might be turned away from
her by the trouble-making efforts of this woman. She rebuts
with anguish the notion that she who is generous should be
so unfairly described as mean. The episode suggests that
from adolescence onwards, Mary Stuart was peculiarly
sensitive to the onslaughts of criticism which she had good
reason to feel were unfair. This feminine and perfectly

understandable sensitivity had dangerous possibilities for
one who was, after all, destined to be a queen regnant: for
there was no certainty that she would always be surrounded with the right sort of advisers to provide a balancing stability of attitude. The suggestion that the young
queen had become positively ill as a result of this domestic fracas is also of interest for her future. She told her
mother that Mme de Parois had almost been the cause of
her death 'because I was afraid of falling under your displeasure, and because I grieved at hearing through these
false reports so many disputes and so much harm said
of me'.[13] This tendency of apparently nervous stress to
show itself in physical symptoms almost approaching a
breakdown was something she clearly inherited from her
father, since the Guises were remarkably free from it: as a
characteristic it was to play a marked part in her later
career.

After a robust childhood, Mary Stuart's general health
began to show cause for concern in adolescence. When she
was thirteen, her uncle thought it necessary to write angrily
to her mother in order to contradict reports that she was
generally ailing; he told her that the verdict of the doctors
was that she would outlive all her relations, although she
sometimes got a certain heartburn or plain indigestion, due
to a hearty appetite, which would certainly lead to her
over-eating if the cardinal did not watch her carefully. 'I
am astonished at what you have been told about her being
sickly,' exclaimed the cardinal, in disgust at the very idea
of such tale-bearing behaviour. 'It can only have been said
by malicious persons out of ill nature.'[14] The truth was
that, despite the cardinal's vehement protests, all her life
Mary Stuart was to suffer from gastric troubles, of which
these were only the first ominous symptoms, and her fierce
appetite, coupled with sickness, stood for something more
sinister than the mere hunger of a healthy adolescent girl.
Other illnesses from which Mary suffered during adolescence included smallpox—possibly for the third time, if
the two other reported attacks in Scotland are correct, but
more probably for the sole occasion in her life. She told
Queen Elizabeth in 1562 that she had been cured and her
beauty preserved by the action of the famous physician
Jean Fernel—certainly in all the tributes to the famous
complexion of the queen of Scots, there is no suggestion

that it was ever marred by the pox. In the summer and
autumn of 1556 she fell ill with a series of fevers, possibly the precursor of the tertian fevers which haunted the
rest of her life, and for all his angry denials to outsiders
the cardinal's letters to Mary of Guise in Scotland show
that he felt extreme concern at the time.[15]

In 1556 peace was once again temporarily established in
Europe by the Truce of Vaucelles: the Emperor Charles v,
anxious to retire from the world and hand over his vast
dominions to his son Philip, agreed to accept the general
results of the war between France and the Empire for five
years. The cardinal of Lorraine was absent in Rome, and
his counsels had not been felt effectively at the French
court for six months; Henry II was swayed in his absence
by the advice of the great rival of the Guises, the Constable Anne of Montmorency. On his return home the
cardinal determined to undo the peace, which meant the
virtual wrecking of his work in Rome, where he had at
last persuaded the aged Pope Paul IV to enter into an alliance with France against the imperialists. As it happened,
even the constable was not totally reluctant to see the
great duke of Guise wasting his reputation in a series of
fruitless Italian campaigns: so that once more war was
resumed, and in Italy, for once, the duke was not immediately successful. The importunity of Philip of Spain to his
wife, Mary Tudor, queen of England, eventually succeeded
in bringing England also into the war on the side of Spain.
In August 1557 the army of the constable, on its way to
relieve beleaguered Saint-Quentin, was routed by King
Philip's army, which included English units. Philip now
captured Saint-Quentin and seemed set to march on Paris.
Once more it was Duke Francis of Guise who came to the
rescue of the French people. By turning the tables of the
war, and finally capturing Calais itself from the English
in January 1558, after 220 years, Francis of Guise not
only confounded those anti-Guise critics who had rejoiced
at his Italian failure, but also elevated the prestige of his
family to new heights.

The victory of Francis of Guise at Calais and the reap-
pearance of the bright star of the Guises had an important
effect on the fortunes of his niece Mary. She was now, in
the spring of 1558, over fifteen, and the dauphin was just

fourteen. By the standards of the age, Mary was marriageable, but Francis only marginally so.* But Henry II now
had two strong motives, both political, to persuade him towards the finalization of this marriage which had been
arranged in theory nearly ten years previously. The words
of the Venetian ambassador Giacomo Sorenzo, writing on
9 November 1557, sum up the situation: 'The causes for
hastening this marriage are apparently two; the first to enable them more surely to avail themselves of the forces of
Scotland against the kingdom of England for next year, and
the next for the gratification of the Duke and Cardinal of
Guise, the said Queen's uncles, who by the hastening of this
marriage, choose to secure themselves against any other
matrimonial alliance which might be proposed to his most
Christian majesty in some negotiation for peace, the entire
establishment of their greatness having to depend on this;
for which reason the Constable by all means in his power
continually sought to prevent it.'[17] Henry sent to Scotland,
to remind the Scottish Parliament that the time had come
to implement their promises. In years gone by, there had
been other matrimonial possibilities suggested for Mary
Stuart, despite her theoretical betrothal to the dauphin.
In July 1556, the French ambassador at Brussels threatened that if the king of Spain married the Archduke Ferdi-
nand of Austria to Elizabeth Tudor, Henry II would give
Mary Stuart to Lord Courtenay, an English aristocrat in
the line of succession to the English throne.[18] The aim of
this dynastic and diplomatic marriage roundabout was to
prevent the house of Austria establishing itself in England,
from which position it was felt it could effectively threaten
France. But in the end Mary Stuart was not forced to ride
on the roundabout. The death of Lord Courtenay, a few
months later, put an end to this interesting possibility.
Mary Stuart was given back her original position on the
chess board of the French king's policy, as the Scottish
pawn, who would help to checkmate England, by marrying
his son.

Commissioners were duly appointed in Scotland to

* It has been suggested, on the evidence of a letter from Henry to
Mary of Guise, that the French king had even contemplated carrying
out the marriage a year earlier, when the bride and groom would
have been only fourteen and thirteen respectively. This letter has
now been convincingly re-dated to the next year, and thus disposes
of the theory that Henry did ever in fact consider such a union of
children.[16]

come to France, in order to carry out the marriage negotiations. The nine envoys thus chosen included three supporters of the Reformation—the queen's half-brother,
James Stewart, the earl of Cassillis and John Erskine of
Dun; for in her anxiety to arrange the marriage contract
of her daughter smoothly, Mary of Guise determined to
exhibit the utmost conciliation towards the reformers, who
might otherwise upset the design to which she attached such
importance. The reformers took full advantage of her
quiescent mood, and as the marriage negotiations proceeded, so did the reformed religion and its preaching
spread in Scotland. The First Band of the Congregation
which pledged the signatories to work for the cause of the
reformed religion in Scotland, was actually signed by
Argyll, his son Lord Lorne, later the 5th earl of Argyll,
Morton, Glencairn and others, in the same month in
which the commissioners left for France.

Unable to leave Scotland herself, Mary of Guise appointed her mother Antoinette to act as her proxy during
the arranging of the marriage contract. As a result the
formal betrothal of the young pair took place on 19 April
1558, in the great hall of the new Louvre, with the cardinal of Lorraine joining their hands together. A magnificent
ball followed, at which Henry II danced with the bride-
elect, Antoine of Navarre with Catherine de Medicis, the
dauphin with his aunt Madame Marguerite, and the duke
of Lorraine with the princess Claude whom he later married. By the terms of the betrothal contract, the dauphin
declared that of 'his own free will and with the fullest consent of the King and Queen his father and mother, and
being duly authorized by them to take the Queen of Scotland for his wife and consort, he promised to espouse her
on the following Sunday April 24'.[19]

Despite the formality of the language, and the political
considerations which had prompted his elders to hurry
forward the match, the young groom does seem to have
felt genuine affection for his bride. His mother, Catherine
de Medicis, and Mary Stuart seem to have been indeed the
only two human beings for whom this pathetic, wizened
creature felt true emotion. Sickly in childhood, he had
become difficult and sullen in adolescence; his physique was
scarcely developed and his height was stunted; furthermore
there is considerable doubt whether he ever actually
reached the age of puberty before his untimely death, when

he was not quite seventeen.* The dauphin showed little enthusiasm or aptitude for learning, although his enthusiasm for the chase astonished the courtiers, considering his frail physique. All the Venetian ambassadors in
turn commented on the fact that he was an invalid, from
Matteo Dandolo who saw him when he was three, to Sorenzo who was at the wedding. Dandolo described him as
being pale and swollen rather than fat, but rather dignified
(as child invalids do often acquire a certain pathetic dignity). Obviously, for better or for worse, he soon became
conscious of his high position: in 1552 he was described
as having a considerable sense of his own importance, and
Capello commented again on the fact when he was eleven:
'He shows that he knows he is a prince', before going on
to say that he spoke little, and seemed generally 'bilieux'.[20]
This taciturn and stubborn character suffered from a
chronic respiratory infection, resulting from his difficult
birth, which cannot have added to his appeal, since it
prompted his mother Catherine at one point to write to
his governor and urge that the dauphin should blow his
nose more, for the good of his health.

However, the same ambassadors who described him as
a rather unattractive and self-important invalid also commented on the real signs of love which he exhibited towards his future bride. Capello wrote that he adored 'la
Reginata di Scozia' who was destined to be his wife, and
whom Capello called an exceptionally pretty child. He
paints a touching picture of the pair of them drawing apart
into a corner of the court, in order to exchange kisses and
childish secrets. When he was eleven, the cardinal referred
to him jokingly as 'l'amoureux', and when he was only
six, he was hoping to joust with the duke of Guise in order
to enjoy the favours of 'une dame belle et honnête', his
niece Mary Stuart.[22] They played childish games of chance
together: on one occasion Mary won 74 sols, and on another lost 45. In short, she was the companion to whom
he was accustomed, and she was in addition young, ro-

* He probably suffered from the condition known medically as
undescended testicles. The Protestant historian Regnier de la Planche
used these words to describe the formation of his body: 'Il avoit les
parties génératives du tout constipées et empeschés sans faire au-
cune action.' Although deeply hostile to the Guises, and thus prejudiced in many of his views of history, la Planche was likely to be
well-informed on this subject through his friendship with Catherine
de Medicis.[21]

mantic and beautiful—increasingly so, in the eyes of the courtiers. It would have been odd indeed if the dauphin had not loved and admired this exquisite and radiant bride being presented to him, who was in addition a comforting friend from his childhood.

What were Mary's own feelings for her bridegroom? First of all it must be said that it is not difficult for the young to be fond of those who are fond of them, and openly display this fondness. Furthermore, as a character, Mary responded exceptionally easily to love all her life. She was used to being loved in the widest sense, since her childhood; she desired to continue being loved, since it was a state she enjoyed; where she saw love, or thought she saw it, she found it easy to bestow her own generous affections in return. The dauphin loved her, of that she felt certain enough in herself, but in any case the Guises and the French court combined were always assuring her that he did. Her feminine wish to charm and please those around her, made her naturally want to show the conventional affection for her bridegroom which was clearly expected of her. And as she showed the affection, the imitative side of her nature made her begin to feel it. To those who have never known the transports of romantic love, companionship and the feeling of general approval are agreeable substitutes: Mary felt that she loved her bridegroom in the most worthy manner, although his infantile physique and immaturity make it unlikely that he actually aroused in her any of the feelings with which most adults would endow the word.

While the two protagonists of the match were thus perfectly content to be united, there were certain political undertones to the arrangements which were considerably more sinister than the innocent childlike emotions of Francis and Mary. Two marriage treaties were in fact signed, one open and one secret. The first official marriage treaty, whose witnesses included Diane de Poitiers, provided terms with which the Scottish delegates were adequately satisfied: the young queen bound herself to preserve the ancient freedoms, liberties and privileges of Scotland; so long as she was out of the country, it was to be governed by the regency of the queen mother, and the French king and the dauphin both bound themselves and their successors, in the case of Mary's death without children, to support the succession to the Scottish throne of

the nearest heir by blood—still the head of the house of
Hamilton, the duke of Châtelherault. Mary was given a
satisfactory jointure. It was further agreed that the dauphin
should bear the title of king of Scotland and that, on his
accession to the French throne, the two kingdoms should
be united under one crown, and the subjects of both
countries should be thus naturalized with each other, in
anticipation of the joint reign. Letters of naturalization
were granted to Henry in June, and confirmed by the parliament of Paris on 8 July. In November the Scottish Estates in their turn granted letters of naturalization to all
the subjects of the king of France. Up till the death of
Henry, Francis and Mary were to be known as the king-
dauphin and the queen-dauphiness. In the case of the
death of her husband, Mary was to be allowed to choose
whether she remained in France or returned to her kingdom; as a widowed queen, Mary was to receive a fortune
of 600,000 *livres;* should there be male issue, the eldest
surviving child should inherit both crowns, whereas if the
couple bore only daughters, owing to the workings of the
Salic Law in France, the eldest daughter would inherit the
Scottish crown alone.

All these terms were nothing more than those the standards of the time dictated, when a female heiress married
the representative of a more powerful kingdom. The only
condition at which the Scottish commissioners demurred
was Henry's suggestion that the crown of Scotland be sent
to France, to be used for the coronation of the dauphin.
As by the following November, the Scottish Estates had
agreed that the dauphin should be granted the crown matrimonial—which gave him equal powers as king of Scotland with his wife as queen—even this objection seems to
spring from an admirably cautious attitude towards sending away a valuable object to a foreign country, rather
than a disinclination towards granting the office itself.
The state documents of Scotland were henceforth signed
by both Francis and Mary jointly: Francis's signature,
however, always appeared on the left hand and Mary's on
the right—the left hand in this case, as dexter in heraldry,
being the more important position, because it was read
first.

At the same time, a second secret treaty was drawn up,
of which the Scottish commissioners were given no official
knowledge. Before the marriage contract was actually

signed, Mary signed three separate deeds by which, first of all, in the event of her death without children, Scotland and Mary's rights to the throne of England were made over freely to the crown of France; secondly, Scotland and all its revenues were made over to the king of France and his successors until France should be reimbursed of the money spent in Scotland's defence; and thirdly, Mary actually renounced in anticipation, any agreement she might make at the Estates' behest, which might interfere with these arrangements. If implemented, these secret agreements would certainly have had the effect of transforming Scotland into a mere French dominion, in the pocket of the French king. To some, the fact that Mary Stuart signed these deeds represents the first blot on her character. Yet surely Mary, aged fifteen years and four months at the time of her marriage, should not be judged too harshly on this issue, and condemnations should rather be saved for the French king and French statesmen who presented her with the deeds. She was given them to sign by an older man whom she had been trained from childhood to love and admire, and by the uncles who had been as parents to her, and had given her for the last ten years every proof of their devotion and welfare. She also had been brought up to believe that although she was virtually born reigning queen of Scotland, her actual destiny was to be queen consort of France. France was her adopted country, and half of her blood was French; as we have seen, little attempt had been made to preserve in her a sense of the true importance of Scotland. Although she had been conscientiously inculcated in statecraft by her uncle, the net result of hearing about her mother's troubles must have been to lead her to believe that Scotland was not much more than a tiresome colony or protectorate; it needed firm government, but had little right to sovereign interests, so long as the French existed to provide it with a wise administration, through the queen regent, and the French officials in power in Scotland.

All Mary's emotional inclinations led her to believe that the happiest fate of Scotland would be to be united with France—this was, after all, the union which she was about to effect by her marriage. She was far from unique in this attitude, in her age. The French panegyrics on her marriage exhibit exactly the same half-patronizing approach towards Scotland.[23] There are conventional tributes to the young queen's charms—she is Helen in beauty, Lucrèce in chastity, Pallas in wisdom, Ceres in riches, Juno in power. But the panegyrists agree that while the bride is beautiful, her country is a minor one, which must consider itself fortunate to be governed for the future by France. The wedding hymn of Michel l'Hôpital puts forward the political gain to France in acquiring new territory and revenues, it is true, but also expresses the view that the Scots will be delighted to gain a new set of rulers in the French. With perhaps a certain overconfidence, he suggests that even Mary's father James v will be pleased to notice Scotland now taking second place to France, as he looks down from his eternal resting-place:

> Nor would he shrink his ancient realm to see
> Ranked second in his regal blazonry.

A work of Estienne Perlin, published in 1558, and dedicated to Henry's sister, the duchess of Berry, observes patronizingly: 'How happy oughtest thou to esteem thyself, O kingdom of Scotland, to be favoured, fed and maintained like an infant, on the breast of the most magnanimous King of France, the greatest lord in the whole world, and the future monarch of that round machine, for without him thou wouldn'st have been laid in ashes, thy country wasted and ruined by the English, utterly accursed by God'.[24]

In such a climate of opinion, it would have needed a woman of maturity, and of stubbornly independent political opinions, not a young girl who had been trained to act in feminine obedience to her powerful uncles, to hold out against the signing of the secret treaties. In April 1558, Mary Stuart can scarcely be blamed for thinking more of the gorgeous pageantry of her wedding celebrations, than of the true implications of the three deeds which she had just been led to sign.

5 Queen-Dauphiness

'Just as we see, half rosy and half white
Dawn and the Morning Star dispel the night
In beauty thus beyond compare impearled
The Queen of Scotland rises on the world'
RONSARD *to Mary Queen of Scots, translated by Maurice Baring*

The French court, in true Renaissance fashion, desired its principals to shine out luminously against a background of endless pageantry; never were its wishes more splendidly gratified than in the marriage ceremonies of Francis, dauphin of France, and Mary Queen of Scots. The wedding itself took place on Sunday, 24 April at the cathedral of Notre Dame. The contemporary *Discours du Grand et Magnifique Triomphe faict du Mariage* gives a full description of the festivities, in which the writer himself seems to be frequently awed by the magnificence of what he is recounting.[1] Already in March, Henry had asked the French Parliament to stay at the convent of the Augustins, in order that its palace could be adequately and conveniently prepared. Notre Dame itself was embellished with a special structure outside in the antique manner, to make a kind of open-air theatre, and an arch twelve feet high inside. The royal *fleur-de-lys* was embroidered everywhere, and positively studded the canopy in front of the church.

The first sign to meet the eyes of the eagerly waiting crowds were the Swiss guards, resplendent in their liveries, who entered the theatre to the sound of tabourins and fifes. Then came Francis, duke of Guise, hero of France, uncle of the bride, and in the absence of the Constable de Montmorency, in captivity in Brussels since the defeat of Saint-Quentin, actually in charge of the proceedings. Then came Eustace du Bellay, the bishop of Paris, who considerately made sure that the view of the common people was not impeded so that they could see the show. Then came a procession, headed by a series of musicians, all dressed in yellow and red, with trumpets, hackbuts, flageolets, violins and other musical instruments. Then followed a hundred gentlemen-in-waiting of the king. Then came the princes of the blood, gorgeously apparelled, to the wonder, and presumably satisfaction, of the onlookers. Then came *abbés* and bishops bearing rich crosses and wearing jewelled mitres, and after them the princes of the Church, even more magnificently dressed, including the cardinals of Bourbon, Lorraine and Guise, and the cardinal legate of France (who had given the bride and groom the necessary papal dispensation for the marriage since they were cousins) and entered with a cross of gold borne before him.*

Now entered the King-Dauphin Francis, led by the King Antoine of Navarre and his two younger brothers Charles, duke of Orleans, and Henry, duke of Angoulême. Finally entered the centrepiece of the occasion, Mary, queen-dauphiness, led by Henry II and her cousin the duke of Lorraine. Mary Stuart, on this the first of her three wedding-days, was dressed in a robe as white as lilies, so sumptuous and rich that the pen of the contemporary observer fell from his hands at the thought of describing it. Since white was traditionally the mourning colour of the queens of France, Mary Stuart had defied tradition to wear it on her wedding-day; it certainly remained a favourite shade with her throughout her youth, and even in later years she loved to have something white about her face and neck: perhaps of all colours she felt that it set off her brilliant colouring to best advantage. On this occasion, her immensely long train was borne by two young girls; tall and elegant, she herself must have glittered like the goddess of a pageant, with diamonds round her neck, and on her head a golden crown garnished with pearls, rubies, sapphires and other precious stones, as well as one huge carbuncle worth over 500,000 crowns.

The young queen was followed by Catherine de Medicis, led by the Prince of Condé, Mme Marguerite, the king's sister, the duchess of Berry, and other princesses and ladies dressed with such grandeur that once again their robes could hardly be described for fear of repetition. The queen of Navarre had brought with her to Paris

* Mary's grandfather, Duke Claude of Guise, and Francis's grandfather King Francis I were second cousins; Mary and Francis were thus fourth cousins.

her six-year-old son, the future Henry IV, who at this wedding had his first sight of the capital which he was one
day to make his own. At a given moment, the king drew
a ring off his finger and gave it to the cardinal of Bourbon, Archbishop of Rouen, who thus espoused the pair,
in the presence of the bishop of Paris; the bishop then
made a wedding oration, described as being both 'scien-
tific and elegant'.

All the while, with typical concern for the reactions
of the populace, the duke of Guise was touring the whole
theatre with two heralds, making sure that the nobles were
not blocking the view of the people in the streets or at
the windows. When he was satisfied the heralds cried out
loudly: *'Largesse! Largesse!'* and threw a mass of gold
and silver pieces to the crowd, at which there was an immediate tumult and clamour as the people scrambled over
each other to help themselves—so much so, that some
fainted, and others lost their cloaks in their greed. Meanwhile all the nobility entered the church itself in the same
order as before, to find another resplendent royal canopy,
as well as gold carpets, within. The bishop of Paris then
said Mass with King Henry and Queen Catherine on one
side of the altar, and King-Dauphin Francis and Queen-
Dauphiness Mary on the other; during the offertory, further sums of gold and silver were distributed outside.
When Mass was over, the fine display of nobility paraded
all over again, with Henry taking the greatest care to show
himself to his people, although in the words of the *Discours*—'Monseigneur de Guise arranged everything'.

A long and Lucullan banquet followed in which only
one jarring note occurred to mar the general rejoicing: in
the course of the meal, the gracefully leaning head of the
queen, on its frail neck, started to ache under the weight
of the heavy crown which adorned it. King Henry had to
command a lord-in-waiting, M. de Saint-Seuer, Chevalier
de Saint-Crispin, to take the crown and hold it. If this
ominous incident portended the danger of placing too
heavy a crown on too young a head, no one at the time
commented on the symbolism. Otherwise nothing untoward
marked the celebrations, except that the Sire de Saint-
Jehan, favourite of the dauphin, had his eye put out during the jousting: but even this minor tragedy was not held
to mar the general sense of accomplishment. At the ball,

Henry danced with Mary, Francis with his mother, the king of Navarre with the Princess Elisabeth, the duke of Lorraine with the Princess Claude, and so on down the royal scale. This was only the beginning: when the ball was over at four or five in the afternoon, the entire court then processed to the palace of the parliament, the gentlemen on horseback and the ladies in litters. In order to give the maximum pleasure to the people, they travelled by a different route, and the crowds who rushed in vast numbers to watch them pass, almost blocking their progress by their density, were rewarded by a sight of the new queen-dauphiness in a golden litter with her mother-in-law Catherine, and the new king-dauphin following on horseback with his gentlemen, their horses adorned with crimson velvet trappings.

A new order of entertainment now followed, organized by the duke of Guise as grand master of the ceremonies: indeed, although the dauphin wrote sadly to the constable at Brussels, regretting that he would be absent on the wedding-day of his *'bon compère François'*,[2] it is doubtful whether the duke of Guise shared his new nephew's sorrow, since the marriage celebrations thus entrusted to him gave him a renewed opportunity to shine in the popular eye. The president, counsellors and officers of the Parliament were all present at the supper which now ensued, their scarlet robes mingling with glittering robes of the court. After a supper, a second celebratory ball was held, even more splendid than the first, and punctuated by an endless series of masks and mummeries, in which the royal family themselves took part. Twelve artificial horses made of gold and silver cloth were brought into the ball-room: the dauphin's brothers, Charles and Henry, the Guise and Aumale children, and other princelings then mounted the horses, and proceeded to draw along a series of coaches with them which contained a number of bejewelled occupants singing melodiously. After this spectacle, in which the fact that the gem-studded passengers were intended to be pilgrims, struck the only conceivable note of austerity, six ships were drawn into the ballroom; their silver sails were so ingeniously made that they seemed to be billowing in an imaginary wind, and the ships themselves gave the impression of truly floating on the ballroom floor. Each of these magic barques had room for

two voyagers, and after touring the ball-room, the noble
gentlemen at the helm selected the ladies of their choice,
and helped them into their boats. Once again, however,
in spite of the delicate fantasy of the scene, choice was
dictated more by court ceremony than by the promptings
of romance. The duke of Lorraine chose Mme Claude, the
king of Navarre chose his wife, the duke of Nemours
chose Mme Marguerite, King Henry chose his daughter-
in-law and Francis chose his mother. The further magnificence of the occasion proved once again to beggar description—for as the author of the *Discours* observed, no one
could really decide which was lighting up the ball-room
more brightly—the *flambeaux*, or the flash of the royal
jewels.

While distinctions of this esoteric nature occupied the
contemporary observers, it is, however, possible for us,
with hindsight, to see behind these elaborate ceremonies,
which continued for several days, and discern the tarnish
behind the tinsel. The land of France was virtually bankrupted by its prolonged struggle against the Empire, which
had involved it in such time-, men- and money-consum-
ing Italian wars. Yet Henry felt it essential to make this
luxurious display, to uphold the prestige of the monarchy
in the eyes of the people, and indeed the nobility. The
king of Navarre whispered malevolently into the ear of
the Venetian ambassador at the celebrations: 'Thou seest
the conclusion of a fact which very few credited till now'
and hinted that the constable had steadily opposed this
Guise marriage. The ambassador commented that the special pomp and display of the occasion was due to the fact
that no dauphin of France had been married in Paris for
two hundred years since they had all brought wives from
abroad.[3] It is, however, likely that King Henry was less
impressed by the historical nature of the occasion than
by his desperate need to wipe out the defeat of Saint-Quentin in the imagination of the populace.

There is no reason to suppose that this canker at the
centre of the gilded apple of fortune which now lay
within her palm was apparent to Mary herself. During the
wedding ceremonies, she had fulfilled the role to perfection for which she had been trained since childhood. Her
new husband loved her, and was scarcely likely to treat
her as Henry had treated Catherine, since the danger of a

Diane de Poitiers was remote in such an immature bride-groom. Boy-husband or not, he was nevertheless the dauphin of France, and Mary thoroughly enjoyed her elevated rank as queen-dauphiness, for which she felt herself to be eminently fitted, being unable to remember a time when she was not treated with deference as a queen in her own right. When she needed advice, her uncles were to hand, anxious to supply it. She enjoyed the feminine friendship of her sister-in-law Elisabeth, or her Aunt Anne of Guise. She was young. She was beautiful. She was admired. An ecstatic letter to her mother in Scotland, written on her actual wedding-day, is almost incoherent with happiness at her new state and mentions how much honour not only Francis but her new father-in-law and mother-in-law continually do to her.[4] Scotland itself seemed far away. Although on her wedding-day, the great cannon of Edinburgh Castle, Mons Meg, was fired, the shot reaching as far as Wardie Moor, not many reverberations of either this or any other Scottish explosion were liable to be heard at the French court of which Mary was the most lucent ornament. The first few months of her new existence as queen-dauphiness were among the happiest and most carefree in a life-span which did not turn out to include many such oases: this was indeed the time when Mary, like Faust, might have addressed the passing moment: 'Linger awhile, you are so fair.'

The legendary beauty of Mary Stuart has been much vaunted. She was praised in her own day by her contemporaries, and in the four centuries since her death her charms have often been extolled in literature and poetry. It is interesting to consider whether she was, in fact, a beauty in the classical sense of the word, or whether her reputation was based on courtly flattery in her own day, and the romantic circumstances of her history ever since. A true estimate of her appearance is the more difficult to make because no authentic portraits of her exist, dating from the years of her personal reign in Scotland. We have no record at all of her beauty or otherwise from the age of nineteen to twenty-five, generally held to be the peak years of a woman's appearance. The authentic portraits of her as dauphiness and queen of France, all done before she was twenty years old, are also comparatively few in number; yet it is on these we must rely in order to acquire an accurate impression of her appearance when she was

in her prime, since the next series of pictures were done
nearly twenty years later and spring from the years of
captivity. Her beauty has sometimes been judged disparag-
ingly on the evidence of these portraits—unjustly so, since
by then it had naturally been somewhat impaired by the
ravages of ill-health, and imprisonment, to say nothing of
middle-age itself. The beauty of Mary Stuart should be
judged firstly on the evidence of the French portraits of
her youth; secondly, since beauty, that insubstantial quality, exists so powerfully in the eye of the beholder, it
should be judged from the verdicts of her contemporaries
who, flatterers or otherwise, had at least an opportunity
of estimating her quality for themselves.

Whether she was a beauty by our standards or not,
Mary Stuart was certainly rated a beauty by the standards
of her own time: even the venomous Knox, never inclined to pay compliments to those with whose convictions he disagreed, described her as 'pleasing', and recorded
that the people of Edinburgh called out 'Heaven bless that
sweet face' as she passed on her way. Sir James Melville,
an experienced man of the world who prided himself on
his detachment, called her appearance 'very lovesome'.
Ronsard paid her superb tributes: he wrote of her hands
which he particularly admired and their long, ringless
fingers, which he compared in a poetic phrase to five unequal branches; he wrote of the unadorned beauty of her
throat, free of any necklace, her alabaster brow, her ivory
bosom. When she was a young widow, he wrote of her
pacing sadly but gracefully at Fontainebleau, her garments
blowing about her as she walked, like the sails of a ship
ruffled in the wind.[5] The word goddess was the one which
seemed to come most naturally to Brantôme in writing of
her: she was *une vraie Déesse* of beauty and grace; he
picked out her complexion for special praise, and described its famous pallor which rivalled and eclipsed the
whiteness of her veil, when she was in mourning. Furthermore Mary had the additional charm of a peculiarly soft,
sweet speaking voice: not only did Ronsard and Brantôme praise her *voix tres douce et très bonne* in France
but even the critical Knox admitted that the Scots were
charmed by her pretty speech when she made her oration
at the Tolbooth at the opening of Parliament, 'exclaiming *vox Dianae!* The voice of a goddess . . . was there

ever orator spake so properly and so sweetly!' It was also
a point on which even the most hostile English observers
commented on her first arrival in that country, including
Knollys and Cecil's own emissary White.[6]

Her effect on the men around her was certainly that of
a beautiful woman: the poet Châtelard fell violently, if
slightly hysterically, in love with her; not only on the eve
of his execution did he call her 'the most beautiful and
the most cruel princess in the world', but on their journey
back to Scotland he exclaimed that the galleys needed no
lanterns to light their way 'since the eyes of this Queen
suffice to light up the whole sea with their lovely fire'. The
Seigneur de Damville was also said to have been so enamoured of the young queen that he followed her to Scotland,
leaving his young wife at home, and if we are to believe
Brantôme, Mary's little brother-in-law Charles was so
much in love with her that he used to gaze at her portrait
with longing and desired to marry her himself after the
untimely death of Francis.[7] In Scotland Mary's beauty
as well as her position was said to have captured not only
the obsessional Arran, but the dashing Sir John Gordon
and the youthful handsome George Douglas. Her first
English jailer, Sir Francis Knollys, although unpromising
material for female wiles, was considerably seduced by
the charming personality of his captive; and although the
later so-called *affaire* with Lord Shrewsbury was undoubtedly the creation of his wife's malicious imagination, nevertheless the fact that the accusation could be taken so seriously by the English court shows that all her life Mary was
considered a beautiful and desirable woman, whose physical attractions could never be totally left out of account. At the time of her illness at Jedburgh when she was
twenty-three, the Venetian ambassador wrote of her being
a princess who was 'personally the most beautiful in Europe'.[8] There seems no reason to doubt that this was the
general verdict of Europe during her lifetime, and that
Mary Queen of Scots was a romantic figure to her own age,
no less than to subsequent generations.

Despite these tributes, a consideration of her physi-
ognomy leads one to believe that Mary Stuart was not a
beauty in the classical sense—to use the language of our
own day, she was an outstandingly attractive woman,
rather than an outstandingly beautiful one. Her most

marked physical characteristic to outside eyes must have
been her height, and it is said that when she fled to England from Scotland after her defeat at Langside, strangers
recognized her by it. In an age when the average height of
the men was considerably shorter than it is today, Mary
Stuart was probably about five feet eleven inches tall, that
is to say, taller than all but the tallest women today. She
grew fast in adolescence, as her grandmother indicated in
her letters. At her French wedding she is said to have
stood shoulder to shoulder with her Guise uncles: obviously she inherited this height from her mother, Mary of
Guise, who in her day was celebrated for her upstanding
stature throughout Europe. Even at the date of her execution, when Mary was humped by age and rheumatics, an
English eye-witness still noted that she was 'of stature tall';[9]
and the figure on her tomb in Westminster Abbey, modelled from details taken immediately after her death, is five
feet eleven inches long. Yet clearly, this stature was never
considered to be a disadvantage, and her height, when described, is always commented on with admiration.* This
may be in part due to the fact that, although tall, Mary
had extremely delicate bones, unlike her mother who had
much sturdier proportions. Mary's height, and the slender-
ness of her youth, which lasted until ill-health and the
troubles of captivity made her put on weight in middle-age,
combined to give an appearance of graceful elongation:
it also made her an excellent dancer, as both Conaeus
and Melville bear witness, and a good athlete, who could
hunt, hawk and even ride at the head of an army, in a
manner calculated to dazzle the public eye at a time when
the personal image of a sovereign was of marked consequence.

The portraits of Mary Stuart show that she had a small,
well-turned head, and beautiful long hands; coins in particular reveal that she had a neck which was positively
swan-like. One of her special charms was her colouring;
the blonde hair of her childhood had darkened by the time

* When Melville told Queen Elizabeth that Mary was 'higher'
than her, Elizabeth remarked jealously that the rival queen must be
'over high'. But, of course, Elizabeth, despite her obsession on the
subject of Mary's beauty, never actually met her: no man who saw
her ever suggested that the queen of Scots was 'over high'.

of her marriage to a shade just lighter than auburn—a bright golden-red. The Deuil Blanc portrait† shows that her eyes were almost the same colour as her hair, a colour like amber, which today would probably be described as hazel, and this colouring was of course certainly set off to brilliant advantage by her incomparable complexion. Curiously enough Mary seems to have had rather similar colouring to her cousin Elizabeth, yet one woman was generally accounted a beauty by her contemporaries, and the other was engaged in a constant, tenacious battle to extract the reassurance of compliments from her courtiers, having been so deprived of them in youth. Possibly it was the quality of the skin which distinguished the cousins as young women: Elizabeth as a young girl was described as having a good skin of somewhat sallow ('olivastra') tint by the Venetian ambassador at the English court—and this was an age when a luxurious skin was considered a prerequisite of beauty.[11]

It was Mary's heavy lowered eyelids, under their delicately arched brows, which gave a brooding almost sensual look to her face, a physical characteristic which was to increase with age. Otherwise her features were extraordinarily firm and regular. The drawing of Mary as dauphiness shows that by the time she was fifteen, the soft roundness of her childish face had formed into a perfect oval. Although her nose was long, it was not yet pronouncedly so, and the slight aquiline tendency is only just perceptible in the drawing. Her chin was well-modelled, her mouth, fashionably small, had a pretty curve; she had a beautiful high 'bombée' forehead, which the caps and veils of the time set off to perfection; and her ears, although large, were elegantly made, and seemed indeed specially designed to bear the lambent ear-rings of the time.

Above all, in her length, her small neat head, her grace, we may suppose that Mary Stuart resembled the contem-

---

†It has recently been pointed out that Mary was not wearing her white mourning in this portrait for Francis II, since the picture was painted some time prior to August 1560 when Throckmorton reported Mary's intention of sending her portrait to Elizabeth, and how she commented to him: 'I perceive you like me better when I look sadly than when I look merrily, for it is told me that you desired to have me pictured when I wore the Deuil.' Mary was therefore in mourning for her father-in-law Henry or her mother, Mary of Guise.[10]

porary Mannerist ideal. A small bronze bust of her in
the Louvre, possibly by Germain Pilon, which is regarded
as an authentic if not necessarily contemporary attempt
at her features when queen of France, shows the lovely
leaning head, the long almond-shaped eyes, and the beautiful disposition of head, neck and shoulder. How significantly she resembled the Mannerist figures of the time, the
elongated figures and angular disposition of Primaticcio's
designs, the long and delicate forms, the tapering limbs,
thin necks and small heads of the figures in the Galerie
d'Etampes at Fontainebleau, or the sculptures of Jean
Goujon. It was the same grace and elegance which her
contemporaries admired in Mary Stuart, the type of
beauty which they were already learning to admire in art,
and could now appreciate in life, all the more satisfyingly
because it was in the person of a princess. Nor must it be
forgotten that to these physical attributes she added the
essential human ingredient of charm, a charm so powerful
that even Knox was openly afraid of its effects on her
Scottish subjects—and perhaps, in his heart of hearts, also
upon himself. It was the charm of Mary Stuart, that
charm which is at once more dangerous and the most desirable of all human qualities, which put the finishing
touches to her beauty in the eyes of her beholders.

Not only the appearance, but also the character of
Mary Stuart made her admirably suited to be a princess
of France in the age in which she lived. The years she
spent in France represented the classical period when art
and architecture flourished there; it was a time when there
was a remarkable flowering in all intellectual fields as
writers and artists began to free themselves from the tutelage of Italy. Not only did Primaticcio and Serlio prosper,
but individual figures appeared like Philibert de l'Orme
whose art was not only classical but genuinely French.
Philibert de l'Orme and Goujon, on the one hand, and
Ronsard and Pléiade on the other, created the first original and independent movements since the Renaissance first
touched France. This culture was firmly centred round the
court, the court at which Mary Stuart glittered, and the
tributes paid to her by the poets of the time make it clear
that she was the ideal star to be shining in the firmament at
this particular moment. She loved their company: 'Above
all,' wrote Brantôme, 'she delighted in poetry and poets,
and most of all in M. de Ronsard, M. du Bellay and M.

de Maisonfleur, who had made such fine poems and elegies
for her, which I have often seen her read to herself in
France and in Scotland, with tears in her eyes and sighs
in her heart.'[12] Mary was exactly the sort of beautiful
woman, not precisely brilliant, but well-educated and
charming, who inspired and stimulated poets by her presence to feats of homage, which were also able to take their
place in the annals of literature. It was an admirable combination of artist and subject, of the sort which occurs
throughout history; and Mary Stuart's own verses, although of a simple and modest nature,* do at least illustrate her love and sympathy for the art of poetry.

The odes of Maisonfleur in praise of Mary Stuart have
vanished from the eye; du Bellay, however, celebrated her
personal attractions in several poems, including a sonnet
in 1557, and a Latin poem celebrating her forthcoming
marriage, in which he described heaven as endowing her
with beauty of spirit and of face, together with royal grace
and honour. With Ronsard the young queen enjoyed a
genuine and long-lasting friendship: the fact that Ronsard had been in Scotland at the court of James v added a
special poignancy to their relationship, since Ronsard understood the very different conditions of the island from
which she had sprung, and to which she might one day
return. In the first verses he dedicated to her, which appeared in 1556, he certainly reminded her of the fact, and
how, since her arrival in France, he had served as her
tutor in poetry, hailing her in lavish terms as 'o belle et
plus que belle et agréable Aurore'. It has been suggested
that it was in response to a request from Mary that Ronsard published the first collected edition of his works in
1560;[14] when she departed from France, he denounced
the cruel fortune which had led Scotland to seize her.
When Châtelard faced the executioner, according to Brantôme, he refused all other consolation except the hymns
of Ronsard, which he had been asked by Ronsard to present the Scottish queen. Four years after her departure,
Ronsard sent Mary his newest volume by the French am-

* The poem most commonly attributed to her, *Adieu, plaisant
pays de France*, has been shown to be the work of an eighteenth-
century French journalist. The authentic poetry of Mary Stuart can
best be judged from the poignant lines she wrote on the death of
Francis, the sonnet by her to Queen Elizabeth in 1568, and the poems
written during her captivity, published by John Leslie.[13]

bassador, and he boasted that he kept her portrait continually in front of him in his library.

It is sad to record that even Ronsard, despite these high-flown sentiments, occasionally deserted Mary's shrine. In July 1565 he published a verse collection *Elegies, Mascarades et Bergeries;* although *Bergeries* is dedicated to the queen of Scotland, the first two portions are dedicated to the queen of England, and contain a quatrain suggesting that Queen Elizabeth rivalled in beauty the queen of Scotland, being two brilliant suns contained within the same island. For this outburst, he received a fine diamond from the queen of England. He may perhaps be forgiven for this temporary disloyalty for the beauty of his sonnet to Mary in captivity: he wrote that nothing now remained to him except the sorrow which unceasingly recalled to his heart the memory of his fair princess, and harangued with anger the queen who had imprisoned her—'*Royne, qui enfermez une Royne si rare*'. It was probably for this pledge of ancient loyalties, romantically renewed, that Mary's secretary sent Ronsard 2,000 crowns and Mary herself responded:

> *Ronsard, si ton bon cueur de gentille nature*
> *Tement pour le respect dun peu de nouriture*
> *Quen tes plus jeunes ans tu as resceu d'un Roy*
> *De ton Rooy alie et de sa mesme loy. . . .**

Her friendship with Ronsard illustrates how fully Mary enjoyed the pleasures of the French court to which she was so well suited. As Castelnau de Mauvissière, an experienced diplomat and man of the world, noted in his memoirs, she turned herself so completely into a French woman, that she seemed not only the most beautiful of all her sex, but also the most delightful, both in her speech and in her demeanour.

There was only one small cloud in this summer's sky— and still no bigger than a man's hand. The exquisite fifteen-year-old queen-dauphiness who danced and hawked and hunted her way through the changing routine of the court's pleasures, was able to pursue these pastimes more

---

* *Ronsard! Perchance a passing note of pain Speaks sometimes to thy heart in days gone by, When he who was thy king did not disdain To do thee honour for thy poesy. . . .*[15]

by the light of will-power than that of robust physical strength. The warning signs of ill-health which had existed during her adolescence had not been successfully brushed away. Her beauty was touched, and possibly enhanced, by a certain fragility. In the spring of 1559, Sir John Mason wrote complacently to Cecil: 'The Queen of Scots is very sick, and men fear she will not long continue.' He added the pious hope: 'God take her to Him so soon as may please Him.' In May, the English ambassador, Throckmorton, mentioned that the queen-dauphiness had been ill again, and when on 24 May the English envoys were conducted before the queen, Throckmorton pronounced a grave opinion: 'Assuredly, Sir, the Scottish Queen in my opinion looked very ill on it, very pale and green, and withal short breathed, and it is whispered here among them that she cannot live long.'[16] In June 1559, she was twice reported as swooning, once she had to be given wine at the altar, and on the second occasion the Spanish ambassador said he had heard that she was suffering from an unspecified but incurable malady. The following autumn Mundt wrote to Elizabeth in London that Mary was 'in a consumption . . .'.[17] Yet whatever the young queen-dauphiness suffered from at this stage, it is clear that despite her pallor, her dizzy spells and her short breath, Mary also brought to her life an intense nervous energy which enabled her to lead an enormously active life when she was not actually suffering. A dangerous accident while out hunting in December 1559 when she was swept off her horse by a bough showed both her reckless courage and the straits to which it could lead her. This combination of a weak physique and overriding will was one which she shared, to some degree, with her husband Francis: it must have led to a bond between them.*

In September 1558 the first sour note was struck in the political existence of the dauphiness. On their way home

* For a discussion of Mary's health in later life and the subject of porphyria see Chapter 22, pp. 512-514. It has been suggested that in youth Mary suffered from chlorosis, or 'green sickness', on the basis of Throckmorton's description.[18] Chlorosis is, however, usually associated with malnutrition and general lack of exercise, fresh air and sunlight in adolescents living in slum conditions. In her upbringing at the French court Mary certainly did not lack proper exercise, fresh air or substantial meals: nor is the puffiness of the face, generally associated with chlorosis, mentioned in any of the contemporary descriptions of her appearance.

to Scotland, the ranks of the nine Scottish commissioners
who had come to France to arrange the marriage contract
were suddenly struck by illness, as a result of which four
of them died in one night, and James Stewart himself fell
ill, although he recovered. In a letter to her mother of 16
September, Mary spoke of this decimation as being God's
will:[19] but at the time another more sinister explanation
was advanced. Knox murmured of poison, either Italian
or French, as did Herries and Buchanan, and even Leslie
noticed 'through suspicion of venom, many wondered'.[20]
It was suggested that the brothers of the queen-regent, the
Guises, had determined to poison the commissioners because they had discovered something about the secret
treaties which signed away the birthright of Scotland. It
is true that it was vital to the Guises' plans that the secret
of the treaties should be preserved; on the other hand, almost every sudden death in this century was attributed
to poison, on principle, by the commentators: if there was
anything to the suspicions at all, it was curious that when
the remaining commissioners presented themselves to the
Scottish Parliament in November, they suggested no further enquiry into the matter, and put no obstacle in the
way of the crown matrimonial being granted to Francis.

Another phrase used by Mary in the same letter to her
mother showed that the realities of the French international situation were beginning to come home to her: she
described how the French court were all 'hoping for a
peace, but this is still so uncertain, that I shall say nothing to you about it, except that they say the peace should
not be arranged by prisoners like the constable and the
Marshal Saint-André'. The summer of 1558 had indeed
been occupied with the general European desire for a peace
settlement. Henry listened the more eagerly to the counsels of the peace party in France, not only because of the
desperate state of his finances, but also because he was
anxious to secure the return of his favourite, the constable, from captivity. The Guises, on the other hand, were
far from anxious for a peace with England and Spain by
which they feared that France would surrender many of
her conquests abroad, and the rival Montmorency would
triumph at home, and as Mary Stuart stressed to her
mother, they felt it unworthy that a prisoner like the constable should have so much say in a peace settlement,
whose main provision seemed to be to secure his return to

France. Even when the negotiations for peace were begun
at Cercamp, the open rivalry between Guises and Montmorencys was a feature of the French king's entourage,
Diane de Poitiers having by now thrown in her lot firmly
with the Montmorencys. The negotiations at Cercamp did
not culminate in peace until the April of the next year,
when the Treaty of Cateau-Cambrésis was finally signed.

In the interval, an event occurred of profound importance in the history of Mary Stuart. On 17 November
1558 Mary Tudor, queen of England, died leaving no
children. Her throne was inherited by her half-sister Elizabeth, an unmarried woman of twenty-five. Until such time
as Elizabeth herself should marry and beget heirs, Mary
was thus the next heiress to the English throne, by virtue of
her descent from her greatgrandfather Henry VII of England.* But the actual situation was more complicated
than this simple statement reveals. Elizabeth was the
daughter of Henry VIII and his second wife Anne Boleyn;
as Henry's divorce from his first wife Catherine of Aragon had never been recognized by the Catholic Church,
so Henry's marriage to Anne was considered void by Catholic standards, and so Elizabeth herself was held by strict
Catholic standards to be illegitimate and thus incapable of
inheriting the English throne. By this process of reasoning, Mary Stuart should rightly have inherited the throne
of Mary Tudor. The actions of Henry VIII himself did not
help to clear up the confusion: in 1536 the English Parliament itself had debarred Elizabeth from the succession as
illegitimate, and the Act which restored her to the succession in 1544 did not remove the stain of bastardy. Yet by
the will of Henry VIII the throne was also debarred from
going to a foreigner—which by English standards also oust-
ed Mary herself from the succession. The troubles over this
will and Mary's claim to have her place in the English succession after Elizabeth, lay in the future. At the moment
of Mary Tudor's death, the troubles were all the other
way about, and involved Elizabeth's right to be queen in
the first place.

Immediately on the death of Mary Tudor, Henry II of
France formally caused his daughter-in-law Mary Stuart to
be proclaimed queen of England, Ireland and Scotland,

* See Genealogical Table in the front of the book for English
Royal succession.

and caused the king-dauphin and queen-dauphiness to assume the royal arms of England, in addition to those of
France and Scotland. Up till the death of Queen Mary Tudor, England had been firmly allied to Spain, through
Mary's marriage to the Spanish king; Henry now hoped
to redress the balance by making a French claim to English
dominion. This eminently political action on the part of
the French king was to be flung in Mary's face for the rest
of her life, down to the moment of her trial in England
nearly thirty years later. Yet it seems certain that she
had even less opportunity for judging the wisdom of her
father-in-law's behaviour on this occasion than over the
matter of the secret treaties. 'They have made the Queen-
Dauphiness go into mourning for the late Queen of England,' commented the Venetian ambassador, who was in
no doubt as to where the initiative for these moves came
from.[21] At the time, the climate of French opinion was
certainly such that Mary's claims were considered no
more than just: the French writers eagerly commented on
the dauphiness's English connection, and celebrated her
accession to the triple crown in enthusiastic verse—as one
of the Pleiade, Jean de Baïf wrote, in a celebratory wedding song: 'Without murder and war, France and Scotland will be with England united.' Ronsard imagined that
Jupiter had decreed that Mary should govern England for
three months, Scotland for three and France for six. In
another nuptial song, René Guillon described the match
as the union of the white lily of France with the white
rose of the Yorkists—an allusion to Mary's Tudor descent.[22]

The letters of the English ambassador were full of details to illustrate the manner in which these infuriating
pretensions were being upheld by the French king: at
the wedding of the Princess Claude at the beginning of
the next year, a feature of the proceedings was that the
dauphin and dauphiness bore the arms of England quartered with those of France. The state entry to the town of
Châtelherault in November 1559 was marked by a canopy
of crimson damask carried over Mary's head with the arms
of England, France and Scotland emblazoned on it. A
canopy of purple damask with the French arms only was
carried over Francis (by now the king of France) and the
arms were painted on the gates of the town in the same
fashion.[23] The English state papers show a definite preoc-

cupation with the subject, understandable in view of the
shaky English policy at the start of a new reign. But Melville also reported in his memoirs that the cardinal caused
the arms of England to be engraved on the queen's silver
plate;[24] a great seal was struck bearing the royal figures
of Francis and Mary, the date 1559 and the inscription
round it referring to Francis and Mary, king and queen
of the French, Scottish, English and Irish. Even while the
treaty of Cateau-Cambrésis was being negotiated the cardinal and others made it their business to say that they
doubted whether they should treat with any of England,
save the dauphin and his wife.

The matter continued to be wrangled over after the accession of Francis. In February 1560 the government in
London decided to point out to the French ambassador
that although the English arms had first been borne by
Mary under Henry II, she had not stopped bearing them
with his death. Throckmorton had a long interview with
the cardinal when he argued over the matter, saying that
despite Mary's admittedly English descent, she ought not
to use the arms without any difference. In March the
Council told Throckmorton to point out to Mary that
'her father, the King of Scots, being higher than she,
never bare the same; nor by the laws of the land is she
next heir'. To this the bishop of Valence, on behalf of the
French king and queen made the somewhat disingenuous
counterpoint that 'the bearing of the English arms by the
French Queen, was thought in France to be done for the
honour of Elizabeth and to show that the French queen
was her [Elizabeth's] cousin'.[25]

However, when peace was proclaimed between England,
France and Scotland in 1560, Elizabeth herself consented
to believe that Mary's 'injurious pretensions' to the English throne sprang from the 'ambitious desire of the
principal members of the house of Guise', rather than the
wishes of either Francis, 'by reason of his youth incapable
of such an enterprise', or the queen of Scots 'who is likewise very young'.[26] The explanation which satisfied the English queen two years later we may also accept as being
the true one. Unfortunately, once political necessity dictated another course, it no longer satisfied either Queen
Elizabeth or her advisers, and the subject of Mary's pretensions to the English throne, made on her behalf by

her father-in-law before she was sixteen years old, continued to haunt her for the rest of her career.

1559, which became a year of death at the French court, seemed destined at its outset to be a year of weddings. The marriage of Princess Claude to the young and handsome duke of Lorraine was celebrated with magnificence in February. The Peace of Cateau-Cambrésis, finally signed in April between England and France on one side and France and Spain on the other, provided that all the French conquests in Italy made during the last eighty years should be surrendered, and made arrangements for two further royal weddings. Mme Marguerite, the long unmarried sister of Henry ii, was to wed the duke of Savoy; Princess Elisabeth at the age of fourteen faced the prospect of marriage to Philip of Spain, freed for matrimony once more by the death of Mary Tudor. Mary Stuart's last summer as dauphiness was spent in planning for the double wedding of these two beloved companions of her childhood, to be celebrated with the full regal panoply to which the French court was so well suited. As the Venetian ambassador commented, nothing was discussed at the French court but handsome and costly apparel.[27]

Beneath these eddies of sartorial rivalry there were the undercurrents of more dangerous enmities. The constable and Diane de Poitiers were now all-powerful with Henry ii, and their own alliance was symbolized by the marriage of a grand-daughter of Diane with the son of the constable. Moreover, the Montmorency faction was beginning to have Protestant affiliations, in contrast to the strong Catholicism of the Guises, since Montmorency's own nephew Admiral Coligny had become a Huguenot. These Huguenot connections were also starting to be shared by the third powerful French family, the Bourbons, through their head, King Antoine of Navarre and his wife Jeanne d'Albret. As the cardinal busied himself with preparations for the double wedding, it must have seemed to him that the fortunes of the Guises had taken a definite downward trend. At this moment, the volatile wheel of fortune, which the Guises had so often observed turning to their advantage in the past, was once again to take a dynamic revolution in their favour.

On 15 June the duke of Alva arrived to claim Elisabeth by proxy for his master Philip ii, and on 21 June the proxy

wedding took place, although as the young bride had not
yet reached the age of puberty, it was decided that she
should not depart for the Spanish court until the autumn.
On 27 June the marriage contract was signed between
Mme Marguerite and the duke of Savoy. There were endless tournaments and festivities, and the culmination of
the double event—the wedding of Marguerite—was only a
few days away. On 30 June, the king, magnificent in the
black and white which he wore because they were the
favourite colours of Diane de Poitiers, mounted his horse
Le Malheureux, entered the lists along with the duke of
Guise wearing red and white, the duke of Ferrara in yellow
and red, and the duke of Nemours commonly known to
be enamoured of the duchess of Guise, in yellow and
black.* The king's love of jousting amounted almost to
a mania. He broke three lances with the duke of Savoy,
the duke of Guise, and Jacques de Lorge, count of Montgomery, a Norman with Scottish blood, who was colonel
of the archers of the guard, and a man of renowned
courage.

All went well until, on a sudden whim, the king chal-
lenged Montgomery to break a last lance with him. Apparently, with some presentiment of evil, Montgomery
tried to excuse himself from the encounter, until Henry
finally commanded him to obey as his sovereign. Now
Catherine de Medicis tried to dissuade her husband, having had two visions of ill-omen about the tournament.
Her daughter Marguerite tells us in her memoirs that on
the previous night Catherine had actually dreamt of the
death of Henry, pierced in the eye by a lance, exactly as
it transpired. Henry merely replied that he would break
one more lance in the queen's honour. Catherine's fore-
bodings were justified: the shock of the meeting between
the two resulted in Montgomery's lance splintering; one
splinter went into the king's right eye, another into his
throat. Throckmorton, the English ambassador, described
the scene; Henry was borne off, 'nothing covered but his
face, he moved neither hand nor foot, but lay as one
amazed'.[28]

* He seemed to be in excellent health at the time although as
Throckmorton had reported to London in May that the king was ill
with vertigo, it is just possible that some giddiness afflicted him to
explain the events that followed.[28]

The king was carried to the near-by Hôtel des Tournelles,
and here lay in a state of virtual unconsciousness for nine
days. On 8 July, in a lucid moment, he ordered Queen
Catherine to proceed with the marriage of Mme Marguerite and the duke of Savoy. The ceremony was bathed
in extreme gloom: the church of St Paul, close by the
Hôtel des Tournelles was hastily decorated and at midnight the young couple knelt at the altar. Catherine sat
alone on the royal dais, in floods of tears, while Francis
and Mary did not even attend, but remained within ear-
shot of the king. Jérôme de la Rovère, bishop of Toulon,
said a Low Mass, trembling all the while lest he should
find the herald at arms announcing the death of the king
at the door of the sanctuary. As Henry felt himself dying,
he called for his son and began 'My son, I recommend
to you the Church and my people . . .' but he could not
go on. He gave the dauphin his blessing and kissed him.
That evening he became paralysed, his breathing was painful, and at 1 A.M. on 10 July he died with grossly swollen
hands and feet, all showing signs of a virulent infection.

Queen Catherine was left to find gloomy consolation in
the fact that the death of Henry II represented a signal
triumph for the art of astrology to which she attached
such importance. The king's death had twice been predicted
accurately, although of course neither prediction had
served in any way to avert the king's fate, this being a
common disadvantage of this absorbing science. Catherine
kept a tame astrologer, Luc Gauric, who predicted the
death of the king in a duel—which was thought at the
time to be extremely unlikely, as a king was seldom to be
found in single combat.*

In 1555 the famous Nostradamus first published his
prophecies, including the rhyme:

The young lion shall overcome the old one
In martial field by a single duel
In a cage of gold he shall put out his eye
Two wounds from one, then he shall die a cruel death.

---

* Gauric also prophesied the death of Duke Francis of Guise correctly, saying that he would be struck down from behind. This met
with annoyance as well as scepticism since Francis thought that the
prophecy carried with it some implication of cowardice. He forgot
that although only the back of the coward is turned towards the
enemy, the dagger of the assassin also strikes from behind.

Afterwards, it was pointed out that the tilting helm strangely resembles a cage, and that the king's visor was actually gilded; the two wounds were held to refer to the splintering of the lance, piercing the throat and the eye. There was actually one outcry demanding the burning of Nostradamus, the man who had prophesied 'so ill and so well'. *

Francis II was now king of France at the age of fifteen and a half, and Mary Stuart queen at the age of sixteen. In one blow of a lance, the fortunes of the Guises had changed. Their niece was now in the very seat of power. The stage was now set for their triumph, however short-lived. The day of Henry's death was referred to afterwards by one wit as 'the eve of the feast of the three kings', and it was commonly asserted that there were now three kings in France, Francis of Valois, Francis of Guise, and Cardinal Charles of Lorraine—'one king in name only and two kings of Lorraine in effect'.[30] Immediately after his father's death, Francis entrusted his father's body to the constable, the Cardinal de Chastillon, Admiral Coligny and the marshal of Saint-André, and entered the coach which had come from the court on the Guises' orders. King Francis entered first, and as Queen Mary hung modestly back, Queen Catherine forced her into the place of honour. The young king was taken to the Louvre, and by the time the deputation from the Parliament arrived, the government was already in the hands of the Guises.

When the Spanish ambassadors visited Queen Catherine to pay her their condolences, they found the room draped in black, the floor as well as the walls.[31] The windows were shut, and there was no light except two candles burning on an altar draped in black. Catherine herself sat in a severe black dress with no ornament except a collar of ermine. The new queen of France on the other hand was dressed in white, the white which she had insisted on wearing for her wedding only fifteen months before, and which

---

* Queen Catherine was not always so fortunate, in astrological terms, in the truth of the predictions which were made to her. When the future Charles IX was born, it was prophesied that he would one day be as great a king as Charlemagne—a prediction which he did very little to fulfil during his days as king. Another son, for whom Nostradamus equally prophesied a brilliant future, died only eighteen months after his birth.

now she could wear in earnest as the colour of mourning. Catherine responded only faintly to the ambassadors' condolences, but the new queen, prompted by her uncles, made a gracious little speech, urging them to come often to court, and asking them to give her compliments to the king of Spain. In the course of her speech she took care to sing the praises of her uncles. At the funeral of Henry II, begun at Notre Dame on 11 August, and completed at Saint-Denis on 13 August, the role of the Guises was even more significant than it had been at the beginning of the previous reign. Cardinal Charles, as abbot of St Denis presided over the interment. Another Guise brother, René of Elboeuf, held the hand of justice, Henry of Guise held the crown, Grand Prior Francis of Guise the sceptre, and the duke of Guise the royal banner of France. By making the young king, as one historian at the Guise family has put it, 'their nephew by alliance, their pupil by necessity',[32] Mary Stuart had fulfilled the ultimate expectations of her family.

6 The White Lily of France

'Alba rosis albis nunc insere lilia . . .'

*Nuptial song on the marriage of Francis and Mary, refer-
ring to the union of the white lilies of France and the white
roses of the Yorkists*

On 18 September 1559, the young Francis was solemnly
crowned king of France at Rheims: his consort Mary had
already been crowned queen of Scotland in babyhood and
unlike previous queens of France had thus no need of
further coronation to confirm her royal state. The weather
was wet and windy. Nor was there any great display of
pageantry on this occasion, owing to the recent and shocking death of Henry II: Throckmorton noted savagely that
the city was scarcely decorated at all 'save that the arms of
England, France and Scotland quartered were brimly
set out in the show over the gate'.[1] Francis himself wore
a coat of black velvet and Mary alone of the ladies who
attended the coronation was not dressed in dark colours.
The day after the ceremony, court mourning was resumed
for a year to mark the late king's death. Although the
ancient crown of St Denis had been placed on his head,
the real power in France was very far from lying within the
puny grasp of Francis II. The English ambassador Throckmorton analysed the situation as follows—the old French
queen (Catherine) had the authority of regent, although
she was not in fact regent in name; in the meantime the
state was governed by the cardinal of Lorraine and the
duke of Guise jointly, the duke having charge of the
war, and the cardinal the ordering of all other affairs including finance and foreign affairs. The Venetian ambassador noted that the Guises now conducted secret inner discussions on matters of policy, just before official meetings
of the Grand Council: these conferences took place either
in Francis's chamber or in that of Queen Catherine.[2]

This political ascendancy had its parallel in the domestic
arrangements of the new king and queen of France:
Guisards were made gentlemen of the bed-chamber to the

THE WHITE LILY OF FRANCE

king, and Mary's new list of domestic officers was headed
by those ladies who were to receive 800 *livres* in wages,
including Antoinette of Guise, Anne d'Esté, the duchess
of Aumale and the marquise of Elboeuf—her grandmother
and her three Guise aunts. One of Mary's first actions
after the death of Henry II as a formal expression of her
joy at coming to the throne was to make a donation to the
grandmother who had contributed so much to her upbringing. The court of France, with Francis, Mary and Catherine at its head, now resumed the endless journeyings
which characterized its way of life. These travels were
prompted by a variety of motives, including the calls of
the chase, domestic convenience and in certain cases the
dictates of security or politics. In the first instance the entire court proceeded to Blois to wait for the signal of the
departure of young Elisabeth to Spain: from Blois the
royal cortège went to Varteuil, and from there to a snow-
strewn Châtelherault, which they entered at the end of
November. On 25 November Queen Catherine finally permitted her child to depart, with grief so extreme that even
the Spanish ambassador was moved by it. Mary herself
was equally distraught at the prospect of the departure
of her friend: she entrusted Elisabeth with a touching
letter to King Philip from his new sister-in-law, saying
that she could hardly bear to part with Elisabeth, were it
not for the fact that she knew Elisabeth would be happy
and contented in her new life. Nevertheless for Mary herself the loss would be irreparable. She ended her letter by
begging the Spanish king to receive it 'as from the person
who loves her [Elisabeth] the most in the world, and who
wishes always to be—*Vôtre bien bonne soeur Marie*'.[3]

With Mary and the royal family immersed in their personal sorrow, the Guise brothers were left to grapple with
the internal government of France, which represented at
this period a problem which other less bold spirits might,
with considerable justification, have shrunk from tackling.
The Peace of Cateau-Cambrésis had not come in time to
save France from cruel inflation, induced by the economic
demands of the Italian wars. It has been estimated that at
the death of Henry II the treasury staggered under a war
debt of forty million *livres:* the theoretical resources of the
crown were ten million *livres,* but the actual income only
amounted to about half this, and the interest on the royal
debt consumed it. At the same time the kingdom was being

rapidly dissected by the presence of two religions, as
French Calvinism became the natural target for discontent
with the central authority.[4] Even if the country had not
been plunged in such grave economic problems, some sort
of regency, *de facto* if not *de jure,* would have been necessary for the young Francis. At the age of fifteen and a
half, when he ascended the throne, his intelligence was
scarcely more developed than his physique. In youth,
like many other boys he had loved to hunt more than he
had loved to learn, but since he was the dauphin of
France, not enough pressure had been exerted to redress
the balance. The result was that his mind, without being
actually feeble, as his body was, had never really developed
to the point when the possibilities of power and government excited him. As a king he lacked the necessary self-
restraint to attend to the business of government when
pleasure offered, his tutors in youth having concentrated
more on the importance of the actual role he would play,
than the importance of the duties which were attached to
it. The enemies of the Guises accused them of encouraging
their nephew in his pursuit of pleasure in order to have
the government of the realm to themselves. But there was
no need to carry out such a policy of corruption, their
work had already been done for them by the over-protec-
tive upbringing of Catherine de Medicis, who had with all
her loving, maternal care, developed only self-importance,
not self-discipline, in her son.

The nature of the king's character was fully appreciated
by the watchful ambassadors at the French court. His
routine was understood to be dominated by his frantic
love of hawking: in December 1559 he was reported as
having retired to Chambord till Christmas, to which the
Chancellor of the Privy Council was obliged to repair in
order 'to arrange his finances for the next year'. In March
1560 when the king refused to see the English ambassadors,
giving out that he was ill, their immediate instinct was to
suspect that he was merely playing truant 'as the king is
wont to go abroad very often to amuse himself for several
days without transacting business'. This was an age when
monarchs were still expected to reproduce in themselves
the personal qualities of greatness, to win the admiration of
their subjects. Duke Francis of Guise owed much of his
prestige to his physical courage: despite her frail health
Mary Stuart was famed for being personally fearless. King

Francis, on the other hand, was timid by nature. He had a certain pathetic dandyism, a love of display revealed by his personal accounts, where swords were made with hilts coloured to match his various costumes; but this was no substitute for the careless courage so attractive in princes.[5] He lived in fear for his personal safety, which made it natural for him to depute the government of the kingdom happily to those he felt best able to secure it.

Francis was demonstrably incapable of ruling without guidance. But the vital regency—as it was in practice but not in name—was not surrendered to his wife's uncles by the other great nobles of France without a struggle. The powerful family of Bourbon postulated strongly that the king was not, in fact, legally of age at all, being only fifteen. Not only had he no right to choose his own counsellers, but being still a minor, he should automatically accept the first prince of the blood as regent: this was of course none other than King Antoine of Navarre, head of the House of Bourbon. Behind this weak and indecisive figure-head stretched the shadow of his restless, ambitious and hot-headed younger brother, Louis, prince of Condé, a recent Huguenot convert, and the sworn enemy of the Guises. An anonymous memoir of October 1559, which detailed these points, not only accused the Guises of trying to cut off Francis from his friends, but of aiming at putting the crown on their own heads, by emphasizing their spurious descent from Charlemagne. A Guise reply *'Pour la majorité du Roy très chrestien François deuxieme'* by Jean du Tillet, bishop of Saint-Brieul, concentrated on the use of texts, laws and customs to prove firstly that the king of France traditionally came of age at fifteen, and thus had the right to choose his own Council, secondly, that the regency in the past had not always been given to a prince of the blood, but on occasions also had been given to queens of France, and to the abbots of St Denis.[6]

King Antoine, having failed to assert his claims, withdrew from the court; the prince of Condé on the other hand took refuge in the Huguenot counter-plots which were the origin of the conspiracy of Amboise. The spring plans of Francis and Mary and their court included a visit to Blois, and then on to the ancient medieval fortress of Amboise, where it was planned that the court should pass the Lenten season. Although this schedule was known to the Spanish ambassador at Christmas, the knowledge somehow eluded the Huguenot rebels, who laid their plans on the basis of finding the king at Blois—an infinitely easier centre to attack than Amboise, where the king was surrounded by his army. Condé was only the 'silent captain' of the enterprise, and did not appear in public as its leader. The ostensible ringleader of these Huguenot anti-Guisards was one La Renaudie; their aim was to seize the person of the king, with the immediate object of freeing him from the tutelage of the Guises, and the ultimate intention of setting up a new and Bourbon regency.

Amboise withstood the siege of the conspirators, and at the instigation of the cardinal of Lorraine the insurrection was punished by hideous reprisals in the streets of the town itself, while the chief rebels, having been tortured, were hung publicly in front of the castle windows after dinner in order that the court might enjoy the edifying sight. La Renaudie died bravely, protesting his loyalty to the king, and maintaining to the last that his only quarrel had been with the Guises. The cardinal, however, adroitly took the opportunity to point out to Francis that the fact that La Renaudie died so defiantly only went to show how cruelly he would have treated Francis if he had succeeded in capturing him. The blood-stained sight from the castle windows did not please every member of the French court. The gentle and tender Anne of Guise was so appalled at what she saw that she wept aloud, and cried out (all too percipiently, as it turned out) what a wealth of vengeance and hatred would fall on the heads of her innocent young sons in consequence. Nor is there any evidence that Mary, who all her life was characterized by a remarkable horror of bloodshed and positive aversion to violence, actually witnessed the hangings. It would have been remarkable if this delicate girl, whose health was a source of constant concern to those around her, and whose swoonings were a feature of court life, should have been considered a suitable spectator for these gruesome scenes.*

---

* The Spanish ambassador, who described how Queen Catherine and the principal nobles of the court were almost always present at the savage questioning of the prisoners, did not list Mary's name among them (although it has sometimes been added to the list inaccurately by popular historians).[7] When Sir John Gordon was executed in Scotland in 1562 and Mary was compelled to witness the scene for political reasons, she fainted and was ill for several days afterwards.

Quite apart from natural affection, there was another
special reason for the great concern which the Guises always showed over the health of their niece. Although the
Guises were accused of wishing to establish a Guise dynasty on the throne of France, it was an infinitely more
practical plan to uphold the existing semi-Guise dynasty
on the throne of France, in the persons of Francis and
Mary, who were not only currently dominated by Guise
influence, but whose children with their share of Guise
blood would one day rule after them. The only flaw in
all this planning was that there was as yet no dynasty,
no clutch of Valois–Guise children to lay up security for
the future—only an adolescent boy and girl both of them
cursed with precarious health. Whether these frail creatures
could be relied on to produce any child at all was very
much open to question.

The question of the consummation of the marriage of
Francis and Mary, owing to the delicate nature of the
subject, rests in the sphere of probabilities rather than that
of certainties. Yet it is of obvious importance in tracing
the development of Mary's character not only in France,
but later in Scotland in the course of her confrontation
with Darnley. The true facts of the situation are somewhat
obscured because contemporary commentators understandably concentrated their observations on the simple
issue of whether Mary was likely to conceive a child by
Francis or not; whereas in the history of Mary, it is of
equal interest to consider whether she had any sort of
physical relationship with her first husband, or whether at
the time of her return to Scotland, she was still in fact
a virgin. There was never apparently any doubt in the
minds of those observers at the French court who had
watched the young king grow up, that the queen of
France would not produce a child, or if she did, as the
Spanish ambassador crudely put it, 'it will certainly not
be the King's'. Regnier de la Planche's derisive comments
on the king's withered anatomy have already been noted
(see footnote on p. 76). Although, to the joy of the
Guises, Francis started to grow up somewhat once he became king, La Planche's description of physical deformity
suggests that there was no real hope of conception, even
if in other respects he could be held to have attained
puberty before he died. The fact that he was unable to
conceive a child was also well known at the court on the

basis of his deformity, for this was an age when the public
nature of royal life meant that problems, even of such an
intimate nature, could not be kept altogether secret from
the watchful ambassadors: when the Spanish ambassador
in Brussels told the English ambassador categorically that
it was out of the question that the Scottish queen should
bear a child, he was probably acting on back-stairs palace
gossip, reliable if scandalous.[8]

This does not altogether rule out the possibility that
the marriage was in some fashion consummated. At the
time of the wedding, the Venetian ambassador at the end
of a long account of the ceremonies, reported that the marriage had in fact been consummated that night, indicating
the respective ages of the young couple. In spite of the
warnings of the doctors, Francis had not died in childhood,
but had grown to the age of fifteen; the Guises presumably
hoped that time would wreak a further miracle with his
physique, and that he would one day be able to procreate
the longed-for Valois and Guise heir. There is evidence
to the effect that, despite the cynicism of the court, Mary
herself believed that her marriage was a complete one. A
month after the death of Henry II, when the Spanish ambassadors came to bid her adieu, they found her extremely pale, and she almost fainted.[9] She received the letters of credit of the duke of Alva swooning and, supported
by the cardinal, was lifted onto the bed of the king.
Chantonay made haste to tell the Spanish king that the
general rumour was that the French queen was pregnant.
Mary herself assumed the floating tunic, the conventional
garb at the time for pregnant women, and the court went
to Saint-Germain for the sake of better air for her health.
However, by the end of September, these interesting rumours perished for lack of further support. Mary abandoned
her floating tunics. There was no further mention of a
royal pregnancy, and it was in fact only three months later
that Challoner was able to report back to England the information which he had received in Brussels from Count
de Feria.

To what then do we attribute these summer vapours of
the young queen? Logically speaking, if there was to be
any question of Mary being pregnant, however mistaken,
the marriage must have been consummated. Unfortunately
this is not an area where logic can necessarily be said to
obtain. The general hope of the court, and the passionate

desire of the Guises, was that Mary should conceive a
child. This desire, which she herself heartily shared, must
have been communicated to her most strongly. In this
case, it seems likely that Mary transformed in her mind
the feeble passion of the king into a true consummation
of her marriage—indeed at the age of sixteen, the natural
ignorance of youth must have made it all the easier for
her to do so. In the same way she transformed in her mind
the symptoms of ill-health into the symptoms of pregnancy:
in the November of the previous year the English ambassador had reported that Mary was 'very ill and looked very
pale and on the 12th kept to her chamber all day long'.[10]
The following autumn, when Mary was actually queen
of France, and the need for an heir increasingly urgent, it
was easy to persuade herself that these symptoms, from
which she had in fact suffered all her youth, had suddenly become those of pregnancy. Yet the king's unde-
veloped and probably deformed physique and generally infantile constitution make it extremely unlikely that anything more than the most awkward embraces took place
between them; whether or not Mary was technically a
virgin when she arrived in Scotland, she was certainly
mentally one, in that her physical relation with Francis
can hardly have given her any real idea of the meaning of
physical love.

Troublesome as was the internal situation in France, the
situation in Scotland was not much better—and here
again religious differences mingled with those of civil
policy. French troops were sent in increasing numbers to
the assistance of the queen regent, and the expedition of
La Brosse, authorized by Francis and Mary in November 1559, included several doctors of the Sorbonne who
were sent with a view to taking part in theological disputes with the Scottish Protestants if the occasion offered.
In their turn, the Scottish insurgents being Protestant
lords of the congregation, appealed for aid from Protestant
England. When in October 1559, the duke of Châtelherault
(the former Arran) joined the party of congregation, he
presented them with a titular leader who had a claim to
the Scottish throne. In October of that year the insurgents even occupied Edinburgh temporarily, announcing
that, since Mary of Guise had brought French troops to
conquer Scotland, it was now lawful to suspend her from

her authority. But the Scots rebels—or reformers—did
not make any true headway until a firmer alliance was
concluded with England in the following spring. By the
Treaty of Berwick, signed on 27 February 1560, between
Scotland as represented by Lord James and the Scottish
lords of the congregation on behalf of Châtelherault in
England, represented by Norfolk, lieutenant of the north, it
was stated that the English were to intervene for the
preservation of the Scots 'in their old freedom and liberties'. Under these auspices English troops now came into
Scotland, and besieged Leith, occupied by the queen regent
and her French troops: significantly, the campaign was
known as 'the War of the Insignia' in England, because of
Mary's use of the royal arms.

The Treaty of Berwick on the Scottish borders had
virtually coincided with the Tumult of Amboise in France:
since Francis was thus unable to provide further military
help for his wife's dominions, it was decided to take the
more sensible course of negotiation. By a commission dated
April 1560 Francis and Mary authorized M. de Montluc,
M. de Pelvé and M. de la Brosse to try to bring back their
Scottish subjects to obedience by peaceful means, including
a promise to forget past wrongs, and also authorized them
to treat with the English queen if necessary. As a result of
these negotiations, culminating in the Treaty of Edinburgh
which was concluded on 6 July 1560, it was agreed that
both English troops and French troops (save sixty in Inch-
keith and sixty in Dunbar) should withdraw from Scotland, and that Francis and Mary by giving up the use of
the English arms should thus recognize Elizabeth's title.
On 15 July the English army moved away, and the French
troops also started to embark; Lord St John was sent to
France to ask Francis and Mary to ratify the treaty. This
ratification was, however, never destined to take place, since
on 11 August, the Scottish Parliament promulgated a
Protestant confession of faith, and five days later abolished
the Pope's jurisdiction, and prohibited the celebration of
Mass under the pain of death for the third offence. In a
historic gesture, the process now known as the Scottish
Reformation was thus officially brought to birth. It was
Parliament, not the queen, that had acted as the midwife:
although constitutionally speaking, the enactment which
produced the Reformation needed the queen's assent, in
fact it never received it. The Scottish Reformation was a

strictly parliamentary affair. Yet at one manifestation of the parliamentary will, the whole image of the Scottish monarchy had been altered in the mind of the people.

This long-term effect, however, was certainly not visible to Mary at the time. From the distance of the French court, it was difficult to realize that Queen Elizabeth had been constituted the protector of Protestantism in Scotland, whether she liked it or not, and that logically the Protestant Scots would turn to England rather than France for help in the future. Still more difficult was it to envisage that if Mary ever returned to her native country, her French Catholic connections would inevitably go against her, that a country which had newly reformed its own religion by act of Parliament without assent of the sovereign would regard the combination of her monarchical power, French upbringing and religious convictions as threatening its *status quo*.*

In the spring and summer of 1560, however, the Scottish insurgency made its chief impression on Mary as a series of appalling troubles which faced her mother, to whom she felt an almost pathetic devotion from a distance. She identified the religious rebels of Scotland with those of France, unaware that the temper of the Scottish people was changing towards the new religion, whereas in France religious opinion was sufficiently if tragically balanced to result in long and stultifying wars. A letter to her mother, describing the coming mission of M. de la Brosse and M. d'Amiens to Scotland, dating probably from the end of March 1560, is lavish in its promises of love and assistance, saying that she swears she will not let her mother down, since the king, she knows, has a passionate desire to succour her, and has given Mary his word that he will do so. Mary begs her mother to care for her health, and to trust in God to help her in her adversities—for God has already helped her so much in all her troubles that surely He will not abandon her now when she needs Him more than ever.[11]

Unhappily the health which Mary so passionately wished

* Already Mary was regarded as a foreigner by many of the people who were in fact her subjects: it is significant that an account of her magnificent wedding written by a Scotsman who was a member of the crowd makes absolutely no mention of the fact that Mary was herself Scottish. The writer proceeds as if Mary had actually been an Englishwoman.[12]

for her mother, eluded her. This gallant woman who faced
an alien people, and attempted to do at least the best she
could in the cause of peaceful administration, was severely
stricken with dropsy. She was seriously ill before November 1559, and by April of the next year was far gone with
the disease. On 11 June, only a few weeks before the final
settlement of the Treaty of Edinburgh, she died, horribly
swollen and in great pain. Knox rejoiced over her end;
he saw in it the hand of God taking vengeance on her
for her behaviour at the siege of Leith, when she was
rumoured to have exulted over the corpses of the Protestant
dead (although such behaviour is more characteristic of
Knox himself than of the merciful Mary of Guise). 'And
within few days thereafter yea, some say that same day,'
wrote Knox, 'began her belly and loathsome legs to swell,
and so continued till that God did execute his judgement
upon her.'

Previously, Knox had described Mary of Guise's assumption of the regency with equal contempt—'A crown was
put upon her head . . . as seemly a sight . . . as to put a
saddle upon the back of an unruly cow.'[13] But in fact
Knox, as often when writing with his pen dipped in acid, did
Mary Guise an injustice as a ruler. In an extraordinarily
difficult situation, she had tried to do her best, and carry
out the advice of her brother the duke of Guise—'To deal
in Scotland in a spirit of conciliation, introducing much
gentleness and moderation into the administration of justice.' On occasions she was even prepared to carry out
these counsels against the advice of her Guise brothers
who had given it to her: as Regnier de la Planche himself
admitted, Mary of Guise's plans for Scotland had always
included acting gently and slowly by the use of Parliament
and it was the Guise males who rejected this course,
saying that their sister might be a good woman, but she
would wreck everything by her tender methods.[14] In her
introduction of French administrators Mary of Guise also
genuinely believed she was benefiting the Scots, since she
was frankly appalled at Scottish administrative methods. As
for Scottish laws she wrote of them that they were the
most unjust in the world, not so much in their provisions,
as in the manner in which they were carried out, and when
one considers the internal state of Scotland in the age in
which she arrived there, particularly in areas like the
borders, where administration was either non-existent or

archaic in the extreme, it is easy to understand how she derived this impression.

Despite her own sincere Catholicism, Mary of Guise also possessed sufficient balance and political acumen not to identify the reformed religion immediately and totally with the forces of darkness. In 1555 D'Oysel's hopes for a good reception among the Scots were dashed by what he described as the totally selfish attitude of the nobility, who wanted each one to be their own petty tyrant. But it was not until the events of late 1557, when the nobility of Scotland refused to fight under her banner against England, that Mary of Guise herself gave way to feelings of angry distrust for these treacherous lords, Catholic and Protestant alike. Even in 1559, when Henry II instructed that heresy was to be stamped out in Scotland, according to Melville, Mary of Guise still protested against her orders: although committed to a policy of French domination, on Mary's behalf, by which she hoped to preserve Scotland for her daughter, Mary of Guise nevertheless attempted all along to implement this policy in the most humane manner. The English certainly both feared and admired her intellectual qualities: Thomas Randolph wrote apprehensively of 'the Dowager's craft and subtleties'. Throckmorton admired her 'queenly mind', and over the peace negotiations wrote to Cecil for the love of God 'to provide that she were rid from hence, for she hath the heart of a man of war'.[15] When she was on her death-bed, Mary of Guise summoned the lords of the Congregation to her side, and in an affecting interview asked them to believe that she had genuinely favoured the weal of Scotland as well as that of France. Whether the lords believed her or not, we can at least accept her word that by her own lights she had done so.

The news of the death of Mary of Guise was known in France on 18 June, but was kept from her daughter until 28 June: with good reason, as it turned out, for Mary Stuart's grief when she finally did receive the news was heart-rending, and she underwent one of the physical collapses which inordinate sorrow was apt to induce in her. Michiel, the Venetian ambassador, had already paid tribute to Mary's devotion to her mother, saying that 'she loved her mother incredibly, and much more than daughters usually love their mothers'. Now he reported: 'The death

of the Queen Regent of Scotland was concealed from the
most Christian Queen [Mary Stuart] till the day before yesterday, when it was at length told her by the Cardinal of
Lorraine; for which her Majesty showed and still shows
such signs of grief, that during the greater part of yesterday
she passed from one agony to another.'*[16] Nor were poor
Mary of Guise's earthly troubles entirely terminated by her
death: for even her wretched dropsical corpse proved a
source of dispute. A funeral oration was made for her in
Notre Dame on 12 August, six weeks after her death, but
it was not until October that her lead-lined coffin was allowed to be conveyed to France, because the Scottish
preachers disapproved of the superstitious rites which they
feared during her obsequies. In March 1561 her body was
removed to Fécamp in Normandy and in July taken to
Rheims, where it was finally buried in the church of the
convent of St Pierre of which her sister Renée was abbess.

Mary's love for her mother spurred her forward in her
knowledge of Scottish politics; her appreciation of French
and English politics was spurred on by her own increasing
estimation of her position as queen of France and heiress—
or rightful possessor—of the English throne. A few days
after Henry II's death, Throckmorton commented that
everything was being done by the queen of Scotland, who
took a great interest in all matters around her. Mary was
also acute enough to send for an inventory of the crown
jewels, many of which had passed into the hands of Diane
de Poitiers, immediately after the death of her father-in-
law, with a view to acquiring what were now her rightful
property as queen of France. Throckmorton's view of
Mary Stuart has a particular interest. As English ambassador he had a definite motive for noting the twists and
turns of her character as it developed: not only did she
claim the English crown for her own, but she was also
more plausibly the heiress to the throne. Life was uncertain, and Elizabeth was childless and unmarried; if Mary
did not actually acquire the English throne by force, she
might easily do so by inheritance. It thus behoved
Throckmorton to keep a watchful eye on the nature and

* A portrait of her mother, brought by Maitland to Scotland in
1563, was carried with her by Mary on all her travels throughout
her captivity, and finally found among her belongings at Fotheringhay.

qualities of this young girl, whom the random chance of
fate might one day establish as his own mistress.

It is significant that the Mary Stuart of Throckmorton's
despatches is a more intelligent and mature girl than the
beautiful wilful delicate creature of, for example, the
Venetian ambassador's reports to his own Italian court.
Mary showed a hint of imperiousness in her words to
Throckmorton concerning her refusal, with Francis, to
ratify the Treaty of Edinburgh. 'My subjects in Scotland
do their duty in nothing,' she told him, 'nor have they
performed their part in one thing that belongeth to them.
I am their Queen and so they call me, but they use me
not so. . . . They must be taught to know their duties.'[17]
Earlier when Throckmorton was taken to have an interview with the royalties in February 1560 the preponderance
of the conversation was had with the Queen Mother
Catherine, but at the end of the interview when Catherine
made an observation to the effect that she wished to be
on good terms with Elizabeth, Mary did intervene. ' "Yes,"
she said, "the Queen my good sister may be assured to
have a better neighbour of me being her cousin, than of
the rebels, and so I pray you signify." '[18] The point may
not have been a good one in terms of power politics—
since Elizabeth might well prefer rebels across the border
to an active young queen, however friendly, however
cousinly—but it was one worth making from Mary's point
of view, and shows that her political intelligence was beginning to emerge from the cocoon of the cardinal's
tutelage.

The cardinal had been the instructor of her youth: but
as queen of France, Mary had a new mentor in the art
of politics—her mother-in-law Catherine de Medicis. It
was no coincidence that Throckmorton had found the
two queens sitting beside each other in February 1560.
The records show that during the seventeen months in
which Francis II reigned as king of France, Queen Catherine and Queen Mary were constantly in each other's
company, and in fact Queen Catherine, far from being excluded from the source of power by the death of her husband, formed a royal triumvirate at the top of the pyramid
of the court; as the mother on whom the king depended
emotionally, and as the queen dowager who had authorized
the Guises to assume power, she was now of infinitely

more account in the counsels of the kingdom than she
had been during the reign of Henry II. There has been
much speculation concerning the relations of Catherine
de Medicis and Mary Stuart: it has been suggested that
Catherine disliked her daughter-in-law so intensely that she
was finally capable of poisoning her son Francis, in order
to bring to an end Mary Stuart's reign as queen of France.
A great deal has been made of the story that Mary openly
despised Catherine for her lowly birth, and described
her contemptuously as nothing but the daughter of a
merchant, the story resting on the word of the Cardinal
de Santa Croce, the papal nuncio in France.[19] Whether or
not Mary, with the imprudence of youth, made this highly
unwise remark, it is certainly easy enough to imagine that
an unattractive older woman should be jealous of an exceptionally attractive younger one, with the additional
complications of a throne to exacerbate their feelings, quite
apart from the traditionally trying relationship of mother
and daughter-in-law. Yet the fact is that whatever her
private feelings, outwardly Catherine exhibited positively
maternal kindness towards Mary during her period as
queen of France, and gave Mary no reason to suppose
that she was anything but most amicably inclined towards
her.

In December 1559 the English envoys reported that
Catherine and Mary listened daily to a sermon in the
chapel, or in their mutual dining-chamber. The interviews
which ambassadors held with the royalties throughout this
period generally found both queens together, with Mary
sitting on Catherine's right hand. Often Mary and Catherine would be installed in one palace while Francis was
away hunting based on another. In April, Mary was
deeply depressed by the bad news from Scotland and it
was Catherine who took it upon herself to comfort her,
just as the previous year Mary had taken to heart Catherine's own grief over the death of Henry. When Throckmorton had an interview with Mary on 6 August, Catherine was present and Mary requested Throckmorton to
speak to the queen mother first.[20] Catherine was also
present at the interview which Francis and Mary granted
to Throckmorton on 15 September at Saint-Germain, and
she was together with the young couple when Condé was
arrested on 31 October. The natural trend of court life
was to throw the two queens together in conditions of

extreme intimacy, a state which appeared to be accepted by both women with perfect satisfaction.

Catherine had indeed been so sternly schooled in the previous reign in the art of maintaining friendly relations with those in positions of power that it would have been inconceivable for her to have displayed any sort of jealousy of Mary in public, while Francis remained on the throne. But to understand the true feelings of Catherine de Medicis towards Mary, it is necessary to appreciate that despite all her cunning, Queen Catherine was fundamentally not a political woman but a mother. The instincts of motherhood, gratified at long last after a hideous period of infertility, remained her strongest emotions. Thus she judged every situation from the point of view of how it might affect the welfare of her children; her desire for political strength sprang from her conviction that the more power she possessed, the more help she could give them. Mary, as ally or rival, was judged primarily from the point of view of Francis. While Francis lived, while Mary was his wife and as such a necessary adjunct to his life and happiness, Catherine would treat her with all the warmth and consideration which was her due; but once Francis was dead, once Mary was no longer the helpmeet of one child but a potential threat to the happiness of another, the picture was liable to be very different. As Regnier la Planche truly observed of Catherine after the death of Francis, when she finally became the official regent of France: for the past twenty-two years she had had plenty of leisure to consider the humours and fashions of the whole French court, so that she understood very well how to play her hand so as to win the game at last.[21]

Mary in her turn did not fail to be influenced by the personality of her mother-in-law. Not only did she imbibe a thoroughly dynastic approach to the business of being a queen, but from Catherine she learnt also that intrigue was a necessary, even enjoyable part of politics. These two thoroughly feminine lessons—that the considerations of the child or unborn child, the continuance of the dynasty, should be placed above all others, and that the most effective weapons in a queen's hand were those of diplomatic intrigue—were impressed on Mary consciously or unconsciously during the seventeen months in which she virtually shared the throne of France with Catherine de Medicis. The second lesson did not fall on particularly

fertile ground: Mary, unlike Catherine, was not by nature
a talented or adept intriguer. Yet she was to become an
enthusiastic one. The effect of Catherine's early lessons can
certainly be discerned in Mary's later career in Scotland
and England.

Despite the temporary victory of the Catholic party at
Amboise, the internal situation in France remained riven
with economic difficulty and religious crisis. In France's
desperate financial situation, it was generally agreed by
August, by Huguenots such as Coligny as well as Catholics
such as the Guises, that the only hope lay in trying to
establish some sort of civil unity. But it was easier to call
for unity than to achieve it. Both sides had their own notions of what was necessary. At a meeting of the Grand
Council, Coligny spoke out boldly in favour of the return
of the Estates, and the diminution of the king's guard,
which he claimed was dividing Francis from his people.
On 26 August, the Estates were convoked for the following December, and a date in January was chosen for a
national synod of the French Church, provided the Pope
should not have already announced an ecumenical council.
But the lost tranquillity of France was not so easily restored. Still fearing for his life, Francis left Fontainebleau
and went first to St Germain-en-Laye for safety, and then
on to Orleans, which, with his wife and mother, he reached
on 18 October. Here, surrounded by his army, he felt his
person to be more secure, unaware that in his case the
ravages of disease were more to be feared than the cold
steel of the assassin. As the Spanish ambassador reported
gloomily to his master that the religious situation in France
was going from bad to worse,[22] the prince of Condé decided to gamble on a personal appeal to King Francis,
whom he trusted to wean from the side of the Guises by
the magnetism of his own physical presence. His trust was
misplaced. On Condé's arrival in Orleans, Francis, on the
instructions of the Guises, reproached him tearfully with
his enterprises against the government. The prince of
Condé was arrested, and on 26 November condemned to
death.

But as the Guises' own fortunes had been transformed
by the sudden death of Henry II, so Condé in his turn
was to be saved by the workings of providence. The danger
of ambitious hopes founded on the frail life of a solitary

human being was once more demonstrated. King Francis announced his intention of setting off from Orleans on a prolonged hunting expedition, in the forests of Chenon-ceaux and Chambord, which would last him until the end of the month. But on Saturday 16 November, while still at Orleans, he returned from a day's hunting in the country, and complained of violent ear-ache. On the Sunday he fell down in a faint while at vespers in the chapel of the Jacobins. The weather had turned unexpectedly icy that November, and the Guises were criticized by the Spanish ambassador for letting the king hunt when the weather was so cold. Nevertheless at first neither the watchful ambassadors, the vultures of the sixteenth-century court, nor the anguished adherents of Condé, had any idea how serious the situation was.

Francis's health had always been the Achilles' heel of the Guises' plans: his breath was foetid; his physical appearance was so alarming, with red patches on his livid cheeks, that it actually gave birth to sinister rumours that he had leprosy; from this rumour spread the still more disgusting gossip that Francis needed to bathe in the blood of young children, in order to cure himself. The peasants thus hid their children from the king as he passed, convinced that otherwise this young Herod would avail himself of their bodies. Subsequently both Catholics and Protestants accused each other of having invented this nauseating calumny: the cardinal was said to have invented it in order to pave the way for the Guises to ascend the French throne, and the Huguenots were accused of trying to blacken the reputation of the Catholic king. The true explanation of Francis's facial condition was probably eczema, caused by the continual irritation of a purulent discharge from his ear; this originated from a chronic inflammation of the middle ear, arising from the constant respiratory infection of his childhood. When the king fell down in a faint on the Sunday, a large swelling appeared behind his left ear, caused by this inflammation spreading to the tissues above and below it.[23]

The Guises, whatever their private fears, were desperate to hide the gravity of his condition, and suspended the posts; they announced to the court merely that the fogs of the Loire had given the king a cold in the ear. The Venetian ambassador was sufficiently hoodwinked by the story to report that the two queens Mary and Catherine were fussing over the king, who was not actually ill. On 19 November the Spanish ambassador asked for, and got, an audience of the king, but was stopped at the door by the cardinal, who said that the king was suddenly worse. Chantonay immediately felt suspicious, and now noticed troubled glances among the Guises. Ridiculous rumours began to fly round the court: that a Huguenot valet had thrown a mortal powder into the king's nightcap, or that an Orleans barber had poured poison into his ear, while doing his hair. Once more the occult art of astrology was called into play to cast light on the situation, and it was recalled that it had been predicted that Francis should not live long—a prophecy, incidentally, which had been made by doctors as well as astrologers—on the grounds of Francis's health by the former, and of his horoscope by the latter. But the Venetian ambassador personally believed that much of Catherine's sorrow was caused by her recollection of these predictions.[24]

The intense interest of the court in the illness of their sovereign was heightened by the fact that the fate of Condé hung in the balance. If Francis died, he would be succeeded by his brother Charles. As Charles was only eleven, there could on this occasion be no question of withholding the regency from the man generally believed to have the best claim to it—the first prince of the blood, King Antoine of Navarre—who was, of course, Condé's elder brother. King Antoine's first act as regent was certain to be the reprieve and release of Condé. If Francis lived, Condé would die. If Francis died, Condé would live. In face of such interest, it was impossible for the Guises to continue to cast a cloud of obscurity over the nature of the king's disease forever. By 20 November, the Venetian ambassador was able to write off a full and accurate description of the king's symptoms. On 27 November, Throckmorton informed Elizabeth that the king's illness was now sufficiently serious for his doctors to doubt his ability to survive it; in any case it was thought that he could not expect to live very long, having wrecked his health in the first place by too much riding and exercise even before this 'evil accident'. The Venetian ambassador now learnt from someone who had been in his chamber, that the king was almost delirious. Even so, there were those who still believed that the illness was nothing more than a device of the

Guises to prevent the supplications of Condé being put
before Francis.[25]

Alas, the wretched little king, far from being the victim
of a Guise plot, was the infinitely more tragic victim of his
own constitution. He alternated between fevers and violent
crises, followed by bouts of speechlessness. In addition to
the natural sufferings of his condition, he also endured pur-
gations and bleedings. On 28 November, a massive dose
of rhubarb brought him some relief, but two days later
the headaches and sickness redoubled. The watch in his
bedroom was maintained ceaselessly by Mary and Catherine, whose joint role in his agony was to act endlessly
as nurses and comforters. On 3 December, it was reported
to Venice by their ambassador that Queen Mary, Queen
Catherine and the king's brothers were taking part in pro-
cessions to the churches of Orleans, to solicit divine aid
for the king's health.[26] Otherwise Mary spent the last
weeks of her husband's life in patient silent nursing in
his darkened chamber. Unlike their niece, the Guises
bore the king's affliction with little patience: their mental
agonies at the prospect opened before them by his illness
seemed almost as acute as the king's physical sufferings.
In their frenzy, they attacked the doctors for doing no
more for the king than they would have done for a common beggar; and in their pursuit of remedies they even
turned to the stone of alchemy.

Neither Mary's patient nursing, nor that of Catherine,
nor the rages of the Guises, nor their manifold remedies,
affected in any way the ineluctable process of the king's
illness. The inflammation was now spreading upwards into
the lobe of the brain, above the middle ear: on Monday,
2 December, there was an apparent improvement in his
condition due to the temporary release of tension when
the tumour was pierced. But the inflammation, having now
reached the brain, formed an abscess within it. With the
formation of the abscess, nothing could save the French
king from death. By the evening of 3 December, Francis
was *in extremis*. On Thursday 5 December, he fell into a
swoon. At some point in his agonies, he is said to have
murmured a prayer taught to him by the cardinal: 'Lord,
pardon my sins and impute not to me those which my
ministers have committed in my name and in my authority.'
But on the Thursday, at a time variously reported to be

five, eleven or ten, by La Planche, Throckmorton and Chantonay, the king's ordeal was at an end. A month off his seventeenth birthday, Francis II was dead.

Calvin wrote triumphantly to Sturm: 'Did you ever read or hear of anything more timely than the death of the little King? There was no remedy for the worst evils when God suddenly revealed himself from Heaven, and He who had pierced the father's eye, struck off the ear of the son.'[27] Calvin's Knox-like exultation reflected the natural view of the French Huguenots who had seen their cause forever swallowed in the voracious Catholic maw of the Guises. Now with the likelihood of Navarre's regency, it seemed that the French Huguenot cause had indeed been presented with a renewed opportunity to triumph through the death of the wretched Francis. The position of Mary was equally transformed by her husband's death: at the age of just eighteen, she was no longer queen but queen dowager of France. Her entire position in Scotland which had been founded on the umbrella-like protection which the French crown had extended to those Scots which it favoured, was likely to be in jeopardy now that her husband no longer sat on the French throne, and her uncles no longer directed French policy. Time would show whether she would evolve a better Scottish policy, or a worse one, but at all events on the death of Francis, Mary Stuart was obliged to work out a different one.

It is doubtful whether these political considerations were uppermost in the young queen's mind during the days before her husband's death, and the days of mourning afterwards. On the contrary, the evidence shows that, almost alone of the central figures at the French court, Mary abandoned herself to passionate grief at the death of the king, a grief founded on deep affection which she had felt for him, rather than the possible upset of her political plans. She had lost the companion of her childhood, the boy-husband who had loved her, and who had shared with her the happy intimacies of their charmed upbringing at the French court. Elisabeth had departed for Spain, Claude for Lorraine. Alone of her close royal companions of her youth, Francis had remained part of her life, and to their childhood intimacy had been added the natural intimacy of husband and wife. Since the first moment of their meeting at St Germain in October 1548, when the five-year-old

Scottish queen had been solemnly presented to the four-year-old dauphin of France, and King Henry II had rejoiced over the immediate love which the children felt for each other, Mary and Francis had never been apart for longer than a few months at a time. They had thus been united by over twelve years of continuous friendship and companionship, and all that happy childhood memories can signify in the mind of a romantic and affectionate young girl. It was only six months since the death of her mother which had induced in her such profound feelings of affliction: now she found herself bereft of a husband, with whom indeed she had led a far more prolonged and contented existence than the few short months she had spent with her mother since babyhood. It was small wonder that Mary gave herself up to transports of true grief.

The sincerity of her feelings was not doubted at the time. Throckmorton commented that Francis had left 'as heavy and dolorous a wife as of right she had good cause to be, who, by long watching with him during his sickness, and painful diligence about him' had worn herself out and made herself ill. The stanzas which Mary wrote on the death of Francis, which struck a chord in the heart of Ronsard, bear witness to the eloquent simplicity of her grief for the lost love of her childhood:

> Si en quelque séjour
> Soit en Bois ou en Prée
> Soit pour l'aube du jour
> Ou soit sur la Vesprée
> Sans cesse mon coeur sent
> Le regret d'un absent
> Si je suis en repos
> Sommeillant sur ma couche
> J'oy qu'il me tient propos
> Je le sens qui me touche
> En labeur et requoy
> Tousjours est prez de moy. . . . *

* Wherever I may be / In the woods or in the fields / Whatever the hour of day / Be it dawn or the eventide / My heart still feels it yet / The eternal regret . . . / As I sink into my sleep / The absent one is near / Alone upon my couch / I feel his beloved touch / In work or in repose / We are forever close . . . / *Translated by the author.*

The political realities of the situation would appear to her later—although some of them may have begun to come home to her, when Catherine asked for the return of the crown jewels, which the date on the order of release and the short hurriedly prepared inventories shows to have been only one day after King Francis's death, in a ghastly parody of events after the death of King Henry, when Mary herself had demanded the return of the jewels from Diane de Poitiers. In the meantime Mary wore white and shut herself in a black room lit by torches to give herself up totally to her sorrow. As the Venetian ambassador commented: 'Soon the death of the late King will be forgotten by all except his little wife, who has been widowed, has lost France, and has little hope of Scotland . . . her unhappiness and incessant tears call forth general compassion.'[28]

7 Mary the Widow

'Since her husband's death the Scottish Queen hath showed
. . . that she is both of great wisdom for her years, modesty
and also of great judgment . . . which, increasing with her
years, cannot but turn greatly to her commendation, reputation, honour and great benefit of her and her country.'

THROCKMORTON *to Queen Elizabeth, January 1561*

By tradition the mourning period of a queen of France
lasted for forty days. The obsequies of the young king
ended when his heart, enclosed in a leaden vase, was
taken to the cathedral of Saint-Denis, outside Paris, traditional resting-place of the kings of France: here amid the
numerous tombs the vase was placed on a pillar surrounded
by sculptured flames, to symbolize that Francis as king
had been as a pillar of flame in the Hebrew desert—a
reference to his stand against the heretics. Immediately
after the death of Francis, Mary, as we have seen, was
prostrated by grief, and kept herself solitary; in any case
visitors during the first fifteen days of her widowhood were
limited by convention to those whose rank was consdered
sufficiently elevated to justify their entrance—the new
King Charles IX, the king of Navarre, her uncles of
Guise and the constable of Montmorency. For more personal consolation Mary depended on her grandmother
Duchess Antoinette. However, once the first fortnight was
over, and Mary's storm of sorrow had abated, it was inevitable that she should consider her future in the world:
more especially did the subject of her future come rapidly
into prominence since ambassadors were permitted to visit
her during the second period of her mourning, and whatever the private unhappiness of a girl of eighteen who had
lost her husband, they at least were untroubled by such
considerations and, like her uncles of Guise, eager to press
on to the burning topic of her future.

There were two possible cornerstones on which such
discussions could be founded: a theoretical second marriage, and Mary's prospective return to Scotland. The Scot-

tish situation was, however, rendered extremely uncertain
by the fact that any sort of royal government had been
in virtual abeyance since the death of Mary of Guise: the
country was now ruled by a Protestant régime containing
both John Knox and the queen's half-brother Lord James
Stewart, under the titular leadership of Hamilton duke of
Châtelherault. Mary was virtually an unknown quantity in
Scotland at the time of Francis's death, and what little was
known of her was feared: she was regarded not only as a
Catholic by a country newly Protestant, but also as a
foreigner by reason of her French upbringing and marriage. It therefore seemed highly unlikely that Mary would
be received back in Scotland unless some foreign army
propelled her there; for this reason her return to Scotland was regarded as being bound up with and dependent
on her second marriage. Consequently during the spring of
1561 it was this marriage which received the full force
of diplomatic and courtly considerations.

The historian Froude, in a trenchant phrase, has accused
Mary herself of speculating on her next choice of husband
before her first husband's body was cold.[1] In fact the
marriage of a queen was unavoidably a political issue in
the sixteenth century; just as Mary's first marriage had
been fervently discussed from the very moment of her
birth, when she was far too young to take any effective
interest in the subject, so now it was natural that the
subject of her second marriage should obsess the conversation and correspondence of ambassadors and courtiers, to say nothing of her Guise relations, quite regardless
of her own personal feelings. The English ambassador,
Throckmorton, made the point with his usual clarity when
he indicated to the Council three weeks after Francis's
death, on the occasion of his first interview with Mary:
'Now that death had thus disposed of the late French king,
whereby the Scottish queen is left a widow, one of the
special things your lordships have to consider, and have
an eye to, is the marriage of that Queen.'[2] His letters are
abundantly filled with rumours on this critical subject. A
whole week before Francis's death when Mary was immured in her husband's sick-room, Throckmorton reported from Orleans that there were plenty of discourses
to be heard already of the French queen's second marriage
and he cited the names of Don Carlos of Spain, Philip II's
heir, the Archduke Charles of Austria, and the earl of

Arran, Châtelherault's heir. After the death of Francis, besides the three front-runners already cited by Throckmorton, who continued to lead the field of gossip, an increasing number of other names were mentioned, including the kings of Denmark and Sweden, the young Lord Darnley, with his desirable inheritance of English royal blood, even the recently widowed duke of Ferrera, who was thought to have a special affection for the Scottish queen. There was always the possibility, mentioned at the Spanish court, that Mary would eventually marry her own brother-in-law, Charles, with a papal dispensation: even the name of her own uncle, Grand Prior Francis of Guise, was canvassed. In short, by the time Mary emerged from her forty days of mourning, possible candidates could be said to include almost any currently unmarried male of roughly suitable age, whose own position could be held to benefit in any way that of the queen of Scots, either by establishing her own throne of Scotland, or by strengthening her claim to the throne of England, or even by re-establishing her on the throne of France.

The torrent of speculation made it inevitable that Mary herself would have to express some sort of personal predilection on the two subjects of re-marriage and Scotland, once she returned to the ways of ordinary life—unless, of course, she was content to leave her affairs and her future in the hands of her uncles as she had done in the past. This, however, she did not seem especially inclined to do, or at any rate, not to the extent which she had suffered herself to be guided during her time as dauphiness and queen of France. It has been suggested that the Guises lost interest in their niece once she no longer occupied the throne from which she could advance their interests: but the evidence of Mary's widowhood in France shows that on the contrary, it was she who attempted to stretch her political wings, and to struggle free as a butterfly from the chrysalis in which the Guises had lovingly contained her. As she was careful to tell Throckmorton just before her departure for Scotland, her uncles did not advise her on Scottish matters 'being of the affairs of France'.[3] Yet in the negotiations for a second marriage, the cardinal showed himself as anxious as ever to guide his niece. It was Mary the widow who was making the first efforts to think for herself, in a way which impressed all those around her.

In the first instance she evidently used the period of her mourning for a serious consideration of her future problems once her first collapse had given way to a more philosophical mood of resignation. Throckmorton visited her on 31 December, and his account of the interview shows us the first glimpse of the new Mary Stuart. There is no question but that the young queen made an excellent impression upon the English ambassador.[4] He wrote back to England that no great account had been made of the queen during her husband's lifetime, seeing that she had been 'under band of marriage and subjection to her husband (who carried the burden and care of all her matters)', and there had thus been no great opportunity to get to know her. But, he continued, since her husband's death she had shown, and continued to do so, that she was 'both a great wisdom for her years, modesty, and also of great judgment in the wise handling herself and her matters, which, increasing with her years, cannot but turn greatly to her commendation, reputation, honour and great benefit of her and her country'. Mary further impressed Throckmorton by professing herself ready to be guided by suitable advisers; 'And for my part,' continued Throckmorton, 'I see her behaviour to be such, and her wisdom and kingly modesty so great, in that she thinketh herself not too wise, but is content to be ruled by good counsel and wise men (which is a great virtue in a Prince or Princess, and which argueth a great judgment and wisdom in her).'

Throckmorton's last comment was of course not only intended to apprise the English Council as to the true nature of the Scottish queen with whom they had to deal: it was also intended as an acid reference to the somewhat less wise and modest conduct of their own Queen Elizabeth. The later reputations of Elizabeth and Mary have somewhat obscured the fact that in the early 1560s, when they were both young women, it was Elizabeth who was considered headstrong, extravagant and stubborn, whereas Mary was generally rated to be modest, intelligent and anxious to do her best as a ruler by taking wise advice. One contemporary described Elizabeth's court at this period as a by-word for frivolity: 'Nothing is treated earnestly, and though all things go wrong they jest, and he who invents most ways of wasting time is regarded as one worthy of honour.'[5]

Only a few months before, in September 1560, Amy Robsart, wife of the English queen's favourite, Robert Dudley, had been found dead in mysterious circumstances. The scandal, which invites comparison with the Scottish court tragedy of Kirk o'Field, although it had a different outcome, was not allayed by Elizabeth's continued association with Dudley and profuse rumours throughout the following winter that she intended to marry him now that he was free. Throckmorton himself was so terrified that his hair stood on end at the very thought, and he declared that he would not wish to live should that day ever come. How different was the conduct of the young queen of Scots, and how infinitely more becoming! It was no coincidence that Throckmorton chose to write to Dudley in the same vein, praising Mary's youthful discretion.[6]

Mary's forty days of mourning were officially ended when she attended a memorial service for Francis in the convent of Grey Friars at Orleans on 18 January. She now withdrew from the strict seclusion of her first *deuil* to a palace a few leagues outside the town of Orleans, which she occupied with her grandmother. By this date Mary had already written to Scotland a moderate temporizing letter, by which she broke the news of Francis's death formally to the Scottish Estates, and assured them that she intended to forget past troubles and differences; she went on to express her desire to return to Scotland as soon as possible, in token of which she asked for royal accounts since the death of her mother, and demanded from the Estates a list of candidates to fill the roles of treasurer and controller in Scotland.[7] The gentle, positively placating tone of this letter was thoroughly in tune with what Mary had also told Throckmorton on the subject of Scotland—that she wished to return home as soon as possible, and hoped it would be at the request and suit of her subjects.

But at this very moment, Mary was also the willing participant in marriage negotiations with Don Carlos of Spain; it is evident that her attitude towards Scotland in the spring, despite her soft words to Throckmorton, was very much one of 'wait and see'. Marriage to Don Carlos, heir to the great throne of Spanish empire, was an infinitely more glorious prospect than a highly speculative return to a distant kingdom. Mary Stuart had been trained to believe herself a worthy incumbent of thrones, and the

Guises had encouraged her in this belief. Don Carlos was a Catholic and could be expected to be supported by Spanish troops. The Spanish marriage was Mary's first choice for her future after Francis's death, and the return to Scotland only assumed its full importance once the prospect of the Spanish marriage faded from the scene for the time being. As has been seen, while Francis lay *in extremis,* there had been rumours at the French court of the possibility of such a match. When the Spanish ambassador visited Mary in the second stage of her mourning, he was thought to have lingered an unconscionably long time 'above an hour together'—too long, thought Throckmorton, for a conventional visit of condolence. The cardinal told Chantonay that his niece only wished for a Spanish marriage. On 10 January Throckmorton reported that 'the house of Guise use all means to bring to pass the marriage between the prince of Spain and the Queen of Scotland'. At the end of January Don Juan Manrique arrived at the French court, and according to the Venetian ambassador 'went to visit the Queen of Scotland, with whom, in the presence of the Duke of Guise and the Cardinal of Lorraine, he held very confidential communications, and, I am assured that, besides his other concerns, Don Juan is also empowered to treat a marriage between her Majesty and the Prince of Spain'.[8]

Don Carlos himself had little to commend him personally as a husband, and indeed in many ways was merely a still feebler version of the wretched Francis, without the advantage of having been well known to Mary in childhood. He was physically undersized, weighing less than five and a half stone. One of his shoulders was higher than the other, he had a marked speech impediment and was also an epileptic. At the time of Mary's first widowhood, he was sixteen, a few months older than his young stepmother Elisabeth of Valois. At the age of seventeen he fell headlong down a staircase, supposedly pursuing a serving maid, and the resulting concussion did nothing to improve his mental state. He lay for a long time, blind and partially paralysed, until an Italian surgeon gave him partial relief by a trepanning operation to cut a triangular piece out of his skull. This relieved the paralysis, but left him in turn prone to fits of homicidal mania: he also subsequently developed a passionate attachment to his young stepmother and a corresponding hatred of his father, the

king.* There was certainly nothing in Don Carlos to inspire any flight of fancy in the mind of a young, recently
widowed queen: it is interesting to note that at this stage
in her career, Mary Stuart's choice of husband was without
hesitation one whose attractions were strictly political
and dynastic. She thoroughly justified Throckmorton's
shrewd estimate of her character in this respect—so commendably different from that of his own wayward mistress
Elizabeth—'As far as I can learn, she more esteemeth
the continuation of her honour and to marry one that
may uphold her to be great than she passeth to please her
fancy by taking one that is accompanied with such small
benefit or alliance, as thereby her estimation and fame is
not increased'.[9]

Fortunately or unfortunately, Mary Stuart was not destined to become another Spanish bride, like her cousin
Mary Tudor. The possible consequences of such an alliance to a strong Catholic power, early in her career, for
Mary herself, for Scotland and indeed the whole British
Isles, lead one down the pleasurable but irrelevant avenues
of speculation. There was an implacable, if unseen, obstacle
in the way of these early negotiations, in the shape of the
hostility of Catherine de Medicis. The death of Francis
had resulted in a real political triumph for the dowager
queen: although it was confidently expected that the
regency of the kingdom would fall into the hands of the
king of Navarre, Catherine had, by a mixture of coercion
and cajolery, cleverly persuaded him to leave it in her
own hands. In return she allowed his brother Condé to
be pardoned, and past misdemeanours on the part of the
Bourbons to be forgotten, and further fobbed off the
king with the title of lieutenant-general of the kingdom. It
was a gesture of supreme political and personal intelligence,
since by retaining the regency in her own hands Catherine
both prevented the warring nobles of the court from

* This passion, which has been enveloped in the mantle of romance by Schiller and Verdi, was in fact more the one-sided fixation
of an idiot than the reciprocated grand passion of their imagination.
One may prefer the notion of the romantic liberal-minded Don Carlos of the opera: but there is no historical evidence that Elisabeth of
Valois ever returned the devotion of her feeble-minded son-in-law,
and she seems indeed to have lived comparatively happily with her
elderly husband, before her premature death.

tearing the kingdom in two, and also promoted the interests of her own family, in the way which was dearest to
her heart. The Guises, who only eighteen days before
Francis's death, had been so confident of Catherine's support, found that their power was considerably and effectively diminished, although Catherine was once again too
clever to go so far as to drive them into open hostility.
Her ultimate object was, after all, the safe rule of her
son over all the nobles in the kingdom, rather than personal revenge.

Catherine's attitude to her son's widow showed the same
judicious mixture of outward conciliation and inward
rigidity on any subject where their interests might clash.
In her letter to the Estates of Scotland, in January, Mary
paid Catherine a warm tribute for her kindness, and said
that she could not have expected more consolation in
her sorrow from her own mother. She also told the Estates
that since France was now ruled by the queen mother,
the Franco-Scottish alliance would be firmer than ever.
Catherine's private letters to her daughter Elisabeth of
Spain tell a very different story.[10] Mary is referred to by the
code name of *le gentilhomme*, a figure of whom Elisabeth
is to be extremely wary. Officially, Catherine was given
no cognizance of Mary's negotiations for a Spanish marriage; but her hostility to the match was none the less
effective for being devious and serpentine, since it allowed
her to maintain a delusive mask of friendliness to her
daughter-in-law. Catherine feared that the house of Valois
would be twice threatened by Mary's return to glory,
through her marriage to Don Carlos. First of all, the star
of the Guises would inevitably rise again, and with their
niece so close to the Spanish throne, who knew what new
twists they might not give to the skein of their ambitions.
Secondly, Catherine feared for the position of her own
daughter Elisabeth on the throne of Spain if Philip
should die and Carlos inherit, in which case Elisabeth might
be pushed aside as she, Catherine, had once been. While
Catherine gave Elisabeth precise instructions on how to
frustrate the match from the Spanish end, Catherine herself complicated the issue by dangling the prospect of
another royal bride for Don Carlos in front of Philip's
eyes—her own daughter Marguerite.

France was not the only country where Mary's Spanish
match was looked on with concern. In England the pros-

pect of Mary Stuart's marriage to a foreign prince, especially a Spanish one, was regarded as scarcely less threatening to the maintenance of English power, and when in
March Elizabeth's minister Cecil wrote a memorial to his
agent in Scotland, Thomas Randolph, on Anglo-Scottish
affairs, the third point on his draft was headed 'the menace of a foreign marriage by the Scottish Queen'.[11] To
Philip, confronted with the firm hostility of Catherine and
Elizabeth of England, and with the prospect of Marguerite
held out before him, Mary no longer seemed so alluring as
a future daughter-in-law. Not only did Philip believe he
would have to establish Mary on her throne by force, but
he would also have to sacrifice his present good relations
with Elizabeth of England. Hitherto Philip had supported
her in calming down her English Catholics, in order to
balance the opposing Franco-Scottish nexus. So long as
Elizabeth did not marry Dudley—and the possibility was
now slightly receding—a Catholic rising in England to
put Mary on the throne was unlikely. Faced with these
considerations Philip understandably preferred the substance of Elizabeth to the shadow of Mary; perhaps he
also shrank somewhat from the prospect of introducing a
Guise cuckoo into the Spanish nest. By the end of April,
Elisabeth of Spain was able to inform her mother that the
Spanish negotiations with Mary had foundered finally, for
lack of interest on Philip's part.

In the meantime Mary naturally continued to be a focus
of interest for other countries, other aspirants. In February, the earl of Bedford arrived on an official embassy
of condolence from Queen Elizabeth of England. Queen
Mary thanked him graciously for her fellow-queen's comfort in her distress and added in her most friendly manner 'considering that the Queen now shows the part of a
good sister, whereof she has great need, she will endeavour
to be even with her goodwill; and though she be not so
able as another, yet she trust the Queen will take her
goodwill in good part'. It was on this occasion that Mary
also took the opportunity to remind Throckmorton that he
had not sent her the portrait of Elizabeth, despite her fervent desire to exchange pictures.* Bedford's next two in-

* Mary's picture for Elizabeth was completed and sent by 1 December 1561. The two queens also exchanged portraits again in the
next year, 1562.[12]

terviews with Queen Mary were, however, on a less gracious, more down-to-earth level, since he had been instructed to ask her yet again to ratify the Treaty of Edinburgh. This treaty, by which peace had been established the previous July between England, Scotland and France, provided for the withdrawal of French troops from Scotland and pledged both France and England to a policy of non-interference there; it had also laid down that Mary and Francis should abandon forever the bearing of the English royal arms. Mary politely but firmly declined to agree to the ratification on the grounds that she must first consult with her Council, in view of her changed status as a widow, but once again went out of her way to show friendliness. She hinted that 'if her Council were here she would give such an answer as would satisfy him', and expressed a strong desire to meet Elizabeth personally, to talk over their differences, for she felt that thus 'they would satisfy each other much better than they can do by messages and ministers'.[13] This desire on the part of Mary to meet Elizabeth face to face, whether prompted by friendship, political wisdom or sheer feminine curiosity, was perfectly understandable; it is also easy to sympathize with Mary's reluctance to ratify the Treaty of Edinburgh so long as Elizabeth declined to recognize her cousin as heiress-presumptive to the English throne. By ratifying the Treaty of Edinburgh immediately, Mary would be discarding a potentially valuable card, for in return for the ratification it was Mary's hope that Elizabeth would set aside the will of Henry VIII from the English succession.

While still at Orleans, Mary received another manifestation of the importance of her claim to the English throne. A young scion of both English and Scottish royal houses, Henry Stuart, Lord Darnley, appeared at the court on an official visit of condolence to his widowed cousin. Darnley, then a youth of only fifteen or sixteen, had not himself provided the impetus for the visit. He had in fact met Mary Stuart briefly once before at the time of Francis's coronation, when his mother Margaret, countess of Lennox, despatched him with a letter to the French court, concerning the restoration of Lennox to the family estates in Scotland. Now his ambitious, striving mother propelled the good-looking boy yet again in the direction of France, with the clear intention of dangling him, royal blood and all, in the path of the newly marriageable young queen.

Darnley was a Catholic, and having been born in England, it could be argued that he was not debarred from the succession by the will of Henry VIII. The Spanish ambassador in England, de Quadra, told his master Philip that if anything happened to Elizabeth, it was understood that the English Catholics would raise Darnley to the throne of England. But in the convoluted world of royal claims and counter-claims, wavering rights were held to be generally strengthened if reinforced by marriage to someone with other wavering rights. The plan was to induce Mary to wed Darnley, with the lure of thus bolstering up her claim to the English throne; Margaret Lennox entered into negotiations with the Scottish nobles at the same time, to the same effect. But, on this occasion at least, the royal fish did not rise to the bait. Mary herself was still involved in her dreams of a glorious Spanish alliance: if Darnley's appearance did make any impression on her sensibilities, this impression was stored away for the future, since her sensibilities at this time were so acutely subordinated to her political activities.

In the middle of March Mary decided to leave the French court, and set off on a prolonged round of visits to her Guise relations. She went first of all to the Guise *château* of Nanteuil, and then on to Rheims, where she made a three-week stay in the convent of her Aunt Renée, abbess of St Pierre, breaking the journey for a brief visit to Paris on 20 March to check over her clothes and jewels. From Rheims, she planned to go to Nancy, in Lorraine, to visit the court of her kinsman, Duke Charles, and her sister-in-law, Duchess Claude; from Nancy she could proceed easily to Joinville, the most outlying of the Guise *châteaux*. Melville, in his Memoirs, attributes the journey to the spite of Catherine, now openly displayed: 'Our Queen, then Dowager of France, retired herself by little and little farther and farther from the Court of France; that it should not seem that she was in any sort compelled thereunto, as of truth she was by the Queen Mother's rigorous and vengeable dealing; who alleged that she was despised by her good daughter, during the short reign of King Francis her husband, by the instigation of the House of Guise.'[14] But Melville is not always strictly accurate in his recollections. Mary had plenty of motives to make such a journey, without the animus of Catherine to inspire her, while Catherine herself understood only too well that hostile intrigues were more easily conducted under the guise of friendship to the victim. Apart from her natural desire to pay a round of visits, to the family of whom she had always been so fond, it seems likely that Mary was also anxious to take part in family conclaves on the subject of her future, which would be easier to arrange away from the confined atmosphere of the French court.

It so happened that while Mary Stuart was on the route from Rheims to Nancy, she received two rival embassies from Scotland, which at the moment when the Spanish negotiations were foundering, opened up new possibilities in terms of a Scottish future. To Vitry in Champagne, came first of all John Leslie, bishop of Ross, Mary's future envoy and historian, representing the party of the Scottish Catholics, and secondly, James Stewart her half-brother, on behalf of the self-constituted Scottish Protestant government. Leslie's suggestions were bold enough: he believed that Mary should detain Lord James in France, and herself disembark at Aberdeen, where he swore she would find 20,000 men levied by her friends in the north of Scotland. She would then be in a position to take Scotland by storm. It is to Mary's credit that she rejected such extremist counsels immediately. The advice was of doubtful value in any case since even the strongest Catholic noble Huntly showed uncertain loyalties at this moment. However, one of the side-effects of Leslie's embassy was to confirm Mary's own view that she would be personally popular once she reached Scotland. (Had she not confidently told Throckmorton that the common people would be glad to see their queen come home?) Leslie told the queen that he expected her to 'overshadow' her subjects with her presence when she returned like a newly-risen sun to scatter the clouds of all tumult shortly from the minds of her subjects.[15] In her interview with her half-brother the next day, Mary retained the bishop's image, while rejecting his advice.

The new emissary with whom Mary had to deal was her half-brother the Lord James. James Stewart was now a man of thirty, some twelve years older than his half-sister. His mother, Margaret Erskine, was that royal mistress who had served for the model of 'Lady Sensualitie' in Sir David Lyndsay's *Satire of the Three Estates;* as the sister of the earl of Mar she ensured her son a place in the network of

Scottish noble families surrounding the crown, in which
the Erskines were honourably situated. From his father
King James v, Lord James inherited the royal Stewart
blood which placed him so close yet so tantalizingly far
from the Scottish throne. One consequence of the importance of kinship in sixteenth-century Scotland was to endow the sovereign's illegitimate children with great natural
importance, because they shared the royal Stewart blood.
It was not quite impossible that a strong male ruler born
out of wedlock might be preferred to a weak female of
legitimate descent. Of the nine known bastards of James
v, three sons—Lord James, Lord Robert and Lord John
Stewart—occupied high positions at Mary's court; and a
daughter Jean Stewart, who married the earl of Argyll, became one of her closest friends, a friendship which originated in their shared blood. James v had even made some
sporadic efforts in 1536, when Lord James was four years
old, to obtain the papal dispensation which would have
enabled him to marry the child's mother, Lady Margaret.
However, the position of Lord James would not have been
automatically clarified by the marriage of his parents: although by Scots law the subsequent marriage of parents
legitimated their offspring, this only applied to parents who
were free to marry at the time of the birth; Lady Margaret
had been married to Robert Douglas in 1527, four years
before the birth of her son in 1531. Lord James might also
have found himself in a disadvantageous position compared to any subsequent children born to James v and
Margaret, who would have begun life as royal princes,
without the stain of bastardy.*

Lacking the charm of his father, Lord James was a man
of solemn manner and appearance; yet this *gravitas,* so
unlike the qualities of the contemporary French nobility,
was to prove highly successful in impressing the English
when he dealt with them. From his Stewart father, James
had inherited at least a subtlety lacking in many of his
contemporaries among the Scottish nobility, which to the
English made him seem a distinct improvement on his
peers—or perhaps this fortunate ability to deal with En-

* Lord James was legitimated in February 1551. But the importance of legitimation in this period was not so much to remove a
social stigma as to correct the fact that bastards could neither leave
nor inherit property. The estates of a bastard descended to the crown
on his death, if he was never legitimated during his lifetime.

gland could be attributed to the fact that he was also one quarter Tudor. The English were delighted to be able to discern in him what they supposed to be a type of new Scotsman, upright, serious-minded and full of conscious rectitude, frequently given public expression, who seemed to them a distinct advance on the self-seeking Scottish nobles of the previous generation. Although more gifted politically than the sons of his fellow-nobles, Lord James was in fact far from immune from that practical avarice so characteristic of the Scottish nobility of this period—nor did he lack the hypocrisy which so often accompanies frequent public statements of the subject of honour. But this temperament, and above all the quality of his religious views, which fitted in so well with those of the English politicians of the period like Cecil, meant that he was always able to deal easily, if not honourably, with his English equivalents, and this was to give him a practical advantage in Anglo-Scottish affairs at a later stage in his half-sister's career.

On his way to France on this occasion, Lord James had stopped in England: he certainly conferred with Cecil, with whom he had an old friendship, and may even have stayed in his house. His interview with Mary, held at St Dizier, was not unsatisfactory to both the participants, despite their widely differing points of view. Lord James had been instructed to ask the queen to embrace the Scottish Protestant faith: this she steadily refused to do. But she did state with some courage that she was prepared to come home without any other restrictions, or a personal armed escort, provided she could have use of her own religion in private. This Lord James himself had already expressed publicly to the Scots as being an acceptable demand. When it was suggested to him that the celebration of any sort of Mass, public or private, within the realm of Scotland would be a betrayal of the cause of God, he replied reasonably enough that this might indeed apply to a public Mass—'but to have it secretly in her (Mary's) chamber, who could stop her?'[16] Mary also allowed herself to be convinced by Lord James that it was politically wise to give the Protestant party its head for the time being in Scotland, although James later told Throckmorton Mary had begun the interview by offering him a cardinal's hat, and several rich benefices in France, if he in turn would forswear Protestantism. The sacrifice of the prospect of

these rich benefices did not mean that Lord James's mind
was altogether concentrated on Scottish affairs, on this occasion, to the exclusion of personal gain, since he almost
certainly took the opportunity to ask his half-sister for the
rich earldom of Moray. Apart from the general understanding which they had reached on the subject of her return, Mary must also have been impressed as a result of
this meeting with the notion that Lord James would constitute her natural adviser in Scotland, by virtue of their
blood connection, as the Guises had done in France. She
had emphasized to Throckmorton that she was prepared
to listen to advice, and even if all Lord James's advice had
not been to her liking, the basis for some tolerable *modus
vivendi*, in the event of her return, had at least been
reached between them.

Yet Lord James was very far from being a Scottish
Guise, in any sense of the word; his next actions showed
that in his order of loyalties he placed the interests of the
Scottish Protestant party, as embodied in an English alliance, well above those of his sister's confidence. Returning
to Paris, he went secretly to Throckmorton's lodgings,
and, in Throckmorton's own words, 'declared unto me at
good length all that passed between the Queen, his sister
and him, and between the Cardinal of Lorraine and him'.[17]
Throckmorton in turn passed the information on to Elizabeth. Although James did actually inform Mary that he
had met Throckmorton, he presumably did not impart to
her the full nature of their discourses. On his way back to
Scotland, Lord James once again stopped in England, and
conferred with Cecil: it has been suggested on the evidence of Camden's Annals, that during his two weeks in
London, James suggested to Elizabeth that she should provide for her religion and her safety by intercepting Mary
on her journey back to Scotland.[18] But in fact, he had little
motive for doing so, so long as Mary showed herself so
adaptable, and so amenable to his advice; his subsequent
actions show that his real intentions were to keep in well
with both queens, rather than secure the captivity of one
by the other. The prospect of a Queen Mary on the throne
of Scotland, dependent on his counsels, and Queen Elizabeth on the throne of England, favourable to his policies,
opened up new and agreeable avenues of ambition to
Lord James. In the meantime James certainly won golden
opinions from Throckmorton as a result of his confidences,

who despite their illicit nature, wrote ecstatically that he
was 'one of the most virtuous noblemen, and one in whom
religion, sincerity and magnanimity as much reign as
ever he knew in any man in any nation'. He also took care
to suggest that there should be a genuinely silver lining
to this cloud of intrigue—in the shape of a distribution
of £20,000 sterling, among the chief men of Scotland, to
include Châtelherault and, of course, Lord James.

James's advice to his sister on the subject of the Scottish
Protestants accorded well with what Mary had already
been told from other sources about the Scottish situation.
Throckmorton heard that even the king of Spain had advised her to be prepared to temporize in matters of religion,
on her first arrival. Melville tells us that all the Frenchmen
who had recently returned from Scotland advised her to
be most familiar with James, Argyll, Maitland and Kirkcaldy of Grange, in short to learn to repose most upon
the members of the reformed religion.[19] Such practical
advice, coloured by tolerance, accorded well with Mary's
own temperament and religious convictions. In religious
matters, her leaning was towards the tolerance of her
mother, rather than the fanaticism of a cardinal of Guise.
As a born Catholic, who had known no other creed, her
faith was to her like her everyday bread, something which
she took for granted, and yet which was essential to her,
and without which she could not imagine her existence; it
was, however, in no sense an Old Testament faith, a fierce
Moloch of a faith, which demanded the sacrifice of all
other faiths to propitiate it, such as animated Philip II of
Spain.

Mary's innate clemency in matters of religion has sometimes been mistaken for lukewarm convictions. The truth
was that she drew a clear distinction between private faith
and public policy. She herself gave Throckmorton the
most explicit avowal of her beliefs, on the eve of her
departure for Scotland:[20] 'I will be plain with you,' she
told him. 'The religion which I profess I take to be the
most acceptable to God; and, indeed, neither do I know,
nor desire to know any other. Constancy becometh all
folks well, and none better than princes, and such as have
rule over realms, and specially in matters of religion. I
have been brought up in this religion; and who aught
would credit me in anything if I should show myself

higher in this case.' This eloquent profession of faith can scarcely be bettered as the personal apologia of a ruler, who at the same time believed in toleration and mercy for those around her. Although Randolph wrote when she was in Scotland: 'She wishes that all men should live as they please',[21] Knox was quick to realize that such permissiveness did not mean, as some suggested in October 1561, that the queen herself should ever be of their opinion. Mary's personal Catholicism was total, her attitude to a state religion inclined to be pragmatic.

Mary's pilgrimage among her Guise relations culminated in a visit to the court of Lorraine, where Duchess Claude, her erstwhile friend, reigned in state. Claude was not destined to atone in public for the private disloyalty of her sister Elisabeth. The princess had grown proud, and used to the adulation of her little court; the widowed queen found little feminine consolation in her company. Nevertheless the Lorrainers gave her a grandiose reception, and 'a magnificent triumph' was planned, with cannons discharged from the city walls of Nancy, in her honour. Bishop Leslie describes how Mary was further entertained with hunting in the fields, and pleasant farces and plays.[22] These diversions did not prevent her falling ill with one of those tertian fevers to which she was so subject. It is possible that the attack was induced by the mental stress of deciding about her future, now that the negotiations for the Spanish marriage were finally halted. The attack was certainly sufficiently severe and prolonged to prevent her arriving at Rheims in time for the coronation of the young Charles IX as she had planned. Instead her grandmother fetched her from Nancy to Joinville, and here even on 25 May, she was still in bed in the throes of a prolonged convalescence, and not allowed to speak to anyone except her doctors. However, by 28 May she had managed to reach Rheims, and was there entertained once again by her aunt the abbess and her uncle the cardinal. On 10 June, Mary finally returned once more to the environs of the French court, from which she had been absent for a critical three months. Her return was accompanied by the formal rejoicings which befitted her rank as a dowager queen of France. She was officially greeted a league outside Paris by the duke of Orleans, the king of Navarre, the prince of Condé and the other princes of the blood, who accompanied her in state into the town. Here she was conducted to her actual lodgings within the palace by the king, the queen mother and the entire court.

Whether Mary's illness was induced by indecision or not, by the time she returned to the court from her wanderings, her mind was evidently made up to return to Scotland. Although a number of factors induced her to reach this decision, it was not the only alternative open to her. Despite the secret hostility of Catherine, Mary's rank in France entitled her to an honourable position at the French court, from which it would have been difficult to dislodge her, if she had been determined to maintain it. Her marriage contract to Francis specifically stated that in the event of his death, she was to be allowed the choice of remaining in France or returning to Scotland. Her marriage portion had made her duchess of Touraine, and her estates there and in Poitou were sufficiently widespread and lucrative to have maintained her in an adequate state; the Guise family, although somewhat blighted, were not totally destitute of power; if she remained on the Continent, it was not likely to be long before some more ardent royal suitor than Don Carlos emerged. To Mary herself must be given the credit of having personally settled for a bold course of adventure, rather than the more placid less demanding existence which it would still have been possible for her to lead in France. The truth was that even as a young girl, Mary showed signs of having a gambling streak, and she was certainly singularly unendowed with conservatism in her nature: the familiar path was never to her automatically the most attractive path while there was another more daring route to be explored. Life in France, as she had known it so gloriously, appeared to have come to an end; but on the horizon, Scotland beckoned, which might provide in time—who could tell, but Mary was an optimist—as many golden opportunities.

As it happened, at the same moment the Scots themselves were beginning to feel more warmly about their absent queen. Among the politicians, it was the quick-witted Maitland with his sense of international values who pointed out that Mary's dynastic claim to the English throne could now work to the advantage of Scotland, rather than France, if she returned to her own country. They suddenly realized that a malleable young ruler, with a strong personal claim to succeed to the neighbouring

throne, and apparently prepared to behave reasonably over
religion was certainly not to be discarded in a hurry. As a
result of these cogitations, Lord James wrote a letter on
10 June which constituted a virtual invitation on behalf
of the Protestant lords to return. Maitland himself wrote
to Mary promising to do all he could for her service.
Scotland for Mary therefore was not a *pis aller,* but a
hopeful venture, in which her Guise blood encouraged her
to expect success.

Neither Moray nor Maitland was especially put out by
the fact that Mary still declined to ratify the Treaty of
Edinburgh: not unnaturally they shared Mary's view that
it was a subject that could be best dealt with once she had
returned to Scotland and could consult her Council.
Throckmorton on the other hand was still desperately hoping to secure the ratification. He sent Somer to Nancy in
April and to Rheims in May: both missions were fruitless.
Now that Mary was returning to the French court, he
begged her with renewed fervour to grant long-withheld
ratification. At an audience of 18 June, Mary pointed out
that her health was still too frail for serious consideration
of such matters, but she went on to say that since in any
case she intended to return to Scotland very shortly, she
would defer her answer until she had the advice of the
Estates and nobles of her own realm. She told Throckmorton that she intended to embark shortly at Calais, and
to this effect d'Oysel was being sent to Elizabeth with a
message asking for a safe-conduct on her route back to
Scotland.[23]

But when d'Oysel had his interview with Elizabeth on
13 July requesting a passport for Mary, the English queen
at once asked him whether he had brought the ratification
of the Treaty of Edinburgh with him. D'Oysel replied that
he had no instructions on the subject. At this he was greeted
by such hostility from Elizabeth—as well as a blank refusal to give the safe-conduct—that when Mary next spoke
with Throckmorton she ironically suggested they should
draw apart, in case he angered her by his speech, as she
herself did not wish to be witnessed giving such a display
of 'choler and stomache' as Elizabeth had shown to
d'Oysel.[24] Elizabeth's behaviour smacks of childish pique
rather than statecraft, and it was not well regarded at the
time, even by her own ambassador. Throckmorton was
frankly amazed at the refusal and said so to Cecil: in his

opinion, the sooner Mary was plucked out of the tangled
web of continental intrigue, into the comparative safety of
distant Scotland, the better it would be for England. The
Scots were appalled, since their avowed aim in the words
of Maitland was to see both queens 'as near friends, as
they were tender cousins', with a view to getting Elizabeth
to recognize Mary as her heir; now here was one tender
cousin treating the other in a way more likely to lead to
distant enmity than near friendship. The Venetian ambassador, a more impartial judge of the situation, described
the refusal as contrary to expectation and certainty, as
well as being in opposition to the dictates of humanity.[25]

Elizabeth's refusal gave Mary Stuart her first public
opportunity of rising magnificently to a crisis. She now
displayed for the first time that quality of cool courage,
when in the public eye, which was to be a feature of her
later career. It was courage which owed nothing to physical well-being. At the beginning of July Mary had a renewed attack of the tertian fever, and when Throckmorton
saw her on 9 July he noted that it had 'somewhat ap-
paired her cheer', although she herself dismissed it lightly
and said that the worst was over. Now, when she received
Throckmorton on 20 July at Saint-Germain, having heard
the news of the denied passport, she was infinitely composed; in a series of speeches to the English ambassador
of fine histrionic power, she showed herself to be not
only brave, but also reasonable and even charitable towards the woman who had thus rejected her—as well as
incidentally having an eloquent command of language.[26]
Like an actress before an audience, the eighteen-year-old
queen seemed to derive strength from the fact that the
eyes of Europe were upon her. Her interviews with Throckmorton lead one to the conclusion that Mary, far from
being daunted by the drama of the situation, was positively
inspired by it.

She began by expressing in polite terms her regrets that
she should have bothered Throckmorton by demanding
a passport which she did not in fact require. She had
reached France in safety, she pointed out proudly, in spite
of the efforts of the king of England to intercept her.
Thirteen years later, she would surely once more reach
her own country with her own people to help her. Mary
also told Throckmorton that she had no intention of ratifying the treaty until she reached her own land, where she

would have the benefit of the advice of the Estates, since
she was bound neither in honour nor in conscience to perform what her late husband had commanded. But as a
proof that she wished to live in amity with the English
queen, Mary also pointed out on the vexed point of the
English arms, that since the death of both her father-in-law
and husband she had borne neither arms nor title.

The next day Throckmorton came to see her again, and
Mary spoke to him with renewed oratorical fervour: 'Monsieur l'Ambassadeur, if my preparations were not so much
advanced as they are, peradventure the Queen, your Mistress' unkindness might stay my voyage; but now I am
determined to adventure the matter, whatsoever come of
it; I trust the wind will be so favourable as I shall not
need to come on the coast of England; and if I do, Monsieur l'Ambassadeur, the Queen your Mistress shall have
me in her hands to do her will of me; and if she be so
hard-hearted as to desire my end, she may then do her
pleasure, and make sacrifice of me; peradventure that
casualty might be better for me than to live,' added Mary
dramatically, although one suspects her real expectations
were somewhat less pessimistic. 'In this matter, God's will
be fulfilled,' she concluded and, in a final superb gesture,
embraced the attendant Throckmorton.[27]

Mary followed up the interview with a friendly letter to
Elizabeth to see if the safe-conduct could still be obtained:
but without awaiting the answer, she forthwith made her
preparations to leave France, passport or no passport. On
25 July, she departed from the court of Saint-Germain,
here bidding adieu to King Charles, Queen Catherine and
the majority of the nobility who had known her throughout childhood, youth and marriage. According to Leslie,
the ancient Franco-Scottish alliance was not forgotten at
this final moment and confirmation was made of 'a perpetual friendship to stand among them, as it had been between their predecessors, by most ancient band and league,
inviolably in all times past'.[28] When the grand farewell
fête, which was held in her honour at Saint-Germain, and
lasted for four days, was over, the young queen set out
for Calais, accompanied by her six uncles and other members of the court. The train stopped at Merly, the constable's house, on their way, where both the cardinal and
duke of Guise fell ill overnight—although in this case
the proverbial rumours of poison which greeted the inci-

dent were made less realistic by the fact that the king of Navarre was also stricken. On 3 August, Mary was still at Beauvais, and Throckmorton then followed her on to Abbeville. Where on 7 August, he had a final interview with the queen, at which both reiterated their former arguments, Mary laying special emphasis on the fact that since she was acting without the advice of her uncles, she genuinely needed to obtain the advice of the Scots before she proceeded further—'I do so much know mine own infirmity that I will do nothing . . . without counsel.'[29]

On 8 August Throckmorton bid the queen a last goodbye. The admiration which the ambassador felt for the queen seems to have been reciprocated. Always generous to those who served her, Mary wrote to Lady Throckmorton the day before she sailed from Calais, saying that she had charged her *maître d'hôtel* to visit her and give her a present as a remembrance of her affection, and a token of the regard which she felt for her husband. Lady Throckmorton subsequently received two basins, two ewers, two salts and a standing cup, all of gilt. A zealous Protestant, whose career in England had been under a cloud during the reign of the Catholic Mary Tudor, when he was tried for complicity in the Wyatt rebellion, in France Throckmorton openly hated the Catholic Guises and admired the Huguenots. Yet he was clearly fascinated by the Catholic queen of Scots, as were so many of Queen Elizabeth's servitors who were to come into personal contact with her. As Mary was beginning to expand in her mind the possibilities of meeting the queen of England face to face, perhaps Elizabeth at the same moment was already digesting the fact that personal contact with the queen of Scots was apt to have an alarmingly seductive effect on the listener.

On the evening of 8 August, Mary rode to the abbey of Forest Monstrier, where she decided to send the lord of St Colme Inch and Alexander Erskine to England, accompanied by Throckmorton's servant Tremaine, for a final appeal for the passport. Before the effects of this letter could be felt—once again its tone was extremely friendly—the preparations for Mary's journey had been completed. The queen and her party were to travel in two galleys, accompanied by two ships. The preparations were not left entirely in the hands of the French. The hereditary Lord High Admiral of Scotland was also involved—this was none other than James Hepburn, earl of Bothwell.

This spirited border lord had already swum into the ken
of the Scottish queen during the previous autumn, when he
had arrived at the French court for the first time. He did
so characteristically, out of financial necessity, abandoning
his Norwegian mistress, Anna Throndsen, in Flanders, while
he made the expedition to seek further funds. Bothwell
had been kindly received by Mary and Francis, and as he
put it himself: 'The Queen recompensed me more liberally
and honourably than I had deserved'[30]—these particular
benefits being a present of 600 crowns as well as the post
and salary of gentleman of the king's chamber. On this
occasion Throckmorton had suspected some political *coup*
and warned his correspondents in London that Bothwell
needed watching, for he was a 'glorious [i.e. vainglorious],
rash and hazardous young man'.[31] He paid a further visit
to France in the spring, and by 5 July was back in Paris
for the third time;* this time he was accompanied by the
bishop of Orkney, himself a seaman of distinction and
Lord Eglinton, no stranger to nautical enterprise in the
sense that he was generally suspected of piracy. As for
Elizabeth, too late she relaxed her fury; by the time she
wrote back to Mary denying any intention of 'impeaching'
her passage, and saying that she had no ships at sea except two or three small barks to apprehend pirates who
were attacking the North Sea fishermen, Mary was no
longer in France to receive the letter.

Mary's departure was not without its tragi-comic elements. The cardinal, for example, suggested that she
should for prudence sake leave her jewels behind in
France, to which Mary, with a flash of wry humour, observed that if she herself were safe to go to sea, why
then so were her jewels. She atoned for this, however, by
giving her aunt the duchess of Guise with characteristic
generosity the day before she finally sailed, a magnificent
necklace of rubies, emeralds and diamonds, from her own
collection, as a token of regard. The company of her own
galley was planned to provide a galaxy of glamour and entertainment to beguile the young queen on her journey; it

---

* Although Bothwell did not travel back to Scotland on Mary's
own galley, it does not seem fanciful to suppose that his return to
France was connected with arrangements for her journey, not only
on grounds of his hereditary office, but also because the contemporary Birrel's Diary specifically states that the queen was 'stolen out
of France by sertain lords'.[32]

included three of her uncles, René of Elboeuf, the duke of Aumale and the Grand Prior Francis, as well as the four Maries, Mary Seton, Mary Beaton, Mary Livingston and Mary Fleming, whose French education was completed, and were now to accompany their mistress back to Scotland, as they had accompanied her to France so many years ago. On Mary's own galley were also to travel the young poet Châtelard and her admiring chronicler Brantôme.[33]

The day of embarkation dawned dull and misty, despite the fact that it was high August. Mary's wavering spirits were not lifted by the fact that a fishing boat in the harbour foundered and went down before the eyes of her watching party, with all its hands drowned. 'What a sad augury for a journey!' she exclaimed aloud. On Thursday 14 August about noon, the servant of ambassador Throckmorton, passing by Calais, saw a stirring spectacle 'haling' out of the haven: two great galleys and two ships. He hastened to give the news to his master. It was news which Throckmorton had been expecting to hear and it cannot have been unwelcome to him. It was a brave sight which the English servant glimpsed at Calais: for it was the queen of Scotland setting forth across the North Sea on the 600-mile journey to her kingdom, unblessed by any passport or safe-conduct from the English queen, whose ships patrolled these seas. As the ambassador faithfully commenced the despatch which would break this piece of news to England,[34] he imagined only the bravado of the gesture which he must have applauded. Even if his watchful eyes had been able to spy into the great white galley and discern the tragic weeping figure on its poop, he might scarcely have recognized this tormented being for his modest self-controlled young queen.

Up till this moment Mary had shown admirable courage and resolution, both in her dealings with Throckmorton, and more profoundly in her decision 'to hazard all she had' by returning to Scotland. But now that the die was cast, now that the ships were actually lying in the harbour of Calais, ready to take her away from all she had known and loved and held dear for that last thirteen years of what seemed to her like her whole life, Mary Stuart's steadfast spirit temporarily deserted her. There was now no great challenge to call forth the resources of her nature, only the prospect of bidding farewell as it might be forever, to

her family, her friends and above all France, France the
beloved land of her adoption.

As the galleys surged forward towards the unknown
coast of Scotland, Mary herself gazed again and again on
the fast receding coast of France; clinging pathetically to
that part of the ship which was still nearest to the French
shores she murmured over and over again in a voice broken with tears: '*Adieu France! Adieu France!*'; again and
again she repeated the words, and as the shoreline gradually faded from her sight, her laments only increased in
fervour. Still mingling with the sound of the wind and the
oars of the sea, her tragic young voice could be heard,
eternally uttering its farewell, melancholy and prophetic.
'*Adieu France! Adieu France! Adieu donc, ma chère
France. . . . Je pense ne vous revoir jamais plus.*'

PART TWO

The Personal Rule

8 The State of the Realm

'Assez fins, astutes et inconstans d'affection'

A judgement on the Scottish people from an anonymous French memoir of 1558

Although Ronsard, in a farewell ode to the queen, expressed the romantic wish that Scotland should fly before her ship, like the floating island of Delos, so that she would never be able to overtake it, in fact the fog-bound Scottish coast loomed out of the mist towards the queen's galleys in a prosaically short time. Queen Catherine wrote coolly to her daughter Elisabeth of Spain on the subject of her daughter-in-law's departure: 'She has set sail . . . and if the winds are favourable, should be in Scotland within the week.'[1] As it happened the journey which had begun under such dramatic auspices turned out to be comparatively uneventful and only lasted five days. Throughout much of its span, Mary's mood of deep depression persisted; her soft heart led her to forbid the customary whipping of the oarsmen, as though in her own state of pain, she could not bear to see further unnecessary suffering inflicted on others.[2]

The encounter with the English ships on the high seas provided the main excitement of the voyage. The English queen had at last despatched a friendly message, in answer to The Commendator of Inchcolm's mission—too late for Mary to receive it in France. Elizabeth now stated that she had no intention of stopping the Scottish queen's passage; in any case she had no fleet in the North Sea, only a few barks who were positioned there to discourage piracy. Cecil subsequently described to Throckmorton how the English ships had found the Scottish queen on the high seas with a tiny brave little train 'not exceeding sixty persons of meaner sort'.[3] Mary, unaware of Elizabeth's volte-face, must have expected a more melodramatic meeting than that which actually took place. The English ships merely saluted the queen's galleys, and allowed them to proceed; they examined the rest of the ships for pirates, and finally detained Lord Eglinton, on suspicion; not long afterwards, however, he too was released and permitted to return to Scotland. The only true casualty of the embargo which Elizabeth had attempted to put on the journey was Mary's own stable of horses and mules which, having landed at Tynemouth, was prevented from proceeding farther by the warden for a full month on the grounds that it lacked a proper passport.

There was a quality of anti-climax about this tame encounter, when so much had been threatened by Elizabeth, so much courage shown by Mary. But it was certainly believed at the time that Elizabeth had intended to capture Mary if she could, and even the English officials in the north of England seemed to be under the same impression that her capture was desirable: on Sunday, 17 August, the earl of Rutland wrote to Cecil that Mary had been seen off Flamborough head, with a great fleet surrounding the royal galleys, including eight galleys and sixteen ships and boasted that if they came ashore Cecil would 'hear good news of their stay'. The next day two great galleys were observed at Flamborough within a furlong of the pier, one all white, the other red, 'well trimmed and appointed', having two flags, a blue one with the arms of France and a white one in the stern glistening like silver. Having let their anchors fall, the galleys each put forth one naked man to swim (what bold spirit of the French party thus tested the bracing pleasure of swimming in the North Sea waters?). All the time at a good distance away, there was apparently visible a large fleet of ships;[4] but as all the contemporary evidence agrees that Mary landed at Leith with only two galleys, it seems likely that this phantom fleet off Flamborough head, far from being Mary's own entourage, was the English fleet hovering round the Scottish queen, uncertain how to proceed as they had no precise commands to intercept her. As for the true intentions of Elizabeth in London, probably she herself was not utterly sure how she would react if an English captain took the law into his own hands and captured the queen of Scots.

Such perplexities of motive and behaviour did not trouble Mary Queen of Scots. The only obscurity which surrounded the journey, from her point of view, once she had determined on it, was the physical obscurity induced by the weather. It had been hazy when the galleys left France, and it continued misty throughout the voyage. On the morning of the day the galleys were due to land at Leith, thick fog descended. A thick fog on the coast of Scotland was not an unexpected hazard, even in the middle of August; yet according to Brantôme the royal party seized on it as another unfortunate omen for the queen's arrival, while John Knox, from the vantage point of Scottish *terra firma,* but with equal pessimism, saw in the fog a symbol of the fact that the queen was bringing with her to Scotland 'sorrow, dolour, darkness and impiety'.[5] Only Mary herself seemed blithely unaware of these gloomy auguries, and determined to put on a smiling face come what might. Her natural buoyancy had helped to restore her spirits towards the end of the journey; now the prospect of meeting her subjects for what was in effect the first time on Scottish soil (discounting childhood memories when she had been queen in name only) presented her with the sort of challenge she especially appreciated— since all her life the sphere of personal encounter represented for her the most probable arena of victory. On Tuesday 19 August Mary Queen of Scots set foot once more on her native soil at the port of Leith, after an absence of just on thirteen years: her head was held high, regardless of any melancholy portents.

Her arrival was unexpectedly early—at about nine o'clock in the morning—as favourable winds had also carried the royal party from France more swiftly than had been anticipated. Nevertheless, by all accounts, her reception was enthusiastic and joyful, even if curiosity played at least as strong a part in it as loyalty. Since Holyrood Palace was not yet made ready for her arrival, the queen was taken first of all to the house of one Andrew Lamb at Leith; here she had a short rest and took her midday dinner, before being conveyed from Leith to Holyrood, on the outskirts of Edinburgh itself. She was conveyed on this short journey by a noble escort of Scottish lords, including the earl of Argyll (one of the leading Protestant lords), the Lord Erskine and the Lord James, her half-brother. The memoirs of Lord Herries give further corroboration of the rejoicings which greeted her arrival, and even Knox admits that 'fires of joy' were lit at night.[6] The nobility might be bound in loyalty to greet their sovereign; they might be fired with the intention of creating a favourable first impression, which would lead to personal advancement later; but the common people were excited by the spectacle in front of their eyes—the 'beauty, youth and stately carriage' of their queen, in Herries's phrase, despite the fact that Mary and her ladies were still in black or black-grey mourning for King Francis, who had been dead less than a year. Mary herself at the age of eighteen, tall, graceful, commanding, was everything in appearance that the popular imagination would have conjured up to fill the role of its newly arrived queen, if it had been allowed to choose.

Brantôme had an acid word to say about the cortège provided for the queen. He looked with contempt on the miserable Scottish horses which were brought to convey her from Leith to Holyrood, saying that these nags were a sorry come-down for a queen who had been used to the finest horses of France. But no doubt the sweet sound of popular acclaim in Mary's ears more than atoned for these deficiencies of transport: at all events she professed herself to be delighted with all she saw. What was more, Mary was able to express her pleasure to her subjects in their own language, for she had not lost her Scots despite the thirteen years spent in France. On her arrival in France as a child, she had indeed been able to speak nothing else, but she soon, by all acounts, learnt to speak French as well as a Frenchwoman, and it was the language which she habitually wrote and presumably thought in. Nevertheless the presence of Scots attendants such as Lady Fleming, her nurse Jean Sinclair or even the Maries must have enabled Mary to practise her Scots: for in August 1560, when she gave Throckmorton an interview, he particularly stated that Mary spoke to him in Scots, and later the papal envoy related how the queen 'began to answer him in Scots',* which she preferred to use to Latin. Although Mary's Scots letters show that she never became fluent in the written language, Knox's history confirms the fact that she was able to converse freely and colloquially in Scots from the time of her first arrival in the country.[7]

* In the sixteenth century the Scots language (as opposed to the Highland Gaelic, which Mary did not speak, since there was no way for her to have learnt it) was generally thought of as being about as different from English as two dialects of the same language: the difference was variously compared to that between Aragonese and Castilian, or the respective dialects spoken in Normandy and Picardy.

At Holyrood Mary was installed in the magnificent tow-
ered and turreted palace which had been extended from
an earlier tower in the reign of her father in the manner
of the Scottish Renaissance; here not only the debt which
the style owed to French architecture, as a whole, but
also the fact that a number of French masons had been
employed in the works, must have commended the whole
building to critical French eyes. Lying on the outskirts of
the city of Edinburgh, outside the actual town walls,
Holyrood also enjoyed the amenities of wild country just
beyond its very windows, as well as the convenience of
having the capital city so close at hand—the ideal palace
for a Stuart sovereign who could combine the pleasures of
sport and politics to an ideal degree. The palace, then as
now, was dominated by the bulk of Arthur's seat: as
Fynes Morison described it at the end of the century,
over Holyrood 'in a park of Hares, Conies and Deare,
an high mountain hangs, called the chaire of Arthur'.[9]
Joined to the palace was the abbey of Holyrood; both abbey
and palace had been burnt by the English at the time of
Hertford's invasion, seventeen years before, but had since
been repaired.

Queen Mary now took possession of those royal apartments in the north-west corner of the palace which were
to play such a significant role in her story. By the standards
of Scotland of the day, they were extremely magnificent:
there was a private chapel, and the ante-room had a fine
heraldic painted ceiling, put up two or three years previously.[10] Security was, however, in no sense neglected at
the expense of elegance: Holyrood in the time of Queen
Mary was reached over an iron drawbridge, and the windows of the state rooms had iron gratings. Mary's first night
at Holyrood was scarcely restful: although for once nobody
seems to have thought of interpreting the disturbances as
omens of what was to come. Having retired to sleep for
the night, the queen was awoken by a night chorus of
five or six hundred amateur musicians, playing what
Brantôme feelingly described as wretched fiddles, and

As one authority puts it, 'any intercepted letter [in Scots] . . . could
be read by an educated Englishman'[8] (although today of course the
transcription of documents in this language presents considerable
difficulties). Mary only spoke English very limpingly before the
period of her captivity, but was able to learn it quickly then.

rebecs,* and singing psalms out of tune. The result was a series of appalling discords, which must have grated at least as much on the ears of the music-loving queen, as they did on those of the outraged Brantôme. However, the next morning, Mary with her usual charm in such small matters, when she wished to please, assured the nocturnal serenaders that it had been a delightful experience, and even went so far, in the words of the critical Knox as to 'will the same to be continued some nights after'.[12]

Despite all Mary's tact, despite her evident resolution to accept any manifestation of her subjects' strange national character with heroic enthusiasm, there is no doubt that the land of Scotland as Mary first saw it, represented something very alien to the land in which she had been brought up. It was not that Scotland lacked links with France—indeed the two French marriages of James V and the subsequent French marriage of his daughter Mary could hardly have failed to have forged such bonds: not only the French servitors of Queen Madeleine and Queen Mary of Guise, but also the French administrators introduced by the latter such as de Rubay, who acted as chancellor, de Bouton, governor of the Orkneys, de Villemore, and d'Oysel existed to prove it. Mary's own marriage, which resulted in the two-way naturalization of Scots and Frenchmen in 1559, also meant that the titular ruler of Scotland lived in France, bringing a growing stream of Scots thither, on matters of administration or, as in the case of Bothwell, of petition.

While a great lord like Lord Seton emulated his master and made a French marriage to Marie Pieris, one of Mary of Guise's ladies-in-waiting, even before this outbreak of Franco-Scottish nuptials, there were links between the universities of Paris and Orleans, and the Scots universities—a great prelate like Cardinal David Beaton had completed his education in Paris. The Scottish Reformation did not break these links but rather strengthened them, since 'earnest and brotherly' relationships developed between the French scholars at universities, and Scottish Protestant scholars: it was even thought worthwhile to

* It is sometimes suggested that Mary's first night's sleep in Scotland was disturbed by the startlingly Scottish sound of the bagpipes. In fact a rebec is a stringed instrument played with a bow. The fault, if any, was in the unskilled nature of the playing, rather than the primitive character of the instrument.[11]

publish the works of Sir David Lyndsay in France. The
education of the sons of the leading Scots lords abroad
was not an unheard-of phenomenon: the son of the Lord
Lovat of the day slain at the Field of Shirts in 1544 was
described as a 'well learned young gentleman, and brought
up with great civility and knowledge in the realm of
France'.[13] James Melville went to France with Mary Stuart
at the age of fourteen to be educated as a page. Maitland
of Lethington was educated abroad after the university of
St Andrews. It is likely that Alexander Scott, the leading
poet of the court of Queen Mary, went to Paris as a student of music.[14] Monks were often educated abroad or
in turn came from abroad. The monastery of St James
of the Scots at Ratisbon, founded by Prince William of
Scotland, brother of King Achaeus, adopted the lively
John Leslie, bishop of Ross, as their patron in this period.
Such centres provided a natural interchange of news and
views between Scotland and the Continent.

In the same way, the trade of the east Scottish seaports
with France provided a more materialistic version of the
interchange—as the merchants of the Scottish burghs ex-
ported linen and wool cloth, skins, and smoked and salted
fish to France, in order to bring back such necessary
luxuries as wine and salt. The courage of the average
Scots as fighters gained them sufficient reputation abroad
to make them in demand as fighters, demonstrated by the
presence of the Scots archers and guards at the French
court, even before the first marriage of James v. The Register of the Privy Seal shows that young Scotsmen went
abroad for military service with enough regularity during
this period to make it a definite feature of Scottish contemporary life. Leslie's comment on the whole subject in
his *History* was that primogeniture often caused sons to
seek their fortune out of Scotland—'Of this comes, that
so many of our countrymen, have such good success
amongst strange Nations, some in the Wars, some in professing of Sciences, and some in merchandise'[15]—admirable
enterprise which time has only confirmed as being an
essential part of the Scottish character.

Unfortunately the adventurous success of the Scots
abroad did not prevent them from being regarded by their
European contemporaries as an extremely primitive, not to
say uncouth, race when at home. An anonymous memoir
on the state of Scotland, written by a Frenchman in 1558,

the year of Mary's marriage, makes this point quite clear.[16] Scotland is described as a poor and infertile land, ill-disposed to strangers, and obsessed with family honour and family disputes. The Scottish manner of living is described as rustic, and the people themselves as '*assez fins, astutes et inconstans d'affection*'. Henri Estienne described the Scots as a simple people 'who consider themselves all to be cousins of the King'. André Thevet, almoner to Queen Catherine, painted a blacker picture: he described them as a lazy, proud, boastful people who, despite their poverty, were swollen with quite unjustifiable pride about their lineage.[17] When Riccio was stabbed to death by over fifty dagger-wounds, Castelnau de Mauvissière, who knew the Scots, commented that such ferocious behaviour was only to be expected from such a nation—he called it 'an extraordinary exhibition indeed, but one often enough to be seen among the Scots, when their spirits came under some sinister influence'.[18] A current French phrase '*poignarder a l'Écossais*' (stabbing through and through) carried the same connotation of violence. It has been pointed out already that the French took a patronizing view of the question of the government of Scotland, and believed that the Scots could only benefit from good sound French administration. Whatever her good intentions, Mary Stuart could not fail to be affected by the prevailing attitude of the land of her upbringing towards the land of her birth —one of condescension not unmixed with scorn.

How far was this picture of a savage primitive people justified, and how far did Scotland in the mid-sixteenth century merit the description '*lourde Écosse*'? The terrain itself must certainly have seemed somewhat dreary to one nurtured in the Loire valley of France, human beings perennially judging beauty by the standards they have known in childhood. Surprising as it may seem to later travellers, Scotland was on the whole a treeless country in the sixteenth century: the great forests of earlier times had disappeared save in the Highlands, and constant legislation on the subject shows that the need of planting trees was considered to be urgent. Although there were still extensive forests round Loch Ness and Loch Maree, the Lowland forests were more in the nature of groups of trees and clearings, and tracts of open country dotted with trees, used for hunting; in the meantime the government endeavoured to force small-holders to plant woods or orchards to cover three acres round their domiciles. Even so, when Sir Anthony Weldon visited Scotland with James VI in 1617, he wrote that Judas himself could not have found a tree on which to hang himself. Scotland was also dissected to a far greater extent than at the pre- sent day by endless and immense watery tracts in the shape of countless lochs and lochans, many of which have now disappeared—in Fife at this period there were for exam- ple twenty lochs or lochans as big as Lochleven.[19]

To add to this impression of bleakness, the climate was not only demonstrably colder, windier and wetter than that of France, for obvious reasons of latitude, but it also so happened that the period of Mary Stuart's personal rule in Scotland coincided with a marked change on the whole weather graph of Europe;* in Scotland this resulted in a series of exceptionally cold winters and stormy wet sum- mers, and a sharp decline in the entire pattern of Scottish weather after 1560. The fact that 1563 and 1564 saw winters of outstanding severity with great loss of stock, 1565 an appalling harvest, and 1567 another unremittingly wet harvest time, can hardly have leavened the rigours of the Scottish climate to those unused to it. Even Bishop Leslie, in his account of the climate of Scot- land, although he loyally denied that it was a cold place, admitted that 'the winds which are North, blow often very vehement swift and with a horrible sound'.[20]

There were of course tracts of Scotland which were ex- quisitely cultivated: Mary of Guise had admired Fife. Les- lie and Buchanan both joined in giving the palm to Lothian, but in Tweeddale Leslie was dramatically excited by the numbers of sheep, and Lithgow described Clydesdale as the paradise of Scotland. However, even the fertile areas of the Merse and Teviotdale were possibly more wonderful to a native-born Scot than to one accustomed to the fertility of France, and since in any case many of the most theoretically cultivated areas in Scotland lay within the border area, where they might be devastated at any moment by English aggression, or straightforward

* The 'Little Ice Age' period of cold climate from 1550–1700 is now established by copious evidence from almost all parts of the northern hemisphere. See H. H. Lamb, *Trees and Climatic History in Scotland*, 1964. In human terms, the first years of the cold period must have been more onerous to endure than the last, when the cold weather was an established, if unpleasant, phenomenon.

free-booting, they did not always present the most luxuriant panorama of growth. Obvious symbols of civilization, such as fruit and flowers, were certainly in much shorter supply in Scotland than in France. Scottish villages and dwellings had always struck outside observers by their meanness: there were no enclosures, no fences or dykes or hedges, for the simple reason, as John Major explained, that the tenants had no permanent holdings, but hired or leased their land for four or five years, and thus had no motive to enclose their land.[21] Even the towns and burghs, whose political power was increasing, lacked stone walls to surround them, and life within them was still essentially medieval. Of the Scottish towns, although Edinburgh with its fair High Street extending the whole length of the town aroused universal admiration even amongst those who had travelled on the continent of Europe, few others could have compared with the French towns of Mary's youth. At the moment of her return, Scotland was in fact on the eve of a population explosion—by the end of the sixteenth century numbers had doubled. But in 1550 the population of Scotland was between five and six hundred thousand, a figure not much greater than it had been in the time before Robert the Bruce, since intervening wars had periodically decimated the nation. The population of France at the end of the 1570s, on the other hand, was between thirteen and fifteen millions.[22]

Communications within Scotland were exceptionally difficult at this period: roads were poor and ill-maintained, as a result of which journeys were considered hazardous and amazing if they were completed without incident. Randolph wrote of his journey from Stirling to Inverness in 1562—'A terrible journey both for horse and man, the countries are so poor, the victuals so scarce.'[23] Norfolk complained of the 'deep and foul ways' even between Berwick and Leith, so that the artillery for the siege of Leith had to go by sea. Coaches were unknown until 1561, when the first one was introduced from France for the royal use. Bridges, like roads, were supposed to be kept up by the people nearest to them, but this was seldom done satisfactorily; ferries played an important part in the kingdom, but again ferrymen were notoriously knavish, as the frequent statutes against them showed. Communications were further threatened by the prevalence of vagabonds on land—whom statutes tried in vain to exterminate—and of pirates on the sea. There were plenty of taverns, but inns or hostels with quarters for travellers were almost unknown, as the nobles journeyed from their own houses to those of their kin, and there was therefore no call for them; a stranger was an object of wonder, if not actual animal hostility.

It was hardly surprising that the different sectors of a country so ill-served by its communications should be very cut off, one from the other. The border peoples, who were comparatively easy to reach, were extraordinarily difficult to subdue for any length of time; as Leslie said, their lives were torn between war and theft, and their own feuds were far more important to them than any dictates of the central government. The Highlands were considered virtually a separate area: John Major drew a stern distinction between the wild Scots of the north and east, and the 'householding Scots' of the Lowlands. Of the so-called wild Scots, half the population only spoke Gaelic, 'the language of savages' Ayala called it;[24] their main contact with the Lowlands was the moving down of cattle to Stirling and the Lowland cattle markets. The Western Isles were so distant that they could, when they chose, opt out of central politics altogether, in favour of local feuds, and play no part in Scottish national affairs. This occurred during the reign of Queen Mary; she never visited them at all personally, and there was no peer of Parliament at this period north of the earl of Argyll at Inveraray. In short, Scotland was a country still struggling painfully within the confines of a medieval framework: it had hardly begun to emerge from this restrictive cocoon, at the date when Mary first arrived from France—a country in which, whatever its other faults of civil strife, this process at least was considerably more advanced.

Parallel with the primitive state of the countryside itself, was the stratification of Scottish society in which notions of kinship were still held to be of paramount importance. It was the great lords, as the heads of clans or the tenants-in-chief of land, who received the true allegiance of the people who were their clansmen and their tenants based either on kinship or on formal bonds of 'manrent' made to them, which promised services in return for protection. These Scottish lords considered themselves to be virtually autonomous in their lands since the system of land tenure gave the crown practically no right to inter-

vene between the tenant-in-chief and his inferiors. The
growth of the lairds, who held their land directly from the
monarch, was a political phenomenon whose importance
was not apparent at the moment when Mary landed in
Scotland. It was true that the lairds had demanded representation during the Reformation Parliament of 1560,
having played a part in the revolution of 1559: but to the
queen the nobles still appeared to block the way for any
real contact between monarch and people. It was therefore with that complex but fascinating body, the Scottish
nobility, that Mary had to deal if she was to deal with
Scotland at all. And, in 1561, the great majority of their
body were scarcely more advanced than the territories over
which they held sway.

This is not to underestimate the power and splendour
of the great magnates, who were just beginning to appreciate the value of display in a civilized society. Many of
them had their own private *poursuivants*. In 1543 the
then earl of Moray gave a banquet to the patriarch of
Venice, at which he caused much fine crystal to be put on
the table, as well as his silver. In order to make the point
that Scotland was over-flowing with such wares, at a given
signal he had one of his servants tug the cloth, so that all
the crystal fell to the ground and was smashed. As the
patriarch was busy murmuring his regrets for this untoward
occurrence, the earl casually had a further store of crystal
brought in of still finer quality. The patriarch was duly impressed and exclaimed that he had seen nothing like it in
Venice (where crystal was perhaps treated with greater
consideration).[25] In 1529 John, 3rd earl of Atholl, a great
feudal magnate with vast dominions, gave King James and
the papal nuncio a magnificent entertainment in the shape
of a hunt, at which the king was 'as well served and eased,
with all things necessary to his Estate, as if he had been
in his own palace in Edinburgh'; the earl had a special
woodland palace constructed of green timber, the floor
strewn with rushes and flowers, and the walls hung with
tapestry and arrases of silk, with actual glass in the windows. The banquet held within this rustic folly, twenty
miles from any dwelling (and which was destroyed when
the banquet was finished, according to Highland custom),
included ale, beer, wine, both white and claret, and *aqua
vitae*, and for food, every kind of meat from beef, mutton
and venison to swan and peacock, fish including salmon,

pike and eels, and even gingerbread. The whole entertainment was supposed to have cost Atholl £1,000 a day,
and the nuncio summed up his reaction in outspoken terms:
he thought it a 'great marvel that such a thing could be
in Scotland, considering that it was named the arse of the
world in other countries'.[26]

Both these anecdotes tell us as much about the swaggering character of the magnates concerned as they do about
the state of Scottish civilization. The list of the belongings
of the earl of Huntly, taken from the castle of Strathbogie
after his defeat and forfeiture in 1562, gives an interesting
glimpse of the furnishings and trappings to be found in
the home of a great lord: the forfeited goods included
elaborate tapestries, beds covered with velvet and hung
with fringes of gold and silverwork, vessels of gilded and
coloured glass, and figures of animals.[27] The Regent
Châtelherault had his castle decorated with painted ceilings. James Stewart, earl of Moray had an excellent library.
The great Lord Seton had gardens and orchards surrounding his castle which the English vengefully sacked in their
invasion of 1544; he enjoyed the sport of horse-racing
and, as recorded in the annals of the burgh of Haddington,
in May 1552 his horse won a silver bell which he himself
had presented. But as a class, the magnates with their
continental affiliations—men such as Lennox and Glencairn who spoke French—must be distinguished from the
mass of the nobility, who were far from appreciating such
refinements. Leslie describes how nobles and commoners
alike wore the same clothes: the chiefs would dress themselves up elegantly in grand clothes to go to court, and
then change back again. The horse was all-important in
the need for show: 'If therefore they have speedy horses,
and wherewith they may dress themselves and their wives,'
wrote Leslie, 'they are not mickle careful for the rest of
their household gear.'[28]

The rough nature of the education which the preponderance of them received may be judged from the fact that
in 1559 it was thought worth delivering considerations
to Parliament that the nobility should be better educated,
so that the ruler should not be forced to advance new men
in their place. Lennox apologized for his 'evil hand';
Huntly and Douglas were scarcely able to write, although
they could do so in times of special crisis, for secrecy;
Lady Huntly and Lady Erroll apparently wrote better

than their husbands. The helpmeets of these men, as Ayala had noticed half a century earlier, were indeed a remarkable race and very often more estimable than their husbands, or perhaps the unbridled spirit is simply more attractive when manifested in the female than in the male sex. Ayala had called them 'really honest though very bold'.[29] The two Lady Huntlys, old and young, of this period, showed a mettle which outstripped their husbands. Despite the almost total lack of education granted to women—it was noteworthy that at the reformation, nuns were almost illiterate, a much higher proportion than of the monks and friars—the wives of the Scottish nobility were from time to time capable of throwing up a figure of genuine intelligence and spirit, such as Jean, countess of Argyll, Jean Gordon, countess of Bothwell, or Agnes, countess of Moray, who put many of their male contemporaries in the shade.

The fortresses which these lords inhabited were in most cases as unpolished as their inmates. They were certainly very different from the fortresses of France to which Mary Stuart had been accustomed. Here she had known the magnificent newly constructed palaces of the French Renaissance, whose size alone dominated the eye. In Scotland she found a few royal palaces of only moderate size, by these standards, some few proper castles, and a plethora of strongholds, which were in effect only domesticated towers. These castles looked more like the elongated castle-houses in a German fairy-story than heavily castellated dwellings of Arthurian imagination. As for the squat tower dwellings, Lethington Tower, the home of Maitland (transformed by the work of later centuries into romantic Lennoxlove) provides an example of this sort of fortified pillar, with its heavily barred door on the ground floor, and nothing but slit windows as high as assailants could reach. When trouble came, women, children and cattle could be driven into the safety of this ground-floor chamber. Normally the house proper began on the upper floors; turrets and dormer windows, corbels and other decorative features could ornament these pillars, but basically they were merely intended for defence; and they represented an obviously stark way of life.

In every sense (except that of unity for a given cause) the Scottish nobility formed a tightly knit body, where feudal and family relationships were interwoven like the

steps of a complicated Highland reel. Intermarriage was
a feature of the situation, making it often as difficult for
the historian to unravel their relationships and loyalties as
it must have been for themselves. Patrick Hepburn, the
fair earl of Bothwell, married Agnes Sinclair, whose mother
Lady Sinclair was born a Hepburn. George, 5th earl of
Huntly, married a Hamilton—Anne, daughter of the duke
of Châtelherault; his sister Lady Jean Gordon was married
to James, earl of Bothwell; his father the 4th earl was
married to Elizabeth, sister of the Earl Marischal; the Regent Moray was married to Agnes, daughter of the same
Earl Marischal; Patrick, Lord Lindsay of the Byres, was
married to Euphemia Douglas, the Regent Moray's half-
sister; Patrick, 3rd Lord Ruthven, was married first to
Janet Douglas, natural daughter of the earl of Douglas
and second to Jane Stewart, daughter of the earl of Atholl,
who had herself been married three times before. Apropos
of another Ruthven-Atholl marriage, an English emissary
wrote to Cecil in 1579, with a mystification which we may
feel we share: 'The Earl of Atholl doth marry the Lord
Ruthven's daughter. It is a question whether by that
marriage the Lord Ruthven will draw the Earl to the devotion of Morton, or the Earl will draw the Lord Ruthven
to his devotion, who is yet an enemy of Morton.'[30] Into
this spider's web of relationships, it was especially hard
for a foreign-bred queen to infiltrate, in order to command any sort of preeminent loyalty. At the same time
Mary's Stewart blood meant that the nobles did not
necessarily regard her, when it did not suit them, as more
than *primus inter pares.**

As a class the nobles had been decimated by Flodden
in 1513, and again a generation later at Solway Moss
and Pinkie Cleugh, in a manner reminiscent of the two
generations of Europe depleted in the World Wars of
the first half of the twentieth century. The nobles with
whom Mary had to deal had in many cases succeeded
early to their estates, through the deaths of their fathers,
and had grown up without the curb of parental discipline.
Their broad lands were generally accompanied by a
singular lack of cash, which left them a prey for the sort

* Sir James Fergusson has pointed out that the saying 'every
Stewart's na sib to the king' gained its relevance from the fact that
so many of them were.[31]

of venal considerations most prone to rob the character of any outstanding loyalties. Lack of money meant that morality was all too often a question of cash rewards, and not necessarily large ones. As de Silva wrote to Philip II, an expenditure of 8,000 crowns brought Queen Elizabeth not only the good will but also secret information from the principal people of Scotland although many of them were Catholics.[32] In other ways than venality, the fibre of the nobles was undeniably coarse. Lyric poets such as Dunbar in an earlier period, and Fethy and Alexander Scott in a later one, spoke with clear and appealing voices where their private inspiration was concerned. Their poetry, closely mingled with the musical traditions of the time, was neither primitive nor cut off from other cultures, often showing direct connections with English courtly lyrics of earlier centuries. But in order to entertain the court in the age before Mary highly lewd verses like the 'Twa Mariit Wemen and the Wedo', containing sentiments of extreme crudity, were produced. In order to please the nobility, the poets had, in the words of C. S. Lewis, to 'lavish their skill on humours now confined to the preparatory school or the barrack-room'.[33] In this respect the court of the French Renaissance at which Mary had been reared cast at least a mantle of elegance over its corrupt morals.

The Scottish nobility included among its number many who were lawless and some who were violent. If the lawlessness merely reflected the general insecurity of an age of transition,* this fact did not make it any more acceptable to their young ruler, or easier to deal with, to one hitherto cut off from such matters in France. As for the violence, there is a natural code of human decency which even insecurity does not excuse men from breaking, and this code was too often set aside by the Scottish nobility of this period, when it suited their convenience. Deeds of villainy were common. The nobles included in their ranks men like Patrick, Lord Lindsay of the Byres, ever prone to use physical assault as a weapon, whether storming the queen's chapel at Mass, or obtaining her

* The Register of the Privy Council from the quantity of its enactments against violence, robbery, murder, etc. reveals the generally lawless state of Scotland in the 1550s, a legacy of the English invasions and the consequent breakdown of civil government.

signature to her abdication by threatening to cut her throat; or there were the two Lord Ruthvens of the age, one of whom was an alleged warlock, a macabre but bloodthirsty spectre at the feast of Riccio's death, and the other behaved with equal ruffianism towards Mary at Lochleven. The Regent Morton was a man of the most boorish calibre: the small greedy eyes in his florid face covered a cruel mind; his pudgy hands grasped avariciously all his life for what rewards and benefits were to be accrued; his slow speech concealed an unpleasant ability to revenge himself swiftly on those who had offended him. His atrocities in his time as regent included the hanging of women still holding their babies in their arms, and the driving of prisoners to the gallows like so many sheep, being pierced through by spears as they ran. Against such a background, the butchery of Riccio, and the explosion at Kirk o'Field can easily be explained, if not condoned.

These lawless nobles were immensely preoccupied with superstition—not the complicated astrological arts of Catherine de Medicis—but the cruder form of witchcraft. Witchcraft first made its appearance in the Scottish criminal code in 1543 when the reformed religion aroused a passionate new desire for purity in such matters. Long before this date, witchcraft played its part in the fabric of Scottish society. There was always a persistent rumour about Bothwell and witchcraft, and he was often accused of having 'enchanted' Mary by her defenders. Janet Beaton, the lady of Buccleuch, and an ex-mistress of Bothwell, was also accused in placards in the streets of having used witchcraft to 'breed Bothwell's greatness with the Queen'. Margaret Lady Atholl was thought to have the power of casting spells, having diligently studied the subject with a magician, and it was she who was rumoured to have cast Queen Mary's pains of childbirth on Lady Reres. One ballad, 'Northumberland betrayed by Douglas', describing the incident when Sir William Douglas handed over the fugitive Northumberland to the English in 1570, even gives the Regent Moray's mother, Lady Margaret Douglas,* as a witch.

* Child, in his edition of Scottish Ballads, thinks that this slur on the regent's mother is unjustified, and that she has been confused with that Lady Janet Douglas, sister of the earl of Angus and wife of Lord Glamis, who was burnt in 1537 on Castle Hill, for meditating the death of James v by witchcraft.[34]

But the main characteristic of the nobles, which applied
to the greater magnates as to the lesser, was that they had
absolutely no sense of the grand design. It was true that a
revolution in religion had been accomplished beneath their
gaze, in which many of them joined, but here the laurels
for purity of spirit, and intensity of theological vision seem
to belong mainly to a lower social class than theirs. Even
the cause of Protestantism did not bind together those
Scottish nobles who were divided by the potent interests
of family ambition. The Scottish nobles were given over to
'particularity' as every commentator at every level in this
period pointed out:

> Neither for king, nor queen's authority
> They strive, but for particularity.

This is how Sir Richard Maitland, father of the politician
Maitland, made the point in a bitter verse, written during
the civil wars of the 1570s.

When Fontenay went to investigate Scotland in 1584 on
Mary's behalf, he commented that money and family ambition were the only two things the Scottish nobles really
understood; in his view, it was mere folly and a waste of
time to preach to them their duty towards princes, the
honour to be found in just and virtuous actions, and the
desirability of leaving a memorial to posterity in the shape
of good deeds done—when the only two things capable
of charming the nobility with any degree of permanency
were 'de biens et de grandeur'. He felt that it was the misfortune of Scotland that the majority of the lords were incapable of taking anything approaching the long or altru-
istic view of any situation—they had, in his view, no wish
to extend their view further than the end of their own toes,
cast not the faintest thought over the past, and still less
towards the future.[35]

Twenty years earlier, it is difficult to avoid the impression that the same combination of goods and grandeur
was already what appealed irresistibly to the Scottish lords.
They were a difficult, intractable, and above all highly unstable class to deal with, since it was impossible to antici-
pate with any certainty in which direction the weathercock
of their purposes would blow from one minute to the next.
They presented an especial problem to a young queen,
brought up in a foreign country, and lacking the knowl-

edge and intuition of how to deal with such men, which
might have been inculcated naturally in childhood had she
been brought up in Scotland. After all, Argyll, Glencairn
and Cassillis were so very unlike Montmorency, Condé and
the king of Navarre, although the former might be said to
have occupied roughly in Scotland the position which the
latter filled in France—a point made by the French memoir of 1558 which directly compared them.[36] Let us not
paint the picture of the Scottish nobility too blackly at the
cost of whitening the aristocracies of other countries.
Ambition and intrigue were certainly not the monopoly
of the Scottish nobility in sixteenth-century Europe. England had her Seymours, and France, as we have seen,
her Guises. In so far as ambition could be held to constitute a vice, the cardinal of Lorraine and the earl of Morton, in both of whom its fires burnt brightly, would be
judged equally for it, before the last Judgement Seat of
heaven. Mary Stuart, on the other hand, was not gifted
with such divine enlightenment. To her, accustomed to the
cardinal with his eloquence, his literary tastes, his designs
by Primaticcio, men of the type of Morton 'unlettered
and unskilful' in Maitland's phrase, presented a very different aspect. She could not fail to find them secretly distasteful as well as baffling because they were so unfamiliar.
The Scottish nobles may not have been impossible by some
absolute standard taking into account all the factors involved: but they were certainly fatally different to the
nobles amongst whom Mary had been brought up.

9 Conciliation and Reconciliation

'Let all thy realm be now in readiness
with costly clothing to decoir thy court.'

ALEXANDER SCOTT: *'A New Year Gift to the Queen Mary,
when she first came home'*, 1562

Exactly how different her new kingdom was from her old
one, the young queen was speedily to discover on her very
first Sabbath in Scotland. Up till that morning there had
been, in Knox's phrase, nothing but 'mirth and quietness',
but on the Sunday Mary, who had been assured by Lord
James of the private practice of her religion, ordered Mass
to be said in the chapel royal at Holyrood.* The preparations for the service were all too familiar to a country
which had only been officially Protestant for one year. The
onlookers exclaimed furiously: 'Shall the idol be suffered
again to take place within this realm?' and speedily resolved: 'It shall not!' Patrick Lindsay, the future Lord
Lindsay of the Byres, went so far as to shout out in the
courtyard that the idolatrous priest should be put to death.
The servant carrying the altar candles was put into a state
of terror when his candles were seized by one of the
crowd, and together with some of the altar ornaments,
either broken or trodden into the mud. The reformers did
not actually penetrate the chapel itself: here at the very
threshold they found the person of the Lord James, barring
their entry: not only had he given his word to Mary that
the private Mass should be respected, but he also had a
devout horror of such extremism. Inside the chapel the
queen, her Guise uncles and her French servants attended
a Mass which was understandably fraught with tension—
the English ambassador reported that the priest was in

* The chapel in which Mary had her Mass said was the private
chapel royal, to be distinguished from the church attached to the
abbey of Holyrood; this became known as the chapel royal in the
reign of Charles II, but at this date was used as the parish church of
the Canongate.

such a state of mortal fear, that he could hardly lift the Host at the Elevation.[1]

If the queen received a rude shock from the incident, she did not allow it to affect her determinedly tolerant religious policy. The next day, Monday 25 August, she issued a proclamation in which she announced that she intended with the aid of her Estates to take a final order, which she hoped would please everyone, to pacify the differences in religion. In the meantime, she charged the whole world, in order to prevent tumult or sedition, to make no alteration or innovation in the state of religion, or to attempt anything against the form of public worship which she had found standing on her arrival in Scotland— under pain of death. She further commanded that no one should molest any of her domestic servants or those who had come with her out of France in the practice of their religion—equally under pain of death.

This proclamation may seem to us, from a modern stand-point, comparatively wise, and certainly singularly free from Catholic bigotry. It aroused, however, the venomous ire of many of the extremist Protestants, and especially that of their leading evangelist, John Knox. The next Sunday Knox took the opportunity of preaching a great denunciation of the Mass from the pulpit: one Mass, he declaimed, was more fearful to him than ten thousand armed enemies being landed in any part of the realm. While still in France, Mary had already formed the most unfavourable impression of Knox, and she told Throckmorton that she believed him to be the most dangerous man in her kingdom. Now she determined to grasp the nettle. She sent for Knox to come to Holyrood, and here took place the first of those dramatic interviews, which as recounted by Knox himself in his *History,* have a positively Biblical flavour.

Knox was now a man of forty-seven; having been rescued from 'the puddle of papistry', as he put it,[2] by George Wishart in the 1540s; he had joined the murderers of Cardinal Beaton in the castle of St Andrews, and after its fall, had done a spell in the galleys. On release he went to England, and from there, on the accession of Mary Tudor, to the Continent where his travels brought him finally to Geneva, where he became a disciple of Calvin. He returned temporarily to Scotland in 1555: the strength of his character and the force of his convictions enabled him to win over many of the greater men to Protestantism by his evangelism when the lesser men had long been interested in it. His main contribution to the Scottish Reformation had thus been made before Mary Stuart's arrival in Scotland, and indeed before the death of Mary of Guise; but his personality ensured that he remained a potent force on the Scottish scene, and it was an unlucky hazard for Mary Stuart that he happened to be living in Edinburgh, the first year of her residence there, to act as a demoniac chorus for all her actions, which good or bad, he presented in the most malevolent light.

Knox's character was compounded of many contradictions. He saw himself as a heaven-sent preacher, whereas in fact he was a bold earthly revolutionary, who openly preached violence, and notoriously considered the death of an unjust ruler absolutely justified. He was a good summarizer of the accepted truth; but he was a savage hater, and obstinate defender of a position once he had adopted it. Lord Eustace Percy in his life of Knox made a sympathetic examination of the reformer's true nature and decided that his real spiritual bent was that of the mystic who was compelled by events to adopt the role of preacher and interpreter: 'In the whole sweep of the Old Testament and the New, what first caught his ear was a voice which almost passes the range of human hearing: neither the words of God to man, nor the words of man to God, but a fragment of the huge soliloquy of God himself.'[3] Knox was an egoist, but his egoism led him to be a cunning politician and excellent lawyer, with an eye to the essentials in any argument. He was not born to the nobility, yet he was immensely brave in his confrontations with the nobles and the queen: as Morton said at his tomb: 'Here lies one who never feared the face of man.' His virtues included a ferocious, rather coarse sense of humour, seen in his writings, very different from Mary's own light ironic sense of humour, it is true, but something which might have enabled them to strike better accord if circumstances had been different; he was also genuinely patriotic, when few men even knew the meaning of the word. Above all, he loved to dominate, as with so many egoists, and it was this need for domination which doomed his relations with Mary from the start. Scotland, and especially Edinburgh, was his stage: he the great preacher, the victor of the Scottish Reformation, was not going to surrender the front of the stage to the young queen, newly come from France. In his imagination he saw even his first encounter with her as a battle, from which he must emerge victorious if the whole Scottish Reformation was not to be imperilled. Knox thus braced himself for the meeting, like an ancient Catholic saint about to wrestle with the devil, not a mature Protestant politician about to meet a young girl who had so far shown herself to be remarkably tolerant in both word and deed. In short, Knox, in his preconceived notions about Mary, was quite as determinedly misguided, if not in such a romantic spirit, as many of her partisans have been since.

Mary's very sex was against her in Knox's opinion: whereas in the sixteenth century it was theoretically considered to be against the natural law for women to rule men, nevertheless most people were content to regard an actual woman ruler as a necessary evil which might have to be endured from time to time. Knox, however, went much further than his contemporaries and in his *First Blast of the Trumpet against the Monstrous Regiment of Women*, published in 1558 against Mary Tudor, declared roundly that to promote any woman—those 'weak, frail, impatient, feeble and foolish creatures'—to any form of rule was the 'subversion of good order, of all equity and justice', as well as being contrary to God and repugnant to nature.[4] Now on 4 September he was confronted in a personal interview with one of these feeble and foolish creatures sitting on the throne of his own country of Scotland.

Lord James was also present at the interview, but tactfully stayed in the background. Mary began by attacking Knox for raising her subjects against her mother and herself, and also for writing *The Monstrous Regiment*. Knox conceded the point about her sex, and said that if she behaved well, and the realm was not brought to disaster by her femininity, he personally would not disallow her rule, on those grounds alone. When Mary struggled with him over the religious issue, however, she found him much less accommodating. Finally Knox agreed to tolerate her for the time being—his phrase, which owed little to courtly flattery, was 'to be as well content to live under your Grace as Paul was to live under Nero'—provided that she did not defile her hands by dipping them in the blood of the

saints of God. But he still firmly asserted the right of the
subject to rise up against the unworthy ruler, who opposed
God's word. Mary was quite clever enough to see the
dangers in this, and quite bold enough to say so: 'Well
then,' she exclaimed, 'I perceive that my subjects shall
obey you, and not me; and shall do what they list and not
what I command: and so must I be subject to them and
not they to me.' When Knox replied that this subjection
to God, as represented by his Church, would carry her
to everlasting glory, Mary pointed out: 'Yea . . . but ye
are not the Kirk that I will nurse. I will defend the Kirk
of Rome, for, I think, it is the true Kirk of God.' But
Knox refused to admit Mary's ability to judge on such
matters: 'Conscience requireth knowledge,' he said, 'And
I fear right knowledge ye have none.' Mary said quickly:
'But I have both heard and read.'[5]

The result of this interview was an *impasse* in terms of
human relations. Knox has been accused of speaking
churlishly to the queen: he certainly spoke to her in a
manner to which she was scarcely accustomed from her
life in France, but she on the other hand seems to have
been stimulated rather than otherwise by his abruptness.
It is true that she relapsed into tears at one moment: but
Randolph thought they were tears of anger rather than
grief. All her life Mary Stuart had a feminine ability to
give herself suddenly up to tears when her sensibilities
were affronted; she seems to have used it as a useful
method of relieving her feelings; it never prevented her
actions from being extremely hard-headed once she had
recovered her composure. Knox himself quickly realized
that Mary was far from being a feeble puppet, which her
career in France might have led him to expect. He told
his friends: 'If there be not in her a proud mind, a
crafty wit and an indurate heart against God and his truth,
my judgement faileth me.' In the same vein, he reported
to Cecil in London that on communication with her he
had spied such craft as he had not found in such an age.[6]

Mary was still being so enthusiastically greeted by her
subjects that an incident in the chapel royal, a rude sermon from Knox, and one brusque interview were not
enough to damp her spirits. She had been received with
elaborate rejoicings on her ceremonial entry into Edinburgh: here were to be seen fifty townsmen dressed up
as Moors, in yellow taffeta costumes, their arms and legs

blackened, and black visors on their faces, and on a stage
at the Tolbooth four fair virgins representing the virtues,
while at Cross, there were four more virgins in 'most heav-
enly clothing', and from the spouts of the Cross wine
poured forth abundantly. Some of the sights had undercurrents of Protestantism—a child who appeared at the
Butter Tron, descending out of a painted cloud from a
temporary wooden gateway, presented her pointedly with
a Bible and a Psalter, and when she reached Holyrood once
more, another child made a speech suggesting she should
put away the Mass. But a scheme for burning an effigy
of a priest saying Mass had been abandoned at the instance of the Catholic Huntly in favour of merely burning effigies of Coron, Nathan and Abiron, the sons of
Izhar and Eliab, to represent the evil of false sacrifices—
a message which it was a great deal easier for the queen
politely to ignore. Indeed Knox thought the welcome
given to Queen Mary so irritatingly lavish, that he remarked indignantly that in their farces, masks and other
prodigalities 'fain would the fools have counterfeited
France'.[7]

After three weeks at Holyrood, Mary set out for a
short progress round her kingdom: here again she was
met with the same combination of enthusiasm, marred by
occasional incidents where the truth of the Protestant religion was suddenly felt to need public demonstration.
She went first to Linlithgow, the palace of her birth, and
after two days on to Stirling. Here she was endangered by
human rather than the divine fire with which Knox had
threatened her: a candle accidentally set light to her bed
curtains while she was asleep. Although the fire was
quickly put out, Randolph took the opportunity to record
an old prophecy that a queen should be burnt alive in
Stirling, which, he said, apparently with some regret, had
proved just about as successful as Lady Huntly's prophecy that Mary would never reach Scotland.[8] On Sunday
there was some sort of incident when her chaplains tried
to sing High Mass in the chapel royal, and it was said
that the earl of Argyll, a leading Protestant, and Lord
James disturbed them; after a fracas some of the priests
and clerks left their places with bloody heads and broken
ears but the most part of the congregation seem to have
taken the incident calmly. At Perth, although the pageants
once more had a sternly anti-Catholic slant, the queen

herself was greeted extremely honourably, and presented
with a golden heart, filled with more pieces of gold.

Despite Mary's determined optimism, and gracious behaviour towards her subjects, whatever their religious
opinions, the events of her journey, her arrival and her
reception had clearly subjected her to considerable strain.
Now that strain inevitably began to tell on her health. The
Diurnal of Occurrents relates that in the streets of Perth
she fell sick and was carried from her horse into a lodging
not far off, with the sort of nervous collapse 'she is often
troubled with, after any great unkindness or grief of
mind'.[9] However, as always, she was quick to recover, and
at Dundee was once more greeted enthusiastically and
given a princely reception. At St Andrews on Sunday 21
September there may have been a religious squabble of
some sort, since a rumour reached Randolph in Edinburgh
that a priest had been slain. Certainly at some point in
the journey Lord James and Huntly had a violent quarrel
about Mass, when the Catholic Huntly said that if the
queen commanded it, he would set up the Mass in three
shires. But the point was that the queen did not command it:
instead she merely continued on her way for a quick visit
to Falkland Palace, and so back to Holyrood, where she
was once more safely installed on 29 September.

Knox reported that Mary remained steadfast in her
'devilish opinions' at the end of her journey, despite the
evidence she had received that most people found them
repugnant; but he had, in his prejudiced attitude to the
queen, missed the point about her attitude to the reformed
religion. It was not a question of her private beliefs, which
were, as she herself had told Throckmorton a few months
previously, steadfastly Catholic. It was a question of the
administration and good government of Scotland. Here the
sights she saw during her progress can only have confirmed her in the conviction which she had already expressed in her proclamation of 25 August—that it was in
the best interests of peace and stability in Scotland that
the Protestant *status quo* should be preserved, so long as
she herself could worship in private in the way she pleased.
When she first arrived, Mary found herself in a curious
situation administratively speaking apropos the structure
of the Protestant Church. In the years leading up to the
Reformation, the power of the Scottish crown over its
native Church had increased with every decade, as royal

control close at hand gradually replaced that of the far-off papacy. In 1535, the Pope conceded the right of King James not only to recommend to but also to nominate to vacant prelacies. Since the income from benefices could now be granted if the king so wished to others than its spiritual incumbent, the whole system developed into a useful method of royal patronage. The process expanded so rapidly that by 1560, in the words of Professor Donaldson, 'There was no financial temptation for the Scottish crown to proceed to a formal breach with Rome because it was already exploiting the Church's wealth with sufficient success'.[10]

But this exploitation of the Church by the monarchy was not brought to an end when the religion of Scotland was officially changed by edict of Parliament in August 1560. This edict was never confirmed by the sovereign, which made it technically illegal. But in any case no provision was made at the time for linking the new religion to the old ecclesiastical régime. By 1561 no financial arrangements had been made for the new ministers. Queen Mary was as free as her predecessors to proceed with the presentation of livings and benefices: there was absolutely no incumbency upon her to present them to the ministers of the reformed Church.* Thus the Scottish crown in the 1560s, freed by the Reformation from the last vestige of papal control, had enormous potential powers of patronage within its grasp. There was an excellent opportunity in this respect for a competent sovereign, well advised, to increase his own strength, since circumstances had conspired to play into the hands of the crown. This applied to a Catholic sovereign as much as to a Protestant one—so long as the Catholic sovereign showed no signs of wishing to restore the Catholic religion to the country. Catholicism as a spiritual force had temporarily retreated into the mists by the time Mary reached the shores of Scotland. One of the factors in this retreat was the remarkable lack of Catholic leadership at the time, which meant that too little was done to rally the Catholics at the moments of crisis. Archbishop James Beaton, for example, who might have constituted a Catholic leader, went to France in 1560 and never returned. Huntly was markedly unreliable as events were to prove. The Protestants, on the other hand, felt a crusad-

---

* There is hardly a single example of a minister being appointed to a benefice before the autumn of 1566.

ing spirit concerning their newly achieved Reformation. When Alexander Scott presented to Mary his 'New Year Gift' of a long poem at the beginning of 1562, his courtly connections encouraged him to address dulcet phrases towards his young queen:

> Let all thy realm be now in readiness
> With costly clothing to decoir thy court.

These same connections did not prevent him warning Mary solemnly that papist idolatry had been newly engraved in certain hearts as a result of her arrival—a development which was to be thoroughly deplored. Yet all the evidence shows that Mary herself was perfectly content to accept the facts of the situation, and had no wish to engrave idolatry anew on any heart, so long as that heart beat loyally towards it sovereign. Very far from being set on re-establishing the Catholic religion in Scotland, she seems to have seen herself as the powerful Catholic sovereign who rules at peace her Protestant people.

In the meantime she was also able to benefit from the breach between Knox and the less extreme members of the reformed Church, those for example who strongly doubted whether it was lawful to resist an ungodly prince as Knox suggested. Knox, strident as his voice might be, did not by any means speak for all members of the reformed religion. As Knox himself angrily reported, the Protestant lords were apt to be seduced from extremism by contact with the gentle and civilizing influence of the court.[11] When the town council of Edinburgh issued an insulting proclamation on 2 October, putting Catholic priests in the same category as prostitutes and whoremongers, Mary managed to get the proclamation suppressed and the council deprived of its privileges, with the full cooperation of both Maitland and Lord James, whom indeed Knox furiously blamed for the whole episode. Then when Queen Mary had a sung Mass in her private chapel on All Hallows Day (1 November), it was finally decided after a conference among the Protestant leaders that the queen should be able to behave as she wished with her household in private. But the actual singing of the Mass caused considerable commotion.

The English ambassador Randolph not only paid tribute to Mary's cleverness throughout her first autumn in Scotland, but indicated that those who had imagined Mary was without wisdom were liable to be surprised, since he himself had detected in her the fruit of the 'best-practised' cunning of France combined with the subtle brains of Scotland.[12] Part of this cleverness on the part of the young queen was to take the financial situation of the ministers of the new Church sufficiently seriously to make provision for them: in February 1562 it was decided that the monetary situation of these ministers was sufficiently desperate for it to be necessary for the crown to take some action. It was therefore decided that while two thirds of the revenues of the benefices were to remain with the existing holders for their lifetimes (probably neither ecclesiastics nor members of the reformed Church), the other third was to be collected by the government, and divided between it and the reformed Church. It was a perfectly acceptable compromise, which showed once again that Mary drew a sharp distinction between the private Mass in her chapel and the public weal in Scotland; and it also helped on the interests of the crown.

As the editor of the Register of the Privy Council at this period has observed, one looks in vain through its pages for any evidence that Mary was a rabid Catholic intent on establishing her own religion in Scotland, and intent on destroying the reformed religion which had replaced it.[13] Both Melville and Castelnau confirm Randolph's opinion that on her first arrival in Scotland Mary's behaviour was designedly accommodating and tactful, never more so than on the subject of religion, as a result of which she was rewarded with considerable personal popularity. Melville wrote that she conducted herself 'so princely, so honourably and so discreetly, that her reputation spread in all countries'; Castelnau indicated that the Scots were delighted with their beautiful young queen and, thanks to her efforts to make herself agreeable to them, they counted themselves lucky to be ruled by one of the most perfect princesses of her time.[14] The Pope wrote to Mary anxiously in December, suggesting that on the subject of Scottish Catholicism she should take Queen Mary Tudor as her model, who 'surely did not defend the cause of God timidly',[15] but Mary Stuart was very far from adopting the methods of her Catholic cousin in England. Her energies at this point were absorbed in an infinitely more worldly design—to get herself recognized by Queen

Elizabeth as her legitimate successor to the English throne
—and in this plan fervently expressed Catholicism could
only work to her disadvantage.

The conciliation of her Scottish subjects was only one
half of Mary's plan: reconciliation with Elizabeth was the
other. Once she was assured that Elizabeth had actually
despatched the safe-conduct—it arrived back in Scotland
four days after she landed—Mary's mood towards her
cousin was as purposely friendly as her mood towards the
Scots had been. Only thirteen days after her arrival, she
commissioned Maitland to go to England and try to treat
with the English queen on the subject of the succession;
Maitland duly set off in September. William Maitland was
the obvious choice for the mission. He had been Mary of
Guise's envoy to London in February 1558, and to Paris
in March 1559, and envoy for the Protestants to London
again in 1560: he was thus by far the most experienced
diplomatist out of the rather limited selection offered by
the Scottish nobility. Maitland can fairly claim to be the
most interesting character in Scotland in the time of
Queen Mary because he represented a type of new man:
aged thirty-three when Mary arrived, roughly the same
age as Lord James, and fifteen years older than the queen
herself, he had been converted to Protestantism by Knox
in 1555. But it was politics not religion which interested
him. His grandmother had been a Seton, and his grandfather died at Flodden, but he himself, one of the seven
children of Sir Richard Maitland, belonged to the new
highly political class of lairds surrounding the capital, who
had been considerably affected by the English occupation
of Haddington in the late 1540s. Maitland had been Secretary of State to Mary of Guise, but did not allow this fact
to prevent him from joining the Protestant insurgents under Châtelherault in the autumn of 1559.

His father, himself in public service of one sort and
another for over sixty years, gave Maitland some Polonius-
like advice at the beginning of his career, *Counsel to
my son being in the court,* in which he admonished him
to be neither a flatterer nor a scorner, to remember the
instability of fortune even in the highest position of government, and in short not to be overconfident in a world
as changeable as the moon or the sea. But as it turned
out, Maitland was not the sort of character to be easily

caught in a fixed position, while the moon and the sea changed round him. His very political abilities led him to exercise a certain pragmatism—did not Buchanan term him the Chameleon?—and his relations with Mary of Guise had already shown that, like a modern civil servant, he did not feel bound to go down with the minister. Yet Maitland was regarded by his contemporaries as having a finesse lacking in others, and an ability which made him 'subtle to draw out the secrets of every man's minds'[16] as Buchanan put it. He was excellently educated and his correspondence is garnished with classical allusions and wit. In other ways, in his lack of ascetic fervour and his emphasis on the practical in politics, Maitland's spirit matched Mary's own. He was even supposed to have carried his cynicism as far as to observe that 'God is a bogle of the nursery'.* In theory at least, he was the ideal adviser for Mary out of the limited selection available in Scotland, and he was certainly the ideal envoy to send to London.

Maitland's interview with Elizabeth took place in London, in the presence of both Cecil, Elizabeth's adviser, and Dudley, her favourite. The Scottish point of view on the subject of the succession had already been put to Elizabeth in a humble letter from Lord James, before Mary even arrived in Scotland. Ratification of the Treaty of Edinburgh was to be given in exchange for Elizabeth's acknowledgement that Mary stood next in line to the throne, after herself and her lawful issue. Maitland pointed out on behalf of Mary that this meant that she could not ratify the Treaty of Edinburgh as it now stood, because the terms of the Treaty called on to surrender not only her present claim to the English throne, but also all further claims after the death of Elizabeth and her problematic offspring. In reply, Elizabeth showed herself nothing if not friendly towards the queen of Scots; although her first impulse was to concentrate on the vexed subject of the treaty ('I looked for another message from the Queen your sovereign') once she realized that the Scots lords, as well as Mary, were in earnest on the subject of succession, she gave herself over to a frank discussion of the whole question.

* His biographer Sir John Skelton could, however, find no contemporary source for this saying.[17]

In the course of this, Elizabeth even went so far as to vouchsafe the information that she herself preferred Mary to all her rivals: she knew of no better right than Mary's, and no one who was strong enough to keep Mary from the throne. At the same time she positively declined to give Mary the acknowledgement she desired. The reason she gave was the impossible burden which it would lay on her own relations with Mary. 'The desire is without example,' said Elizabeth, 'to require me in mine own life, to set my winding sheet before my eyes. Think you that I could love my own winding sheet? Princes cannot like their own children, those that should succeed unto them. . . . How then shall I, think you, like my cousin, being declared my Heir Apparent?' She also put forward a more practical, less personal reason of her own safety: 'I know the inconstancy of the people of England, how they ever mislike the present government and have their eyes fixed upon that person that is next to succeed.' And she quoted in Latin: 'They are more prone to worship the rising than the setting sun.' Elizabeth went on to describe her own experiences as a focus of opposition during the reign of Mary Tudor. With these personal revelations, and an unresolved situation, Maitland had to be content. However, Elizabeth made one concession in that she agreed to accept a certain modification of the treaty, so that Mary should not have to sign away her claim, beyond the period of Elizabeth's life and that of her lawful offspring. Elizabeth also suggested that Maitland and Cecil should correspond privately on the subject, although under the supervision of the two queens; the situation, if fluid, seemed also full of promise. In this auspicious atmosphere Maitland returned to Scotland at the end of September.

The truth was that Elizabeth was in a more complicated situation apropos her successor than might appear from a first glance at the Tudor family tree. Mary Stuart, the obvious successor, had as we have seen been theoretically debarred by the will of Henry VIII, which precluded foreigners from succeeding. Maitland, in the course of his mission, did not enter into controversy concerning the will of Henry VIII, but merely made the point that Henry VII, in wedding Margaret Tudor to James IV, had not intended to deny her the succession; Elizabeth herself, by saying that she knew of no better right than Mary's, showed that she was not allowing her father's will to enter her calculations. But in 1561 Mary was extremely unpopular in England, being considered virtually a Frenchwoman and a Guise, as well as a Catholic, and she was especially disliked by the English Parliament, which was strongly Puritan in tone; Elizabeth, in her personal favour towards Mary, was certainly in contradiction to the majority of her subjects at this period. There were other claimants, whom the English as a body might be thought to prefer: Margaret, countess of Lennox, mother of Darnley, was a grand-daughter of Henry VII; although her claim was inferior to Mary's as she descended from Margaret Tudor's second marriage, yet she was an English subject, which gave her an advantage in some English eyes. On the other hand her legitimacy could be questioned, since her father Archibald Angus had divorced her mother on grounds of pre-contract. Then there was the twenty-five-year-old Henry Hastings, earl of Huntingdon, who descended from the countess of Salisbury, niece of Edward IV, and last representative of the Plantagenets. His strength was in his sex—in 1560 the Spanish ambassador de Quadra reported: 'the cry is that they do not want any more women rulers.'[18] He was also Dudley's brother-in-law, he was a Protestant, and was lieutenant for Leicestershire where he had strong connections.

By far the most serious counter-claimant was Lady Catherine Grey, the twenty-three-year-old sister of the ill-fated Lady Jane Grey. Catherine Grey, like Mary Stuart, was a great-grand-daughter of Henry VII, but she descended from his young daughter Mary Tudor who had married the Duke of Suffolk. By 1561 Lady Catherine had already led a checkered matrimonial career, by which she had incurred the spiteful enmity and personal dislike of Queen Elizabeth. Her first marriage to Lord Pembroke's son was dissolved. She then secretly married Lord Hertford in late 1560, but without the queen's permission, which had been made necessary by an act of 1536. In the summer of 1561, her obvious pregnancy forced her to admit to the marriage, as a result of which both she and Hertford were clapped in the Tower. On 24 September, at roughly the same moment as Maitland's mission to Elizabeth on behalf of Mary, she gave birth to a son, Edward Seymour. This piece of unwelcome parturition roused Elizabeth to a pitch of vindictive fury. She referred to the unpleasant subject bitterly to Maitland when she alluded to those who, by showing themselves not to be barren, had declared to the world that they were more worthy of the throne than herself or Mary. Elizabeth had both mother and father cross-examined, and as they could provide no witnesses of their wedding or find the priest involved, the marriage was finally declared invalid in May 1562. Despite this stern lesson in the unwisdom of illicit romance, the unhappy Lady Catherine managed to have sufficient contact with her husband within the confines of the Tower to give birth to a second son Thomas in February 1563. By the findings of Elizabeth's commission, both these sons were of course illegitimate, somewhat reducing Lady Catherine's desirability as a candidate for the throne.

Nevertheless in the 1560s it was Lady Catherine who was regarded as the most likely successor to Elizabeth by the English Parliament, on the grounds that she was Protestant and she was English. So strong were her claims thought to be that Philip II of Spain is even supposed to have worked out a scheme by which he would have abducted her, in 1560, and married her off to that famous putative bridegroom Don Carlos, in order to establish her immediately on the throne of England, on the grounds that she was legitimate, and Elizabeth was not.[19] However, when Lady Catherine was revealed to be a Protestant, Philip lost interest in her. Mary Stuart on the other hand was the subject of various English attacks at this period. 'Garboduc' attacked her right to succeed as an alien; in the Parliament of January 1563 Sadler made a speech against Mary the foreigner succeeding to the throne: 'Our common people and the very stones in the streets should rebel against it.' In October 1562, when Elizabeth was gravely ill with smallpox, de Quadra reported that there was absolutely no certainty about the succession, the Protestants being divided between Catherine Grey and Huntingdon, and the Catholics between Mary and Margaret Lennox. Under the circumstances it is easy to understand why Mary believed that the personal favour of Elizabeth constituted her best hope of being recognized. Mary believed that Elizabeth could and would override the will of Henry VIII. Elizabeth's dislike of Catherine was blighting her chances. Elizabeth's love of Mary—if it was sufficiently stimulated—might be the making of her fortunes. Throughout the autumn and spring, Mary devoted all her efforts to bringing about the personal meeting between the two queens, by which she felt certain she could win the all-important affections of Elizabeth.

Mary was not deluding herself on the subject. In the opinion of one of Elizabeth's modern biographers, Sir John Neale, 'There is no resisting the conclusion that Elizabeth was prepared virtually to assure Mary of the succession, assure her of it on conditions that are easy to guess: no league with France, friendship with England, an acceptable marriage, and probably ultimate conversion to Protestantism'.[20] The first three of these conditions would not have been difficult to fulfil for a Mary so set on being acknowledged as heiress, and the last one lay only in the sphere of possibilities. The important point, which Mary had ably grasped, was that she herself should inspire Elizabeth with confidence, so that she would be armoured by Elizabeth's favour against the hostility of the English Parliament, and presumably many of the English Protestants. By far the best way of inspiring this confidence was to meet the English queen face to face: had she not won the golden opinions of Throckmorton? Surely it would be no more difficult to win the affections of Elizabeth, with whom she had in common not only their cousinly relationship, but also the mutual problems of government in the hands of the weaker sex. As she had told Bedford, when she was first widowed: 'We are both in one isle, both of one language, both the nearest kinswoman that each other hath, and both Queens'.[21] In view of Mary's known success in the sphere of personal contact, her steady aim to meet Elizabeth must be regarded not as the caprice of an inquisitive woman, but as a sound piece of political reasoning.

Once Maitland was back in Scotland, he corresponded with Cecil for the rest of the autumn and winter, according to Queen Elizabeth's suggestion. At the same time Elizabeth herself sent Sir Peter Mewtas to Scotland, officially to greet Mary on her arrival in Scotland, unofficially to demand ratification of the treaty. Mary diplomatically suggested in reply that as so many matters in the treaty had concerned her late husband, the whole subject should be considered anew: in November she put forward the names of new commissioners. All Mary's letters to Elizabeth throughout this period have the same attitude of friendliness which would seem positively sugary to our ears, were it not for the high stakes which were to be won by cajolery. Mary means 'nothing more earnestly than continuance of tender amity and good intelligence' between the two of them; she finds that Mewtas has 'so wisely and discreetly uttered and expressed the sincerity of your [Elizabeth's] affection towards us'.[22]

Elizabeth still evinced a personal desire that the whole affair should be conducted secretly, or through the medium of Randolph; thus on 23 November she replied to Mary's gracious letter, turning down the idea of new commissioners. Maitland now tried in vain to discover privately from Cecil what the next approach should be from the Scottish queen. But as Cecil did not take the hint, Mary's answer had to be framed without any secret advice from England. Mary's letter of 5 January is skilful, and once again tolerant and loving; she cannot imagine what lack Elizabeth has found in her letter and her answer to Mewtas, she now fully accepts Elizabeth's own suggestion that she should communicate 'privily' to Elizabeth's envoy Randolph instead of relying on a new set of commissioners, 'Or rather'—and here once again Mary is hammering on her favourite theme of personal contact—'by our own letters to you.' 'We will deal frankly with you,' cries Mary to Elizabeth, 'and wish that you deal friendly with us; we will have at this present no judge of the equity of our demand but yourself.'[23] Mary was well aware of the value of flattery. If Mary was dealing with some other prince on the whole question, there is no one whose advice she would rather take than Elizabeth's—'such opinion have we conceived of your uprightness in judgement'. She injects a note of appeal: 'We will require nothing of you, but that which we could well find in our heart to grant unto you, if the like case were ours.' Once again Mary suggested that she would ratify the treaty immediately, if only her ultimate right could be recognized, but she ended by proposing her pet objective, a personal interview: 'If God will grant a good occasion that we may meet together, which we wish may be soon, we trust you shall more clearly perceive the sincerity of our good meaning than we can express by writing.' It was a masterly letter, a tribute to the political cunning of Maitland, and the propitiatory temperament of Mary.

Mary did not rely only on the seductive quality of her letter: she also wooed the English queen with gifts and

even verse. Randolph reported in February that Mary intended to send Elizabeth a fair ring with a diamond in
it, made like a heart, and this ring seems to have been
finally conveyed to England by du Croc in the summer.[24]
According to Bishop Jewel the ring was further enhanced
by 'flattering and elegant verses'; these may have been in
French in which case they were by Mary herself, who was
fond of saluting such occasions with poems of her own
composition, or alternatively they were Latin epigrams
composed by George Buchanan, who included two such
in his works, suitably inscribed from the queen of Scotland to the queen of England. It was in return for this
gift that Elizabeth sent a fine ring to Mary the next year
via Randolph, which was by his account 'marvellously esteemed, oftentimes looked upon, and many times kissed'.

The effect of these advances upon the English queen was
just as Mary hoped. Elizabeth rose to the bait. In late
December Cecil wrote to Throckmorton that he found a
great desire in both queens to have an interview, although
he gloomily feared the worst from two such different
women meeting.[25] When Elizabeth finally replied to Mary's
letter of 5 January, she certainly did not object to the
proposed interview. Mary and Maitland took this lack
of negative for a positive acquiescence in their plans; although Maitland had hoped to get some of the outstanding issues settled first, it was decided that he should return
once more to London, to negotiate for the meeting, the
prime impulse being still the urgent desire of Mary that
it should take place. Her relations with Elizabeth were
indeed a subject on which she allowed herself to dwell
with fantasy as well as affection; one of her favourite jokes
at this period was the notion that if the queen of England
had been a man, she would have willingly married her.
'This Queen wished that one of the two were a man, to
make an end of all debates,' reported Randolph, adding
perhaps rather unnecessarily, 'This . . . I trowe was spoken
in her merrie mood.' This little pleasantry of the volatile
queen of Scots had, however, already occurred a year earlier to the serious-minded Sir Nicholas Throckmorton.
Then in the full flush of his admiration for Mary Stuart
as widow of France, he wrote: 'Methinketh it were to be
wished of all wise men and her Majestie's good subjects,
that one of these two Queens of the Ile of Britain were

transformed into the shape of a man to make so happy a marriage, as thereby there might be an unitie of the whole and their appendances.'[26]

In the absence of any signs of such a miraculous transformation, however, the negotiations for the interview continued. On 19 May Mary persuaded the Scottish Council to agree to it in principle, although they were understandably worried about the safety of her person, in view of the fact that it was less than a year since the English queen had been threatening to imprison her if she landed on English soil. There were other considerations to dampen the ardour of the Scottish Protestants: such meetings were notoriously expensive, and the Scots did not especially wish to send so much money into England and leave it there. Not only that, but they feared that if Elizabeth was seduced by Mary's charm she might cease to keep them under her protective wing. The Scottish Catholic party were concerned that their queen, who had shown a disappointing lack of interest in their case, should be further corrupted by a meeting with the Protestant Elizabeth and were correspondingly opposed to the whole project. But Mary's will prevailed. Maitland was sent to London on 25 May and reached it on 31 May. Her enterprise bore dividends. Elizabeth now showed herself positively favourable to the whole project of the meeting and Maitland brought Cecil round to his way of thinking that on balance a meeting of the two ladies would be advantageous to their respective countries. The English Council were less enthusiastic and, like their Scottish counterpart, pleaded the expense—they reckoned that the whole undertaking would cost at least £40,000. Not only the two councils but the face of heaven itself seemed set against the meeting, since the summer of 1562 was so wet as to make many of the roads between the two countries virtually impassable.

Despite these setbacks, articles for the proposed meeting were agreed on, and duly ratified by Elizabeth. In the articles, York was suggested as the best venue, and the dates mentioned were between 20 August and 20 September. Later, Sheffield House, which was to feature again in the years of Mary's captivity, was put forward as a possible site, before Nottingham was fixed upon in the preliminary arrangements. Maitland optimistically termed

Elizabeth to be 'earnest bent' on the project; on 10 June
she wrote a letter to this effect to Mary, which pleased the
Scottish queen so much that she placed it sentimentally
in her bosom, next to her skin. When Maitland returned
to Mary in Scotland with the good news, he brought with
him Elizabeth's portrait. Mary, with typical female curiosity, asked Randolph whether the likeness was a good
one, to which Randolph replied that soon she would be
able to judge for herself. Mary explained that this was
what she most desired—she hoped that they would strike
such deep accord at the meeting, that afterwards the most
painful thing which could happen to either of them would
be that they had to take leave of each other.[27] In London
the prospect of the encounter was considered sufficiently
certain for the actual masques to be devised which were
to entertain the two queens, the chosen allegorical theme
being the punishment of False Report and Discord by
Jupiter at the request of Prudence and Temperance. The
detailed and long-winded plans for the masques—three
nights of them—were vetted personally by Cecil and
much courtly care was exercised in the delicate task of
balancing the allegorical compliments to both royal
ladies.[28]

Unfortunately False Report and Discord were in the
end never destined to be consigned to the prison of Extreme Oblivion at the instance of Prudence and Temperance. At the very last minute, with that element of unhappy fatality which never seems far absent from the story
of Mary Stuart, the meeting had to be put off—through no
lack of keenness on the part of Elizabeth, or the objections of the English Council, but owing to the explosive
situation in the rest of Europe. It was to be France, the
country for which Mary felt such poignant affection, the
country she still secretly thought of as her native land,
whose chaotic affairs proved a sudden stumbling-block in
the way of the long-desired meeting. On 1 March 1562
the duke of Guise ordered his followers to fire on a Protestant prayer-meeting at Vassy; the next month Catholics
and Huguenots in France were at war with each other. The
natural sympathies of Mary would have been supposed to
lie with her Guise uncles and the Catholics; the natural
sympathies of Elizabeth with the Huguenots. It was a
point Throckmorton made from France, when he instantly

urged Elizabeth to back the Huguenots, as Spain was likely
to intervene on behalf of the Catholics. But although Mary
might weep, torn between anxiety for her uncles and fear
for her English negotiations, throughout the summer she
had not allowed her sympathies with France to override
her political designs on England. Elizabeth answered her
Council personally when they tried to use the urgency of
the French situation to dissuade her from meeting the
half-French Catholic queen of Scotland at such a juncture.
Cecil continued to hope very practically that the interview might at least lead to a number of benefits for England—the confirmation of the Treaty of Edinburgh, the
breaking off of the Franco-Scottish alliance, or even the
conversion of Mary from the 'Roman Religion'.[29] On 25
June peace was agreed in France and on 6 July Elizabeth
finally settled that she should set out for the meeting as
arranged. On 8 July Cecil prepared a safe-conduct for
Mary. But on 12 July the French peace collapsed, the war
was renewed; Elizabeth had to admit that it was no longer
possible for her to set out for the distant north of England with civil strife raging so closely just across the
Channel, in which at any moment England might have to
intervene, if Spain did likewise.

Mary first heard the news of the sudden débâcle of her
plans from Maitland. She took refuge in a violent flood of
tears, and kept to her bed for the rest of the day, nursing
the cruel and unexpected disappointment. The next day
she received Elizabeth's envoy, Sir Henry Sidney, who
had been despatched to Scotland on 15 July to acquaint
her with the course of events. Sir Henry brought with him
a more consoling piece of intelligence: Elizabeth offered
to plan the interview for the next year, 1563, between 20
May and 31 August, at York, Pomfret, Nottingham, or
some other place nominated by Mary. Mary allowed herself to be comforted by the thought that the meeting was
only postponed, not cancelled, and her spirits revived.
After all, her personal energy and enthusiasm, aided by the
skill of Maitland, had been within an ace of achieving
this great diplomatic coup, and only circumstances, not
Elizabeth's own intentions had prevented it. With the natural optimism of her nature, she convinced herself that in
the mirror of the future, that dark and cloudy surface, she
could see reflected the image of success, only a year away.
Little did she know that this image was merely an illusion

—that the meeting between Elizabeth and Mary, which has been so often fabled by poets and dramatists, the possible consequences of which are incalculable, but must surely have been immensely favourable to Mary, was destined never to take place.

10 Governor Good and Gracious

'Be governor both good and gracious
Be loyal and loving to thy lieges all'

LORD DARNLEY *to Mary Queen of Scots*

While Mary negotiated for the throne of distant England, the boisterous spirits of her Scottish nobles presented her with certain very different problems at home, involving not only the public peace but her own physical safety. While Lord James, whom Mary considered to be her natural protector, was away on the borders dispensing justice, there was a sudden alarm that Châtelherault's eldest son, the eccentric earl of Arran, intended to abduct the queen. Although the court sprang to the alarm, it subsequently turned out that rumours of the plot had originated in a chance remark of Arran's; in fact that the only true stability that the nervous and highly-strung man showed in his wavering career was in his neurotic fixation on his cousin Mary. The next crisis had more substance to it. A mutual hatred existed between James Hepburn, earl of Bothwell, and the Hamiltons, and Bothwell decided to win the favours of an Edinburgh girl Alison Craik ('a good handsome wench' said Randolph)[1] in order to practise a crude revenge on Arran 'whose whore the said Alison was suspected to have been'. Bothwell, Mary's half-brother Lord John Stewart and her Uncle René of Elboeuf (who lingered on in Scotland after the departure of her other Guise relations) gained entry to the house of Alison's step-father, an Edinburgh merchant, on the first night wearing masks; the second night, they were denied admittance, either because Alison did not choose to betray Arran with his political enemies or because she simply did not care to repeat the experience. Whereupon Elboeuf and Bothwell forced their way in. The result was an uproar. The Church Assembly presented a horrified petition to the queen and the Protestants seized the opportunity to sug-

gest that such conduct was typical of a Catholic degenerate like Elboeuf. Mary herself had a prudish horror of
such bawdy behaviour: it ill accorded with her own re-
fined interpretation of court life, and she administered a
stern rebuke to Elboeuf and Bothwell.

Undismayed by this rebuke, Bothwell and Lord John
boldly threatened to repeat the offence the next night, and
defied anyone to stop them. At this the Hamiltons took
furious umbrage and assembled aggressively in the market-
place armed with spears and jacks. It was now Bothwell's
turn to gather up a muster of his own adherents. At the
prospect of what looked like being an ugly affray, the
townsmen were summoned by the common bell, and Elboeuf's Gallic spirits were so roused that he declared ten
men would not be able to hold him back from the battle
(but as he was within the royal gates of Holyrood, and
the main action was centred between the Cross and the
Salt Tron, in the city itself, the prospect of his intervention was somewhat limited). At the last minute it was
Lord James, Argyll and Huntly, rushing down from the
court, who managed to disperse the assailants. The whole
incident illustrated the swift rough passions which ran so
high in Mary's nobles; in these disputes, animated by long-
held family hatreds, the queen appeared in the role of an
outsider.

The third incident once again involved Arran and Bothwell. At Christmas Mary had been unable to reconcile
them, and Bothwell had been obliged to leave the court in
the general interests of peace. Towards the end of March,
these two contentious nobles were once more on amicable
terms, largely as a result of the good offices of John Knox.
No sooner had the reconciliation taken place than Arran
went to Knox with a disreputable story about Bothwell.[2]
Bothwell, he said, had suggested to him that they should
join together in a conspiracy, by which James and Maitland would be slain, and the queen herself abducted by
force to Dumbarton Castle. After that, he, Bothwell,
would share the rule of the kingdom with Arran. Not content with his revelation to Knox, Arran wrote a full account of the matter to Mary and James, who were then at
Falkland, saying that Bothwell's true motive in the matter
was to bring about the ruin of the House of Hamilton by
devious means. Arran's sanity had long been a matter of

common speculation and family concern; as Randolph put it, the earl was 'so drowned in dreams and so feedeth himself with fantasies, that either men fear that he will turn into some dangerous and incurable sickness or play some day some mad part that will bring him into mischief'.[3] To his distracted father, it now seemed that he had finally opted for this latter alternative, and had well and truly involved himself in a most dangerous piece of mischief; Châtelherault forthwith shut up the wretched Arran. However, with the determination of lunacy, Arran managed to smuggle out a second letter in code to Randolph, which Randolph duly passed on to the queen.

Just as Queen Mary was digesting the news of the plot, which at best must have greatly perplexed her, at worst alarmed her for her own safety, Gavin Hamilton, Arran's kinsman, panted up with the news that Mary must not credit anything that Arran might have written or would report, for it was all false. Lord James acted with despatch on Mary's behalf: making short work of Hamilton's excuses, and those of Bothwell, he had them both arrested on suspicion of conspiracy. Arran proved the more slippery to hold of the two: half-naked, he managed to escape out of his window from his confinement in his father's castle, 'with cords made out of the sheets of his bed'.[4] He then made his way to the home of Kirkcaldy of the Grange at Stirling. Here he gave himself to the ravings of madness, howling and shrieking of devils and witches, and protesting that everyone wanted to kill him. His passion for Mary was transformed by his addled brain into a series of delusions, in which he believed himself to be her husband, and lying in her bed. From Stirling, he was brought to St Andrews, and kept in close confinement, until he was finally confronted with Bothwell, in the presence of Mary and the Privy Council. Here, obsessed by his fantasies, he charged Bothwell with high treason; Bothwell, characteristically, wanted the matter settled by single combat, but since this was obviously impossible under the circumstances, suggested a court of law. This suggestion was ignored. Instead Arran, still refusing to withdraw his accusations, was taken back to St Andrews and almost immediately to Edinburgh Castle, where he was put into the charge of James Stewart. It was certainly no age to be mad in: he does not seem to have been kindly treated, even by the low standards of the times towards lunatics, since Stewart was later 'ill-bruited for the rigorous entertainment' he gave to him. He never fully recovered his sanity; in 1564 he was described by Randolph as mad, jaundiced, lying, eating little and desiring only solitude, suspicous of all around him. And in May 1566, he was liberated on a caution of £12,000, and was allowed to reside quietly with his mother.*

Although there was no proof of his guilt except the word of a madman, Bothwell was sternly treated. He was left to languish a prisoner in Edinburgh Castle without trial, Mary being persuaded by James that it would be highly politically embarrassing to bring the incident out into the open, since if Arran was shown to have borne false witness, he would have to be executed, and he was too near the throne for this to be desirable. It was also put to Mary that Bothwell had been intriguing with the English. Mary had the keen dislike of ingratitude sometimes found in those who themselves have generous natures, and therefore particularly hate to feel themselves treated any differently by other people. She was annoyed that the man to whom she felt she had been so good, should show himself so false, and she quoted pointedly to Buchanan in Latin a maxim from Livy: 'It is safer not to accuse an evil man, than to pardon him'. Châtelherault was in a pathetic state over the whole incident: Mary was moved to see the tears pouring down the old man's cheeks like those of a child who had been beaten. Nevertheless he had to surrender the castle of Dumbarton, as the price for his supposed political treachery.

The episode, with its mixture of pathos and brutality, has a twofold interest. Firstly it shows that the abduction of Mary's person was a subject of comparatively common discussion—since it arose twice within the first six months of her arrival in Scotland—and certainly not a novel idea in April 1567 when it was finally achieved. It is true that there is absolutely no tenable evidence against Bothwell except the babblings of a lunatic: but it is just possible

---

* Arran plays no further part in the story of Mary Queen of Scots. Yet he lived on, unhappy invalid, for nearly half a century, and did not die until 1609, when all the actors in his story were long since dead, and the son of the woman he had once loved with the obstinate passion of an idiot was securely established on the throne of England.

that there was something more sinister at the back of it all, and that Bothwell did make some chance remark to Arran, which acted on Arran's mad passion for Mary, and set him off on the whole disastrous train of thought. One must bear in mind the possibility that Bothwell was at least toying with the idea of an abduction so early in the period of Mary's personal rule. Secondly, the episode reveals how closely Mary's lot was joined with that of Lord James. At this point, she was making no attempt to rule the Scottish nobles by balancing them against each other, now advancing one faction, now promoting another. On the contrary, she was clearly backing Lord James in whatever he chose to do. This policy would be perfectly satisfactory so long as the interests of Lord James and Queen Mary coincided; should they ever diverge, the queen might find that she would need the other strong nobles in the kingdom to support her, whom she was now allowing her half-brother to put down as he willed.

Shortly after her arrival Mary had chosen her Privy Council, the chief nobles of the kingdom, six of whom were to be in constant attendance on her, to help her despatch routine business. The Privy Council was vested with full executive powers, sat in the royal palace, and its members were traditionally chosen by the sovereign. However, the true direction of affairs was firmly vested in the hands of Lord James and Maitland; Randolph described them as being above all others in credit with the queen, and contrasted their two techniques of dealing with her: Lord James treated her according to his nature in a homely and blunt fashion, whereas Maitland approached his young mistress more delicately and finely. The practice of having the six nobles in attendance soon lapsed. Since the Acts of the Privy Council had the same force as Acts of Parliament, it was on the Privy Council and its directors that the full administrative business devolved. The role played by Parliament in this period on the other hand was comparatively remote: this was more especially true since between Parliament and the sovereign stood a committee called the Lords of the Articles, to which was delegated its actual business. The Lords of the Articles were an expedient which had grown up out of the remissness of some members of Parliament in attending sessions, as well as the difficulties of prolonging their attendance. Parliament only assembled in practice to vote approval or disapproval of the acts presented to it for sanction by this committee.[5]

As the Lords of the Articles in their turn tended to be amenable to whatever ruler or strong faction was in power, it will be seen that the potential powers of the Scottish crown within the constitution at this period were widespread. The problem was the implementation of these powers in a backward country, rather than the nature of these powers themselves. There were some hopeful signs for the monarchy for the future: although the great magnates held the great offices of state, transmitted by a more or less hereditary title from father to son, there were other lesser posts such as advocate, justice-clerk, treasurer and secretary to be filled by the lesser gentry—the secretaryship for example was Maitland's post; these positions could be personally attached to the sovereign. Against the strength of local justice administered by the lords could now be balanced the endless officials attached to civil and consistorial tribunals, belonging to the central legal order, at the head of which stood the supreme court. The lesser burgesses and lairds who were first called into life at the time of the Reformation Parliament would grow to challenge the great magnates: and the crown might expect to benefit from their challenge.

It will be seen in the civil government, as in the ecclesiastical structure, that the possibilities of the crown under Queen Mary were extensive, if the potentialities of her royal position were ever converted into actualities. But apart from the obvious disadvantage of the strength of the nobles, the crown had two other great weaknesses. It had no standing army—and bitterly had the Scottish nobles resented it when Mary of Guise tried to establish such a thing; the crown, should it be involved in action necessitating war, had to depend on the locally raised hosts of other loyal nobles, with the consequent dangers of personal vendettas being involved in royal policy. Secondly, the financial resources of the Scottish crown were cripplingly restricted. Mary Stuart received an annual income of 40,000 *livres* as her jointure as queen-dowager of France, although there were constant troubles over the payment and administration of this sum, which became acute during the years of her captivity. But the lands and properties of her father had been largely squandered by the expen-

sive English wars during her minority.* Other royal lands
had been apportioned to the nobles during Mary's minority, although by the ancient law of minority of lesion,
she would have a right to resume these on her twenty-fifth
birthday, in six years' time. The royal income therefore
depended, apart from the lease on its own lands, on wardships of minors and heiresses, export dues derived from
duties on trade at the burghs† and ecclesiastical revenues.
The entire income from the collectory of crown property
amounted to about £18,000 Scots.[6]

Apart from her personal resources, the resources of the
crown were meagre indeed and economic organization
correspondingly backward. The method of collecting taxes
in Scotland in the sixteenth century has been compared
unfavourably with that of twelfth-century England, taxes
being farmed out for collection to sheriffs whose offices
had become hereditary. In any case, the only instance of
national taxation during the six years of Mary's personal
rule was a levy of £12,000 for the baptism of Prince
James. The total royal revenue in 1560 was around
£40,000 Scots or about £10,000 sterling.[7] Compared to
this, that of Queen Elizabeth was £200,000, rising to
£300,000 in the last ten years of her reign:[8] yet Elizabeth was always notoriously conscious of poverty. It is
hardly surprising that in Scotland the treasurer's deficit
amounted to £33,000 in 1564, and was up to £61,000
in 1569.[9] Indeed, Queen Mary would have been hard put
to it to pay a standing army had she been endowed with
one. In short, one problem Mary Queen of Scots faced
throughout her personal rule was that of frustrating royal
poverty. It was no wonder that the French memoir of
1558 on the state of the country dwelt vividly on the poverty of the Scottish monarchy, which it ascribed to the lack
of a proper royal domain, and the absence of any means
of imposing taxation. Mary, like her grandfather James

* At this point the finances of the crown had become so critical
that the most intimate royal treasures had to be sold, including the
gold and crimson coat worn by James v in Paris during his courtship of his first wife Madeleine, the crystal and agate cup which had
been made for Queen Madeleine as a child, and the dresses left behind by the summer queen; even the cap sent by Pope Paul III to
James v vanished as did the historic cup from which Robert Bruce
used to drink.[10]

† Fiscal business had of course been greatly interrupted by the
English wars, with consequent loss of revenue to the crown.

IV, could fairly be described as 'in want of nothing . . .
but not able to put money into his strongboxes'.[11]

At the same time, during the second half of the sixteenth century prices were rising fast all over Europe due
to the influx of silver from the New World. From this
desperate need for money resulted the strange 'treasure-
hunter's' economics of the period[12]—the persistent search-
ings for gold and silver deposits, which unfortunately lay
in Scotland only in small and scattered pockets and involved high working and transport costs. For much of her
reign Mary was also too poor to issue a coinage, although
this had been done yearly from 1529 to 1542. At the same
time the Register of the Privy Council shows that it was
the policy of Mary's government to try and make French
currency legal tender, and to discourage the entry of
currency from England, which was made treasonable—although the English currency was getting a reputation for
purity from the developing commerce with the Hanse
towns and the Low Countries. Another economic expedient was developed when the government realized that considerable profit could be derived from the issue of a silver
coinage, at a considerably greater face value than its true
value in silver: ryals began to be issued with a nominal
value of thirty, twenty and ten shillings, but costing much
less to mint. Naturally, such debasements had the effect
of only encouraging hoarding and speculation. During the
period of Mary Stuart's personal rule, it would be true to
say that just as the crown suffered from straitened finances
it was incapable of curing, so the country suffered from
economic difficulties for which the government also could
supply no certain remedy.

Despite these gloomy considerations, for the first years of
her life in Scotland Mary Stuart made a fair attempt to re-
create the conditions of the French court and to enjoy the
native resources of Scotland. Fortunately she had a natural
appetite for pleasures of many different types, as well as
being blessed with youthful high spirits and enthusiasm,
which enabled her to create pastimes where she did not
find them; in particular she had a positive mania for outdoor pursuits—all her life her physical constitution demanded a daily ration of fresh air and exercise if she was
to feel herself well. Although later in her life, this was
to mean that she suffered cruelly from the conditions of

close confinement, it meant that now she was well suited to the conditions of life in Scotland, where she was destined to spend nearly half her life in the saddle, progressing about her dominions. In the Scottish countryside she also had endless opportunities for the hawking and hunting which she loved as had her father James V, and later her father-in-law and husband. Falkland Palace in Fife was a favourite centre for royal sport, having been rebuilt for this purpose by James V, with new stables built in 1531, so that it occupied rather the same role as Balmoral Castle in the life of Queen Victoria as a holiday and hunting retreat. It was surrounded with parkland and to the north lay the Forest of Falkland. It was not left to chance that the royalties should enjoy good sport: roebucks and stags were actually brought in litters along with the court, from their last stopping place; they were then temporarily released for the chase. When the court moved on again to Edinburgh, the deer were rounded up, and brought on to be released once more in the royal park at Holyrood. Wild boar, to be hunted among the oaks of the forest, were specially imported from France. Hawks commanded good prices: James IV had paid £189 for a trained bird, Mary herself acquired hawks from as far as Orkney and Zetland, and in 1562 hawks were among the presents she sent to Elizabeth, £80 being paid for conveying them to London.

To Mary, a fearless rider who loved the excitement of the chase, not only hawking but deer-hunting was a popular pastime; anti-poaching laws had to be made to preserve the deer for the royal delectation, since on one occasion it was found that 'the deer [were] so destroyed that our Sovereigns can get no pastime of hunting' when they had repaired to a special piece of forest on purpose for the chase. Deer-hunting was far from being the solitary hardy stalking of modern times: the deer were actually beaten in to where the lords would be lying, their heads and antlers appearing over the hill 'making a show like a wood', as Taylor described it in his *Penniless Pilgrimage*.[13] It was a primitive sport by our standards, the cries of the men, with their arrows, javelins and clubs, mingling with the barking of the dogs, often Irish wolf-hounds, who were used to catch the beasts. In 1564 an especially magnificent deer-hunt was organized for Mary by the 4th earl of Atholl; Mary camped for the occasion on the shores of Loch Lochy, on the east side of Beinn a' Ghlo, on a spot now traditionally known as Tom Na Banrigh, or the queen's hillock. One of Queen Mary's retainers described how 2,000 Highlanders (or 'Wild Scots' as he noted that they were called) were employed for two months to drive all the deer from the woods and hills of Atholl, Badenoch, Moray and all the counties about, into a special area—'As these Highlanders use a light dress, and are very swift of foot, they went up and down so nimbly that . . . they brought together 2,000 red deer, besides roes and fallow deer.' The queen and the other great men waited in the glen as the deer thundered towards them, led by one magnificent leader who thrilled Mary's heart, until Atholl warned her that if this leader, either in fear or in rage, turned in their direction, the entire herd would follow and they might be stampeded. This did in fact happen to some of the Highlanders, when Mary let her dog loose on a wolf and the stag bolted; in spite of throwing themselves flat in the heather, two or three Highlanders were killed, and others injured.[14]

In his *History of Scotland*, Leslie emphasizes the importance of hunting to the Scots as a national pastime: in her enthusiasm for it, Mary certainly met with the full accord of her subjects. Archery—for which she would wear a velvet glove—also appealed to her, and she had butts set up in her private gardens at Holyrood, where one spring day she was surprised by Randolph shooting with the vigorously Protestant Master of Lindsay against Lord James and one of her ladies, showing that it was easier to be friendly with the turbulent Lindsay on the common basis of sports than on that of religion.[15] She played at golf and pall-mall (croquet). With her penchant for fresh air, she loved to walk in the gardens surrounding her palaces, and frequently held audiences of her ambassadors there—Randolph even mentions one interview taking place in the garden of Holyrood in February. Here there were two gardens, a north and a south, into which Mary is said to have introduced on her own initiative a young sycamore from France, which was to become the parent of all the groves celebrated in Scottish songs. The other palaces of Linlithgow, Stirling and Falkland also had their gardens and parks, the gardens of Stirling lying far below the castle on the level ground, so that the butts could be surveyed from the castle walls.

Mary Stuart had her resplendent side, when she appeared to her subjects as Diana the goddess of the chase; but she also had another charming and touchingly domesticated side to her character in marked contrast to this dazzling public *persona*. This paradox is stamped on many of her actions, which hover between the imperious deeds of the woman born a queen, who loved to shine in the eyes of her people, and the more clinging reactions of a woman, who was after all markedly feminine, in temperament as well as in sex. She adored small dogs, as well as the great hounds of the chase, and this trait did not wait for the cramped conditions of her captivity to manifest itself: there is mention in her inventories of pretty blue velvet colours for the queen's little dogs; a daily ration of two loaves of bread was set apart for them; payment was made to the boys who looked after them, and occasionally they were sent to France. She loved to embroider, and is described as sitting at her Council, placidly plying her needle, a model of the compliant female. Mary Stuart was also marked all her life, in its early no less than in its later stages, by extreme attachment to her servants, particularly her own personal attendants, with whom she felt she could share her joys and woes without fear either of their presumption or of their disloyalty. Mary's court therefore had an agreeably intimate character, which spread outwards from the feminine side of its queen's own nature. There were certainly indoor pleasures enough to be enjoyed. The queen had a gambling streak, as her mother had had before her, and loved to play at cards or at dice, losing a jewel of crystal set in gold to her father-in-law Lennox on one occasion. She enjoyed biles or billiards, and in Lent 1565, before they were married, Mary and Darnley together lost an agate ring and brooch worth 50 crowns to Mary Beaton and Randolph, a debt which Darnley gallantly paid. Mary enjoyed backgammon, and also chess, her library including *The Rules of Chesse* translated from French by William Caxton in 1474. She loved to watch the plays of puppets, a new fashion which had lately spread out of Italy.[16]

Mary was also a considerable linguist, and the number of languages which she had learned as a child in France was reflected in her reading-matter. Besides French, Latin, Scots books, and a few English volumes, there were books in Italian and Spanish—while the presence of books in the original Greek suggest that the queen either understood a

smattering of Greek herself, or else had at least an interest
in the culture of the Greeks. At all events her library was
extensive: from the two incomplete lists of it made at
Holyrood in 1569 for the Regent Moray, after she had
fled to England, and in 1578 at Edinburgh Castle, it is possible to form at least some impression of her literary
tastes.*[17] Her library was kept at Holyrood in a green-
carpeted room, and by 1566 her collection of Greek and
Latin books had grown sufficiently large to be left by her
in her will to the university of St Andrews. There were
a quantity of Latin books in the original, not only the
Livy which we know from Randolph that she read daily
after dinner with George Buchanan, but also Horace, and
a quantity of medieval and modern Latin prose, including
the famous copy of Buchanan's translation of the Psalms.
This was dedicated by him to Queen Mary in Latin in
lines which are strangely poignant when one recalls that it
was later Buchanan who was to be Mary's chief traducer:

> Lady, whose sceptre (yours by long descent)
> Gives Scotland now a happy government
> By beauty, virtue, merit and sweet grace
> Queen of your sex, star of our age, our race—
> Accept (light task) done in the Latin tongue
> The glorious Psalms the prophet-king once sung. . . .†

Greek authors represented included Homer, Herodotus,
Sophocles, Euripides and Plato, and there were French
translations of the classics such as Suetonius, Plutarch,
Ovid and Cicero. Italian books numbered the *Decameron,*
Ariosto's *Orlando Furioso,* Petrarch, and Marcus Aurelius
translated into Italian.

By far the greatest proportion of the books is, of
course, in French. English books are rare, but include
the Acts of Parliament of Queen Mary Tudor, less frequently browsed over one feels than the volumes of history and French poetry, which seem to have been Mary
Stuart's real loves. Brantôme bore witness to her genuine

---

* The libraries of her ancestors had been destroyed at the time
of the sack of Holyrood in 1544, so that previous kings cannot be
credited with the listed books. On the other hand, the Edinburgh
Castle list does include the childhood books of James vi.

† Translated by James Michie.

passion for poetry—her library includes the works of
Clément Marot, du Bellay and Ronsard, all poets she had
known and loved in France. Mary seems to have had a
preference also for medieval romances either of the Arthurian legends or the story of Roland. Melville reports
that when she had leisure from the affairs of the state
'she read upon good books, the history of diverse countries'[18]—books such as the chronicles of the emperors and
kings of Austria, found in the list of Edinburgh Castle, and
histories of the medieval kings of France. The colourful
mixture of event and character to be found in history
evidently appealed to her—it is obvious from her answers at her trial in England, and her conversations with
Paulet at the end of her life, that she had read and pondered on English history. In short, her library shows the
typical all-round tastes of what might be termed an educated Renaissance woman who enjoyed reading widely as
her fancy listed—as well as the individual touches to be
found in any library, such as The Book of Hunting (the
sort of book which might also be found in the fine library
of any eighteenth-century English gentleman), a book on
astronomy, and dutifully enough the bound sermons and
prayers of her uncle the cardinal of Lorraine.

There are three books on music listed: for music Mary
Stuart would seem to have had a profound feeling which,
like her love of poetry, appealed to the romantic, rather
than the inquisitive, side of her nature. She herself played
on both the lute and virginals, and as she plucked her
lute strings she loved to display those long white fingers,
which Brantôme and Ronsard admired. Although Melville
in his famous interview with Queen Elizabeth described
Mary as playing only 'reasonably well' for a queen, the
verdict of Mary's contemporaries who did not have to discuss the matter with her jealous rival is more generous.[19]
Mary had a charming soft singing voice which, like her
speaking voice, won the admiration of her listeners, and
on whose natural ability Conaeus commented. Musical
talent played its part in the selection of her valets of the
bed-chamber—later it influenced the choice of Riccio; in
1561 she had five violas and three players on the lute,
and some of the valets of the bed-chamber also played
and sang, so that Mary could beguile the long dark Scottish winter evenings with the sort of little musical supper
parties which she had enjoyed in France. The queen also

loved to have music to accompany her Mass; at first this
presented a problem, since the chapel organs had been
destroyed at the time of the Reformation as being pro-
fane instruments, with the exception of that at Stirling
which the mob could not reach. In 1562 Randolph reported
her as being desolate because no one would play at her
mass on Christmas Day;[20] however, by April 1565 she had
a band of musicians, and at Easter High Mass Randolph
furiously noticed that 'she wanted now neither trumpets,
drum, nor fife, bagpipe or tabor'.[21]

The skill of Mary Stuart for which Knox had a particular loathing, which summed up to him everything he detested about her character, education and upbringing, was
her dancing. There was a genuine and irreconcilable difference of attitude. To Knox, dancing seemed truly an invention of the devil, something which good women never
practised; in his opinion, the activities which Mary got up
to whenever she was alone with her 'French fillocks, fid-
dlers and others of that band' made the whole atmosphere
more like a brothel than a place for honest women. If we
are to believe Knox, in December 1562 Mary danced ex-
cessively 'beyond midnight' out of glee, because she had
received the news that the persecution of the Huguenots
had begun again in France.[22] He immediately resorted to
his favourite weapon of the denunciation of the pulpit, as
a result of which Mary summoned him to their second interview, some eighteen months after the first.

She received him in her chamber, attended by Lord
James, Maitland and Morton. Knox proceeded to qualify
his condemnation of dancing with certain provisos—he
said that he was prepared to tolerate dancing if the principal vocation of the dancer was not neglected, and that the
dancers took care not to dance as the Philistines did, for
the pleasure they took in the displeasure of God's people.
If they did fall into either of these two heinous errors,
they should 'receive the reward of dancers, and that will
be drunk in hell, unless they speedily repented'. Mary
Stuart on the other hand had been brought up in France
to dance, and she danced well and elegantly; in the words
of Melville, once more jealously cross-examined by the
queen of England, she danced 'not so high and disposedly'
as Elizabeth, but in Conaeus's less inhibited phrase she
danced most 'gracefully and becomingly'. With Mary Stuart, dancing was a natural expression of her pleasure in

life, as well as an artistic performance; it is small wonder therefore if the young queen, just nineteen, dancing with the ladies of her court in a carefree but hardly unseemly fashion, should have felt that of the two of them it was Knox, and not her, who was the Philistine.

In her dress, at least, Mary Stuart was able to give the femininity of her nature full reign, because to be magnificently attired was expected of a sixteenth-century queen, by all except the most bigoted and puritanical. Even in childhood, she had been distinguished by a keen interest in clothes when she teased her governess into letting her have as splendid gowns as the princesses of France. When she grew up, and had what virtually amounted to a constitutional duty to dress herself elegantly, she did so with innate good taste—lacking her cousin Elizabeth's inclination to bedizen herself ostentatiously, possibly because she was conscious that unlike Elizabeth she had the sort of beauty which was best set off by rich simplicity. Of course a large proportion of her time as a young woman was spent in mourning—for her mother, her father-in-law, and finally for her husband. The outward signs of grief were taken extremely seriously at this period—it has been noted that she was wearing black when she first arrived in Scotland—after Francis had been dead a year, in December 1561, the court went into half-mourning but Mary herself did not totally cast off her mourning until she married Darnley four years later. Perhaps she understood how to make her many black accoutrements a dramatic foil for her red-golden hair, white skin and golden eyes; for the same reason, white appears and reappears throughout the list of dresses in her wardrobe there being perhaps no better setting for a glowing complexion than a white dress: the list of her robes, with their descriptions and colours, fully explains how she came to be known as 'la reine blanche' in France. Indeed her detailed wardrobe books show the intense interest which Mary Stuart took in every detail of her clothes: there are lists of all the articles delivered from the wardrobe at Holyrood each month from the beginning of 2 September 1561 to June 1567 when the nobles took arms against her.[23] Ordinarily, she wore dresses of camlet (a sort of mohair), damask or serge, stiffened in the neck with buckram, and mounted with lace and ribbons; the queen was also fond of loose dresses ('à l'Espagnole'); her riding skirts and cloaks were of

Florentine serge, often edged with black velvet or fur. Beneath her gowns were 'vasquines', stiffened petticoats or farthingales to hold out her skirts, expanded with hoops of whale bone to give a crinoline effect. Her underwear included silk doublets, and there is mention of 'brassières' of both black and white silk. Her 'woven hose' often were made of gold and silver, and it is specifically mentioned that they were of silk. Her hats and caps were of black velvet and taffetas—her veils of white.

On state and ceremonial occasions, the queen's clothes were universally glittering. The inventory of the queen's dresses made at Holyrood in February 1562[24] lists 131 entries, including sixty gowns, of cloth of gold, cloth of silver, velvet, satin and silk. There are fourteen cloaks, five of which are in the Spanish fashion, and two royal mantles, one purple velvet and the other furred in ermine. There are thirty-four vasquines and sixteen devants or fronts (stomachers), mainly of cloth of gold, silver and satin. The dresses themselves ranged from the favourite white—often with silver fringes and embroidery—and preponderant black, to crimson velvet, orange damask embroidered in silver; the embroidery was so rich and detailed, that it was often passed from dress to dress, and listed separately among the jewellery.

Not only Mary's dresses, but also her jewels were of enormous importance to her: these of course represented something more than adornment, since by being treated as solid financial assets, they could be given as presents, held for security, or sold to pay troops, if necessary. In her childhood, Mary Stuart was decked by her attendants in those jewels considered fit for an infant queen; in Scotland she enjoyed the enhancement of a series of romantic gems; later in her life, her jewels were to enjoy a career as checkered as her own, as they were stolen, seized, sold to Elizabeth, or pawned, all to her violently expressed anguish. The inventory of her jewellery, made also in 1562,[25] contains 180 entries, an increase of twenty-one over the inventory of the queen's jewels made at the time of her departure from France—new acquisitions include a cross of gold set with diamonds and rubies which Mary had just redeemed for £1,000 from the hands into which it had been pledged by Mary of Guise. She had also acquired some new Scottish pearls from an Edinburgh goldsmith, for Scottish pearls were held to share with Bo-

hemian pearls the honour of being the finest in Europe,
although still rated as inferior to the pearls of the Orient.
As she loved white, so the queen seems to have had an
especial affection for pearls—it was noted that she was
wearing two of a group of twenty-three pearls in her ears
at the actual moment when the inventory is taken. But
rubies she also seems to have admired, as she loved to
wear crimson velvet; and among her profusion of rings,
necklaces and earrings, there is mention of enamel, cor-
nelian and turquoise, as well as, of course, gold and diamonds.

The queen paid fashionable attention to the care of her
hair, and the elaborate dressing of it, according to the
caprices of the time. We know that among her Maries,
Mary Seton was an especially skilled hairdresser, having
learnt the art in France. Even in her youth, when she had
lovely thick glistening hair—those tresses 'si beaux, si
blonds, si cendrés' wrote Brantôme—the dictates of the
mode led her to use perukes or false hairpieces. Later in
her life her glorious hair darkened, and the sorrows and
illnesses of her captivity caused it to thin and go grey
prematurely. Then, false pieces of hair were to be essential,
but now in her heyday, she made use of them equally:
there is repeated reference to her perukes or the bags
to keep them in, in her wardrobe lists. By 1569 Nicholas
White mentions that she had them of all different colours,
and Sir Francis Knollys was impressed by the pretty
fashions created on her head by Mary Seton when she first
arrived in England (he considered the art a novelty although Queen Elizabeth herself had no less than eighty
perukes). Queen Mary's perukes were among the first
necessities which she sent for from Lochleven, and as can
be seen by the awe of Knollys, these much-travelled hand-
maidens of beauty, were despatched to Mary at Carlisle by
her wardrobe master Servais de Condé only a month
after she reached it herself.[26]

The queen of Scots had a childish love of fancy dress
and dressing-up which she preserved throughout her life.
It has already been mentioned that she loved to adopt
Scottish national dress in France, and even had herself
painted in it, according to Brantôme, although the portrait
does not survive. In Scotland, with a romantic love of
the Highlands, reminiscent of her descendant and admirer
Queen Victoria, Mary adopted the costume of wearing

the so-called 'Highland mantles'—these were not plaid, but loose cloaks reaching to the ground, and generally embroidered. In this she followed her father, who had had himself made a Highland suit in 1538, including 'variant coloured' velvet to be a short Highland coat, and 'Highland tartan' to be hose—trews and a belted plaid being the contemporary form of Highland dress rather than the later kilt.* Queen Mary had three cloaks, one white, one blue and one black embroidered in gold.[27] In Scotland also, Mary loved to adopt male costume, and wander about the streets, enjoying the sort of romantic incognito among her subjects which has always been considered the perquisite of adventurous royalties. With her height and long legs, she must have made an engaging picture: and would surely have earned the admiration of Brantôme, who wrote that only a lady of perfect beauty with perfect legs should attempt such a disguise, in order that no man should be able to tell 'to which sex she really belonged, whether she was a handsome boy or the beautiful woman she was in reality'.[28] At one banquet given to the French ambassador, the queen appeared with her Maries, all dressed as men; riding against the rebels in 1565, she dressed up as a man to ride at the head of her army, the cynosure of every loyal eye. On Easter Monday 1565, Mary and her women dressed themselves up like burgesses' wives, in Stirling, and ran up and down the streets, according to Randolph, gathering money for the banquets; later they all banqueted where Randolph himself was lodging, to the wonder of the common spectators.[29] Three weeks before she married Darnley, they both sauntered about the streets of Edinburgh in disguise until supper-time, and did the same thing again the next day, causing a certain amount of gossip.

In all these pranks and escapades, of the type in which royalty have always indulged to escape the gilded bird-cage of their existence, it is unnecessary to discern more than natural high spirits and youthful love of pleasure. Certainly there were no sexual scandals surrounding the sovereign, as there had been in the time of Mary's father,

---

* Tartan is also not to be understood in the modern sense: it was the name given to a certain material, which in the sixteenth century was not necessarily checkered. During his visit to the Highlands at the beginning of the next century, John Taylor still did not describe Tartan more specifically than as 'a warm stuff of divers colours'.[27]

and in so many monarchs before and since. Mary, who throughout her first years in Scotland was an unattached and beautiful girl, with no restraints except those of prudence to hold her back from the wildest excesses had she wished to indulge in them, was as clearly *sans reproche* in her court life, as she was *sans peur* in the hunting field. The only scandal to be seen was the scandal, in the eyes of Knox at least, of the spectacle of human enjoyment. Mary conducted herself in a thoroughly innocent, somewhat hoydenish fashion, somewhat like the Shakespearian heroines whom she so much resembles—like Rosalind, rejoicing in her boy's attire in the Forest of Arden, but fainting at the sight of Orlando's blood on a handkerchief. Certainly, like Rosalind, although caparisoned like a man, she did not have a doublet and hose in her disposition, but retained all her female impulsiveness.

Mary Stuart's simple sense of fun—what Randolph called her 'merry mood', fitted in well with the boisterous sense of humour of her Scottish subjects at this time, although this was certainly more bawdy in its most outspoken manifestations. The sixteenth-century Scots did not necessarily see the reformation of their religion as leading to the end of those hearty crude bucolic games and sports which they had long enjoyed; they loved the favourite May game of Robin Hood, with its Abbott of Unreason and its Queen of the May. When these games were forbidden by the magistrates in May 1561, for the disturbance they caused, the ban caused public riots, and Robin and his men patrolled the streets all the same, in defiance. One of Robin's companions was arrested, condemned to death and carried to the gibbet, until he was rescued on the verge of the hanging by his fellow-rioters. The people who enjoyed this sort of entertainment naturally loved the pageantry brought to the country by Mary and her court. On Sunday 30 November, a few months after Mary's arrival, her uncle Elboeuf, and her half-brothers Robert and John Stewart took part in 'running at the ring', two teams of six, one disguised as women, and the other as strangers in fancy dress. Elboeuf did well, but the 'women', led by Lord Robert, won; the queen watched it all with great enjoyment. A week later, on Saturday 5 December, the anniversary of Francis's death was marked by the solemn presentation of a huge wax candle draped in black velvet; the next day possibly because it was two days off

Mary's own nineteenth birthday, there was 'mirth and
pastimes' upon the seashore at Leith, a romantic, if chilly,
prospect upon the winter sands, at which the queen was
present.[30] Court life was enlivened by numbers of paid
jesters, often female. One, known as 'La Jardinière', had
her own keeper or *gouvernante*, Jacqueline; La Jardinière
was given a green plaiding coat, handkerchiefs, and linen
for underclothing. Another favourite of the queen, Jane
Colquhoun, received a red and yellow coat in 1566. A
special canvas bed was made for another of Mary's female fools, Nichola, 'La Folle', whom she brought from
France, and who stayed with the queen until her imprisonment in England, when Lennox paid generously for the
'fool's' return to her native land.[31]

Among the special features of the social life of the time
were the weddings of the nobility, which were nearly
always the occasion for banquets and masques. Mary seems
to have had a wistful love of weddings, and loved to give
not only feasts but also bridal dresses to her favourites.
Two significant weddings took place in her first year in
Scotland—in January 1562 Lady Janet Hepburn, Bothwell's sister, married Mary's half-brother, Lord John, at
Bothwell's own castle of Crichton; both Queen Mary and
Lord James came to the castle, with Bothwell acting as
host, and the English ambassador was duly impressed by
the sports and pastimes which were indulged in. Four
weeks later Lord James's own nuptials to Lady Agnes Keith
were celebrated in Edinburgh with great splendour. He
was created earl of Mar the day before the marriage,
which was held in St Giles Cathedral, with Knox preaching the sermon. A long train of nobles witnessed the rites
and then went to Holyrood, for the first instalment of
three days' banqueting—on which Knox commented sourly
that 'the vanity used thereat offended many godly'.[32]

The series of masques included that held after the
wedding of Argyll's sister at Castle Campbell in midwinter
1563, at which shepherds appeared wearing white damask
and playing sweetly upon the lute. Perhaps the most
splendid of all the banquets was that which Mary herself
gave at Shrovetide in 1564 when she was just recovering
from an illness. It was reported by Randolph that no
Scotsman had ever seen anything like it, except at the marriage of a prince: it lasted for three days and all the attendants, as well as the queen herself, her ladies and her

gentlemen, wore classical black and white. Randolph himself echoed the prevailing mood of carefree enjoyment, when he told Cecil, that until the arrival of the French ambassador, du Croc, in May 1563, who brought in the sterner atmosphere of outside affairs, all those at the Scottish court 'did nothing but pass our time in feasts, banqueting, masking and running at the ring and such like'.[33]

Through all this tapestry of court life, ran the bright threads represented by the four Maries. Knox, ever eager to repeat scandals about the court if he could learn them, concentrated much of his attention on the Maries and the queen's women in general, presumably because scandal about them could be held to smear the queen. For example, he repeated one actual case which had come to public knowledge at the beginning of Mary's rule; of a 'heinous murder' committed in the court—'yea, not far from the Queen's own lap'. A French woman who had served in the queen's chamber was said to have 'played the whore' with the queen's apothecary and in the course of the liaison unwisely conceived a child. Father and mother then conspired together to murder the infant: 'Yet,' to continue Knox's account of it all, 'were the cries of the newborn bairn heard; search was made, the child and mother both deprehended, and so were both the man and the woman damned to be hanged upon the public street of Edinburgh.' But Knox did not mention what Randolph reported, that it was the queen herself, with her profound disgust of immorality in sexual matters, who insisted on the death sentence being carried out. Instead he went on to add that it had been well known that 'shame' hastened the marriage between John Semple, called the Dancer, and Mary Livingston, surnamed the Lusty. Having delivered this Parthian shot, he still could not resist saying it was well known what shocking reputations the Maries and the rest of the dancers at the court enjoyed: 'The ballads of the age did witness, which we for modesty's sake omit.'*[34]

* From this anecdote of Knox it used to be deduced, notably by Sir Walter Scott, that the beautiful and melancholy ballad of the Queen's Maries with its haunting refrain:

Last night the Queen had four Maries
Tonight there'll be but three

But *pace* Knox, the four Maries had in truth simple
natures: like their mistress they were easily pleased by
court festivities and enjoyments, and their reputations certainly did not deserve to be besmirched by his slurs. Their
faults, if any, sprang from the natural light-heartedness
and frivolity of youth, rather than anything more vicious.
Mary Livingston owed her nickname of the Lusty to her
energetic habit of dancing rather than to any raging
physical appetites: there is no other contemporary evidence
other than the venomous suggestion of Knox that her
marriage was hastened by pregnancy, and her eldest child
was indeed born a year after her marriage. Mary Livingston
was considered reliable enough to be given special charge
of the queen's jewels, and her nuptials in fact at her family
home at Falkirk seem to have been the occasion for special
and long-planned rejoicings, which do not accord with the
notion of a shameful union. The truth was that Mary
Livingston was a girl of high spirits and exceptional vivac-
ity, two qualities which were scarcely likely to commend
her to Knox.

Although the first to marry, Mary Livingston was not
the *belle* of the quartet: this honour was always accorded
to Mary Fleming. Originally it was her royal blood, which
set her apart from the other Maries: later, as her beauty
bloomed, her remarkable combination of looks and vitality
made her in the opinion of Leslie, 'the flower of the flock'.
At the Twelfth Night festivities of 1564 Mary Fleming,
dressed as Queen of the Bean in cloth of silver, her neck,
shoulders and what seemed like the whole of her body
set with jewels, so dazzled the gaze of Thomas Randolph
that although Mary Beaton was his acknowledged favourite

There's Mary Seton and Mary Beaton
And Mary Carmichael and me.

applied to the court of Mary Stuart, despite the fact that the Maries
of the ballad were named Mary Beaton, Mary Seton, Mary Carmichael and 'me' (Mary Hamilton) whereas Queen Mary's last two
maids were of course named Mary Fleming and Mary Livingston.
The ballad has subsequently been traced to a scandal at the court
of Catherine the Great in early eighteenth-century Russia, where one
of her maids of honour of Scottish origin, Mary Hamilton, was executed for the murder of an illegitimate child, after having had a love
affair with Catherine's husband, the Tsar Peter. The ballad, which
Child dated between 1719 and 1764, evidently made use of the well-
known fact that Queen Mary in the sixteenth century had employed
four girls named Mary to serve her, and grafted it on to the tragedy
of Mary Hamilton in Russia.[35]

among the four he expressed the opinion that 'the fair
Fleming' was surely chosen by Fortune to be a queen,
and not for Twelfth Night only: assuming the mantle of
Paris, he compared her in lyrical terms to Venus in beauty,
Minerva in wit and Juno in worldly wealth—the two
former being given her by nature, and the third he assumed
to be at her command within the kingdom of Scotland.
Buchanan too extolled the praises of this queen-for-the-night
in Latin verse, terming her Queen 'Flaminia' to whom
virtue itself had already supplied a sceptre.[36]

Mary Beaton seems to have been the most classically
beautiful of the four,* but she lacked the flowering fascination of Mary Fleming, which the fair Fleming owed
perhaps to her share of Stuart blood. Like Mary Fleming, Mary Beaton's beauty and worth were praised by
Buchanan in verse, but her character was cast in a less
flamboyant mould. The meekest of the four, Mary Seton,
a daughter of one of the grandest houses in Scotland, was
naturally pious and more devoted to the service of her
mistress than to the pleasures to be derived at the court, as
her subsequent history showed.

Whatever Knox's feelings about the Maries, and whatever his strictures on masques and similar diversions, we
may be sure that Mary's subjects themselves thoroughly
enjoyed such display since it was twenty years since
there had been anything in Scotland approaching proper
court life. Randolph described what a pretty sight the
Maries made as they rode with their mistress to Parliament in 1563—'virgins, maids, Maries, demoiselles of
honour, or the Queen's *mignons*, call them as you please,
your Honour'—wrote the English ambassador;[37] the effect
was the same: they made a pleasing spectacle. The burgesses' wives who were reported to find the queen's dresses
too rich were probably nonetheless happy to be able to
watch them go by. To the argument that Mary was extravagant, it may be answered that she was considerably less
extravagant than her cousin Elizabeth in both her dress
and her progresses. Not only was Mary used to infinitely
more prodigal expenditure at the court of France, but
also much of her glamour consisted in her personal charm.

---

* There are no contemporary portraits of the four Maries to be
seen. One picture once thought to be that of Mary Beaton showing
her with fair hair and dark eyes is now thought to date from the
late seventeenth or early eighteenth century.

In any case, such display on the part of a sovereign was an essential part of personal and monarchical government —as one Elizabethan contemporary observed—'in such ceremonies, does the art of good government much consist'.[38] The result, as even Buchanan, later to be her harshest critic, admitted, was that this pretty, high-spirited creature, with her hunting, her hawking, her masques, her clothes, her jewels, was able to charm those members of the Scots nation who were there to be charmed. She indeed 'fleet the time carelessly, as they did in the golden world' in her own particular Forest of Arden. Buchanan himself wrote of this period in her life:[39] 'Apart from the fascination of her varied and perilous history, she was graced with surpassing loveliness of form, the vigour of maturing youth, and fine qualities of mind which a court education had increased or at least made more attractive by a surface gloss of virtue.'

11 The Fall of Huntly

'Far o'er the crashing forest
The giant arms lie spread:
And the pale augurs murmuring low
Gaze on the blasted head'

LORD MACAULAY

On 11 August 1562, Mary Queen of Scots rode north on her first visit to her Highland dominions. She had long intended to visit these wild and individual territories: a ceremonial visit to Aberdeen had been planned for Eastertide as early as January, but had apparently been delayed by the English negotiations. Now that the interview with Queen Elizabeth was temporarily postponed, the queen of Scots was free to resume the plan; but in the interval since the progress was first mooted, it seemed that her purpose had altered. Her primary intention was no longer to extend her knowledge of her kingdom, nor merely sporting (as the date might suggest to modern eyes); it had now become distinctly punitive. The might of the Gordons, under their magnificent but unpredictable head, George, 4th earl of Huntly, had long loomed over the north-east of Scotland like the shadow of a great eagle which might at any moment sweep on its prey. This fact in itself, however disquieting, would not have inspired a martial expedition—quite apart from the fact that Huntly's state approached that of an independent monarch, he was in any case the leading Catholic magnate. Firstly, it might be dangerous to attack him, and secondly, it might be unwise. But in the course of the summer, Huntly's third son, Sir John Gordon, became involved in an unsavoury scandal, and provided the queen with a *casus belli* against one Gordon at least, if she needed one.

In June Sir John severely wounded Lord Ogilvie in a street brawl in Edinburgh as a result of which he was thrown into prison. The feud with the Ogilvies had arisen because the Ogilvie of Findlater had disinherited his own son James Ogilvie of Cardell and left his lands, including

the castle of Findlater, to Sir John in his place. The disinheritance was at the instance of Ogilvie's second wife, who
persuaded Ogilvie that his son had made amorous advances
to her, and thus deserved punishment. The step-mother
herself now became the mistress or 'pretended spouse' of
John Gordon, who was not only a bold cavalier but good-
looking also, and as Buchanan put it 'in the very flower of
youth'. Public opinion was outraged and the scandalous
alliance did the poor woman little good in the end, for
when Sir John could not secure from her all the lands he
wanted, he shut her up in a 'close chamber' and both discarded her as a mistress and disowned her as a wife.[1] But
matrimony was much on the mind of the ebullient Sir John:
as a scion of the Catholic Gordons, he had been suggested
as a possible husband for the queen herself. He himself
seems to have been confident (on little foundation) that
his dashing good looks had already caught her eye. Now
his volatile temperament could not long endure the incarceration of prison. He escaped, and fled northwards to
the safety of his father's domains.

Mary did not view his offence with either a merciful
or an indulgent eye. He had escaped justice, and he had
also possessed himself of the lands of her own master of
the household—none other than that James Ogilvie of
Cardell, who had been so cruelly dispossessed by the accusations of his step-mother. Mary now determined to
pursue Sir John in the course of her northern progress,
and James Ogilvie was among the courtiers who accompanied her on the journey. Scandal apart, Mary also intended to demonstrate that the Gordons could not behave
as they pleased with impunity. Huntly had been out of
favour with the queen since January, since he had made
no secret of his disapproval of her cool policy towards the
Scottish Catholics. Not only had Mary rejected his plan of
a Catholic rising at Aberdeen, when she was still in France,
but ever since she had refused such provocative offers as
'setting up the Mass in three shires'. The untrustworthy
temperament of the 4th earl made him indeed a delicate
subject to handle either in conflict or alliance—as Randolph observed unpleasantly, were it not for the fact that
'no man will trust him either in word or deed', he would
have been capable of doing a great deal of mischief.[2]

The character of the 4th earl belongs to that great tradition of independent Highland lords who throughout his-

tory have posed such problems for the central government—since their policies, which have seemed so strangely
inconsistent from the viewpoint of the centre, have in fact
been consistently bent towards the aggrandizement of their
own clans. Huntly had powerful royal connections: as the
grandson of James IV by his natural daughter Margaret
Stewart, he was, although thirty years older, Mary Stuart's
first cousin (she always addressed both him and his son
as 'cousin' in her letters), and since his own father died
when he was a baby, he was actually brought up with
King James V. Two of his nine sons were married to two
daughters of the duke of Châtelherault. His power extended across the north-east of Scotland in a formidable
array of tangible castles, and intangible but effective
family alliances. Not only did he hold the royal castles of
Inverness and Inverlochy, but he was further supported
by his own castles of Strathbogie, Bog of Gight, Aboyne,
Ruthven in Badenoch and Drummin in Glenlivat; from
1549 onwards, he was allowed to hold the large and
profitable earldom of Moray under the crown. At different
dates, the local Fraser lords of Saltoun and Lovat had
made bonds of manrent to him, as had the captains of
Clan Cameron and Clan Chattan. The grandeur of his
household impressed even Mary of Guise's French court
when they came north. Now, at fifty, grown corpulent with
age, like a great northern bear, he seemed the very pattern
of the Highland patriarch.

The past career of this patriarchal figure had, however,
been somewhat checkered. As one of the leaders of the
Scots army at Pinkie Cleugh (where his white and gilt
armour dazzled the eye) he had been captured by the
English; although Leslie tells the story of his romantic
escape from Morpeth while his jailers were playing cards,
in fact he procured his release by the more down-to-earth
method of signing an indenture with Somerset to pursue
the cause of King Edward VI in Scotland. He was imprisoned by Mary of Guise in 1555, but restored to favour
to become lieutenant-general of the kingdom two years
later. Yet her favour and his Catholicism did not prevent
him defecting to the reformers briefly in April 1560: his
motives seem to have been his notorious 'doubleness and
covetousness' since he was careful to stipulate that he
should continue in supreme authority in the north as before. When his castle of Strathbogie was sacked, among its

contents was found a large proportion of the ecclesiastical
ornaments of Aberdeen Cathedral which Huntly was said
to have stored away for use when Catholicism was restored.[3] Yet his defection at this critical moment virtually
wrecked the Catholic cause. Now Huntly was once more
openly professing the faith of his fathers, but Mary's
caution towards this unstable character can readily be
imagined, since not only she but all his contemporaries
generally reckoned him to be totally untrustworthy in the
final analysis, in all except that which intimately concerned
his own clan.

There was a further complication between Huntly and
the central government: although Huntly, free from interference in the north, had profited from the revenues
of the lands of the earldom of Moray ever since 1549, the
title itself had been given secretly to Lord James at the end
of January 1562 by the queen. At his wedding in February
Lord James had actually been invested earl of Mar, but
when Lord Erskine protested that this earldom was an
Erskine perquisite, Lord James resigned it a few months
later, retaining only the secret Moray earldom; nevertheless despite this private assurance of Moray from the
queen to Lord James, the news was not broken to Huntly.
It has been suggested that the prospect of the formal acquisition of the earldom of Moray provided a sinister motive for Lord James to drag his sister northwards, and
persuade her to strike down the overmighty Huntly. It was
true that Lord James was quite as avaricious as most of
his contemporaries: certainly his best chance of publicly
acquiring the earldom which he had already acquired
secretly was to proceed north with an adequate force,
and possess himself of it. In this, he clearly needed the
assistance of the queen. But it is equally certain that
when Mary and James set forth for the north in August
1562 they were perfectly united in their aims. For the last
year James had been Mary's chief adviser and she had accepted all his lessons. James did not need to drag Mary
north: she herself was anxious to make her progress and
in doing so restore the errant Sir John to the arms of
justice. As for the earldom of Moray, one of the points of
the gift was intended to be the curtailment of Huntly's
expanding powers. With regard to Mary's ultimate intentions towards Huntly, the evidence suggests that in August
the queen had made no positive decision, but was content

to see how Huntly would react to her northern progress
before judging whether he was indeed an over-mighty subject, or merely a convenient Catholic viceroy. The focus
was therefore for better or for worse on the behaviour
of Huntly.

Queen Mary arrived at Aberdeen, via Stirling, Coupar
Angus, Perth and Glamis, on 27 August. Here in this
Huntly-dominated town, she paid the visit to the university which must have provided the inspiration for the
bequest of Greek and Latin books to its library in her
will of 1566. At Aberdeen she was also greeted by the
countess of Huntly, who was surrounded by a splendid
train of attendants. This remarkable and vigorous woman
had been born a Keith, a sister of the Earl Marischal, and
was incidentally aunt to that Lady Agnes Keith whom
Lord James had recently married. Clearly the strain provided a series of redoubtable helpmeets, for Elizabeth,
countess of Huntly, not only provided the decision which
her husband often lacked, but was also not above turning
to the aid of her tame 'familiars' or witches, when inspiration from any other source was lacking. Now she pleaded
as a mother with the queen to overlook Sir John Gordon's
indiscretion and pardon him. Queen Mary, with the strictness with which she seems to have regarded all scandalous
misdemeanours, insisted that Sir John must return to ward
at Stirling before he could be pardoned. The gallant Sir
John was thus temporarily induced to surrender himself—
but shortly afterwards his turbulent nature reasserted itself,
and escaping once more, he gathered a force of 1,000
horse about him.

The Gordons were traditionally skilful horsemen. With
this force, Sir John now proceeded impudently to harry
the queen's train as she proceeded north. He later admitted that this was done with the deliberate intention of
abducting her and, unlike Arran, he seems to have been
gaily certain that the queen would accede to the arrangement. His confidence in his powers of physical attraction
was unfortunately misplaced. This flagrant defiance of her
royal authority enraged the queen, who promptly refused
to visit the Huntly stronghold of Strathbogie, on her road
to Inverness. Caution as well as anger may have played
its part in the decision: for it was highly uncertain what
might befall her once inside the Gordon stronghold, in
the grasp of the unstable Huntly, to say nothing of the

mercurial Sir John. It was afterwards suggested that had
Mary stopped at Strathbogie, Huntly would have had Lord
James, Maitland and Morton killed and established a
Catholic coup. He would most likely have completed the
operation by marrying off Mary—to be 'kept at the devotion of the said Earl of Huntly'—to his son. Mary certainly told Randolph indignantly later that among Huntly's
crimes had been the fact that he would have married her
off 'where he would'.[4]

In the meantime Huntly was given no chance to put
these dastardly plans, if indeed he held them, into effect.
Queen Mary by-passed Strathbogie, and taking a more
western route to Inverness, she stopped instead at Darnaway Castle. Here in this stronghold a few miles from the
sea, set aloft amid surrounding forests in the centre of the
earldom of Moray ('very ruinous' complained Randolph,
except for the hall which was 'fair and large') she took
the opportunity to announce that Lord James had been
granted the earldom in place of that of Mar. She also issued
an order against John Gordon for his efforts to 'break the
whole country, so far as is in his power', as well as failing
to return to ward.[5] When Mary finally reached Inverness
on 11 September, she had brusque confirmation of Huntly's attitude towards her. The keeper of the castle, Alexander Gordon, another of Huntly's numerous offspring
(he had nine sons and three daughters), refused her entrance, although it was a royal, not a Gordon, castle, being only committed into Huntly's charge by virtue of his
position as sheriff of Inverness. This was not so much in-
solence as actual treason, whether by Huntly's specific orders or not, and in the queen's mind certainly lent colour
to what he would have done if Mary had stopped at
Strathbogie. Huntly, on hearing that the rest of the Highlanders were rallying behind the queen, took alarm at the
situation, and sent orders to his son to admit the queen.
Mary Stuart then entered Inverness Castle, and its captain
was promptly hanged over the battlements for his defiance.[6]

Installed at Inverness Castle, Mary was now able to taste
the sweets of Highland life, which has commended itself
to so many royalties since: the sport, the freedom, the
beauty of the scenery all appealed to her romantic temperament. She felt a childish happiness to feel herself
among this strange people dressed in their skins (half of

whom only spoke Gaelic, a language she could not speak),
so tough that they habitually slept out in the heather, said
Leslie, but now came down from their distant glens to
gaze on this beautiful young creature they were told was
their queen. In order to please them, not only did the
queen herself adopt Highland dress, some of it acquired
hastily in Inverness according to the royal accounts, but
plaids were also purchased locally for several of her
courtiers. To Inverness came the local lords: the young
gentlemen of the Fraser clan were presented to her, at
their head their seventeen-year-old chief Lord Hugh of
Lovat, nephew of that Lord Lovat who had perished with
his eldest son and so many of the Fraser men eighteen
years before in a clan battle on the Field of Shirts at Loch
Lochy. The newly be-plaided courtiers were impressed
by this muster of Highlanders, having never seen such
an abundance of them before, and the queen showed
particular favour to the good-looking young boy. As a result young Lord Hugh, 'not a little vain' of the dash which
he had cut, offered the services of his Frasers to the queen
against the Gordons, in order to avenge the deaths of his
forbears at the Field of Shirts. The queen tactfully replied, however, that she was loath to give cause for a
further quarrel between the clans. When Queen Mary departed from Inverness, Lord Hugh and his Frasers merely
conveyed her to the banks of the Spey—and sad to relate
for the self-confidence of youth, a number of Frasers ended
by fighting against the queen for the Gordons.[7]

Although Randolph grumbled dreadfully at the appalling journey from Stirling to Inverness, and though
the surrounding power of the Gordons was to say the least
of it menacing, all in all Mary Stuart had never seemed
more blithe. She evidently looked on the Highlanders as
noble savages, a category she found more sympathetic than
their opposite numbers, the savage nobles, in the south.
Randolph was amazed at her happiness and her health:
'In all these garbullies,' he wrote, 'I never saw her merrier,
nor dismayed, nor never thought that stomache to be in
her that I find! She repenteth but, when the lardes and
other at Inverness came in the mornings from the watch,
that she was not a man to know what life it was to lie all
night in the fields, or to walk upon the causeway with a
jack and knapscall [helmet] a Glasgow buckler and a
broad sword.'[8] In short, Rosalind was in her element: the

very spice of danger, provided by the fact that Sir John still hovered impudently in her wake, far from upsetting, merely stimulated the queen.*

From Inverness, Mary still dogged by Sir John proceeded to the seat of the Catholic bishop of Moray at Spynie. It was suspected that Sir John might finally choose to attack as the royal party crossed the Spey, and Mary's scouts reported that up to 1,000 Gordon horsemen were concealed in the woods. But no attack came. As the queen passed the castle of Findlater, the former Ogilvie stronghold, she called on it to surrender; but since there was no response, and the castle could not be captured without cannon, owing to its sea-girt position, she abandoned the effort, and passed on back to Aberdeen. Here, on 22 September, she was received with a rapturous and loyal welcome, whatever intrigues Huntly might be meditating at near-by Strathbogie. The great question which now faced the queen and the new earl of Moray† was how next to proceed against Huntly: was he to be allowed to maintain this mighty sway over the north of Scotland, so complete that his son temeritously dared to defy the queen outside her own castle of Inverness, and another son, an escaped criminal, harried the queen's troops, with impunity, while he himself apparently planned a state of near-independence? Mary, spurred on by Moray, now sent for 120 harquebussiers, and experienced soldiers such as Lord Lindsay, Kirkcaldy of the Grange and Cockburn of Ormiston (all incidentally keen Protestants), as well as some cannon. She also forwarded a message to Huntly asking him to surrender his own formidable cannon, which stood in the courtyard at Strathbogie, in order to menace the Highlanders into subjection.

* In all Queen Mary made two expeditions to the Highlands: it was on the second occasion, in the summer of 1564, that she made her way north to Ross-shire once more through Inverness. *En route* to Dingwall, the chief town of the earldom of Ross, Mary stopped at the priory of Beauly, founded in the thirteenth century by monks of the Valliscaulian order, and taking its name from the beauty of the place, commemorated in its Latin charter—*Monasterium de Bello Loco*. The name seemed apt also to the queen three hundred years later, and inspired her to a royal play upon words: *'Oui, c'est un beau lieu'* she is said to have exclaimed, with gracious good humour.[9]

† As Lord James will be referred to in the future to distinguish him from Mary's son James.

A prolonged game of cat-and-mouse now ensued with Huntly; the earl himself drawn two ways, was clearly not yet quite sure in his own mind whether he was engaged in a rebellion or not; 'letting I dare not wait upon I would', he temporized by sending his eldest surviving son Lord Gordon to consult Gordon's father-in-law Châtelherault in the south. Knox wrote later that Gordon actually tried to raise the south to the same effect as his father was raising the north, and to this effect even contacted Bothwell, who had just escaped from his own imprisonment in Edinburgh Castle. But in the meantime Huntly offered to join with the queen to pursue his errant son John Gordon, provided he could appear with an armed force to support him. The queen understandably did not trust the appearance of Huntly surrounded by his Gordons, and Huntly equally declined to appear alone. Frightened of being captured, the great earl now took humiliatingly to sleeping every night under a different roof (easy enough in Gordon territory) but spending his days at Strathbogie. When the queen's army got to hear of this, Kirkcaldy set out from Aberdeen with a small party of twelve men in order to surprise Huntly at his midday dinner and hold the entrance to Strathbogie until reinforcements arrived. Unfortunately the reinforcements proceeded both too quickly and too noisily, and Kirkcaldy was still parleying with the porter for an entrance to the castle when the clatter of their approach alerted the watchmen. Huntly had time to abandon his half-eaten meal, rush through the castle to the back and escape over a wall on to a waiting horse, without boots and without sword, but nevertheless still free. And on this fresh horse he soon outdistanced his pursuers.

Lady Huntly was now compelled to welcome the royal emissaries in Strathbogie at last: they found it stripped bare, except, rather touchingly, for the chapel, which had been left completely furnished with all its candles, ornaments and altar-books, in readiness for the queen's visit, when it had been expected that she would use it. But as Huntly and John Gordon had both now disappeared, and the latter had recently captured fifty-six harquebussiers from a company near Findlater, which rendered him still more dangerous, it was considered by the government that the final stage of rebellion had been reached. On 16 October, by orders of the Privy Council, both Huntly

tainted. The body, still unburied, was then deposited in
the Blackfriars Priory in Edinburgh, and it was not until
April 1566 that it was allowed to be carried back to the
north, to be laid in the family tomb of the Gordons in
Elgin Cathedral. The fate of the gay young Sir John
Gordon was shorter and sharper. On 2 November he was
executed, in the presence of the queen herself, who was
compelled to attend in order to give the lie to stories that
she had encouraged him in his affections and his wild
matrimonial schemes. Having a horror of bloodshed, she
was extremely reluctant to do so, and as it turned out the
reality was even worse than her imaginings. Sir John cried
out that the presence of the queen solaced him, since he
was about to suffer for love of her. But the executioner
was clumsy at his task and the spectacle reduced the queen
to passionate weeping; she was indeed so horrified by her
ordeal which resulted that she ended by breaking down
completely, and had to be carried to her chamber, where
she remained all the next day, in a state of nervous collapse.

Two of Huntly's sons, Alexander and John, having been
sacrificed in the general holocaust of his family's fall
from grace, Mary proceeded to spare the life of the eldest
son George, Lord Gordon; he had not been involved in
the final battle, having been away in the south consulting
Châtelherault, and after being officially condemned with
his father, he was pardoned and merely put into free ward
at Dunbar. Huntly's youngest son, Adam Gordon, was
also spared. The rich vestments from Aberdeen Cathedral
stored at Strathbogie since 1559 were taken down to
Holyrood, where it seems the queen treated them more
as Gordon spoils rather than as the ecclesiastical heritage
they were, for they were probably among the gilded vestments in her belongings turned to secular uses in the
spring of 1567 making a rich bed for Darnley and a doublet
for Bothwell. The spoils of Strathbogie Castle were either
taken by the queen or given to Moray for his new castle
of Darnaway. Besides the earldom of Moray, whose
revenues were estimated by Randolph at 1,000 merks a
year, Moray also received the sheriffdoms of Elgin, Forres
and Inverness. Hence the tumbling-down of Huntly's
power in the north left an empty space which Moray,
rather than the crown, was able to fill; while the disappearance of the leading Catholic magnate from the

Scottish scene could not fail to weaken the Catholic cause there, and in turn benefit the reformed religion.

It has sometimes been argued that Mary made a fundamental mistake in allowing the balance of power to be upset in this way. The north of Scotland, which conceivably could have been a Catholic *bloc* under a friendly Huntly, to play off against a Protestant south, was now broken up into different units; and when the attainer was removed three years later for Huntly's son, the properties were too dissipated for him to become the magnate his father had been. But even before 1562 Mary had never shown any signs of supporting Huntly either as a magnate or as a Catholic, and had repeatedly snubbed his overtures in favour of the Protestants. Her attitude towards Huntly was very much affected by her general policy since her arrival in Scotland, of leaning upon the advice of Moray and Maitland; her aim was to quieten down all possible Catholic insurrections, in favour of general peace, the maintenance of the royal authority and the *status quo*. It may well be argued that Mary's policy was unwise, compared to the more serpentine procedure of backing each noble in turn, and luring them in some fashion to destroy each other, until the crown should be left triumphant. By this reasoning Huntly should have been skilfully built up, rather than bloodily laid low. Certainly the 'pale augurs' might well murmur low over his 'blasted head', when they reflected how critical Mary's situation could be if Moray's loyalty faltered. There was, however, an obvious difficulty in the way of pursuing this policy of checks and balances, quite apart from Mary's own inexperience of Scottish affairs; this was the character of Huntly—so manifestly unreliable.

Mary herself was in no doubt afterwards that Huntly's treachery had been proved by the evidence discovered after his death, and the confessions of Sir John and Huntly's servants (one of them made before the battle of Corrichie): all of which suggested that in his last moments Huntly did have some wild ill-conceived plan of seizing Mary's person, and upsetting the Protestant régime, in favour of a Catholic one. Mary continued to regard Huntly as a double-dyed traitor, and when she wrote to her uncle in France and to the Pope in January 1563, protesting her continued devotion to the Catholic faith, she clearly felt no regret that circumstances had compelled her to lay low

her greatest Catholic subject—it had been an unpleasant
duty which it would have been dangerous not to have carried out.[15] By denying her entrance at Inverness, refusing
to join her in the hunt against his son, and finally in taking
up arms against her with the possible object of abducting
her, he had certainly made it extremely difficult for her to
support him against Moray, even if she had so wished.
Thus Moray was easily able to gratify his natural avari-
ciousness, and acquire the rich spoils in the north, having
no need to work out any more subtle conspiracy. It is
significant that Maitland himself, on his way back to
southern Scotland, revealed that he was finally convinced
of Huntly's treachery: 'I am sorry that the soil of my
native country did ever produce so unnatural a subject as
the Earl of Huntly hath proved in the end against his
Sovereign,' he wrote. 'Being a Princess so gentle and
benign. . . . Well, the event hath made manifest his in-
iquity, and the innocence as well of her Majestie as of her
ministers toward him.'[16] In short, it was the character
and temperament of Huntly which made it possible in the
final analysis for any dependence to be put upon him.

Chastened in spirit by her experiences, and by the chilling
fate of Sir John Gordon, Mary made her way southwards
again and was back in Edinburgh by November: here,
along with Maitland, she fell victim to the fashionable new
disease, influenza, lightly dubbed 'the New Acquaintance',
but was otherwise not directly threatened by any personal
danger for the next few months, at least. In the spring of
1563, however, she was to be the subject of a more intimate assault than the projected abduction plans of either
Arran, Bothwell or Sir John Gordon. Among the train of
French courtiers who accompanied the queen to Scotland
from France in 1561 was a certain Pierre de Châtelard:
well-born, charming-looking and gallant, Châtelard was also
a poet, a fact which naturally commended itself to Mary.
He was attached to the suite of the son of the Constable
de Montmorency, Damville, who was also counted among
Mary's admirers, to the extent that he was supposed to
have desired to abandon his wife, still in France, out of love
for the Scottish queen. Mary certainly wrote to the Constable when he departed that she found his son the most
agreeable company.[17] Châtelard himself speedily followed
suit by professing the sort of wild lyrical passion, suitable
in a chivalrous man of literary aspirations for a lovely

young queen. It was the sort of admiration—light, courtly
and elaborately meaningless—which Mary Stuart particularly enjoyed, because it committed her to nothing (unlike the more vigorous proposals of a John Gordon) and it
was something to which she had long and agreeably been
accustomed at the court of France. It was after all much
more to her taste to be celebrated in verses, than dragged
into a Highland fastness and forcibly married. There was
no suggestion at the time of anything at all scandalous in
her attitude to Châtelard, and Knox's insinuations (written
after the event) that she had been over-familiar with him
can safely be attributed to his vicious desire to put
everything the Queen did in the most evil light—he was
also incidentally probably unaware of the gallant license
allowed to poets at the French court, and if he had been
aware of it, would have regarded it as a further proof of
French devilry. Châtelard ended his visit to Scotland with
his master Damville, and returned to France.

In the autumn of 1562, however, he decided to revisit
the Scottish court; on his way through London, he confided that he was about to visit 'his lady love', and soon
he was back with Mary's court at Aberdeen, with a letter
from Damville, and a book of his own poems. Mary received him in her usual friendly way, and with the com-
pulsive generosity which she showed to those who pleased
her, presented him with a sorrel gelding which had been
given her by her half-brother Lord Robert, as well as some
money to dress himself as befitted a young gallant: these
favours were still absolutely no more than she showed
at many times in her life to those around her, nor was there
even now the faintest suggestion of impropriety in this
conventional relationship of beautiful queen and platonic
admiring poet. All this made Châtelard's next move
particularly incomprehensible. On the night when Maitland
was about to set forth again for England, at the queen's
request, Mary, Moray and Maitland all conferred together
until past midnight. Châtelard seized the opportunity to
dash into her bed-chamber unobserved, and hide under
the bed. Luckily he was discovered by two of her grooms
of the chamber, making their routine search of her tapestries and bed, and thrown out. The queen was not told
of the incident until the morning, but immediately the
news reached her, she ordered Châtelard to leave the
court.

Châtelard, however, was either self-confident enough or crazy enough to follow the queen to St Andrews. The next night he proceeded to burst in on her, when she was alone with only one or two of her women, and according to what Randolph first heard, made such audacious advances to her that the unfortunate queen cried out for help. Her brother Moray rushed in, and Mary, in a state of near-hysteria, begged him to run his dagger through the man to save her. Moray, with greater calm and prudence, soothed his sister, and persuaded her that it would be better if Châtelard's life were temporarily spared, so that he could face a public trial. Randolph later heard that Châtelard's intentions in making this second foray into the royal apartments had been merely to explain away his first intrusion, on the grounds that he had been overcome by sleep, and had sought the first convenient resting-place.[18] Whether he attempted to advance this implausible explanation or not, Mary's reaction to the whole incident was highly hysterical, and no spinster ever reacted with more horrified indignation to the presence of a man in her bed-chamber, than the already once married queen of Scots.

Châtelard was sent to the dungeons of St Andrews, and after a public trial sentenced to execution on 22 February. Romantic to the last, just before his execution, he read aloud Ronsard's Hymn to Death there and then in the market square of St Andrews. The beautiful last lines of the poem must have seemed strangely ironical to those of the bystanders who understood enough French to appreciate them:

Je te salue, heureuse et profitable mort . . .
. . . puisqu'il faut mourir
Donne-moi que soudain je te puisse encourir
*Ou pour l'honneur de Dieu, ou pour servir mon Prince . . .**

In fact, it was far from clear for whose honour, or in whose service, Châtelard was dying. Just before he died, his last words echoed out: 'Adieu, the most beautiful and

* I salute you, happy and profitable Death . . .
   . . . since I must die
   Grant that I may suddenly encounter you
   Either for the honour of God, or in the service of my Prince . . .

the most cruel princess of the world'—words which are
given slightly differently by Knox—'In the end, he concluded looking unto the heavens, with these words "O
cruel Dame".' The sense, however, is in both cases the
same, despite Knox's efforts to give the common French
word *dame* a more sinister import: 'That is,' he wrote,
'Cruel mistress. What that complaint imported, lovers may
divine.'[19] Châtelard's general behaviour and these rhetorical
last words all lead one to suppose that the young poet
was a victim of one of those unbalanced passions for a
royal personage, to which princesses have been subject all
through history, royalty being notoriously a great aph-
rodisiac to an unstable mind. Châtelard had mistaken
Mary's gracious reception for something more humanly
passionate, and died for his error. The queen's outraged
withdrawal from his advances makes it quite clear that
she never reciprocated them in her own mind—as indeed
does the method by which Châtelard chose to approach
her, since if they had been lovers already or intending to
become so, she would presumably have arranged a more
convenient rendezvous and one which was less likely to
be interrupted.

But it is possible that there was a more sinister explanation for Châtelard's advances. Publicity seems to have been
one of the main features of his attempt on the queen's
virtue: if Châtelard's wits were not actually wandering, he
must have realized that he was all too likely to be discovered in her bed-chamber by her attendants. The ugly
speculation arises whether this was not in fact Châtelard's
intention, and whether his ultimate aim was to blacken
Mary's reputation rather than win her love. According to
Maitland, Châtelard had confessed to Mary that he had
been despatched by persons in a high position in France
expressly to compromise her honour, and the duchess of
Guise hinted at the same thing to the Venetian ambassador.
Mary mentioned the name of Coligny's first wife, and
told Maitland there were other names involved she could
not trust to paper. The nuncio at the French court heard
that the incident had been arranged to give Mary a bad
name.[20] In the circumstances, it is significant that Châtelard himself turned out to be a Huguenot. Even his casual
remark in London about his lady love may have been intended to draw attention to his relationship with the queen.
Whether Châtelard was an emissary of the French Hugue-

nots or a lovesick fool, the one certain piece of evidence which emerges from the whole affair is that Mary's reaction to the escapade was markedly severe. Death was after all a high price for Châtelard to pay for an amorous adventure: it is true that Mary may have justified his subsequent execution in her mind by the knowledge of the plot which had been woven around her: yet both Randolph and Knox confirm that her first reaction to his entry had been to demand for him to be killed by Moray. There was no hint here of the loose easy-going morals of the French court, which it has sometimes been suggested that she acquired along with her education.

It was a sad spring for the young queen. Two or three days after Châtelard's execution, her uncle Duke Francis of Guise was shot down by a Huguenot assassin, Poltrot, who knew him by the white plume in his hat, and attacked him from behind—thus fulfilling the prophecy of Luc Gauric that he would die from a wound in his back, which the duke had once angrily repudiated as being a slur on his courage. On 15 March came the news that he had died. Mary was overcome with grief and her ladies shed tears 'like showers of rain.'[21] Only a few weeks later another uncle, the Grand Prior Francis, also died. Mary, upset by these repeated sorrows in the only family she had really known, melancholy after the Châtelard episode, so distasteful to her nature, exhausted in health by the long Scottish winter and bouts of illness, burst out to Randolph that she was really almost destitute of friends; she outlined her many adventures and vicissitudes since her husband's death, and confessed that the burden suddenly seemed too much for her to bear. In an access of feminine weakness, she read Queen Elizabeth's letter of sympathy with tears in her eyes, and exclaimed to Randolph that neither of them could afford to turn down a possible support—how much better everything would be, if the two queens were indeed friends! 'For I see now that the world is not that that we do make of it, nor yet are they most happy that continue longest in it.'[22] These were gloomy sentiments for a young girl just turned twenty-one: Mary Stuart had now been a widow for over two years. Since the Châtelard incident Mary Fleming had been taken to sleep in her room for company and protection. But it was high time that she made a serious attempt to share the load of her responsibilities with a proper part-

ner, especially since her naturally dependent nature inevitably turned to a masculine adviser, as a sunflower
turns to the sun. Neither James Stewart, earl of Moray, in
her counsels, nor Mary Fleming in her bed-chamber were
adequate substitutes for the wise, strong, loyal husband
whom she now more than ever needed to support her.

12 A Husband for a Girl

'. . . The case was different for an heiress to a kingdom, who by the same act took a husband to herself and a King to the people. Many were of the opinion that it was more equitable that the people should choose a husband for a girl, than that a girl should choose a King for a whole people.'

BUCHANAN *on the marriage of queens*

Mary Stuart was young, beautiful and attractive: she was also a queen, and she could offer an independent kingdom as a dowry to any husband. On the surface, it would seem that it should not have been too difficult for her to find a suitable candidate, since she had none of the psychological problems of an Elizabeth Tudor, and was sufficiently conventionally feminine to long for a male partner on whom to depend. In theory therefore she had a wide choice of possible husbands: but, in practice, so many considerations had to be taken into account, that while the field was not exactly reduced—since many candidates met one or other of the requirements—it was impossible to declare a clear winner, since none of them met them all. This was true if only because many of the requirements were actually contradictory. The only point on which everyone agreed was that the choice was an important one, not in terms of Mary Stuart's happiness, but because whomever she married would inevitably expect to become king of Scotland—not merely a titular consort in the more modern sense. Francis had always been known as king of Scotland, and had also been granted the crown matrimonial: any future consort might expect to enjoy the former privilege and hope to enjoy the latter. Under the circumstances, Buchanan's views on the subject of an heiress to a kingdom may be appreciated: by the same act she 'took a husband to herself and gave a King to the people. Many were of the opinion that it was more equitable that the people should choose a husband for a girl, than that a girl should choose a King for a whole people.'[1] However, Mary had no intention of consulting her people on this subject, which she considered to be essentially a matter of royal prerogative: it was now the subject of anxious consultation between herself and Moray and Maitland, in Scotland, while her French relations the Guises held and acted on views of their own in France.

The first problem was that of religion: was Mary to marry a Catholic like herself, as was generally assumed to be her intention, an Archduke Charles of Austria for example, or even her cousin Henry of Guise? Or would she perhaps attempt the more daring policy of binding together her subjects by wedding someone of their own religion—even the name of the prince of Condé was put forward at one point. Both courses had obvious dangers: a Catholic marriage would inevitably upset the balance she was so carefully maintaining between her private religion and the public religion of her country, by emphasizing that she was very much a Catholic at heart whatever her outward tolerance to the Protestants; a Protestant marriage on the other hand would be difficult to explain to her Catholic relations and allies on the continent, on whom she still depended.

Apart from the religious question there was the question of status: was she to marry an independent prince with a kingdom of his own, a king of Denmark or Sweden, or even her ex-brother-in-law the twelve-year-old King Charles of France, whose name was mentioned in this connection despite his youth and their previous relationship? Don Carlos, as sole heir to the mighty Spanish dominions of Philip II, also came into this category. Or was she to marry a subject within a kingdom: an Englishman such as her cousin, Henry, Lord Darnley, or even the duke of Norfolk, a Scot—a Hamilton, a Gordon or some other scion of a powerful clan—or a Frenchman such as the duke of Nemours? Once again there were obvious disadvantages to both courses: an independent ruler with a kingdom of his own could not fail to treat Scotland as a satellite, and could scarcely be expected to put Scottish interests above those of his own country; the raising-up of a mere subject to royal rank, on the other hand, would certainly arouse jealousy and dissension among the Scottish nobles, who scarcely allowed their actual sovereign the prerogatives of monarchy, and would certainly view the elevation of one of their own rank most unfavourably.

As Archibald Douglas had noted long ago, when the queen
was a baby, the ideal thing might seem to be a second
son of 'France, Denmark, or England if such a thing
existed . . . that one of the second sons might thereby be
King of Scots, and dwell among them keeping the Estate
of Scotland which evermore hath been a realm of itself'.[2]
The trouble with this solution, quite apart from the comparative shortage of second sons among the European
royal families at this date—none in England or Spain, and
those in France still mere children in 1563—was that such
a candidate might easily combine the disadvantages of both
the foreign prince and an inferior subject: his foreign
nationality would inevitably involve Scotland in certain
alliances and commitments in which her own interests
might not be paramount, and his own status might not
be sufficiently impressive to cow the Scots.

Among all these imponderables, there was the matter of
the views of Queen Elizabeth on the subject. So far,
while Mary's domestic policy had been towards the maintenance of peace and order, and the religious *status quo*,
her foreign policy had been directed towards getting herself recognized as Queen Elizabeth's successor on the
throne of England. In this endeavour, in which so far no
real progress had been made, Mary's putative husband
was obviously a trump card: yet once more how was this
card to be played? Was Elizabeth to be asked to nominate
a husband of her own choice, which Mary would meekly
accept in order to show herself satisfactorily pliant to
Elizabeth's wishes, and thus worthy of the recognition
which she desired? Or was the prospect of a foreign
Catholic husband hostile to England to be held over
Elizabeth's head, to blackmail her into granting the recognition, lest her own problems with her English Catholics
should be thus increased. Again there were drawbacks
to both courses: if Elizabeth nominated the husband,
but still refused to give formal recognition until after the
marriage, Mary would have surrendered her advantage,
with no certainty of gain: if Mary carried through her
threat and married a strong Catholic, then Elizabeth
might understandably announce that Mary by her actions
had excluded herself forever. Still on the tack of the
English royal succession, might it not be more to the point
if Mary attempted to bolster up her English claim (still
strongly rebutted at this date by the English Parliament,

and with the shadow of Henry VIII's will lying across it) by marrying someone else in whose veins also ran the vital blood which brought them within the English royal family tree. It could be argued that marriage to a Darnley, for example, or even one of Geoffrey Pole's sons, would reinforce Mary's own claim by a sort of royal osmosis. But here again, Elizabeth's attitude to the subject would clearly be vital, for although such a marriage might impress the English Parliament, Elizabeth herself might feel that her actual throne, rather than the succession to it, was being threatened.

In the face of so many unknown or unknowable elements, so many possible avenues of action, each one barred by some sort of obstacle, so many diplomatic negotiations, both secret and open, some merely the reported rumours of ambassadors, others the declared (but not necessarily sincere) intentions of monarchs, the marriage of Mary Stuart took on a very different appearance from the simple matching of a nubile and beautiful young girl, with an excellent worldly position to offer her husband. In face of the chaos and tragedy in which these negotiations ended, it is legitimate to question whether there was indeed *any* happy solution to the marriage problems of Mary Queen of Scots: one may perhaps return to the 'merry' wish of Mary and the devout wish of Throckmorton—how much simpler if one of the queens had been a man, so that they could have married each other.* The consort was indeed the perennial problem of the female ruler in this century: it is significant that the one queen who emerged in the eyes of the people as having never made a mistaken match was Queen Elizabeth—who made no match at all, despite negotiations which lasted for three-quarters of her reign.

The first negotiations on the subject which Maitland undertook in the spring of 1563 revealed that Mary's personal attitude to marriage had not changed since the early days of her widowhood as queen of France: Don Carlos was still the object of her desire, and as it was Spanish prestige—backed up by troops and Spanish money—which

---

* Confronted with such a problem, it was perhaps regrettable that the solution of the royal family of Egypt was not open to that of Scotland: Dr A. L. Rowse once suggested that if Mary had been able to marry her half-brother Moray, as Cleopatra married Ptolemy, she might have fared much better.

made him so desirable, it is evident that Mary saw marriage at this point very much in terms of power politics. Just after the Châtelard incident, Maitland was sent again to London, on the ostensible excuse of offering Mary's mediation between Queen Elizabeth and the warring French; his instructions also bade him pursue the subject of Mary's claim to the English throne after Elizabeth, but secretly he was commissioned to reopen the negotiations for a Spanish marriage with de Quadra, Philip II's ambassador in London, by hinting that the alternative might be a match with the young French king. The mere mention of this prospect was enough to terrify Philip sufficiently to start up discussions of the subject once more— although he did stipulate that the utmost secrecy should be preserved if the negotiations were to have any chance of success. The true attitude of Moray and Maitland towards this Spanish marriage can only be guessed at: it is impossible to be certain whether they actually approved of a Catholic bridegroom for the queen, hoping to be able to rule an independent Protestant Scotland for themselves once more, with Mary safely installed on the throne of Spain as she had once been installed on the throne of France; or whether they were merely attempting to bluff Queen Elizabeth into showing her own hand over Mary's projected marriage. In any case the Spanish negotiations now went forward once more.

Despite Philip's plea for secrecy, the news of these discussions began to leak out in France: here they naturally caused the same apprehension in the breast of Catherine de Medicis as the prospect of a French marriage had caused in that of Philip of Spain. The Guisards themselves with the traditional French jealousy of Spain would have infinitely preferred the prospect of the Archduke Charles, brother of the emperor: and Mary's uncle the cardinal took it upon himself to enter negotiations for his hand, of his own accord, parallel with the Spanish negotiations. But there is no reason to suppose that Mary herself ever seriously considered the archduke—at one point the queen grew quite angry with her uncle for thus embroiling her without definite authority. Archduke Charles had one important defect, in that he was generally thought in Scotland to be too poor to maintain the state of consort, especially for a queen who was hard put to it to manage her own finances; even if his brother gave him a large allowance, as was suggested, he still would not have the army behind him, which his cousin Don Carlos could command as heir to the Spanish throne.

Naturally the news of these negotiations also came to the ears of Queen Elizabeth herself—Maitland was after all conducting them under her nose in London, and Throckmorton took care to repeat all the gossip from France. Before Maitland returned to Scotland, Elizabeth took the opportunity to inform him that if Mary married either Don Carlos or the Archduke Charles, or indeed any other imperial candidate, she could not avoid becoming her enemy; if on the other hand Mary married to her satisfaction, Elizabeth sweetly added, she would surely be a good friend and sister to her, and in the course of time, make her her heir. This was the crux of the problem: how was Mary to marry to Elizabeth's satisfaction, if Elizabeth did not express any definite choice? Now, from the autumn of 1563 onwards, Elizabeth began to drop broad hints as to who her personal choice might be. The only trouble was that Elizabeth's choice of candidate was sufficiently eccentric to arouse serious doubts as to whether it was a genuine suggestion, or whether on the contrary she was merely trying to prevent Mary in the end making any marriage at all.

The husband whom Elizabeth apparently had in mind was her own favourite Lord Robert Dudley. She had first mentioned his name to Maitland in the spring of 1563, when he arrived in London: jokingly, as it seemed to Maitland, she observed that Lord Robert Dudley would make a good husband for the queen of Scots. Maitland could indeed hardly fail to treat the suggestion as a pleasantry since at first sight Dudley had absolutely no obvious advantages as a husband, and a great many obvious disadvantages. His stock, far from being royal, was actually tainted by treason, his father the duke of Northumberland having been beheaded, and the title put under attainder; he himself was generally considered to be Queen Elizabeth's paramour, and whatever the truth of their relationship, her familiarity with him had certainly caused scandal throughout Europe, and continued to do so; thirdly, his first wife Amy Robsart had died under the most suspicious circumstances, which, it was generally believed, left him free to marry Queen Elizabeth, if she would have him, and the country would accept it. Now Maitland was asked to consider this controversial figure as a husband for his own mistress, a born queen, the widow of another king, and herself highly conscious of her own position, as well as being the bearer of an unblemished character. Maitland showed himself at his diplomatic best when he answered Queen Elizabeth that it was a great proof of the love she bore to the Scottish queen 'as she was willing to give her a thing so dearly prized by herself', but that Queen Mary would hardly wish to deprive Queen Elizabeth of the joy and solace of Lord Robert's companionship. In a further vein of witty invention, he suggested that Elizabeth herself should marry Dudley, and then bequeath both her husband and her kingdom to Mary when she died.[3]

In September 1563, the Scots had perforce to take the suggestion more seriously: Randolph was instructed to approach Queen Mary, newly arrived at the castle of Craigmillar near Edinburgh, after a western progress, and hint broadly at Queen Elizabeth's own wishes on the subject of Mary's marriage; he was to indicate a husband, the English queen added in her own hand to the instructions, *'perchance as she would hardly think we would agree to'*.[4] Randolph of course mentioned no actual name of an English noble, but he did confirm to Mary that the continuance of friendship with Elizabeth was impossible if she married into either imperial family. In November Randolph was given further instructions on the subject—but still he did not officially name Lord Robert Dudley, contenting himself with pouring cold water on 'the children of France, Spain or Austria', and telling Mary that her late husband, the king of France, had been a perfect example of whom *not* to marry.[5] Mary replied that she could only give a vague answer to such vague propositions: she needed after all to know the names of suitable bridegrooms, not unsuitable ones. It was not until the end of March 1564 that Randolph was authorized officially to offer Lord Robert Dudley, as most suitable among the English nobles, a year after Elizabeth's first hint to Maitland. Mary's outward reaction was meek: she listened graciously once more, and suggested as she had done previously in the autumn that a conference should be held at Berwick between English and Scots. Inwardly, however, she can hardly have regarded the notorious Lord Robert as an acceptable husband—she who still longed for the heir of the Spanish empire—unless of course he brought with him a definite recognition of her title to succeed Elizabeth as a dowry.

While Mary pursued a Catholic marriage abroad, her policy at home continued to favour the reformed religion as it had done ever since her arrival. She herself certainly felt that she had absolutely no choice in the matter. At an interview with the papal nuncio Gouda in the summer of 1562, Mary told him that she could not even promise him a safe-conduct while he was in Scotland, and advised him to stay indoors as much as possible and not attempt to deliver the Pope's briefs—unless he wished to die violently. She herself, explained Mary patiently, would be quite powerless to help him if anything untoward occurred. Nor did Gouda feel that Mary's apprehensions were unjustified: she made an excellent personal impression on him, and he accepted her word that she intended privately to live and die a Catholic, whatever the ways of her kingdom. Mary also refused quite flatly to consider sending Scottish priests to the Council of Trent: once again she protested her personal devotion to the Catholic cause, but said that the despatching of a Scottish deputation would be quite out of the question under the present circumstances. Equally, when a college for training Catholic priests was suggested to her, Mary dismissed it in one word as 'impracticable'.[6] The truth was that Mary, from the vantage point of Scotland, could perceive realities about the religious situation there not readily understandable by the distant papacy or even by her uncle in France, the cardinal. Her continual aim in her letters abroad was to explain this dichotomy she was obliged to practise in order to preserve the peace—devotion to Catholicism in private, tolerance towards Protestantism in public. But, of course, it was a dichotomy which it was not easy to convey in letter to those who had never visited the country.

In 1563, Parliament, with the queen's agreement, provided that Protestant ministers should have the use of manses and glebes and that churches should be repaired. Symbolical of Mary's desire to preserve religious amity and peace in her country (at the expense of those zealous Catholics who still hoped she would fight for their cause) was her renewed attempt to win the friendship or at least the approval of John Knox. In the middle of April 1563 the queen was staying on the island of Lochleven with

Moray's mother Lady Margaret Douglas and his half-brother, Sir William Douglas. Here, in this ill-omened fortress which was to play such a significant part in her future story, she sent for Knox. Together queen and reformer took part in a long and fairly friendly dispute in the great hall of the castle. Mary asked Knox to abate the persecution of the Catholics, especially in the western regions of Scotland, where it was fierce, and Knox in return asked her to administer the laws of her kingdom, which had made Catholicism illegal. The next morning, as she was hawking near Kinross, the queen sent for Knox again, and among other topics she raised were the fearful quarrels between the earl of Argyll and his wife—Mary's beloved but wayward half-sister, Jean Stewart, who was, as the queen herself admitted 'not so circumspect in all things as that she wished her to be', and much preferred the delights of Holyrood life to a quieter existence in the west of Scotland with her husband. Now Mary attempted to charm Knox by asking him to mediate in this domestic dispute, which was becoming a scandal of court life: and although Knox said later that the whole conversation showed how deeply Mary Stuart was able to dissemble, in fact he did write a stern letter to Argyll on his matrimonial problems.*[7]

The news of Mary's Spanish negotiations, however, provoked a sterner reaction from Knox. A Catholic match was the very last thing he could be expected to countenance and he thundered forth from the pulpit on the subject in Edinburgh, in front of a large congregation of the nobility, assembled in the city for Parliament, despite Maitland's somewhat disingenuous assertion that 'such thing never entered in her [the Queen's] heart'. This public rebuke was too much for Mary. She sent for Knox to come to Holyrood and in 'vehement fume', exclaimed that no prince had ever been so treated—had she not borne with him more patiently than any other ruler 'in all your rigorous manner of speaking both against my self and my uncles; yea,' she continued indignantly, 'I have sought your favours by all possible means. I offered unto you presence and audience whensoever it pleased you to admonishe me; and

---

* The earl and his countess were never permanently reconciled despite the good offices of Knox and the queen: they were finally divorced and Argyll married again.

yet I cannot be quit of you.' She added in a voice choked
with 'howling' in Knox's immortal trenchant phrase, and
tears (so many tears that the chamber boy, Knox says,
could scarcely find enough napkins to mop them up) that
she would be revenged upon him.[8]

Knox tried to justify himself by saying that it was his
duty to speak plainly but Mary burst out again and
again: 'What have you to do with my marriage?' and
finally in a surge of irritation: 'What are you within this
commonwealth?' which gave Knox the opportunity for
the crushing reply: 'A subject born within the same,
madam.' He proceeded to speak again at length on the
horrors of a Catholic marriage, which only brought forth
further floods of angry tears from the queen. Erskine of
Dun tried to calm her by tactfully praising her beauty and
charms and suggesting that any prince in Europe would be
glad to marry her, but Mary was not to be smoothed with
fair words; furiously she requested Knox to leave her presence, regardless of the fact that he solemnly assured her
how much he disliked tears, since even the tears of corrected children wounded him. Knox departed, characteristically taking the opportunity on his way out to point out
to the maids of honour in attendance, that their 'gay gear'
would little avail them at the impending coming of the
Knave Death.

That summer the queen made her progresses in west
and south-west Scotland, visiting the local castles, seeing
and being seen by her subjects and last but not least enjoying the pleasures of the chase. The court made ready
their 'Highland apparel' for the tour and the English ambassador Randolph, not to be outdone, fitted himself out
'in outer shape . . . like unto the rest'.[9] In July, Mary
was actually guest of the earl of Argyll, the warring husband of Jean Stewart, at Inveraray; in August she toured
the south-west, staying first with Lord Eglinton, on to
Dunure Castle, at St Mary's Isle by mid-August, then to
Dumfries and so to Drumlanrig; by 27 August she was at
Peebles. As the queen hunted and harmlessly enjoyed the
sight of some of the most beautiful scenery of her dominions, back in Edinburgh Knox was enraged to hear that
she was having the Mass said constantly on her route.
Nothing daunted by the interview in the spring, Knox took
the opportunity to preach energetically against Mary once

more: 'Deliver us, O Lord, from idolatry.' Such defiance could not pass forever unchecked. But as the year wore on, Knox dared to go even further. Two militant Protestants forced their way into the chapel royal in Mary's absence and broke up the Mass of her household. They were arrested but Knox took the line that their trial should be an occasion when the congregation showed its solidarity in favour of the accused, in order to protect them from condemnation. To this effect, he wrote round Scotland, urging the members of the congregation to attend the trial. It was a flagrant insult to the authorities and to the queen. As a result, in December, Knox was summoned before the Council on a charge of treason. He arrived with an enormous following, and when the queen saw him sitting there bare-headed at the end of the table, she burst out laughing, and in an access of high spirits, her angry tears dismissed but not apparently forgotten, she exclaimed in her broad Scots: 'Yon man gart me greit [made me weep] and grat never tear himself. I will see if I can gar him greit.' However, although Knox admitted having written the offending letter, the Council voted that he had not committed treason; so far from being made to weep by Mary, the following spring Knox merely succeeded in angering her further—and pleasing himself. As the burgesses of Edinburgh gossiped, the fifty-year-old reformer married, as his second wife, the seventeen-year-old Margaret Stewart, daughter of Lord Ochiltree, and as such one of Mary's own kin—'of her own blood and name'.[10]

It was hardly surprising that throughout the autumn of 1563 the courtiers noted that the poor queen frequently succumbed to fits of weeping and depression, alternating with bursts of merriment. Her French physician attempted to cure her by putting her on a diet. But the death of her uncle, the slow progress of her marriage plans, her own loneliness, to say nothing of the loquacious hostility of the uncharmable Knox, were all enough to produce a pattern of nervous ill-health. In December she took to her bed with an unidentified pain in her right side—which was to recur for the rest of her life; Randolph suggested that her collapse might have been due to exhaustion after dancing too long on her twenty-first birthday, and she herself put it down to praying too long in an icy chapel after Mass, in a bitterly cold winter.[11] By mid-January she had recovered. The whole attack may well have been exacerbated by Mary's tension at the lack of conclusion over her marriage plans.

Although Elizabeth had nominated Lord Robert in spring 1564, Mary continued to hope rather for success in the direction of Spain until August: then Philip II, changing his mind once more on the subject, and having procrastinated once again for nearly eighteen months, indicated to his ambassador that the negotiations were once more closed (a decision in which the growing insanity of his son must have played some part). Even so, in the autumn of 1564 Mary despatched James Melville to London, with the vain hope of revivifying the plan of the Spanish match: in fact Melville's main occupation was to charm Queen Elizabeth with his courtly manners and enjoy in return a prolonged display of her accomplishments, in order that he should thus estimate her more highly than her rival queen of Scots. Melville was, however, also called upon to witness a significant rite by which Dudley was created earl of Leicester and baron of Denbigh, which honours were specifically intended to fit him to wed Queen Mary, although one unrehearsed detail of the rite—by which Elizabeth tickled her favourite's neck in the midst of the ceremony—may have been considered by Melville to have had the opposite effect.[12]

Nevertheless the Dudley negotiations still wound on, and in November 1564 a conference was finally held at Berwick on the subject between Moray and Maitland on one side, and Randolph and Bedford on the other, without, however, anything definite being promised by the English with regard to the recognition of Mary's title in return for the Leicester marriage. As the Scots naturally regarded this recognition as the vital *quid pro quo* for a match which they had no other reason to desire, by December, as Randolph reported to Cecil, they were beginning to clamour for some sort of frankness on the subject from the English. But in reply Cecil was far from frank; on the contrary, he took refuge in phrases of much obscurity more suitable for an oracle than a statesman: let their negotiations so full of promise, not 'be converted to a matter of bargain or purchase' he wrote, since the English crown 'if it be sort for, may sooner be lost than got, and not being craved, may be as soon offered as reason can require'.[13]

This sort of riddle was all very well, but it was now nearly two years since Mary had started her second serious round of marriage negotiations, and still the English party were taking refuge in saws and sayings and making no definite commitment. In short, Mary was no nearer getting either a husband or the succession to the English throne, although she had been a childless widow over four years, as a result of which there was still no direct heir to the Scottish throne closer than the Hamiltons. Under the circumstances, the impatience of the Scottish party who wrote to Cecil of his 'many obscure words and dark sentences' is understandable; Maitland and Moray pointed out to him quite plainly that if Elizabeth would not establish 'the succession of her crown' it would be quite impossible for them to induce Mary to marry an Englishman, and she would then make her own choice.[14] Yet still no promise came. Not only that, but the next emanation from England—the appearance of young Lord Darnley himself mysteriously granted permission to travel to Scotland in early February 1565—cast serious doubt over the whole straight-forwardness of the English point of view.

It was an interesting enigma why Darnley, young, eligible and handsome, with the royal blood of England and Scotland in his veins, should be suddenly allowed to return to Scotland at this very moment, by permission of Queen Elizabeth. The name of Darnley had always played a minor part in any discussion of Mary's possible suitors because of his position in both the Tudor and Stuart family tree, and because he was roughly the right age to be Mary's bridegroom. The match had certainly always been in the mind of Darnley's ambitious striving mother Margaret, countess of Lennox, and it was not for nothing that she had sent him hotfoot to France to condole with Mary on the death of Francis.* In September 1564 the earl of Lennox, who had long been banished from Scotland for trying to capture Dumbarton Castle in 1544 with English troops, was allowed to return to Scotland ostensibly to look to his estates. None other than Queen Elizabeth her-

* Dr Strong has pointed out that the double portrait of Darnley and his brother, from which Eworth copied his own picture, is in the unusual medium of tempera painted on linen, which suggests that it was designed for travelling: it may therefore have formed part of the ambitious countess's plans for bringing her handsome son to the notice of the queen of Scots.[15]

self pleaded with Queen Mary to receive him. According
to Melville, Elizabeth's motive in thus smoothing Lennox's way was quite definitely to promote the Darnley marriage: Elizabeth told Melville Darnley was one of the
two that she had in her head to offer unto the queen, as
born within the realm of England.[16] In the course of the
ceremony by which Leicester was invested with his titles,
Elizabeth also teased Melville that he would prefer to see
Darnley, who was standing by, as a husband for his queen
rather than Leicester. The presence of her husband in the
rival camp did not dim the ardour of Margaret Lennox in
forwarding the claims of her son: the Lennox Jewel, for
example, once thought to commemorate Lennox's death
in 1571, is now thought on grounds of style to date from
this earlier period, and in any case contains no memorial
details of Lennox's life, such as might be expected in a
commemorative piece. Margaret Lennox certainly took
advantage of the return of Melville to Scotland to send
jewels to her husband in 1564: she may have taken the
opportunity to create an elaborately emblematic *objet d'art*,
whose complicated symbolism would convey messages to
her husband on the subject of her matrimonial schemes,
too dangerous to commit to paper.* When Mary wrote to
Elizabeth in December 1564 asking that Darnley might be
allowed to come north to join his father, neither Elizabeth
nor her advisers can have been in any doubts that Darnley was now a strongly fancied runner in the Scottish
queen's matrimonial stakes. The Spanish contendent had
recently vanished from the race, and in view of Elizabeth's behaviour Leicester was still not a certain starter:
the odds on Darnley, who was Catholic, semi-royal, and
apparently approved of by Elizabeth, now dramatically
shortened.

It was popularly believed at the time by the Scots that
Elizabeth herself had launched Darnley, in order to trap
Mary into a demeaning marriage, although, as Randolph
indicated in his letter of 12 February, it seems to have
been Leicester and Cecil who combined together to get
the boy his licence to come north.[17] Elizabeth's part seems
to have been a passive one: having an extraordinary inability to make up her mind on matters of emotion, she

* See G. H. Tait, F.S.A., 'Historiated Tudor Jewellery', *Antiquaries
Journal*, 1962.

probably did not know herself whether she desired the marriage of the beloved Leicester and Mary. This inability nearly always turned out fortunately for her, since it allowed others to take the action, and in doing so, it was they who made the mistakes. In this particular case, it is likely that Leicester and Cecil, encouraged by indecisive passivity of Elizabeth, launched Darnley as a sort of Trojan horse into the Scottish queen's kingdom. Queen Mary could not fail to be interested in such an obvious candidate for marriage: as Melville put it, she might prefer Darnley 'being present' to Leicester 'who was absent'; and of Leicester and Cecil it was of course Leicester who had a further personal motive to embroil the negotiations —he may well have been anxious not to have them concluded while Elizabeth herself still remained unmarried. Elizabeth later told de Silva that it was Leicester who had refused to consent to the match, and thus wrecked it.[18] The Scots, who were becoming obstreperous in their desire for some sort of concrete result, would become confused between Leicester and Darnley. Mary herself would dither between the two claimants and continue to remain unwed. The English therefore would be able to continue in that policy of masterly inactivity which best suited their own interests over the marriage of the Scottish queen; as for Elizabeth, she could continue to use the unmarried and therefore uncommitted state of Mary as an argument for not recognizing her place in the English succession. This seems to have been the tortuous reasoning of the English at the beginning of February when Henry Stuart, Lord Darnley, left London, by specific permission of the English queen.

Darnley was on the borders of Scotland by 10 February, and at Dunbar the next day, from whence he went on to Haddington, finally reaching Edinburgh on 13 February. Here he spent three days, in the course of which he was most warmly received by Elizabeth's envoy Randolph, who lent him his own horses, as Darnley's had not arrived. Darnley was entertained by Lord Robert Stewart at Holyrood where, according to Randolph, his pleasant social manner made an agreeable impression. Mary was away hunting in Fife. Here on Saturday 17 February, at the house of the Laird of Wemyss, the first meeting for four years between the ill-starred couple took place. The young man whom Mary saw before her was eminently

handsome. Although Melville had assured Queen Elizabeth that he found him almost too effeminate—'beardless
and lady-faced' were the words he used—this was more
evidence of Melville's wish to please Elizabeth, than of
Darnley's lack of attraction.[19] The contemporary portraits
by Eworth, standing with his younger brother, or painted
alone three-quarter length, show that Darnley at the age
of eighteen* was nothing if not outwardly good-looking.
In these portraits Darnley appears at first sight like a
young god, with his golden hair, his perfectly shaped face
with its short straight nose, the neat oval chin, and above
all the magnificent legs stretching forth endlessly in their
black hose. But on closer inspection the god appears to
be more Pan than Apollo: there is something faun-like
about his pointed ears, the beautiful slanting hazel eyes
with their unreadable expression, and even a hint of cruelty
in the exquisitely formed mouth with its full rosy lips. It
was Darnley's height which was considered at the time
to be his main physical characteristic—had not Elizabeth
called him 'yon long lad' when she pointed him out to
Melville?—and he was fortunate in being slender with it,
or as Melville put it, 'long and small, even and straight'.
His elegant physique could hardly fail to commend itself
to Mary for two reasons. Firstly, beautiful as she was,
Mary was nevertheless tall enough to tower over most of
her previous companions, including her first husband Francis. The psychological implications of this height can only
be guessed at, but as Darnley was certainly well over six
feet one inch† Mary for once could feel herself not only
overtopped at dancing, but also physically protected by
her admirer if she so wished; as a novel sensation it could

---

* Hay Fleming pointed out that there is a mystery about the actual
date of Darnley's birth. This is usually given as 7 December 1545.
But Knox's Continuator states that Darnley was not yet twenty-one
at the time of his death (10 February 1567). In March 1566 he was
specifically stated by Mary's own messenger to the cardinal of Lorraine to be nineteen years old.[20] It seems that the earliest date he
could have been born to fit with this evidence was 11 February 1546.
If the 7 December birthday is accepted, however, Darnley must have
been born on 7 December 1546: he was thus four years younger
than Mary, not three.

† His height has been calculated to have been between six foot
one and six foot three inches on the evidence of his reputed thigh
bone in the museum of the Royal College of Surgeons. See *Skull
and Portraits of Henry Stuart Lord Darnley*, Karl Pearson, F.R.C.S.

hardly have failed to be pleasant. Secondly, as Mary was also a woman of strong aesthetic instincts, she would tend to appreciate the effeminate beauty of a Darnley more than the masculine vigour of some of her Scottish nobles.

The handsome youth had been well-trained in all the arts considered suitable for a gentleman—or princeling— of the period; he could ride a horse, hunt, dance gracefully and play the lute extremely well. In this respect he took after his father Mathew, earl of Lennox, who had been one of the most gallant figures at the Scottish court before his English marriage. The aim of his ambitious mother had been to make his courtly ways as winning as his outward appearance. To his internal qualities she had unfortunately paid less regard. It was true that his education was in the impressive mould of royalty at the time of the Renaissance: when he was only eight he was accomplished enough to send a letter to Queen Mary Tudor in which he asked her to accept 'a little plot of my own penning' which he termed Utopia Nova. He is traditionally supposed to have translated the works of Valerius Maximus into English. Better attested is the fact that he wrote some pleasant poems, a talent he must have inherited from his mother, herself a poetess;[21] the subjects Darnley chose for his verses included fittingly enough a long address 'to the Queen' on how to treat her subjects, in which he adjured her somewhat priggishly:

> Be governor both good and gracious
> Be loyal and loving to thy lieges all
> Be large of freedom, and nothing desirous;
> Be just to the poor, for any thing may fall. . . .

But whatever the veneer of education lovingly applied to his surface, it had in no sense left Darnley an intellectual. Throughout his short life he showed remarkably little interest in any matters of the mind, and a single-minded concern for the pursuit of pleasure. The truth was that Darnley was thoroughly spoilt: he was the product of a striving mother and a doting father, and even the most rigorous education would probably have left little impact on a personality which from his earliest years had been encouraged to regard himself as the important centre round which the world revolved.

As a character there was very little to commend him

despite or more probably because of all the maternal solicitude which had been expended on him—on his first arrival in Scotland Randolph did not want 'a little cold'
which he was suffering from, to get to the ears of Lady
Lennox, lest she should be alarmed.[22] Apart from being
spoilt, he was headstrong and ambitious; but he was ambitious only in so far as his mind could hold any concept
for long enough to pursue it, since above all he desired
the palm and not the race. It was the outward manifestations of power, the crown, the sceptre and the orb, which
appealed to him: the realities of its practice made no appeal to his indolent and pleasure-loving temperament. Vanity was by far the strongest motive which animated him.
It was vanity which made him seek out evil companions,
such as the profligate Lord Robert Stewart, even from the
first moment of his arrival in Edinburgh, and seek solace
in the admiration of low company. If the pursuit of pleasure led him inevitably on to fresh excitements, and thus
to more vicious enjoyments as simpler pleasures failed, it
was his vanity which brought about his quick touchy
temper, and his fatally boastful nature; finally, his vanity was the fatal flaw which made Darnley incapable of
assessing any person or situation at its true worth, since
he could not help relating everything back to his own
self-esteem. The kindest judgement made about him was
that of the cardinal of Lorraine—'un gentil huteaudeau'[23]
(an agreeable nincompoop)—but such lightweight figures
had a way of becoming dangerous if they were inserted
into serious situations.

None of this was apparent to Mary Queen of Scots at
her first meeting with her cousin in Scotland, at Wemyss
Castle. She merely saw and admired his charming exterior,
which, like a delightful red shiny apple ready for the eating, gave no hint of the maggots which lay inside. Her
reaction was instantaneously romantic: she told Melville
that 'he was the properest and best proportioned long man
that ever she had seen. . . .'[24] Although the long man went
on to see his father Lennox who was at Dunkeld with
his kinsman Lord Atholl, he was back at the queen's side
on the following Saturday, in order to cross over the
queen's ferry with her towards the south. From now on,
he was scarcely allowed to be away from her side. On
Monday Darnley listened to Knox preach, dined with
Moray and Randolph, and finally at Moray's instance

danced a galliard with Mary—the tall graceful young
couple looked so suitable together that at this point Randolph reported: 'A great number wish him well—others
doubt him, and deeply consider what is fit for the state of
their country, than, as he is called "a fair jolly young
man".'[25] Yet the tide was running very strongly in favour
of the fair jolly young man—more especially since in mid-
March Randolph was finally instructed to tell Mary that
the Leicester marriage would definitely not be exchanged
for her succession rights. Mary was deeply depressed by
the news, and wept bitter tears: but it had the inevitable
effect of focusing her attention still more strongly on
Darnley now physically present by her side, as Elizabeth
and her advisers must surely have anticipated when they
sent the final crushing message.

In the meantime marriage was in the air of Mary's little Scottish circle. During the previous autumn Mary's
secretary Maitland had begun to court the dazzling Mary
Fleming, he being a recently widowed man of forty, and
she a girl of twenty-two. Maitland was clearly fascinated
by her radiant youth and vitality, although Kirkcaldy
scornfully described her as being about as suitable for
him 'as I am to be pope'.[26] Maitland's passion became an
open subject for discussion at the court, and in February
Maitland confessed to Cecil that his passion brought him
at least one 'merry hour' out of the four and twenty, whatever the troublesome affairs of the kingdom, even advising
Cecil himself to turn to such amorous sport for relaxation since 'those that be in love, be ever set upon a merry
pin'.[27] Randolph was scornful over Maitland's infatuation
which he described in withering terms, but Randolph himself, a forty-five-year-old bachelor who observed the gam-
bolling of the Maries with gallant approval, was himself
an unsuccessful admirer of Mary Beaton, and his account
was probably tinged with jealousy. In the end it was not
the acknowledged *belle* Mary Fleming who was to be the
first Marie to wed, but, as we have seen, her energetic
agile companion, Mary Livingston, who chose as her
bridegroom a younger son of Lord Sempill. The marriage took place on Shrove Tuesday, 6 March 1565. The
queen was not only party to the marriage contract and
gave the bride a dowry of £500 a year in land, but also
paid for the wedding gown and bridal banquet, as was her
custom with her favourite ladies. As the first of the Maries

to marry, the wedding of Mary Livingston naturally attracted a great deal of attention, and the French and English ambassadors give many details of the impending ceremonies for two months before hand (the detailed preparations certainly give the lie to Knox's suggestion of a hurried ceremony). Randolph described Sempill as 'a happy Englishman' for winning the estimable Mary Livingston as a bride. Mary Stuart's own views on the subject were best expressed by the French ambassador in his report to Catherine de Medicis: 'She has begun to marry off her Maries, and says that she wishes she herself were of the band.'[28]

Up to this point, however much Mary had enjoyed the company of Darnley, she had not shown any evidence of passion for him: Randolph weighed up the favour she had shown him as proceeding 'of her own courteous nature' rather than anything more serious. In March Mary still seems to have regarded Darnley as a suitable candidate for marriage only because of his English and Scottish royal blood and his religion, and not for any more personal reason. But in April the situation dramatically changed. Darnley fell ill—an illness which was to transform his fortune and that of Mary Queen of Scots. The illness itself was of no great moment: it began with a cold, which Darnley attempted to cure by sweating it out, and then turned into measles. The young man was incarcerated in his sick-room in Stirling Castle. It was the situation of his sick-room which was the crucial fact about his illness. Inevitably, within the confines of the enormous fortress, like a private town hanging above the plain of Stirling, the young queen found her way with increasing frequency to the bedside of her handsome young cousin. She began to visit him continually and at all hours, and she even took to staying past midnight. She constituted herself his nurse. When measles was succeeded by an ague, the distracted girl refused to ride forth to Perth until Darnley was recovered, and her care was redoubled. Under the influence of the proximity of the sick-room, and the tenderness brought forth by the care of the weak, the suffering—and the handsome—Mary had fallen violently, recklessly and totally in love.

There can be no doubt that whether Mary herself realized it or not, her feelings for Darnley were overwhelmingly physical. The demanding nature of her passion can easily be explained by pent-up longings which were the

result of an inadequate first marriage, which had aroused
few physical feelings in her and satisfied none. In the years
since Francis's death she had led a life of celibacy, allowing herself courtly flirtations but nothing more, and had
been seemingly horrified at any more crude confrontation
with life, such as Châtelard presented to her. Her thoughts
about marriage had been concentrated on the power it
would bring her, for Don Carlos as a bridegroom could
have offered few other consolations, and she had shown little interest in the prospect of that great lover Robert Dudley as a possible husband. Now at one touch of Darnley's
hand, the caution, the concentration on the issue of her
marriage in which Elizabeth's approval was so vital, the
discretion and wisdom which all had praised in her during her four years as queen of Scotland—all were swept
away in a tide of tumultuous feelings which Mary Stuart
can scarcely have known she possessed.

13 The Carnal Marriage

> 'Nuptiae carnales a laetitia incipiunt et in luctu terminantur'
> ('Carnal marriages begin with happiness and end in strife')
>
> CECIL'S *comment on the marriage of Amy Robsart and Leicester*

In March Darnley had been one possible candidate among the many from whom the queen of Scots might choose her consort. In April he became the one man she was determined to have beside her as husband. From Stirling she took a keen interest in the intrigues on the subject in Edinburgh. The faithful Maitland was promptly despatched to London to acquaint Elizabeth with the news and, as it was hoped, win her approval—this sanction being doubly necessary because Darnley was not only a member of the English royal family through his Tudor descent, but also held to be an English subject. At this point Mary genuinely believed that she would receive this approval. Her confidence was easy to understand: Darnley had come north with the official blessing of England, and he was an English noble of the type whom Elizabeth had often observed that she wished Mary would marry. From hearsay Mary had reason to suppose that Darnley was one of Elizabeth's own candidates, if the Leicester marriage failed. Maitland reached London on 15 April. But at this point the honeyed trap—as Darnley now turned out to be —was sprung. Mary to marry Darnley! Darnley, the great-grandson of Henry VII, with a claim of his own to the English throne! No indeed, Elizabeth, made newly aware of the disapproval of the Scottish Protestants for a Catholic bridegroom and anxious to dissociate herself from the project, now took the line that the whole idea of the marriage was preposterous, and represented a renewed attempt on Mary's part to acquire the English throne for herself. In London Margaret, countess of Lennox, was first commanded to keep to her room and later sent to the Tower. Regardless of the fact that Lennox and Darnley had gone north with her express permission, Elizabeth exploded with anger and demanded their instant return. When neither paid any attention to her angry bulletins, Throckmorton was sent north to dissuade Mary from the disastrous, nay, menacing course of marrying Darnley.

Mary in Scotland was in no state to listen to the advice of even the sagest counsellor. Love was rampant in her heart for the first time, and she could hear no other voice except the dictates of her own passionate feelings. In the words of a poem of the period, it was a case of 'O lusty May, with Flora Queen' at the court of Scotland.[1] Randolph wrote back to Leicester in anguish of his 'poor Queen whom ever before I esteemed so worthy, so wise, so honourable in all her doings', now so altered by love that he could hardly recognize her. To Cecil he described a queen seized with love 'all care of common wealth set apart, to the utter contempt of her best subjects'.[2] Randolph was in a particular state of despair at the whole situation because it was being widely stated in Scotland that Darnley had been deliberately despatched by Elizabeth to trap Mary into a mean marriage: and he only wished that there was not so much concrete evidence to back up these suspicions.

Darnley himself reacted predictably. In the same breath as he bewailed his once-honoured queen's infatuation, Randolph reported that Darnley was now grown so proud that he was intolerable to all honest men, and already almost forgetful of his duty to Mary—she who had adventured so much for his sake. Darnley's health had taken an unconscionable long time to recover, and even while on his sick-bed he had struck the ageing duke of Châtelherault on his pate to avenge some fancied slight. By 21 May he had only been seen outside the four walls of his room once, and was still more or less confined to his bed. Well before Darnley's final emergence Throckmorton managed to see Mary at Stirling and put to her as strongly as possible Queen Elizabeth's dislike of what she considered to be a hasty manner of proceeding with Lord Darnley.

At this point Mary would surely have been wise to have taken serious thought. It was true that the approval of Philip II of Spain for the match was sought and won; Charles IX of France was approached through Castelnau and approved; her Guise relations were informed (al-

though Mary's beloved Anne of Guise must have been
somewhat surprised by the development since only in September she had given it as her opinion that Mary's innate
pride was far too strong to permit her to wed a mere
subject—'her heart was too great to debase it').[3] All these
approvals were as nothing compared to the approval of
Elizabeth: for after all Elizabeth could offer Mary what
none of these other potentates had it in their power to
extend—the reversion of her own throne. Over the question of Mary's marriage, hypocritically as she might behave, maddeningly as she might procrastinate, Elizabeth
was still in the position of paying the piper and therefore
calling the tune. Only the rashest and most impetuous of
women would have proceeded now on the same determined
course without taking heed of Elizabeth's declared disapproval—but this was what love had apparently made
Mary Stuart. She and Throckmorton argued fruitlessly,
while Mary tried to put her own point of view, finally
Throckmorton concluded that the queen was so far committed in this matter with Lord Darnley, as it was irrev-
ocable, and 'that there was no point in exercising any
persuasion and reasonable means any further'. Gloomily
the courtier who had once so much admired Mary for her
discretion in her first widowhood in France, and had
wished that Elizabeth could behave more like her, concluded that she had been captivated, either by love or cunning, or rather, 'to say truly, by boasting or folly'.[4]

Darnley's recovery did nothing to dim the queen's love.
Now she was so infatuated that many began to suggest
that Darnley had actually bewitched her, looking for a
supernatural explanation of her great love when a natural
one was only too obvious. At the beginning of June Randolph moaned again to Leicester that Mary and Darnley
were still exchanging great tokens of love every day, and
Mary seemed to have laid aside all shame in her behaviour.
He even suggested that passion had caused the queen to
lose her looks somewhat—but perhaps he merely meant
that her dignity had been laid aside in favour of the reckless glowing aspect of a woman in love.[5] Darnley's pride
waxed with the queen's affection: to show his virility, he
launched out characteristically with blows towards those
whom he knew would not dare to retaliate. On the day in
May on which he was created earl of Ross, he drew his

dagger on the wretched justice clerk who brought him the message, because he was not also made duke of Albany as he had expected. It was the typical gesture of the spoilt and vindictive child. By the beginning of July, Darnley was held in such general contempt that even those who had been his chief friends could no longer find words to defend him. Randolph made the gloomy, but as it proved singularly accurate, prophecy: 'I know not, but it is greatly to be feared that he can have no long life among these people.'

The truth was that even if Darnley had spoken with the tongues of men and of angels, Mary Stuart would have had sufficient problems in persuading her court to accept him as her bridegroom. In the course of the summer Darnley wooed Mary with a light and courtly love poem:[6]

> If langour makes men light
> I am for evermore
> In joy, both even and morrow . . .
>
> The turtle-dove for her mate
> More dolour may not endure
> Than I do for her sake . . .

If such felicitous pleadings recalled to Mary pleasantly the far-off days of the French court, her advisers were singularly unimpressed by them. To the Scots now around the queen whatever Darnley's poetic talent, his arrogant nature was merely the final disaster in a long train of possible disadvantages. Firstly there was the attitude of England, crystallized in the discussion of the English Privy Council on 4 June, where the two great perils of Mary's marriage were laid down as firstly the plain intention of Mary by such a match to occupy Elizabeth's throne now rather than later, and secondly, 'the increase and credit of the Romish religion in England'. The avowed hostility of England was naturally fuel to the smouldering flames of Scottish hostility: Moray, for example, had viewed the match with great gloom from the start, since he had little desire to see the rival Lennoxes raised up, and his own credit and influence with his sister, built up over four years, debased. Added to which, Darnley had made it clear that he regarded Moray's spreading dominions in Scotland as surprisingly and disagreeably extensive, and even passed unpleasant remarks on the subject to Moray's brother, Lord Robert Stewart, an unwise choice of confidant.

Moray withdrew from the court at the beginning of April, on the ostensible excuse that he did not wish to witness the popish ceremonies at Easter. The whole benefit of his advice and approval which Mary had enjoyed for so long, was thus removed from her, at one swoop, as Moray now proceeded to indulge in a series of confused but hostile manœuvres, whose intention was to demonstrate his opposition to Darnley, without breaking into open rebellion, until he should be assured of English support for his cause. But there were other Scottish nobles, quite apart from Moray, who had ancient, feudal or hereditary reasons for disliking and fearing the Lennoxes: to many Scots Darnley seemed to combine the disadvantages of both the subject and the royal prince as a husband. The Hamilton faction was newly united with Knox in their disapproval of the marriage.* Even the Maries were said to be against the match—and to be out of credit with the queen in consequence. The only name mentioned as encouraging it, was that of David Riccio, the queen's new secretary for her French correspondence, and Darnley's boon companion.

All the while Mary was caught fast in the tangled bonds of passion. So vehement did her love seem, and so overweening the pride of Darnley, that it was even rumoured that they had been secretly married in early July. It is very probable that the queen had gone through some betrothal ceremony with Darnley at the beginning of May, in the very first ecstasies of love, betrothals then resembling marriages in the sense that much greater liberties were allowed between the betrothed pair. But an actual secret marriage is rendered unlikely by the fact that Mary deliberately and impetuously married Darnley before the arrival of the papal dispensation from Rome. The dispen-

---

* An unpublished letter in the Register House, Edinburgh, from Mary to John Spens, her advocate, on a legal matter, dated from Stirling on 9 April, contains a passionately scribbled postscript in the queen's own hand, in which she directs the advocate to find out more concerning certain 'secret gatherings' said to be held in the evenings in Edinburgh between Knox and Gavin Hamilton: 'I pray you endeavour to learn what is done or said and inform me thereof, using all the diligence you can, but take good care that no one learns that I have written anything to you on this matter. . . .'[7]

sation was necessary because they were step-first cousins, and Mary was acting on the presumption that the dispensation had already been granted in Rome even if it had not yet arrived in Scotland. She was certainly in no mood for hole-in-the-corner ceremonies.* On 22 July Darnley was at last given the coveted title of duke of Albany. On 29 July the heralds proclaimed that Darnley (or Prince Henry as he was termed) should henceforth be named and styled 'King of this our Kingdom'. This was Mary's ultimate proud pursuit of her own desires, since rightly she should have asked Parliament to give Darnley the coveted title of king. By bestowing it herself, she was pledging her full authority in the cause of her future husband. Finally on Sunday morning 29 July, between five and six o'clock in the morning, a radiant Mary was conveyed to the chapel royal at Holyrood, on the arm of her future father-in-law the earl of Lennox, and the earl of Argyll, there to await her chosen consort once the young Lord Darnley, now King Henry of Scotland.

For this wedding, however, there was to be no dazzling white marriage robe for Mary Stuart, whatever the romantic passion which inspired her: she wore on the contrary a great mourning gown of black, with a wide mourning hood attached to it, which apparently much resembled the costume which she had worn on the burial day of Francis. This was to indicate that she came to her new husband not as a young and virgin girl, but as a widow, a queen dowager of France. Having been led into the chapel, she remained there until her future husband was brought in by the same lords. They exchanged the vows of marriage service according to the Catholic rite and three rings were put on Mary's finger, the middle one a gleaming diamond. Darnley then left Mary alone to hear Mass, abandoning her with a kiss, and himself going straight to her chamber to await her. With the marriage completed, Mary was now at last by custom required to cast off her mourning

---

* But Mary was wrong in supposing that the dispensation had already been granted. The dispensation was granted in Rome some time after 1 September and before 25 September; it arrived in Scotland several weeks after that—but was not of course published, since the marriage had already taken place on the assumption of its existence, and to publish its actual date would have been embarrassing to the queen.[8] Unless Mary and Darnley went through a further marriage ceremony after the date of its granting (of which there is no record) their marriage was technically invalid.

garments, and signify that she was about to embark upon
'a pleasanter life'. In Randolph's words, after 'some
pretty refusal'[9] which with some reason he believed was
more for form's sake than from any genuine reluctance to
abandon her widowed state, she allowed everyone standing
round to take out one pin; then, giving herself into the
hands of her ladies, she changed out of her black clothes.

There then followed the usual dancing and festivities
of a nuptial celebration; if they did not compare with the
grandiose ceremonies which had accompanied Mary's
marriage to Francis, they were at least considered magnificent by Scottish standards, and seven years was perhaps
long enough for the memories of such far-off grandeurs
to have faded in Mary's mind. There was a banquet for
the full court of nobles, the sound of trumpets, largesse
scattered among the crowd and money thrown about the
palace in abundance. After the dinner there was some
dancing, and a brief respite for recovery, before the supper, as magnificent as had been the dinner. Finally, as Randolph reported, 'and so they go to bed'. It is to be hoped
that Mary Stuart, who had sacrificed so much for this
match, found at least this part of the ceremony to her
satisfaction: there is no evidence to prove that she had
anticipated the marriage ceremony and become Darnley's
mistress in the course of the summer, beyond the bawdy
rumours of their enemies, who said that they had lain together at Seton. It is significant that Randolph, who had had
every opportunity of observing the young couple throughout the summer, specifically advised the English Council
to the contrary:[10] 'Suspicious men,' he wrote, 'or such as
are given of all things to make the worst, would that it
should be believed that they knew each other before that
they came there [to bed]. I would not that your Lordships
should so believe the likelihoods are so greatly to the contrary.' Certainly the wildness of Mary's infatuation seems
to point to tormenting and unslaked physical feelings
rather than the comparative satisfaction of a liaison.
Throughout her four and a half years of widowhood, Mary
Stuart had displayed a strong sense of her own 'majesty'
where the attentions of young gallants were concerned;
in the course of the last year she had seemed in addition
obsessed by the subject of marriage. Darnley had long
been one of those on her list of possible husbands. Therefore when she finally fell in love with him in the Easter

of 1565, she had no reason to surrender herself to him outside the bonds of marriage, when there was the prospect of connubial bliss with him in the future.

Knox wrote of the prolonged rejoicing after the marriage ceremony: 'During the space of three or four days, there was nothing but balling, and dancing, and banqueting.'[11] The pen of Buchanan, who owed feudal allegiance to the earl of Lennox, was pressed into service for the many masques which followed; in one Diana complained that the foremost of her bright band of five Marys had been taken from her by the envious powers of love and marriage and in another the four remaining Marys offered oblations to the goddess of Health.[12] To many, the most significant ceremony which followed was that which took place the next day. On Monday 30 July, Mary deliberately had the fact of Darnley's new title of King Henry* announced once more by the heralds, with the further proclamation that hence-forward all documents and proclamations would be signed by them jointly in the two names MARIE and HENRY, that is, 'set forth in the names of both their Majesties as King and Queen of Scotland conjunctly'. At this news, there was a heavy ominous silence among the nobles of Scotland. Not one as much as said 'Amen'. Only the happy doting father, Lennox, at seeing his darling thus glorified, cried out aloud: 'God save his Grace!'

Cecil had commented on the ill-fated marriage of Leicester and Amy Robsart that *Nuptiae carnales a laetitia incipiunt et in luctu terminantur*—Carnal marriages begin with happiness and end in strife.[13] Mary was allowed little enough time to enjoy the happiness of her own 'carnal marriage' before the first presages of strife were made apparent. Already, before her wedding, Moray had indulged in behaviour which was at best menacing, at worst plainly re-

* The title of Lord Darnley was a courtesy title, which he bore as the elder surviving son of the earl of Lennox, according to the English custom (in Scotland at this period Darnley would have been known as the master of Lennox). Darnley was created earl of Ross in May and duke of Albany in July, before being proclaimed as 'King Henry' by the queen. In the present work, however, which already contains three King Henrys—Henry VIII of England, and Henry II and III of France—he will still be referred to as Darnley for the sake of clarity. But it is important to realize that Darnley was universally referred to as 'the king' in Scotland at the time.

bellious; he declined to attend the convention of the nobility called at Perth at the end of June on tne grounds
that he was ill, and lurked at Lochleven; from here he
spread a rumour that the Lennox faction was planning to
assassinate him. It was a time when rumours were spreading freely—the Lennox party in their turn suggested that
Moray intended to kidnap Lennox and Darnley and ship
them back to England, but the existence of this plot has
never been concretely proved. Moray was also involved in
more practical schemes: on 1 July he asked Randolph
for a subsidy of £3,000 from Elizabeth to support the
Protestant religion in Scotland, and the English alliance.
Furious with Mary for her choice of Darnley as a husband, Moray's intention was to show that she was endangering the Protestant religion. But in her desire to win
support for the Darnley marriage, Mary had on the contrary taken the trouble to court the favour of the reformers. Nor was Darnley himself, although now a professed
Catholic, a shining example to the other members of his
Faith: in England he had acted as a Protestant, and once
back in Scotland, he had happily listened to the sermon
of John Knox in St Giles Church, as well as avoiding the
nuptial Mass to his own wedding, which Mary had attended: Darnley's faith appeared to have a chameleon
quality about it, which enabled it to assume whatever colour seemed convenient at the time. Mary's conciliatory attitude on the subject of religion showed up Moray's rebellion for what it was—a jealous disaffection springing from
feudally inspired hatred of the Lennoxes, with religious
overtones introduced for the sake of English subsidies,
rather than a genuine revolt of conscience.

On 6 August Moray was put to the horn or outlawed,
having refused to put in any appearance before his sister
to explain his behaviour, despite promises of safe-conduct
for himself and eighty of his followers. His two most powerful allies, Châtelherault and Argyll, were informed that
they would be outlawed in their turn if they gave him any
further assistance. Mary now acted with admirable promptness. The properties of Moray, Rothes and Kirkcaldy were
seized on 14 August; on 22 August Mary announced that
she intended to march against the rebels, and ordered a
muster of troops (to pay for which she pledged her
jewels). In order that Moray's rebellion should be seen
for what it was—the foray of a rebellious noble rather

than a religious crusade—Mary once more announced
that no religious change was intended. Atholl was made
lieutenant in the north, in order to hold Argyll at bay.
On 26 August Mary rode out of Edinburgh towards the
west of Scotland, with Darnley swaggering at her side in
gilt armour: she was swearing revenge on Moray, but the
vivid emotion brought such a sparkle into her spirits that
in the course of the campaign even Knox's narrative expressed admiration of her as she rode at the head of her
troops: 'Albeit the most part waxed weary, yet the Queen's
courage increased man-like, so much that she was ever
with the foremost.'[14]

In her absence, Moray, Châtelherault, Glencairn and
Rothes entered the city; but they discovered that there
was little support for them there, from Protestants and
Catholics alike, Mary having by now made herself extremely popular with the ordinary people—who in the
course of her four years in Scotland had seen no evidence
that she intended to deprive them of the practice of their
new religion, and their minds set at rest on this subject
positively enjoyed the acquisition of a young and beautiful
queen, who understood better how to reach the hearts of
her humbler subjects than those of her nobility. Threatened by the guns of Edinburgh Castle, manned by Lord
Erskine, now earl of Mar, Moray departed. In Glasgow,
Mary decided to wait until her northern levies should
reach her at Stirling at the end of September before finally
attacking Moray. In the meantime she issued another
proclamation promising a definite settlement of the religious question. Randolph heard that Mary was putting
such enthusiasm into her cause, that she frequently rode
with a pistol at her saddle, outriding all her ladies and
gentlemen except 'one stout lady'.[15]

It was left for Moray and his associates to appeal endlessly for the help from England which they believed had
been promised to them by Elizabeth, but by the end of
September the most Moray had got out of Elizabeth was
the promise of an asylum in England, if he should need it.
Meanwhile the English Council dithered and finally came
down against him. Early in October, Moray realized his
cause was hopeless, and on 6 October fled across the border
from the south-west of Scotland, as Mary prepared to
attack him. In London he underwent the humiliating experience of being told by Elizabeth, in the course of a per-

sonal audience, duly witnessed by the French ambassador,
that he had done very wrong in rebelling against Mary.
Having publicly exculpated herself from the charge of
abetting the Scottish rebels, Elizabeth, in a triumph of
double-talk, said that she would intercede with Mary for
the return of Moray. Moray now settled down at Newcastle, to brood on the possibility of more favourable developments in Scotland.

It is difficult to explain Moray's conduct in terms of
statesmanship: not only was Mary not threatening the
Protestant religion at the end of July, but it was actually
his rebellion which enabled Mary to send an emissary to
Rome in September asking for a papal subsidy to assist her
in the conflict. Mary had understandably been experienc-
ing some difficulty in the past two years in convincing
the Pope that she truly had the cause of Scottish Catholicism at heart. Yet papal money continued to be a golden
lure as was papal approval to one who might at any moment need foreign Catholic support: now Moray's rebellion, so publicly stated to be in the cause of Protestantism,
presented the Scottish queen with a perfect opportunity to
present herself in Rome as a champion of the Catholic
faith. But the truth was that Moray, in his revolt, was no
more championing Protestantism, than Mary was championing Catholicism by attacking him. The composition of
their respective parties shows how strongly feudal and
family alliances still acted in Scottish politics.

Moray had Châtelherault on his side, because the Hamiltons were perennially opposed to the Lennox Stewarts,
who contested their claim to be the next heirs to the Scottish throne; Mary in turn reacted to Moray's revolt by
pardoning young Lord Gordon, Huntly's son, who was
released from ward, and restored to his father's title on
3 August, for the very good reason that the Huntlys were
now the sworn enemies of Moray. Even Bothwell was now
allowed back into royal favour because his enmity against
the Hamiltons could be relied on keeping him loyal to
the queen: the crude insults which he was said to have
bestowed on Mary after his escape to France (she was
the 'cardinal's whore', and she and Elizabeth between
them did not add up to one honest woman)[16] were conveniently forgotten in the need to suppress Moray. The
presence of the keen Protestant and traditional Hamilton

ally, Argyll, on the opposing side meant that Atholl could
be relied on to act against him on Mary's side to preserve
the balance of power in the north of Scotland. Indeed
during the Chaseabout Raid, Argyll took the opportunity
to despoil Lennox and Atholl, which he considered evidently a more important task than supporting Moray
against the queen. Lastly the 'slow and greedy' earl of
Morton, head of the Douglas clan, supported the queen,
because Lennox's wife Margaret had been a Douglas, and
Darnley was thus 'mother's kin' to the Douglases.

The Chaseabout Raid, as Moray's abortive rebellion was
called, marked a significant change in Mary's attitude to
her Scottish nobles, which may not have been politically
wise, but whose genesis was certainly easy to trace. She
certainly did not despair of the Scottish people—indeed
her experiences during the raid only confirmed her in
her prognostication to Throckmorton when still in France,
that she would manage to appeal to 'the common people'
of Scotland. But in the course of four years, her two
major subjects had both revolted against her, in the interests of their own power, as it seemed to her. She had
defeated them both, married the man of her choice, and
had been able to re-establish herself as a champion of the
Scottish Catholic cause abroad, without in fact making
as yet any significant concessions to the Catholics in Scotland—in short, she was riding high. None of these experiences had taught her to trust her own nobility at any
point where her interest might conflict with theirs: she
therefore took the natural step of relying more and more
on those who had no mighty Scottish lands and clans to
back them up, no family feuds to sway them, and who
did not belong to the spider's web of Scottish family relationships. In her newly important relations with the papacy,
her vast correspondence with her French relations, and
even with Spain, Mary began to make use of a sort of
middle-class secretariat. These rising stars were not even
lairds as Maitland had been but, in Randolph's term, 'crafty
vile strangers'[17]—although Mary saw them as loyal and
discreet servants. It was a move which was passionately
resented by the nobles who saw themselves about to be
edged out of the centre of a stage they had occupied
so tempestuously and for so long.

Randolph, in his discussion of the subject, mentioned

two Italians, Davy and Francisco (Francisco de Busso), and an Englishman called Fowler. Others who were complained of were Sebastian Danelourt and the Scottish lawyer James Balfour: in his criticism of Mary, Moray had mentioned that she relied on such men, rather than take what he chose to term 'the wholesome advice and counsel' of her barons. Of these men, Davy or David Riccio* was the most interesting character. He had first arrived in Scotland in 1561 in the train of the ambassador from Savoy, and he came of a good but impoverished Savoyard family; he was of course a Catholic, although no evidence has ever been found in the Vatican to confirm the suggestion of his enemies that he was at any time a papal agent. He was now aged about thirty-five; but otherwise the only fact on which everyone agreed about this cuckoo in the royal nest—which appears in every contemporary record whether of friend or foe—was that Riccio seemed extremely ugly by the standards of the time,† his face being considered 'illfavoured' and his stature small and hunched. Although he had a Latin love of fine clothing —after his death an extravagant peacock's wardrobe was discovered—Buchanan commented spitefully 'indeed his appearance disfigured his elegance.'[18] Riccio also seems to have been avaricious, since a cache of £2,000 was discovered among his effects, which would have been difficult to amass out of his yearly pay of £80 and lends colour to the accusations of his enemies that he took bribes. Riccio, however, first came into Mary's service on a more spiritual level.

Ugly as he might be, avaricious as he might be suspected to be, Riccio was generally conceded to be a fine musician. Music as we have seen was Mary's private passion. Riccio entered Mary's employ when she needed a bass singer to make up a quartet with the valets of her household. Although Riccio was clearly a talented performer,

* The correct spelling of his name: Rizzio seems to have originated from Rizio in the first printing of Knox's *History* in 1644.

† The portrait usually given as that of Riccio, from which many engravings have been made, showing a soulful gentleman fingering a lute, with fine eyes, a chiselled mouth, a neat beard, certainly does not depict him as ugly; but it is an imaginary portrait, dating from the late seventeenth or eighteenth century, and has no connection with his true appearance.

there is no concrete evidence to prove that he combined these talents with those of a composer.* Riccio, apart from his musical talent, was also an amusing conversationalist; to a queen who was in Melville's phrase 'of quick spirit, curious to know, and get intelligence of the estate of other countries and would be sometimes sad when she was solitary, and glad of the company of them that had travelled in other parts',[19] Riccio provided an agreeable opportunity to discuss the Europe they had both once known.

When Mary's French secretary Raullet died at the end of 1564 Riccio was appointed in his place; this meant that he was nominally responsible for her French correspondence, as opposed to Maitland, who was her secretary of state and responsible for all her affairs. But by the autumn of 1565 Randolph was able to observe spitefully about Maitland that he had been sufficiently pushed out of the centre of affairs to have the leisure to make love— to his coy mistress, Mary Fleming.[20] Melville paints a picture of Riccio standing at the entrance to Mary's chamber, smiling at the nobles as they went by, and being glowered on in return.[21] Certainly Maitland, in terms of power politics, had reason to resent the advancement of Riccio, since it had led to his own decline. But to Mary the loyalty of Riccio at least was beyond reproach, and she had a natural horror of disloyalty, especially when it was accompanied by ingratitude. As Mary wrote to de Foix, the French ambassador in London, in November 1565, in a long letter pleading with him to get her mother-in-law Lady Lennox released from the Tower, the ingratitude of Moray seemed to her fantastic: here was a mere subject on whom she had showered honours and goods, trying to prevent her marrying whom she pleased. Again and again

* He was credited with the composition of the music for seven Scottish songs—The Lass of Patie's Mill, Bessie Bell, The Bush Aboon Traquair, The Bonnie Boatman, And Thou were my Ain Thing, Auld Rob Morris and Down the Burn David, in the 1725 edition of Orpheus Caledonius; later James Oswald attached his name to certain songs in the Caledonian Companion, and was accused of having done so for the sake of publicity. In fact the legend of Riccio the composer rests on tradition only, and as such can be neither proved nor disproved—although it seems infinitely more likely that a native Italian would be interested by, collect and play, rather than actually compose such characteristically Scottish melodies. See John Glen, Early Scottish Melodies, for a balanced discussion of the whole subject.

she reverted to the topic as she utterly refused to allow the release of Lady Lennox to be made conditional on her pardoning Moray and his fellow-rebels.[22] In a memorandum on the reasons for her second marriage, she bitterly related how Moray had deliberately agreed to the idea of Darnley at first, in order to spite the pretensions of the Hamiltons, under the impression that he could scotch the match whenever he wished.[23]

Mary had *au fond* an unhypocritical and undissembling nature: in this respect she was curiously unlike her contemporary queens, Elizabeth Tudor and Catherine de Medicis, who had after all been brought up from childhood in far harder schools of learning than the idolized young queen of Scotland. Although Mary enjoyed the prospect and motions of intrigue, and took a keen interest in letters, schemes and news, she lacked the disposition of the true intriguer: the born double-agent, by not knowing which interest he really wants to come out on top, except his own survival, is able to take advantage of every new twist of the situation and thus in the end always survive—both Elizabeth and Cecil had something of this temperament. Mary on the other hand was by nature frank and open, as she knew herself; she was also passionate, quick to love, quick to hate, easy to weep, easy to laugh. This meant inevitably that she had a love of being committed: she preferred action, whatever the cost, to inaction, whatever the gain. Her fluctuating health may well have played some part in this; it was infinitely easier for one of her nervous energies to galvanize herself to spring forward than to rally her strength for a debilitating period of waiting. But such tendencies marked Mary off from the real plotters. Her love of commitment meant that in turn she felt bitterly betrayed when those around her seemed to neglect her interests for their own, showing no equivalent commitment to her. Her fiercest hatreds were always reserved for those whom she had raised up and who now let her down—Moray was now in this category and Darnley was shortly to enter into it.

Unfortunately this July marriage, begun in the high summer of love, did not preserve its warmth into the cooler temperatures of autumn and winter. At first, as Melville said, Mary was so delighted with her new acquisition, Darnley, that she did him great honour herself, and willed everyone who desired her favour to do the like and wait upon him. But after the honeymoon was over—a honeymoon spent as it happened virtually on the field of battle, defending Darnley as a choice of husband—Mary was ready to return to the more serious business of ruling Scotland. In her work, she was only too happy to have Darnley beside her—for his signature, that of 'King Henry', was together with hers on every document, as she had promised, and even the summons to serve in the field at the time of rebellion was sent out jointly in their two names. It was true that Mary signed on the left (the position of honour because it was read first) and Darnley on the right* (unlike Francis who had occupied the left). But his signature was nevertheless always present with one exception—that of a safe-conduct to England; Elizabeth refused to accept it on grounds that she did not acknowledge Darnley as king but on the contrary as 'a subject and an offender', and after a debate in Council, Randolph did manage to get Darnley's signature left off ('notwithstanding all the former promises made to him').[24] Apart from this single victory of expediency over principles, Mary throughout the autumn continued to bolster up the power of 'King Henry'.

Yet Darnley was obviously not much interested in the process of government. He continued sulkily to demand the crown matrimonial (egged on by his father Lennox), and wished to spend more money than Mary, perpetually embarrassed in this respect as we have seen, could easily provide: the crown matrimonial, which Francis had enjoyed, could only be granted by Parliament, at the instance of Mary, but it would have ensured that Darnley's power was equal with Mary's while she lived, and continued after her death, if Darnley survived her. Darnley's way of showing himself worthy for this high honour was a strange one: Knox's Continuator summed it up neatly: 'As for the King, he past his time in hunting and hawking and such other pleasures as were agreeable to his appetites, having in his company gentlemen willing to satisfy his will and

---

* The six documents among the state papers in the Register House at Edinburgh dated from July 1565 to May 1566 signed by Queen Mary and Darnley after their marriage invariably show their signatures in this position; on at least two occasions, however, Darnley asserted himself by making his signature considerably larger than that of the queen.

affections.'[25] Darnley's continued love of the chase and sport in particular meant that governmental measures were often held up by his absence, since they demanded the joint signature. In the second half of November, when the queen was seriously ill with the recurring pain in her side, Darnley spent about nine days hunting in Fife: this was the occasion when an iron stamp or seal was made of his signature to prevent delays. Even Darnley's partisan, Buchanan, admitted that Darnley raised no objection to the practice: the queen told Darnley that while he was busy hawking or hunting, matters of importance were unseasonably delayed—and 'he consented to this proposal as he did not wish to offend her in anything . . .';[26] the seal was duly given into the custody of David Riccio. At all events, to those accustomed to the double signature at the end of a document a stamp of one of the signatures would hardly have been noticed.†

At the beginning of December, Mary went to the palace of Linlithgow to convalesce after her recent indisposition. Perhaps her illness had been exacerbated by other more fruitful symptoms: she must by now have been about two and a half months pregnant with the future James VI.* The birth of an heir—preferably male—was of vital importance to Mary's plans; if she gave birth to a son, she would automatically be placed in a much stronger position with regard to the English succession than a mere childless queen. Randolph, in the manner of courtiers, watched the queen eagerly for signs of pregnancy, and was avid to pick up court gossip on the subject. By 31 October, he was reporting to London: 'It is given out by some of her own

† In England signatures by wooden stamp were used from the reign of Henry VI onwards.

* James was born on 19 June 1566. By the law of averages, he was therefore conceived on or about 19 September 1565. The circumstances of his birth might seem to suggest that he was premature, since his mother had endured such hardships during the pregnancy. But after the murder of Riccio, Mary specifically declared in her letter to Archbishop James Beaton of 2 April 1566,[27] that she had been nearly *seven* months pregnant at the time of the assassination (9 March 1566). Yet a calculation based on James's birth shows that she was in fact only approaching *six* months pregnant. This seems to show that Mary in April believed her pregnancy to be more advanced than it was. It certainly disposes of the notion that James was premature, since by Mary's calculations James was born late rather than early. One therefore returns to the most likely date of on or a little before 19 September 1565 for conception.

that she is with child, it is argued upon tokens I know not what, annexed to the kind of them that are in that case.' By 12 November Randolph wrote that it was now commonly said that 'she is with child, and the nurse already chosen. There can be no doubt and she herself thinks so.' Mary's November illness temporarily persuaded Randolph that the rumours of pregnancy were false, especially as on 1 December, he reported her as being up once more, and 'taking as much exercise as her body can endure': although she herself believed she was pregnant, those around thought it to be 'something worse'. However, when Mary set out for Linlithgow, it was not on horseback but on a litter, in Randolph's words 'being with child, as the rumour is again common among us'.[28] By 19 December Lady Lennox in the Tower in London, knew the happy news of her impending grandchild and by the spring the queen's pregnancy was an undeniable fact.

The prospect of motherhood—much as she must have desired it for dynastic reasons—did not increase Mary's affection for Darnley. In view of the four-year gap in their ages, there may originally have been something quasi-maternal in Mary's feelings for the beautiful young Darnley, which she was now able to satisfy more conventionally in the prospect of impending motherhood. It is significant that her confidant Leslie, in his *Defence of her Honour* deliberately chose to refer later to her 'very motherly care' for her husband—'for besides all other respects, though they were not very different in years, she was to him not only a loyal Prince, a loving and dear wife, but a most careful and tender Mother withal'.[29] In addition ill-health was obviously causing her discomfort which may in turn have caused distaste for the more physical aspects of married love. Certainly her violent infatuation for Darnley had not survived the onsets of pregnancy, and she could after all no longer share the pleasures of hunting and hawking which both had once enjoyed so keenly. On 20 December, Bedford from Berwick reported that, 'The Lord Darnley followeth his pastimes more than the Queen is content withal; what it will breed hereafter I cannot say, but in the meantime there is some misliking between them.' On 25 December Randolph noted that 'a while ago there was nothing but King and Queen, now the Queen's husband is the common word. He was wont in all writings to be first named: now he is placed second.' The relative

placing of the two names Henry and Mary was at the
heart of the mysterious matter of the silver 'ryal', a new
denomination of coin introduced shortly after their marriage at a nominal value of thirty shillings. This 'ryal'
showed the heads of Mary and Darnley facing each other
on one side, and on the other in Latin a reference to their
marriage—'Whom God has joined together, let no man
put asunder'. In December Randolph also reported that
this coin had been withdrawn from circulation in Scotland,
because the names of the royal pair were engraved on it in
an unusual order as HENRICUS & MARIA D. GRA. R. & R. SCOT-
ORUM. Randolph represented Mary as now regretting the
prominence given to Darnley's name, which for once pre-
ceded that of the queen.[30]

The best summary of the points of difference between
Mary and her husband is provided in the memoirs of
Lord Herries: Mary believed 'all the honour and majesty
he had came from her: that she had made choice of him
for her husband by her own affection only, and against the
will of many of the nobility'. Darnley, on the other hand,
was complacently convinced that 'the marriage was done
with the consent of the nobility who thought him worthy
of the place; that the whole kingdom had their eyes upon
him; they would follow and serve him upon the fields,
where it was a shame a woman should command'. And as
the memoirs added: 'These conceits [were] being continuously buzzed in the young man's head.'[31] It was, however, quite one thing for Mary to get on badly with her
husband, and for Darnley's young head to buzz, and
quite another for this disagreement to be put to savage
use by Mary's enemies. Darnley by himself was powerless, whatever his posturings. Darnley as the tool of Mary's
opponents could have a cutting edge. For it was a regrettable fact that by the beginning of 1566 there were quite
a number of Scottish nobles who were inclining to put
themselves in the category of the queen's enemies. Their
disputes with the queen had quite different origins from
those of Darnley, and formed very different patterns. But
the combination of two forces of disaffection was capable
of proving very dangerous for Mary—and fatal for her
servant David Riccio.

14 Our Most Special Servant

'Some of our subjects and council by their proceedings have declared manifestly what men they are . . . slain our most special servant in our own presence and thereafter held our proper person captive treasonably.'

MARY QUEEN OF SCOTS *to Queen Elizabeth of England,* *15 March 1566*

In January 1566 Mary Queen of Scots was in her own estimation riding high, with her courage unimpaired and her resolution only strengthened by the recent ordeal through which she had passed with such success; the future, bringing with it the prospect of the birth of an heir, looked bright to a woman whose nature combined spirit and optimism with tenderness. But there was no denying that the opposition which was building up against her both within and without Scotland had an ugly aspect to it: if she had appreciated its real extent, even Mary in her most buoyant mood might have experienced some unquiet moments while she speculated just how and when such thunder clouds would break into the fury of the storm. First of all there were set steadily against her those Protestant lords temporarily in exile, such as Moray; their primary desire was to return to Scotland, but their hostility to Mary was given a new edge when she threatened, in addition to banishment, to attaint them and declare their properties forfeited at the forthcoming session of Parliament, to be held in the spring.

Then there were the Kirk and Knox who feared to see Mary take advantage of her new strength since the defeat of Moray to advance the claims of the Catholic Church; this they also suspected she might try to accomplish at the coming parliamentary session. As it happens, the contemporary rumours that Mary was about to join a Catholic League with other foreign Catholic powers have been shown to be groundless—no record having been found of such a League, let alone Mary's intended participation in it*—and what plans if any Mary had for helping the Catholics at the forthcoming Parliament will never be known. At most she would probably have asked for toleration of the Mass for Scottish Catholics, rather than the rabid attacks to which the Mass and priests were subjected when detected; Mary was certainly modern enough in thought to wonder why the Catholics should not enjoy the free practice of their own religion, which she had so unquestioningly granted to the Protestants from the first moment of her arrival in Scotland. But of course Knox, like all those who have accomplished a revolution, was hysterically fearful to see its effects undone, and any ideas of mutual tolerance would have fallen on very deaf ears indeed. In January an emissary came from the new Pope Pius v, with an extremely friendly if somewhat over optimistic message for the queen on the subject of the recent revolt: 'Most dear daughter—We have heard with the utmost joy that you and His Highness, your husband, have lately given a brilliant proof of your zeal by restoring the due worship of God throughout your whole realm. Truly, dearest daughter, you understand the duties of devout kings and queens . . .' The Pope went on to encourage her to weed out completely 'the thorns and tares of heretical depravity . . .',[1] and promised all the help possible in this worthwhile task. Although Pius v seemed to have but little idea of the true state of affairs in Scotland, Mary was quite acute enough to send her own emissary, the bishop of Dunblane, for the second time to ask for a papal subsidy—since the Pope's mention of 'all the kind offices that paternal love can suggest' certainly spelled financial aid to Mary, always extremely conscious of this problem.

Added to these two groups were those other Protestant nobles within the confines of Scotland, such as Morton and Maitland, who hated to see Mary's other 'base-born' advisers advanced to the detriment of their own position. It will be seen that Riccio, as chief representative of this despised and hated class, was the natural scapegoat for all the sections of the community opposed to the queen. He was also of course the obvious suspect on whom Darn-

---

* See Pollen, *Papal Negotiations*, p. xxviii, where Mary's involvement in a Catholic League, as a result of the meeting of the Catholic sovereigns at Bayonne in July 1565, has been shown to be a chimera of the Protestant imagination, just as any Protestant League in Europe was equally a figment of Catholic fancy.

ley could pour his rage and jealousy against his wife—if such a jealousy could be focused on the hunched figure of the little Italian. It was now the work of Mary's opponents at court to incite the foolish bombastic Darnley into such a state of frenzy that he might be persuaded to join in their own more serious enterprises. In order to do so it was necessary to present to Darnley that in the opinion of many Scottish nobles he, not Mary, would make the most suitable ruler of Scotland. This was the notion which was now 'buzzed' in Darnley's excitable brain.

The extreme cynicism of such behaviour should not be overlooked—the Scottish nobles, including Moray, were now proposing a scheme which involved the coronation of Darnley, the very man against whose elevation they had rebelled in August. Darnley was still nominally a Catholic, and since Christmas 1565, when he ostentatiously went to Mass to score a point over his wife, he had been flaunting his faith in the face of his compatriots for some reason of his own. On the Feast of the Purification, he processed through the streets of Edinburgh with lighted tapers, a notably Catholic gesture; on another occasion he asked Lords Fleming, Livingston and Lindsay whether they would be content to go to Mass with him 'which they refusing, he gave them all evil words'.[2] Bedford reported that Darnley would have liked to have shut up the noblemen in their chambers and forced them to go to Mass. Yet this Catholicism was apparently of no account to the Protestant Lords Moray, Ochiltree, Boyd and Rothes now that their persons and properties were threatened by the oncoming session of Parliament: Darnley's qualities and religion, so distasteful in July that he could not be tolerated as a royal consort, were in February apparently sufficiently worthy to make a candidate for supreme power, with the backing of the Protestant lords.

It was now plainly suggested to Darnley that his wife was Riccio's mistress, and the waning of his own power was due to the machinations of the Italian. It was not difficult to arouse the jealousy of a man of Darnley's vain temperament, and Darnley's cousin Morton seems to have done much of the trouble-making. Mary, conscious of her innocence, added fuel to the flames by openly finding pleasure in Riccio's counsels and his company. Could there have been any truth in the story? Neither Riccio's

age, height nor his ugliness would have been any certain
bar against a woman finding him desirable, since attraction
follows its own rules. It is true that Mary Stuart herself
did not appear to find men of this sort appealing—Darnley, young, elegantly beautiful and outwardly romantic
was the type she apparently admired; all we know of
her relations with Riccio, including her behaviour at his
death, seems to fit into the pattern of ruler and confidant,
rather than mistress and lover. But what really militates
against the possibility of Mary having had a love affair with
David Riccio is the timing of it. Later the reproach was
to be flung in the face of James vi that he was actually
'Davy's son'.* In January Randolph wrote dolefully to
Leicester: 'Woe is me for you, when Davy's son shall be a
King of England',³ but as this was only a few weeks before
he was asked to leave Scotland by Mary, and as ever since
her marriage to Darnley his reports on her behaviour had
been openly laced with spite, too much attention should
not be paid to the scandalous prophecy. In order for the accusation to be true the queen would have to have been
indulging in a secret love affair with Riccio throughout
that same summer in which she was so obviously infatuated
with Darnley; she would then have had to conceive a
child by Riccio less than two months after her marriage
to Darnley, when to outward observers she was still deeply
in love with her husband. It seems that the worst that Mary
can be accused of, with Riccio, as with Châtelard, is a
certain lack of prudence which was very much part of her
character, rather than some more positive indiscretion.

The character of Darnley was like a tinderbox, on which
it was all too easy for the disaffected nobles to strike a
flame, using Riccio as a flint. Early in 1566 the Order of
St Michel was brought by a French envoy M. Rambouillet
to Edinburgh, to bestow upon Darnley on behalf of the
king of France. When asked what arms should be placed
upon Darnley's shield, Mary coldly 'bade them give him his
due',⁴ as Knox's narrative has it: the fact that she did not
specify the royal arms was a further unwelcome indication that she did not intend to bestow the crown matrimonial upon Darnley in the coming Parliament. Darnley

---

* In later years King Henry iv of France (Henry of Navarre) observed that James could indeed claim to be the modern Solomon,
since he was the son of David.

retaliated with a series of debauched and roistering
parties, which caused considerable scandal in Edinburgh;
in the course of them, he made several of Rambouillet's
suite hopelessly drunk. Quite apart from the intoxication
he spread about him, Darnley's own drunkenness was
beginning to constitute a public problem. At the home of
an Edinburgh merchant, he became so wild in Mary's
presence that she tried to halt his drinking, at which he
insulted her, and she left the house in floods of tears.
Nor was his drunkenness his only weakness: he searched
for his pleasures in many different corners of human experience; on the one hand there were rumours of love affairs
with court ladies. On the other, in a letter to Cecil in
February, Sir William Drury hinted at something so vicious
which had taken place at a festivity at Inch-Keith, too dis-
graceful to be named in a letter, that Mary now slept apart
from her husband.[5]

Despite the anxiety caused by Darnley's behaviour,
Mary persisted in her plan to hold a Parliament in March
at which the Protestant lords who had rebelled would be
attained and their properties forfeited. She turned a deaf
ear to any suggestions that they should be pardoned, with
the exception of Châtelherault, who had been forgiven on
condition he went into banishment for five years. Under
these circumstances the two-pronged conspiracy to restore
these lords and give Darnley the crown matrimonial went
forward. On 9 February Maitland, who now clearly
despaired of the pardoning of Moray, and feared for his
whole Anglo-Scottish policy, wrote to Cecil that since the
rebels were not to be readmitted, there was nothing for it,
but 'to chop at the very root'.[6] This sinister phrase seemed
to hint at least at the possibility of removing Mary from
her throne—and it might of course mean something more
violent directed towards her actual life. On 13 February
Randolph sent a communication to Leicester on the whole
subject, which casts an even more lurid light on the secret
intentions of the conspirators: 'I know for certain that
this Queen repenteth her marriage, that she hateth Darnley
and all his kin,' he wrote. 'I know there are practices in
hand contrived between father and son to come by the
crown against her will. I know that if that take effect
which is intended, David, with the consent of the King
[Darnley] shall have his throat cut within these ten days.
Many things grievouser and worse than these are brought

to my ears, yea, of things intended against her own person.'[7] Let us not forget, what was surely ever-present in the minds of Lennox and Darnley, that if Mary vanished from the scene, and her unborn child never saw the light of day, Darnley had an excellent chance of becoming king of Scotland in his own right. It was a propitious moment for the Lennox Stewarts, since the head of the Hamiltons was abroad in disgrace; this might prove the ideal opportunity for them to stigmatize the Hamilton claim to the throne as illegal once and for all.

A bond was now drawn up by those conspirators active in Scotland; these included Morton, George Douglas the Postulate, his illegitimate half-brother, Ruthven and Lindsay, both married to Douglas wives. The former Protestant rebel lords who signed included Ochiltree, Boyd, Glencairn, Argyll and Rothes, as well as Moray, who signed it at Newcastle on 2 March. Maitland did not actually sign the bond, from whatever motives of caution or self-preservation, although Randolph listed his name among the conspirators. In this bond, the declared intentions were to be the acquisition of the crown matrimonial for Darnley, and the upholding of the Protestant religion, and the return of the exiles. The lords were careful to obtain Darnley's signature, in order that he should be as thoroughly implicated as themselves; but in all the clauses of the bond there was no mention of any sort of violence or of David Riccio—only Item Five had a faintly menacing ring: 'So shall they not spare life or limb in setting forward all that may bend to the advancement of his [Darnley's] honour.'[8] One aspect of the conspiracy which seemed to rob it still further of any possible content of idealism was the fact that it was known about in London beforehand. In February Randolph's known agent had been caught *flagrante* supplying money to the rebels; Mary had sent for Randolph, furiously upbraided him, and then ordered him to leave Scotland; from Berwick, however, he still remained thoroughly in touch with the seething atmosphere of Edinburgh. On 25 February he was able to write a full report of the conspiracy and its known adherents to London; Elizabeth reacted characteristically to a situation which she saw about to put Mary at a new disadvantage: on 3 March she wrote her a threatening letter, criticizing Mary's treatment of both Moray and Randolph, although one was an ambassador caught bribing rebels, and another a Scottish subject who had rebelled against his queen.[9] Elizabeth also sent £1,000 to Moray at Newcastle.

Yet Mary herself seemed to have no inkling of what was about to happen—or else she had gained sufficient self-confidence in the past year to believe that she would weather the storm. The spreading panoply of court life continued to flower on majestically, ignorant of the fact that its roots were threatened. On 24 February the marriage of Bothwell and Lady Jean Gordon, sister to Huntly, was celebrated with considerable pomp. The significance of the match was the dynastic union of two of Mary's firmest adherents. In token of her approval, Mary herself supplied the eleven ells of cloth of silver for Lady Jean's wedding-dress, although Bothwell firmly insisted on the marriage taking place according to the Protestant rite. Love does not seem to have played much part in the match: Lady Jean had a cool detached character, warmed by a masculine intelligence—'a great understanding above the capacity of her sex' as her son later put it.[10] Her long clever face with its firm nose and rather bulbous eyes lacked beauty and softness: she was hardly the type to appeal to Bothwell, judged from the standard of those women with whom he had been involved up to the present. She did, however, possess one definite attraction in her solid dowry, provided by her brother Huntly, and Lady Jean herself proved to have an excellent appreciation of the values of the property —later she managed to hold on to her lands through thick and thin despite Bothwell's attainder. The real love of her life, the man for whom she reserved affections which Bothwell never touched, seems to have been Alexander Ogilvy of Boyne: two months after Lady Jean's own marriage, he was wedded to the beautiful Mary Beaton.*

In the meantime the behaviour of Riccio, like that of Darnley, played into the hands of the conspirators. Froude has given the most sympathetic interpretation of Darnley's fatal incursion into Scottish politics—he was 'like a child who has drifted from the shore in a tiny pleasure boat, his sails puffed out with vanity . . .'.[11] But if Darnley was a

---

* It is pleasant to relate that this relationship had a happy ending rare in the annals of the time: Lady Jean and her lover were finally united in marriage over thirty years later when both Mary Beaton and Lady Jean's second husband, the earl of Sutherland, were dead.

child, Riccio was like the bullfrog in Aesop's fable, inflated
by his own arrogance. The astrologer Damiot tried to
warn him of the dangers of his situation, and told him to
'Beware of the Bastard'; Riccio assumed this referred to
Moray and replied confidently: 'I will take good care that
he never sets foot in Scotland again'—forgetting that the
description could apply to a number of other people in
sixteenth-century Scotland. Damiot talked of his unpopularity. Riccio said grandly: 'Parole, parole, nothing but
words. The Scots will boast but rarely perform their brags.'
Mary took the same line. Melville tried to warn her also of
what was going on, saying he had heard 'dark speeches',
and that there were rumours current that they should hear
some unpleasant news before Parliament was ended. Mary
replied that something of the sort had also come to her
own ears, but she had paid no attention since 'our countrymen were well-wordy'.[12]

On Thursday 7 March Parliament assembled. Mary went
personally to the Tolbooth for the election of the Lords
of the Articles, glittering in a silver head-dress. Bothwell
bore the sceptre, Huntly the crown and Crawford the
sword. Darnley pointedly did not accompany her, in token
of his displeasure at not being granted the crown matrimonial. Parliament was put under considerable pressure
by Mary to draw up a bill of attainder against Moray, and
Tuesday 12 March was fixed as the date at which the bill
was to be passed. The fixing of this date automatically induced the climax of the conspirators' plans. On the evening
of Saturday 9 March, the queen was holding a small supper party in her own apartments at the palace of Holyrood; advancing pregnancy and ill-health had made her increasingly disinclined to go about in Edinburgh, preferring
the company of her intimates at home. Those present with
her all fell into this cosy category—her half-brother Lord
Robert Stewart, her half-sister and confidante Jean, countess of Argyll, her equerry Arthur Erskine, her page Anthony Standen, and of course her secretary and musician,
David Riccio himself. Perhaps there was to be music later,
or perhaps this was to be one of those evenings, which
Darnley said he so much resented, when the queen and
Riccio played at cards until one or two in the morning.
At any rate, the atmosphere was innocuous and domestic
rather than exciting. At the time of his death, Randolph
reported that the dandyish Riccio was wearing 'a night-

gown of damask furred, with a satin doublet and a hose
of russet velvet'.[13] It used to be suggested by critics that
the fact that Riccio was in his 'night-gown' proved an unlawful degree of intimacy with the queen: but in the sixteenth century the word 'night-gown' was used in its literal
sense to denote informal evening dress, the sort that might
be expected to be worn on this sort of occasion.*

The true story of the dramatic events which interrupted
this supper party has to be pieced together from the many
differing accounts of it. Two people among those present
wrote their own eye-witness accounts of what happened,
within a few weeks of the murder: Queen Mary wrote a
letter to James Beaton, archbishop of Glasgow, her ambassador in Paris, on 2 April giving her version of the
affair, and Ruthven, one of the murderers, wrote an account of it with Bedford at the end of March for English
consumption.[14] Although both accounts must be expected
to suffer from partiality, the queen to accuse and Ruthven
to excuse, at least these letters represent fairly instan-
taneous reactions. Mary's later account of it all, to be
found in Nau's Memorials of Mary Stuart, was told by
her to her secretary when she was in captivity, long after
the death of both Riccio and Darnley; although valuable
for narrative detail, the motives it sometimes attributes
to the participants must be regarded with reserve, since
Mary's emotion, recollected in tranquillity, has by no
means decreased in fervour.† Of all other accounts it must
be remembered that the writers concerned were not present
(although Melville was in the precincts of Holyrood) and
therefore dependent on second-hand information.

One of the most important aspects of the affair is the
scene in which it was set. Mary's apartments in Holyrood
lay in the north-west corner of the palace, on the second
floor; the rooms were four in number—a large presence
chamber at the head of the main staircase, draped in black
velvet, with the arms of Mary of Guise on the ceiling, a

* Ruthven suggested that Riccio was also wearing his cap in the
presence of the queen—which does seem to denote remarkable familiarity. But it is significant that Randolph, who was at pains to
find out the most suggestive details possible, does not mention this
one. Ruthven is the only source which mentions the subject of the
cap.

† Claude Nau did not join the queen's service until 1575; his Memorials were written in 1578.

bed-chamber of considerable size lying directly off it, and off that again two very small rooms in each corner, not more than twelve foot square, one a type of dressing-room, the other a supper-room hung in crimson and green. Beneath these apartments, on the first floor of the palace, lay Darnley's rooms, which were roughly equivalent to the queen's. The two sets of apartments were connected by a narrow privy staircase which came out in the queen's bedroom, close to the entrance to the supper-chamber. The intimacy of the occasion has already been stressed. But although in one sense the supper-room was totally cut off from the outside world, except for the privy staircase, in another sense it was not a very secure place to choose to perform a murder.* The heart of Mary's apartment was indeed a curious place from which to choose to pluck one of her own servants, since there were the guards surrounding the queen's person to be taken into account. How much simpler it would have been to kill a mere servant in some other less public place. After all Riccio went normally and unguardedly about his business in Holyrood. Earlier there had been some story that George Douglas had offered to Darnley to throw him over the side of the boat while they were fishing at Castle Douglas,[15] but Darnley had jibbed at the idea; such a scheme, quick, secret and unprovable would certainly have made more sense as regards the elimination of a mere servant. The question arises why the choice of the queen's own rooms was deliberately made instead. Ruthven, in his narrative, attributed the choice of location to Darnley, who, he said, wanted to avenge the public insult to his honour by a public coup. But this time Ruthven was busy piling all the blame possible on Darnley. The king was after all a weak character, notoriously easy to sway. The fact that the murder was deliberately planned to take place in the presence of the queen when she was nearly six months

* Although Holyrood was restored and extended in the reign of Charles II, Queen Mary's apartments can still be seen in much of their original state, as they were at the time of the murder: indeed, they form the most dramatic visual link to be found today with her life story, so many of the buildings connected with her now lying in ruins. But the staircase which can now be seen connecting the king's apartments with the queen's has no connection with the six-teenth-century privy staircase. This is still in existence, but concealed behind the Charles II panelling.

pregnant points to some malevolent intentions towards her own person (as Randolph prophesied in February), as well as the elimination of a presumptuous servant.

Although it was Lent, meat was served at the queen's supper party, since her condition permitted her to ignore the fast. As the supper was being served, to the great surprise of all those present, the figure of Darnley suddenly appeared up the privy staircase; although he was by now a comparative stranger to these domestic occasions, preferring to go his own way in pursuit of pleasure in the streets of Edinburgh, he was still welcomed as the king. But a few minutes later there was a far more astonishing apparition up the staircase—Patrick Lord Ruthven, with a steel cap on, and with his armour showing through his gown, burning-eyed and pale from the illness of which he was generally thought to be dying on his sick-bed in a house close to Holyrood. So amazing was his emergence at the queen's supper party, that the first reaction of those present was that he was actually delirious, and had somehow felt himself pursued, in his fever, by the spectre of one of his victims. Ruthven—who did in fact die three months after these events took place—was a highly unsavoury character, popularly supposed to be a warlock or male witch, or at any rate in Knox's phrase to 'use enchantment'. However, his first words left the queen in no doubt as to what had brought this death's head to her feast. 'Let it please your Majesty,' said Ruthven, 'that yonder man David come forth of your privy-chamber where he hath been overlong.' Mary replied with astonishment that Riccio was there at her own royal wish, and asked Ruthven whether he had taken leave of his senses. To this Ruthven merely answered that Riccio had offended against the queen's honour. On hearing these words, the queen turned quickly and angrily to her husband, realizing the Judas-like quality of his visit. She asked him if this was his doing. Darnley gave an embarrassed reply. Ruthven, by his own account, launched into a long and rambling denunciation of Mary's relations with Riccio, reproaching her for her favour to him, and for her banishment of the Protestant lords. Riccio had been shrunk back into the large window at the end of the little room, but when Ruthven made a lunge towards him Mary's attendants, who seem to have been stunned into inaction, at last made some sort of protest. 'Lay not hands on me, for I will not be handled,' cried Ruthven, with his hand on his dagger: this was the signal for his followers, Andrew Ker of Fawdonside, Patrick Bellenden, George Douglas, Thomas Scott and Henry Yair, to rush into the room, also from the privy staircase. In the ensuing confusion the table was knocked over and Lady Argyll was just able to save the last candle from being extinguished by snatching it up as it fell (although presumably the flickering light from the large fireplace still filled the little room). While Riccio clung to the queen's skirts, Ker and Bellenden produced pistols, and others wielded daggers. Finally the fingers of the little Italian were wrenched out of the queen's skirts, and he was dragged, screaming and kicking, out of the supper-room, across the bed-room through the presence-chamber to the head of the stairs. His pathetic voice could be heard calling as he went: *'Justizia, justizia! Sauvez ma vie, madame, sauvez ma vie!'*[16]

Here he was done to death by dagger-wounds variously estimated at between fifty-three and sixty: a savage butchery for a small body. Mary was convinced later that the first blow had been struck over her shoulder: at all events, the first knife-wound was made by George Douglas the Postulate, Morton's illegitimate brother, thus fulfilling the prophecy of Damiot concerning the Bastard; he carefully used Darnley's own dagger for the bloody deed in order to involve him still further in the crime. Riccio's serrated and bleeding corpse was now flung down the winding main staircase. Here as it lay on a chest it was stripped of its belongings by a porter, who moralized as he did so in truly Shakespearian fashion: 'This was his destiny,' he soliloquized, 'for upon this chest his first bed when he came to this place, and there he lieth a very niggard and misknown knave.' By now such commotion, such screams and cries had alerted the rest of the palace. Mary's own domestics came rushing to her assistance from the outside, with their own weapons of sticks and staves, without knowing exactly what peril threatened her. At the same time, up the wider outside staircase could be heard cries of 'A Douglas, a Douglas' as the rest of the clan rushed to support the inner conspirators. Ruthven later blamed the ensuing commotion for the death of Riccio, saying that the assassins feared he would otherwise be rescued; he stated that their original intention had been to bring him before Parliament. But the excuse seems thin, in view of the violent nature of the attack. Mary herself, by her own account, originally offered in the supper-room to let Riccio appear in Parliament, if he had done wrong, yet Ruthven dismissed the notion as worthless.

For the rest of her life, Mary Stuart was to believe that her own life also had been threatened in the course of the tumult in the supper-room and that Darnley, her own husband, had intended to compass her own destruction, and that of her unborn child. It is indeed impossible to understand her later attitude to Darnley without taking into account this steadfast inner conviction on the queen's part. After the birth of James, she burst out angrily to him: 'I have forgiven, but never will forget! What if Fawdonside's pistol had shot, what would become of him and me both? Or what estate would you have been in? God only knows, but we may suspect.'[17] In her account of events, she laid great stress on the violence which had been shown to her personally. This violence she laid at the door of Darnley, believing that she and her child had been about to be sacrificed at the altar of his ambition to become king of Scotland. In her mind she obviously believed that she had only escaped this fate through her own resolution and because her will was stronger than Darnley's—a conviction backed up by the fact that she was now to escape entirely through her own courage and daring. It was only too natural for a woman six months pregnant, having undergone such a traumatic experience of a pistol pointed at her stomach, to be imbued with these feelings. Even for us, the desperate circumstances of the murder make it hard to believe that something violent if unspecific was not meditated against her—perhaps it was hoped that the shock of the murder would cause her to miscarry and die (the death of the mother was then the end of most late miscarriages).

But at the time the quality of Mary Stuart's spirit was proof even against such an appalling experience, despite her condition. Far from shrinking from the danger, she turned furiously on Darnley, now left with her in the supper-chamber, and upbraided him. Then Ruthven returned from the carnage and, sinking onto a chair, called for wine to revive him; although the queen herself was still standing she still did not lose her poise and defiance. Gazing at the wine, she enquired acidly: 'Is this your sickness, Lord Ruthven?' In the course of a three-cornered wrangle between herself, Ruthven and Darnley, in which Ruthven called in question once more her behaviour as a wife the queen refused to be cowed in any way; if one report is to be believed, she even told Ruthven that she had 'that within in her belly' which would one day be revenged upon him.*[18] In the course of the conversation, she had to deal with still further threats to her person: the disturbance at Holyrood had alerted the people of Edinburgh and the alarm bell of the city had been sounded. In order to quiet the townspeople, Darnley went to the window and spoke to them reassuringly in his familiar voice. When Mary strained to make her own voice heard, Lindsay brutally threatened to 'cut her in collops' if she made another move in the direction of the window. Finally Ruthven left and Darnley too departed. Mary sent one of her ladies for news of Riccio's fate. When she was told that he was dead, she wept for a moment; but a moment later, drying her tears, observed calmly: 'No more tears now; I will think upon revenge.'[19] She also retained her composure sufficiently to send a lady to Riccio's room to recover a black coffer, with her ciphers and writings in it.

As Ruthven informed those left in Holyrood that the former Protestant rebels were now on their way back to Edinburgh, Mary was left to spend the night alone, without any sort of medical attention or a midwife, which might have been thought necessary, and only old Lady Huntly, widow of the 4th earl, to keep her company. So far, the conspirators seemed to be in complete outward command of the situation, except for the annoying fact that of their other intended victims, Bothwell and Huntly had escaped by jumping out of the back windows of the palace, past the lion pit. It had originally been projected to slay these two and Lords Livingston and Fleming as well as Riccio, and hang Sir James Balfour as being all adherents of the queen. Now they contented themselves merely with the death of a Dominican priest, Father Adam Black. This very night, when the conspirators' triumph

* If true, it was certainly an accurate prediction. It fell to the future James vi to put to death both Ruthven's son and his grandson, the 1st earl of Gowrie in 1584, and the 2nd earl in 1600, at the time of the Gowrie conspiracy.

seemed certain, was crucial in the history of Mary Stuart.
At some point in the course of it she took the bold decision
to choke down her feelings of revulsion for Darnley and
win him over on to her side, reasoning that the character
of Darnley might now be the weakness of the conspirators'
cause, as it had once been the weakness of her own. Since
she had survived the slaughter, it will never be known
exactly what plans the lords now had for the queen. She
herself, presumably getting the news from Darnley, afterwards said in her letter—and amplified it to Nau[20]—that
they intended to hold her in prison in Stirling until she
gave birth to her child, and afterwards indefinitely, 'in
the meantime the king could manage the affairs of state
with the nobles'. Lord Lindsay was supposed to have remarked callously that she would find plenty of pastime
there at Stirling in nursing her baby and singing it to sleep,
shooting with her bow in the garden, and doing her fancy
work. Although Lord Lindsay added that he happened to
know that such things delighted her much, it was a tame
prospect for one who had been queen of Scotland all her
life, and thoroughly enjoyed the business of ruling.

Therefore when at daybreak the next morning, Sunday,
Darnley went once more to her chamber, he found his wife
calm rather than tearful, resolute rather than reproachful.
Darnley himself seems to have been comparatively hysterical as a result of Riccio's death, and the queen told Nau
that he pleaded with her with the old familiar endearments
to forgive him for what had happened: 'Ah, my Mary,' he
said (as he was wont to address her). In the meantime
old Lady Huntly showed herself a resourceful companion
of the first order, trained no doubt by the old days as the
wife of the 4th earl. She offered to smuggle a rope ladder
in between two plates and continued to suggest other
schemes for escape until Lord Lindsay, breaking abruptly
into the room (as the queen sat on her *chaise percée*),
ordered her to depart. Even so Lady Huntly managed to
take a letter to her son in her chemise (her outer clothing
was searched), ordering him to stand by at Seton the
following night. As escape by towels or ropes out of her
window was clearly out of the question, because she was
guarded above, Mary had a simpler and more intelligent
plan. At some point in the course of Sunday she won back
the facile Darnley by convincing him that his own prospects

were as bleak as hers under the new régime, and that if
he was not careful, they would both end up in ward in
Stirling Castle. It was a triumph of a stronger character
over a weaker one.

Armed with the knowledge of Darnley's new treachery,
Mary was able to greet the conspirators the next day,
Monday, with composure and even charm. She promised
pardon, and that she would overlook recent hideous events:
she even drank to the compact, although she could not
quite bring herself to drink to Ruthven. Moray, apprised
of what was about to take place, had set off from Newcastle: he arrived back in Edinburgh on the Monday, the
day before his attainder had been due to be passed by
Parliament. At this point Mary was unaware of Moray's
complicity in the plot, and memories of their old intimacy,
those early days in Scotland when the brother had seemed
the natural loving protector of the younger sister, flooded
back. Mary flung herself in his arms, crying: 'Oh my
brother, if you had been here, they had not used me thus.'
But when Moray in return chose to treat her to a sen-
tentious lecture on the virtues of clemency Mary not unnaturally fired up and pointed out tartly with reason
that 'ever since her earliest youth, her nobility and others
of her people, had given her frequently opportunities of
practising that virtue and becoming familiar with it'.[21] As
she felt her indignation overcoming her, she was compelled
to feign the pangs of labour in order to preserve secrecy
about her intentions, and she ordered the midwife to attend to her, whom the lords themselves had appointed on
Sunday. This midwife unwittingly played her part in helping Mary's escape, for some of the lords remained suspicious of Mary's true feelings, despite her promise of pardon; however, the woman, who was their nominee, assured them of her own accord that the queen was extremely
ill and in danger of her life, as a result of what she had
been through. At eight o'clock on the Monday evening
Mary carried the second stage of her plan into effect
by sending for Stewart of Traquair, the captain of the
royal guard, Erskine, her equerry, and Standen, one of
her pages; she then begged them in the name of chivalry
to assist her not only as a defenceless woman, but also
as the mother of the future king of Scotland. These gallant
gentlemen proved susceptible to her appeal, and promised

to stand by her escape, in the manner she now outlined.

At midnight the queen and Darnley made their way down the privy staircase up which the assassins had filed only fifty-two hours before. Darnley's acquiescence meant that Mary could now use the staircase as an escape route; they then made their way through the back passages and servants' quarters of Holyrood, where Mary's French servants would not betray her escape, and finally past an outside cemetery, close to the abbey of Holyrood. Here, by Mary's account, Darnley gave an involuntary sigh at the sight of a newly dug grave, and confessed to his wife that she was practically treading on the burial ground of the wretched Riccio*—'In him I have lost a good and faithful servant,' said Darnley, 'I have been miserably cheated.' These gloomy reflections were checked by the need for silence. Outside the abbey to meet the royal couple were Erskine, Traquair, Standen and two or three loyal soldiers with horses. Mary mounted pillion behind Erskine. Darnley took a horse of his own. In a short while, under the friendly cover of darkness, they were clear of the town.

The plan was to go to Dunbar Castle, pausing at Seton to pick up the nobles who had been alerted via Lady Huntly. The ride was of necessity fast, and as furious as possible. Even so, Darnley, in a panic of fear at being hunted down by the men he had so recently betrayed, kept spurring his own horse and flogging that of the queen, shouting: 'Come on! Come on! By God's blood, they will murder both you and me if they can catch us.' Mary pleaded with him to have regard to her condition, at which Darnley only flew into a rage and exclaimed brutally that if this baby died, they could have more.[23] By the time they reached Dunbar Castle, on the coast, twenty-five miles from Edinburgh as the crow flies, the long night was almost over. For a woman in an advanced state of pregnancy, a five-hour marathon of this nature must have been a gruelling ordeal. Even now, the queen's formidable courage

---

* It seems inconceivable that Mary should then have told Darnley bluntly that he himself would go the same way before a year was out—as Lennox announced in his own narrative,[22] written after Darnley's death. Even if Mary nourished the thought, she would scarcely have chosen such a dangerous moment to give it expression, when she was still within the bounds of Holyrood, and still dependent on the goodwill of Darnley.

did not desert her: she is said to have sent for eggs to cook breakfast. Here at Dunbar* Mary set herself about the task of consolidating the advantage which her liberty had given her.

On 15 March she dictated a long and passionate description of her experience, to be sent to Queen Elizabeth in London. She described the butchery of her secretary before her very eyes. 'Some of our subjects and council by their proceedings have declared manifestly what they are . . . slain our most special servant in our own presence and thereafter held our proper person captive treasonably. . . .'[24] She appealed to Elizabeth to beware of similar betrayals, which might lead to similar horrifying ordeals. She ended with the note that she had intended to write the letter in her own hand, to make it all seem more immediate, but 'of truth we are so tired and evil at ease, what through riding of 20 miles in five hours of the night, as with the frequent sickness and evil disposition by the occasion of our child' that the task had proved beyond her. Nevertheless, whatever physical reaction the queen was suffering after the event, she appeared to be once more triumphing over her enemies, as decisively as she had done in the previous August—and once more as a result of her own boldness and promptitude. The escape of Bothwell and Huntly proved decisive. Atholl, Fleming and Seton also came to her at Dunbar. Men began to flock to the queen's side at Dunbar, stirred up by these loyal agents. Soon there were 4,000 men at her command. On 17 March Mary issued a proclamation from Dunbar calling for the inhabitants of the surrounding districts to meet her at Haddington next day with eight days' provisions. On 18 March she was able to re-enter Edinburgh victoriously at the head of 8,000 men, only nine days after the murder which had caused her to flee from the city so precipitately.

Darnley rode beside her, like a sulky page. At the news of his defection, his fellow-plotters had fled from Edinburgh on the morning of 17 March realizing that their re-

---

*It was at this moment in history that the important wardship of Dunbar Castle was transferred from the laird of Craigmillar to the earl of Bothwell, to punish the one, and to reward the other for their respective roles in the Riccio affair—this transfer led to the dramatic part played by Dunbar Castle in Mary's abduction by Bothwell in the following year.

bellion no longer had any focal point. Morton, Lindsay, Ker of Fawdonside and Ruthven went to England; Maitland, who had certainly known of the plot, although he had not wielded a dagger, went to Dunkeld; John Knox, who may not have known in advance what was proposed, but certainly applauded Riccio's killing as a goodly deed, went to Ayrshire. Moray alone remained in Edinburgh since he had cunningly arrived in the city too late to be implicated in the bloody events of the night of 9 March, and the fact that he had signed the pre-murder bond was of course unknown to the queen. Mary was also reconciled to Glencairn and Argyll. In any case, in her new grim determination to avenge the butchery of Riccio and pursue his killers to the utmost limits of her power, Mary was now prepared to forgive the previous rebels of the Chase-about Raid. Time's revolutions—and the treachery of Darnley—had combined to effect the pardon of Moray, which Mary had once strenuously refused to grant, despite the pleadings of her own nobles, and the admonitions of the queen of England.

15 Breakdown

'He misuses himself so far towards her that it is an heart-
break for her to think that he should be her husband.'

MAITLAND: *On the relations between Mary and Darnley,*
October 1566

It was easy enough, once Mary was back in Edinburgh,
to rescue the body of Riccio from its common grave, and
have it reburied according to the Catholic rite he had professed, in her own chapel royal.* Ten days later Riccio's
brother, Joseph, a boy of eighteen, was made French
secretary in his place. Mary, being anxious not to rule
over a torn kingdom on the eve of the birth of her child,
also took the trouble to reconcile Moray, Glencairn, and
Argyll, recently allowed back into her favour, with Huntly,
Bothwell and Atholl; together these two groups were now
to make up the effective body of the Privy Council. Mary's
vengeance was thus officially reserved for the brutal
murderers of her servant who had actually burst into her
apartments—Morton, Ruthven, Lindsay and their minions.
But as they were now safely escaped to England, the only
two lives which were actually forfeited for the crime
were those of two of Ruthven's retainers—Tom Scott,
under-sheriff of Perth, whose official position made his
crime of 'warding the Queen within Holyrood' especially
reprehensible, and Henry Yair who had killed the Dominican priest Father Black shortly after the murder of the
Italian, and was executed the following August. Two other
underlings, Mowbray and Harlaw, were released at the
scaffold when the queen, characteristically moved by
mercy, 'gave them their lives'.[1] Yet the murder of the
Italian had marked a turning-point in the affairs of Mary
Queen of Scots, and the memories of the affair were

---

* Not, as Buchanan suggested, in the royal vault with Mary's father; this lie was finally nailed in the seventeenth century when the
king's tomb was opened.

not so easily laid in peace and forgotten, as his poor lacerated corpse.

The most obvious result of the affair was Mary's abiding hatred of Darnley. She had either concealed this in order to escape from Holyrood or else she did not at this point realize the full extent of her husband's complicity. Although she told Nau that Darnley had admitted to her on the Sunday that he had signed a bond to procure the crown matrimonial, and Leslie repeats the story, she did not mention the fact in her letter to Beaton of 2 April.[2] Whether Mary knew beforehand or not, the conspirators now took the understandable if vindictive step of sending the bond to the queen, so that she should see for herself the full extent of her husband's treachery. Yet once more Mary was obliged to put a good face upon the situation for the time being, and issue a public statement of his innocence at the market cross. It was not within the compass of her thoughts to take any action against her husband before the birth of her child, since Darnley was quite capable of casting doubts upon the child's legitimacy, if it suited his purpose. Although there were already rumours of a divorce between the two by the end of April —Randolph said Thornton had gone to Rome to treat about it—Mary, like all the Scots, had heard far too many arguments over the legitimacy of heirs, as the result of the subsequent divorces of their parents, to risk considering the subject before her child was actually born. In May there was another rumour from Randolph that Darnley would leave Scotland after the birth of the baby, and go to Flanders. He described Darnley's new situation thus: 'He is neither accompanied for, nor looked for by any nobleman, attended by certain of his own servants, and 6 or 8 of his guard, he is at liberty to do or go what or where he will.'[2] In his reflective moments Darnley must have realized that this aimless freedom might in fact be the deceptive liberty of the marked man. Of the powers that then existed in Scotland—the queen, Moray and his associates, Bothwell and the loyalist nobles, he had betrayed them all or tried to attack them at one or other point in his career. Should these potential enemies flag, there was also a whole new ferocious band of them headed by Morton, now in England, who might not stay there forever.

Mary's relations with Darnley settled down into an uneasy truce until the birth of her child. Darnley had not reformed his behaviour: during her confinement he 'vagabondised every night'.[3] In these circumstances it was natural that Mary should come to rely increasingly for political advice on those nobles who had proved themselves loyal to her throughout the two crises which she had faced in the past year.* Into this category fell notably James Hepburn, earl of Bothwell, who as he leapt clear of the lion-pit at Holyrood, and rode off to summon Mary's subjects successfully to her assistance, seemed to display that combination of resource, loyalty and strength which Mary had so persistently sought among her Scottish nobles. Now that he was reconciled with Moray, and firmly allied by marriage to Huntly, he seemed set in Mary's estimation to form a useful loyal member of the Scottish polity. Yet Bothwell in his character seemed to sum up those very paradoxical contrasts which made it so difficult for anyone not brought up among them to understand the nature and behaviour of the Scottish nobles. For whereas Darnley by reason of his English royal blood and English upbringing was atypical of the Scottish nobility, Bothwell shared the turbulent contentious characteristics of his class—and it was this class whose motives and actions Queen Mary was never able to predict successfully. In the past she had been baffled and angered by Huntly, puzzled and hurt by Moray, appalled and shocked by Morton. Now she was once again, by the unwitting fault of her French upbringing, to make a mistake of judgement, and see in Bothwell the mirage—it was no more than that—of a strong wise protector, able to solve her problems by holding down the other nobles under his heel.

Bothwell was not a stupid man; he had been well educated by his kinsman the bishop of Moray, as his letters and writings show, and his books included volumes on both mathematics and the arts of war. He was well traveled: in Denmark he had picked up a Norwegian mistress, Anna

---

* Mary's well-known memoir in which she expressed a preference for the services of a loyal 'man of low estate' to those of the nobility, is attributed by Prince Labanoff to the period directly after Riccio's death. But as it is in Nau's handwriting, it seems more likely that Mary dictated it to her secretary later during her captivity.[4]

Throndsen, whom he had seduced under promise of marriage; and it was seeking funds to support himself on this occasion that he had first met Queen Mary at the French court. He had made several expeditions to France, and spoke French himself. He was adventurous by nature, and his life (he was at this date about thirty) had already been full of ups and downs; apart from his imprisonment in Edinburgh Castle he had done a spell in the Tower of London in 1564 while trying to escape to France. When Mary sent for him at the time of the Chaseabout Raid, he arrived in a fishing boat from Flushing, eluding capture by the English. He came of the great border family of Hepburns, and in feudal terms his power stretched across the south-east of Scotland, with certain specifically family dominions, and the wards-ship of other royal castles (such as Hermitage and Dunbar) dependent on royal favour. Bothwell, like all his class, was keenly interested in the acquisition of such royal castles for the family interest, and official positions such as lieutenant of the borders had the natural corollary for him of the extension of his family's power. His family, and indeed he himself, suffered from the proverbial pennilessness of the contemporary nobles, and his marriage contract to Jean Gordon shows that he was heavily in debt at the time. In the past there had been something amounting to a family tradition for the Hepburns to attempt to improve their fortunes by favour of widowed queens. Bothwell's own father, Patrick, the Fair Earl, had courted Mary of Guise throughout the winter of 1543* in a ludicrous competition for her affections with Lennox (by a curious coincidence, to be Mary Stuart's father-in-law) in which fine clothes played an important part. An earlier Patrick Hepburn had been linked with the widow of James I, and an Adam Hepburn with

---

* There is, however, no evidence that their relations were consummated, and still less reason to suppose that Earl Patrick had a liaison with Mary of Guise early in 1542; yet the scandalous rumour that Bothwell was 'near sib' to Mary Queen of Scots, could, as Professor Donaldson points out,[5] only be explained if Earl Patrick had been her natural father, making Bothwell her half-brother. In the absence of any other support for the theory, the rumour must surely be dismissed along with the many other scandalous rumours concerning the parentage of famous persons which abounded during this period.

Mary of Guelders. After the battle of Pinkie Cleugh Bothwell's father even negotiated with the English to marry an English princess in return for handing over the castle of Hermitage. In their marriage projects the Hepburns had tried without success to become the Habsburgs of Scotland.

Yet the effect of Bothwell's concentration on the possibilities of the main chance was in fact to give him a far better record of loyalty to the central government—in the shape of Mary of Guise and her daughter—than most of his contemporaries. In the same way his religious attitudes showed a real degree of consistency. He refused to marry Jean Gordon according to the Catholic rite, despite Queen Mary's pressure, and was described by Randolph as being one of those very strong against the Mass.[6] His critics retaliated by accusing him of being interested in the black arts which he was thought to have acquired during his education in France. La Mothe Fénelon told Charles IX that Bothwell had principally used his time at the schools in Paris to read and study sorcery and magic. At any rate his ambition was certainly boundless: as the memoirs of Lord Herries put it, he was a man 'high in his own conceit, proud, vicious and vainglorious above measure, one who would attempt anything out of ambition'.[7] But his brain and methods were the reverse of Machiavellian, and to consider his political acumen in the same category as that of Cecil, in the sense that he now became the adviser on whom Mary relied, as Elizabeth relied on her secretary, is to demonstrate how very retarded sixteenth-century Scotland was, in political terms, compared to sixteenth-century England.

It was significant that at two crucial moments in his career—in November 1560 serving Mary of Guise against the insurgents under Châtelherault, and in June 1567 before Carberry Hill—Bothwell issued a challenge for personal combat with his enemies; as a feudal baron, and primarily a soldier, he was apt to choose the quick, if bloody, solution to any problem. It was true that during his brief spell as the queen's husband Bothwell showed signs of a certain administrative ability, as a soldier can sometimes make a successful politician in a crisis; in the same way the coarse-grained Morton made not a bad showing as regent from the administrative point of view. But Bothwell's personal qualities negated his usefulness in any delicate situation, and made him the last person to unite successfully that essentially disunited and suspicious body, the Scottish nobility. For one thing, Bothwell's violence and his boastfulness (when Throckmorton called him a 'glorious, rash and hazardous young man' he was of course using the word glorious in the derogatory sense of vainglorious) scarcely led to popularity. Violence in matters of policy was accompanied by a streak of roughness, verging on bullying in private life. His servant Paris testified that he had kicked him in the stomach when Paris tried to argue with him.[8] He was certainly not a man who was prepared to try using charm to gain his objectives: as Mary told Nau, 'he was a man whose natural disposition made him anything but agreeable or inclined to put himself to much trouble or inconvenience to gain the goodwill of those with whom he had been associated'.[9]

Bothwell's relations with women fell into the same adventurous but straightforward pattern as his career. Although interested in women, he drew a sharp and effective distinction between sex and marriage: Anna Throndsen never did secure the marriage contract she desired and departed disconsolately to her home some time in 1563. His name was also linked with that of the legendary Janet Beaton, aunt of the queen's Marie, made famous as Sir Walter Scott's Wizard Lady of Branxholm, who could bond to her bidding 'the viewless forms of air': this remarkable lady enjoyed five husbands—the last at the age of sixty-one—and a number of lovers in the course of a long and full life. When she became Bothwell's mistress, he was twenty-four and she many years older, her unfading beauty generally attributed to the practice of magic, a subject she may have had in common with her lover. Despite the difference in their ages, they may have gone through some sort of ceremony of 'hand-fasting', Bothwell being fascinated by her combination of audacity, determination and sexuality. But it was finally Jean Gordon, the comparatively rich sister of the powerful Huntly, whom Bothwell actually married, the marriage contract making it clear that it was the bride who was making the settlement on the groom rather than the other way round. Bothwell evidently regarded lust as a simple sensation to be quickly gratified. The deposition of Thomas Craigwallis at the time of his divorce gave an evocative

picture of his relations with his mistress, pretty little black-
eyed Bessie Crawford, the blacksmith's daughter—a fifteen-
minute rendezvous in the steeple of the abbey at Haddington, and another tryst in a mid-chamber of the kitchen
tower at Crichton (Thomas remaining at the door); a subsequent encounter took place 'in a chamber within the
cloister' according to Pareis Sempill's evidence 'and when
my lord came forth his clothes were loose, and Patrick
Wilson helped him up therewith'.[10] Marriage on the other
hand was a more serious business to be undertaken for the
positive motive of gain.

In appearance Bothwell lacked the hermaphrodite beauty
of a Darnley; he was only of middle stature, compared to
Darnley's slender height—his mummified corpse at Dragsholm measures five feet six inches. Although those who
had reason to deplore his influence over Mary Stuart, like
Brantôme and Buchanan, rather childishly described him
as having been hideously ugly—'like an ape in purple'
said Buchanan—another of Mary's partisans, Leslie, said
that he was of great bodily strength and beauty, although
vicious and dissolute in his habits.[11] The only known
portrait traditionally said to be of him—a miniature now
in the Scottish National Portrait Gallery—shows a face
which is certainly not conventionally handsome; there is
even something simian here to confirm Buchanan's insults;
the complexion is swarthy, the nose appears to have been
broken, the ears large and slightly protruding, the lips
under their carefully trained mustache with its curling
ends are full and sensual, the eyes look suspiciously out
of the picture like those of a watchful animal. It is the
face of a man who might well prove attractive to certain
types of women, because it is strong and vital, yet from
another point of view it gives the impression of one to
whom the defence of the rights of the weak would seem
a thorough waste of time.

At the beginning of June Mary began to make detailed
preparations for the birth of her child: at the wish of her
Council, she had been lodged in Edinburgh Castle since
early April, since the great castle frowning on its rock over
the town below was evidently felt to be a safer locality for
this important event than Holyrood, so recently demonstrated to have the flimsiest defences; it would also be
understandable if Mary herself had been reluctant to give

birth to her child in the same apartments where her servant
had been butchered. In view of the hazards of the time
towards any mother and child in the process of labour, let
alone one who had been through the Scottish queen's experiences in March, it was particularly important that
Mary should make a will. This testament, of which she
made three copies, one to keep, one for those who were
to execute it in Scotland, and one to send to France,
provides an interesting commentary on her state of mind
on the eve of this critical occasion.[12] The lords also signed
a document binding themselves to adhere to the queen's
testament, in view of the fact that she was (through imminent childbirth) 'in peril and danger of her life': in
this semi-governmental measure, which was presumably
directed against Darnley, it is significant that Bothwell's
signature was now high up and prominent among the other
loyal lords.[13]

Mary's first thought is for her child, to whom, if it survives her own death, everything is to be left without further
distinctions. But in the event of their joint death, she lays
down minute provisions for the disposal of her jewels,
in which her foremost concern is the establishment of a
rich inheritance for the Scottish crown itself: her choicest
gems, including the Great Harry, are to be annexed to
the Scottish crown in perpetuity by Act of Parliament, in
remembrance of herself, and the Scottish alliance with
the house of Lorraine. Darnley is included in the will, as
befits the queen's husband, and is left twenty-six bequests,
among them a diamond ring enamelled in red of which
the queen notes in her hand-writing 'It was with this that
I was married; I leave it to the King who gave it to me';
although Buchanan later stated quite erroneously that
Darnley had been totally ignored in the will, not only does
Mary acknowledge the conventional claim of her husband
to be remembered but she also leaves minor bequests to
both Lord and Lady Lennox, as her father- and mother-
in-law.

However, it is to her French relations, who seem to
have possessed her true heart, that her most affectionate
and detailed bequests are made: she still feels herself
sufficiently a member of the house of Guise to outline a
gift of rubies and pearls, to be handed down from generation to generation as the legacy of its first-born. The family

of Duke Francis and Duchess Anne, whom she had known
so well as little children, and who had grown to adolescence
since her departure, are left rich jewels, the most precious
going to the youngest son, Francis, namesake and godson
of Mary's first husband;* Duchess Anne, Mary's beloved
aunt and correspondent, herself receives splendid jewels
and another aunt, the Abbess Renée, for whom the queen
seems to have felt a daughter's affection after her mother's
death, receives a number of bequests including a portrait
of Queen Elizabeth in the frame of a mirror. Other Guise
children, those of the Elboeuf and Aumale families, all now
growing up, are remembered with Mary's own namesake
and god-daughter, young Mary of Elboeuf, receiving again
a specially large share. To the cardinal of Lorraine goes
an emerald ring.

In Scotland, it is her illegitimate Stewart relations whom
Mary treats as her own family; not only her confidante and
half-sister, Jean Argyll, but also Moray, his wife Agnes
and their daughter are mentioned; Mary's godson Francis,
son of her half-brother Lord John Stewart and Bothwell's
sister, is given special consideration. One of Mary's
charming traits was a fondness for young children as this
will shows. The queen seems always to show a particular
affection for this boy, reminiscent of her later fondness
of Arbella Stuart; owing to the early death of his father,
he became her ward as well as her nephew and godson;
she heaped him with honours and lands until in captivity
she could do no more.† Other legatees included the two
Lady Huntlys, young and old (young Lady Huntly being
the only Hamilton to be mentioned in the will), and Privy
Councillors then in favour including Argyll, Atholl, Huntly
himself and of course Bothwell. Otherwise Mary's innate
concern seems to have been for her servants—not only
the four Maries, but also an endless string of other ladies-
in-waiting, maids-of-honour, women of the bed-chamber,

---

* It is interesting to note that the name Francis was introduced
into Scotland by the godchildren and namesakes of Queen Mary's
first husband.

† This child whom Queen Mary befriended was to become the
notorious Francis Stewart, earl of Bothwell, of the reign of James VI;
being Bothwell's nephew through his mother Janet Hepburn, he was
given his uncle's title in 1581 by James VI.

and equerries are remembered, including the faithful Arthur Erskine, behind whom she had ridden to Dunbar, Riccio's brother Joseph, to receive a ring to be delivered to a secret destination (perhaps some relation or dependent of David Riccio, of whose existence Mary knew), and Mary's favourite bed-chamber woman Margaret Carwood, who had entered her service in 1564. Like all servants at court, Mary's attendants tended to form a tight little circle who were both related to each other and who married each other—as Erskine had recently married Magdalene Livingston, a royal maid-of-honour who was also the sister of the grander 'Marie', Mary Livingston. Their intimate little world of service is here commemorated in the queen's will.

According to the custom of the time, the queen took to her lying-in chamber ceremoniously on 3 June to await the confinement. Already in May the midwife Margaret Asteane had been provided with a special black velvet dress for the coming occasion; an enormous and sumptuous bed hung in blue taffeta and blue velvet had been prepared for Mary's use, and as much as ten ells of Holland cloth commissioned to cover the baby's cradle.[14] The apartments Mary now inhabited in Edinburgh Castle were in the south-east corner, within the old palace, and thus over-looked the town; the actual room in which the birth took place was extremely small, like so many of the important rooms of this period, and lay off the chamber now known as Queen Mary's room. On 15 June a false alarm about the birth gave rise to premature rejoicings; but it was not until four days later that the labour actually began. This was long, painful and difficult, and the queen was 'so handled that she began to wish that she had never been married'. This was despite the efforts of Mary Fleming's sister Margaret, countess of Atholl, to cast the pangs of childbirth upon Margaret, Lady Reres, by witchcraft; Lady Reres lay in bed, suffering likewise with her mistress, but Mary's pangs do not appear to have been solaced in consequence. The baby prince was finally born between ten and eleven on the morning of Wednesday 19 June, with a thin, fine caul stretched over his face. Despite this hazard, and despite the length of the labour, he was an impressively healthy child, as Killigrew, the English ambassador noticed five days later when he was shown the naked infant. Killigrew first saw the baby sucking at the breast of his wet-nurse—Lady Reres, who was perhaps given the

post as a consolation for her earlier ordeal—and the baby
James was later unwrapped for his inspection, much as
Mary herself had been displayed in infancy to Sir Ralph
Sadler. Although Mary could only manage to speak to him
faintly with a hollow cough, Killigrew concluded that her
child was likely to prove 'a goodly prince'.*[15]

The birth of a male heir was signalled with immense rejoicings in Edinburgh, and now five hundred bonfires were
lit, to illuminate the city and the surrounding hills with their
festive fire. The whole artillery of the castle was discharged, and lords, nobles and people gathered together in
St Giles church, to thank God for the honour of having
an heir to their kingdom, the fact that St Giles was the
main Protestant church demonstrating the great legacy of
goodwill which awaited any queen who gave birth to a
healthy prince in this era. Sir James Melville, given the
good news by Mary Beaton, rode off to London an hour
later to break it to Queen Elizabeth. The English queen
reacted with her famous outcry, the primitive complaint of
the childless woman for a more favoured sister: 'Alack,
the Queen of Scots is lighter of a bonny son, and I am
but of barren stock.'[18] It was true that the birth of James
duly enhanced Mary's merits as a candidate for the English throne. A strange little incident about the time of
Mary's accouchement involved an English spy, Rokeby, who
was supposed to have lured Mary in Edinburgh into un-

* This is the appropriate moment to dispose of, briefly, the imaginative notion that Mary's child died at birth, and another Erskine
baby, child of the countess of Mar, was substituted. This tale is
backed by no contemporary reference, and the present (13th) earl
of Mar and Kellie has told the author that he can find nothing in
his extensive family archives to support the theory of an Erskine
family tradition. The story has arisen apparently as a result to two
events—firstly, in 1830 a skeleton, rumoured to be that of a child,
was found in the wall of a chamber in Edinburgh Castle by some
workmen; the bones were wrapped in a woollen cloth (not cloth of
gold with a royal cipher or a *fleur-de-lys* on it, as is sometimes
stated); secondly, at the end of the last century, it was noticed that
James vi, in the portraits of his maturity, bore an undoubted resemblance to the 2nd earl of Mar, who would, if the story were true,
have been his full brother.[16]

These two slender threads have been woven into a tissue of fantasy, by which it is suggested that Mary arranged the substitution
after the death of her own child, in order to prevent Darnley seizing
the throne. It ignores the fact that Mary was a young woman, able

wise pronouncements concerning her future on the English
throne—although even Rokeby admitted in his report to
Cecil that Mary 'would be content that she would have it
after. . . .' Others were not so discreet as to wait for
'after'. In a poem of thanksgiving for James's birth,
Patrick Adamson in Paris even went so far as to refer
to him as 'Serenissimus princeps' of Scotland, England,
France and Ireland, a gesture which not only infuriated
Elizabeth in London, who ordered her envoy Bedford
to make a protest about it at James's christening, but also
produced angry outbursts in the English House of Commons; Adamson finally underwent six months' imprisonment for his indiscretion.[19] The birth of a son, however,
strengthened Mary's hand over the English succession for
the future in a way which was obvious, and which even
the English Commons could not obliterate by intemperate
speeches.

The birth of an heir also inevitably moved the child's
own father, Darnley, further down the line of succession
for both English and Scottish thrones. Queen Mary, aware
of the temperament with which she was dealing, took
care to display the baby to him publicly and announce:
'My Lord, God has given you and me a son, begotten by
none but you.' She went on, uncovering the child's face:
'Here I protest to God as I shall answer to him at the
great day of Judgement, that this is your son and no other

---

to have more children, quite apart from the difficulties of arranging
such a substitution within the confines of Edinburgh Castle, filled
with nobles of conflicting loyalties, including the Archbishop Hamilton, who would scarcely have stood by while the claims of his own
house were set aside. Nor can any special importance be attached to
the fact that Lord Mar was shortly afterwards made the governor
of Prince James, since this office was, as has been seen, hereditary
in the Erskine family. This leaves the question of the resemblance
of James and the 2nd Lord Mar, on which two points should be
noted: firstly, the interrelation of the great Scottish families which
was such a feature of this period, meant that such a resemblance
could emerge quite naturally, as such resemblances do not always
descend directly from father to son—the grandmother of the 1st Lord
Mar had in fact been a Lennox Stewart. Secondly, the portrait of
James VI as a child by Honthorst is so strikingly like that of his legal
father Darnley as a young man by Eworth, as to make further arguments on the subject surely unnecessary. In short, the little skeleton
in the wall—if child it truly was, and this point was never officially
stated at the time of the discovery[17]—is far more likely to be the
sad relic of a lady-in-waiting's peccadillo, than a queen's conspiracy.

man's son. I am desirous that all here, with ladies and others bear witness.' She added, as though to clinch the matter by a note of contempt for her husband: 'For he is so much your own son, that I fear it will be the worse for him hereafter.'[20] Having thus, as she hoped, preserved her child from the stigma of illegitimacy, Mary devoted the rest of her time in Edinburgh Castle to his care, having the baby to sleep in her own room, and frequently watching over him at night. A few days after the birth, she sent for Anthony Standen, the faithful equerry who had helped her escape from Holyrood, and had him knighted by Darnley. Pointing to the child in its cradle, she announced in words which showed how far Mary was from forgetting the events after the murder of Riccio: 'For that you saved his life. . . .'[21]

The birth of James had two dramatic effects upon Mary Stuart: she no longer had any pressing motive for demonstrating a public reconciliation with Darnley, and at the same time her own extremely precarious health had its balance finally destroyed. There is no evidence that she ever really recovered it before her extremely serious illness at Jedburgh four months later, and this illness in turn led to a prolonged phase of highly nervous almost hysterical ill-health which lasted right until her incarceration on Lochleven the following June. But for her actions and movements during the next eight months, the critical period from the birth of James in June 1566 until the death of Darnley in February 1567, it is extremely important to distinguish between information and reports written at the time—that is to say before the death had taken place—such as ambassadors' comparatively impartial reports on the state of Scotland, and Mary's own letters posted to France, which could not be altered by *arrière pensée,* and those accounts written long after the event, specifically to prove Mary's guilt with Bothwell. These later accounts include the *Book of the Articles* written by Buchanan as an accusatory brief at the time of her trial in England, two years later, and Buchanan's own *History,* and his *Detection of Mary Queen of Scots.* The point of Buchanan—who was bound by allegiance to Lennox, and therefore to Darnley—is to prove as salaciously as possible that Mary had enjoyed an adulterous liaison with Bothwell from the birth of her child, and even possibly

before. But in the course of making his charges, Buchanan
allowed himself the luxury of so many glaring inaccuracies
that it is difficult to take his opinion on any aspect of the
situation seriously—of these the comment on the queen's
will is only a minor example: the tale of Bothwell hauled
up by a rope unwilling and half-naked out of one mistress's
bed directly into that of the queen by James's wet-nurse
is probably the most ludicrous.[22]

It is a remarkable fact that there is no uncontested
evidence among the letters or reports written *before* Darnley's death, whether French, English or Scottish, to show
that Mary was involved in a sexual affair with Bothwell
while her husband was still alive. There are on the other
hand a number of pointers to the fact that she was not.
The picture of the Scottish court through the autumn and
winter of 1566, built by contemporary comments, is of a
queen to whom her husband was becoming an increasingly
distasteful problem, and a nobility to whom he was becoming an increasingly urgent one. Not one observer made
any attempt during this period to connect the queen's
growing scorn for Darnley with her growing affection for
Bothwell, although the point would have been one which
the ever-watchful ambassadors would have been delighted
to make if they had felt it to be true. Of the couple, Mary
and Bothwell, Mary was wracked in health, not in itself
very conducive to romance, and desperate to solve her
marital problems; she was also well aware by now that
she had created these problems for herself originally
through her physical infatuation for Darnley; the very last
intention in her mind was to tread so soon again down the
treacherous paths of passion. Bothwell on the other hand
was steadily bent on his own personal advancement in
Scottish government affairs. It is questionable whether the
one had the energy, and the second the inclination for the
time-wasting business of an adulterous love affair when
there were so many important matters to hand.

Before the end of July, Mary left Edinburgh for New-
haven, to see if a change of air would restore her lost
health, and from there went on by sea to Alloa, the seat
of Lord Mar. She particularly enjoyed the pleasure of sea
travel—as Buchanan put it, she 'joyed to handle the
boisterous cables', but on this occasion she made the journey alone, unaccompanied by either Bothwell or Darnley.

Darnley, having not been informed of her departure, later followed Mary to Alloa but stayed there only a few hours, as Bedford duly reported back to England. In the same letter Bedford also noted that Bothwell's arrogance was making him so unpopular with his fellow-nobles that he believed that there might be some plot in hand against him. A few days later Bedford reported again that Bothwell was now as much hated as Riccio had ever been, and also that the queen was not getting on well with her husband.[23] It was significant that Bedford made no attempt to connect the two facts: on the contrary, by mid-August it was Moray's influence over his half-sister which was said to be causing Darnley to sulk: Bedford wrote that his jealousy was such that 'he could not bear that the Queen should use familiarity with men or women, and especially the ladies of Argyll, Moray and Mar, who keep most company with her'.[24] Mary now went hunting in the extreme south of Peeblesshire, with Bothwell, Moray and Mar, but without Darnley.

Reunited in each other's company at the house of Traquair, home of John Stewart of Traquair, captain of the queen's guard, the royal couple apparently gave way to their most open and shocking disagreement. Romantic Traquair, said to be the oldest inhabited house in Scotland, guarding and guarded by the Tweed, lies amid rich park lands ideal for hunting. A stag hunt was planned for the next day, in which both Mary and Darnley were expected to take part. But at supper, the queen begged to excuse herself on the grounds that the exertion would be too much for her health. When Darnley refused to listen, she whispered in his ear that she suspected she was again *enceinte*. Darnley answered aloud, in roughly the same words he had used before during the ride to Dunbar: 'Never mind, if we lose this one, we will make another,' at which Traquair rebuked him sharply for his un-Christian behaviour. Darnley (who was probably drunk) then exclaimed coarsely: 'What! ought not we to work a mare well when she is in foal?' The anecdote comes from Nau,[25] and in relating it to him the queen may perhaps have allowed time to have overcoloured Darnley's brutality. But the possibility that Mary could have been *enceinte* once more—it was now two months since the birth of Prince James—is an interesting one in view of Buchanan's accusations that Mary never again admitted Darnley to her bed after the child's birth. A ballad written in 1568 after Mary had fled to England, called *The Earl of Bothwell,* represented her as vowing after the murder of Riccio

. . . for a twelve month and a day
The king and she would not come in one sheet

In view of Mary's conviction that Darnley had aimed at her death and that of her child, her refusal to grant him his conjugal rights would be easy to understand: but of course it could scarcely be expected to lead to happier relations between them. It is noticeable that his humiliation as a husband was one of Darnley's main points of complaint on the occasions when he voiced his grievances. Taking into account Mary's ill-health, the most likely state of affairs between them during July and August would seem to be an occasional reluctant acquiescence on the part of the queen to her husband's embraces, which did little to convince Darnley that she either loved or respected him. After Mary's illness, and especially once the matter of a divorce had been broached at Craigmillar, her abstinence from any physical relationship was certainly total: by then she clearly wished to have nothing more to do with him as a husband, and would therefore hardly have run the risk of another pregnancy.

On her return from Traquair to Edinburgh, the queen arranged for the transference of the little prince to Stirling Castle, the traditional nursery of royal princes. His cortège accordingly set off with four or five hundred harquebussiers round it for protection, and the prince was handed into the care of the Erskine family as his hereditary governors. In delegating the upbringing of her child in this manner, Mary Stuart was in no way deviating from normal practice, and certainly not showing herself a cold or unfeeling mother. Fosterage was on the contrary the standard custom of the Scottish noble families, who handed over their children in babyhood, and the custom of fosterage, being regarded as a mark of aristocracy, gradually came to be copied lower down the social scale. Mary, in her anxious watching over James's cradle, and her immense solicitude for the grandeur of his christening ceremony, which it was within her power to arrange, showed an almost pathetically strong maternal anxiety, borne out by her

touching fondness for all other small children with whom
she came in contact throughout her life. The preparations
for his first nursery at Stirling were both detailed and
sumptuous, done to the queen's personal command: there
were to be buckets of gold and silver 'the finest that can
be gottin', lengths of blue plaiding for the baby's cradle,
fustian for his mattress, feathers for his bolster; his room
was to be hung with tapestries, as well as adequately provided with blankets. The needs of Lady Reres in her
capacity of wet-nurse were not overlooked: she too was to
have plaiding to cover her bed and a canopy to go over
it. The instructions were to be carried out without any
delay, because it was all 'very needful to be had'.[26]

In September, Maitland, long out of favour with the
queen, was reconciled to her, and returned to court; he
was also reconciled with Bothwell. At the end of September there was a confrontation between Mary and Darnley
in front of the French ambassador and many of the nobles, in which both stated their grievances. The emphasis
was all on Darnley's status within the kingdom, and
whether Mary was still allowing him his rights as king.
Lennox first brought the matter up in a letter to Mary of
29 September when he told his daughter-in-law that Darnley was now so humiliated by his position that he intended
to go abroad, having a boat all prepared for the journey.[27]
As a result Mary faced Darnley the next day in front of
the Council and du Croc, and made him a *'fort belle
harangue'* in which she asked him in what respect she
had offended him, and pleaded with him, with hands joined
together, not to spare her anything, but to tell her the
truth. The lords then joined in asking Darnley how they
had offended him, and even du Croc chimed in with the
view that if Darnley went abroad it would be an offence
to the queen's honour. Darnley made little of this opportunity for airing his grievances against his wife, but
merely said flatly that he had no particular cause for offence; his sting was in his deliberately melodramatic departure from the queen's side, without kissing her, and
vowing in sybilline fashion that she would not see him
again for a long time. Whereupon the lords and du Croc
crowded round the queen and told her to continue in her
present course of wise and virtuous behaviour, and the

truth between her and Darnley would soon be generally
known.*

Two weeks later du Croc wrote to Catherine de Medicis
of the newly excellent relations which existed between
Queen Mary and her subjects, through her own efforts and
good qualities—they were 'so well reconciled with the
Queen as a result of her own prudent behaviour, that now-
adays there was not a single division to be seen between
them'. Darnley, on the other hand, was equally ill-regarded
by both parties; having apparently learnt nothing from
his recent experiences, he still wanted to rule everything;
yet there was not a single noble who did not take his cue
for his behaviour towards Darnley from the queen. Du
Croc noted that preparations were already being made
for the christening of the little prince, £ 12,000 being
raised by direct taxation to pay for it, and he represented
Catholics and Protestants as being equally enthusiastic
about the coming celebrations. Indeed, he attributed much
of Darnley's spoilt and sulky behaviour to the fuss which
was going on about the christening: not only was Darnley
jealous of Mary's reconciliation with the Protestant lords,
but he was also fearful lest strangers should witness his
obvious fall from favour at the ceremony—a prospect
which was intolerable to his 'haute et superbe' temperament.[28]

To the queen's attitude to the official religion of her
country, as much as to the birth of an heir, must be attributed much of this Indian summer of warm relations
with her nobility. The tender green shoots of a pro-Catholic policy which she had put out in the spring of 1566 had
been rudely blighted by the sharp frost of Riccio's murder,
which among other things demonstrated the strength of
the Protestant lords who could even storm her apartments.
For the rest of the fifteen months of her personal rule,
Mary made no attempt to help the Scottish Catholic

* It is surely inconceivable that Darnley or Lennox would not
have mentioned the subject of Bothwell's relations with the queen
during the course of this long discussion on the troubles between
Darnley and his wife, if indeed they had constituted a major source
of dispute between the couple. Yet Bothwell's name was never introduced into the conversation. Describing the scene afterwards to the
French court, du Croc did not mention it either.

Church, but showed on the contrary a renewed warmth
towards the organization of the reformed religion. On 3
October an Act of the Privy Council ordained that benefices worth less than 300 merks annually were to go to
the Protestant ministers, and there were now some instances of ministers being appointed to benefices. On 13
December a further law was enacted to help the Protestant
administration; and on 20 December the Church received
from the queen a direct gift of £10,000 as well as provisions.[29] Such an attitude to the religion which the majority
of her subjects professed may seem to us today pragmatic
in terms of government and admirable in terms of tolerance and good order. There could after all be no doubt of
Mary's personal attachment to the Catholic faith, since
quite apart from her early words to Throckmorton, she
never wavered from the holding of her own personal Mass
in Scotland, even at the times when it would have been
most expedient to do so, and the Mass itself as we have
seen was a most detestable symbol to the fervent Protestants. One may therefore applaud her far-sighted policy,
all the more remarkable in one born after all in the year
in which the Spanish Inquisition was founded. But of
course Pius v, in distant Rome, could not be expected to
view the situation in the same detached light: indeed, to
him the flagging of his spiritual daughter's newly kindled
zeal was a painful prospect, and one to be combated with
the double weapon of a papal mission and a papal subsidy. A papal nuncio, the bishop of Mondovi, was despatched, bearing 150,000 crowns in gold from the Pope,
intended to help the queen combat the heretics; but now
as before, Queen Mary showed an absolute disinclination
to receive the nuncio on Scottish soil, on the grounds that
his arrival would occasion 'great tumults'.[30] Mondovi was
in fact lingering in France, awaiting permission to land,
when the news came of Mary's serious illness at Jedburgh.

   Jedburgh was one of the important towns in the Scottish border country, lying on the edge of the wild terrain which led across to the Anglo-Scottish border itself.
Here Mary had arrived in early October to hold a justice
eyre. She inhabited a 'bastel-house', or fortified dwelling,
in the main street, still visible today in its original form.
While she was in the midst of administering justice, news
came that her lieutenant on the borders, Bothwell, had
been seriously wounded in a foray there, and was now

lying in danger of death at the castle of Hermitage. The queen did not immediately take any action, but five or six days later, when her business had been completed, she decided to pay Bothwell a visit, not so much to express her sympathy, as for the practical reason that he was her lieutenant and one of her chief advisers, especially on the perennially vexed border questions, and she needed to consult with him. Bedford, reporting the incident, and the earl's recovery, commented that the queen of Scots would certainly have been sorry to lose Bothwell, but made no remotely bawdy suggestion about the loss, which was by implication a strictly political or administrative one.

On 16 October, the queen, accompanied by her half-brother Moray and a large number of her court, as well as a quantity of soldiers, decided to ride over to the Hermitage, visit Bothwell, and since this border fortress was not prepared to receive the luxurious burden of a royal stay, return to Jedburgh that same day. Hermitage Castle was a thirteenth-century fortress, gaunt and forbidding in appearance, in the centre of Liddesdale. Lying on the left bank of the Hermitage water, twelve miles south of Hawick, it was a true military outpost, where up to 1,000 men and 200 horsemen could be stationed in times of danger. Already it had acquired cruel and mournful memories from earlier violent scenes in Scottish history, and being close to the English border, it was understandable that the queen should not wish to linger there overnight. In any case the day's journey meant a ride of only a little over fifty miles. Although a good day's ride at the time was considered to be thirty to forty miles, it was always considered possible to ride more than fifty miles in emergencies: the ride was not an outstanding hardship to a queen accustomed to daily hunting and riding hard in the saddle all her life, who had ridden twenty-five miles pillion to Dunbar when six months pregnant. The decision to make the visit within the day was certainly a practical one under the circumstances.*

* On 16 October 1966, the 400th anniversary of Queen Mary's ride, an equivalent ride was mounted from Jedburgh to Hermitage and back, following the route which she was believed to have taken: Banchester Bridge (via the queen's well), Earlside, Stobs Castle, Barnes Farm, Priesthaugh, the rough country between Priesthaugh and Hermitage known as the queen's mire (where the enamelled

However, on her return from Hermitage Queen Mary
fell violently and seriously ill. Undoubtedly the ride contributed to the final impetus of her collapse, but she had
evidently been sickening in her habitual and, as it seemed,
nervous fashion for some sort of breakdown for weeks,
since the situation with Darnley seemed to admit no solution. In a confidential letter to Archbishop Beaton, Mary's
ambassador in Paris, Maitland attributed her illness entirely to her disagreements with Darnley—'he misuses himself so far towards her that it is an heartbreak for her to
think that he should be her husband. . .'.[31] Physical and
mental stress now apparently combined to produce an attack of illness so severe that many of those who observed
Mary in the throes of it formed the opinion that she was
unlikely to recover, even if she was not already dead. First
the queen was seized by a prolonged fit of vomiting—'more
than sixty times'—so long and severe that she several times
fell into unconsciousness; two days later, she could neither
speak nor see, and had frequent convulsions. There was a
temporary recovery, but by 25 October she had become
so rapidly ill again—'all her limbs were so contracted, her
face was so distorted, her eyes closed, her mouth fast and
her feet and arms stiff and cold'—that she was once more
considered to be on the verge of death. Since she was generally believed to be sinking, Mary was publicly prayed for
in the churches of Edinburgh as Knox's *History* testifies.[32]
By her own account to Nau, Mary's servants thought she
was dead, and started to open the windows of the little
room where she lay; Moray was accused of trying to lay
his hands on silver plate and rings; mourning dresses were
ordered and funeral arrangements discussed. In Maitland's
more laconic account to Cecil, it was admitted that her
life had actually been despaired of for half an hour. The
situation was saved by the queen's physician, Arnault,
who seeing some signs of life in her arms, bandaged her

---

watch now in the museum in Queen Mary's House was later found)
and finally Hermitage Castle which was reached at 12 noon, the
expedition having left Jedburgh at 7 A.M. The return journey took
from 1 P.M. to 7 P.M. The weather on this occasion was misty, and
visibility was down to fifty yards over the queen's mire. But Miss
Elizabeth Millar, twenty-six, who took the part of Queen Mary, not
at the time accustomed to long hours in the saddle (unlike her pro-
totype) told the author that she did not feel particularly tired at the
end of the journey, and was able to attend a banquet in the evening
without undue exhaustion.

very tightly, including her toes and legs from the ankle upwards, and then having her mouth opened by force, poured wine down it. He then administered a clyster, the queen vomited an amount of corrupt blood, and subsequently began to recover.[33]

Out of these facts, dramatic enough in themselves, Buchanan wove a lecherous fairy story in which the queen rode like a maniac to be by Bothwell's side the moment she received the news of his mishap (which as we have seen is quite contradicted by the facts), fell ill through having thus gratified her unlawful passions during her short stay at Hermitage (Moray's presence at the interview is ignored) and subsequently had Bothwell moved into the room below hers at Jedburgh, so that they could continue their love-making conveniently during their mutual convalescences[34]—once again almost ludicrously far from the truth. In fact, the queen was occupied at Jedburgh far away from Bothwell, once more in making provisions for her kingdom in the event of her death. When she felt herself to be *in extremis* she called the nobles into her room, including Moray, and attempted to dictate some sort of settlement which would ensure a calm inheritance for her son—for it is the son who is to succeed, not the father, and Mary specified that Darnley was not to seize the crown 'to which he laid claim by right'. Her first concern is for the young prince, who is to have no evil company around him during his 'youth head'—here perhaps Queen Mary was influenced by the example of Darnley, who often tried to excuse his failings on the ground that he had been corrupted by bad companions. Darnley is once more castigated for ingratitude: 'My lords, you know the goodness that I have used towards some whom I have advanced to a great degree of honour and pre-eminence above others; who, notwithstanding, has used . . . ingratitude towards me, which has engendered the displeasure that presently most grieves me, and is also the cause of my sickness. I pray lord mend them.' Perhaps her most interesting words of all were on the subject of religion, where she pleaded for the tolerance which she had shown during her life to the Protestants, to be shown after her death to the Catholics: 'I have pressed none of you that professes religion by your conscience . . . I pray you, brother earl of Moray, that you trouble none.' When Father Edmund Hay, a Jesuit in Paris on his way to Scotland reported

the scene round the bedside of the apparently dying woman
in a letter to St Francis Borgia of 6 November[35] he said
that, although she affirmed her desire to die in the (Catholic) religion which her predecessors, the kings of Scotland, had practised for 1,364 years, yet she frankly admitted that she had been neglectful not only in government
of the realm, but also, and chiefly, in promoting the Catholic religion.

Throughout this period of illness, Darnley scarcely
showed himself as the devoted husband. He was in the
west of Scotland when Mary fell ill and did not, as Buchanan and Knox afterwards stated, come rushing to his
wife's side. He paid the queen a brief visit eleven days
after she first fell ill, and then returned to Glasgow. The
queen's apologists have sometimes cited this in turn as an
example of callousness; however, the Diurnal of Occurrents, an unbiased chronicle of events, suggests that as he
was hunting and hawking, he did not even hear of the illness until 27 October, whereupon he rode to Edinburgh
and the next day to Jedburgh.[36] At Jedburgh he received
some fancied slight, of the sort Darnley was quick to perceive—so that he went back to Edinburgh and thence to
Stirling. Possibly no special messenger had been sent to
advise him of the illness: at any rate the picture of a
breach in their relationship is a complete one.

The next episode in the mounting tragedy of Darnley
took place at the end of November at the castle of Craigmillar, an enormous baronial edifice, founded by the Pres-
ton family, in the parish of Liberton, on the outskirts of
Edinburgh. Mary was still in the hands of her physicians,
since her illness, and was apparently in a state of deep depression. Du Croc, the French ambassador, wrote to
Beaton in Paris that she often repeated the words 'I could
wish to be dead'. Du Croc commented that no future understanding could be expected between the queen and her
husband for the two reasons of his arrogance and her suspicion: 'The first is, the king will never humble himself
as he ought; the other is, the Queen cannot perceive any
nobleman speaking with the King, but that she presently
suspects some contrivance between them.'[37] Ever since the
murder of Riccio, Mary evidently regarded herself as permanently threatened by some possible conspiracy on the
part of Darnley. But Mary's chief nobles, lodged with her

at Craigmillar, were equally resolute in their hatred of
Darnley, who had betrayed them over Riccio, and was
yet still left nominally able to lord it over them as king
of Scotland. Experience had not curbed Darnley's arrogance: nor were nobles of the temperament of Moray,
Argyll, Bothwell and Maitland likely to forgive and forget.

According to the 'Protestation' of Huntly and Argyll
(written in January 1569 when Huntly and Argyll formed
part of the Marian party), Moray and Maitland now
broached the subject of a divorce to Argyll; Huntly was
then brought in, finally Bothwell; then the queen was approached. Maitland opened up the argument by saying
that means would be found for Mary to divorce Darnley,
if she would only pardon Morton and the other Riccio assassins (who were still in exile). The queen promised her
consent, but said that the divorce must be legally obtained
without prejudice to her son. Maitland then suggested
'other means', and in a famous phrase told the queen that
'Moray would look through his fingers'. At this the queen
quickly asked them to do nothing against her honour, and
Maitland replied: 'Let us guide the matter among us, and
your Grace shall see nothing but good, and approved by
Parliament.'[38] This was in effect to be the case of Mary's
supporters in later years, to prove her innocence over the
death of Darnley. They maintained that the queen, although anxious to rid herself of Darnley, could not have
known that the nobles actually intended to kill him, since
Maitland had assured her that whatever happened would
have parliamentary approval. But of course Mary was not,
and was never intended to be, one of the executive conspirators; the details of the deed were not within the province of her concern. At Craigmillar she made it clear that
she wished to be rid of Darnley, much as Henry II had
once exclaimed: 'Who will rid me of this turbulent priest?'
of Thomas à Becket; she made two further points of vital
interest to her—firstly that her child must not run the risk
of bastardy, and secondly that 'her honour' was not to be
impugned. Maitland reassured her on both these points:
but it was difficult to see what 'other means' he was con-
templating except perhaps a treason trial of Darnley before
Parliament, which would result in his execution. Mary,
however, did not examine the situation so candidly in her
own mind. She was a queen and a woman; as a woman she
wished to be rid of an intolerable marital situation; as a

queen she expected her nobles to help in a difficult governmental problem of order; there could be no benefit to her
thinking too far or too clearly into how the nobles proposed to carry out her wishes. If Moray was quoted as intending to 'look through his fingers', Queen Mary on the
other hand, intended to keep her own hands tightly across
her eyes.

It seems virtually certain that a bond was then drawn up
and signed at Craigmillar by those nobles who intended to
get rid of Darnley, including Maitland, Bothwell, Argyll,
Huntly and James Balfour, with Morton signing later on
his return to Scotland, much as a bond was signed before
the murder of Riccio. Following the parallel with the Riccio bond, it is unlikely that the murder was specifically
mentioned, for the death of Riccio had never been alluded
to in the official document. The project could be put more
vaguely, especially as Sir James Balfour, who had a legal
training, probably played an important part in drawing
it up. The hostile *Book of Articles* described the bond as
follows: 'It was thought expedient and most profitable for
the common wealth, by the whole nobility and lords un-
derscribed, that such a young fool and proud tyrant should
not reign or bear rule over them; and that for diverse
causes, therefore, that these all had concluded that he
should be put off by one way or another; and whosoever
should take the deed in hand, or do it, they should defend
and fortify as themselves.'[39] But the actual bond does not
survive for inspection, although its existence was mentioned in the confession of Bothwell's henchman, John
Hepburn of Bolton, who said that Bothwell showed it to
him, and later Ormiston, another henchman, executed in
1573, described it in his death-bed confession to a priest.
The queen later told Nau that when she parted from Bothwell for the last time before the battle of Carberry Hill,
he pressed into her hand a piece of paper and told her to
guard it well, since it was the evidence of the complicity
of the other lords in the murder—those very lords who
were now drawn up in battle array against them, and accusing Bothwell alone of the crime. If this account is accepted, the incriminating paper must have been taken from
her after her capture and destroyed. Moray's part in the
whole affair remains obscure: he did not sign the Craigmillar bond although he certainly knew of its contents. He
afterwards protested that he had taken part in, and ap-

proved of, nothing that was illegal. In view of Maitland's assurance to Mary that Moray would 'look through his fingers', it seems likely that it was Moray's intention to leave the actual execution of the deed to others, while approving the result and hoping to benefit from it. If he believed that it was intended to seize Darnley for trial for treason, and kill him in the act, he could perhaps stretch his conscience sufficiently to cover the statement that he had approved of nothing illegal.* Moray was therefore several degrees closer than Mary in his knowledge of what was planned, although in their general attitudes to the subject, the responses of brother and sister were not dissimilar.

In December the queen was able to turn her mind from her vexatious problems with her husband, to the happier matter of her son's baptism. Shortly after the birth, messages had been sent to the king of France, the duke of Savoy and the queen of England to act as godparents. Darnley objected to the inclusion of Elizabeth, because of her animosity against him, but his objections were overruled by Mary who visualized a golden future for James if Elizabeth's goodwill could be secured. On 17 December the ceremony took place, according to the Catholic rite, in the chapel royal of Stirling Castle. The little prince, now just on six months old, was carried in the arms of the count of Brienne, proxy for the king of France, from the royal apartments to the chapel between two rows of courtiers, the whole scene lit by flaring torches. M. du Croc represented the duke of Savoy. The procession was followed by a list of Catholic nobles, bearing the various official accompaniments of the Catholic christening—one the cierge, one the salt, one the basin and laver and one the rood. At the entrance of the chapel, the cortège was received by the archbishop of St Andrews and other Catholic prelates.

Queen Elizabeth had sent a magnificent gold font, weighing two stones according to the Diurnal of Occurrents,[41] as a present for her godson. But as Bedford, her emissary, was a leading English puritan, he could not stand proxy for her at the font. Jean, countess of Argyll, the child's aunt, acted as proxy godmother for Elizabeth, and held

* This is the explanation for Moray's behaviour and his subsequent protests advanced by his biographer Maurice Lee. But Professor Donaldson points out that so long as Darnley remained king, it was still illegal for the nobles to arrest him for treason.[40]

James in her arms. Prince James was duly christened according to the full Catholic rite, except that the queen refused to let the priest spit in his mouth as the custom then was, saying according to a later story, that she was not going to have 'a pocky priest' spitting in her child's mouth. The Diurnal of Occurrents merely reported that the queen 'did inhibit' the use of the spittle. Throughout the ceremony, Bedford and the other Scottish Protestant lords stood outside the chapel.

The accomplishment of the ceremony was celebrated with all the magnificence which Queen Mary could command. She clothed the nobility at her own expense for the occasion, 'Some in cloth of silver, some in cloth of gold, some in cloth of tissue, every man rather above than under his degree'.[42] Moray was clothed in green, Argyll in red and Bothwell in blue (Buchanan afterwards chose to report that Mary had deliberately clothed Bothwell alone). There were fire-works and masques, with verses written by George Buchanan himself, evidently still at this date an admirer of the queen. The English party took offence at one masque in which some French-born satyrs deliberately turned in their direction and 'put their hands behind them to their tails which they wagged with their hands'.[43] This insult apart (and the English believed it sprang from uncontrollable Gallic jealousy of the honour which was being done to their national rivals) the merriment was general, and Bedford, puritan as he might be, graciously allowed the young gentlemen in his train to join in the dancing at night.

In all these rejoicings, there was only one mysteriously absent figure, that of the baby's father, 'King Henry' himself, although he was actually present within the castle of Stirling at the time. It has been suggested that his absence was due to his continued bad relations with Queen Elizabeth (who had never officially countenanced his marriage) and because Bedford had been instructed not to give him his due as king of Scotland. But no such instructions have been discovered. It seems more likely that Darnley, as du Croc suspected, hated the idea of the English, from whose ranks he sprang, whom he had once scorned, seeing how far he had fallen in prestige at the Scottish court; it would certainly be in his character to avoid any occasion of public humiliation, real or imaginary.[44] The change in his position was made all the more obvious to him, because on

the day of the christening itself du Croc three times declined to give him an interview. The reason given was especially irritating. As Darnley was not now 'in good
correspondence' with Mary, the French king had instructed
du Croc to have nothing further to do with him. At the
end of December, Darnley left Stirling abruptly, and went
to Glasgow, in the west of Scotland, the traditional centre
of Lennox Stewart power, where he hoped to be more
royally treated.

16 The Murder of Darnley

'I'll pity thee as much' he said
'And as much favour I'll show to thee
As thou had on the Queen's chamberlain
That day you deemedst him to die'

BOTHWELL *to Darnley, from the ballad* Earl Bothwell

In October at Jedburgh Mary Queen of Scots had nearly
died. At Glasgow in the New Year Darnley in his turn
fell extremely ill. At the time it was given out that he had
smallpox, but it seems more likely that he was actually
suffering from syphilis. Bothwell, on his own narrative of
events written during his captivity in Denmark, *Les Affaires du Conte de Boduel,* took the trouble to cross out
the words *petite vérole* (smallpox) and inserted *roniole*
(syphilis) in his own hand-writing. The Diurnal of Occurrents, a contemporary diary probably written by a minor
official of the court, referred to the 'pox', a word often
used at the time for syphilis, and Pitscottie stated that the
king was stricken with 'a great fever of the pox'.[1] Darnley's skull, now in the Royal College of Surgeons at London, was analysed by Sir Daniel Wilson, at the request of
Dr Karl Pearson, and discovered to be pitted with traces
of 'a virulent syphilitic disease'.[*2] The queen did not immediately visit her husband, but she did show her habitual
humanity: she sent him her doctor to Glasgow, and in
early January, according to the accounts, gave orders for
the royal linen to be cut into ruffs for the king's night-
shirt.

Yet despite Mary's careless kindness—so typical of her
nature—clearly she was still pondering in her mind legal

* W. Armstrong Davison, in *The Casket Letters,* advances the further theory that Darnley was already suffering from syphilis when
Queen Mary nursed him, apparently for measles, in April 1565. He
states that it was by no means rare in the sixteenth century for a
measles-like eruption to be succeeded by a smallpox-type eruption
twenty-one months later, and for both to be symptoms of syphilis.[3]

ways and means of ridding herself of this degenerate creature as a husband. On Christmas Eve she duly pardoned
Morton and his associates—a fact which lends conviction
to the story of the Protestation that Mary believed herself
to have struck a bargain with Maitland and other nobles:
now that she had allowed Morton to return, it was up to
these nobles to rid her of Darnley in such a way as would
be 'approved by Parliament'. The return of Morton and
his friends also of course substantially increased the numbers of Darnley's potential enemies within the boundaries
of Scotland. A further step taken by the queen before
Christmas shows that she was still considering the question of a divorce: the Catholic Archbishop Hamilton of
St Andrews was temporarily restored to his consistorial
jurisdiction from 23 December until some date before
9 January, when the privilege was again removed. The intention was presumably to allow the archbishop to pro-
nounce decrees of nullity between the queen and her husband. The brief restoration suggests that the queen was
still casting around for ways to come about a decent divorce which would not compromise Prince James, and did
not regard the subject as totally closed by Maitland's ad-
verse advice; after all as a Protestant Scot he did not
necessarily represent the views of Catholic Rome, which
had not yet been officially sounded. In any case the marriages of royal persons were by Canon Law reserved for
the consideration of the Pope himself, as *causae majores*.
However, divorce for royal personages was by no means
unthinkable in the sixteenth century, even within the
structure of the Catholic church. There had been some
significant divorces in the French royal house. Mary and
Darnley's mutual grandmother, Margaret Tudor, had been
divorced from her second husband, the earl of Angus; and
the marital problems of Henry VIII, which he had originally attempted so hard and so long to solve within the
structure of the Church, were only a generation away.

For Darnley, with his teeth drawn, and threatened from
so many quarters, was still in some respects a dangerous
animal. He did not cease to intrigue as well as boast. He
was clever enough to see that he had a possible line of attack against Mary in her determinedly *laissez-faire* policy
towards the Scottish Catholic Church: he was unscrupulous enough to contemplate blackening her reputation in
the eyes of the Catholic powers abroad with the aim of

elevating himself, as the champion of the Catholic faith,
in Scotland. In the summer of 1566 there had been some
crazy story that he contemplated inhabiting the Scilly
Isles and from there attacking England.[4] On 22 October
Robert Melville reported to Beaton in Paris that Darnley
was trying to use his threat to leave the country to demand the dismissal of Maitland, Macgill and Bellenden, all
strong Protestants, from the queen's counsels.[5] On 13 November, de Silva, the Spanish ambassador in London, reported to Philip II that Queen Mary had heard in Scotland
that Darnley had written to Philip, the Pope, the king of
France and the cardinal of Lorraine, that she was 'dubious
in the faith'.[6] Nearly a year before Darnley had pictured
himself in possession of the coveted crown matrimonial.
Now his ambitions were strong enough still to picture
himself set up as Catholic king of Scotland, at the will of
a strong foreign Catholic power, ruling as guardian of
his infant son—with his wife of course overthrown.

It will never be known exactly how much of this 'Catholic' plot existed in the imagination of Darnley, or indeed
Darnley's enemies, and how much reality there was behind the rumours and the suspicions. But certainly at the
turn of the year there were whispers that Darnley was once
more intriguing against his wife which were loud enough
to reach not only the queen's ears in Edinburgh, but also
those of Beaton in Paris. In the words of the historian
F. W. Maitland, it is very hard to remember that events
now long in the past, were once in the future. In January
1567 it was Darnley, out of the royal couple, who had
been shown to be the plotter, who had aimed at the crown
matrimonial and perhaps more, by a conspiracy. So far
Queen Mary had only been plotted against during her
reign, and ever since the Riccio affair had kept, as du
Croc pointed out, an extremely wary eye on Darnley for
'further contrivances'. Now she believed she had stumbled on news of such contrivances: she wrote to Paris
in January to tell Beaton that there was a rumour of a
plot by Darnley to seize the person of Prince James, and
thus control the reins of government.[7] The story had been
brought to her at Stirling by a servant William Walker:
'How it was not only openly bruited, but also he had
heard by report of persons whom he esteemed lovers of
us [the Queen] that the King, by assistance of some of
the nobility, should take the Prince our son and crown

him, and being crowned, as his father, should take upon him the government. . . .' Walker gave as his reference another servant, William Hiegate. But Hiegate, when questioned, denied the whole thing, and merely repeated a rumour to the opposite effect, that he had heard how the king was about to be put in ward by the nobles.

The queen duly conveyed this atmosphere of plot and counter-plot to Beaton in Paris. But at the end of her letter she merely concluded rather dourly that God knew how her husband had behaved towards her, and the outside world knew as well as God; as for her subjects, she did not doubt that they too, in their hearts, condemned him for the way he had treated her. Darnley was always enquiring for news about her doings, and in Mary's view, both he and his father Lennox, with their adherents, would be delighted to do her some mischief, if their strength were equivalent to their wishes. Luckily, wrote Mary, God had seen to it that their power was moderated, so that they had little means to execute their evil intentions. In any case Mary declared herself sceptical as to whether any in Scotland—beyond the immediate Lennox party—would truly approve of an action against their queen. Despite Mary's boasted self-confidence, she did take one precaution against the possible malevolence of Darnley: she had the little Prince James brought out of Stirling Castle, where he was considered to lie too close to the dangerous Glasgow area. On 14 January he was installed with his mother in the palace of Holyrood. Other rumours of danger to the queen had already reached Beaton in Paris, before the arrival of her letter; these came in the form of a hint from the Spanish ambassador that 'there be some surprise to be trafficked to the Queen's contrary'. The Spanish ambassador in London heard from the same source that there was a plot forming in Scotland against the queen.[8] Beaton's reaction to these innuendoes was to send Mary a warning letter, in which he begged her to re-establish good relations with her husband, lest some peril ensue from him in the future to destroy her. Unfortunately this letter, full of good sense, reached Mary too late, when Darnley was already dead.

On 20 January Queen Mary set off for Glasgow to bring back her sick husband on a litter to Edinburgh, to finish off his convalescence in her own company. In view of the dispassionate contempt which she quite openly

expressed for him in her letter to Beaton, written on the
very day of her departure, it is necessary to consider exactly what prompted her to make the journey. It is true
that Mary had always displayed courteous kindness towards Darnley's sufferings; but some more compelling
argument than sheer humanity must be advanced to explain her actions—and also to explain what is every bit as
mysterious, why Darnley so readily agreed to follow her
back. One must therefore examine the actions of the conspirator nobles during the period in January leading up to
the queen's expedition. It was on 6 January—the last
Twelfth Night that the queen of Scots who loved these
celebrations so much was ever to spend outside prison
walls—that Maitland at last achieved his wish and married the voluptuous Mary Fleming in the chapel royal at
Stirling. By this marriage to the chief of the Maries, the
queen's own kin, Maitland was further entwined in Mary's
inner court circle, to which he had been re-admitted in the
previous September. In January also some sort of conference took place at Whittingham, one of the Douglas
castles, between Bothwell, Morton, newly returned to Scotland, his cousin Archibald Douglas, and Maitland. The
exact truth of what happened at this conference is impossible to establish, since afterwards, once the nobles concerned were on different political sides, each accused the
other of having raised the subject of Darnley's murder.

Morton, in his confession, some fifteen years later, said
that Bothwell suggested the killing of Darnley to him, at
which Morton begged himself off on the grounds that he
had only just recovered from his disgrace over Riccio—'I
am but newly come out of a great trouble. . . .' According
to Morton, Archibald Douglas was then despatched to
Edinburgh to see if the queen would give some written authority for the despatch of her husband, but Douglas returned with the quite definite answer: 'Show to the Earl
of Morton that the Queen will have no speech of the matter.'[9] Bothwell, on the other hand, represented himself as
being anxious 'for rest and a peaceful life after the imprisonment and exile I had suffered', whereas it was Morton who was determined to spur him forward to annihilate
Darnley, as a revenge on him for his treachery.[10] There
is little to choose between these two versions of the same
story, and it is hardly necessary to decide which of these
two ambitious and daring men should be given the honour

of first broaching the subject. But it is important to notice that neither party suggested that the queen had any fore-knowledge of their plans; according to Douglas, she had even gone further and specified that she wanted to hear nothing more about such a blood-thirsty enterprise. The queen's dissent, combined with her known merciful character and clemency, which made her ever ready to pardon those who were sometimes best left unpardoned, gave the conspirators a strong motive for the future in not involving her in their plans. She had a horror of violence: as she said of herself years later, she would rather pray with Esther than take the sword with Judith. Yet the nobles had every reason to believe, after the conference at Craigmillar, that she would approve the end result. The argument for proceeding with their plans without informing the queen further was overwhelming.

There was, however, one detail in which the queen could help them: their plan did demand that Darnley should be in Edinburgh or thereabouts, rather than Glasgow; there he was surrounded by his own Lennox Stewart adherents, in feudal fashion, but Morton's Douglases and Bothwell's Hepburns were at a distance. It is possible that Maitland indicated to Mary that in practical terms it was unwise to allow Darnley to remain in Glasgow where he might manage to work up an effective conspiracy against her. During the period leading up to the murder, according to Nau, a man called John Shaw came to the queen and told her that Ker of Fawdonside, whom she particularly loathed for his part in the Riccio murder—it was he who had held the pistol to her stomach—was back in Scotland: 'He having boasted to certain persons . . . within fifteen days he assured them, there would be a change at court, and he would be more than ever in credit; and then he enquired boldly how their queen was.'[11] Or it may have been Bothwell who dropped the hint—Bothwell, whose record of loyalty was impeccable in the last two years. Equally the queen herself may have needed no particular prompting to see that it was safer to have Darnley under her own eyes where experience had taught her that it was easier to control him, than loose in the countryside, either plotting or breeding dissension with his wild schemes. At all times during the past year, she had shown herself to be extremely upset when Darnley broke loose from the court and wandered off by himself presumably because she trusted him even less, once he was outside the sphere of her influence. Her journey to recall the errant Darnley made sense in terms of her own personal security, whether prompted or not by one of her nobles. But being both frank and feminine, or in her own phrase 'undissembling', Mary, in her letter to Beaton, made no attempt to pretend a passionate love for Darnley which she was by now far from feeling.*

If her motives are plentiful enough, the question still arises exactly how Mary induced her husband to accompany her back to Edinburgh: for it is clear that once Mary arrived in Glasgow, she experienced no difficulty in persuading him to make the move. Darnley freely consented to the plan, and this despite the fact that he had heard some rumour of what had transpired at Craigmillar, as his servant Crawford later deposed. Darnley had learned apparently that something had been plotted against him in the autumn, but that Mary had refused to be a party to it: in Crawford's words,[12] he knew that 'a letter was presented to her in Craigmillar, made by her own device, and subscribed by certain others, who desired her to subscribe the same, which she refused to do. And he [Darnley] said that he would never think that she [the queen] who was his own proper flesh, would do him any hurt. . . .' Darnley's confidence in the gentle nature of his wife on eighteen months of marriage is significant. However, this confidence in itself would not have been enough to persuade him to return from Lennox-dominated Glasgow to Edinburgh, inhabited not only by the queen but by many nobles with far from gentle natures. The promise which Mary seems most likely to have held out to Darnley was the resumption of full marital relations on his return to Edinburgh.

* The only documents ever produced which were supposed to date from the period before the murder, to prove that the queen enjoyed an adulterous liaison with Bothwell, were the highly dubious Casket Letters. These will be considered in Chapter 20. In order to explain the many inconsistencies in these letters (whose originals have vanished) some sort of theory of interpolation has often been adopted, i.e. genuine letters from Mary interposed with passionate love letters to Bothwell from another woman. If this theory is correct, then the so-called Long Casket Letter, supposed to be written while at Glasgow by the queen to Bothwell (although containing the unnecessary reminder 'remember you . . . of the Earl of Bothwell') might be the draft of another similarly frank letter from Mary describing her feelings for Darnley, interpolated with a genuine love letter to Bothwell from another woman.

Mary's coldness as a wife had been one of Darnley's complaints against her: it wounded his vanity as a man, and also, he felt, threatened his status as a king, there being more to the embraces of a queen than the mere feel of her arms round him. This promise would have been enough to rouse Darnley's ambitions all over again, to rekindle his hopes of future grandeur as king: in this way he went willingly out of his own feudal domain of influence into hers. The attitude of Mary to the journey was totally different: convinced that Darnley was once more plotting against her, convinced also that Darnley had once attempted her own death and might do so again, she felt little love or any emotion of any sort for her husband, as her letter to Beaton shows. Nevertheless it still seemed safer for herself and her child to have him lodged in Edinburgh under her own eyes, than let him loose in the west of Scotland, free to plot. Mary led Darnley to Edinburgh with kind words and hints of happiness as once before she had won him over on the dramatic day after Riccio's murder, for the same cogent reasons of self-preservation.

The only subject on which the queen and king now disagreed was the place where Darnley should spend the rest of his convalescence: he needed constant baths to improve his condition, and his face was still shrouded with a piece of taffeta. Mary had intended to bring him to the castle of Craigmillar a little way outside Edinburgh, that same castle where the bond had been signed. Darnley, however, declined to enter the stronghold, as his own servants testified. Perhaps he was afraid to do so. He chose instead— and once again there is general agreement that the choice was his, not the queen's—a house of moderate size on the outskirts of Edinburgh town proper, but still lying just inside the town wall. It was situated within the quadrangle attached to the old collegiate church of St Mary-in-the-Field, as it had once been called, which was now known as the Kirk o'Field, and it was about three quarters of a mile distant from Holyrood palace, along hilly streets. This house, known as the old provost's lodging, because it had once been the house of the provost of the collegiate church, now actually belonged to Robert Balfour, brother of Sir James Balfour, but was often said to belong to Sir James himself. Within the same quadrangle lay the considerably larger Hamilton House, belonging to the

duke of Châtelherault. Darnley's servant Nelson, while
agreeing that Darnley himself made the choice of Kirk
o'Field, stated in his deposition that Darnley had been expected to be lodged in Hamilton House and was surprised
to find himself in the old provost's lodging.[13] But no other
mention is made of Darnley's surprise, whereas there is
general agreement that Darnley made the choice after the
royal cortège left Glasgow. In addition one may doubt
whether Darnley would actually have wished or expected
to be lodged in the house of his hereditary family enemies,
the Hamiltons. The main point to be grasped about the
old provost's lodging, apart from the Balfour connection
of the house, is that the venue of Darnley's lodging had
been changed suddenly and unexpectedly at his own request: therefore any plans centred on his dwelling would
necessarily have an improvised and makeshift quality,
since they could not have taken longer than a few days
to both plot and put into action. This need for speed at
the cost of efficiency may explain some of the confusion
of the tangled events which followed.

But of course the many seemingly irreconcilable contradictions of what followed at Kirk o'Field—the most debatable, as well as surely the most worked over murder
in history—have a deeper cause than the essentially makeshift nature of the crime. They arise principally from the
extraordinarily untrustworthy nature of the evidence. The
basic difficulty in the way of reconstructing the truth about
Kirk o'Field is the fact that the lesser executive criminals
were subsequently executed for the crime at the instance
of the great nobles who had approved or inspired it. There
is thus a veil of unreality over the depositions of these
minor figures, as in the trial of criminals in some twenti-
eth-century totalitarian state, since their words had to be
carefully tailored not to incriminate the men then in power
in Scotland. Equally it was desirable to throw all the blame
possible on one noble who had vanished from the scene,
after quarrelling with his former associates—Lord Bothwell. The evidence is affected further by the circumstances
of Mary Stuart's own trial in England in late 1568: as
with her alleged adultery with Bothwell, it will be found
that once again the *Book of Articles* related a series of
demonstrable untruths, the intention of which was to keep
her in captivity in England while Moray remained regent

safely in Scotland. In short, the unreliability of the depositions, many of them made under torture, and the political 're-writing' of history which went on at the time of Mary's trial means that the detailed story of Kirk o'Field can only be guessed at, or pieced together, rather than established with total certainty.

The house in which Darnley now settled for the last days of his recovery was in many ways ideally suited for the state of convalescence. According to Nau, a raven had hovered over the royal caravan on its way from Glasgow, and now settled on the roof of the lodging. But there were certainly no other evil omens to be discerned in the actual structure of the building. The house lay on a slight eminence, overlooking the Cowgate, and the site was open and healthy compared to low-lying Holyrood; as Leslie said, the air was thought by the doctors to be the most salubrious in the whole town.[14] The quadrangle in which it lay and its recent connection with the university must have given the lodging something of the atmosphere of a house in a cathedral close in an English provincial town. It was far enough from Holyrood for the king's illness not to be an embarrassment to him, yet it had the security of lying just within the town wall, which had been begun to be built round Edinburgh at the time of Flodden. Edinburgh during this period had a nightly town watch, numbering a total of thirty-two men, of whom twelve were stationed at the various gates, or the Leith Wynd gap in the wall, and ten perpetually perambulated the streets—providing a considerable sense of security to its citizens, and a continual threat to anyone who might stray in its streets by night without a lawful excuse to do so. This town wall, six feet wide at its base, and tapering to a flat top, skirted the back of the house; and the characteristic gallery which extended off the first floor chamber of the lodging rested on it.* The house had its own east garden, with a door into it, and on the other side of the town wall lay further gardens and orchards, once part of the

---

* There is no trace of St Mary, Kirk o'Field, its quadrangle and the little houses round it in modern Edinburgh. The site of Darnley's last lodging lies somewhere beneath the Adam-designed quadrangle, which is the central establishment of the University of Edinburgh, off South Bridge Street.

fields, but divided off by the building of the wall. All these
details can be clearly distinguished in the sketch of the
scene after the murder sent to Cecil in London, which is
also vital to our own understanding of the geography of
Kirk o'Field. From it, it can be seen that the old provost's
lodging lay on the south side of the quadrangle; two of
the other sides were occupied by smaller houses, still standing in the sketch, and the third contained slightly larger
houses such as Hamilton House. The quadrangle has been
estimated to be eighty-six feet by seventy-three feet.†

Although Buchanan tried to make out that the lodging
itself was ruinous and uncomfortable—in order to blacken
the character of Queen Mary who was erroneously stated to
have chosen it—it was in fact a pleasant house of moderate size, by the standards of the day. Mahon calculated
the house to have been about sixty-one feet long and
twenty-five feet deep compared to King James's Tower
at Holyrood, containing all the state apartments, which is
seventy-four feet by thirty-seven feet. Besides the door into
the east garden already mentioned, the house had two
other doors, into the quadrangle, and through the postern
gate in the town wall (visible in the sketch) into the alleyway beyond. No trace has ever been found of a secret
tunnel connecting the lodging with Holyrood: when Lennox furiously and crazily accused the queen of coming
disguised in men's clothing to witness his son's murder
by 'secret ways', in his Narrative,[15] he was presumably
thinking not of a tunnel, but of the back streets of Edinburgh. The obvious route from Holyrood to the provost's
lodging lay down the Canongate, through the town wall
at the Netherbow Port, down the Blackfriars Wynd, crossing the Cowgate, and so to the purlieus of St Mary's. But
sixteenth-century Edinburgh was a network of smaller
streets, off the main thoroughfares, and it would have been
possible to take an altogether more circuitous route, along
the back wall of the south Canongate gardens to St Mary's
Port, and thence, where the town wall was as yet unbuilt,

† By Major-General Mahon, whose *Tragedy of Kirk o'Field*, 1923,
contains by far the most detailed investigation into the geography
and circumstances of the events now to be related. Later writers,
whether they agree with his conclusions or not, must acknowledge
a debt of gratitude for his painstaking consideration of even the
minutest aspect of the crime.

through the gardens and fields of the old Blackfriars Priory
to the east garden of the Kirk o'Field house. This would
avoid the town wall, and the challenge of the watch; the
only remaining problem would be the curious eyes of the
ten watchmen nightly patrolling the streets of the city.

The lodging contained two bedrooms for Darnley and
the queen, Darnley's lying directly above that of his wife,
a presence chamber (or *salle*), two *garde robes*, a kitchen
and vaulted cellars beneath. The drop from the gallery,
which extended out of Darnley's bedroom on to the town
wall, to the ground, was only about fourteen feet, since
the level of the ground beyond the wall was higher than
within the quadrangle. The house was not only pleasantly
situated and healthy, with gardens, but it was also well if
hastily furnished for Darnley's benefit, once he had selected
it, from the store of royal furniture at Holyrood. The inventories testify not only the suddenness of the decision
to use the provost's lodging, but also the amount of furniture and ornaments now brought down from Holyrood.[16]
A series of seven pieces of tapestry representing the 'Hunting of the Conies' were brought for the *garde robe,* as well
as a canopy of yellow taffeta to enclose the *chaise percée.*
Five pieces of tapestry were brought for the *salle.* For
Darnley's bedroom, six pieces of tapestry, originally taken
from Strathbogie after the defeat of Huntly, were ordered,
a little Turkish carpet, two or three cushions of red velvet,
a high chair covered in purple velvet, and a little table covered with green velvet (which had also once belonged to
Huntly), as well as a bed which had once belonged to
Mary of Guise, which Mary had given her husband in the
previous August—hung with violet-brown velvet,* em-

---

* It is characteristic of the confused nature of the evidence about
Darnley's death that Buchanan later in his *History* accused Mary of
deliberately having her own bed changed in order to save it from
the blast: this contradicted not only his own story in the *Book of
Articles,* but also the deposition of Darnley's servant Nelson (who
said that it was Darnley's bed the queen had changed). Nelson reported that a new black velvet bed was sent away in favour of an
old purple-brown one; in fact the black bed was probably lying at
the lodging when Darnley arrived at short notice, and was later
changed for Darnley's favourite royally-ornamented purple-brown
bed. The inventories record that this was specially brought down
from Holyrood; they record no other exchanges made on a later
date.[17]

broidered with ciphers and flowers, trimmed with cloth of gold and silver, and having three coverlets, one of them blue quilted taffeta. A bath stood beside the bed— baths being a necessary part of the convalescence—and one of the makeshift aspects of the visit was the fact that one of the doors of the house was taken off its hinges to serve as a lid when it was not in use. The chamber beneath that of Darnley, which had a window looking north over the quadrangle, contained a small bed of yellow and green damask with a furred coverlet, in which the queen could sleep if she so wished.

Darnley took up residence in his new dwelling on Saturday 1 February. The last week of his life was pleasant and almost domesticated. Queen Mary felt confident that her husband had for the time being no opportunity to weave any plots against her, especially as his father Lennox, so often his evil genius in feeding his childish vanity with praise, was still in Glasgow. The mass of courtiers, Privy Councillors and attendants who inevitably moved with the queen as she progressed through Edinburgh, settled into a routine of visiting Darnley at Kirk o'Field and then returning to the royal palace at Holyrood for the other formal ceremonies of court life. Relations at this point between Darnley and his wife were perfectly amicable. On the Wednesday the queen spent the night at Kirk o'Field in the chamber beneath Darnley's. According to her own account, propinquity now led to newly friendly relations between them. They had certainly seen little enough of each other lately: when Mary fetched Darnley from Glasgow at the end of January she had not seen him since his abrupt departure from Stirling at the end of December; in October and November she had been ill, and separated from her husband. On the Friday 7 February Darnley was actually inspired by this novel amity to discuss with his wife some information he had of plots against her. He begged her in touching language to beware of the people who tried to make mischief between them, adding with self-righteous horror that it had even been suggested to him that he should take his wife's life.* This sort of volte-

---

* Buchanan's *Book of Articles* and his *Detection,* both luridly accusatory, later tried to turn the whole incident round to the queen's disadvantage, accusing Mary of trying to work up a quarrel between Darnley and Lord Robert Stewart on this Friday, a fracas to which Moray also was supposed to have been a witness.[19] Although the

face was typical of Darnley: Mary, being the stronger character of the two, was always able to win his loyalty for the time being by force of personality, provided they were face to face, as the denouement of the Riccio affair had demonstrated. It was on this very Friday also, according to Lennox, that Darnley wrote to his father concerning the improvement of his health, which had occurred so much sooner than he had expected, through the kind treatment of 'such as hath this good while concealed their good will, I mean my love the Queen, which I assure you hath all this while and yet doth use herself like a natural and loving wife'.[18] It would seem therefore that Friday, from the point of view of the husband and wife, was outwardly another day of uneventful convalescence. The Friday night was once more passed by the queen at the old provost's lodging, under the same roof as her husband.

Is it possible to construct out of Darnley's outburst of penitence to his wife, Mary's suspicions and the warnings received from abroad, evidence of an actual plot by Darnley against Mary, based on his residence at Kirk o'Field? It has been suggested that Kirk o'Field was in fact a monstrous conspiracy against Mary, which reacted in the end against its own perpetrator, Darnley.† Darnley was certainly by nature an intriguer and an ambitious one. But the fact that he was plotting in general is not evidence that he was plotting in particular at Kirk o'Field. He was here, impaired in health, virtually confined to his bed, with few of his supporters about him, surrounded by those of the queen, in the house of the brother of one of the nobles who hated him. Mary, far from being the immobile pregnant woman of a year back, was now active and energetic, flitting between Holyrood and Kirk o'Field, whereas Darnley was stationary. This was not a roundabout age in the manner of its killings. Kings and nobles died violently, but they died openly. The regent Moray died at the hand of an assassin, who shot out of the window into the street;

_____

Book of Articles made out that Mary's intention was to get her husband killed accidentally, it is notable that Moray made no mention of this remarkable scene, at which he was alleged to have been present, either at the time, or in any later indictment against Mary.

  † Principally by Major-General Mahon, *op. cit.* R. Gore-Brown, in *Lord Bothwell*, follows Mahon in believing that Darnley planned the explosion against Mary, while admitting that Bothwell actually ignited it, having discovered Darnley's treachery in the nick of time, and determined to pay Darnley out with his own coin.

the Riccio plot had aimed at the queen's life in the crudest possible manner. Queen Mary, who rode freely and frequently among her people, would at all times present an excellent target for an assassin: if gunpowder had been in Darnley's mind, it would have been aimed at a dwelling where there was not the faintest doubt that the queen would be present, at a time when he was in perfect command of himself. Kirk o'Field was so very far from being the ideal situation for Darnley to plan to kill Mary that, in the absence of concrete proof that he did so, it is surely more logical to regard the crime as aimed straightforwardly at the man it did in fact kill—Darnley. It is in the participants and the accessories to the crime, rather than the intended victim, that the complexities of the plot lie.

For while Darnley and Mary jogged through their last week of marriage in comparative peace, the conspirators had been hard at work to compass the death of one and the deliverance of the other. Friday seems to have been the critical day. Darnley could not be expected to stay in the lodging forever and Holyrood with its guards obviously presented more of a problem from the point of view of assassination than Kirk o'Field. Sir James Balfour told the lords in the summer, when he made his peace with them, that he first knew of the plot on Friday. Morton admitted in his own confession years later that he first knew of the plot from Archibald Douglas a little before, possibly on the Friday. The *Book of Articles* went further and said that this was the day originally intended to perform the murder, but the preparations were not ready. John Hay of Tallo in his deposition stated that it was on Friday that Bothwell said to him: 'John, this is the matter. The King's death is devised. I will reveal it unto you for if I put him not down, I cannot have a life in Scotland. He will be my destruction!'[20] John Hepburn, Bothwell's kinsman and henchman, deposed that the original purpose had been for certain of the nobles to kill the king by each sending two of their servants 'to the doing thereof in the fields'—[21] this corporate fate, so characteristic of gang vengeance, whether in Scotland or Sicily, would not only have wiped out Darnley's treachery but would also of course ritually involve all the nobles in the act, much as Riccio himself had received over fifty dagger-wounds in his body including Darnley's own dagger planted by George Douglas.

It would thus not have been possible later for some of the nobles to have denied their involvement.

The dagger being the natural murder weapon of the time, it is interesting to speculate what made Bothwell change his plans and turn to the much less malleable weapon of gunpowder. The reason he gave John Hepburn was probably the true one—because it was the obvious one. With servants openly at work, the death of Darnley in the fields would inevitably have been pinned upon the nobles who had concocted it. Bothwell was already in his agile opportunist's mind aiming at the position of king. He knew Mary had formally indicated that she wanted no violence done to Darnley. It was no part of his plan to be blamed for the crime: he certainly did not wish to suffer for it, merely to enjoy the result. Ironically enough, the use of gunpowder, and the blowing-up of the house which gave its incredibly flagrant character to the crime—and made Mary's cheerful tolerance of the perpetrators give such appalling scandal throughout Europe—seems to have been planned in simple good faith that a hearty explosion would cover the tracks of the killers, and make it impossible afterwards to prove who had done it, even if it was only too easy to guess. Such bold but straightforward reasoning was typical not only of Bothwell but of the age in which he lived.

The testimony of the page 'French' Paris (although extremely suspect, because it was wrung from him by torture) does at least confirm that Kirk o'Field was not a subtly planned crime.[22] Paris, once Bothwell's servant, was now in the queen's service, and attended her at the old provost's lodging. It was on the Wednesday or Thursday that Bothwell came into the queen's chamber, below that of Darnley, and told Paris that he found himself ill of his 'usual illness' which was a flux of the blood. He asked Paris whereabouts in the house he could 'faire mes affaires', and Paris, in view of the urgency of the situation, found Bothwell a corner; it was here, as Bothwell availed himself of the slight privacy to relieve himself, that Bothwell outlined to Paris that he had in mind to kill the king. Paris hesitated. Bothwell told him angrily that he was an utter fool if he thought that he Bothwell would enter such an enterprise all on his own—Bothwell then named Maitland, Argyll, Huntly, Morton, Ruthven and Lindsay as his accomplices. Paris enquired about Moray, Bothwell replied that he was neutral.* When Paris resisted Bothwell's demands, Bothwell only exclaimed impatiently: 'Why did I put you in the Queen's service if not to help me?' and it was at this juncture that Paris pointed out that Bothwell had bullied him for more than six years, kicking him in the stomach to make him do what he wanted. Paris was, however, insistent that Bothwell wanted the keys of the house of lodging from him—a point which incidentally points to the innocence of the queen, since she could presumably have provided them easily herself, had she been aware of the details of the plot. On Saturday, 8 February, Paris had apparently obtained these keys while no one else was in the room and taken them to Bothwell at Holyrood.

Sunday, 9 February was to be the last day of Darnley's convalescence. It was announced that he would return to Holyrood early on the Monday. It was also the last Sunday before the beginning of Lent, and, as such, a day of carnival and rejoicing; two events typical of the life of Queen Mary's court were planned to take place. In the morning Mary's favourite valet Bastian Pages married Christiana Hogg; being a Catholic it was his last opportunity to do so before the beginning of Lent. The wedding dinner took place at noon, and the queen was present: Bastian was an amusing high-spirited Frenchman, who shared the queen's own love of masques. It was he who had devised that masque at the baptism of Prince James, with the satyrs wagging their tails, which had so much enraged the English visitors that Hatton exclaimed that if it had not been for the presence of the queen, he would have put his dagger in the heart of 'that French knave Bastian'. The second court event was a formal dinner given at four o'clock by the bishop of the Isles in the house in the Canongate for the returning ambassador of Savoy. The queen attended this dinner, accompanied by her chief nobles, Argyll, Huntly, Bothwell and Cassillis—but not Moray. He had that very morning slipped out of Edinburgh, on the excuse that his wife was sick with a mis-

---

* By the date this deposition was made, later in 1568, it must be remembered that Moray was regent of Scotland: Paris's interrogators would have a strong motive for not wishing to incriminate their ruler.

carriage. Maitland was also absent, and Morton was not
yet sufficiently in the queen's personal favour to be admitted to court events. This duty accomplished, the queen
and her court rode down to the provost's lodging again,
in order to spend the evening with Darnley. The queen
planned to sleep Sunday night at Kirk o'Field once more,
at the end of her day of revelry, as she had done on the
Wednesday and the Friday.

There was a crowded scene at Kirk o'Field, as there
had been on many previous evenings there during the previous week. The royal entourage—'the most part of nobles
then in this town' said the queen[23]—crowded into the
king's chamber. The nobles, including Huntly, who had
been at the bishop's dinner, played at dice on that little
table with a green velvet cloth which had once belonged
to Huntly's father, still in their carnival costumes. Bothwell
was an especially striking figure in black velvet and satin,
trimmed with silver. The queen chatted pleasantly to the
king. There was probably some music, a song in the background to the sound of the lute or the guitar. It was the
sort of evening the queen much enjoyed whether at Holyrood or any of her other Scottish palaces: she may even
have appreciated the comparative adventure of sleeping
at the Kirk o'Field. But at ten or eleven o'clock her intention to do so once more was forestalled. Something—or
someone—reminded Queen Mary that it was the hour of
Bastian's wedding masque which she had promised to attend. Queen Mary was unable by nature to resist this sort
of obligation and Bastian's masque was of special importance in view of the fact that he had designed one for
her only six weeks previously. It now seemed unnecessarily
inconvenient to return once more to the provost's lodging
after the masque, to sleep there, since Darnley was coming
back to Holyrood early the next morning, and the queen
herself had also planned an early ride to Seton—according to Lennox's Narrative, it was 'Bothwell and others,
who seemed to bear a good countenance', who reminded
her of this last point. Darnley was sulky at the idea of
the change of plan, making the petulant demur of a sick
man, from whom the centre of amusement was being suddenly swept away. According to Moretta, the Savoyard
ambassador, the queen lightly gave him a ring as a pledge
of her goodwill.[24] She then bid him good-bye. Down the
staircase went the queen, out to the door where the horses

of the court were ready to bring her back to her palace. As she stood to mount her horse, she paused for a moment puzzled. She saw in front of her own page, Bothwell's former servant, French Paris. 'Jesu, Paris,' said the queen. 'How begrimed you are!'[25]

Little did the queen know that her innocent observation touched at the core of the secret happenings within the provost's lodging. For at some point during the day which the queen had spent in the formal court ritual of a servant's wedding and an ambassador's dinner, with the prospect of another court masque ahead of her, enough gunpowder had been placed in the vaults of the cellar of the house to blow it sky-high, and reduce it to the heap of rubble to be seen in the Cecil sketch. It is impossible to be sure with any accuracy exactly when the gunpowder was introduced and by whom. The henchmen employed in carrying out the practical details of the plot were apparently nine in number: John Hepburn, John Hay of Tallo, kinsman of Bothwell, William Powrie, his porter, George Dalgleish, his tailor, French Paris, his former servant, James (Black) Ormiston and Hog Ormiston, two further kinsmen, and Pat Wilson. At no point do their subsequent depositions seem more improbable than on the subject of the gunpowder.

According to the official story given by the arrested criminals later, the gunpowder was brought openly through the streets of Edinburgh by William Powrie, during the evening of Sunday, since it had been for some unaccountable reason stored in Bothwell's apartments at Holyrood in a barrel. The gunpowder was supposed to have travelled in two trunks. But William Powrie subsequently changed his story from one journey with two horses, to two journeys with one horse.[26] There was incidentally no explanation given as to why Bothwell should have already brought gunpowder from Dunbar, well before the Friday when he was first supposed to have broached the idea of an explosion. Powrie took the gunpowder to the gate of the Blackfriars Priory and helped to carry the gunpowder in 'polks' or bags over the wall. According to Paris's story, the gunpowder was now placed openly in a heap on the floor of the queen's chamber (with the entire court, in Buchanan's words, 'a great attendance', revelling in the room above). Bothwell himself was even supposed to have come down in the course of the evening and seen how matters were progressing. Powrie now made his way back up the Canongate accompanied by Wilson; together they conveyed the empty trunks; as Powrie went, he saw the torches of the queen's party flaring ahead of them, and heard the hooves of the royal horses clattering on the cobbles.

This whole story is so improbable that too much time need not be wasted in demolishing it: in any case it has been constructed out of depositions which are in many respects mutually contradictory. But certain salient points should be noticed: firstly the amount of gunpowder which could have been conveyed on horseback in two trunks was certainly not adequate to demolish the house at Kirk o'Field. At most, this amount could not have been more than two hundredweight.[27] The strength of gunpowder in the sixteenth century was also considerably weaker than today. Yet it was suggested that this amount of gunpowder, loosely placed in a heap on the floor of the queen's bedroom (the ground floor of the house), was sufficient to produce an explosion which by every contemporary account reduced the whole house to rubble. If the gunpowder was to produce any sort of blast, it would have had to have been tamped in rather than left in a heap; it would also have needed to be placed in the vaults of the house rather than on the ground floor. Left in a loose heap on the bedroom floor, there was no certainty it would have produced any sort of explosion at all: it might merely have flared and burnt itself out. It therefore becomes clear that the detail concerning the heap of gunpowder on the floor of the queen's bedroom was particularly inserted in Paris's deposition in order to incriminate her: for quite apart from the impossibility of producing an explosion from there, the heap of gunpowder would only too easily have attracted the attention of Darnley's servants as they passed to and fro on their way to the kitchen. Not only Darnley's attendants but the entire court were thronged into the room above, and there was no guarantee that they would all stay peacefully within the confines of the upper room. Like Bothwell on a previous occasion, they might have searched out the *garde-robe*.

The second point to notice in the depositions is that Holyrood Palace would have been an extraordinary place to choose to store gunpowder: not only was it patrolled by the royal guards, but the conspirators inevitably risked

detection once more when they had to convey the gunpowder through the streets of Edinburgh, patrolled in turn
by night watchmen, to the distant Kirk o'Field. Thirdly
the movements attributed to Bothwell present him with
an impossible schedule to fulfil, since he had already a full
list of engagements to carry out in the course of the day,
in official attendance on the queen. The figure who was
far more involved in the practical details of the crime than
the depositions revealed was Bothwell's then close associate Sir James Balfour. The reason for the obscurity which
was cast over his actions is not difficult to find: by June
1567 he had abandoned Bothwell's side for that of the
lords in power, and they therefore had an excellent motive for keeping his name out of trouble, and at the same
time blackening that of Bothwell still further. This remarkable but unlikable man was later described by Queen Mary
as 'a traitor who offered himself first to one part and then
to the other'[28] and his career seemed certainly to justify
her condemnation. Balfour had every reason to know the
geography of the old provost's lodging, since both it and
the house next door (the new provost's lodging) belonged
to his brother.* A few days after the explosion Drury reported to Cecil that James Balfour was known to have
bought powder to the tune of £60 Scots.[30] If any explosion was planned, it would certainly have been infinitely
more practical to bring the gunpowder, in sufficient quantities, from some comparatively obscure house much
nearer the provost's lodging than from Holyrood Palace.
The inconsistencies of the depositions make it clear that
others involved were being shielded, and although it cannot be proved, Balfour seems the most likely candidate
for the chief accomplice whose name was afterwards
shielded. It would have been easy for Balfour to store the
large quantity of gunpowder needed in the vaults of his
brother's house, and from there transfer it silently to the
vaults of the house next door. With his knowledge of
Darnley's house and of the district, he could have chosen
the time and place at his leisure, when he and his assist-
ants were not likely to be detected.

* The Continuator of Knox's *History*, writing at a later date, had
come to believe that Balfour himself owned the house where Darnley died, having 'lately bought it'.[29]

Queen Mary, in happy ignorance that the house in which she had just spent a relaxed evening, was in fact heavily mined with gunpowder—if she had known, one can hardly believe that she would have rested in it so contentedly—now proceeded down the Canongate to Holyrood. Here she attended the masque in honour of Bastian's marriage. She did not stay particularly long there, having made her *acte de présence,* and in any case the party seems to have been almost over when she arrived: it was time to put the bride formally to bed, according to the custom of the period. Mary now went to her apartments, where she took part in a long and earnest conversation until about midnight with Bothwell and John Stewart of Traquair, the captain of her guard. What was the subject of this conversation? No record was ever kept, and no contemporary suggestion ever made. But of one thing we can be certain— Bothwell did not take this opportunity to impart his plans for the destruction of Darnley to the queen. There could be no conceivable point in doing so at this juncture. The conspirators had no need to drop the slightest hint to the queen, so long as she fell in unconsciously with their plans. What could be their motive in informing her of the conspiracy at this late hour? If Mary showed signs of lingering at Kirk o'Field, it took only a gentle reminder from a courtier to recall Bastian's masque to her attention, a ceremony which she would be loath to miss. On the Friday the conspirators may have supposed that the masque would keep her away from the lodging altogether on the Sunday evening. Now that the lodging was heavily mined and Mary safely stowed at Holyrood, there could be no hitch in their plans—unless of course they chose to make a last-minute revelation to the queen. Mary, with that soft heart, that horror of bloodshed, that inclination towards mercy, to say nothing of love once felt towards Darnley, extinguished perhaps from the senses but not from the memory, might suddenly experience a last-minute feminine revulsion for what was proposed. She still had it in her power to wreck everything, with a lightning message of warning to Kirk o'Field. The arguments for not implicating her were now, as they had been previously at the conference at Whittingham, overwhelming. Queen Mary retired peacefully to sleep in her apartments in Holyrood. It was a cold evening; there had been a new moon at six o'clock that morning; outside a little snow powdered the streets and fields between Holyrood and the old provost's lodging.

It was now time for Bothwell, released from the royal presence, to join his underlings at the scene of the crime to supervise the lighting of the fuses. Going to his room, he changed out of his splendid silver and black carnival costume; his black velvet hose 'trussed with silver' were exchanged for a sober plain black pair, and a canvas doublet. He wrapped his riding cloak around him: George Dalgleish, with his tailor's eye, added in his deposition that it was of that 'sad English cloth, called the new colour'.[31] He collected the unwilling Paris, who by his own account showed no enthusiasm for the dangerous project. He now had the problem of reaching Kirk o'Field undetected, or at any rate comparatively so. We may dismiss the stories given in the depositions, which related that Bothwell now marched boldly down the Canongate and through the town wall at the Netherbow port. Here he was supposed to have answered the challenge of 'Who goes there?' from the watch with the piece of blatant self-advertisement: 'My lord Bothwell's men.' Bothwell who had abandoned the dagger and turned to gunpowder had obviously no desire to have the crime pinned on him. It is more likely that Bothwell went to Kirk o'Field by back streets, perhaps availing himself of the unbuilt section of the town wall, and thus approaching the lodging through the east garden, into which as we have seen, the house had its own door; of this door, Bothwell had either been given the keys by Paris as the servant deposed, or else had had false keys made by an Edinburgh blacksmith, as one of the anonymous placards after the murder suggested. Bothwell was now ready to supervise the lighting of the fuses. He was not the only nobleman present among the gang of conspirators. The movements of Sir James Balfour are obscure, but from the near-by Douglas house came Archibald Douglas and some of his men; although the Douglases were kinsmen to Darnley (through his mother Margaret born a Douglas) they were under the leadership of Morton, and were sworn to the destruction of the man who had betrayed them over Riccio. It was said that Archibald Douglas left one of his velvet slippers —'his mule'—at the scene of the crime: but at Douglas's trial in 1586, his servant John Binning said that after supper, Douglas, wearing secret armour and a steel helmet, took Binning and another servant by the back door of his house to the scene of the crime and Douglas was rightly able to pour scorn on the idea of wearing velvet slippers with armour.[32] It is far more probable that the gang of Douglases were heavily armed as they thronged round the house, either in the east garden, or the alleyway beyond the town wall.

Meanwhile within the doomed house, Darnley sulkily made preparations for his early departure the next morning to Holyrood. He ordered the 'great horses' for 5 A.M. For an account of how he spent his last hours, we are dependent on the narrative of his father Lennox.[33] Lennox paints an affecting picture of the lonely young boy (his 'innocent lamb') reciting the Fifth Psalm with his servant, 'My voice shalt thou hear in the morning, O Lord; in the morning will I direct my prayer unto thee, and will look up.' It is, however, a picture which ill accords with Darnley's known tastes during the rest of his life. More in keeping with his character was the fact that he called for wine from the kitchen downstairs, presided over by the cook Bonkil. Did he repeat to his servant, as Lennox suggested, some ominous words of the queen's that evening— 'It was about this time of year that David Riccio was killed . . .'? It seems likely that, as with the psalm, this dramatic detail sprang from Lennox's imagination. They were not at Holyrood, after all, where Riccio was killed, and it was a full month off the Riccio anniversary. There would have been little point in the queen taunting her husband on the subject, and in any case there is general agreement that their last interview was polite and friendly. One of his servants suggested that he should play the lute, but Darnley said that his hand was not given to the lute that night. They compromised on 'a merry song'. Darnley then retired for the night, with Taylor his valet sleeping in the same room, and Nelson, Symonds and Taylor's boy sleeping in the adjoining gallery, which overhung the town wall. Two grooms, Glen and MacCaig, were in attendance. There was a light burning in the window of Hamilton house, within the quadrangle, otherwise outward calm and silence over the Kirk o'Field.

At two o'clock in the morning, or thereabouts, the silent

air was rent by an explosion of remarkable proportions. The Keeper of the Ordnance afterwards likened it to thunder. Paris said that the air was rent by the 'crack', and that every hair of his head stood on end. The Memoirs of Herries described it thus: 'The blast was fearfull to all about, and many rose from their beds at the noise.'[34] At distant Holyrood, the queen in her bed was wakened as by a sound likened at the time to that of cannon fire and sent messengers to find out what had happened. Her guards heard it, and said: 'What crack was that?' People in the near-by Blackfriars Wynd came rushing out into the streets in fear to see what had transpired. We know from the Cecil sketch the sight which met their eyes—the house in which their king was lodged, totally reduced to a pile of rubble. Obviously the first immediate reaction was to imagine that the king had been killed. The first man to rush out into the street—a Captain William Blackadder, a henchman of Bothwell—was promptly arrested, although he swore he had merely been drinking in the near-by house of a friend. But now it was seen that on the top of the town wall, which was still standing, stood Nelson, one of Darnley's servants, who had survived the blast, calling to the people for help. If Nelson had survived, why so might the king. The next discoveries put an end to this hope. In the garden outside the town wall lay the dead bodies of the king and his servant Taylor. The king was still in his nightgown, and naked beneath it. Beside him was a furred cloak, a chair, a dagger and some rope. There was no mark or mutilation on either body, 'no fracture, wound or bruise' as Buchanan put it[35]—and no sign of the work of the blast. The king and his servant had been strangled.

The famous gunpowder plot of Bothwell had proved in the end all in vain—although Bothwell himself may not have known it as he returned to Holyrood once more. Indeed, he himself looked like perishing in the ruins of Kirk o'Field at one point, alongside Darnley. Having lit the fuses, he retired to watch the explosion; but, according to John Hepburn, as the train of gunpowder did not 'take fire so quickly as the Earl had expected', Bothwell impatiently began to approach the house once more. 'Thereupon the train suddenly emitted fire', and Hepburn, noticing it, was able to drag back his master in the nick of

time, before the whole house collapsed upon him.* With
the explosion completed, it was time for Bothwell to return to Holyrood once more; if the depositions are to be
believed, Bothwell answered the challenges of the watch
with the same self-advertisement, as he made his way
through the town back to the royal palace. According to
Paris, the keys of the house were dropped down a deep
well the day after the murder. But Bothwell scarcely
needed to perform this symbolical action to expunge any
guilty feelings concerning the death of Darnley. From the
point of view of a border adventurer and bold warrior, it
had been a satisfactory night's work, in which an eye—
Darnley's—had been given for an eye—Riccio's. Bothwell's own personal fortunes also stood to gain from the
enterprise. The paradoxical almost ludicrous element in
the whole situation—that Bothwell had not actually killed
Darnley by his mighty explosion—was probably unknown
to him at the time when he sank thankfully into his bed
at   ood.

For Darnley in fact died at other hands than those of
the earl of Bothwell. Something frightened Darnley, as he
lay within the mined house, and frightened him so badly,
that he escaped out of the provost's lodging in only a
nightgown, and attempted to make his way across the
gardens beyond the town wall to safety. He had had no
time to dress himself, and although his servant clearly
picked up a cloak, Darnley was not wearing it when he
died. They had one dagger between them. The chair and
rope indicate the improvised method of their escape—a
chair let down by a rope out of the gallery window into
the alleyway—a drop of only fourteen feet as we have
seen, and so through the next gate into the garden. There
had been no time to alert the grooms (who died in the
explosion) or the other servants. Darnley acted with the
speed of panic.

The most likely explanation of Darnley's precipitate departure would be that he was originally wakened by some
noise (possibly the laying of the gunpowder train within
the bowels of the house); he then looked out of his win-

* Related by John Hepburn in prison 'in the very agony of death'
to a fellow-prisoner, Cuthbert Ramsay. Ramsay told this story nine
years later, when he was giving evidence in Paris for the nullification
of Bothwell's marriage to Mary.[36]

dow, and saw the gathering of Bothwell's men and the Douglas faction in the east garden, on to which the window looked directly. Gunpowder would not have immediately sprung to mind (unless some hint of it had already been dropped, which now fell into place in his conjectures) but fire would. Burning the enemy's house over his head was a comparatively common sixteenth-century Scottish practice. The sight of Bothwell and his Hepburns and the hostile Douglases milling outside his house would certainly have suggested some imminent danger of fire, if not assassination to Darnley. Put at its mildest, there were no arguments to linger. But for Darnley, even once outside the house, there was no escape. The fleeing figures in their white nightgowns were discerned by some of the Douglas men who pursued them into the gardens. Here they were quietly and efficiently strangled, even as the house itself exploded in a roar of flames and dust. Some women living in the near-by houses said afterwards that they overheard the wretched last plea of Darnley for mercy to the Douglas men who were after all his relations: 'Pity me, kinsmen, for the sake of Jesus Christ, who pitied all the world . . .'[37] The plea went unanswered. Darnley died, a boy of not yet twenty-one, as pathetically and unheroically as he had lived.

17 The Mermaid and the Hare

'Certain stars shot madly from their spheres
To hear the sea-maid's music'

SHAKESPEARE *in* A Midsummer Night's Dream (*said to be
a reference to Bothwell and Mary*)

At the palace of Holyrood Queen Mary was woken from
her sleep by a noise like twenty or thirty cannon. Shortly
afterwards messengers brought her the news that the house
at Kirk o'Field had been totally destroyed, and her husband's dead body found lying at a distance of sixty to
eighty paces. Her first reactions were horror and shock—
horror at what had happened and shock at the feeling that
she herself had had such a narrow escape. Bothwell described her in his narrative as *'fort épleurée et contristée'*.[1]
She wrote the same day—Monday, 10 February—to her
ambassador Beaton in Paris, pouring forth her amazement
and distress, although it is noticeable that her conventional
grief for Darnley is outweighed by her conviction that the
conspiracy had been aimed at her personally; shortly after
the event, the Venetian ambassador in Paris also reported
that the crime was the work of heretics (Protestants) who
had intended to kill Mary too.[2] 'The matter is so horrible
and strange,' wrote the queen, 'as we believe the like was
never heard of in any country.'[3] She retailed Darnley's
fate (still apparently unaware that he had been strangled,
and not killed by the blast) and reported the utter demolition of the building 'with such a vehemency, that of the
whole lodging, walls and other, there is nothing remaining,
no, not a stone above another, but all carried far away,
or dung in dross to the very groundstone. It must have
been done with the force of powder, and appears to be a
mine.' The queen did not yet know who was responsible,
but is certain that with 'the diligence our Council has begun already to use . . . the same being discovered . . . we
hope to punish the same with such rigour as shall serve
for example of this cruelty to all ages to come'. She continued: 'Always who ever have taken this wicked enter-

prise in hand, we assure our self it was dressed always for us as for the King; for we lay the most part of all the last week in that same lodging, and was there accompanied with the most part of the lords that are in this town that same night at midnight, and of very chance tarried not all night, by reason of some mask in the abbey; but,' the queen concluded piously, 'we believe it was not chance but God that put it in our head.'

It is evident that at the moment when she wrote this letter, a few hours after the crime, it had not yet struck the queen that any of her chief nobles were involved in its execution. The sheer outrageousness of the explosion had distracted her from considering the known enmities between Darnley and many of the nobility—as Bothwell must have planned that it should; nervously convinced that she herself had only escaped death by a miracle, the queen was at first more inclined to ponder on her own enemies than on Darnley's. The official letter sent to France by the lords of the Council on the same day also emphasized the danger to the queen. So far, then, Bothwell's strategy had succeeded. He himself was officially notified of what had happened when George Hackett came and woke him from his bed at Holyrood, with the news that the king was dead. 'Fie, treason!' exclaimed Bothwell, jumping out of bed, and pulling on his clothes, which he had discarded only an hour before.* As sheriff of Edinburgh, it was now Bothwell's duty to lead a party of soldiers from Holyrood to the scene of the crime; whereupon the king's body, bearing as Knox said 'no mark of fire', was carried into the next door new provost's lodging. Here it was inspected by surgeons, then members of the Privy Council, and also by the general public, who were allowed to exercise their natural curiosity. It was at this point that the news that Darnley had in fact been strangled began to spread abroad —the variety of rumours on the nature of the weapon included his own belt, the sleeves of his shirt, his garters, a serviette, a napkin steeped in vinegar (Lennox's lurid contribution), and waxed cord. The old women in the Blackfriars Wynd—who were later examined by the Coun-

* In his own narrative, *Les Affaires du Conte de Boduel*, Bothwell announced that he had spent the whole night in bed with his wife— the classic alibi of the criminal.[4]

cil and dismissed for involving too indiscreetly the names
of the great—began to chatter of the men they had
seen round the house and that last poignant cry of Darnley.
His body was now carried on a board to Holyrood, embalmed by an apothecary and a surgeon, and laid formally
in state for several days, before being buried in the vaults of
the chapel royal, as was his due as a king of Scotland.

So far the royal widow had behaved with perfect correctness. She ordered the court into mourning, for which
£150-worth of black was ordered. Although, according
to Knox's *History* Mary showed no outward sign of joy or
sorrow when shown the corpse of Darnley, her strange
composure—so unlike her usual ready tears—may well
have been due to simple shock.[5] She herself embarked
heavily on the traditional forty days' mourning for her
husband, permitting herself, however, to attend the wedding of Margaret Carwood, her favourite bed-chamber
woman on the Tuesday after the murder; she had paid
for the wedding-dress—£125—[6] and either considered a
promise to a beloved servant too important to break, or
else was too dazed to realize the significance of what had
just happened. Her spirits had never recovered properly
from her Jedburgh illness; at the time of James's baptism
at the end of December du Croc had prophesied gloomily
that her nerves would give them some trouble yet—'nor
can I be brought to think otherwise so long as she con-
tinues to be so pensive and melancholy . . . She sent for
me yesterday and I found her laid on the bed, weeping sore. She complained of a grievous pain in her
side.'[7] Now her nervous health became so critically
weakened by the shock of the crime that, according
to Leslie, the Privy Council were earnestly exhorted
by her doctors to let her get away from the tragic and
gloom-laden atmosphere of Edinburgh for a while, lest
incarceration in the closed chamber of the widow
should cause a total breakdown—the doctors emphasized
'the great and imminent dangers of her health and life, if
she did not in all speed break up and leave that kind of
close, solitary life and repair to some good wholesome
air'.[8] Accordingly, the queen went to Seton, one of her
favourite haunts close to Edinburgh, a week after the murder, and spent three recuperative days there. Although
Mary's enemies subsequently accused her of dallying at

Seton with Bothwell, it was the task of Bothwell and
Huntly, as chief nobles of the kingdom, to remain at Holyrood to guard the person of Prince James.

In the course of her further reflections, once the first
distressing impact of the murder wore off, it could not fail
to occur to Mary that this was no hideous outrage by unknown assassins, but a deliberately planned coup on the
part of those nobles who had hated Darnley, and who had
openly discussed his removal with her at Craigmillar. It
must now have become apparent to her that she herself
had been in no personal danger, but that Darnley had paid
the penalty for his treachery in the violent and blood-
thirsty manner which she had by now come to associate
with Scottish vengeance. Possibly she taxed Bothwell with
complicity or possibly she was informed of it from another
source; but in any case by the mere process of reasoning
she could hardly have been ignorant as to who were the
authors of thè crime, when the first shock had subsided. In
the meantime rumours as to the truth of the matter, and
the fact that Mary's chief nobles had been involved, began
to reach both England and France. By March the Venetian
ambassador in Paris had heard a comparatively accurate
account of events from Moretta, the returning ambassador
of Savoy, and commented further: 'It is widely believed
that the principal persons of the kingdom were implicated
in this act, because they were dissatisfied with the King',
amongst whom he singled out Moray for having had a
quarrel with Darnley.[9] Both Catherine de Medicis and
Elizabeth reacted predictably to these rumours: a king
had been killed; Mary's leading subjects were said to be
involved in the crime; it was now up to Mary herself to
dispense public justice with a heavy hand, whether it was
directed towards the true criminals or not being less important than the fact that justice should be seen to be
done. The two queens, French and English, wrote long
admonitory letters to the third Scottish queen to this
effect.

Rumours were not only rife on the Continent and in
England: they were also percolating rapidly round Edinburgh itself. A quantity of people, many of them servants,
had been involved in the murder; it was hardly likely that
an outrage of this magnitude would remain a total mystery
for very long. Tongues wagged. There were dark hints, and
others a good deal plainer. One story said that Sir James

Balfour had had one of his underlings killed, because he threatened to reveal the truth out of a crisis of conscience.[10] Placards began to appear in the streets—the art of the anonymous placard having being recently imported from France. The first placard was nailed up on 16 February, a week after the murder, naming Bothwell and Balfour, and asserting that the queen had consented to the murder, as a result of the witchcraft of Janet Beaton, the lady of Buccleuch. The second placard on 18 February took a more xenophobic line, naming three foreigners in Mary's household—Bastian, Francisco, and Joseph Riccio. In a letter of 28 February to Cecil, Drury spoke of other bills bestowed upon the church doors, even of one posted upon a tree which mentioned a smith who would step forward if necessary and say he was the maker of the false keys for the house (if the man existed, it casts further doubt on Paris's deposition in which he said he was instructed to steal the keys of Kirk o'Field).[11] The sound of voices crying that Bothwell was the murderer of the king was heard through the night in the streets of Edinburgh. On 1 March the most famous and most virulent of all the placards appeared: it showed Queen Mary as a mermaid, naked to the waist, with a crown on her head, and Bothwell as a hare—the crest of the Hepburns—crouching in a circle of swords. The implication behind the use of the mermaid was not romantic, as might appear to modern eyes, but deliberately insulting, since the word was commonly used in the sixteenth and seventeenth centuries to denote a siren, and thus by analogy a prostitute.*

This was the supreme moment for Mary to show herself the prudent and ruthless sovereign, and benefit from the actions of others to make her own position thoroughly secure. Her Achilles' heel in Scotland—her husband Darnley—had been eliminated from her path by her own nobility. She had not known of the crime beforehand, and was not implicated in its details. Now her best course was

* The description of a mermaid was one which was thought especially applicable to Mary: Shakespeare used it in *A Midsummer Night's Dream* when he wrote of
    A Mermaid on a dolphin's back
    Uttering such dulcet and harmonious breath . . .
  [that] Certain stars shot madly from their spheres
    To hear the sea-maid's music.
The stars were intended to represent Bothwell.

to pursue the so-called murderers with public vengeance, in order to establish once and for all her own innocence of any possible complicity. After all, once the nobles came to power they took good care to produce some criminals publicly, as we shall see, in order to exculpate themselves; Mary herself should have been at least as practical while she still had the opportunity. Even if she could not go so far as arraigning Bothwell himself, there were underlings to be sacrificed. As it was, her conduct bordered on madness. The Privy Council had announced a reward of £2,000 for the capture of the criminals, immediately after the deed; there had been vague questionings of Nelson and the old women; but beyond that no further steps were taken to secure any arrests. Neither the placards, the rumours, the letters from abroad, nor Lennox's furious denunciations of his son's murderers—about whose identity he was personally in no doubt—seemed to have the power of penetrating Mary's passive state of despair and melancholy. Since health and shock had clearly robbed her of any shred of political judgement, she was exceptionally dependent upon her advisers. But the advisers who surrounded her were all for one reason and another incapable of pointing out the true facts of the situation; never was Mary Stuart's pathetic lack of loyal disinterested consultants more disastrous to her than in the period immediately after Kirk o'Field.

Moray's first concern was to clear himself of any possible guilt in the eyes of his English friends: Moretta, after all, had believed Moray implicated above all others because of his notorious hatred for Darnley. In a letter to Cecil of 13 March, Moray anxiously excused himself and also asked for a passport so that he could come to London.[12] In this crisis of his sister's affairs, Moray was eager to put as much distance as possible between himself and the Scottish court, partly so that he should not be involved in the contentious struggle for power which he saw coming, in which the strength of the hated Bothwell seemed to be growing hourly, partly so that he could ingratiate himself in England. He departed for London at the beginning of April—incidentally making his sister guardian of his daughter, in his will. Queen Mary wept at his departure, and wished 'he were not so precise in religion'.[13] Of the queen's other possible advisers, Maitland had been involved in the plot, and could therefore scarcely advise

her to pursue its punishment vindictively. Bothwell was
hardly likely to counsel a course so alien to his own interests. There was thus no force to conjure the queen out of
her mood of lassitude and melancholia. Her foreign correspondence ceased—that immense flood of letters to her
Guise relations, in whom she had taken such a touching
detailed domestic interest ever since she left France, dried
up; there is no more poignant evidence that Mary Stuart
had fallen into a state of despair. The Scotland of her
dreams and early happiness now seemed to her a cruel
and barbarous country where deeds of violence succeeded
each other in remorseless succession; her secretary and
now her husband had been done to death within a year,
not by low assassins but by the chief men of the kingdom.
The renewed bloodshed less than twelve months after the
death of Riccio horrified her. In her sad passivity, she
allowed herself to lean increasingly on the one man close
to her who still showed strength of purpose, energy and
determination—and was also only too anxious to direct
the affairs of state. Unfortunately for Mary, that man was
Bothwell, who, whatever his dominating qualities, was also
the chief suspect of her husband's murder.

On 8 March, the queen received a formal visit of condolence from Killigrew, Elizabeth's envoy. He found her,
by his own account, 'in a dark chamber, so as I could
not see her face, but by her very words, she seemed very
doleful, and did accept my sovereign's letters and messages in a very thankful manner . . .'.[14] On 14 March, an
effort was made to punish the author of the defamatory
placards, and James Murray of Tullibardine was accused of
having 'devised, invented and caused to be set up certain
painted papers upon the Tolbooth door of Edinburgh,
bending to her Majesty's slander and defamation'.[15] On
19 March, Bothwell began to show his mettle as director
of Mary's policies: it was time for Prince James to be
returned to the royal nursery at Stirling, from which his
mother had plucked him a month before, when there were
rumours that Darnley was threatening his safety. While
Argyll and Huntly conveyed him there, his governor, Lord
Mar, was presented with the governorship of Stirling
Castle. This meant, in turn, that Mar could be deprived of
the vital governorship of Edinburgh Castle—which he had
held loyally for the queen in August 1565. This fortress
Bothwell now bestowed on his own ally Sir James Cock-

burn, but later, even more fatally, gave to his associate
Sir James Balfour—presumably as a reward for his part
in the murder.

Bothwell's ambitions to become effective ruler of Scotland, which one may conjecture he had nourished since
the summer of 1566, had been given a further fillip at
the end of February by the serious illness of his wife Jean
Gordon: she hovered on the brink of death, and one ambassador went so far as to announce that she had actually
died. There is no need to attribute poison to Bothwell to
explain the illness, since divorcing Jean later proved extremely easy—but it must surely have had the effect of
sending his thoughts racing forward to his future plans.
His finances were also no better than before and in
February he had to sell more land to Alexander Home,
which gave him another powerful motive to press forward
towards a position in which his finances would be at least
unassailable. By the end of March, a story had reached the
English ambassador in Paris that a marriage might be
forthcoming between Mary and Bothwell and, at roughly
the same date, Drury reported to Cecil in London that
'the judgement of the people' was that Mary would marry
Bothwell.[16] For once more in her history, as at her birth,
and after the death of Francis, the queen's new marriageability made her a target for any ambitious man who
wanted to make himself a king. And Bothwell was certainly such a man inspired either by family tradition of
advancement through queens, or plain personal ambition,
unmarked by any trace of sentiment or sensitivity.

On 23 March, the fortieth day after Darnley's death, the
queen's period of mourning officially came to an end with
a solemn Mass of Requiem and a dirge for Darnley's soul.
In fact her sorrows were only just beginning. The vociferous demands of Lennox for vengeance had reached a pitch
when even Mary, advised by Bothwell, felt herself unable
to ignore them. In a letter of 24 March she agreed to allow
him to bring a private process in front of Parliament
against Bothwell as the slayer of his son, and the process
was set up by an Act of the Privy Council on 28 March
to take place on 12 April. It was hardly surprising that
in two letters of 29 and 30 March, Drury reported the
queen to be in continuous ill-health—'She has been for
the most part either melancholy or sickly ever since, and

especially this week upon Tuesday or Wednesday often swooned . . . the Queen breaketh very much.'[17] The trial of Bothwell was not even instituted officially by the queen, but allowed to stand at the private petition of Lennox. But Lennox understandably shrank from appearing in Edinburgh with the six followers permitted to him by law, in view of the fact that the city was swarming with 4,000 of Bothwell's adherents.

On the appointed day, Bothwell rode magnificently down the Canongate, with Morton and Maitland flanking him, and his Hepburns trotting behind. The queen, with Mary Fleming, now Maitland's wife, watched them go from the window at Holyrood. Although the due processes of justice were observed at the trial—which lasted from noon till seven in the evening—the absence of the accuser Lennox meant that Bothwell was inevitably acquitted; the wily Morton excused himself from the jury, on the grounds that he was kin to the victim, and thus cunningly, with an eye to the future, did not partake in Bothwell's acquittal. The Diurnal of Occurrents, written by a comparatively impartial court observer, commented sourly that Bothwell was 'made clean of the said slaughter, albeit that it was heavily murmured that he was guilty thereof'.[18] Another omen for the future was the fact that a last-minute messenger from Elizabeth arrived at Holyrood at 6 A.M., and attempted to get the trial postponed, presumably until Lennox could be present. The messenger was, however, not admitted to the Scottish queen's presence, and treated with little courtesy.

Bothwell reacted characteristically and braggartly to his acquittal: he sent a crier round the town, and had bills stuck on the town gates and the Tolbooth, emblazoned with his arms, offering to defend his innocence with personal combat. However, that night, an anonymous acceptor of his challenge on a placard offered to prove that Bothwell was the 'chief author of the foul and horrible murder by law of arms', showing that the Scots spirit was not to be bullied. The next Wednesday, the queen rode to Parliament, with Bothwell carrying the sceptre, Argyll the crown and Crawford the sword once more as a year ago: but on this occasion, her nerve had evidently gone sufficiently to surround herself with hagbutters, no longer trusting the bailies of Edinburgh. At this Parliament, the proceedings of Bothwell's trial were officially declared to be just according to the law of the land; all subjects were ordered to live in unity, despite their religious differences, and even more significantly, grants of land towards certain nobles were confirmed—the lands that went with Dunbar Castle were confirmed to Bothwell, and Huntly and four other Gordons were confirmed in their estates, although unofficial restitution had been made two years before. These were the practical aspects of the fall of Darnley.

Bothwell's next move was absolutely in keeping with his character and the conditions of the time: if he was to make his power even more effective by occupying the position of king, he needed the support of at least some of his fellow-nobles. The contemporary expedient of a bond was once more called into play, as twice before over the murder of Riccio and the murder of Darnley. In order to secure adherents for this new bond, on Saturday 19 April, at the end of the sitting of Parliament, Bothwell duly entertained twenty-eight of the nobles and prelates then in the capital to a lavish feast—contemporary reports differing as to whether this banquet took place in his own apartments at Holyrood, or in Ainslie's Tavern in the town itself. What was sure was that at the end of this momentous supper party, Bothwell produced a long document, the main point of which, apart from his own innocence of the murder of Darnley, was that the queen was now 'destitute of a husband, in which solitary state, the commonwealth may not permit her to remain'.[19] It continued ingenuously: if the 'affectionate and hearty service of the said Earl, and his other good qualities' might move the queen to select him as a new husband—and the document suggested that another reason for such a choice, quite apart from Bothwell's noble nature, might be the fact that Mary would prefer 'one of her native-born subjects unto all foreign subjects'—then the signatories were to promise themselves to promote the marriage by counsel, vote and assistance. To this remarkable manifesto, known by the name of the tavern as the Ainslie bond, eight bishops, nine earls and seven barons now put their signatures including Morton, Maitland, Argyll, Huntly, Cassillis, Sutherland, Glencairn, Rothes, Seton, Sinclair, Boyd and Herries.* Although the

* Although one contemporary report said that Moray also put his signature to the bond, this seems unlikely as he was by now in London.

motives and loyalties of some of the signatories must be considered to be highly suspect—for surely to Morton and Maitland King James Hepburn would be no more acceptable than King Henry Stuart had been—nevertheless Bothwell now had in his pocket the document he considered he needed for his next bold move forward.

The queen having gone to her favourite Seton, Bothwell now followed her there with Maitland and Bellenden. According to Queen Mary's own story, it was here that he first paid suit to her, suggesting both that she needed a husband, and that he was the best man to fill the role, since he had been selected to do so by her nobles. This direct request threw the queen into a state of confusion: 'This poor young princess, inexperienced in such devices,' wrote Nau,[20] 'was circumvented on all sides by persuasions, requests, and importunities; both by general memorials signed by their hands, and presented to her in full council, and by private letters.' We can certainly believe Mary's account that she did not know what to do, especially when Maitland assured her what she knew only too well, that it had become absolutely necessary that some remedy should be provided for the disorder into which the public affairs had fallen for want of a head. Now her chief nobles were apparently pleading with her to accept Bothwell—'a man of resolution well adapted to rule, the very character needed to give weight to the decisions and actions of the council'. However, Queen Mary always asserted afterwards that she refused Bothwell's proposals at this point, on the grounds that there were too many scandals about her husband's death, despite the fact that Bothwell had been legally acquitted of complicity by Parliament.

With this refusal still uppermost in her thoughts, the queen proceeded to Stirling to pay a visit to her baby. She arrived on Monday 21 April, and spent the whole Tuesday enjoying the company of her child. James was ten months old. The queen played with him in peace, happily unaware that this was the last meeting she was ever to have with her son. While she was at Stirling, she also wrote to the former papal nuncio, the bishop of Mondovi, now back in Turin, protesting her devotion to Scotland, to the Pope, and the Holy Catholic Church—in which she intended to die.[21] It is difficult to know for certain what thoughts of the future inspired this strange guilty little letter, but Mondovi's reaction, written before he had heard news of her abduction and marriage to Bothwell, is significant: he prophesied that unless the queen of Scots was given strong support by the papacy, she might give way to the natural impulse of a young woman and seek support elsewhere from a husband instead; as a candidate for this post, Mondovi put forward the name of Bothwell 'who has ever been the Queen's most trusty and obedient adherent'.[22]

On the Wednesday Mary started back to Edinburgh. The visit to Stirling had ostensibly been a secret one, and she had with her only Maitland, Huntly, James Melville and about thirty horsemen. Mary's health was still poor. On the road back she was seized with a violent pain and had to take rest in a roadside cottage. That night she slept at the palace of Linlithgow, the peaceful palace overlooking its lake, where she had been born. The next morning, Wednesday 24 April, the ninth anniversary of her marriage to Francis, the queen and her little troupe started back on the road for Edinburgh. But as they reached the Bridges of Almond, about six miles from Edinburgh, close to the point where the Gogar Burn joined the Almond River, and travellers were ferried across, Bothwell suddenly appeared with a force of 800 men. He had spent the night at the near-by castle of Calder, apparently on his way into Liddesdale. Bothwell rode forward, put his hand on the queen's bridle, and told her that since danger was threatening her in Edinburgh, he proposed to take her to the castle of Dunbar, out of harm's way. Some of Mary's followers reacted disagreeably to the sudden appearance of Bothwell, but the queen said gently that she would go with the Earl Bothwell rather than be the cause of bloodshed. Docilely, without more ado, she allowed herself to be conducted about forty miles across the heart of Scotland, skirting the capital itself; she seemed to accept Bothwell's story so totally that she made no attempt to seek rescue from the country people as she passed. Her only positive action was to send one James Borthwick to Edinburgh to issue a warning of possible danger. When Borthwick told the provost what had happened, a very different view was taken of the disappearance of their sovereign. The alarm bell was rung and the citizens were begged to attempt a rescue. But by this time there was little that they, or anyone, could do. At midnight, the queen was within Dunbar Castle, surrounded by a force of Bothwell's men. The gates of the castle were firmly shut behind her.

This abduction—if the word can truly be applied to anything so calm and placid as these proceedings at the Bridges—represented a typical example of Bothwell's thinking. Even if earlier hints of Bothwell's predilection for abduction, in Arran's story, are disregarded, Bothwell clearly had the mentality which considered that a sufficiently public outrage covered in some curious way a multitude of sins. This had been his reasoning over Kirk o'Field. Now he confidently believed that an abduction would not only put an end to further consultation and discussion about the marriage—in which his reasoning was perfectly correct—but also distract public attention from his connection with Darnley's death by the very flagrancy of the act; here of course his reasoning was disastrously wrong. Was Queen Mary enlightened in advance as to her prospective fate? Although we cannot have the certainty of definite proof, the contemporary evidence points strongly to the fact that Mary knew of the plan beforehand, and agreed to it weakly, as a possible way out of the morass in which despair brought on by ill-health seemed to have landed her. The intended abduction was certainly widely known about beforehand among her nobles. Lennox knew about it on the Tuesday, and Kirkcaldy of Grange, Bothwell's bitter enemy, mentioned it on Wednesday, the day it actually happened.[23] In a fury at Bothwell's rising eminence, Kirkcaldy wrote to Bedford in the same letter that the queen had been overheard saying that she would go to the end of the world in a white petticoat with Bothwell—but as Kirkcaldy did not reveal by whom or under what circumstances this extraordinary declaration had been overheard, and as he subsequently became one of Mary's loyalest followers, it seems likely that he was allowing his dislike and jealousy of Bothwell to taint his imagination. Maitland must surely have known of the plan. Paris, in his deposition, said Bothwell's man, Black Ormiston, came to Linlithgow Palace secretly the night before the abduction and had a long earnest conversation.[24] It seems inconceivable that the scheme should not have been outlined also to the queen, if only to secure her cooperation. Mary, still envisaging Bothwell as her help and support among the nobles, and not as the reprobate adventurer whom his enemies later built up in their writings, felt in no position to withstand this latest proposition; it was presented to her by Bothwell, using the same arguments which he had used to himself, as a convenient solution to her difficulties.

Once within the castle of Dunbar, Bothwell made his second planned move—an equally characteristic one, although in this case the queen was not consulted beforehand. He decided to complete his formal abduction of her person by the physical possession of her body. His intentions in this aggressive act were as before perfectly straightforward: he intended to place the queen in a situation from which she could not possibly escape marrying him. Bothwell was certainly not in love with Mary, although he may have accompanied his actions with some sort of protestations, such as he thought suitable to the occasion. But in the course of the gratification of his ambitions, rape was not the sort of duty from which Bothwell was likely to shrink. Melville, who was present in the castle at the time, and only allowed to go free the next morning, was quite certain that the ravishment had taken place: 'The Queen could not but marry him, seeing he had ravished her and lain with her against her will.'[25] It was Melville who tells us that Bothwell had already boasted that he would marry the queen—'who would or would not; yea, whether she would herself or not'. A fortnight later Mary gave a very vivid description of her experiences to the bishop of Dunblane, who was instructed to explain her hasty marriage to Bothwell to the French court: first of all Bothwell 'awaited us by the way, accompanied with a great force, and led us with all diligence to Dunbar' and there, in words which seem positively touching, 'Albeit we found his doings rude, yet were his words and answers gentle.' Now Bothwell, not accepting her promise to marry him, refused to have the consummation of the marriage delayed, but kept up a continuous barrage of importunity, 'accompanied none the less by force' until 'he has finally driven us to end the work begun at such time and such form as he thought might best serve his turn'.[26] It is interesting to note that Bothwell's and Mary's contemporaries believed instantaneously and strongly that the abduction scheme had been a rigged one and intended to save the queen's face. Within three days Drury wrote that although the manner seemed to be forcible, it was known to be otherwise.[27] But it was also widely believed that Bothwell had completed his scheme by ravishing the queen, and that this was probably against her will. These were the conclusions drawn by those able to observe at first hand the bold and scheming character of Bothwell, and the markedly straitlaced attitude of Queen Mary to 'matters of sexual morality.

It is sometimes suggested that Mary found a sexual satisfaction with Bothwell which she had not experienced with either of her previous husbands. This may or may not be true: it can certainly never be proved, since the queen herself certainly never ventured any opinion upon the subject, and to the end of her life always firmly attributed her marriage to Bothwell to reasons of state rather than dictates of the heart. In fact, the events leading up to her marriage to Darnley point far more clearly to the workings of physical infatuation, than those leading up to the Bothwell marriage. In spring 1565 Mary Stuart was a young and beautiful woman, healthy and energetic, long widowed, eager to be married; in spring 1567 she was broken in health, distraught, nervously concerned about the future of her government in Scotland. Quite apart from the evidence of events, it seems extremely doubtful whether they were the sort of couple who would have been drawn to each other if political considerations had not been involved. Practical ambition had driven Bothwell to woo the queen: this elegant, coquettish, literary-minded, slightly cold woman, with her graceful, leaning figure, her red-gold hair, her laughing flirtatious ways, her demand for obeisance to which she had been accustomed from her earliest years, was not the type to appeal to Bothwell, the lover of the lusty Bessie Crawford, the dominating courtesan Janet Beaton or the plaintive submissive Anna Throndsen. Of all Mary Stuart's qualities, her courage and gaiety, her ability to make quick decisions and pull herself rapidly out of an untenable situation were those most likely to appeal to Bothwell: but these had been strangely in abeyance since her virtual nervous breakdown at Jedburgh. The important fact about Mary Stuart in Bothwell's eyes was that she was queen regnant of Scotland, with the power to make her husband king consort and effective ruler of the country.

Of course it would not be essential for Bothwell to love Mary for her to respond to him: she might even have experienced some perverse satisfaction in domination by this straightforward and brutal man, so different from her other husbands, and her potential courtly lovers. Bothwell's intellectual curiosity certainly extended into matters of sex. Apart from the common contemporary rumours of his vicious life, there was a *canard* that he practised homosexuality.* The feelings which Queen Mary felt for Bothwell can only 'be estimated in terms of the importance which as a woman she gave to the whole subject of sex. In early youth she naturally paid little attention to such questions, and during the period of her first widowhood also was remarkable for the discretion with which she conducted herself. Her disastrous marriage to Darnley, springing from physical attraction, gave her every reason to adopt an extremely suspicious attitude towards passion and its consequences. If, despite all these considerations, she experienced some genuine fulfilment in Bothwell's embraces, it is remarkable how little effort she made to keep in touch with her husband, once she was in captivity: from the moment of her abdication onwards, she seems to have lost all interest in Bothwell, as though he belonged to some previous, unsuccessful, political phase in her life. Another interesting aspect of her captivity is that she made absolutely no attempt to quench any desires of the flesh, if indeed, she felt them, during the whole nineteen years: there is no rumour, which bears investigation, of the sort of liaison which would surely have occurred had she become, under Bothwell's tuition, the *grande amoureuse* of so many imaginings. On the contrary, from the age of twenty-five onwards, the queen led a life of total chastity.

Whatever Mary's inner feelings for Bothwell during the short period of their concubinage—three weeks from Dunbar to the marriage, and four weeks thereafter—their union was certainly not founded originally on the flimsy basis of passion. Mary's confessor Mameret later solemnly swore to the Spanish ambassador in London that, until the question of her marriage to Bothwell was raised, he had never seen a woman of greater virtue, courage and uprightness—

---

* A broadside ballad published in Edinburgh after Mary's abdication, *An Declaration of the Lord's Just Quarrel*, written by Robert Sempill, an extremist Protestant, exclaimed:

>   *Such beastly buggery Sodom has not seen*
>   *As ruled in him who ruled Realm and Queen.*[28]

and he therefore, with all the intimate knowledge of her character gained in the confessional, utterly believed that Mary had only taken up with Bothwell in order to settle the religious situation in Scotland.[29] In fact the queen had not one but three pressing and—as it seemed to her—good reasons for giving her consent to the marriage with Bothwell. In the first place he had succeeded in convincing her that he would at last provide her with the able and masterful consort whom she had so long sought to share with her the strains of the government of Scotland. He had subjugated her by the undoubted strength of his personality at a time when broken health had induced in her a fatally indecisive, even lethargic state of mind, so that faced with the reality of Bothwell and his positive aims, she was unable to see clearly where her own best interests lay. Secondly, Bothwell was able to show to Mary the Ainslie bond which proved to her satisfaction that the majority of her nobility—not only Seton and Huntly but also the more contumacious Morton and Argyll—were prepared to accept him as their overlord. Mary had married Darnley defiantly against the advice of most of her nobles: she did not intend to make the same mistake twice. The Ainslie bond, and the apparent approval of the nobility were worth more to Bothwell in furthering his suit than all the magic arts and enticements with which he was afterwards credited by Mary's partisans in order to explain his seduction of her.* Thirdly, Bothwell had effectively ensured that the queen would not be able to go back on her word once she was back in her capital, by the act of physical rape which he had performed at Dunbar. The union had already been consummated: it remained to transform it into a legal marriage.

Having secured the queen's acquiescence, Bothwell now faced the problem of ridding himself of his existing wife, to whom he had been married just over two years before. This did not prove difficult, since Jean Bothwell seems to have raised no objections: her marriage had been brought about by political considerations, and she was now content to have it dissolved for the same good reasons.

---

* Both Leslie and Lennox, from different sides, accused Bothwell of using black magic to seduce the queen. Today he would probably have been accused of drugging her. In his *Confession*, a suspect document, Bothwell admits to using magic to secure the queen's affections.[31]

There were already rumours by the end of March that
her brother Huntly had agreed in principle to the deal. On
3 May Lady Bothwell was given judgement against her husband in the Protestant commissary court, which had replaced the old church courts in matrimonial cases: the
grounds given were his adultery with Bessie Crawford. In
order to make assurance doubly sure, their marriage was
then formally annulled on 7 May by the Catholic Archbishop Hamilton, on the grounds that they had not received
a dispensation for their marriage, although they were
within the fourth degree of consanguinity, Bothwell's great-
great-grandfather having married a Gordon. The cynicism
of this gesture may be judged by the fact that not only
had a dispensation actually been given, but it had been
given by Archbishop Hamilton himself.[30] Despite the ease
of the divorce, Bothwell's servants took the opportunity in
the course of it to threaten violence to Master John Man-
derstoun, canon of Dunbar collegiate church, who was
told that if matters did not move fast enough 'there shall
not fail to be noses and lugges [ears] cut, and far greater
displeasures . . .'.[32] On 6 May Bothwell brought the queen
back into Edinburgh: at the end of April she had received
an offer of rescue from Aberdeen, which she had rejected.
She was now regarded as firmly committed to Bothwell's
rule. The couple entered Edinburgh by the West Port and
then rode up the Bow towards the castle. Both Huntly and
Maitland were in their train. Although the artillery of the
castle shot off magnificently for the queen's arrival, it was
generally remarked that Bothwell's power was now absolute. The Diurnal of Occurrents recorded that the Earl
Bothwell led the queen's majesty by the bridle of her
horse, as though she were a captive.[33]

As Queen Mary moved in a trance towards her public
union with Bothwell, already the forces of aristocratic reaction were coalescing against his meteoric rise. Furious
at the realization that Bothwell—one of their own number—had made himself a virtual dictator, on 1 May a
party of dissidents gathered at Stirling. They vowed in yet
another communal bond to strive by all means in their
power to set their queen at liberty, and defend her son
Prince James. In this meeting at Stirling, it is significant
that the key figures were Morton, Argyll and Atholl—all
three of whom only a week before, out of either cunning
or weakness, had signed the Ainslie bond promising to

forward Bothwell's suit of the queen. Bedford was now
asked by Kirkcaldy to write to Moray and ask him to return, and Robert Melville wrote for English support against
Bothwell, threatening French support if it was not forthcoming. The pattern of Scottish politics was forming once
more into the same shapes of family alliances and feuds,
in which the power of one noble could not be allowed to
grow unchecked, and in which English help was like the
joker in the pack of cards. The Stirling conspirators di-
verted themselves with a drama called The Murder of
Darnley and the Fate of Bothwell—in which the boy
actor who played the part of Bothwell was hanged so
realistically that it took some time to restore him to life.
These same nobles sent a message to Mary offering her
their support against the Lord Bothwell. But since Bothwell was firmly governing all matters around her, the queen
could scarcely credit that he had already lost the support
of the fickle Scottish lords: it was after all only a few
weeks since the signing of the Ainslie bond, which had
convinced her that the majority of her nobility especially
desired this Bothwell marriage.

The days passed with horrible speed towards her
wedding-day. When John Craig, Knox's colleague in the
parish church of Edinburgh, refused to proclaim the bans
of their marriage without a writ from the queen, he was
brought a command signed by her personally saying that
she had been neither ravished nor yet retained in captivity.
But when Craig did make his proclamation, he was still
brave enough, on 9 May, to express contemporary disgust
at the speed of events, by a denunciation in front of the
Privy Council of Bothwell's behaviour: 'I laid to his charge,
the law of adultery, the ordinance of the Kirk, the law
of ravishing, the suspicion of collusion between him and
his wife, the sudden divorcement, and proclaiming within
the space of four days, and last the suspicion of the King's
death which her marriage would confirm.'[34] Angrily Bothwell threatened to hang Craig: but Craig spoke no more
than what the common people of Edinburgh, once so devoted to Mary, their dream figure, their beautiful young
queen, felt themselves at seeing her thus recklessly and
carelessly allow herself to be trampled in the mire of Bothwell's ambition. On 12 May Mary created Bothwell duke
of Orkney and lord of Shetland (titles once borne by his
ancestor, the 1st earl) and placed the ducal coronet on his

head with her own hands. Four of his followers were knighted, including Black Ormiston of Kirk o'Field fame. To many the queen seemed like a mindless zombie under the power of Bothwell's authority: Beaton in Paris was naturally growing distracted at the madness or folly of his young mistress, but Clernault reported to him on 14 May that Mary neither listened to nor inspected any communication he brought her from Beaton or others of her advisers abroad.[35] On the same day the queen officially pardoned those nobles who had signed the Ainslie bond.

On Thursday 15 May, twelve days after his own divorce, just over three months after the death of her own husband, Mary and Bothwell were married in the great hall at Holyrood. Lines from Ovid were posted upon the gates of the Palace—'*Mense malas maio nubere vulgus ait*'—or as the people murmured significantly: 'Wantons marry in the month of May'.* A greater contrast to the two previous weddings of the queen could hardly be imagined. The very fact that the ceremony took place according to the Protestant rite showed how much the queen had lost control of her destinies, although it is possible that she herself heard a Mass earlier in the day, out of which her adherents later tried to construct a story that they had been married under both forms. At the service, Adam, bishop of Orkney, preached a sermon in the course of which he chose to announce Bothwell's penitence for his former evil and wicked life. After the wedding, there were no masques as there had been at the Darnley wedding, or 'pleasures and pastimes' as there had always been before when princes married.[36] There was merely a wedding dinner, at which the people were allowed to watch Mary eating her meal at the head of the table, with Bothwell at the foot.

Equally significant of the queen's state of mind is the fact that there were no rich presents for Bothwell as groom as there had been for Darnley, and certainly no lavish replenishment of her own wardrobe. Whereas Darnley had received violet velvet, furs, a cupboard for perfumes,

---

* There was a rooted prejudice in Scotland against May marriages —or, as a similar Scottish saying had it: 'Marry in May and regret it for ay'; and the records show a remarkable decline in the number of marriages practised during that month. Ovid's line (from the fifth book of the Fasti) described the similar prejudice of the ancient Romans, said to have been due to the fact that the *Lemuralia*, or three-day feasts to appease the spirits of the dead, began on 9 May.

cloth of gold for his horse's caparison, blue bonnets with
feathers for his fools, and other tokens of Mary's love,
Bothwell merely received some genet fur from one of Mary
of Guise's black cloaks for his dressing-gown—his solitary
present. Furthermore, the queen seems to have paid no
attention to the subject of her own clothes, once so important to her. There are only two entries in the inventories
of her wardrobe in May 1567—one being for Bothwell's
fur—compared to thirty in July 1565, the month in which
she married Darnley.[37] Her sartorial preparations were confined to having an old yellow dress relined with white
taffeta, an old black gown done up with gold braid and a
black taffeta petticoat relined. Of all the sad events in the
life of Mary Stuart in Scotland, this squalid hurried
wedding, of a rite she did not profess, without any of the
preparations she so loved, is surely the most pathetic.

Judged from the comments of observers, Mary's brief
married life with Bothwell brought her absolutely no personal happiness. Already on their wedding-day, du Croc reported that a strange formality was noticed between the
queen and her new husband. Mary tried to excuse it, by
saying that she did not wish to be merry. To Leslie, she
was more explicit: she sent for him, and in floods of tears
told him how much she already repented of what she had
done, especially her Protestant marriage ceremony.[38] She
promised him desperately she would never do anything
again opposed to the Catholic Church. In front of others,
Mary's sadness was even more fearful and more desperate.
Melville heard her actually ask for a knife, to kill herself
in front of Arthur Erskine, her equerry, the day after the
wedding, and when he remonstrated with her, the queen
threatened to drown herself.[39] It has been suggested that
Mary's unhappiness was due to the fact that Bothwell now
made some revelation to her about his past—his guilt at
Kirk o'Field, for example, or even his father's supposed
liaison with her mother Mary of Guise. But Mary Stuart's
state of mind was now too immediately disturbed for such
past scandals to be able to affect her, and Bothwell's involvement in her husband's death was certainly no surprise
to her at this point. The hysterical nature of Mary's reaction shows not only how far she was from feeling any kind
of personal love for Bothwell, but also how desperately
close her nerves were to the surface and how far her self-
control had vanished. As it began to dawn on her that she

might have betrayed her whole reputation in order to marry a man who was no more suited than Darnley to advise her, control the nobles, or govern Scotland, her future began to look very black indeed.

Melville reported that Bothwell's beastly and suspicious nature was such that 'not one day passed' during their time together without the queen shedding abundant tears. Maitland told du Croc a little later that since the day of the queen's marriage there had been no end of tears and lamentations, since Bothwell was furious and jealous if she looked at anyone except him—he accused her of having a pleasure-loving nature, and liking to spend her time in frivolous worldly pursuits, like any other woman.[40] In short there was now no lute-playing, hunting and hawking, as in the early days with Darnley. Even before their marriage, Bothwell's unkindness had led to half a day's quarrel between them. Bothwell's language was said to be so filthy that even Melville was constrained to leave his presence. Gossips in London suggested that Mary suffered tortures of jealousy because Bothwell's former wife Lady Jean still remained installed in his own castle of Crichton. Maitland helped to stir up trouble by telling Mary that Bothwell had written to Jean several letters assuring her that he only regarded Mary as his concubine—Jean was still his only lawful wife. Du Croc took care to pass the story on to the French court, adding spitefully: 'No one in this kingdom is in any doubt but that the Duke (Bothwell) loves his former wife a great deal more than he loves the Queen.'[41] In fact property was probably at the bottom of Bothwell's relations with Jean: it is unlikely that he could have turned her out of Crichton, even if he had so wished, since her dowry had redeemed the mortgage, and Jean Bothwell, as we have seen, had a commendable sense of property values.

But Bothwell in his treatment of Mary was less concerned with the niceties of their legal relationship, than in the power that it brought him. In their bond of 16 June, the lords announced that Bothwell had kept Mary as the virtual prisoner of his ambition. None of their number had been able to speak to her, even on lawful business, without Bothwell being present; so suspicious had Bothwell become, that he kept the queen's chamber door perpetually guarded by his own men of war. Drury reported on 20 May that the queen's distress was the talk of the court:

never, it seemed, had a woman changed so much in appearance in so short a space of time. It was even rumoured that she was suffering from the falling sickness (epilepsy) to explain her deranged behaviour.* The mermaid and the hare were evidently as ill-suited to live together as might be expected of a half-fairy sea creature and a wild animal of the earth.

One of the first tasks the queen and Bothwell had to face after their hasty marriage was that of explaining it away to both the French and English courts. Mary's instructions to the bishop of Dunblane,[43] who was entrusted with the mission to France, and the letter he sent along the same lines to Beaton, have a strongly apologetic note, as though she was all too aware of that unpleasant French proverb, *qui s'excuse, s'accuse*. Apart from her accounts of events leading up to the marriage, already quoted, she stressed her continued loyalty to the Catholic Church—she would not 'leave her religion for him, nor for any man at all'—aware that her actions had once more cast this seriously in doubt. Her instructions emphasized Bothwell's loyal service to the Scottish crown, and glossed over their previous disagreements which she attributed to the jealousy of other nobles. 'As envy follows virtues, and this country is of itself somewhat subject to factions; others began to mislike his proceedings, and so far by reports and misconstructing his doings, went about to put him out of our good grace. . . .' Then Mary stressed the fact that Bothwell had won over the other nobles to the marriage project —'He obtained an writing subscribed with all their hands, wherein they not only granted their consent to our marriage with him, but also obliged them to set him forward with their lives and goods.' Finally she described her own helpless and broken spirit, how she felt herself inadequate to deal with the Scottish situation single-handed—'this realm being divided in factions as it is, cannot be contained in order, unless our authority be assisted and forthset by the fortification of a man who must take upon his person in the execution of justice . . . the travail thereof we may no longer sustain in our own person, being already

---

* From this comment Mahon argues that the queen suffered from mild epileptic seizures all her life, citing her dementia, stupour and apathy after Kirk o'Field as signs of temporary post-epileptic insanity. But the evidence of her captivity—when her health was closely observed and recorded—does not confirm the epileptic diagnosis.[42]

wearied, and almost broken with the frequent uproars and rebellions raised against us since we came in Scotland'. Despite this plea for sympathy in her situation, which has the ring of truth, Mary felt it necessary to outline answers to two possible objections—the lawfulness of the marriage she defends by saying that Bothwell's previous marriage was dissolved, and her failure to bring the nuncio to Scotland she defends by saying rather ingenuously that she had done all she could in this respect, and that if the nuncio had arrived such terrible events might not have happened.

Robert Melville's instructions for breaking the news to Queen Elizabeth ran along very similar lines.[44] The difficult quarrelsome nature of the Scottish people is once more emphasized, as is Mary's personal exhaustion and despair for lack of a husband to support her in this impossible situation. Mary met the principal objection of Elizabeth— that she had married the man suspected of her husband's death—with the point that he had been formally acquitted of the crime by the Scottish Parliament. Despite the fact that Mary accompanied her instructions with a personal and charming letter to Cecil, begging him to help her cause with Elizabeth, neither the English queen nor the French queen allowed themselves to be distracted by Mary's excuses from the patent facts of the case. From the point of view of either France or England, the Scottish queen had totally lost her head in thus allowing herself to be wedded to the disreputable Bothwell. The only real line of defence was after all that which Mary took in her letter to Beaton: 'The event is indeed strange and otherwise nor (we know) you would have looked for. But as it is succeeded, we must take the best of it.'

Ironically enough, if the Scottish situation had not been so factious, if Bothwell had not by the flagrant manner of Darnley's death provided such a convenient handle against himself, if he had understood in any way how to persuade his fellow-nobles into accepting him as consort—as he attempted unsuccessfully to do through the Ainslie bond— he might not have made a bad ruler of the country. The union of Mary and Bothwell might have turned out a marriage of convenience, if not a love match. Bothwell had strength and he had intelligence; as for his tendency to search for violent solutions to problems, he was certainly not alone in possessing this failing in this epoch.

He showed reverence for the queen's position if not her person, refusing to cover himself in her presence until she took his cap and put it on. When they rode abroad together, they put up a good public front of content. Bothwell's actions during his five weeks as consort were positively encouraging for the future of the country, were it not for the fact that his fellow-nobles were by now seething in almost open revolt. The machinery of the Privy Council, for example, was overhauled to provide for more regular attendance; a law was passed against bringing false money into Scotland; more important still, on 23 May the proclamation concerning the religion of the country which Mary had enacted on her first arrival in Scotland in 1561, was re-enacted formally to reassure the troubled minds who had heard false rumours about its validity. It was pointed out that by allowing certain persons to practise their own (Catholic) religion, the queen had intended no violation of the Act. Scotland was still very much officially Protestant. All this was done with the advice of Mary's 'dearest husband, James Duke of Orkney, Earl Bothwell, etc.' Bothwell's own letters to France and England, backing up Mary's explanations of their marriage, revealed a certain native diplomatic ability. To Queen Elizabeth, Bothwell wrote: 'I will thus boldly affirm that, albeit men of greater and birth and estimation might well have been preferred to this room, yet none more careful to see your two Majesties' amity and intelligence continued by all good offices. . . .' He wrote in the same vein to Charles IX of France; Archbishop Beaton he tactfully requested to excuse him in so far as some of his behaviour might seem rather unceremonious and lacking respect.[45] Such intelligence might have stood Mary in good stead, if she had ever been allowed the time to enjoy it. It was in exchange for his strength and support in the future that Mary had endured the humiliation of her wedding-day to Bothwell. But the cruelty of fate ensured that she was never allowed the time to enjoy her part of the bargain.

Fast as events had moved before Mary's wedding, the speed only increased after the ceremony. By the end of May the clouds of war were gathering round Bothwell's head with such menace that on 30 May the queen and duke were constrained to summon their people to meet

them at Melrose on 15 June, with a view to taking arms.
The granting of Tantallon to Morton and Edinburgh Castle
to Balfour made neither of them more agreeable to see
Bothwell elevated above them. Mary described the genesis
of a new conspiracy in Scotland to Nau as follows:[46] 'It
may have originated in some secret feuds among the lords
of recent date, or possibly from grievances of remoter
origin which though long hidden, at last came to scatter
their poison on the surface.' What distinguished this new
fracas from the Huntly affair, the Chaseabout Raid, the
Riccio killing and even the murder of Darnley, was that
it now proved convenient to bring in a new dimension of
morality, in order to blacken the case against Bothwell,
and gloss over the previous commitments of Morton and
Maitland. Undoubtedly the hatred of Bothwell and Maitland for each other proved a telling point in the rallying of
the nobles against the queen. This animosity was so well
known, that Maitland was actually rumoured to have been
killed by Bothwell at Dunbar. In the end Maitland placed
his feelings for Bothwell above his loyalty to Mary, and
on 6 June finally left the royal court for the west. He told
Cecil that he had been in fear of his life, since Bothwell had
tried to kill him in a fit of ungovernable rage in the
queen's own presence, and would have succeeded in doing
so, if Mary had not rushed to Maitland's assistance. Maitland refused to admit that his disappearance at this critical
juncture involved any disloyalty. To Cecil he explained
smoothly that he had only remained at Mary's side for so
long, with so many hazards to his life and honour, because
of his ancient affection for the queen. Now he could endure no more.[47]

Many of the conspirators, such as Kirkcaldy, belonged
to the old Protestant party of Moray, who had hated Bothwell since Chaseabout days and before. Bothwell had many
virulent enemies. After Home and Murray of Tullibardine
joined, Tullibardine brought in his brother-in-law Mar,
the more inclined to come over because Bothwell had deprived him of Edinburgh Castle. The allegiance of Atholl
was the easier to procure because his wife was sister to
Maitland's wife Mary Fleming; Morton also dangled the
prospect of the marriage of his rich young ward the
countess of Angus with Atholl's son before the earl's eyes,
although in the end the young lady was married off to Mar's
son instead. In this network of allegiances and betrayals the

treachery of Sir James Balfour surpassed that of anyone else: for he, the closest involved in the murder of Darnley, who had probably drawn up the Craigmillar bond, and who had been granted the custody of Edinburgh Castle as a reward for his complicity, now secretly treated with the conspirators and agreed to support their cause, on condition that his custody of the castle was confirmed. Yet another bond was made in which Sir James Balfour promised to put Edinburgh Castle at the disposal of the nobles, on the grounds that Bothwell was wickedly keeping their sovereign's person in thrall. A further condition of Balfour's adhesion was a total indemnity for any past crimes he might have committed up to the present moment —which included of course his participation in the murder at Kirk o'Field.

On 6 June, Bothwell took Mary from Holyrood to the castle of Borthwick, a stark twin-towered fifteenth-century fortress, set down beneath a low hill in a valley watered by a tributary of the Esk, about twelve miles to the south of Edinburgh. The lord of Borthwick was Bothwell's neighbour and ally: from the battlements of Borthwick, the tip of Bothwell's own castle of Crichton, only two miles away, could be discerned. Mary evidently considered her stay would be tranquil enough, for the Demoiselle de Courcelles specially brought down the royal silver hand-basin for the queen to use while she was there.[48] Her hopes were disappointed. Borthwick was surrounded by the insurgents. Bothwell, with his military knowledge, realized that it was ill-situated to withstand a siege, and therefore slipped away through a postern gate, with only one companion, the son of the laird of Crookston. The boy was captured, but Bothwell galloped clean away, leaving Mary to hold the castle. The besiegers called up to the queen to abandon her husband and accompany them back to Edinburgh. When she proudly refused, they shouted insults up the steep and forbidding walls, of a nature 'too evil and unseemly to be told', wrote Drury in a letter to London, as he described the new plight of 'this poor princess'.[49] The poor princess had not, however, lost all her old spirit. She sent two messengers to Huntly for help, both of whom fell into Morton's hands. The besiegers felt unable to attack without the arrival of Mar and Lindsay, and decided to return to Edinburgh. In the meantime Mary disguised herself as a man, and escaped out of the castle by night

to the near-by Black Castle at Cakemuir, which belonged
to the Wauchopes, also neighbours and adherents of Bothwell. Here she met Bothwell, and together they made their
way to Dunbar, by Fala, skirting the Lammermuir hills to
the north to avoid detection.

It was at Dunbar that the ultimate treachery of Balfour
revealed itself: for it was his message to the queen that
she would do better to return to Edinburgh, where the
guns of the castle, under his command, would support her,
which brought her out of this comparatively safe place,
before the royal forces had mustered to anything like a
secure strength. In answer to this reassuring summons,
Mary and Bothwell now issued forth from Dunbar, with
200 hagbutters (musketeers), sixty cavalrymen, and only
three field guns taken from the castle itself. All the queen's
belongings and wardrobe had been left behind in Edinburgh or at Borthwick from which she had escaped in her
male disguise: she was now dressed in clothes hastily borrowed at Dunbar: a short red petticoat, a muffler, velvet
hat and sleeves tied with bows, such as the women of
Edinburgh wore. Her charm and dignity were undiminished
by her costume: it was her reputation which no longer
had its pristine purity in the minds of her ordinary subjects
and, in a tragic phrase, as the royal cortège passed, 'the
people did not join as was expected'. By the time the queen
reached Haddington she had about 600 horses—the faithful Seton had joined her, but Lord John Hamilton and
Fleming did not appear; as they still debated the best
route to take, Huntly and the rest of the Hamiltons stayed,
either dispiritedly or indecisively, within Edinburgh Castle.
Bothwell found himself relying on the inferior contingents
of border lairds such as Ormiston, Langton, Waughton,
Wedderburn and Bass. At Gladsmuir, those royal supporters to be seen were treated to a proclamation saying that the
conspirators, under the pretext of saving the life of Prince
James, were trying to dethrone the queen, in order that they
might rule in their own fashion. Queen Mary was therefore compelled to take up arms, and those faithful subjects who had come to her assistance would be rewarded
with the lands and the possessions of the rebels. The army
then marched on to Leith, and reached Prestonpans, where
they spent the night. Mary and Bothwell passed the night—
their last together—at the palace of Seton, the house which

Mary had loved so long and happily in her six years in Scotland.

At 2 A.M. on the Sunday morning, 15 June 1567, the confederate lords marched out of Edinburgh towards Musselburgh. In the van of their procession was borne a white banner showing a green tree, with the corpse of Darnley lying underneath it, and his infant son kneeling before him, with the legend: 'Judge and avenge my cause, O Lord': otherwise the rebel lords were each marked by the banner of their family. A few hours later, the royal army under Bothwell also moved out, and took up a commanding position on Carberry Hill. About eight miles east of Edinburgh, above their heads flew not family banners, but a series of banners bearing in each case the cross of St Andrew; and the position of the queen herself was marked by the solitary rampant red lion of Scotland. These nobles now took up their position on a hill opposite—Morton and Home with the cavalry, and behind them, Atholl, Mar, Glencairn, Lindsay and Ruthven with the main body of troops. It was a blazing hot day. Both parties suffered from thirst although by one account the lords had the advantage of some wine to sustain them. In between these two armies, neither of them exactly certain as to how they should proceed, the queen lacking troops, and the nobles lacking authority, there appeared the figure of du Croc, the French ambassador, who had panted out from Edinburgh after the insurgents.[50]

Du Croc was now deputed by the rebels to beg Mary to abandon Bothwell, at which they were to restore her to her former position, while they themselves would continue to be her loyal subjects. This Mary absolutely and furiously declined to do. She pointed out in a passion of indignation to du Croc that these same lords had signed a bond recommending marriage with the very man they were now opposing so vehemently—'It was by them that Bothwell had been promoted' she kept repeating. By her own account, Mary had no inkling at this point that the lords intended to charge Bothwell with the murder of Darnley: but certainly she felt absolutely no temptation to desert Bothwell. In the first place, Bothwell, with all his faults, had shown himself loyal to her throughout her adversities and his own, and was pledged to her support; she felt no such confidence about the behaviour of men of the calibre of Morton, Lindsay and Ruthven. Secondly, the queen, who miscarried a child at Lochleven in the middle of July, must by now have realized herself to be pregnant by Bothwell. The fact could not fail to seal their union in the mind of such a philoprogenitive woman. A single child was scarcely enough to ensure the royal succession of Scotland—or England—as history had all too often proved: it was no coincidence that Mary's marriage contract to Bothwell had specifically stated one of the objects of the match to be: 'that of her royal person succession might be produced'.[51]

As Mary refused to relinquish Bothwell, both sides now gave themselves up to a series of chivalric parleys, reminiscent of medieval warfare, in which challenges to personal combat were given and taken with great enthusiasm, but no actual battles took place. The first challenge came from the lords, who probably thus hoped to delay matters, until their reinforcements reached them. Bothwell, whom du Croc described as being in high spirits—'a great Captain, speaking with undaunted confidence, and leading his army gaily and skilfully . . . he could not count on half his men, and yet was not dismayed'—accepted the challenge and rode out in front of the troops, sending a herald forward. James Murray of Purdovis was the first to step forward, but the queen refused to tolerate the encounter, on the grounds that his rank was so much inferior to that of the duke. Bothwell then indicated the sly Morton as a suitable recipient of his challenge. Morton characteristically delegated the job to the spirited Lindsay, who took off his armour and rested his limbs in preparation for the combat. Morton then clasped round his waist the great sword which had once belonged to his ancestor Archibald Bell-the-Cat. But even as these parleyings and preparations were proceeding, the royal troops were melting away, as can be seen in the contemporary sketch of the battlefield. This was probably the intention of the rebels, for in the end, despite these splendid preparations, no one ever did come forward to meet Bothwell's challenge. Like an ancient hero he stood alone while his troops vanished. It was too late now to attack his enemies up hill, and his men were insufficient. There was no sign of the Hamiltons, who it was hoped might reinforce them.

At evening the rebels decided to press their advantage with a new parley. Atholl and Maitland both lacked the courage to confront the queen they had betrayed, but

Kirkcaldy rode forward. Bothwell's spirits were very far from being either broken or cowed: but as a good general he was aware that the royal party suffered from a striking lack of troops. It would be highly unwise to choose this moment to challenge the lords, when there was a possibility of rallying much more support to Mary's side in other parts of the country. He therefore suggested to Mary that they should retreat to Dunbar: first of all the castle had a strong, virtually impregnable position on the sea; secondly, it would serve as a rallying-point for new supplies of royalists. But Mary could not believe that the situation was so desperate. She still believed in Kirkcaldy's honour. She considered that the wisest course for her to pursue in the interests of peace and the avoidance of bloodshed was to accept a safe-conduct for Bothwell, and trust herself to the confederate lords, whom she now apparently thought would investigate everything anew by Parliament. Kirkcaldy assured her that the crown as such was not being attacked; afterwards Mary told Nau that both Maitland and Atholl had assured her privately that they were not with the rebels at heart.[52] Bothwell, it was agreed, would gallop off to Dunbar, either to raise further troops, or to await parliamentary developments in the capital. With renewed trust in her nobles, Mary bade farewell to the man for whom she had sacrificed so much in terms of honour and reputation. They embraced in full view of both armies. It was at this point that Bothwell entrusted to Mary the bond signed at Craigmillar, which gave her the proof of Morton's and Maitland's complicity in the murder; perhaps because he had been raised among them he had less optimism than his wife about her future at the hands of the rebels. At sunset Bothwell mounted his charger, and after five weeks of power galloped away down the road to Dunbar. It was the last sight Mary was ever to have of him.

The queen of Scots was now thoroughly alone. And her entry into the camp of the rebels immediately and rudely jolted her confidence in the love which she still believed her subjects bore for her. Here was no enthusiastic reception, no cheers, no protestations of devotion. On the contrary, the soldiers shouted crude insults at her. The queen's spirit still held. She said loudly and openly to Morton: 'How is this, my lord Morton? I am told that all this is done in order to get justice against the king's murderers.

I am told also that you are one of the chief of them.'[53]
Morton slunk away. But Mary Stuart needed all her
courage to endure the ordeal before her, for which she
seems to have been ill-prepared. She, who all her life had
been greeted publicly with adulation and enthusiasm, now
heard the soldiers shout: 'Burn her, burn the whore, she
is not worthy to live,' as they conveyed her along the road
into Edinburgh. 'Kill her, drown her!' they cried. Close
to Mary's side rode Drumlanrig and Cessford, two notorious
young thugs, who joined their insults to the soldiers' as
they rode. Amazed, almost stunned, the queen allowed tears
of shock and humiliation to pour down her cheeks, as she
rode forward in the clothes she had acquired at Dunbar—
now 'all spoiled with clay and dirt'. For the first time she
began to realize what the effect had been on the ordinary
people of Scotland—the people who had once loved her—
of her reckless action in marrying her husband's assassin,
and of those weeks of propaganda by the enemies of Bothwell. To them she was now no longer their young and
beautiful queen, but an adulteress—and an adulteress who
had subsequently become the willing bride of a murderer.

In Edinburgh, the queen was not taken to either of her
own residences, Holyrood or Edinburgh Castle, but to the
house of the laird of Craigmillar, the provost of Edinburgh, who was Maitland's brother-in-law. The nobles sat
down to a hearty supper, but the queen retreated in a daze
of horror at her experiences into her bedroom—even here,
however, she could not find peace, since the guards insisted on remaining with her inside the room, so that she
could not even undress. Mary now lay down on the bed,
deprived of any furniture or bedding proper to her station
as a queen, still in the red petticoat in which she had come
from Dunbar, and gave herself up to the wastes of despair.
There seemed no hope, and certainly no honour in Scotland, since the nobles, to whom she had freely surrendered,
now held her a humiliated and unconsidered captive. Looking out of her window, she caught sight of Maitland—
Maitland of Lethington who had risen so high in her
favours, Maitland, her earliest counsellor, Maitland, her
secretary, 'her Lethington' who owed so much to her for
kindnesses in the past. In a piteous voice, and through
her tears, she cried out the name: she called him: 'Lethington, Lethington.'[54] But Maitland pulled his hat over his
ears and pretended not to hear her. In the meantime that

cruel white banner was stationed in front of her window, with its corpse and its legend, which had accompanied her all the way to Edinburgh, the first thing to meet her impassioned gaze.

By the next day Mary's self-control had utterly collapsed. She came to the window, and cried out to the people that she was being kept in prison by her subjects who had betrayed her. The sight of her brought about rioting outside and more mockery and more insults. The lords pulled her back, saying that shots might be fired, and that they could not guarantee her safety. But before they did so, many of her subjects had seen the distraught woman, as she showed herself at the open window—her hair hanging down about her face, her clothes torn open so that the upper half of her body was almost bare, her beauty ravaged, her courage gone.[55] Where now was the exquisite princess who had fascinated the French court and half Europe, the 'belle et plus que belle' of Ronsard's poetry, in this wretched near demented creature hanging out of the window of an Edinburgh prison, half naked, her bosom exposed, shrieking out that she had been betrayed? The people of Edinburgh, their innate decency overcoming their moral disapproval, were shocked into pity and compassion at the sight. It was four weeks since Mary's marriage to Bothwell, and not quite two years since her boldly triumphant marriage to Darnley, attended by all the panoply of the Scottish court. This was the nadir of Mary Stuart.

18 Lochleven

'How the Mouse for a pleasure done to her by the Lion, after that, the Lion being bound with a cord, the Mouse chewed the cord, and let the Lion loose. . . .'

AESOP'S *Fable of the Mouse and the Lion, quoted in the deposition of a servant after Queen Mary's escape from Lochleven*

The confederate lords were aware that they were on extremely delicate ground with regard to the queen's imprisonment, since this imprisonment had followed ruthlessly on her own voluntary surrender in the interest of civil peace. Mary herself had genuinely, if naïvely, expected a parliamentary investigation into the murder of Darnley to follow her surrender. Under these circumstances, the lords decided that it would be too dangerous to keep the queen in ward in Edinburgh itself. The people of the city regarded the queen's wretched state with sad astonishment: it would certainly be easier to keep their moral disapproval of her behaviour at feverpoint during her absence, when rumours of her depravity could be spread without fear of contradiction. But even *in extremis* Mary retained enough of her former decisiveness to send a message to the captain of Edinburgh Castle, begging him to keep 'a good heart' towards her, and to preserve the fortress from the rebel lords. There is no proof that Mary wrote to Bothwell on the night of her arrival swearing to be true to him: Melville believed the story was invented by the lords themselves to lend colour to the theory of the queen's infatuation;[1] in any case no such letter has ever been found. The queen did succeed in having an interview with Maitland on Monday evening (she told Nau that, in the course of it, he was never able to meet her eyes) in which she continued to demand a full enquiry into the circumstances of the late king's death.[2] It was just this enquiry which Morton, Maitland and Balfour in particular had good reason to fear, and against the possibility of which they were so determinedly blackening the name of their former colleague Bothwell. All things considered, it was clearly in their interests to remove the queen as fast as possible to some secure prison, where she could no longer make these inconvenient demands, or if she did so, her utterances need not necessarily be reported accurately beyond the bounds of the four walls which would confine her.

On the Monday evening, therefore, the queen found herself being taken down to her own palace of Holyrood, where she was reunited with her own women including Mary Seton and Mary Livingston (Sempill). Some supper was prepared for her. This was the first meal she had eaten since before her surrender at Carberry Hill, for she had been at first too upset, and later too frightened by the idea of poison, to eat anything while she was in the provost's house. Morton stood behind her chair while she ate. In the middle of the supper he sent a message to find out if the horses were ready and, on hearing that they were, told the queen to leave her meal and get ready to ride on horseback. At this point, Mary had some vague idea that she was being taken to Stirling Castle, to join her son. She was not allowed to take any of her ladies-in-waiting with her, but only two *femmes-de-chambre;* nor was she allowed to take any clothes, not even a nightdress or linen. At this news, the women around her set up a great wailing. Against the background of this melancholy sound and under cover of darkness, the queen was once more conducted out of her palace.

Mary found herself being taken at great speed not to Stirling, but fifty miles north, to Kinross-shire. The two lords whom she had most reason to fear for their previous boorish conduct to her—Ruthven and Lindsay—were put in charge over her. Still scarcely able to credit what was happening to her, Mary had got as far as Leith, which was posted full of soldiers, when a rumour reached her that the Hamiltons were going to mount a rescue attempt. The queen tried to slow down the pace of her horse, but the gesture was in vain, since her escorts whipped it on. Late at night Mary reached the vast waters of Lochleven. Here, on one of the four islands in the middle of the loch, lay the dour castle of Sir William Douglas. Douglas was a most trustworthy jailer from the point of view of the lords: he was the half-brother of Moray, being the son of Moray's mother Margaret Erskine by her legal husband

Robert Douglas; he was the nephew of the earl of Mar, Margaret Erskine's brother; he was cousin and heir-presumptive to Morton. The lords could certainly rely on his interests being bonded to theirs. The queen was now rowed across the bleak waters of the lake. On arrival she was conducted quickly and unceremoniously to the laird's room; it had in no way been prepared for her visit, and lacked any sort of furniture, equipment or even bed suitable to her rank and condition. Mary sank once more into a stupor in which sickness, aggravated by pregnancy, despair and exhaustion, all played a part. She remained in this semi-coma for a fortnight, neither speaking to any-one nor, as she remembered afterwards, eating or drink-ing, until many of those within the house actually thought she would die.

Beyond the laird himself, the inmates of Lochleven con-sisted of his mother Lady Margaret—'the old lady' as she was known—who as the mother of the bastard Moray by Mary's own father, James V, was said to bear a natural, if illogical, grudge against the queen for occupying the throne from which fate had debarred her own son. Also within the castle was one of the old lady's younger sons, George Douglas who was nicknamed 'pretty Geordie', a hand-some and dashing young man, very unlike his half-brother Moray both in appearance and in the roman-ticism of his character. Mary had visited the castle itself previously under happier auspices, using it as a centre from which to hunt in Kinross-shire: it was here in its great hall that she had debated with Knox in the spring of 1563. But by nature, Lochleven was indeed more suited to be a prison than a pleasure haunt.* In the six-teenth century, the island on which it stood was so small that it hardly extended beyond the walls and garden of the fortress—the present-day slightly larger island being the result of a considerable fall in the water level of the lake in the last century. Its dominating, square main tower, from which an excellent view of the shore was to be ob-tained, stuck up out of the lake like a signpost pointing to its inviolability. This tower had been built in the late fourteenth century, and contained five storeys, with the

---

* Later the earl of Northumberland was also imprisoned there by Morton when he fled to Scotland in 1570 after the failure of the northern rebellion.

entrance only on the second floor; in this tower the laird
and his family lived. The castle also contained another
round tower, built in the corner of the courtyard, and
here the queen was eventually incarcerated, on the grounds
that this would make it more difficult for her to signal to
the shore. The lake itself, then twelve miles across, was a
bleak place even in August, with the Lomond hills lower-
ing over it, and the flat grey waters punctuated only by the
occasional dark trees of the islands; during the winter, the
winds and rain would sweep across the lake and make it
a desolate place indeed. It was certainly a prison from
which escape would prove a virtual impossibility without
connivance from the inside.

On 16 June the warrant for the queen's imprisonment
was signed by nine lords including Morton, Glencairn and
Home, who only eight weeks before had put their signatures to the Ainslie bond supporting the Bothwell marriage. The lords left in power in Edinburgh—for Lindsay
and Ruthven remained at Lochleven to guard the queen—
like robber barons, did not fail to take possession of the
queen's silver plate, jewels and other goods which she had
involuntarily left behind her. Calderwood wrote that the
lords went through her belongings, as well as overthrowing
the religious furnishings of her private chapel, as soon as
she was gone to her prison. Mary herself told Nau that the
silver and furniture and her multitudinous wardrobe were
handed over to the lords by the treachery of one of her
Italian servants—who probably felt himself unable to resist the new powers in the land. Certainly by 10 July arrangements were made for twenty-seven pieces of the
queen's plate to be delivered over by her chamberlain, Servais de Condé, to be melted down into silver coin.[3] In
view of the fact that the previous bond of the rebel lords
had expressly referred to their intention of releasing Mary
from the thraldom of Bothwell, and restoring her to liberty to rule as before, it was small wonder that the queen
now felt herself totally betrayed—being in closer thraldom
than ever, with her belongings sequestrated and her liberty far more grievously curtailed than it had ever been in
the days of her marriage to Bothwell.

In the meantime Bothwell himself was still at liberty.
From Carberry Hill he had gone to Dunbar, but on hearing of the queen's imprisonment, he sallied forth from the
castle, and during his remaining two months within the

bounds of Scotland attempted with great energy and single-mindedness to raise some sort of support for her. At first he enjoyed a certain success, with the Hamiltons at Linlithgow, and then at Dumbarton which Lord Fleming still held for the queen; Argyll and Boyd actually rejoined the royal cause, showing once more the chameleon-like character of Scottish family allegiances. The speed of Bothwell's movements defied capture by the lords, even after 1,000 crowns was offered for his apprehension as a result of the protests of the Assembly of the General Kirk; he was able to make a quick visit to the borders, where he hoped to be able to galvanize his family adherents.

He was now called to the Tolbooth officially to answer for murdering Darnley, kidnapping the queen, and making her promise to marry him: having ignored the statutory three weeks' notice to appear, Bothwell was formally declared an outlaw and a rebel, with his titles, offices and dignities forfeit. The outlawry cracked the somewhat weak nerves of the royalist party, who feared for their own possessions: Seton and Fleming withdrew from the connection; Huntly, whom Bothwell visited at Strathbogie, discerned how little backing Bothwell now had in the Lowlands and lost heart at the idea of raising the Highlands; his sister Jean Bothwell shortly afterwards abandoned the castle of Crichton and returned to her mother at Strathbogie, pausing on the way to inform the countess of Moray that she wished to have nothing more to do with her outlawed ex-husband. With the queen immured silently at Lochleven, the royalist party crumbled away, despite all Bothwell's energetic foraging for support from one end of Scotland to the other. Bothwell was eventually compelled to withdraw to the palace of his kinsman, the bishop of Moray, at Spynie in the far north. Here he was betrayed to his enemies by the bishop's illegitimate sons, but even so, managed to make his way to the Orkneys, where as their duke, and also as lord high admiral of Scotland, he hoped either to rally support once more by sea, or at least to continue to elude capture.

Unlike Mary herself, the lords now took care to pursue with relentless ferocity those of Bothwell's underlings who had been involved in the murder of Darnley. This process, which continued throughout the rest of the year, was intended to distract public attention from the complicity of

the new governors of Scotland, Morton, Balfour and Maitland, in the crime. William Blackadder—he who maintained he had merely run out of a near-by tavern when
he heard the explosion at Kirk o'Field—was the first to be
captured; he was hung, drawn and quartered, and his
limbs posted up on the gates of the leading burghs of Scotland. William Powrie, who had been in charge of trans-
porting that suspiciously small amount of gunpowder
through the streets of Edinburgh, was caught; under threat
of torture he provided two separate depositions, contradicting each other in many respects, and he was finally
hung. Bastian and Francisco Busso were imprisoned in
the Tolbooth. Another of Bothwell's men, John Spens, was
given his life, in return for handing over the coffers full
of his master's money. John Hepburn and John Hay of
Tallo were caught and executed before the turn of the
year; in each case they made self-incriminatory depositions before the end. It was another year before the lords
managed to lay their hands on 'French' Paris—he who
described how he had been kicked and bullied by Bothwell
into participation in the murder; by this time Mary was
in an English prison and Moray securely installed as regent; Paris's deposition therefore proved the most fruit-
fully damning of them all. But when Cecil sent a request
from London that Paris should be sent down for cross-
examination, the page was promptly hanged in Scotland.
Black Ormiston was hung in 1573, after making a highly
dubious deathbed confession to a priest. Pat Wilson and
Hob Ormiston were never caught.

The most dramatic capture, from the point of view of
the future, was that of the tailor, George Dalgleish, he
who had watched Bothwell while he changed his carnival
clothes to a cloak of 'sad English cloth'; his seizure was
afterwards said to have marked the first appearance of
those most debatable of all controversial documents—the
Casket Letters. The alleged circumstances of their discovery were not made public until eighteen months later, at
the Conference of Westminster in December 1568, in a
declaration given by Morton. But it is worth giving the
declaration's story in detail here, at the moment in history at which these events were afterwards said to have
taken place, in order to see how far this later declaration
fits in with the happenings of the time. The story of Dal-

gleish's apprehension was given by Morton as follows:[4] on 17 June Morton was dining with Maitland in Edinburgh Castle when a spy reported to them secretly that Dalgleish was known to have come into the castle from Dunbar, with the parson of Oldamstocks. Archibald Douglas was sent to catch the clergyman, but Dalgleish himself had almost escaped when his whereabouts were betrayed. Dalgleish protested that he had only arrived on a simple errand to fetch his master's clothing, but after being threatened by torture he changed his story, and according to Morton's statement, led his interrogators to a house in the Potterow where he produced from under his bed a silver casket. This was the first appearance of the famous silver casket in which the Casket Letters were said to have been discovered, and it will be seen how dubious the circumstances of its discovery were from the first, with the threat of torture playing a sinister role. Morton's declaration went on to state how on 20 June he had the casket formally opened; the papers within it were presumably read, but no note was taken of their contents, beyond the fact that the documents pertained to Bothwell. There was absolutely no mention of the queen, or of letters in her hand-writing. Morton sealed up the casket again and took it into his own possession, where it remained.

The strange fact about this declaration, and the whole affair of George Dalgleish's capture was that absolutely no mention was made of these remarkable facts at the time. According to Morton's December 1568 statement, the lords were from 20 June 1567 onwards in full possession of the vital evidence of the Casket Letters; but although these letters thoroughly incriminated Mary in Darnley's murder, it was remarkable that the lords still made no mention of her guilt three weeks later when they made a series of accusations against Bothwell at the Tolbooth. As has been seen, throughout the summer of 1567, the blame for Mary's downfall was heaped by the lords on Bothwell; the queen's crime was considered to be her refusal to abandon him; there was no suggestion that she had participated personally in Darnley's death. Yet the lords were nothing if not anxious to retain the queen in her prison at Lochleven; it seems inconceivable that they should not have used this damning evidence against her at this point, if indeed they possessed it. More extraordi-

nary still, if Morton's declaration was to be believed, was
the matter of George Dalgleish's deposition.[5] The unfortunate tailor, although later described as so instrumental
in its discovery, was asked no questions at the time about
the silver casket, nor cross-questioned in any way about
its contents. His interrogators concentrated entirely on the
subject of Darnley's murder. By the time the subject of
the Casket Letters was raised in England, eighteen months
later, George Dalgleish had long since been executed.

It was hardly likely that such untoward events in Scotland would pass unnoticed or undigested in England and
France. Queen Elizabeth's first reaction was strong distaste
for such unmannerly treatment of queens, and her second
characteristic reaction was to see what advantage could be
obtained from the situation for England. She sent Throckmorton north to parley with the lords, and also to see if
there would be a possibility of obtaining the wardship of
the little Prince James whom she now suggested could be
brought up conveniently in England by his grandmother
the countess of Lennox, conveniently forgetting that day
when Elizabeth had flung her into the Tower out of rage
at the marriage of James's parents. The French were animated with the same happy idea of bringing up the young
prince; the discussions over his welfare were strongly reminiscent of the arguments over Mary's own custody during
her infancy. Throckmorton reached Edinburgh before the
middle of July; his letters back to London provide a valuable insight into the state of affairs in the Scottish capital,
since he brought the fresh mind of an outsider to his
commentary. It is more difficult to assess Mary's own state
of mind during the crucial early weeks of her captivity:
none of her own letters from this period has survived,
with the exception of two or three smuggled out of the
island towards the end of her stay there; it is more than
probable that the strict conditions of her confinement
simply did not permit her to write them. The narrative of
her secretary, Nau, dictated by the queen while in captivity
in England, is the only guide extant to her personal feelings, and it suffers from the obvious disadvantage of having been written many years after the events in question
took place, by one who had not himself been present on
the island.

The first fortnight of Mary's incarceration was an agonizing experience, not only on account of her wretched health. Throckmorton heard that the queen was kept 'very straightly'; the lords did not intend that there should be any dramatic moonlight flitting from Lochleven. After a fortnight her total nervous collapse seems to have drawn to an end; Drury heard from Berwick that she was 'better digesting' her captivity, and could even take a little exercise. Bedford heard about three weeks later that her health was improving.[6] With the return of her strength, some of her personal magnetism seemed also to be exerting itself, since Lord Ruthven, son of that Lord Ruthven who had appeared like a vengeful ghost at the murder of Riccio, was considered by his colleagues to be falling under her spell, and was removed from his post. According to the queen's own account,[7] he made advances to her, throwing himself on his knees near her bed, promising that he would free her, if only she would love him. From the amorous behaviour of this former enemy of Mary's can be deduced either the glamorous effect of her personal presence or, more cynically, the quickness of Ruthven's wits. He may have realized already that the departure of Bothwell made the queen once more potentially marriageable, with all the advantages likely to ensue from such a match.

The queen still absolutely refused to hear of divorcing Bothwell: her reasons for this, as before Carberry Hill, were twofold. Her pregnancy by Bothwell was now thoroughly established in her own mind, and she feared more than ever to compromise the legitimacy of her unborn child; secondly, her extreme suspicion of the intention of the lords towards her own person had only been deepened by their behaviour since Carberry Hill. Although Maitland told her that if she agreed to divorce Bothwell she would be restored to liberty and freedom, Queen Mary must have doubted whether the lords would have carried out their part of the bargain. Why should the same men who had planned to ward her in Stirling Castle eighteen months before have agreed to release her now, even if she put away Bothwell as they suggested? Her return could not fail to threaten their newly acquired power, as well as bringing out into the open once more the events leading up to the death of Darnley. Had the lords really wished to re-establish her, they had an excellent opportunity after

Carberry Hill, instead of which they locked her up on
Lochleven. The existence of the infant Prince James, held
at Stirling Castle under the governorship of the earl of
Mar, one of the principal confederate lords, which had
once seemed to promise so much for Mary's future, now
told as strongly against her. A long royal minority, with a
series of noble regents, was traditionally regarded by the
Scottish aristocracy as a time for aggrandizement. It should
be borne in mind that on 8 December 1567 Mary herself
was approaching her twenty-fifth birthday, on which date
it was possible by custom for a sovereign to call back
wardships and properties given out during his or her own
minority. To the Scottish nobility, the rule of the thirteen-
month-old James was an infinitely preferable prospect to
that of his twenty-five-year-old mother, whether she divorced Bothwell or not.

It is noticeable that Throckmorton was deeply shocked
by the brutal attitude of the Scots towards their sovereign
on his arrival from England. He was genuinely convinced
that her life was in danger, and believed that it was his
appearance and intervention which actually saved her;
otherwise she too might have died as violently as Riccio
and her husband. The common people too he found to
be highly hostile to their queen, especially the women:
Tullibardine took the opportunity of explaining to him
that Mary would be in danger of death if they released
her. But of course this attitude was only increased by the
propaganda of the nobles in her enforced absence: what
especially shocked Throckmorton was to find that noble
families like the Hamiltons, who had a vested interest in
the succession, were ready to join the lords if Mary died,
and on 18 July he wrote to England that the Hamiltons
would concur with the confederate lords in all things,
'yea, in any extremity against the Queen', as long as they
were assured that Darnley's younger brother, Charles,
would not be preferred in the Scottish succession over
them, if Prince James died.[8] On 7 August Murray of
Tullibardine went as far as to tell Throckmorton that the
Hamiltons, Argyll, Huntly and others in their groups only
refrained from joining the confederates because they had
so inconveniently allowed the queen to live. The Hamiltons were ambitious enough to see how their chances of
succession were greatly improved with the disappearance
of Mary; there was now only the little king to be elimi-

nated 'and then we are home'.[9] The behaviour of Maitland was as before highly ambivalent: Throckmorton accused him also of threatening the queen's life, and pointed out to him that her death, apart from being an outrage, would only clear the way for the Hamiltons; Maitland in turn accused Throckmorton of having liberty in his mouth but not in his heart. At all events, by 9 August Throckmorton was convinced that his intervention had saved the Scottish queen's life and that 'this woefull Queen' would not now die except by an accident, although he could not forbear from commenting, when he heard of the new agreement between the lords and the Hamiltons, that he hoped their accord would not be like that of Herod and Pilate who agreed to put Christ to death.[10]

On one point the lords were adamant: Throckmorton should not visit the queen personally, despite his many requests to do so. He was thus compelled to depend on their own bulletin as to her state of mind. They assured him that Mary was still madly infatuated with Bothwell, and said in addition that she would be willing to abandon her kingdom for him and live like a simple damsel (a statement for which there was no other confirmation and on which Mary's subsequent career casts considerable doubt). On 16 July Throckmorton heard that the queen was in great fear of her life, and had said to some of the lords about her that she would be well contented to live in a close nunnery in France or with her grandmother, Antoinette of Guise.[11] These sentiments, if indeed Mary expressed them, must be regarded as coming out of the depths of her despair and physical weakness. More importance can be attached to her first communication to Throckmorton, which he reported on 18 July, when she sent word that she would in no way consent to a divorce from Bothwell 'giving this reason, that taking herself to be seven weeks gone with child, by renouncing him, she should acknowledge herself to be with child of a bastard and forfeit her honour'.[12] It was now some eight weeks since the queen's marriage to Bothwell: in her letter she therefore suggests that the baby had been conceived subsequent to the marriage. But at some date before 24 July, no doubt as a result of privations and stress, she miscarried the child, and according to Nau, who inserted the phrase very carefully as an afterthought on the page, found herself to have

been bearing 'deux enfants'.[13] If the twins had been conceived at Dunbar, on or about 24 April, they were about
three months old at the moment of miscarriage, and the
double gestation would have been easily recognizable.
Even at eight weeks, the foetus is just over one inch in
length; but at twelve to thirteen weeks, the foetus is three
and a half inches long, which would have made the recognition of 'deux enfants' perfectly possible. On balance of
probabilities, it seems likely therefore that the queen conceived the twins at Dunbar at the end of April, and that by
Carberry Hill, at least, if not earlier, knew for certain that
she was pregnant by Bothwell; uncertainty on the subject
could have been a factor in hastening on her actual wedding date in May.

What is virtually impossible is the suggestion, sometimes made since by historians, that the queen could have
conceived twins by Bothwell in January before Darnley's
death, and carried them in complete secrecy, without the
faintest contemporary report of her pregnancy, throughout the vital months following the Kirk o'Field tragedy.
It was mid-June before Bedford heard that the queen was
pregnant; although Guzman, the Spanish ambassador in
London, wrote to Philip II on 21 June, saying that the
Scottish queen was five *months* pregnant,[14] he probably
mistook five months for five weeks, since there is no reference of any sort through March, April and May to the
royal pregnancy, which would have been becoming rapidly
more apparent as the queen's figure changed. This was an
age in which such facts were speedily known by the accurate news service of servants' gossip: as a girl queen in
France, Mary's prospects of becoming a mother had been
intimately assessed by the ambassadors at the court. Randolph's extraordinarily early reports of Mary's pregnancy
with James in the autumn of 1565 will be recalled—he
heard the first rumours of her condition about five weeks
after conception, giving as his reference such 'tokens . . .
annexed to the kind of them that are in that case'.[15] The
spring months following the Kirk o'Field tragedy were
among the most critical of Mary's existence, in which her
every word and action were watched, checked and reported: how inconceivable is it then that an event of
such moment as her growing pregnancy outside the bonds
of marriage should have passed quite unnoticed until the

sixth month, by observers who would certainly have
grasped joyfully at such a convenient weapon to destroy,
if not Mary, at least Bothwell, the child's father.*

The queen's miscarriage proved a turning-point in her attitude to Bothwell, for it removed one important obstacle
in the way of divorce. By 5 August Throckmorton no
longer despaired of securing her consent to the divorce,
as he had done previously.[17] It has occasionally been supposed that Mary did not in reality miscarry the child, but
merely concealed her pregnancy; according to this legend,
she gave birth to the baby—a daughter—in the following
February; the little girl was smuggled away to France and
there grew up as a nun in the convent of Notre Dame de
Soissons. Alas, nothing would have been more impracticable than for the Scottish queen to have concealed her
condition in the confined space of Lochleven, quite apart
from the fact that there is no contemporary evidence to
back up the story.† It is also highly unlikely that Mary
would have ignored the continued existence of such a
daughter—next heiress after James to the Scottish and
English thrones—in the later years of her captivity when

* Dan McKenzie in his short article on the subject, 'The Obstetric
History of Mary Queen of Scots at Lochleven', *Caledonian Medical
Journal,* suggests that the time of conception might be 'about the
time of Darnley's murder' (9 February) on the evidence of Guzman,
although he does not make any suggestion as to how the queen concealed all signs of her condition until mid-June. Professor Donaldson, although giving McKenzie as a reference, goes further and suggests that Mary 'knew or feared' she was pregnant on 20 January,
when she went from Edinburgh to Glasgow to fetch back Darnley,
and this provided her with the motive for the reconciliation.[16] This
of course suggests a conception date of early January, which makes
her concealment of her condition until six months later still more
remarkable.

† The story was first given credence in the edition of the memoirs
of Castelnau, with notes by Le Laboureur, written in 1659, and published in 1731; Le Laboureur added the information in a footnote.[18]
On the grounds that Le Laboureur occupied a post of confidence at
the court of France as counsellor and almoner of the king, and
therefore might have special access to this sort of information, Lin-
gard accepted his story, as did Prince Labanoff, in his edition of the
letters of Mary Queen of Scots. The whole story has been the subject of a historical novel—*Unknown to History* by Charlotte M.
Yonge—in which sphere it rightly belongs.

she quarrelled with her son. Such a daughter could have
been introduced with effect into her last testaments.

It was while the queen was lying in bed after her miscarriage, by her own account 'in a state of great weakness'
having lost a great deal of blood, and scarcely able to
move, that Lindsay came to her and told her that he
had been instructed to make her sign certain letters for
the resignation of her crown. Mary now believed herself
once more to be in great personal danger, on this tiny
island, in the midst of an enormous lake, whose waters
could claim any victim silently without the circumstances
of their death being ever properly known. Despite her
fears the queen was outraged at the monstrousness of the
request, and continued to demand that she should be taken
in front of her Estates for the parliamentary enquiry which
had been promised to her; but Lindsay's rough words on
the subject, that she had better sign, for if she did not,
she could simply compel them to cut her throat, however
unwilling they might be to do so, only convinced her further of her own personal danger. She had no allies to
assist her, except the two *femmes-de-chambre* she had
been allowed to bring from Holyrood. In a state of terror
and despair, she declared that she refused to leave the
house. When Lindsay threatened her with forcible removal
she replied that she would have to be dragged out by the
hairs of her head.

It was at this point that Robert Melville hinted to Mary
that by no means every member of the Douglas family
was as hostile to her as the laird of Lochleven himself: his
brother, for example, the young debonair George Douglas,
was already showing himself susceptible to the charms of
the beautiful if unfortunate prisoner: he showed his sympathies by persuading the servants of the house to rise up
in rebellion at the project of her removal. But from the
actual signing of the letters of resignation there was no
escape. Mary told Nau later that Throckmorton had managed to smuggle her a note in the scabbard of a sword,
telling her to sign to save her own life, as something so
clearly signed under duress could never afterwards be held
against her.[19] Certainly if duress was ever held to affect
questions of legality there could be no possible legality
about such a document, by which Mary signed away the
crown she had inherited twenty-four and a half years ago,

in favour of her own son, and a regency of her half-brother, on a lonely island, without any advisers and surrounded by soldiers, under the command of the new regent's own brother. Shortly afterwards, Mary fell seriously ill again: her body began to swell up, chiefly in one arm and leg; her skin turned yellow, and she broke out in pustules, so that she began to believe she might have been poisoned. This disease, which seems to have had something to do with the liver, was relieved by bleeding, and a potion which was said to strengthen the heart.

As a result of the instruments which his mother had been compelled to sign in this manner, on 29 July James was crowned king of Scotland at the Protestant church, just outside the gates of Stirling Castle, at the tender age of thirteen months. The oath was taken on his behalf by Morton and Home. The circumstances strongly recalled those of Queen Mary's own coronation twenty-four years before: once more the Scottish crown was in the grasp of a puny child, hedged round by a grasping nobility, whose powers seemed to have been curtailed very little in the intervening years. Letters of commission signed by the ex-queen were read out—one established a regency in the name of Moray, and after him Morton, during the king's minority; one resigned the crown and kingdom on Mary's behalf; a third appointed a Council to act with Moray. On the day of the coronation, the gloomy peace of Lochleven was disturbed by all the artillery of the house being discharged; the queen, sending to find out what the matter was, discovered that bonfires had been lit in the garden, and that the laird was celebrating riotously at the news. He asked her mockingly why she too was not making merry at the coronation of her own son, at which Mary started to weep and went indoors.[20]

No further excitements disturbed the queen's close imprisonment, until her half-brother returned to Scotland to assume the position of regent. Some of Mary's supporters had hoped that Moray's arrival would result in some amelioration of her condition, remembering the many benefits which she had bestowed upon him in the past. George Douglas, falling further under the spell of Mary's charm, chose to remind Moray of how he had been used to call himself the queen's 'creature'. But Moray had now no call to term himself anyone's creature, with the prospect ahead of him of at least twelve or fourteen years' rule

of Scotland, during his own nephew's childhood. When he
arrived at Lochleven, it was in a cold and punitive mood.
To Mary's surprise, her brother was now addressed as
'Grace', a title usually reserved for kings or their children.
In their first interview, he chose to harangue her in a tone
of angry condemnation, which justified Throckmorton's
description of him as leading his people like the ancient
prophets of Israel. It was true that Moray's lofty sermon
on Mary's past imprudences, unattractive as it might be,
contained many observations which were most applicable
to her case: he told her that the Scottish people were dissatisfied with her conduct, and even though innocent before God, she should have had regard to her reputation in
the eyes of the world, 'which judges by the outward appearance and not upon the inward sentiment'. On the subject of her marriage to Bothwell, and the rumours it had
aroused concerning the death of Darnley, he observed perfectly correctly that it was not enough to avoid a fault,
but also the occasions of being suspected of it. Such admirable pieces of advice would have been the more effective if the lords associated with Moray in the government of the realm had not been far more practically implicated in the death of Darnley than the unfortunate queen.

Moray gave a full account of his interview to Throckmorton on his return to Edinburgh.[21] Sometimes, he said,
Mary had wept bitterly, sometimes she acknowledged her
imprudence and misgovernment, some things she did confess plainly, some things she did extenuate. Almost certainly Moray went so far as to threaten Mary with execution, for their interview took place on two consecutive
days, and the first night, as he told Throckmorton, he left
her with the hope of nothing but God's mercy. Throckmorton was impressed with Moray's grave and pious character—as the English almost universally were—and praised
his sincere qualities to Queen Elizabeth. But in fact there
was little to admire in such cruel hectoring of his sister,
who on Lochleven was totally at his mercy. Nevertheless
the ruse worked. Mary once more passed a night of horror
and fear; now even her own brother seemed to have turned
against her; the next day she begged Moray to accept the
regency. Moray told Throckmorton that Mary kissed him
and asked him not to refuse it. She had of course ex-
torted no concessions of any sort from him in return for
the offer—neither the promise of liberty nor any other hint

that she might enjoy freedom in the near future. In the meantime Moray was able to assure Cecil on 30 August that his new public state was neither welcome nor pleasing,[22] and even repeatedly assured Mary herself that he had no personal wish to assume the regency for his own private tastes led him to shun such grandeur and ambition, as she well knew. He might, however, be able to be of service to her as regent, where another in the same position would ruin her. Mary's own account of the interview to Nau put herself in a less desperate, more spirited light than Moray's account to Throckmorton. Although more reliance should be placed on Moray's account since it was delivered immediately, Mary did deliver herself of one significant aphorism on the subject of ruling Scotland. She warned Moray that if she, a born queen, was rebelled against by her people, how much more would the people rebel against him, a bastard by birth and origin. She quoted the maxim: 'He who does not keep faith where it is due, will hardly keep it where it is not due.'[23]

On 22 August James Stewart, earl of Moray, was proclaimed regent of Scotland. One side-effect of his new status was the opportunity which it gave him to take possession of Mary's rich hoard of jewellery. It was a subject on which the queen felt strongly, and continued to do so for the rest of her life: the rape of her jewels by Moray caused her as much indignation as any other single injury he did to her. Moray was cunning enough to tell Throckmorton that Mary had actually begged him to take charge of her jewels on Lochleven in order to preserve them for herself and her son: but Mary afterwards accused Moray of simply stealing them. According to Nau, Mary pointed out to her brother not only that she wanted many of the jewels to be permanently united with the crown of Scotland (as she had specified in her will of 1566) but also that a preponderance of the jewels had been given to her by King Henry of France, or her husband Francis, and were therefore her own private property. Strong feelings on all sides were roused by the thought of this glowing prize. On 10 September Melville reported that Moray's acquisition of the jewels had 'colded many stomaches among the Hamiltons'.[24] The one thing which Moray did not do with the jewels was to unite them permanently to the honour of the Scottish crown, as Mary intended. He gave some to his wife. Others he sold to Queen Elizabeth

the following April in order to remedy his forlorn finances.
The latter action may perhaps be justified, if not excused, as an act of state—but the former cannot. The
pearls, which were shown to Elizabeth on 1 May 1568, in
front of Pembroke and Leicester, consisted of six rows,
strung like rosaries, and separate pearls as large as black
grapes. They were thought to be of 'nonpareiled' beauty;
there were also rings of lesser value, and a piece of heavily bejewelled narwhal tooth; the pearls seem to have been
those intended in Mary's will to be divided between the
crown of Scotland and the house of Guise, and the narwhal tooth for her favourite nephew Francis Stewart.
From France Catherine de Medicis scented out the secret
disposal of the pearls she had once admired and envied
round her daughter-in-law's white throat at Fontainebleau,
and tried in vain to obtain them for herself.

The proclamation of Moray as regent, coupled with the
disappearance of Bothwell from the Scottish scene, led to
a period of comparative calm on the little island of Lochleven. The queen's health gradually returned, after her
privations and her miscarriage, since the enforced seclusion, however odious, did at least ensure her the rest
which she so grievously needed. With health and the sinking away of hysteria returned also resolution and calm
positive thinking. By the beginning of September, she was
able to write to Robert Melville far more in her old vein
of practical decisiveness, as though the year from the
birth of James onwards had been lived under some black
and disastrous shadow, now fortunately rolled away. She
asked for materials, silks to embroider, and clothes for
her ladies including her favourite Mary Seton who had
recently been allowed to join her—'for they are naked'.[25]
On 23 September Moray was able to tell Bedford that her
health was good, and she herself was 'merrily disposed'.[26]
The question of her clothes was now better resolved: much
of her gilded wardrobe was gone forever, seized by the
confederates, and not a great deal of attention seems to
have been paid to her luggage-less state until after the arrival of Moray, when Mary accused him of bringing her
some old and mean garments, very roughly made up, in
place of her own clothes.

But the private aide-mémoires of her chamberlain, Servais de Condé,[27] show that even in June some clothes were
of necessity brought, to supplement the clothes in which

she had travelled: such as a red satin petticoat furred with marten, some satin sleeves, a cloak of Holland, a pair of black silk tights, or *chausses,* and more practically, some pins and a box of sweetmeats. In July she received another box of sweets, various stockings and garments of a utilitarian nature, such as leather shoes and wool chemises as well as a little red velvet box with crossed Fs on it in silver. From August onwards she began to receive supplementary provisions, the lists of which sound like any parcels sent to prisoners of war or state in any century: boxes of sweets, more pins, lengths of Holland material to make clothes, soap, Spanish silk and gold and silver thread for embroidery to while away the hours, handkerchiefs, an embroidered peignoir and a little blue box of taffeta full of *'poudre de santeur'*. In October she received what must have been a welcome parcel—her perukes of false hair, and other accessories to arrange her coiffure. In November she received a striking clock with an alarm or *'réveille matin',* more pins and linen. To a queen accustomed to the lavish grandeur of royal state since childhood, this was the diet of captivity. There was certainly no mention of the gorgeous dresses of the earlier inventories of the royal wardrobe in these lengths of Holland for her ladies to make up clothes. But, as captivities go, it was not particularly stringent, and on Lochleven, once her health was recovered, the queen began to develop those harmless, agreeable but petty activities with which royal prisoners while away their time—an unwitting dress rehearsal for the long years of imprisonment which lay ahead. She began to dance once more, and played at cards. She embroidered. She walked in the garden. She also looked out of the window towards the dark sedge of reeds along the distant edge of the lake and fed by the prisoners' fare of hope pictured the moment when she too would be standing on that wind-blown shore, once more at liberty.

If the queen dreamt of freedom, in the manner of all prisoners, it is unlikely that she also dreamt of Bothwell. Melville's hint to her concerning George Douglas had borne fruit. The young man was personable, gallant, and only too happy to see in his sovereign a frail and helpless woman, the victim of a cruel fate. Her fragile beauty drawn with suffering, coupled with her romantic history, could not fail to move him further; Cecil said afterwards that he fell into 'a fantasy of love' with the queen. By

August, the queen was attempting to draw over the inhabitants of Lochleven to sympathize with her by the exertion of her famous personal charm and gentleness; even
Lady Margaret was thought to be succumbing. By the
end of October, even Drury from Berwick was able to
report to Cecil in London that there was a nasty suspicion of over-great familiarity existing between the queen
and Mr Douglas.*[28] Although George Douglas's heart was
genuinely stirred by the presence of this romantic heroine,
Mary's aim in this relationship, however much she appreciated the admiration, was quite clearly to escape from
Lochleven; she now hoped to have found in George Douglas the weak link in the Douglas chain. But she was also
able to extend her allure and her promise beyond even that
of her own affections: for as Bothwell had now disappeared, there was in theory no reason why George Douglas should not aspire to her hand. This in turn did not
necessarily displease his ambitious mother Margaret, who
could imagine a worse future for her younger son than
seeing him the husband of the queen of Scotland, with her
other son the regent, able to restore his sister to power at
any moment. As these projects buzzed in the minds of its
inhabitants, during the autumn the island of Lochleven
ceased to be an absolute slough of despair for the imprisoned queen of Scots.

The disappearance of Bothwell was the key to this new
hope, as it was also to the temporary stability of Scotland.
Beyond the confines of the island, Bothwell had been pursued to the Orkneys by his inveterate enemy Kirkcaldy
of Grange, who promised to bring him dead to Edinburgh
or die himself. In the event, neither death took place, for
although Bothwell's capture was scheduled to take place
before the end of August, at the beginning of September
Moray was still obliged to observe warily on the subject:
'We cannot merchandise for the bear's skin before we
have him.'[29] Kirkcaldy lived on, to become later one of
the queen's most loyal adherents; Bothwell escaped to the

---

* Out of this statement, an absurd story has been built, quoted by
Bishop Burnet in his *History*, that Mary Stuart conceived and bore
a son by George Douglas while on the island of Lochleven. This
son was said to have been the father of Robert Douglas, the coven-
anting divine who preached at the coronation of Charles II at Scone
in 1651. There is no contemporary evidence whatsoever to support
this story which is, in terms of time alone, scarcely possible.

Karmoi sound on the coast of Norway, but here had the misfortune to encounter some kinsmen of his former mistress, Anna Throndsen, as well as some creditors from his previous Scandinavian travels. The combination resulted in him being officially captured and taken to Bergen on 2 September, with two ships and 140 men. By the end of September he was being held in Copenhagen Castle, since King Frederick, joint sovereign of Denmark and Norway, quickly perceived in his uninvited guest a useful pawn in international politics, who as the husband of the queen of Scots, heiress-presumptive to the English throne, could certainly be used against the English queen. Although Moray pressed for his extradition, and Bothwell himself wrote anxiously to the king of France, asking for help, he was destined to remain in a series of Danish prisons, of increasing squalor, for the rest of his life.*

Throckmorton returned to England at the beginning of September, having never succeeded in achieving that audience with Queen Mary on Lochleven which he had so earnestly desired. On instructions from the English queen, he refused the silver plate given to him on his departure in the name of King James, on the grounds that Queen Elizabeth did not acknowledge Queen Mary's abdication from the throne of Scotland; nor did she acknowledge the regency of Moray, despite his many friendly overtures to England. Despite this disapproval from across the border, the Marian party in Scotland seemed temporarily in abeyance: Huntly and Herries had recrossed to Moray's side; Dunbar surrendered to the regent; Dumbarton, in the west of Scotland, was the only fortress left, and its effectiveness was considerably annulled by the fact that it lay in the centre of Lennox country. By the middle of October, Moray was able to write to Cecil that Scotland was quiet.[30]

Scotland might be quiet, and no part of it quieter than the tiny island in the middle of Lochleven which held the imprisoned queen. Nevertheless the course of Mary's for-

* It was while in the castle of Copenhagen that Bothwell wrote his own narrative, *Les Affaires du Conte de Boduel,* referred to earlier over the events of Kirk o'Field. Completed by 5 January 1568, it was intended to procure his release. It is to be distinguished from his so-called death-bed *Confession,* a dubious document which was probably written much later on Mary's behalf to secure her release. Bothwell would in any case have been unable to write a death-bed confession, since he died insane.

tunes did not stand still. The winter of 1567 was remarkable for an unpleasant new development in her affairs. The governing lords found that circumstances dictated they should change their attitude both towards her and towards the official reasons for her imprisonment. It was not enough to keep Mary incarcerated, having procured her abdication; the lords needed to provide some further public justification for their behaviour towards her. Originally they had claimed to be freeing Mary from Bothwell's tutelage at Carberry Hill—there was no question of implicating Mary personally in Darnley's murder. But now that Bothwell had disappeared from the Scottish scene and Mary was in prison at Lochleven, they could hardly continue to criticize her on the score that she was unduly influenced by Bothwell. Some other reason had to be put forward to justify her continued confinement. It was time for the lords to gloss over the deep implication of some of their number in the murder at Kirk o'Field. The Craigmillar bond of November 1566, to get rid of the king, had been signed by Maitland, Morton and James Balfour amongst others; now this was conveniently forgotten. In December 1567, nearly a year after the event, Mary was herself publicly blamed for the death of Darnley.

The existence of certain documents which implicated Mary in the crime was mentioned for the first time in front of the Privy Council on 4 December.[31] The text of these writings was not quoted, nor were the actual documents produced; but their existence was used to justify a new Act of Council which stated that the official cause of Mary's detention was her involvement in her husband's death. Mary was said to have encouraged the outrage 'in so far as by divers her privy letters written and subscribed with her own hand and sent by her to James Earl Bothwell, chief executioner of the horrible murder'. At the Parliament convened by Moray on 15 December, Mary's abdication of the government was said to be 'lawful and perfect'; James's investiture and coronation was described as being valid as those of his ancestors, since it was to be considered as though his mother were actually dead. Moray's appointment as regent was confirmed, and the lords who had taken up arms at Carberry Hill were formally vindicated in that Queen Mary had been 'privy, art and part of the actual devise and deed of the fore-named murder of the King her lawful husband'. [32] This was quite a new departure from the line which the lords had actually taken on the eve of the battle. Then all the talk had been of Bothwell's guilt; now for the first time the subject of Mary's guilt was introduced. It was a change of emphasis which boded no good for Mary's future.

Although Mary herself on her island was unaware of the turn which matters were taking, the news that Moray was summoning a Parliament was enough to cast her into a state of fervour agitated by frustration. She addressed a long letter to her brother, asking that she should be allowed to vindicate herself before it, as previously arranged; she touched on her relationship to Moray, the favours she had shown him, his promises to the French court to support her, and earnestly suggested that she would submit to any law, even laying aside her queenly rank, if only she could be allowed a hearing; Queen Mary also pointed out pathetically her past virtues as a ruler—how she had never been extravagant or embezzled her subjects' money, like so many sovereigns.[33] To this *cri de cœur*, in which can be heard the desperation of the captive who will promise anything, if only he or she can be allowed a hearing from the outside world, Moray sent only a few lines of acknowledgement. On his next visit to Lochleven, when he brought James Balfour and Morton, relations between the brother and sister were cold and quarrelsome. Yet by mid-winter the graph of Scottish loyalties was rising once more in Mary's favour. For one thing, the Hamiltons were annoyed that Moray had assumed the regency, which they thought belonged rightfully to their family, as in the past, and did not attend the December Parliament. Kirkcaldy and Maitland were both privately concerned lest Mary's abdication under duress might be considered illegal in the future. It was not long before Maitland began to display his usual political ambiguity: in her prison the queen received secretly an engraved ring representing Aesop's fable of the lion and the mouse.[34] The gift was said to come from Mary Fleming, but at the time it was generally believed that its true significance was the promise of future support from her husband Maitland—the grateful mouse who would gnaw through the bonds of the lion, Mary.

The Scots people, who had been told that their queen had been removed for complicity in Darnley's murder, could see for themselves that many nobles, far more in-

timately involved than she, were not only at liberty, but
forming part of the government of the country. Moray's
persistent hunting down of the lesser criminals was intended to distract attention from this patent fact: but when
John Hay of Tallo was publicly executed at the beginning
of January, he stood up on the scaffold and declared boldly
to the large crowd assembled that Huntly, Argyll, Maitland
and Balfour had all subscribed the bond for Darnley's
murder. This scarcely helped on the process of distraction.
The hacked-off limbs of Hay, Powrie and Hepburn were
in turn posted up on the gates of the leading Scottish
towns, twenty-two shillings being paid to the boy who
went on his way from Edinburgh to Leith, Haddington and
Jedburgh bearing the grisly burden of a pair of legs.[35] But
such public expenditure, such improving sights, still did
not prevent Queen Mary's erstwhile subjects from clam-
ouring against the lords in the government, that they
too should 'suffer for their demerits'.

The marriageability of the queen became once more a
matter of public comment and private speculation. Drury
thought Mary asked her brother if she might marry George
Douglas as early as December[36]—fresh evidence of the
unenduring quality of her feelings for Bothwell; the regent
was said to have refused on the grounds that his half-
brother was an 'overmean' marriage for the queen. George
Douglas had the advantage of being able to press his suit
in person. Other names, some of them strange indeed in
the context, were mentioned, including a Hamilton, son
of the duke of Châtelherault, Argyll's brother, and a
young Stewart (Lord Methven). The most optimistic
rumour was that which advanced the name of Morton
himself, although it was agreed that the queen might not
take easily to the notion. The *junta* of nobles in power, in
between scheming privately for their relations or themselves to marry the queen, jested publicly about what
would befall them if the queen managed to escape.

As spring came to Lochleven, Mary was able to smuggle out a few letters to France describing her plight and
appealing for aid. They have a determined and desperate
tone. She begged Queen Catherine de Medicis, in a letter
(written while her jailers were at dinner) which stressed
her wretched condition, to send some French soldiers to
deliver her—'it is by force alone I can be delivered. If you
send never so few troops to countenance the matter, I am

certain great numbers of my subjects will rise to join them; but without that they are overawed by the power of the rebels and dare attempt nothing of themselves'.[37] She managed to write to Archbishop Beaton, her ambassador in Paris, describing her sufferings, but begged him to burn her letters, lest they be discovered and get some of her supporters, who had helped her smuggle them out, into trouble.[38] She also wrote to Queen Elizabeth, a letter dated 1 May, in a large sprawling hand-writing, very unlike her usual even lines, showing the ravages of despair after ten months' captivity: she described movingly *'la langueur du temps de mon ennuieuse prison'* and the cruel slights of those to whom she had done nothing but good; how her brother Moray had taken all she has (this letter was written on the very day on which Queen Elizabeth was viewing those 'nonpareiled pearls', a fact of which Queen Mary was fortunately in ignorance). Mary also attached great importance to the ring which Elizabeth had once sent her, and considered it as a talisman which would bring good luck to their relations. To her great distress she had not managed to persuade Robert Melville to part with the jewel, for fear of Moray's vengeance, so that she could not despatch it to England as she wished to move Elizabeth's heart with pity. The letter ended pathetically: *'Ayez pitié de votre bonne soeur et cousine.'*[39]

Yet within twenty-four hours of writing this anguished letter, the queen was able to escape from her prison largely by her own generalship, ably assisted by George Douglas and an orphan member of the Douglas household whom she had won over by her kindness and captivated with her charm. Her active temperament fortunately allowed her to cast about ceaselessly for some practical means of terminating her confinement, like the lioness pacing its cage to which Maitland had compared her, while at the same time pouring forth as many appeals for outside help as she could smuggle out of the island. In the end it was inside rather than outside assistance which proved effective. So long as George Douglas remained on the island itself, there was not a great deal he could do to help his heroine beyond organizing her correspondence by bribing the boatman. But in the spring George Douglas quarrelled with his brother the laird (they both seem to have had their share of the peppery Douglas temper) and was ordered out of the house and off the island. This gave him

the necessary opportunity to alert on the queen's behalf
lords such as the faithful Lord Seton, on whose loyalty
she knew she could rely. Not only did George Douglas
incur his brother's wrath, but his rumoured plans to
marry the queen seem to have also brought down the anger
of Moray on his head, so that he was in a mood of fair
rebellion towards his family, and the established government of Scotland, by the spring. Queen Mary was able to
turn this to full advantage. The attitude of his mother Lady
Margaret was more ambivalent; Melville hinted that she
had been 'upon the counsel' of the plot, although if Nau's
account is accepted, she was left in total ignorance of it
all.[40] As a mother, she would be torn between ambition
for one son, George Douglas, and fear for the fate of
another son, Sir William Douglas, if Mary escaped from
his custody—for this would surely bring down the wrath
of a third son, Moray the regent.

Queen Mary's chief female companions during her incarceration were the laird's wife, young Lady Douglas,
who often slept in her room, and generally accompanied
her throughout the day, old Lady Margaret Douglas, and
two young Douglas girls of fourteen and fifteen, daughter
and niece of the laird. These girls conceived a hero-worship
of their captive, and the younger one especially was so
obsessed by her presence that thoughts of the queen filled
her imagination, even when she was asleep. In the late
spring, however, young Lady Douglas gave birth to a
child. This gave Queen Mary a little more liberty during
the period of the lying-in; she determined to avail herself of the opportunity to effect her escape. One romantic
attempt, variously placed at the end of March or the end
of April, involved the queen disguising herself as a laundress, and escaping by boat with a bundle of washing
while Mary Seton took her place in the castle.[41] Unfortunately one of the boatmen, mortified at the way she refused to show her face, tried to take down the muffler
with which she kept it covered. Instinctively the queen put
up her hand to stay him. The whiteness of the hand—
that hand with its long fingers like five unequal branches
which Ronsard had once praised—betrayed her. She was
returned to her quarters, although the boatman kept his
silence and did not report the attempt to the laird.

The key element in any escape was obviously the crossing of the water itself. Having suborned the boatman,

George Douglas's first idea was to carry off the queen in a box; but the boatman dissuaded him, and together they agreed that it would be far easier to abduct the queen in disguise. There was by now another spy within the castle dedicated to the queen's cause—young Willy Douglas, an orphaned cousin of the house called 'the little Douglas', who was also by now devoted to her interests, won over by the charm and kindness she had shown to him. Willy became involved in smuggling out the queen's correspondence, for which he received a number of gold pieces, and incurred suspicion as he flaunted them about. There were other similar minor hazards to overcome: the laird's daughter noticed Willy Douglas delivering some letters to the queen, one of which she dropped on the ground; as a result the girl had a nightmare in which she saw Willy Douglas bringing a black raven into the house which flew away with her precious queen from the edge of the loch. The girl was so distressed at this that Mary was frightened she might arouse suspicion, and had to make her promise not to mention either the letters or the dream, on condition that the queen would take her with her when she escaped. But, Mary quickly added, of this escape she had at present neither hopes nor means. The laird of Markyston, a notorious wizard, also predicted that the queen would have escaped by the beginning of May and made a bet on it: as a result of which unhelpful piece of prophecy or sportsmanship her guard was increased.

George Douglas now asked permission to revisit Lochleven in order to say farewell to his mother, using the pretext that he intended to leave Scotland altogether and go to France. Both his mother and brother were deeply upset at this decision, and tried to persuade him to live instead with his half-brother the regent; they even enlisted the queen to write to him to this effect, and it was in this letter, which the queen obligingly wrote at their request, that she was able to send George Douglas a secret message urging the need to act swiftly before young Lady Douglas recovered from her confinement. The day fixed for the attempt was 2 May, but the fact that Mary took the trouble to write to both Queen Elizabeth, quoted earlier, and Catherine de Medicis, appealing once more for assistance by French troops, on 1 May, shows that there was a great deal of doubt in her mind at least as to whether the escape would be successful. As spring stole

towards summer, life on Lochleven became somewhat less
bleak, and there were even modest boating expeditions on
the lake; in the course of one of these, in which the laird
accompanied the queen, her servants played a joke pretending their mistress had escaped, and in the ensuing
fracas, half-playful, half-serious, some of the crowd on
the shore of the island were wounded, and had to be attended to by the queen's surgeons. This incident was
later considered by the queen to have distracted attention
from the plots of George Douglas in Lochleven village
itself.[42]

As George Douglas remained on shore in this village,
having alerted Lord Seton of what was on hand, Willy
Douglas took charge of arrangements on the island. His
first idea was that the queen should leap a seven-foot wall
in the garden, but when a gallant lady-in-waiting attempted
the drop as an experiment and severely injured her foot,
the plan was abandoned. Willy Douglas decided that the
only safe course was for the queen to march boldly out
of the main gate of the castle. On 2 May he therefore
organized a May-Day pageant, with himself as Abbot of
Unreason; in the manner of such celebrations, the queen
was made to swear to follow the abbot about all day;
whereupon Willy Douglas gave a splendid exhibition of
drunken fooling, as a result of which by the afternoon the
queen declared herself to be so exhausted that she must
sleep; she then flung herself down on her bed, not exhausted but desperately excited. As she rested, she heard
a woman in the next room chattering and saying that a
great troupe of horsemen had passed through the village
of Lochleven that day, including Lord Seton, saying that
they were going to an assize, and also that George Douglas had been seen in the village that day.

There were still some dramatic dangers to be overcome: for example Lady Margaret insisted on discussing
the question of the queen's escape, saying how she would
ruin the Douglases if she did so and, in the midst of the
actual conversation, noticed some horsemen on the shore:
she would have raised an immediate outcry if the queen
had not distracted her by fulminating bitterly against
Moray. The laird himself looked out of the window and
noticed Willy putting pegs into the bottoms of all the
boats on the shore except one (to hole them against pursuit); he began to exclaim against Willy's idiocy, without

exactly understanding what he was up to, until the queen pretended to faint, and the laird was compelled to go and fetch her a glass of wine. He was still sufficiently suspicious to ask to be near the window at dinner so that he could keep an eye on the loch and the village. Finally George Douglas bade farewell to his mother before his theoretical journey to France. One of the queen's maids then brought her one of the pearl earrings which she habitually wore, saying that George Douglas had recovered it for her from the boatman who had found it and had wished to sell it to him; but George Douglas had recognized the earring as belonging to the queen. This little piece of by-play was the signal that everything was now ready for the escape.

The queen retired into her room an hour before supper and put on a red kirtle belonging to one of her women, and one of her own long mantles over it. Then she went into the garden to walk with Lady Margaret. The queen was served her own supper by the laird, according to custom; next the laird went across the courtyard into the main tower, to eat his own supper with his family. Drysdale, the chief soldier of the island's guard, who generally stayed in the queen's room, went too and played at handball (thus reinforcing contemporary suspicions that he was in the plot).* The queen now had to rid herself of her faithful escort of the admiring young girls; she went to the upper room of her own tower, announcing that she wanted to say her prayers; this was not solely an excuse to absent herself, since she did indeed pray fervently for the success of her venture. Here she cast off her own mantle and put on a hood like those worn by the country-women; one of her *femmes-de-chambre* dressed herself similarly; the other stayed below and tried to allay the suspicions of the girls, who kept asking why the queen was so long upstairs.

In the meantime Willy Douglas dexterously removed the laird's keys as he was handing him his evening drink at supper.† He then gave a sign through the window to the

---

* But these suspicions do not seem to have been justified. A later letter written by Mary from England shows that she continued to dislike and fear Drysdale.[43]

† Some doubt has been cast on the possibility of this feat, which is related by Nau. But the story is confirmed by a report, received in Paris by the Venetian ambassador at the time of the escape, via John Beaton.[44]

queen's woman that all was ready. The queen, in her disguise, boldly crossed the courtyard, although it was full of servants passing to and fro, and went out of the main gate; having relocked the gate, Willy Douglas threw the keys into a cannon near at hand. The queen and her attendant stood for a time in the shadow of the castle wall, fearing they might be seen from the windows of the house, before finally going to the boats. Here the queen laid herself down beneath the boatman's seat, partly to be hidden, partly to avoid cannon shot. Several washerwomen by the boats recognized her, and one of them made a sign to Willy that she had done so; but the boy called out to the woman to hold her tongue. Even now the last hazard was not at an end: as they neared the opposite shore, Willy thought he saw an enemy lurking. It turned out to be one of George Douglas's servants who was a stranger to him. Finally they landed.

Mary was welcomed by the faithful George Douglas and by John Beaton. By a piece of ironic justice, Beaton had with him the best horses belonging to the laird of Lochleven, stolen out of the laird's own stables, which lay on the mainland. The queen mounted and taking only Willy Douglas with her—even her *femme-de-chambre* was left behind for the time being—she set off to meet Lord Seton, the laird of Riccarton and their followers, about two miles away. They then crossed the sea at Queensferry, and were at the Seton palace of Niddry by about midnight. The country people, who recognized the queen, cheered as she passed, and even the laird's uncle, who saw her, did not try to stop her. The music of popular acclaim sounded sweetly in Mary's ears after her confinement: there is a tradition that when she greeted her people outside Niddry the next morning, her long auburn hair was still flowing about her shoulders, for in her eagerness to show herself, she had not even paused to have it dressed.

Queen Mary was once more at liberty after ten and a half months of captivity on a tiny island. In the meantime a countryman of lesser loyalty had rowed back to Lochleven to report her escape. Her disappearance had already been made known by the eager young girls, who found the queen's mantle in the upper room and thought she was hiding. The laird of Lochleven fell into such a passion of distress that he tried to stab himself with his own dagger.* But it is pleasant to record that those two other Douglases, George and Willy, who had placed devotion to their queen above family interest, were duly rewarded by her continual gratitude in later life, for as Mary herself wrote later to Beaton, asking him to forward George Douglas's cause in France, 'tels services ne se font pas tous les jours'[45] (such services are not performed every day). The dashing George continued in Mary's employ during her English captivity; although he did not succeed in winning the hand of the queen he loved, his romantic aspirations might not have been so quickly extinguished if she had remained longer at liberty in Scotland. As Moray's brother, a Protestant and a member of the powerful Douglas clan, he would have represented a good compromise candidate as a husband. Willy Douglas, the boy Mary plucked from Lochleven, whom she called 'her orphan', remained attached to her service until death, and was mentioned in her last will at Fotheringhay.

* The laird later sent on the queen's belongings from Lochleven, and in a report on her character to Morton said that there was no vice in her. This still does not prove that he connived at the escape, as has been suggested. While Mary was on Lochleven, he had good reason to fear the wrath of his half-brother Moray if he failed in his trust; once she was at liberty, she was once more queen of Scotland in many people's eyes, and it would be worth trying to win her favour.

PART THREE

The Captivity

19 In Foreign Bands

'And I'm the sovereign of Scotland
 And mony a traitor there
Yet here I lay in foreign bands
 And never-ending care'

ROBERT BURNS: Queen Mary's Lament

On Lochleven Mary had been compared by Maitland to a
captive lion; the feelings of the Regent Moray on hearing
that his sister had escaped from her prison may be compared to those of Prince John, regent of England, when
he learnt that his brother King Richard was on his way
home, and 'the lion was unloosed'. The Regent Moray was
sore amazed, said the Diurnal of Occurrents,[1] more especially because he happened to be at Glasgow when he
learnt the evil news, and by now Mary herself had
reached near-by Hamilton from Niddry. The regent's first
instinct was to desert the unhealthy area of western Scotland—where such loyal Marian lords as Herries and Maxwell held sway in the south, and Argyll, now also a Marian, in the north, to say nothing of the menacing prospect
of the key fortress of Dumbarton, still firmly held for the
queen, to the west beyond Glasgow. But prudence prevailed: the regent decided to stand firm, rather than let the
whole west unite for the queen; as it turned out, he was
amply repaid for the steadfast nature of his decision.

Supporters were flocking to the queen, as a result of
the series of proclamations in which she once more sought
her subjects' allegiance. On 8 May nine earls, nine bishops,
eighteen lairds and over 100 other lesser supporters declared for her in a joint proclamation. Despite this impressive show of loyalty and strength, Mary was not without her problems. The Hamiltons seized this ripe opportunity of emphasizing their own claims to the succession
if both Mary and James disappeared—and their right to
act as governors if only Mary did. Another particularly
virulent Marian proclamation, thought to be the work of
Archbishop Hamilton, referred to Moray as 'an bastard

gotten in shameful adultery' and Châtelherault as the
'Queen's dearest father adoptive . . . head of the good
house of Hamilton'. Although it is unlikely that this proclamation was ever published,[2] its tone certainly makes it
clear why Mary feared to remain overlong at Hamilton.
Having escaped her Lochleven bonds, she did not wish to
become the puppet of another Scottish house. She therefore determined to march towards Dumbarton and here on
neutral ground try to draw her subjects back to her. Mary
was certainly not particularly anxious to fight Moray before she reached Dumbarton, seeing no advantage in con-
fronting him at the head of a Hamilton force when she
might in the future be able to face him backed up by a
more truly national army. In her desire to be restored to
her throne at all costs, Mary was even prepared to treat
with Moray; but the regent refused to enter into negotiations.

The Marian party had by now reached impressive proportions—twice as many as that of the regent, said the
queen.[3] Estimates vary from 6,000 royalists to Moray's
4,000, to 5,000 and 3,000 respectively; but all agreed that
Mary's party had considerable numerical superiority. This
preponderance had the fatal effect of encouraging the
queen's army to skirt Glasgow narrowly on their route
to Dumbarton, in the hopes of drawing the regent into a
fight and thus annihilating him. The Hamiltons had, after
all, suffered much at Moray's hands; his occupation of the
regency was a flagrant insult to their ancient position in
Scotland; they now saw an excellent opportunity of oblit-
erating their enemy under what seemed to be ideally
weighted conditions. As the Marians reached the small village of Langside, the vanguard under Lord Claud Hamilton stormed forward. Moray was established beyond Langside on the Burgh Muir. He appeared to accept their challenge, despite the Marian numerical superiority. But
Moray was fortunate in having two experienced and skilful soldiers beside him—Kirkcaldy of Grange and Morton. Morton remained at Moray's side, in charge of the
main battle, while Kirkcaldy rode forward with his hagbutters to harry the royal troops as they entered the narrow main street of Langside.

Under the regent's attack, the border horsemen under
Lord Herries did valiantly, and Hamilton's men fought
their way gallantly forward. But by an evil chance, the

main command of the royal army had been given to
Argyll, now made 'Lieutenant of the Kingdom'[4] on the
grounds that he had supplied by far the largest amount
of men. And now the main body of the royal troops under Argyll's personal command entirely failed to follow
up their van. It was said afterwards, to explain his defection, that Argyll had actually fainted, or else had had an
exceptionally ill-timed epileptic fit; his enemies pointed out
that as he was Moray's brother-in-law and erstwhile com-
rade, his failure of generalship might have the less medical and more sinister explanation of pre-arranged treachery. Whatever its origin, the temporary suspension of Argyll's faculties proved fatal to the cause of Mary Queen of
Scots at Langside. As Kirkcaldy's pikemen fell upon the
Hamiltons, they found themselves totally unsupported by
Argyll's men who, leaderless and unable or unwilling to
withstand a full charge, broke away from it, and fled back
towards their native Highlands. The crossfire of the hagbutters, the depredations of the pikemen, and the failure
of Argyll combined to bring about a colossal defeat for
the queen in which only one member of Moray's side was
even killed by Herries's gallant charge (although Lords
Home and Ochiltree were injured). Over 100 of the
queen's party were slain, mainly Hamiltons, and over
300 were taken prisoner, including the faithful Lord Seton, Sir James Hamilton and many other members of his
clan.

The queen watched this gloomy contest from a near-by
hill. For once might had been allied with right; but sadly,
the combination had worked out to the advantage of
neither. Mary's servant John Beaton told Catherine de
Medicis later that Mary had mounted on her own horse,
and like another Zenobia ridden into the battle, to encourage her troops to advance; she would have led them
to the charge in person, but she found them all quarrelling
among themselves, insensible to her eloquence and more
inclined to exchange blows with each other than to attack
the rebel host.[5] Once the battle was clearly decided in
favour of Moray, the queen had more pressing problems
to deal with than the feuds of her own supporters. She
had now to ride, not like Zenobia into battle, but like
any fugitive away from the scene of her defeat, and away
from the scaring sweep of Moray's men. Dumbarton was
the obvious target for her—Dumbarton, from which

French help could be introduced into the country, or from which France itself could be reached, if the situation became so desperate that the queen had to flee. But Dumbarton was cut off by hostile Lennox country and Moray's forces; guided by Lord Herries, the queen decided to flee south instead, into the south-western territories of Scotland which were still extremely Catholic in feeling as well as loyal to Mary, under the feudal sway of two Catholic magnates, Herries and Maxwell.

The journey itself was rough and wild; the conditions of travel were primitive in the extreme. Afterwards the queen seemed to remember so little about this nightmare flight in her account of it to Nau, that his narrative, so free and detailed during the period of her captivity at Lochleven, degenerates into a mere list of headings. Once she was in captivity, perhaps Mary preferred to throw a veil in her own mind over these last Scottish sufferings, which had been a prelude to the long years of English imprisonment. Immediately after the flight, in June 1568, she gave a description of it to her uncle in France: 'I have endured injuries, calumnies, imprisonment,' she wrote, 'famine, cold, heat, flight not knowing whither, 92 miles across the country without stopping or alighting, and then I have had to sleep upon the ground and drink sour milk, and eat oatmeal without bread, and have been three nights like the owls. . . .'[6] Queen Mary fled first to Dumfries, a journey of about sixty miles; by tradition Lord Herries led her down through the unfrequented passes of the Glenkens and along the west bank of the River Ken. They paused to rest at the head of the valley of the Tarff, at a point now named Queen's hill. The Dee was crossed just beyond the village of Tongland, where her escort destroyed the ancient wooden bridge to avoid pursuit; close by, at Culdoach, Mary received the reviving bowl of sour milk which she mentioned to her uncle.* Having rested at Herries's own castle of Corrah on the way, the queen finally reached the Maxwell castle of Terregles.

It was here at Terregles that the critical decision was

---

* Tradition has it that the old woman received the freehold of her croft—for which she had previously paid rent—for this Samaritan deed. This was probably through the good offices of Lord Herries, who was the principal local landowner, and in a position to make such a gesture.

taken to flee further on into England. The decision was
made by the queen alone. She herself described dolefully
to Archbishop Beaton in Paris how her supporters had
cautioned her piteously not to trust Queen Elizabeth, since
the English in the past had savagely imprisoned a Scottish
sovereign, in the shape of James I, and even her own father
had not trusted himself to meet Henry VIII at York. The
general view was that she should either stay in Scotland
—where Herries guaranteed that she could hold out
for at least another forty days—or go to France and hope
to rally some support there. In retrospect, either course
would seem to have been more sensible than seeking an
English refuge. We cannot tell what considerations
weighed with Mary Stuart to choose it nevertheless, what
dreams of friendship and alliance with Elizabeth still possessed her; yet the siren song of Elizabeth's friendship, the
mirage of the English succession, were still strong enough
in this moment of decision to blot out the stable image
of the proven friendship of France, where Mary had actually lived for thirteen years, and which could still be
so easily sought from a western port of Scotland, the sea-
route past Wales and Cornwall which Mary had taken
years before as a child. In France Mary had the inalien-
able estates and incomes of a queen dowager of the country; as a Catholic queen fleeing from a Protestant country,
she had every reason to expect the support of her brother-in-law, Charles IX, and Queen Catherine, to say nothing of her Guise relations, of whom the latest scion Henry,
duke of Guise, was just rising into a manhood which
promised to be as glorious as that of his father Duke
Francis. Even if Elizabeth had shown stronger support
for Mary against her rebels in the short interval since
Carberry Hill than the French king, the patent fact that
Mary was a Catholic whereas her insurgents were mainly
Protestants meant that the French would always have
a vested interest to help the Scottish queen as their co-
religionist.

In place of friendly France, Mary Stuart chose to fling
herself upon the mercy of unknown England, a land
where she had no party, no money, no estates, no relatives except her former mother-in-law, Lady Lennox, who
hated her and Queen Elizabeth herself, whom she had
never met personally, and whose permission she had not
even obtained to enter the country. As decisions go, it was

a brave one, a romantic one even, but under the circumstances it was certainly not a wise one. No human character is static. Different circumstances develop different aspects of the same personality. Perhaps ten months in prison had served to bring out in Mary's nature that streak either of the romantic or of the gambler, which leads the subject fatally on ever to prefer hope and high adventure to the known quantity, and which Mary Stuart passed on so dramatically to many of her later Stuart descendants. From now on, like all captives, Mary Stuart was to live of necessity far more in the world of dreams, than in that of reality. Her confinement in Lochleven seemed to have already begun the process of attrition in her powers of judgement. The queen herself summed up the subject of her fatal decision in a sentence at the end of a letter to Beaton towards the end of her life as sad as any she ever wrote: 'But I commanded my best friends to permit me to have my own way. . . .'[7]

The decision once taken, Herries wrote to Lowther, the deputy governor of Carlisle, asking permission for the Scottish queen to take refuge in England. But Mary did not even wait for the return of the messenger. She was now in borrowed linen, and in clothes and a hood lent by the laird of Lochinvar. The hood was especially necessary because her head was shorn of its beautiful red-gold wealth of hair as a precaution against recognition: one of Nau's most poignant headings reads: 'How she caused her head to be shaved.'[8] In this disguise she made her way west from Terregles to the abbey of Dundrennan, lying among trees in a secluded valley at the end of winding roads from Kirkcudbright and Castle Douglas, which finally led down to the coast. Dundrennan, a twelfth-century Cistercian foundation, was one of the most beautiful abbeys in Scotland: but the queen had little time to admire its beauties or even to listen to the soft roar of the sea a mile away. Her mind was on the future and on England. She sent yet another letter to Elizabeth from Dundrennan—'After God, she has now no hope save in Elizabeth. . . .'[9] But having so firmly fixed her earthly hopes on the English queen, Mary seemed to find no point in waiting for an answer to her letter.

On the afternoon of Sunday 16 May she went down to the little port at the mouth of the Abbey Burn from which the monks of Dundrennan used to trade with the continent.

From this undistinguished sea shore, she could actually
see the coast of England across the Solway Firth. Perhaps
the sight encouraged her, for at three o'clock in the afternoon the queen of Scotland embarked in a small fishing
boat, with only a tiny party of loyal followers—Lords
Herries, Maxwell and Fleming, Lord Claud Hamilton and
about sixteen other attendants. In this humble fashion,
Mary Stuart, who had been born in such magnificence in
the palace of Linlithgow, a princess of Scotland, left her
native country in a common fishing boat, never to return.

According to one tradition, during the four-hour journey
the queen had a sudden premonition of the fate which
awaited her in England, and ordered the boatmen to take
her after all to France; but the winds and tide were against
her, and the boat went remorselessly on towards England.[10] Nau mentions no such vacillation: when Queen
Mary arrived at the small Cumberland port of Workington
at seven in the evening, she seemed as elated as ever by
the heady wine of optimism. Queen Mary stumbled as
she first set foot on English soil: this omen, which might
have been interpreted in a sinister light, was on the contrary taken by her followers as a sign that their queen
was coming to take possession of the country. At Workington, the queen rested and was given supper, while Lord
Herries sent a message to Sir Henry Curwen of Workington Hall, whom he knew of old, to say that he had with
him a young heiress whom he had carried off from Scotland with the hope of marrying her to Sir Henry's son.
The answer to this inviting proposition came back that
Sir Henry was in London but that his house and servants
were at Lord Herries's disposal. Already Mary's surprising
and sudden arrival at the small port, combined with her
marked height and dramatically beautiful appearance,
were leading the inhabitants to guess only too easily that
they had the famous Scottish queen in their midst. One of
the Curwen servants, who was French, did not even have
to guess: he recognized Queen Mary immediately and told
Lord Fleming that he had seen her majesty before 'in better days'.

The next morning the deputy governor, Lowther, already warned by Herries's letter, arrived with a force of
400 horsemen. In the absence of the governor, Lord
Scrope, who was at that moment in London, he planned

to conduct the queen back to Carlisle. Queen Mary told Lowther calmly that she had come to England to solicit the assistance of the queen of England against her rebellious subjects. She had already in her brief space of freedom in Scotland sent John Beaton to Elizabeth in London with the famous diamond to which Mary attached such importance; she had written to Elizabeth from Dundrennan; now Mary wrote a third letter from Workington asking for help. The queen was taken to Cockermouth the next day, where she lodged in the home of Master Henry Fletcher, and by 18 May was installed in semi-captivity at Carlisle Castle. On her route she encountered the French ambassador to Scotland, Villeroy de Beaumont, on his way back to France after having had his train plundered by Moray's followers. The news he gave Mary of the fate of her own supporters in Scotland was discouraging: Mary was confirmed in her gloomy supposition that she would need English aid if she was ever to make her own way back to Scotland.

Lowther had reported that the attire of the Scottish queen was 'very mean':[11] once more in Mary's history a hurried escape from danger, in disguise, had left her with nothing in the way of a change of clothes. However, Fletcher, who was a merchant, is said to have presented her with a length of velvet for her wardrobe and a black dress was made for her on credit. Also Lowther, noting that the Scottish queen had so little money with her that it would scarcely cover the costs of clothing she so sadly needed, gallantly ordered her expenses at Cockermouth to be defrayed, and provided geldings of his own accord, to convey the queen and her train to Carlisle. Lowther was evidently genuinely puzzled as to exactly how he should treat this strange bird of rare plumage which had so confidently flown into the English aviary; but he was determined to err if anything on the side of courtesy, not knowing from one minute to the next whether his guest might not be summoned to London and there received with every honour by Queen Elizabeth herself. As a result, at this point Mary's own confidence in the rightness of her decision was unshaken, and in a letter to the earl of Cassillis dictated from Carlisle on 20 May she described herself as 'right well received and honourably accompanied and treated' in England; she expected to be back

in Scotland at the head of an army, French if not English,
'about the fifteenth day of August'.[12]

Puzzled as Richard Lowther might have been as how to
treat his royal visitor, whether as queen or captive, or a
nice combination of both, his bewilderment was as nothing compared to the perturbation of Elizabeth's advisers
in London. Here Queen Mary's arrival, romantic foolish
gesture as it might be, had caused a flutter from which
the English court would take time to recover. After all,
how was Queen Elizabeth to treat the royal fugitive? She
had not captured Queen Mary, nor sought to do so. Mary
had arrived of her own free will, expressly seeking English assistance, as her own letters immediately before
and after her arrival testified. It is a point worth emphasizing, since it was to be raised by Mary again and again
during her years as an English prisoner, last of all, with
pardonable bitterness, at her own trial in England. Yet
Queen Mary's request to be restored to her own throne
posed Elizabeth a whole series of problems which she
could hardly ignore. It was unthinkable in fact for the
Protestant English queen to take arms against Scotland
on behalf of her Catholic cousin; on the other hand if
Elizabeth did not do so, there was nothing to stop Mary
making the same request of the French, who might seize
with enthusiasm upon this new opportunity for entry on
to the British mainland. Therefore, to allow Mary to pass
freely through England to France was hardly good politics
from the English point of view.

Was the Scottish queen to be received at the English
court, and permitted to enjoy full liberty in England? The
Venetian ambassador in Paris sanguinely reported that a
palace was being specially prepared for Mary in London,
with great pomp;[13] but this was an equally obnoxious
prospect from the angle of English statecraft. Mary Stuart
at liberty might prove an unpleasant focus for the loyalties of the English Catholics. Mary herself might have
forgotten that ten years before as dauphiness of France she
had claimed to be rightful queen of England, rather than
heiress-presumptive to the throne. But Elizabeth's principal adviser, Cecil, had not forgotten her pretensions, and
there was no guarantee that the English Catholics had
either. Mary at this point knew nothing at first hand of the
remarkable character of these people: their obstinacy,

their heroism, their fineness of spirit which made them, paradoxically, for all their attitude to the new official religion of the country, among the most admirable of the Elizabethans. But to the prudent Cecil, the possible reactions of the English Catholics to Mary had to be taken into account.

Taken all in all, the most politic course from the English point of view was to temporize, until sufficient assessment had been made of the interior situation of Scotland. In the long run, Elizabeth felt, it would probably be wisest to despatch Mary back to her difficult subjects, rather than let her loose in either England or France, and furthermore there was that other consideration that subjects should not be encouraged to rebel against queens. But of course there was no question of restoring Mary by the force of an English army; the terms on which the Scots would accept Mary back would have to be discovered by cautious enquiries—and, if possible, negotiated to Elizabeth's own advantage. In the meantime it would be best to keep Mary in the north not exactly a prisoner, but not exactly free, not exactly debarred for ever from Elizabeth's presence, but certainly not welcomed into it.* The only course which was emphatically to be debarred to Mary was that of seeking French help: as Elizabeth's instructions of 18 May stated, Mary was to be told plainly that as Elizabeth intended to assist her herself, any attempt on the Scottish queen's part to bring in the French as well would be regarded as merely renewing old quarrels.[14] Fortunately Mary had not arrived in England with an unbesmirched reputation: there was that unresolved matter of Darnley's death, and the scandal she had caused by marrying the chief suspect. The cloud of old scandal round Mary's head now provided a convenient excuse for putting her off from Elizabeth's presence, until she should have been cleared of all guilt. And in such a work of arbitration, who would be more suitable to act as judge between Mary's cause and that of her nobles than the English queen herself?

Queen Elizabeth's next move was to send her trusted

---

* From the point of view of the succession, there was something to be said for having Elizabeth's nearest relative under lock and key; acting on this principle, the emperors of Ethiopia used to incarcerate all the princes of blood royal on a mountain near Gondar, until the time came for one of them to succeed.

counsellor, Sir Francis Knollys, north to treat with her guest-captive along these delicate lines. Knollys was the husband of Catherine Grey, Lord Hunsdon's sister, who was Elizabeth's first cousin through the Boleyns, as well as being her intimate friend. The Knollys had an enormous family, to whom Sir Francis was a punctilious father. He was now about fifty-five, a man of the highest honour, and a leading Puritan, who had fled to Germany during the reign of Mary Tudor. Despite their religious differences, Mary made an immediately favourable impression upon this experienced courtier. He discovered in her a woman of innate intelligence, blessed with an eloquent tongue and full of practical good sense; to these qualities, she also joined considerable personal courage. A little later, when he felt he knew her better, Knollys ventured on a further and even more favourable character sketch of the Scottish queen:[15] to begin with she was a 'notable woman' because she had no care for ceremonies beyond the acknowledgement of her royal estate (possibly a sly dig at Queen Elizabeth); then she spoke freely to everyone, whatever their rank and 'showeth a disposition to speak much and to be bold and to be pleasant to be very familiar'. Furthermore not only was she brave herself, but she was also delighted by valour in others, 'commending by name all approved hardy men of her country, although they be her enemies, and she concealeth no cowardice even in her friends'. In short, 'For victory's sake pain and peril seem pleasant to her and in respect of victory, wealth and all other things seem to her contemptible and vile'. Knollys metaphorically scratched his head as he concluded by wondering what on earth was to be done with such a spirited creature: Was 'such a lady and princess' to be nourished in the English bosom? He questioned his correspondents in London whether it was indeed 'wise to dissemble with such a lady'.

The answer came back from the south that it was indeed wise to dissemble, since it was for the moment the most politically advantageous course open to the English. Knollys was therefore instructed to tell Queen Mary that she could not be received at the English court until she had been purged of the stain of her husband's murder, and this purgation could only be achieved if she submitted herself to the judgement of Elizabeth. Tears flowed from Mary's eyes at the news; in a passion of rage at the injustice, she pointed out that both Maitland and Morton had assented to the murder of Darnley 'as it could well be proved, although now they would seem to persecute the same'.[16] Knollys himself was impressed by her arguments: he wrote to Elizabeth that as Mary had easily convinced those around her in the north of her innocence, it might be better for Elizabeth's honour to offer her the choice of remaining in England (to be cleared by Elizabeth of complicity in the crime) or returning once more to Scotland of her own volition. The worst that could happen, thought Knollys, was that Mary would decide to go to France, and in any case Moray would probably put a stop to that from Scotland. But in London Queen Elizabeth found it wiser to concentrate on Mary's honour than on her own—and this honour, she persisted in pointing out, had been too besmirched for her cousin to be released before the formality of an English investigation. Mary and Knollys were left together at Carlisle, with Knollys under orders to get his captive to agree to submit herself to this process.

On 30 May they argued on the subject of Mary's deposition; when Mary inveighed against Moray for his behaviour, Knollys maintained that if princes could be deposed for being mad so they could also for common murdering. Both crimes were the result of evil humours, he continued, with characteristic sixteenth-century preoccupation with the subject, one coming from melancholy (madness) and the other from choler (murder). Poor Mary wept and tried to excuse herself. But Knollys only seized the opportunity to press her further and say that she should now allow herself to be tried by Elizabeth, and thus officially purged of her crimes.[17]

Mary's state within Carlisle Castle was on Knollys's own admission far from luxurious. Her chief lack was of waiting-women: she who had been surrounded all her life by ladies of the highest rank to attend her, now had only two or three to help her, and they were 'not of the finest sort'. Her gentlemen included the romantic-minded George Douglas who had followed the queen into exile: he was one of the three or four allowed to sleep within the precincts of the castle, the rest of the gentlemen leaving the castle at sunset and sleeping within the town, with the rest of her train, down to cooks and scullions, making a total of between thirty and forty. Another serious lack was of horses—for the queen had of course arrived without any at all, and with her enthusiasm for physical exercise she felt the deprivation keenly. There were heavy iron gratings across Mary's windows and a series of three ante-chambers packed with soldiers led to her own chamber. Although Mary was able to attend football matches organized by her own retinue on the green—Knollys noted with surprise that there was no foul play—whenever she walked or rode she was attended by a guard of a hundred men, lest George Douglas's fancy should once again turn to the subject of escape. Her one attempt at hare-hunting was her last: it was thought too risky to let her ride abroad even under the pretext of sport.

The arrival of Mary Seton, the remaining unmarried Marie of happier times, provided a welcome relief, more especially as Mary Seton was an expert hairdresser: Knollys noted with admiration her skill in the art of 'busking', as he termed it, excelling anything he had seen previously—'among other pretty devices, yesterday and today she did set such a curled hair upon the Queen that it was like to be a periwig that showed very delicately; and every other day she hath a new device of head dressing, without any cost, and yet setteth forth a woman gaily well'.[18] Such feminine skills were all the more necessary since the queen had chopped off her own hair during the flight from Langside; it never grew again in its old abundance and in any case was frequently cut to guard against persistent headaches; it seems that for the rest of her life Mary was dependent on wigs and falsepieces. Despite Mary Seton's endeavours, the queen's clothing remained a problem. Queen Elizabeth, appealed to for some help out of her own copious wardrobe, responded with gifts of such mean quality—some odd pieces of black velvet and old dresses—that the embarrassed Knollys tried to explain them away by saying that they had been intended for Mary's maids. Moray was scarcely more generous: when he despatched three coffers of his sister's clothes from Scotland, the queen noted angrily that there was but one taffeta dress amongst them, the rest merely cloaks, and 'coverage for saddles'—ironically useless to a captive. She had to send for sartorial reinforcement from Lochleven. In July she did receive from her own chamberlain in Scotland a number of belongings, mainly accessories including gloves, pearl buttons, tights, veils, coifs of black and white, and twelve *orillettes* or bandages, to place over the ears when asleep, no doubt to cut out from the royal consciousness the heavy tread of the hagbutters in the three rooms outside.[19]

To Mary these feminine considerations of dress and hair, and even the conditions of her confinement (which shocked Montmorin, the French ambassador) were secondary to her grand design to reach the presence of Queen Elizabeth. From her arrival at Workington towards the end of May, until the end of the conference at York, and its removal to London, Queen Mary wrote over twenty letters to Queen Elizabeth, most of them extremely long, well thought out, intelligent pieces of pleading, all elaborations on the same theme of Mary's need for succour to regain her Scottish throne, and her trust in Elizabeth to provide it. Mary even summoned her poetic gifts to her aid: she wrote a poem to her '*chère soeur*' of which both an Italian and a French version survive, expressing the mingled pleasure and pain which the subject of their meeting produced in her heart, torn as she was between hope and doubt. She likened herself to a ship blown backwards by contrary winds just as it was entering the harbour, the poem ending with a prophetic fear that Fortune might once more turn against her in this as in so many things:

> *Un seul penser qui me profficte et nuit*
> *Amer et doux change en mon coeur sans cesse*
> *Entre le doubte et l'espoir il m'oppresse*
> *Tant que la paix et le repos me fuit . . .*
>
> *J'ay veu la nef relascher par contraincte*
> *En haulte mer, proche d'entrer au port,*
> *Et le serain se convertir en trouble.*
> *Ainsi je suis en souci et en crainte*
> *Non pas de vous, mais quantes fois a tort*
> *Fortune rompt voille et cordage double.**

* A longing haunts my spirit, day and night
  Bitter and sweet, torments my aching heart
  'Twixt doubt and fear, it holds its wayward part,
  And while it lingers, rest and peace takes flight . . .

  Ah! I have seen a ship freed from control
  On the high seas, outside a friendly port,
  And what was peaceful change to woe and pain:
  Ev'n so am I, a lonely trembling soul,
  Fearing—not you, but to be made the sport
  Of Fate, that bursts the closest, strongest chain![20]

Other variations on the theme in letters were the evil plight of her supporters in Scotland under Moray's cruel persecution, and the monstrous nature of her subjects' rebellion against her, a tendency which surely no sovereign queen would encourage. One of the most poignant of the pleas, on 5 July, expostulated: 'Alas! Do not as the serpent that stoppeth his hearing, for I am no enchanter but your sister and natural cousin. If Caesar had not disclaimed to hear or heede the complaint of an advertiser [soothsayer] he had not so died. . . .' And with still more anguish, on the subject of the personal interview: 'I am not of the nature of the basilisk and less of the chameleon, to turn you to my likeness.'[21] Mary was of course writing not only to Elizabeth, but also to France, to Catherine de Medicis, to Charles IX, to whom she protested that she was suffering for the true religion, the duke of Anjou, and her uncle the cardinal. Some of these letters touched naturally on the vexed subject of money, the perennial preoccupation of exiled royalty: Mary now desperately needed the income of her French estates to provide for herself and her household, having arrived without a penny. But her instructions of 30 May to Lord Fleming, whom she despatched to London, made it clear that if Elizabeth did not agree to help her, then help was to be sought immediately from France, and that Mary herself in these circumstances would arrange to depart thither as soon as possible.[22] Fleming, however, was not allowed to proceed from London to France; and the instructions were never able to be carried out. On 8 June Mary received a visit from Middlemore, Elizabeth's emissary to Scotland, on his way north. Middlemore handed her a letter in which Elizabeth promised to restore Mary if she consented to have her innocence proved by Elizabeth's enquiry. Mary wept and stormed. In vain she tried to tempt Middlemore with the notion of the confidences she would make personally to Elizabeth if only she was allowed to meet her: 'I would and did mean to have uttered such matter unto her as I would have done to no other. . . . No one can compel me to accuse myself, and yet if I would say anything of my self, I would say of myself to her and to no other.'[23] To such beguilements, Elizabeth was deaf.*

* It has sometimes been conjectured from these words that Mary intended to reveal to Elizabeth the full truth about the murder of Darnley. But Mary's words have the unmistakable ring of the cap-

In Scotland Middlemore found that Moray and his supporters had quite independently reached the same conclusion as Elizabeth, to which they had been working since the previous winter: Mary's guilt over Darnley's death and her subsequent marriage to Bothwell were the points to be stressed if Mary was to be kept where Moray would most like to see her—in an English prison. The difference between Elizabeth and Moray was that Elizabeth at this point intended ultimately to restore Mary to Scotland, and only wished to delay the process; Moray on the other hand had no wish to see Mary back on the throne on any terms whatsoever. To Moray, the viciousness of his sister was no moral issue, it was a question of his own survival as governor of Scotland. Moray was therefore determined to go much further than the English and make the mud already thrown at Mary stick so hard, that there could be no question of this besmeared figure returning to reign.

It was significant that Cecil himself, in one of those private memoranda he was so fond of drawing up for his own guidance giving the *pros* and *contras* of any given situation, could find Mary's alleged moral turpitude the only true excuse for keeping her off the Scottish throne, and in an English prison.[24] In favour of setting Mary at liberty were the following arguments: that she had come of her own accord to England, trusting in Elizabeth's frequent promises of assistance; that she herself had been illegally condemned by her subjects, who had imprisoned her and charged her with the murder of Darnley, without ever allowing her to answer for her crimes either personally or through a lawyer in front of Parliament; that she was a queen subject to none, and not bound by law to answer to her subjects; lastly there were her own frequent offers to justify her behaviour personally in front of Queen Elizabeth. It was indeed a hard case to answer; it was certainly not answered by Mary's opponents at the time, nor has the passage of time and the unrolling of history made it seem any less formidable as an indictment of England's subsequent behaviour. The case which Cecil put *contra* Mary's liberty was entirely based on the assumption that she had been an accessory to the murder of her husband, and gone on both to protect and to marry the chief

---

tive, to be heard increasingly from now on in her utterances and letters, who will make any promise, hold out any lure, in order to achieve liberty.

assassin, Bothwell—apart from a somewhat dubious argument that since Darnley had been constituted king of Scots, and by Mary herself, so he was 'a public person and her superior', and therefore her subjects were bound to search out his murderer. This argument ignored the fact that Darnley had never in fact received the crown matrimonial, without which, despite his title of king, he could scarcely claim to be Mary's equal, let alone her superior.

It was under these circumstances that, shortly after Mary's flight to England, the first salvoes in the new campaign to blacken her reputation once and for all were fired by the men who now occupied the throne from which they had ejected her. The queen's 'privy letters,' of which nothing had been heard since the Parliament in the previous December, and which had apparently lain the while untouched in Morton's keeping, now made a new appearance on the political scene. It was interesting to note that these letters seemed not only to swell in importance, but also actually to grow in number as the campaign mounted in fervour. In England at the end of May, Lennox presented his own supplication to Elizabeth, wildly inaccurate in many details and poisonously accusatory of his former daughter-in-law; it referred to one letter only written by Mary by which she was supposed to have lured Darnley to his death. On 27 May Moray commissioned George Buchanan, Lennox's feudal vassal, to prepare a *Book of Articles* to denounce Mary. These articles, to whose inaccuracies reference has already been made in Chapter 15, were originally in Latin, and contained a short reference to Mary's 'letters'. But this term did not necessarily imply that there was more than one letter: the Latin word was *litterae* which was used to denote one letter as well as several, and in sixteenth-century English, also, the term 'letters' was always used to describe a solitary letter. The Latin *Book of Articles* was ready by June. On 21 May, five days after Mary's flight, Moray despatched his secretary John Wood to London, gnawingly anxious to prevent Elizabeth showing favour to Mary; Wood's instructions were to 'resolve' Elizabeth's mind of anything she might 'stand doubtful to'.[25] A little while later, translated copies of an unspecified number of the queen's writings were sent on to Wood from Scotland; as copies of letters said to have been written originally in French and now translated into Scottish they were, of course, of little value as evidence. But

Wood was to show them secretly to the English establishment, in order to hint what big guns Moray might be able to bring against his sister, if only the English would encourage him to do so.

The encouragement which Moray needed was an assurance from Elizabeth that she would not restore Mary to her throne in the event of her being found guilty of the murder. On 22 June, therefore, Moray despatched an extraordinary letter to Elizabeth in reply to her request to explain his rebellion; he virtually asked to be assured in advance that the verdict of Elizabeth's judges would be guilty *if* Moray was able to produce some of Mary's own letters, and *if* he could prove they were genuine. The English were asked to make up their minds on the basis of the translated copies of the letters now in London in order to resolve Moray's dilemma for him. Moray continued the letter on a note of near indignation at his difficulties: 'For what purpose shall we either accuse, or take care how to prove, when we are not assured what to prove, or, when we have proved, what shall succeed?'[26]

Moray's letter was a remarkable document. It may be thought to show more regard for the principles of statecraft than those of justice; it certainly outlined the problems of Moray and his supporters. For it was of no avail to accuse Mary of murder, and even prove it by fair means or foul, if she was subsequently to be restored to her throne, whatever the English verdict. Her vengeance might then be expected to be fierce upon those who had accused her. At this critical juncture, it seems likely that in response to Moray's anxious enquiries, Cecil did in fact give some private unwritten assurances to John Wood in London, to pass on to Moray: whatever Elizabeth might say in public, in order to lure the Scottish queen into accepting her arbitration voluntarily, it was not in fact intended to restore Mary to Scotland if she was found to be guilty.[27] At all events, Moray received some sort of satisfactory answer to his problems at the end of June, for he now began to endorse the plan of an English 'trial' with enthusiasm.

While Mary's emissary in London, Lord Herries, treated with Cecil and Elizabeth over the possibility of the English holding such a 'trial' if Mary would agree to it, Mary herself suffered a change of prison. It was decided to re-

move her to Bolton Castle in Yorkshire. Carlisle was
dangerously near the Scottish border. From the moment of
Mary's arrival there, other more secure places of confinement for her had been discussed, including Nottingham and Fotheringhay. The move was complicated by
the fact that Mary was still not officially a prisoner. When
the suggestion of a change was first broached to Mary,
she quickly asked Middlemore whether she was to go as a
captive or of her own choice. Middlemore tactfully replied
that Elizabeth merely wished to have Mary stationed nearer
to herself. To this Mary countered with equal diplomacy
that since she was in Elizabeth's hands, she might dispose
of her as she willed.[28] But when the actual moment came
to leave Carlisle, Mary showed less composure. She began
to weep and rage with a temper which was rapidly quick-
ening with the frustrations of her unexpected imprisonment. Knollys had to exercise all his patience to get Mary
to agree to proceed, since he did not wish to practise
duress. Eventually Mary saw the threats and lamentations
were achieving nothing, whereas gentleness might win her
some advantage. She therefore withdrew her objections
to departure, like a wise woman, said Knollys, and allowed
herself to be removed quite placidly, on condition that she
should be permitted to despatch messengers to Scotland.
The journey took two days, with a night at Lowther Castle and a night at Wharton. On arrival, Mary was pronounced by Knollys to his satisfaction, to be very quiet,
tractable, and 'void of displeasant countenance'.[29]

There was, however, much to displease Mary's countenance in the intrigues which were now being spun between
Edinburgh and London. In spite of her incarceration, she
had some inkling of what was taking place, and her knowledge of Scotland led her to guess more. Some messages
from Wood in London to Moray fell into her hands by
chance in June and uncovered some of the regent's plotting. The news that some of her own letters were to be
used against her reduced her to a state of nervous collapse,
and she ended one letter to Elizabeth with a plea to excuse
her 'bad writing, for these letters, so falsely invented, have
made her ill'.[30] The move away from Carlisle proved to be
a severe handicap. Carlisle was at least the capital of the
western portion of the English borders, a frontier town
with administrative connections, easy of access for travellers. Bolton was an isolated castle in a remote corner of

the North Riding of Yorkshire, looking over the broad
pastoral valley of Wensleydale; it had no town of its own to
surround it, and lay forty miles from York, and over fifty
miles from Carlisle. The castle itself was comparatively un-
furnished on her arrival, and hangings and other belongings had to be borrowed from Sir George Bowes's house
some distance away. Far more serious to Mary's cause than
these minor discomforts was the fact that she was from
now on placed physically outside the mainstream of political life, although mentally she remained very much part
of it. Mary had never been well-endowed with advisers, although she was a woman who wished by nature to lean
upon others for advice; for the next nineteen years she
was deprived of any sort of proper worldly contact by
which to judge the situations which were reported to her.
Her own servants, although loyal, were no match in intelligence for the English politicians with whom they had
to deal. A Herries certainly could not hope to worst a
Cecil: in any case the mistress of one presided at liberty
over an illustrious court, whereas the mistress of the other
pined in enforced seclusion.

Herries came to Bolton from London at the end of
July and put the English proposals to his queen; it is easy
to understand how Mary, lit up by false hopes of restoration at Elizabeth's hands, agreed at last to the prospect
of an English 'trial'.* The fact that the English had no
right to try her seemed now less important than the fact
that Elizabeth had promised to restore her whatever the
outcome, although if the lords proved her guilt, it was
stipulated that the lords themselves should go unpunished
for their rebellion. If the lords brought no evidence against
Mary, on the other hand, or if their evidence was not held
to be valid, then Mary was to be adjudged innocent in any
case and restored as before, on condition that she renounced her present title to the crown of England during
the lifetime of Elizabeth and her lawful issue. Other conditions made were the abandonment of the alliance with
France, and the substitution of an alliance with England,

* The English were careful to avoid using the word 'trial', aware
that they had no possible right to try the queen of another country,
for a crime said to be committed there. But of course the proceedings were a form of trial, and the word is used hereafter without
inverted commas.

the Mass in Scotland to be abandoned by Mary and common prayer after the English form to be practised instead and the ratification at last of the Treaty of Edinburgh. Believing herself to be on the eve of liberty, Mary even bade her partisans in Scotland cease fighting on condition that Moray's would do the same.

The climate in the outside world was harsher than Mary, within her prison walls, remembered. Whether or not Mary's partisans did lay down their arms—at any rate at the Parliament of 16 August Moray swiftly declared the forfeiture of the Hamiltons, Fleming and the bishop of Ross, before ever the boasted English trial had taken place. More damaging still to Mary's cause, on 20 September Elizabeth wrote privately to Moray promising him what Cecil had already divulged in secret: whatever impression Elizabeth might have given Mary, the Scottish queen would not in fact be restored to her throne if she were found guilty in England. This letter, following on Cecil's hints to Wood, was crucial to the development of Moray's behaviour. On 23 September Cecil repeated the same information to Sussex.[31] Moray had now every impetus to prepare the blackest possible case against his sister. The queen's 'privy letters' had therefore become the central plank of his accusatory edifice.

The English translation of Buchanan's *Book of Articles*, prepared for the coming trial in September or October, contained a much expanded reference to these letters. Instead of the brief phrase in the Latin version written in June, there was now a long postscript specially devoted to the subject. Mary's own supporters also began to appreciate that these writings were to be the testing-point not only of her own guilt or innocence, but also of the whole future government of Scotland. The Marian nobles, gathered together at Dumbarton, took the opportunity to declare publicly that '. . . if it be alleged that her Majesty's writing, produced in parliament, should prove her Grace culpable, it may be answered, that there is in no place mention made in it by the which Her Highness may be convicted; albeit it were in her own hand-writing, as it is not'.[32] Only Mary herself, wrapped in her little prisoner's world, believed, trusting Elizabeth, that the trial was a mere formality, and that she would be set free in any case.

Under these inauspicious circumstances, the conference

of York was set up. It was decided that the trial should
take the form of examination of the evidence by an English
panel, headed by the duke of Norfolk. Both Mary and
Moray were to be allowed commissioners. Moray's commissioners included himself and Maitland; Mary's included among others John Leslie, bishop of Ross, and
Lords Livingston, Boyd and Herries. Her instructions to
her commissioners illustrate Mary's personal conviction
that the conference was only being held in order that
Elizabeth might in the future restore her to her throne,
having accomplished 'the reduction of our said disobedient
subjects to their dutiful obedience of us'. With such rising hopes to illuminate her horizon, even captivity at Bolton
seemed tolerable to Mary. She occupied herself learning
to write English under the tuition of Knollys. It is obvious
from his letters that propinquity led Knollys to fall a little
in love with his glamorous prisoner. Exercising her arts
of fascination on those around her in charming little ways
was second nature to Mary Stuart: to Knollys she wrote
her first letter in English when he had been absent from
Bolton for two or three days. The letter, which is indeed
exceedingly misspelt and scarcely intelligible as English
at all, announces that she has sent him a little token,
asks after his wife, and ends touchingly: 'Excus my ivel
vreitn thes furst tym. . . .'[33]

Knollys also applied himself enthusiastically to trying
to persuade his captive of the delights of the English religion which he himself practised. Knollys reported happily
that Mary was now at Bolton growing to a 'good liking
of English common prayer, had received an English chaplain, and had listened to his sermons which had happened
to deal severely with the pharisaical justification of works
by faith, as well as all kinds of papistry, with 'attentive
and contented ears'. Her replies were gentle and weak
and Knollys reported complacently that 'she does not
seem to like the worse of religion through me'.[34] Mary was
by now surrounded by Protestants: her cousin Agnes
Fleming, Lady Livingston, joined her in August and both
Livingstons belonged to the reformed Church, as did
Herries; they may have added their influence to that of
Knollys. It is possible also that she felt some genuine and
laudable intellectual curiosity concerning the doctrines
which the majority of her subjects practised, and that her
enquiries helped to while away the captive hours. But the

true motive behind this suspicious docility was now as ever
her desire to win the good opinions of Elizabeth, for whom
Knollys was merely a stalking-horse. At the end of August
Knollys put his finger on the point when he reported how
marvellously polite Mary had been of late 'as though she
conceived I could persuade her Highness to show her
great favour'.[35] The *beaux yeux* of Knollys, that good
family man, who worried over the welfare of his daughters
in London ('experience teaches what foul crimes youthful
women fall into for lack of orderly maintenance' he pronounced in an anxious letter), were quite incidental to
Mary Stuart's plans.

Mary's apparent Anglicanism did not pass unnoticed in
England. Towards the end of September Mary heard that
the local Catholics believed she was turning away from
the old religion, and were very upset by the news; immediately in the great hall of Bolton, in front of a full assembly, she professed herself as fervently Catholic as ever before, her arguments, according to Knollys, being 'so weak,
they only showed her zeal'. To Knollys alone she attempted
to make capital out of the incident, saying pointedly that
she could scarcely be expected to lose France, Spain and
all her foreign allies by seeming to change her religion,
and yet still not be certain that Elizabeth was her 'assured
friend'. But her letter to her girlhood friend, Elisabeth de
Valois, queen of Spain, at the end of September shows
that her heart was evidently as Catholic as ever beneath
its convenient show of Anglican interest.[36] Mary invokes
the memory of their common childhood, the food they
had shared in the past which had nourished an indissoluble
friendship, to plead for Spanish aid. She tells Elisabeth
that she has been offered '*de belles choses*' to change her
religion, but whatever Elisabeth may hear to the contrary,
Mary will never abandon the Faith, but merely try to accommodate herself to her changing circumstances. In the
meantime Mary hoped somehow to smuggle out her little
son James from Scotland to marry one of Elisabeth's
daughters. By the time this letter reached Spain, Elisabeth
was already dead in childbirth (incidentally leaving Philip
II, that ever recurring prospective bridegroom, once more
free to marry). But in November Mary wrote angrily in the
same vein to Philip himself, saying that she was considered
too closely related to the queen of England to enjoy the
services of a Catholic priest, but that it should not be

believed on that account that she had given up the beliefs
of her religion, as well as the practice.[37]

The point was a good one. It was perfectly true that on
her first arrival in England Mary had asked Lord Scrope
for a Catholic priest to attend her and he had replied
firmly that there was none left in England. It was also
true, as Mary told Philip, that if Knollys introduced a
Protestant preacher into her chamber, she could hardly
prevent him. Nevertheless Mary always felt somewhat sensitive in later life on this point of her alleged Anglicanism,
not so much out of intellectual distaste—for her own
strong but primitive faith seems to have remained perfectly unaffected by all the assaults made upon it—but
for the good practical reasons she outlined to Knollys.
By such aspersions on her Catholicism, she feared to forfeit the support of her Catholic allies. On the eve of her
death, she still took trouble to justify herself for having
listened to Protestant sermons when she first came to England. One may perhaps detect in these protestations the
murmur of a faintly guilty conscience; possibly Mary did
feel later that she had compromised herself a little in this
respect in her desire to please Elizabeth. This very minor
essay into the realms of Protestantism on the part of
Mary may be ascribed in part to the wishful thinking of
the ardent Puritan Knollys, in part to the natural curiosity
of the captive cut off from contact with her own religion,
but mainly to Mary's devouring obsession with the subject
of Elizabeth.

Knollys worried himself constantly over the prospect
of his prisoner escaping: he even sent a map of the castle
down to London so that his security arrangements could
be approved. The royal train at Bolton now consisted of
Leslie, Herries, the Livingstons, the Flemings, Gavin Hamilton, the master of the household John Beaton, Bastian
Pages and his wife, Mary Seton and young Willy Douglas,
a corps of loyal supporters. Bolton was only sixty miles
to the south-west Scottish border as the crow flies. Escape
might or might not have been possible. Knollys's forebod-
ings indicate that Mary might with luck have eluded her
captors. But at this point there were positively no attempts
at escape, no disguises as a laundress, no stolen keys, no
corrupted guards; Mary herself made it clear that this
was at her own wish. She saw no reason to try and escape
when she hoped for so much from Elizabeth. It suited her

too to pretend to be a guest, not a captive. At the beginning of October Mary warned Knollys that things might be very different in the future: 'If I shall be holden here perforce, you may be sure then being as a desperate person I will use any attempts that may serve my purpose either by myself or my friends.'[38]

In the meantime, with the prospect of the successful conference of York in front of her, Mary was content to stay where she was. Knollys really had no need to fear those hare-hunting expeditions across the moors—'the wind never so boisterous' which made him feel so nervous because he constantly imagined a dozen or so Scots would ride over the moors and carry off their queen. In his mind's eye he saw them riding over mountains and heaths with spare horses, avoiding villages and towns, and rescuing this Diana—'for she hath an able body to endure to gallop apass'. Knollys believed that the country folk would certainly not stop her: they would laugh in their sleeves to see her go.[39] Mary on the other hand no longer saw herself in this romantic and impulsive light. In mid-September she wrote proudly to the king of France, saying that the fact she had had no response to any of her letters to him pleading for assistance no longer worried her, since now Queen Elizabeth her good sister had promised to do all things to her honour and grandeur and restore her to her estate.[40] In October Mary pinned all her hopes on that conference to open at York, the result of which she believed, win or lose, guilty or innocent, could not fail to be her restoration to the throne of Scotland.

'By divers her privy letters written wholly with her own hand . . . it is most certain that she was privy, art and part of the actual devise and deed of the fore-named murder of the King, her lawful husband.'

From the Act of the Scottish Parliament, 15 December 1567

The conference of York, which opened in October 1568, was remarkable from the first for the confusion of aims among its participants. Elizabeth had already left conflicting impressions upon Mary and the Scottish nobles as to what she regarded the desirable outcome of this conference to be. Their own intentions were equally at variance. Of those present, only Moray was able to show true singleness of purpose, in that he intended to prove the queen of Scotland's guilt up to the hilt in order to prevent her return north; with this object in view he officially took custody from Morton of the debatable 'privy letters' in their silver casket on 16 September, before setting out for England. However, the incriminating documents had signally increased from the solitary letter of Lennox's supplication, and the briefly mentioned *litterae* of Buchanan's June *Book of Articles*. They were now named in the receipt as 'missive letters, contracts or obligations for marriage, sonnets or love-ballads, and all other letters contained therein'.[1] Buchanan's English translation of his *Articles,* prepared at the end of September for use in front of the commission, also contained an additional long postscript on the specific subject of the letters, in contrast to the single phrase used three months earlier.

Moray's supporters were much less single-minded than their chief in their aims; Maitland in particular still dangled after his old scheme of Anglo-Scottish union, in which a restored Mary could play her part. Nor were Mary's own commissioners, including John Leslie, bishop of Ross, and Lord Herries, as resolute in their determination to prove her innocence as was the queen herself;

having lived through the troubled times of the queen's marriage to Bothwell, they conceived their role as rather to secure some sort of compromise by which Mary could be brought back to Scotland, than to shout out Queen Mary's freedom from guilt from the house-tops. As for the English 'judges', the earl of Sussex, Sir Ralph Sadler and the duke of Norfolk, it soon transpired that they too were not immune to private considerations. Norfolk had recently been widowed; he was England's leading noble, and himself a Protestant, although he had many Catholic relations; the queen of Scots was now generally regarded as once more marriageable, despite the fact that divorce from Bothwell was not yet secured, and Norfolk's name had been mentioned in this context, even before the opening of the conference. As a 'judge', therefore, Norfolk might be supposed to be somewhat *parti pris*.

Under these circumstances, it was hardly surprising that the conference at York seemed at first to achieve but little. On 11 October Moray decided to make a bold essay to resolve matters. Copies of the 'privy letters' were secretly shown to the English commissioners. Maitland, however, seems to have leaked the news to Mary's own commissioners for the next day they rode over to Bolton and informed her of this development, although they had not actually seen the letters themselves. Moray was still acting cautiously: Norfolk reported back to London that the letters had not been shown to them officially as commissioners, but merely 'for our better instruction'.[2] Moray asked Norfolk to find out how Elizabeth would react to the letters, and whether they would be considered sufficient proof to condemn the queen of Scots of murder. Despite the judicial irregularity of Moray's behaviour, Norfolk professed himself to be horrified by the contents of the letters; although he had only seen copies, he expressed the view that so many letters could hardly be counterfeited; in asking Elizabeth's advice on how to proceed next, he gave the opinion that conviction of the Scottish queen would scarcely be avoided, if indeed the letters were written in her own hand.

Elizabeth's reaction to this communication was to send for the whole conference to start again at Westminster. It was felt that away from the frenetic atmosphere which seemed to have developed at York, calmer counsels might prevail, and some solid solution emerge from out of this

morass in which, as Sussex truly pointed out, the crown
of Scotland was being tossed about on wave after wave
of private feud and interest. Elizabeth was as yet unaware
that only five days after Norfolk wrote in such shocked
terms concerning Mary's letters, he had had some private
conference with Maitland in which it seems likely that
Maitland held out to him the bait of Mary's hand in marriage. From Maitland's point of view, the marriage of
Mary with a leading English Protestant noble was an excellent step forward in his plans. It had been suggested that
at this point Maitland must also have revealed to Norfolk
that the so-called Casket Letters were not all they seemed,
and that the allegations against Mary as a murderess were
not really to be taken too seriously. After all, in this
strange quasi-judicial world of a trial which was not a trial,
guilt might also be considered non-guilt. At all events,
Norfolk now allowed himself to be involved secretly in
certain schemes for a marriage between himself and Mary.

Sussex, another English commissioner, did not seem
to take the letters particularly seriously himself. In a letter back to London, he neatly summed up the course
future developments might be expected to take, if Mary
was allowed to appear before the tribunal at Westminster:[3]
she would obviously deny the authenticity of the letters
in toto as a result of which she could never be convicted on their evidence; after this Elizabeth would be
compelled to acquit her, and set her free. If on the other
hand, Mary was not allowed to appear personally, the
whole matter could probably be 'huddled up' with some
show of saving Mary's honour, and yet without exposing
the Scottish lords as forgers; after this Mary could still
be kept in prison. It was a shrewd summary, and with
its emphasis on the need to prevent Mary making a personal appearance at Westminster, a prophetic one. Knollys,
from Bolton, put his finger on the same urgent necessity
to condemn Mary somehow or other, if she was to be kept
in captivity: he could not see how Elizabeth could with
honour and safety detain Mary, unless she was utterly
disgraced to the world and 'the contrary party [Moray]
thoroughly maintained'.

Knollys's solution to the problem of Mary was to marry
her off to his wife's nephew, and Queen Elizabeth's own
cousin, young George Carey, Lord Hunsdon's son. This
handsome young man had called on Mary at Bolton in

September, on his way north to join his father, the newly appointed governor of Berwick. The visit was probably prompted by Knollys's match-making. Carey was courteously received by Mary, although her mind seems to have been more on politics than on dalliance: she spent most of their conversations retailing to him a list of messages to give to his father about border matters, where conditions were by now exceptionally turbulent, as always during a period of governmental unrest in Scotland. Mary was still blithely unaware of the cool conclusions which Sussex had drawn concerning the paramount need to prevent her appearing personally in London. To Cassillis in Scotland she wrote quite confidently on 23 October of the 'good procedure' at York where nothing had been proved against her. At first puzzled by the transference of the conference, she then consoled herself with the thought that from the first she had always wanted Elizabeth to take personal control of the whole matter, and now she was achieving her wish. Her letter to Elizabeth of 22 October was a model of docility: 'Since you, my good sister, know our cause best, we doubt not to receive presently good end thereof; where through we may be perpetually indebted to you.'[4]

The commission of Westminster opened officially on 25 November. It was a considerably enlarged body from that of the three commissioners at York, and now included both Leicester and Cecil. Shortly before its opening, on hearing that Elizabeth was constantly receiving her rival plaintiff Moray into her presence, Mary wrote commandingly to her own commissioners saying that they were on no account to take part in the conference if she Mary were not allowed to attend it on exactly the same footing as Moray; nevertheless she still does not seem to have believed that this right could actually be denied to her throughout the proceedings.[5] On 29 November, Moray presented his 'Eik' or list of accusations, followed by the presentation of a personal accusation by Lennox. It was not, however, until 1 December that Mary's commissioners put in their first protest, that Mary also should be allowed formal access to the court, since Moray was personally appearing in it; they demanded that Mary should be allowed to speak in her own defence in front of the English Council and the foreign ambassadors. Elizabeth, however, refused the request on the ingenious grounds that no proofs had as yet been shown against Mary (the Casket Letters had not yet been produced in court); there was therefore no point in her appearing at this juncture, when as far as Elizabeth knew, it might never be found necessary at all, and Mary might be able to be declared innocent *in absentia*. Winter had come early that year. Thick snow piled the ground between London and distant Bolton, 250 miles and days of hard riding away. Mary's enforced isolation proved once more a disastrous hindrance to her cause. For without consulting her, her commissioners continued to try and bring about some sort of compromise to restore her to Scotland, in spite of the fact that Moray in his Eik had openly accused the queen of murder. They thus acted in direct contradiction of Mary's specific instructions to break off from the conference if she personally was not allowed to appear on the same terms as Moray: 'since they have free access to accuse us'.

On 6 December Mary's emissions made their first protest on the subject; but the English still retained the Marian commissioners within the conference, by the expedient of arguing over the conditions of withdrawal. Moray was now asked to produce additional proofs to his Eik; he exhibited the December 1567 Act of Parliament, and Buchanan's *Book of Articles*. Finally, on 7 December the casket itself was produced by Moray and his supporters in front of Mary's own commissioners. According to the Journal of the Commission for that day, the tribunal saw 'a small gilded coffer not fully one foot long, being garnished in many places with the Roman letter F. set under a royal crown'.[6] The circumstances of its finding, outlined earlier in Chapter 18, were now solemnly declared by Morton. Before the casket's contents were exhibited, however, the tribunal were shown two marriage contracts which were not included in it: after this the first two letters from the casket were produced. The next day seven letters out of the casket were displayed, all said to be in French, written in the Roman hand. The English tribunal, according to their account, duly had the letters copied out for themselves, collated the copies with the originals, and then, at Moray's own request, handed him back the originals. This done, Moray produced the cases against Bothwell's servants, Hepburn, Hay, Powrie and Dalgleish, including their depositions.

The next day, 9 December, while Mary's commissioners

made renewed attempts to withdraw from the conference, which had for them become a travesty of justice, since they were not even admitted to the proceedings, the tribunal continued to examine the copies of the letters they had taken and the sonnets 'written in French, being duly translated into English'. Morton made a further official declaration about the finding of the casket, and the evidence of Darnley's servant Nelson, and one of Lennox's servants, Thomas Crawford, was also produced. It was now decided to enlarge the tribunal still further with other leading English nobles including Northumberland, Westmorland and Shrewsbury. On 14 December the new tribunal was given a *resumé* of proceedings up to date. In the meantime Elizabeth gave Mary at Bolton three choices: she could answer the accusations through her own commissioners, in writing herself, or personally to some English nobles sent expressly to Bolton for that purpose. To all these alternatives Mary returned an indignant negative: she could hardly be expected to answer accusations based on evidence she was not allowed to see, or surrender the traditional right of the prisoner to face her accusers. But Elizabeth said that if Mary refused these three alternatives: 'it will be thought as much as she were culpable'.[7]

At last Mary was beginning to have some inkling of the treacherous nature of the quagmire into which she had so unwarily walked. Her frantic state of mind at this point, cut off at Bolton, dependent on slow-moving letters for news from London, may be judged from her letter to the earl of Mar in Scotland, in which she begs him to guard the infant James well at Stirling, and not allow him to be either brought by agreement to England, or snatched away from him by surprise: Mary adds a postscript in her own hand, reminding Mar that when she handed her son over to him, *'comme mon plus cher joiau'*, he promised never to hand him over to another without the queen's consent.[8] On 19 December she belatedly drew up her own Eik for the accusation of Moray, presented on 25 December. Naturally she waxed especially furious over the accusation that she had planned the death of her own child to follow that of his father: the nobles 'cover themselves thereanent with a wet sack; and that calumny should suffice for proof and inquisition of all the rest; for the natural love of a mother towards her bairn confounds them'. Beyond that Mary dwelt on her previous troubles with the lords—the murder of Riccio when they would have 'slain the mother and the bairn both when he was in our womb', and the manifest illegality of Moray's regency.[9]

Despite Mary's counter-accusations, and despite her continued requests to be shown the writings which were said to arraign her, the conference at Westminster was officially ended by Elizabeth on 11 January without either Mary or her commissioners being allowed to glimpse these debatable documents. The verdict of the tribunal was indeed as ambivalent as the rest of the proceedings: it was decided that neither party had had anything sufficiently proved against them. Mary had not proved that her nobles had rebelled against her—'there has been nothing deduced against them as yet that may impair their honour and allegiances'. But on the other hand, all the prolonged inspection of the so-called Casket Letters had not apparently convinced the tribunal of the guilt of the Scottish queen. Elizabeth pronounced on the subject of the evidence brought forward by the Scottish nobles that 'there had been nothing sufficiently produced nor shewn by them against the Queen their sovereign, whereby the Queen of England should conceive or take any evil opinion of the Queen her good sister, for anything yet seen'.[10] In short, neither side was adjudged guilty at the end of the 'trial', the only difference being that whereas Moray was now allowed to depart for Scotland, after a personal interview with Elizabeth—and incidentally with a £5,000 subsidy in his pocket—Mary was still held at Bolton, with preparations afoot to move her to a still more secure prison.

Now at last Elizabeth offered to let Mary have copies of the writings produced against her, provided she would promise to answer them. (The originals had of course gone back to Scotland with Moray.) But at this point Mary's commissioners, who all along had shown themselves so little match for the English politicians, rallied sufficiently to point out that since Moray had by now left England for Scotland, and the conference had no other judicial basis except in so far as it was supposed to judge between Mary and Moray, it was far too late for Mary to answer Moray's accusations. Mary's commissioners were themselves allowed to return to Scotland on 31 January. Thus ended what was surely one of the strangest judicial proceedings in the history of the British Isles, with a verdict of not proven given to both parties, yet one plaintiff allowed to return freely to rule in the place of the other plaintiff, who in the meantime continued to be held a prisoner.

It is time to consider the Casket Letters themselves, those debatable documents, and see how much if anything they genuinely prove against the moral character of Mary Stuart —her adulterous liaison with Bothwell before the death of Darnley, and her guilty foreknowledge of his murder. It is an interesting point that Mary Stuart's contemporaries apparently attached a great deal less importance to the Casket Letters than has been given to them ever since by the studies of historians. In the four hundred years since their appearance, more ink has been spilt on the subject— textual difficulties, language difficulties, theories of author- ship, theories of interpolation—than on almost any other textual mystery. Yet at the time when the actual letters were exhibited it has been seen that not only Norfolk took a sufficiently *degagé* view of the whole matter to pursue marriage to Mary ardently thereafter, but Sussex, another Englishman, was of the opinion that as proofs, the letters alone would never be sufficient to condemn the Scottish queen. Subsequently, due to yet another revolu- tion in Scottish internal politics, Maitland himself be- came one of Queen Mary's most ardent champions in Scotland, apparently undismayed by the depths of villainy she was said to have revealed in the letters. Despite this contemporary reaction, succeeding generations of his- torians have attempted to do what Elizabeth's tribunal specifically did not do, and give a verdict on Mary's char- acter based on these letters. Yet every modern argument concerning the Casket Letters, and indeed every argument on the subject since the conference of Westminster in 1568, has of necessity to leave out of account the most important consideration in any discussion of letters said to be forged —the question of hand-writing—for the Casket Letters now disappeared from sight as mysteriously as they had ap- peared.

In January 1569, they were taken to Scotland by Moray, to whom they had been re-delivered by the tribunal. On 22 January 1571, they were handed over once more to Morton: although what should have been twenty-two docu- ments (eight letters, two marriage contracts and twelve son-

nets making up one poem) had mysteriously become only
twenty-one, raising a doubt that one document might
have been left behind in England. Copies were once more
made, but these copies vanished immediately and have
never been seen since. After Morton's execution, the letters passed to the earl of Gowrie, who was executed in
turn in 1584, after which the original letters were never
seen again from that day to this, despite repeated efforts
on the part of Elizabeth to get hold of them, ranging from
bribery to suggestions of theft.*

Today, in order to consider the authenticity of the Casket
Letters, we are dependent on two sources: firstly those
contemporary copies made by the clerks at Westminster
which have survived. Some of these copies are in the original French, others in the English translation made for
the use of the tribunal; all of these contemporary copies
(with the exception of one) are in the Elizabethan 'secretary' hand in marked contrast to Mary's infinitely more
legible Roman or Italian hand. There are four of these
contemporary copies in the Public Record Office, and four
others among the Cecil Papers at Hatfield House; a contemporary copy of one of the marriage contracts is among
the Cotton MSS at the British Museum.[13] These are the
only 'original' manuscripts available for the study of the
Casket Letters—all of them purporting to be only contemporary copies. Otherwise we are dependent on the
secondary published sources—and in the case of two of
the letters, the twelve sonnets, and one of the marriage
contracts, for all of which not even a contemporary copy

* The only link with the Casket Letters which remains to be seen
in Scotland is the beautiful silver casket in the Lennoxlove Museum;
although not garnished all over with the roman letter F. under a
crown, as the Journal of the Commission described it, it is the right
size, and a French work of the early sixteenth century; its lock is
also stricken up in the manner Morton described. There is room for
two crossed Fs and a crown where the Hamilton arms are now engraved; alternatively the Journal's description may have been mis-
leading, and the Fs may have been embroidered on the velvet cover
of the box, as in another velvet coffer sent to Mary on Lochleven.[11]
The Lennoxlove casket has a long provenance: it was purchased
some time after 1632 from 'a Papist' by the marchioness of Douglas, daughter of the 1st marquess of Huntly. After her death, her
plate was sold but her daughter-in-law Lady Anne Hamilton, later
duchess of Hamilton in her own right, purchased it back, and, at her
husband's request, had the Hamilton arms engraved on the casket,
in place of those of Douglas.[12]

survives totally dependent on them. The contemporary published versions consist of Buchanan's Latin 'Detection' which appeared in 1571, and gave three of the letters; in the same year a Scottish version of the 'Detection' also appeared, giving all eight letters, with the first sentence in the original French; the next year an Anglicized version of the Scottish translation appeared, following the same principle. In 1573 a French edition was published giving seven of the letters; this was not the original (as can be seen by comparing it with the contemporary manuscript copies)—merely a French version retranslated out of the Scots or English. This re-translation leads to considerable differences between the two French versions.

Quite apart from the lack of originals, the situation over the letters is complicated by the fact that none of them has any dates attached to it and none has any proper beginning or ending or signature; the fact that none is signed by the queen makes the letters particularly remarkable, compared to the rest of Mary's correspondence, since Mary, in all her other letters, always took especial trouble with her endings, and the individual phrase before the characteristic signature MARIE was always carefully suited to the receipt. Furthermore there is not one letter which does not have some internal problem of its own, either of dating or of sheer sense, so far as one can judge from the copy. As forgeries, then, if forgeries they were, these were no smooth and expert job, but botched up—even patched up—efforts, done in a hurry by men who were trying to prove something, and because they had to prove it quickly, were not too particular about details, so long as the broad facts of the case appeared as they wished. These are of course exactly the sort of results which might be expected to emerge from the events of the summer of 1568—Queen Mary's unexpected flight to England, Moray's desperate need to keep her there, his anguished enquiries to the English as to what sort of evidence they would accept, and his final secretive, deliberately 'unofficial' production of the letters at York to Norfolk. The Casket Letters were to be regarded then as a collection of accusing briefs in a trial: in this context it is significant that the contemporary copies are all endorsed at the top in an English hand, sometimes that of Cecil himself, with a sentence giving the exact point they were said by the lords to prove. But regarded as a bundle of love letters, the Casket Letters are not only quite incomprehensible, but also in places manifestly absurd when applied to the relationship possible between Queen Mary and Bothwell.

Letter I,[14] of which no contemporary French copy survives, only a contemporary English translation, is marked at the top 'proves her disdain against her husband'. It is, however, not a love letter, but a calm and practical communication, from its style evidently written by Queen Mary herself at some point, although not necessarily 'From Glasgow this Saturday morning', as it states at the head of the letter—a phrase easily added. In it, Queen Mary refers to 'the man' who is 'the merriest that ever you saw, and doth remember unto me all that he can to make me believe that he loveth me. To conclude: you would say that he maketh love to me, wherein I take so much pleasure that I never come in there but the pain of my side doth take me.' This 'man' is to be brought by Mary to Craigmillar on Wednesday. From the endorsement, it is clear that the lords maintained this 'man' was Darnley whose advances at Glasgow, when Mary went to fetch him towards the end of January, were causing Mary a pain in her side. But the dates do not fit with Darnley's journey: he could never have expected to reach Craigmillar on the Wednesday; the person whom Mary did take on a journey also in January from Stirling to Edinburgh, arriving there on Wednesday, 15 January, was her son James. And it has been pointed out that Mary's language makes it at least possible she was talking of her baby son, 'the merriest that ever you saw . . . you would say that he maketh love to me . . .'; just as the term 'the man' makes more sense as a mother's fanciful term for a little boy, than as Mary's description of Darnley, to whom in all other letters even to her most intimate relative she refers impersonally as 'the King'. However, these details were not likely to bother the English tribunal. At a rough inspection, prodded on by the Scottish lords' explanations, such a letter could easily be held to prove the queen's disdain of Darnley at Glasgow nearly two years back. It was easy to add the phrase 'From Glasgow . . .' at the head of the letter to give verisimilitude; and a phrase about Paris being commanded to bring back medicine was probably interpolated in the middle of the letter for good measure—Paris being by now a notorious guilt-inferring name in the history of Mary–Bothwell relations. But of course, in the absence even of a French contemporary copy of this letter, it is impossible to be certain about this.

Letter II,[15] the famous 'Long Casket Letter' is an extraordinary document which must have baffled the English judges if they had ever considered it in detail almost as much as it has baffled historians ever since.* Once again, no contemporary French copy survives to guide us, only the contemporary English copy and the Scottish version later published by Buchanan. The English copy was endorsed by the clerk: 'The long letter written from Glasgow from the Queen of Scots to the Earl Bothwell.' This letter is susceptible of almost any interpretation except that of being one single letter, written on a single occasion from Mary Stuart to Bothwell. It is extremely long—over 2,000 words altogether. The contemporary English copy runs to seven pages of manuscript with a long unexplained gap on the fifth page. As before, it begins without any salutation: 'Being gone from the place where I had left my heart; it may easily be judged what my countenance was . . .', but after these first few affectionate but not amorous sentences, it turns into a long account of Mary's journey to Glasgow to fetch Darnley, her meeting with a gentleman of Lennox's, and other meetings *en route* with James Hamilton and the laird of Luss. The letter now gives a long intimate account of Mary's interview and relations with Darnley while at Glasgow: Darnley pleads with Mary to lodge 'nigh' unto him, blames his sickness for Mary being 'so strange unto him', and attacks Mary for her cruelty who will not accept his 'offers and repentance'. These phrases ring very true of what is already known of Darnley's character, and Mary's relations with him, especially when he begs Mary to forgive him on grounds of his youth and inexperience: 'May not a man of my age, for want of council, fail twice or thrice, and miss of

* See the Appendix, p. 643, for the two versions of this letter. The full text of all the letters has most recently been published in *The Casket Letters* by M. H. Armstrong Davison, London 1965, to which the reader is recommended for a more prolonged survey of this complicated subject. The full text is also to be found in A. Lang, *The Mystery of Mary Stuart,* London 1901 and T. F. Henderson, *The Casket Letters,* London 1890.

promise, and at the last repent and rebuke himself by his
experience. . . .' The words echo the phrases, related by
Nau, which Darnley used to Mary after the death of
Riccio.

Mary now taxes Darnley with his plans to depart in an
English ship, and the rumours of his plotting spread by
Hiegate—matters which we know from her letter to
Beaton just before she left for Glasgow were very much
on her mind. The conversation ends with Darnley pleading with Mary to spend the night in his lodging, and
with her refusing to do so until he is 'purged' of his disease;
Mary then offers to bring Darnley to Craigmillar where he
can be cured, and she can be near her son—an offer
which we know did take place. She also promises to resume physical relations after he is cured. To this Darnley
asserts that he knows Mary will never harm him, and as
for the others, he will sell his life dear enough—sentiments
which again fit neatly with Darnley's character and with
his continued trust of Mary, proved by the fact he did
accompany her to Edinburgh. Up to now it is evident
that we are receiving from Mary a frank report on her
relations with Darnley at Glasgow, written to some close
confidante. But in the next phrases the tenor of the letter
changes and the sense becomes more obsure. Mary writes
of Darnley's attempts to win her: 'Fear not, for the place
shall continue till death. Remember also in recompense
thereof not to suffer yours [Bothwell's heart] to be won
by that false race that would do no less to us both. . . .'
Later she writes: 'We are tied to two false races; the goodyeere untie us from them. God forgive me, and God knit
us together for ever for the most faithful couple that ever
he did knit together. This is my faith. I will die in it.'

These phrases which, on quick reading, seem to show
that Mary was cold-bloodedly planning Darnley's murder
with Bothwell, her lover, with a view to marrying him,
make no sense on a second reading, if applied to the
Mary–Bothwell relationship. Who was the 'false race'
which might win Bothwell's heart, and to which he was
tied, to the exclusion of Mary? Not the Gordons surely,
who were now among Mary's most faithful adherents;
Huntly, Bothwell's brother-in-law, had been Mary's loyal
supporter over the Chaseabout Raid, and the Riccio
murder, and was to continue as such throughout his sister's

divorce proceedings (to which he agreed with alacrity) up to and beyond Carberry Hill. As for the rest of his family, after July 1565 Mary had no more devoted adherents; his mother was one of her chief ladies; his sister Jean allowed herself to be divorced with incredible speed in order that Bothwell might marry the queen. Yet throughout the rest of the letter, there is a theme of constant, agonizing jealousy on the part of the writer, for some other woman in Bothwell's life, who, from the angry references to Huntly as 'your false brother-in-law' is clearly Bothwell's wife Jean Gordon. This 'false brother-in-law' is making mischief between the writer and Bothwell, and is to be given no credit 'against the most faithful lover that ever you had or shall have', to please whom the writer will 'spare neither honour, conscience, nor hazard nor greatness'. It would have been quite impossible in January 1567, or indeed at any other date, for Mary to have referred to Huntly in those terms.

It becomes apparent therefore that some letter, or draft of a letter, written by Mary herself, has been loosely and not particularly skilfully run together with a love letter written to Bothwell by some other woman. There is more than one possible candidate for the role of the other woman: Anna Throndsen in particular had every reason to consider herself badly treated by Bothwell and tricked out of a promise of marriage; but as she had left Scotland by the date of Bothwell's marriage it seems that the charge of writing these tortured jealous letters cannot be laid at her door, although they fit with what we know of her character. However, Bothwell had many mistresses previous to his marriage: in the autumn of 1565 Randolph referred to some mysterious French mistress imported by Bothwell to Scotland. Bothwell did not marry Jean Gordon until the spring of 1566, and the match could well have aroused the most poignant jealousy in some discarded mistress, seeing herself passed over in favour of the rich and powerful Huntly connection. Whereas it is highly unlikely that Bothwell would have retained an incriminating letter from Mary written before Darnley's death among his papers, he might easily have preserved a bundle of love letters of no political implications, from an insignificant but passionate mistress; these could have been seized either in June 1567 from George Dalgleish, or at any other

point after Bothwell's departure from the Scottish scene
and before October 1568, during which time the lords
were totally in power in Scotland.

The interpolation of a love letter from the other woman
makes sense not only of the inordinate length of this letter
—and Mary, who was only at Glasgow two nights, was already supposed to have written one letter from thence to
Bothwell—but also of the strange activities she described
herself as doing there: she writes on two separate occasions in the same letter of a bracelet she is making for
her lover, a bracelet which she is staying up late to finish
in secret, amazing occupation for Queen Mary to adopt in
the course of her critical mission to Glasgow. The pleading tone of the latter half of the letter is also strangely at
variance with Mary's character: 'Alas, and I never deceived
anybody but I remit myself wholly to your will, and send
me word what I shall do, and whatever happens to me I
will obey you. . . .' Bothwell is said to be almost making
Mary a traitor—an odd phrase for a queen to use, who
could hardly be accused of treason towards herself. Still
more puzzling, if the whole letter had indeed been written
by Mary, is the concluding sentence: 'Remember your
friend and write unto her and often.' For not only have
no love letters from Bothwell to Mary survived (it is
surely strange that the allegedly reckless Mary should have
been so much more prudent than the theoretically cold-
blooded Bothwell), but also Mary was about to return to
Edinburgh, where she would actually sleep under the
same roof as Bothwell at Holyrood; Bothwell being here
in constant attendance on her, she would surely have no
need for these constant communications for which the
writer cravenly begged.

If parts of this long letter are dismissed as interpola-
tions of another hand, this still leaves the problem of Mary's
own highly confidential letter, and to whom it was addressed. One piece of internal evidence points to the fact
that it might have been Moray: the queen compares Darnley's evil breath (due in fact to syphilis, although she did
not know it) to 'your uncle's breath'. Bothwell has no
uncles, and only one great-uncle, the bishop of Moray,
whom Mary had met once over four years ago. His personal hygiene can scarcely have been so vividly in her
mind. But Moray's uncle, the earl of Mar, was a prominent courtier, had been so over a number of years, and

was now guardian of the queen's son. Mary would have every reason to know such an intimate detail about Mar. Another piece of internal evidence suggests even more strongly that the queen's part of the letter was not intended for Bothwell: at the very end of the published Scottish version of the letter there follows a mysterious list of headings: 'Remember you . . . of the purpose of Lady Reres, of the Inglismen, of his mother, of the Earl of Argyll, of the *Earl Bothwell*,* of the lodging in Edinburgh.' These headings were clearly intended to remind the writer of certain points she was to raise: but Mary would hardly remind herself to raise the subject of the Earl Bothwell in a letter written to Bothwell himself. These are not the only headings in the letter: half-way through the letter occurs a further list of headings, referring back to subjects already discussed. The existence of two such groups of memoranda lead one to suppose that Mary's part of the Long Casket Letter might have been only a draft for a letter which was never in fact sent. As a draft, it would have remained in her possession, and might therefore have been seized among her other papers when she was taken to Lochleven.

Whether such a draft was intended for Moray, or possibly even one of Mary's French relations, who would all have uncles known to her, to follow up her letter to Beaton the day before is less relevant than the light this letter casts on Mary's state of mind at Glasgow. The report of the Spanish ambassador in July 1567, the statement in Parliament in December of the same year, Lennox's supplication to Elizabeth in May 1568, and Buchanan's early mention of *litterae* applicable to a single letter, show that quite early on in their rule of Scotland, the lords did feel they possessed some sort of written evidence against Mary—to be distinguished from the actual Casket Letters themselves. It is quite possible that this evidence was the draft of Mary's letter from Glasgow, in which she discusses her relations with Darnley with such candour, and relates her own promise to renew their married life once he was cured. It is significant that Crawford's deposition to the English tribunal was apparently tailored from the Marian parts of this letter, to the extent of virtually copying it.

* Author's italics.

Darnley's docile acceptance of his removal from Glasgow, into what he must have known was danger, is one of the more puzzling aspects of the Kirk o'Field tragedy. It has been seen that Mary more or less certainly suspended physical relations with her husband from the late summer onwards: perhaps the promise of renewal was made to bring the invalid to Edinburgh. This still incidentally provides no proof of Mary's adulterous liaison with Bothwell, merely of her own desire to get Darnley to Edinburgh, by promise if not threats, and under her influence once away from his own conspiracies. When the lords came to present their evidence to the English tribunal, they too did not find this draft letter sufficiently damning, and therefore laced it with a few classically villainous phrases— such as a suggestion that Darnley's 'physic' at Craigmillar should be poisoned—as well as interpolating, very roughly, another love letter to Bothwell.

Letter III,[16] of which a copy in the original French survives, is marked 'to prove the affections' in a clerkly hand. No attempt was made by the lords to date it, which would indeed have been very difficult, and it is of course not signed. It is quite inconceivable that it should have been written by Mary to Bothwell at any point in their relationship: the writer appears to have followed Bothwell's fortunes over a long period (as he is said to know) and have been brought into 'a cruel lot' and 'continual misadventure' as a result. Nothing was less true of Mary, to whom Bothwell brought good fortune up to the last moment, after which she was not able to write love letters to him. There is a reference to a secret 'marriage' of bodies, which the writer hugs to her bosom, until their marriage can be made in public—the classical delusion of the girl who has been seduced. For all Bothwell's unkindness, the writer will in no way accuse him: 'neither of your little remembrance, neither of your little care, and least of all of your promises broken, and of the coldness of your writing. since I am so far made yours, that that which pleases you is acceptable to me.' This is hardly the pattern of Bothwell's relations with Mary: he broke no promises to her, was never cold, but acted for many years as a loyal servant and lieutenant before he aspired—his aspirations, not hers—to become still more powerful as her consort. Letter III, on the other hand, comes from the pen of someone who has had a long, passionate and unhappy love affair with Bothwell, over many years—in short, the other woman. If it be true that in all love affairs, *il y a un qui baise et l'autre qui tend la joue,* with the other woman and Bothwell it was always she who kissed and he who extended the cheek. Mary Stuart's relations with Bothwell took place on the less fanciful plane of politics: and it was Bothwell, as the seeker after power, rather than Mary as the fount of it, who was the aggressor in their relationship.

Letter IV[17] refers to that mysterious incident which Buchanan also mentioned in his 'Detection' (but to which Moray never referred although said to be a witness of it) in which Mary was supposed to have incited Lord Robert Stewart to quarrel with Darnley, with a view to getting him neatly killed in the course of the dispute.[18] This letter was marked by the English clerk: 'Letter concerning Holyrood House'—a mistake for the house at Kirk o'Field. Apart from backing up Buchanan's dubious story which seems to be its main point in the lords' scheme of accusation, it is an extraordinarily obscure letter, despite the existence of both French and English contemporary copies, suggesting that the copyist found the original difficult to decipher, or else that the original was somewhat clumsily forged. It is a long letter—which makes it implausible that Mary should have written it to Bothwell on 7 February, two days before Darnley's death, during a week when Bothwell was in constant attendance on her both at Holyrood and at the provost's lodging. Again, many of the references are quite out of keeping with Mary at this point, including the reiterated theme of the 'ill luck' of the writer (quite inconsistent with Mary's fortunes at this date) and her jealousy of some rival who has not 'the third part of the faithfulness and voluntary obedience that I bear unto you'. Who was the rival who in February 1567 had the advantage over Mary in Bothwell's affections? The only possible answer was his wife Jean Gordon. Yet the writer of the letter deliberately compares herself to Medea, the first wife of Jason, whom he deserts to marry Glauce— the implication being that the writer, unlike Queen Mary, had been first in the field with Bothwell.

The letter concludes with the most enigmatic phrase in the entire Casket documents: in the French copy it reads: '*Faites bon guet si l'oiseau sortira de sa cage ou sens son per comme la tourtre demeurera seulle a se lamenter de l'absence pour court quelle soit.*' This translated literally as

'Beware lest the bird fly out of its cage, or without its mate like the turtle-dove live alone to lament the absence however short it may be.' The only possible implication is that the writer is the bird who may fly out of her cage, if badly treated, or else go into a decline out of melancholy. But, of course, such a sentiment could hardly be applied to Mary. Therefore the contemporary English translation, presumably at the instruction of the Scottish lords present, tries to make Darnley the bird who may fly out of the cage, and by mistranslating *per* (mate) as father (*père*), implies that the absence of Lennox is making Darnley mourn like the dove. The published Scottish version, on the other hand, while making Darnley the bird who may fly out of the cage without his mate, makes the writer the dove who will remain alone to mourn his absence, an interpretation which fits neither the French nor Mary's alleged disdain of Darnley—since there was no reason why she of all people should mourn the absence of Darnley.

Letter V,[19] of which the contemporary French copy survives, is endorsed: 'Anent the dispatch dismissal of Margaret Carwood; which was before her marriage; proves her affection.' This endorsement is indeed essential to explain the production of this letter, which is otherwise of little guilty import in the history of Mary's relations with Bothwell. The writer—whose style one has now come to recognize as that of the other woman—expostulates against the folly and ingratitude of a certain woman who has made trouble between her and her lover: 'I beseech you that an opinion of another person be not hurtful in your mind to my constancy . . .' and whom she now detests in consequence. There is as usual no signature and no proper names are mentioned. In point of fact Margaret Carwood was never in any disgrace with Mary: she was married from her service and as has been seen her wedding was attended by Queen Mary herself on the Tuesday after Darnley's death, a mark of signal favour; the queen also paid for her wedding-gown as the inventories show. There was certainly no question of her 'dispatch' from Mary's service. These facts were either forgotten or ignored by the lords presenting the ladies, in their inspiration at fitting this particular letter into the scheme of things, or else they rightly banked on such details of Scottish court life nearly two years before being unknown to the English tribunal.

Letter VI[20] is ostensibly written from Stirling where Mary went on 22 April to visit Prince James. It was on her return journey that she was abducted by Bothwell, and the letter is thus endorsed: 'From Stirling before the ravishment—proves her mask [pretence] of ravishing.' It exists in the contemporary French copy, and the English translation among the Cecil MSS at Hatfield House. Once again this love letter contains many internal references which make it impossible to have come from the pen of Mary. The external theme of jealousy on the part of the other woman for her rival is once again present: Bothwell is accused of having 'two strings to his bow', and Huntly is once more described as 'your false brother-in-law' who has come to the writer and warned her that Bothwell will never marry her 'since being married you did carry me away'. Yet Huntly at this point had just signed the Ainslie bond, backing Bothwell's marriage to the queen, and he certainly never seems to have been morally troubled by the abduction in any way. Furthermore, the other woman repeatedly reproaches Bothwell with being a negligent suitor, who has promised to resolve everything, but in fact: 'Vous n'en avez rien fait.' Yet Bothwell in April 1567, as far as Mary was concerned, was a man of consummate vigour and resource, as the organization of the Ainslie bond itself goes to prove. Clearly the lords were struck by the coincidence of the phrases concerning Bothwell carrying his mistress away, referring in fact to some other earlier adventure, and adapted the letter to their own purposes.

There is, however, one interesting point to note about the contemporary copies of this letter: the original French copy at Hatfield is in an italic hand, in contrast to the 'secretary' hand of all the other copies. This hand, while clearly distinguishable from Mary's on close inspection (the c's and d's are completely different, the writing is smaller and neater), is nevertheless of the same Roman type, and might even be taken for it at a quick glance, particularly by a group of men used to dealing with a very different type of hand-writing. Why should this one letter survive in the Roman hand? No explanation has ever been offered. But its existence does seem to argue that it may quite possibly be one of the original Casket Letters, masquerading as a clerk's copy; perhaps the prudent Cecil took one of the originals away with him, in place of a copy, as a piece of wise reinsurance bearing in mind always Queen Mary's close relationship to the English throne, which might at any minute, by the premature death of Elizabeth, make her his sovereign. The fact that the twenty-two documents had mysteriously sunk to twenty-one by the time they were handed over to Morton in 1571 may be explained by this piece of abstraction, which was not noticed at the time.

It is a fascinating, if speculative, thought. If this Hatfield letter is accepted as one of the original documents shown to the English tribunal, it still leaves us no nearer knowing whether this Roman hand was that of a Scottish forger, or that of the other woman, who, being brought up on the Continent, happened to write in very much the same manner as Mary herself. The Hatfield group of Casket documents were only discovered at Hatfield House in 1870 by Mr R. Gunton, private secretary and later librarian to the 3rd marquess of Salisbury. They were first published in the Calendar of the Historical Manuscripts Commission in 1883. If any further copies of the text were ever discovered in French, in this same hand-writing, akin to Mary's but not hers, or in any other Roman hand, fresh light might yet be cast on the whole complicated subject of the Casket Letters.

Letters VII and VIII,[21] for which no contemporary copies exist, are like Letter VI supposed to have been written from Stirling during the day and two nights Mary spent there before her abduction. Letter VII has a genuine Marian ring: the tone is regal in contrast to the self-abasement of the others, and Bothwell is here addressed very much as the faithful servant—the role which he occupied also to outward eyes in April 1567. If Letter VII is accepted in its entirety as being written by Mary from Stirling, then it certainly proves that she had foreknowledge of the abduction. Mary writes that she leaves 'the place and the time' to Bothwell. As for marrying her afterwards, Mary believes that Bothwell will deserve a pardon for his behaviour through 'your services and the lang amities . . . if above the duty of an subject you advance yourself', especially if he gives as his motive the need to preserve the queen from a foreign marriage. This need to save her from the arms of a foreign-born prince was one of the arguments Mary always gave afterwards for believing that Bothwell was the nobles' own choice of consort. This let-

ter also stresses another point on which Mary was known
to be anxiously concerned at the time: Bothwell is firmly
adjured to make sure of the support of the lords, and to
take particular trouble to smooth down Maitland (Bothwell's known antagonist). This eminently practical letter,
which Bothwell would have good reason to preserve
among his most important papers, lest he could be accused
of treason in that he had abducted the queen against her
will, is another possible candidate for the queen's incriminating 'privy letters' which the lords might have discovered
in the summer of 1567.

Letter VIII, on the other hand, although also said to
have been written from Stirling, must have been written by
Mary at some other date, since it refers to Huntly as
'your brother-in-law that was'. The divorce of Bothwell
and Jean Gordon did not take place until after the abduction; at Stirling Huntly was still very much Bothwell's
brother-in-law; it was a mistake which Mary could not
possibly have made. Letter VIII is once more a Marian
letter, calm, without words of passion, warning Bothwell
of various problems, and hoping in unemotional terms to
see him soon: 'pray God send us an happy interview
shortly'. The letter would seem to have been written to
Bothwell some time after their marriage, the most likely
date, as Dr Armstrong-Davison suggests, being 8 June
when Bothwell had gone to Melrose to raise help against
the rebels, and Mary was in Edinburgh. It won a place in
the dossier, however, through the wording of this passage:
'there be many folks here, and among others the Earl of
Sutherland who would rather die, considering the good
they have so lately received of me, than suffer me to be
carried away'. Although the apprehensions of the 'folks'
applied to Mary's probable fate at the hands of her rebels,
the lords tried to interpret the words as applying once
more to the abduction, ignoring the erroneous description of
Huntly.

The twelve love sonnets, as they were termed, consist
in fact of one long love poem of twelve verses. We are dependent on the published French and published Scottish
versions for their text, since no contemporary copies have
survived.[22] Brantôme and Ronsard, who both had intimate
knowledge of Mary's earlier verses, indignantly denied
that these poems could have been by Mary Stuart. These
long rather turgid verses are certainly remarkably unlike

Mary's known poetic efforts, her early simple poems and
her later more complicated poetry, which tends to be extremely courtly in phrase and analogy, as might be expected from the atmosphere of the High Renaissance in
which she had been educated. But style apart, these verses
contain sufficient material to convince one once more that
they are the works of the other woman. This unhappy
poetess has abandoned all her relatives and friends for her
lover, unlike Mary who neither did nor was asked to do
any such thing. There are references also to Bothwell's
wealth, which were unthinkable for Mary to make. To her,
Bothwell was a comparatively poor man, who had to be
subsidized with grants of money from their earliest meeting; it was she who encouraged the profitable Gordon marriage on his behalf, and finally she gave him grants of
money after their marriage. Furthermore, the habitual
theme of jealousy pervades the whole long poem. The only
lines in the total of 158 which might seem to apply to
Mary, and Mary only, are those in which she describes
how she has subjected herself, her son, her country and
her subjects to Bothwell:

> *Entre ses mains & en son plein pouvoir*
> *Je mets mon fils, mon honneur, & ma vie,*
> *Mon pays, mes subjects, mon ame assujetie*
> *Et tout à lui, & n'ai autre vouloir.*

Apart from the fact that Mary neither placed nor tried to
place James in Bothwell's hands (it was a favourite accusation of her enemies but untrue: throughout the Bothwell marriage he remained in the care of the earl of Mar),
the third line has an odd ring, as if the words *'mes subjects'* (so pointedly applicable to Mary, so inapplicable to
any other woman) had somehow been substituted for another shorter word in a line which already ended *'mon ame
assujetie': 'mon coeur'*, for example, fits the rhythm much
better. Although erasions and substitutions are impossible
to describe with any certainty in a poem of which only
a published version survives, the natural inference is that
here once again the interpolator has been at work. In order to apply a melancholy rather verbose love poem to
the particular case of the queen of Scots and Bothwell,
the interpolator has altered one small word—not difficult
to do—on the same principle as the words 'From Glasgow

this Saturday morning' were added to the head of Letter I, to adapt it to the fatal fetching of Darnley.

There remain the two marriage contracts which the lords produced. One of these, in French, is a manuscript from among the Cotton MSS in the British Museum.[23] It has been argued in the past that this is the original document, which was somehow never redelivered to Moray, using the previously cited alteration in the number of documents handed over to Morton in 1571. But the Journal of the Commission specified that this contract was 'written in a Roman hand in French'[24]; unless the Journal was mistaken, the Cotton contract cannot possibly be the original, since it is in an Elizabethan not Roman hand, whose salient feature is the thick backward strokes given to certain letters. Moreover, the signature MARIE R at the end of the contract is a manifest forgery, if indeed this is the original contract shown to the tribunal. The most marked characteristic of Mary Stuart's signature, seen on letters and documents throughout her life, is the even level of all the letters, including the first letter M; there is sometimes a slight rise in the level of the word towards the end, on the R or I, but M is never of greater height than the A. The Cotton signature on the other hand is conspicuous for its capital M, which is twice the height of the other letters.

The lords themselves exhibited this French contract with some doubts and the explanation: 'although some words therein seem to the contrary, they suppose [the contract] to have been made and written by her before the death of her husband'. Certainly some words do seem to the contrary, for the queen specifically refers in the text to 'my late husband Henry Stuart called Darnley', before declaring herself once more free to marry, in consequence of which she chooses Bothwell. If an original French contract in her own hand-writing, signed by her, did ever exist, this might well have been a document written and signed by the queen at Dunbar at Bothwell's dictation, shortly after her abduction; in which case, Bothwell would certainly have preserved it among his papers. The absence of any date would be explained by the fact that the lords lopped it off, thus optimistically hoping to incriminate the queen by pretending the contract had been signed before Darnley's death, despite the wording of the contract which states to the contrary. The fact that Mary, in the contract, says that she makes her promise to marry Bothwell 'without constraint' does seem, on the principle of *qui s'excuse s'accuse,* to suggest that this document was drawn up at Dunbar.

The second contract does not survive in a contemporary copy but was printed by Buchanan.[25] It is said to be a marriage contract signed on 5 April at Seton, between Mary and Bothwell, at a time when he was not yet 'cleansed' of Darnley's murder. It is a long document in official language, quite unlike the other contract, said to have been witnessed by Huntly and Thomas Hepburn, parson of Oldamstock: the fact that Huntly should have witnessed such a contract made nonsense of many of the other letters, but these details were obviously considered unimportant. It is reminiscent of Queen Mary's actual wedding contract, signed on 14 May, and binds the queen to marry Bothwell, rather than some foreign prince, once Dame Jean Gordon, his 'pretended spouse', shall have been removed from his matrimonial path. Although Mary, Bothwell and Huntly were all at Seton on 5 April, it seems highly unlikely that she would have signed such a document before Bothwell had been divorced. It has been suggested that the clerk, as sometimes happens with official documents, mistook the month, and this contract really dated from 5 May, when marriage preparations were very much under way. If this coincidence is dismissed, the most likely explanation of the contract is that Bothwell and Huntly drew it up at Seton, but only presented it to the queen for signature at Dunbar nineteen days later; otherwise her signature might have been quite plainly forged, as on the copy—this being impossible to tell without a sight of the original document.

So much for the Casket Letters on which Mary's reputation was so thoroughly blasted in later centuries, although Queen Elizabeth herself understandably found nothing in them which was proof against her dearest sister. Compounded of Bothwell's previous love letters, some textual interpretations from other letters and a certain amount of inexpert forgery, all glossed over by a great deal of optimistic explanation on the part of the lords who presented them, they were certainly never intended to be exposed to the fierce glare of criticism and discussion which has been directed on to them ever since. The intensity of this discussion results from the fact that they are the only direct proof—inadequate as they are—of

Mary's adultery with Bothwell before Darnley's death. Yet a rational consideration of the letters, in so far as is possible from mere copies, shows that at most Mary can be accused of two 'crimes', neither of them anything like as serious as the murder of her husband. In the first place it is likely that she induced Darnley to leave Glasgow for Edinburgh with the promise of resuming physical relations with him once he was cured of his pox; but this does not in itself constitute a proof of adultery with Bothwell, and Mary's partisans might even point out in her defence that there was no proof that she would not have implemented her promise if Darnley had lived. Secondly, and much more cogently, she can be accused of foreknowledge of her own abduction by Bothwell. Once more this is not criminal so much as unwise behaviour and has no specific bearing on the death of Darnley six weeks earlier. It reflects much more acutely on Mary's total inability at this point to deal with the internal politics of Scotland without leaning on some sort of support, and in the event she chose the wrong sort of support. These aspects of Mary Stuart's behaviour in the first half of 1567 are certainly not enough to brand her as a murderess or even as a scarlet woman, deserving the vengeance of society.

As to the hand of the forger, the finger of accusation must inevitably point in the direction of Maitland. He, who had been Mary's secretary for so many years, must have known her hand-writing by heart; it would have been an easy task to produce something of sufficient verisimilitude to convince men who were not in themselves experts on hand-writing. The collation of the writings does not seem to have been particularly prolonged: the passage in the Journal is in any case ambiguous and it is just possible that the collation refers to Morton's two declarations rather than the queen's hand-writing;[26] even if such a hasty collation were made, Leicester and his company were certainly inexperienced in the delicate science of judging forged hand-writing. Furthermore, as Queen Mary herself stated, her hand-writing is a particularly easy one to forge for anyone who had made a study of her letters.* Of course, if it is accepted that Maitland performed the forgery, he

* Lang prints some examples of modern forgeries of Mary's handwriting impossible to tell from the originals printed beside them, in The Mystery of Mary Stuart.

still should not be blamed utterly for the ruin which fell
upon the queen as a result of the use made of the letters:
Maitland, like his contemporaries, certainly did not foresee
the enormous prominence which history was to give to
these botched-up documents; the mere fact that he subsequently supported Mary shows what a swift temporary expedient was the production of the famous letters. On the
other hand, even if Maitland is acquitted of performing—
or directing—the forgery, he cannot be acquitted altogether of participation in the fraud: from the first moment
he set eyes on the letters he must have realized that they
had not in fact been written by his mistress, since of all
the Scottish nobles it was Maitland who had the most profound and sympathetic knowledge of Mary, from the years
of service spent with her.

It has been further adduced against Maitland as being
the forger that he was married to one of the queen's ladies,
Mary Fleming, who would have been able to assist him
in the task. Once again Mary Stuart herself hinted, in her
declaratory statement on the subject before the conference
at York, in September 1568, that her ladies might be able
to counterfeit her hand-writing[27]—'There are divers in
Scotland, both men and women, that can counterfeit my
hand-writing, and write the like manner of writing which
I use, as well as myself, and principally such as are in
company with themselves,' she pronounced, before going
on to add (surely with truth) 'I doubt not, if I had remained in my own realm, but I would have gotten knowledge of the inventors and writers of such writings before
now. . . .' All her Maries had been educated like herself
in France and therefore wrote in different forms of the
italic hand. The hand-writing of Mary Beaton is the most
similar to that of the queen; furthermore Mary Beaton was
at this point involved in a dispute with her former mistress
over some jewels. This dispute has led some students to
suggest in turn that Mary Beaton was the actual forger. It
would be sad indeed if Mary Stuart, who always loved
and nourished her attendants with a quasi-maternal passion, was rewarded by this ultimate treachery at such a
critical moment in her fortunes, by one of those who had
once been nearest and dearest to her. But there is no proof
against Mary Beaton or indeed Mary Fleming except the
merest supposition: Mary Fleming like her husband Maitland subsequently became one of Queen Mary's keen ad-

vocates in Scotland itself. Furthermore it would surely have been highly indiscreet to have involved one of the Maries in such a confidential business, when ancient loyalties might so easily have prevailed later and unloosed the tongue of the forger at some future date to reveal her own villainy and that of her confederates. There were those much closer home, in the heart of the nobles' party, foremost among them Maitland, who could do the job as well as any former Marie. In any case, as Queen Mary herself was never shown the letters, she at least never knew for certain the answer to that classic conundrum of history—who wrote the Casket Letters? Had she seen them, the result would surely have been, as she herself put it: 'to the declaration of my innocence, and confusion of their falsity.'

21 My Norfolk

'Our fault were not shameful: you have promised to be
mine and I yours; I believe the Queen of England and
country should like of it.'

MARY QUEEN OF SCOTS, *to the Duke of Norfolk*

As the last farcical acts of the conference of Westminster
were taking place, preparations were already afoot in far-
away Yorkshire to move Queen Mary to a more secure
prison at Tutbury in Staffordshire. This time Mary could
hardly persuade herself that she was no longer a prisoner,
or that restoration to her throne was imminent, since the
news that Moray had been allowed to return to Scotland
unscathed represented an undeniable blight to even her
most timid hopes. In December Mary had told Knollys
that she would have to be 'bound hand and foot' rather
than be removed from Bolton.[1] In January Knollys was
still her jailer, although arrangements were being made
to hand the queen over to the earl of Shrewsbury, owner
of a magnificent string of dwellings across the midlands of
England; here it was felt that Mary could be contained in
safety, equally distant from the London of her desire and
the dangerously Catholic northern counties. In the meantime Knollys had his own troubles: his wife was sinking
fast in the south, and died in the midst of all the commotion involved in the removal.

The journey itself, in icy winter weather through the
north of England, was frightful. Lady Livingston fell ill *en
route* and had to be left behind; two days later the queen
herself also collapsed between Rotherham and Chesterfield,
and the cortège had to be halted while she recovered. Then
a message was received by Knollys to say that as Tutbury
had not yet been made ready for the queen of Scots' arrival, they would have to lodge temporarily at Shrewsbury's
own house at Sheffield. But before they could reach Sheffield, another bulletin arrived to say that since all the
Sheffield hangings had already been sent to Tutbury, Shef-

field itself was uninhabitable—so it was once more on to Tutbury.

This medieval castle, which Mary finally reached on 3 February, was of all her many prisons the one she hated most. She always maintained afterwards that she had begun her true imprisonment there,[2] and this in itself was sufficient reason to prejudice her against it; but Tutbury quickly added evil associations of its own to combine with her innate distaste. The castle, which was large enough to be more like a fortified town than a fortress, occupied a hill on the extreme edge of Staffordshire and Derbyshire from which the surrounding country could be easily surveyed. Although Plot in his *History of Staffordshire* written a hundred years later waxed eloquent on the subject of Tutbury's view, comparing the castle to Acrocorinthus 'the old Castle of Corinth whence Greece, Peloponnesus, the Ionian and Aegean seas were semel and simul at one view to be seen', it is doubtful whether the weary royal party and the mourning Knollys would have appreciated the comparison when they finally arrived: for since the early sixteenth century, the structure originally built by John of Gaunt had been virtually falling down, and as a Dutch surveyor reported in 1559, 'only indifferently repaired',[3] hence the powerful need to bring hangings and furnishings from Sheffield. Not only was Tutbury in many parts ruined (as the English government from the vantage point of London never seem to have realized), but it was also extremely damp, its magnificent view of the midlands including a large marsh just underneath it from which malevolent fumes arose, unpleasant enough for anyone and especially so for a woman of Mary Stuart's delicate health. Later on, when Mary had reason to know full well the evils of Tutbury, she wrote of its horrors in winter, and in particular of the ancient structure, mere wood and plaster, which admitted every draught—that *'méchante vieille charpenterie'*, as she put it, through which the wind whistled into every corner of her chamber. As for the view, Mary herself, in words very unlike the raptures of Plot, described Tutbury as sitting squarely on top of a mountain in the middle of a plain, as a result of which it was entirely exposed to all the winds and *'injures'* of heaven.[4]

Nevertheless Mary had perforce to make the best of her new accommodation—her comfort not increased by the

fact that her jailers had not even any money to provide
for her, and Knollys wrote desperately to London for an
immediate grant of £500, since they were destitute.[5] She
now made the acquaintance of George Talbot Earl of
Shrewsbury, and his famous or infamous second wife,
known to history as Bess of Hardwicke. Shrewsbury, who
was to act as the queen's jailer, with only short breaks,
for the next fifteen and a half years, was a man of about
forty. He himself was a Protestant although his father had
been a fervent Catholic and he had many Catholic relations. He was immensely rich and possessed an enormous
range of properties across the centre of England; but like
many rich men he was obsessed with the need to preserve
his inheritance, so that in the course of his ward-ship of
Queen Mary, his letters to the English court began to
sound like one long complaining account book of rising
prices, servants' keep and inadequate subsidies. But
Shrewsbury had long proved his loyalty to Elizabeth, and
his character, fussy and nervous, constantly worrying
about the reactions of the central government to his behaviour or that of his prisoner, made him in many ways
an ideal jailer, for a state captive. Despite these suitable
attributes of a public servant, Shrewsbury was not a strong
character; at the time when he took charge of Mary, he
was totally dominated by the redoubtable Bess.

Bess was now forty-nine, eight years older than her husband, and over twenty years older than Mary. She had
been married three times previously, and by her second
husband Sir William Cavendish of Chatsworth had had
eight children. It was no mere flight of fancy that led her
third husband Sir William St Loe to address her in letters
by the name of this Cavendish mansion, which she herself
inherited—the salutation which she often used of 'my honest sweet Chatsworth' gives a more realistic indication of
the attention which this remarkable lady bestowed upon
material possessions than of her actual qualities of nature.
Bess's practical streak led her to marry off two of her
Cavendish children, Henry and Mary, to Shrewsbury's heir
Gilbert Talbot and his daughter Grace, in order to preserve as much wealth as possible within the bounds of the
family. She was also, in the words of Lodge, 'a builder, a
buyer and seller of estates, a money-lender, a farmer and
a merchant of lead and coals and timber'.[6] Apart from
this financial acumen, in private life the 'honest sweet

Chatsworth' occupied the role of a termagant, for as Lodge painted her, she was 'a woman of masculine understanding and conduct, proud, furious, selfish and unfeeling'. In short, Bess was in character the exact opposite of her new charge, Mary Stuart, who was so feminine in both brain and intuition, and, if proud, was also full of generosity and feeling towards others.*

However, at first meeting, the queen and her new captors got on agreeably enough. The queen spoke 'temperately' to Shrewsbury, and Shrewsbury spoke *'de belles paroles'* to her, as each graciously admitted. Mary was allowed to set up her cloth of state to which she attached such importance, and a certain Sir John Morton was introduced into her *ménage,* who was in fact a Catholic priest, a fact of which Shrewsbury was either ignorant or agreed to turn a blind eye; in any case Mary must have been pleased by the innovation. The queen and Bess were even described by the fond husband Shrewsbury as sitting peacefully together embroidering in Bess's own chamber where, with Agnes Livingston and Mary Seton, they delighted in 'devising' fresh works to carry out. 'They talk together of indifferent trifling matters,' reported Shrewsbury happily, 'without any sign of secret dealing or practice, I can assure you.'[8] It was during this first visit to Tutbury and the early honeymoon period of Mary's relations with Bess that much of the joint embroideries attributed to them, at Hardwicke Hall, Oxburgh Hall and elsewhere, must have been completed.

Embroidery was to prove the great solace of Queen Mary's long years of captivity. It was a taste she had already acquired as a young queen, and it has been seen that one of her first actions on Lochleven was to send for her sewing materials. Now, with all too ample leisure at her command, the taste was to become a passion and almost a mania. Pieces of embroidery, lovingly and hopefully done with her own hand as though the needle could pierce the stony heart where the pen could not, were to prove the basis of the gifts which Queen Mary sent to Queen Elizabeth; Norfolk was similarly honoured with

* A letter from Bess in the unpublished Bagot papers illustrates her attitude to those who stood in the way of her schemes: an elderly widow who is failing to agree to some project which is to Bess's advantage (but not her own) is described as 'behaving very badly'.[7]

an embroidered pillow. An inventory of her belongings six months before her death included many items of embroidery not yet finished, including bed hangings and chair covers, as though the captive had set herself the Penelope-like task of ornamenting every object in her daily life. Into her embroidery the queen put much of herself, including her love of literary devices and allusions, which she had first acquired at the French court, and which had led her during her first widowhood, to adopt two anagrams of her own name as devices: TU AS MARTYRE and TU TE MARIERAS (both of which were in a manner of speaking prophetic). This enthusiasm for devices was also shared by Elizabethan society, having reached England from Italy, where it had been introduced by the French invasions at the beginning of the century;[9] thus Mary's passion was able to find an answering echo in the heart of Bess—she who was to have E S (Elizabeth Shrewsbury) so firmly carved round the pedestals of the new Chatsworth. But quite apart from the contemporary delight in such conceits, which today might be satisfied by the more mundane pursuits of crossword puzzles and acrostics, they seem to have appealed to the romantic streak in Queen Mary's nature, a child-like love of intrigue and secrecy. This was a strain only encouraged by captivity and her attitude to codes, secret messages and the like can be compared to her love of emblems and devices; it is as though having been captured at the age of twenty-four, and cut off from outside society before she had fully reached maturity, Mary remained in some ways frozen in curiously youthful and even naïve attitudes.

In 1614 William Drummond of Hawthornden gave a full and marvelling description of the joint embroideries of Mary and Bess in a letter to Ben Jonson; these panels, which in most details can be equated with the hangings now at Oxburgh Hall,* contained a series of *impresas*, or allegorical pictures with text, in which the words expressed one part of the meaning, and the emblem another. One panel consisted of a lodestone turning towards a pole and the name MARIA STUART turned into the anagram SA VERTUE M'ATTIRE which Drummond preferred to

---

* See *Embroideries by Mary Stuart and Elizabeth Talbot at Oxburgh Hall,* by Francis de Zulueta, for a discussion of the authenticity of these tapestries. Also *English Secular Embroidery,* by M. S. Jourdain, for a further discussion of Queen Mary's embroideries.

the other anagram of her name VERITAS ARMATA. A phoenix in flames was said to be the emblem of Mary's mother, Mary of Guise, and the words accompanying the device were that now famous motto of Mary Stuart: *En ma fin est mon commencement*. About the same date Cecil's emissary White noticed this motto also embroidered on Queen Mary's cloth of state.†[10] Some emblems referred to Queen Mary's past—the crescent moon and the motto *Donec totum impleat orbem* for Henry II, the salamander for King Francis I. Others alluded more directly to Mary's recent fortunes and her future hopes from Elizabeth—for example two women upon the wheels of fortune, one holding a lance, and the other a cornucopia with the motto FORTINAE COMITES. A lioness with a whelp and the motto UNUM QUIDEM SED LEONEM referred to Mary and her son James. At Oxburgh, one panel just below the centrepiece, which is yet another monogram of Mary Stuart, has a large monogram GEORGE ELIZABETH beneath a coronet, and is surrounded by the legend GEORGE ELIZABETH SHREWSBURY in full—representing a unity later to be crudely disrupted by the marital disputes of Mary's jailers, just as the unity between Mary and Bess, embodied in these hangings, was also to be torn asunder by Bess's venomous accusations. It seems also that Mary's early French life was never to be forgotten: the cipher combining the Greek letter Phi and M—for Francis and Mary—which the queen had used on her own signet ring after her return to Scotland, is also to be found in the corner of at least four of the Oxburgh panels, yet it was now half a generation since the death of Francis.

In captivity Mary's health was her most obvious problem, apart from her desire for freedom. It was often the old pain in her side which put a final end to a day's embroidering. Her health was only worsened by the discomfort of Tutbury. In March Shrewsbury noted that she was once more severely ill from what he termed 'grief of the spleen' and which his doctor told him was *'obstructio splenis cum flatu hypochondriaco'*: the queen's symptoms

† These famous words have always been taken to refer to Queen Mary's religious beliefs and the victory of the soul after death; but if Drummond is correct in reporting that they were attached to the emblem of Mary of Guise, they originally had the more philo-progenitive meaning that in the end of the mother was the beginning of the child.

were pains, said to be the result of 'windy matter ascending to the head' strong enough to make her faint.[11] Even a move from odious Tutbury to the more salubrious Shrewsbury dwelling of Wingfield Manor did not effect the desired cure. At the end of April, the queen went into such a decline at hearing of the dreadful fates of some of her friends in Scotland that her whole face swelled up, and she sat weeping silently and uncontrollably at supper. By 12 May the queen was critically ill once more; at Chatsworth—'my wife's house', as Shrewsbury put it—where she was taken for the cleansing or 'sweetening' of Wingfield, she had to be seen by two doctors.[12] As it happened Shrewsbury's own health suffered that summer, for he had both gout and 'the hot ague', to the extent of announcing that he no longer wished to live; his physician Dr Francis was deeply concerned over the many hot choleric vápours which had apparently found their way up to the patient's head from his stomach, when Shrewsbury took a fever after drinking too much cold water. But whereas Shrewsbury suffered occasionally from bouts of painful ill-health, Queen Mary's health now became a chronic problem for her and her jailers, only exacerbated by the conditions of captivity, and there are few of her letters in the ensuing years which do not refer in some manner to the physical pain she had to endure.

It was at the end of February 1569 that Nicholas White, who was journeying to Ireland on Cecil's behalf, broke his journey at Tutbury in order to report on the state of the Scottish queen. From his letter back to his master, it is clear that he found her as dangerously fascinating as had Knollys nine months earlier—although White, like Knox, had a rather less chivalrous reaction to the spectacle of her beguiling charms.[13] He too observed that the queen spent much of her time embroidering, telling him that 'all the day she wrought with her needle and that the diversity of colours made the time seem less tedious'. They also had a pleasantly intellectual discussion on the comparative artistic merits of carving, painting and embroidering, in the course of which Queen Mary expressed the view that painting was the most commendable of the three. At which White, who had already unpleasantly and most unfairly told Mary that she was responsible for the death of Lady Knollys by keeping Sir Francis away from her side (although there was surely nothing Mary would

have liked better than for Knollys's duties to have been
ended by her own release), replied rudely that he had
read that painting was a false truth—*Veritas Falsa*. Mary
understandably drew the audience to a close at this
brusqueness, and withdrew to her own room.

Nevertheless for all his churlishness—and he may have
feared to be seduced by this famous basilisk—White fully
took in the physical appearance of Mary, informing Cecil
that he found her hair dark, although Knollys had warned
him that she often wore false hair of different colours.*
And the percipient White added: 'She hath withal an alluring grace, a pretty Scotch accent, and a searching wit,
clouded with mildness. Fame might move some to relieve
her, and glory joined with gain might stir others to adventure much for her sake.'

White's words concerning the inducements there would be
to rescue Mary were prophetic. Indeed, already the thought
of 'glory joined with gain' had led Norfolk to go forward
in the negotiations to marry the Scottish queen, the project
first mentioned to Mary before the York conference.
Mary's captivity in England had after all no legal basis,
and even her abdication from the throne of Scotland had
been made under duress, which robbed it of its validity;
in the meantime her blood relationship to Queen Elizabeth,
and her possible succession to the English throne—cast
into further prominence by the death in 1568 of the unfortunate Lady Catherine Grey, the main Protestant Tudor
candidate—made her a rich prize. Elizabeth's disapproval
was by no means a foregone conclusion: after all she herself had suggested Norfolk as a possible bridegroom for
Mary before her marriage to Darnley. Under these circumstances the secret moves to marry Mary to Norfolk, and
then presumably restore her to the throne of Scotland,
neatly linked to a Protestant English bridegroom, proceeded apace. Maitland was involved, and shares with
Mary's envoy, John Leslie, bishop of Ross, the possible
credit or discredit for having first initiated the plan; many
of the Scots were said to look on the scheme with favour,
and even Moray himself appeared to play along with the

* White may have been deceived by false hair in this instance.
Mary in youth had light red-golden hair. Although hair darkens
with age, it could never have reached a really black tint naturally.

idea of the marriage for the time being, although he soon
had an opportunity of publicly showing his strong disapproval of any notions of Mary's restoration. Many of
the English nobles, who themselves disliked the dominance
of Cecil within the English Privy Council, and in addition
felt that his foreign policy, so intensely hostile to Spain,
was against England's best commercial interests, saw in
the elevation of Norfolk as Mary's bridegroom a convenient way of dealing with Cecil's rising influence. This particular question in English internal politics had been
brought to a head in the winter of 1568–9 when Elizabeth
confiscated three Spanish treasure ships at Cecil's instigation, and to the violent disapproval of many others within
the council.*

The actual part played by Queen Mary herself in all the
cobwebs of intrigue and counter-intrigue which followed,
was negligible: considerations of Anglo–Spanish commercial rivalry become somehow enmeshed with rival considerations of Scottish internal politics; England's foreign policy
towards France and the attitude of the Pope towards
Queen Elizabeth and the English Catholics were likewise
issues which became firmly entangled in the simple topic
of Mary's marriage to Norfolk. Yet throughout all these
negotiations, whether secret or open, Mary remained a
comparatively isolated captive, and her personal role was
therefore a minor one, except in so far as her mere existence made her, as Elizabeth angrily wrote at the end of
it all, 'the daughter of debate that eke discord doth sow'.
But Mary could hardly be blamed for her mere existence
and as for her captivity, which made such an apple of discord in the centre of England, there was no one more anxious to end it than Mary herself. In all the first attempts
or conspiracies to procure her release, Queen Mary
adopted exactly the same attitude: since her imprisonment
was illegal, she would consider herself free to try and
achieve her liberty by any means in her power, as she
had warned Knollys that she would in October 1568. As a
'sovereign princess' over whom Elizabeth had no jurisdiction, she never considered that any schemes, letters of instruction, however damning from the English point of

---

* These ships, however, continued to be held, and were not in fact
released till 1572.

view, could possibly be fairly held against her by English justice.

This was her personal point of view on the subject of
escape. There were refinements to it: for example Queen
Mary was strongly predisposed towards any scheme that
sounded as if it might have the backing of a major power,
and strongly disinclined to consider any hare-brained
scheme which had exactly the opposite ring. At the head
of her list of major powers who she thought might help
her was still Elizabeth—whom Mary still hoped would
achieve her restoration to Scotland in the end. Beyond that
Philip of Spain was one possibility and Charles IX of
France another. With the latter in mind she early established a code with which to correspond with the French
ambassador in London, Mothe de la Fénelon. But Elizabeth was still, and continued to be so for the next three
years at least, the person from whom Mary hoped the most
effective succour. It was the blood tie which joined them,
which Mary always felt must surely in the end influence
Elizabeth to assist her; and Elizabeth's approval or disapproval, so far as she could guess at it, was something
Mary always took into account in any project which was
outlined to her. Mary was therefore a catalyst rather than
the chief conspirator in the two plots which followed.

Mary's new potential bridegroom, Thomas Howard, 4th
duke of Norfolk, now a man of thirty-three and a widower,
was not an especially glamorous figure by any standards:
an anonymous admirer described him in 1569 as being
'no carpet knight . . . no dancer or lover knight', while
going on to boast that he came of the race of Howards
who could never be made to hide their face from the enemy.[14] Mary never actually met him, and most of her information on the subject of his personal attractions seems
to have come from his sister, Lady Scrope, in whose
charge she had been placed at Carlisle, and with whom
Mary had become extremely friendly.* In spite of being
no carpet knight, Norfolk had other more solid qualities
to commend him: he came of ancient lineage (he was in

---

* It is sometimes suggested that Mary and Norfolk did meet briefly while she was at Carlisle, staying with his sister. But there is no
proof of this, and if so, it is strange that neither of them ever referred to the incident in their correspondence. Certainly, Norfolk
himself was always emphatic that he had never met Mary.

fact the only duke in England) and a territorial magnate
on a grand scale, who was able to tell Elizabeth that he
was 'as good a prince in his bowling-alley at Norwich'
as Mary would have seen in the midst of her own country
of Scotland.[15] He was also an experienced administrator,
who had been English lieutenant-general in the north from
1559 to 1560, before becoming chief commissioner at
York. Mary's part in the marriage negotiations—conducted
in strict secrecy from Queen Elizabeth whose temper on
the subject of any marriage, and especially royal ones, was
notoriously uncertain—was confined to writing a series of
affectionate and even loving letters to Norfolk; yet since
she had never met their object, these letters belonged very
much to the world of pen-friendship and dreams rather
than to that of reality. He was now to Mary 'my Norfolk', to whom she emphasized her unhappiness and the
desire for liberty. 'My Norfolk,' she wrote charmingly on
occasion, 'you bid me command you, that would be beside
my duty many ways, but pray you I will, that you counsel
me not to take patiently my great griefs. . . .'[16] She also
underlined the fidelity she would show to him: 'I trust
none that shall say I ever mind to leave you,' she wrote,
'nor to anything that may displease you, for I have determined never to offend you, but remain yours. I think all
well bestowed for your friendly dealings with me, all un-
deserved.' The famous pillow which Leslie later revealed
Mary had sent to Norfolk was embroidered with the motto
VIRESCIT IN VULNERE VULTUS, and the arms of
Scotland, to signify Mary's courage. Norfolk himself sent
Mary a fine diamond, which was brought to her by Lord
Boyd and Mary prettily vowed in a letter of thanks to
keep it hung round her neck unseen 'until I give it again
to the owner of it and me both'.[17]

Yet it is clear that despite these affectionate demonstrations, in the Norfolk negotiations Mary was very much following the line of conduct presented to her by her advisers,
rather than leading them forward; this was in part due to
her captivity, and the conditions which made her dependent on the reports of others to estimate any other situation.
It was also due to her natural suspicion of the whole state
of marriage which had brought her into such a parlous
condition at the time of her marriage to Bothwell. She had
believed Bothwell to be the choice of her nobles and he
had turned out to be their bane; she had believed Darnley

to be the choice of Elizabeth, but she had been rewarded for marrying him by the virulent fury of the English queen. It was hardly surprising that she greeted the first approaches over the Norfolk match with considerable doubts. When she finally gave her consent, it was on the strict understanding that Elizabeth's approval would be secured: 'she wished them first and foremost to get the Queen's assent, lest the matter might turn to her hurt and the Duke's whereof she had had experience before in her marriage with Lord Darnley contracted without her (Elizabeth's) assent.'[18]

But Mary managed to convince herself in her prison, or was persuaded by John Leslie, bishop of Ross, that Elizabeth did approve these negotiations, or would approve them when she was informed. As late as January 1570 (when she had had considerable evidence to the contrary), she wrote confidently to Norfolk that their marriage would be generally approved: 'Our fault were not shameful: you have promised to be mine, and I yours; I believe the Queen of England and country should like of it.'[19] In the following August Leslie told the Spanish ambassador that Mary had been much importuned over the marriage, but had been driven to it by necessity, since she believed Elizabeth wanted her to marry an Englishman. Therefore, despite Mary's formalized sentimental attitude to Norfolk, her wearing of the diamond which he sent to her, for which Mary sent in exchange a miniature of herself set in gold, it is evident that Mary was seeking an honourable exit from her cage approved by Elizabeth rather than involvement in a life-and-death conspiracy.

In the summer of 1569 Elizabeth showed further encouraging signs of favour to Mary by testing out a series of restoration proposals with the Scots. There were three possibilities: that Mary might ratify her abdication, and live in England; that Mary and James should rule jointly; and, thirdly, that Mary should be restored with certain religious guarantees, and a promise for the security of Moray. The English nobles and Leslie also secretly imagined that the Norfolk marriage would fit neatly into this third solution, the only one, as Leslie proclaimed, which would be tolerable to his mistress. Already in the previous October Mary had expressed herself willing to be divorced from Bothwell, and messengers had been sent to him in Denmark to sign the necessary documents. Now, with a view to proving that there had been no marriage, emissaries were sent to Rome to institute a suit of nullity on two grounds; firstly, it was said that Bothwell had never been properly divorced from Jean Gordon, so that Bothwell could not have rightly married Mary; secondly, it was suggested that Bothwell had used force to effect his marriage to Mary, which was in itself a cause of nullity. In June 1569 Lord Boyd was given authority by Mary to treat with Moray on the subject, and a written mandate to apply for the divorce.[20] Such negotiations made it clear not only that passion for Bothwell had well and truly waned —if indeed it had ever existed—but also that Mary was prepared to suit her marital situation to anything which she imagined might lead to her restoration in Scotland.

These restoration proposals, to which Elizabeth herself seems to have been genuinely well-disposed, were turned down by the Scots themselves, led by Moray, at the Perth convention at the end of July, when the idea of Mary's return was rejected by forty votes to nine; among the nine who voted for Mary's return on certain conditions were Atholl, Huntly, Balfour and Maitland. Six weeks later Moray's position was made still more secure when Queen Elizabeth discovered the Norfolk marriage plot. Her rage was extreme. Mary found herself moved back to the hated Tutbury, and given an additional jailer in the shape of Huntingdon, the man whom she particularly disliked and even feared because she always believed his own pretensions to the English throne (he had Plantagenet blood) might lead him to do away with her. Her suite was cut down, and Elizabeth angrily ordered that Mary should neither give nor receive messages to the outside world; Mary complained to Elizabeth that her rooms had been roughly searched by men armed with pistols. Norfolk was imprisoned in the Tower. Elizabeth even turned, through his servant John Wood, on Moray, amazed to discover that he too had apparently been favourable to the notion; but Moray quickly informed Elizabeth's Governor Hunsdon at Kelso that he had never done more than tell Norfolk that if Bothwell were dead or Mary divorced, and if Elizabeth agreed to the match, then he would approve.*

---

* It is difficult to believe that Moray ever really countenanced the match, which would have been dangerous to his prospect. Moray's biographer, Lee, suggests that all along Moray relied on Elizabeth to prevent the marriage once she heard of it—as indeed she did.[21]

The northern rising in November, under the Catholic
earls of Northumberland and Westmorland, did nothing to
improve Queen Mary's lot. This rising, ill-prepared and
ill-organized, was more in the nature of a separatist movement on the part of northern Catholics, than a revolt
on behalf of Mary Queen of Scots. Queen Mary herself
disapproved of it, not only on the grounds that she hated
violence and wished to avoid the risk of the slaughter of
innocent people, but also on the very sensible grounds
that she did not believe it would do her cause any good,
since the moment was hardly ripe for such a demonstration. Leslie later testified that she had asked him to try
and get Northumberland to stop or stay the rising. Yet
whatever her own wishes, a Catholic Queen was the inevitable rallying-point for such an enterprise. Mary was hastily
taken to Coventry for the time being in order to be geographically still farther away from the rebels; here she had
to be temporarily lodged in an inn, since Coventry Castle
had been uninhabited since the Wars of the Roses and was
therefore destitute of furniture—the government in London
being as usual in ignorance of conditions in the midlands.
The idea of the inn infuriated Elizabeth when she learned
of it, since she thought it implied too much dangerous social life for the queen of Scots. Mary was then removed
to a house in the centre of the town;† here she in turn was
annoyed to hear that Huntingdon, her jailer, had been listening to some sermons containing 'lewd preachings'
against her, which she herself understandably refused to
attend. Yet the see-saw nature of English noble attitudes
and alliances at this time may be judged by the fact that
Huntingdon now took the opportunity to press the suit
of his own brother-in-law, Leicester—Mary's former suitor
Robert Dudley under a new name—on the grounds that
Queen Elizabeth was now considering the duke of Anjou
as a husband, which left Leicester free for Mary; Mary,
reporting this back indignantly to Norfolk, said that Huntingdon's next proposal was that his own claims to the
throne of England should be recognized in return as being
next to those of Mary and James.[23]

In the meantime events in troubled Scotland were about

† Local legends suggest that she was kept in the upper room of the
building known as 'Caesar's Tower' (now rebuilt) which adjoined
St Mary's Hall.[22]

to take another dramatic turn: on 11 January 1570, the regent Moray fell dead, struck down by the bullets of an assassin in the main street at Linlithgow; the story that he fell a victim to the vengeance of a poor man whose wife he had driven out into the snow, to meet her death, has long since been exploded. In fact his assassin was a Hamilton, and the Hamilton archbishop of St Andrews had at least foreknowledge of the plot. The death of Moray drew to an end the career of one who had aimed high: it will never be known exactly how high, or whether the pretensions by which his enemies accused him of aiming at the throne itself had any substance.* Mary certainly came to believe that he had aimed at the throne, and paid his assassin a pension. At all events, under Moray's brief regency Scotland had not more, but much less, stability than in the early years of Mary's rule, and there was nothing in his conduct of affairs to justify his ejection of his sister from the throne on administrative grounds. It was no coincidence that he was struck down by a Hamilton, a member of a rival family: Scotland was by now, and continued to be throughout the minority of James, a hotbed of warring factions; Scots with long memories might have looked back to the minority of James's mother Mary and seen that little outward progress had been made.

The death of Moray meant the search for a new regent, to whom most parties would agree. It was not until the summer that the choice finally fell upon James's grandfather, Lennox, largely as a result of the favour of Elizabeth, who supported him as being a likely tool for English policy. In the meantime Mary herself made frantic efforts to maintain some sort of maternal contact with her little boy, now three and a half. Just before Moray's death she sent him a little pony of his own, and a saddle, with a pathetic little note to accompany them: 'Dear Son, I send three bearers to see you and bring me word how ye do, and to remember you that ye have in me a loving mother that wishes you to learn in time to love know and fear God.' Mary wrote in vain: for neither her letter nor her presents were allowed by Elizabeth to pass to Scotland, to the son who could not remember Mary; and James himself far from being taught to remember his duty 'anent

---

* A popular rhyme current at the time of the conference of Westminster suggested that Moray was a traitor trying to seize the Scottish crown on the pretence of his mother's lawful marriage.[24]

her that has born you in her sides' as his mother hopefully
put it, was being instructed by George Buchanan and
others that his mother had cold-bloodedly murdered his
father to marry her lover. These teachings did not augur
well for Mary's future relationship with James.

In the summer of 1570 there was some scheme promoted by Elizabeth for bringing James to England (that
old desire of the English to acquire a Scottish princeling);
the Scots never agreed to it, but Mary was enthusiastic
at the opportunity of bringing her child a little nearer.
She swallowed her pride and even contacted her former
mother-in-law and established enemy, Lady Lennox, on
the subject, seeking her grandmotherly advice about
James. 'I have born him and God Knoweth with what
danger to him and to me both, and of you he is descended,
so I mean not to forget my duty to you,' she wrote. But
this scheme came to nothing. In the autumn of 1571 Mary
was still pleading with Elizabeth to let her correspond with
her son, or at least find out how he was faring, in her
own words, from the point of view of a 'desolate mother
whose solitary child has been torn from her arms'.[25]

In May 1570 Mary was once more taken back to Chatsworth, and here a fantastic plot was hatched on the part
of some romantic local squires to rescue her. At the time
of the northern rising, Mary had been offered a possible
chance of escape by Leonard Dacres, Northumberland's
cousin, and had refused the bait, because she felt herself
committed to Norfolk and her plans in that direction; Norfolk had pointed out that an escape would ruin everything, and leave no chance of Elizabeth's approval. By
May the papal bull *Regnans in Excelsis,* which had been
promulgated by Pope Pius V in Rome in February, had
reached England, and had been posted up on the door of
the bishop of London by a Catholic hand. This bull was
to have an enormous effect on Mary's future, since it
formally excommunicated Elizabeth and declared that her
Catholic subjects were released from their loyalty to her.
But at Chatsworth this summer Mary still remained damp-
ing towards the ardour of her supporters who wished to
compass her escape.

The fabric of the plot was revealed in the examinations
of those involved after they had been arrested; it seemed
the protagonists were Sir Thomas Gerard, a local Catholic
squire (father of the future Jesuit missionary John Ge-

rard), two brothers, Francis and George Rolleston, one
John Hall and two Lancashire magnates, the brothers Sir
Thomas Stanley and Sir Edward Stanley. But the most
searching cross-examinations could never make the actual
practical details of the plot amount to very much, and Sir
Edward Stanley strongly denied that he had had any effective part in it, giving the ingenious excuse that he had
been away in the north at the time courting a Mrs Strickland. Gerard's idea was that the queen of Scots having
escaped from Chatsworth should be shipped away to the
Isle of Man by the good offices of Thomas Stanley; but he
put his finger on the main trouble with any private rescue
plot to do with Mary Stuart during all her years of captivity, when he said that he had 'feared to make any man
privy thereof for danger of discovery, and unless many
were made privy, the thing could not be done'.[26]

Finally Hall and Rolleston did manage to have a cloak-
and-dagger meeting with the master of Mary's household,
John Beaton, on the high moor above Chatsworth at the
conspiratorial if chilly hour of 5 A.M. Beaton told them
he would have to consult the queen herself, but he could
give them in advance her general answer to such proposals:
'So would she wish that no man should go about that matter, unless they were assured to put her in surety.' The plot
was finally betrayed by George Rolleston, and Thomas
Gerard was arrested and spent two years in the Tower.
Francis Rolleston in his examination showed how frail
the structure of conspiracy had been when he said that
Chatsworth had been chosen as a good escaping ground
because the queen could be carried off as she took the air
on the moors, but it was never decided what to do with
her next 'because the matter never grew to any determination or likelihood' since everyone had been in doubt of
everyone else.[27] Hall's examination was especially significant on the subject of Mary's attitude to the whole project:
Beaton had thought that the escape should take place at
night, despite the fact that the queen's servants were then
locked into their rooms, but he admitted that Mary herself
remained distinctly unenthusiastic since 'she nothing
doubted but that the Queen's Majesty [Elizabeth] at the request of the Kings of Spain and France would restore her
to her former dignity hereafter, the which she rather
minded to expect, than to adventure upon a mere uncertainty, by such means to work her own delivery, which

might if the matter miscarried, turn her to confusion and all her partakers'.[28]

This was a commendably prudent reaction. Beaton was never able to be arraigned for his part in the conspiracy since by the time it was uncovered he was dead, and buried (a sad expatriate Scot but a loyal servant) in the parish church at Edensor, close by Chatsworth. Mary's words showed that her eyes were sternly fixed on where the power lay, on the help of monarchs, not a handful of local lords, whose number of horsemen varied from 100 to 200 to 'a few', and at times apparently intended to ship her beyond the seas and at other times imagined 'they might keep her in some secret place undiscovered, if she could not have ready passage'. She showed no more interest when there was an attempt to revive the plot the next year. Mary was by now a woman of nearly thirty, on the verge of middle-age by the standards of the time; the old impetuosity of her youth was gone. She was chronically sick, alone in a country she did not know; it was a different matter to elude the bars of her own palace of Holyrood and ride to Dunbar through her own kingdom of Scotland, than to travel in disguise through unknown England, a foreign queen among foreigners. Under the circumstances Mary preferred to pin her hopes to more substantial targets.

In August 1570 Norfolk was released from the Tower. His release proved the signal for a further and much wider conspiracy, in which he was once more involved, under the inspiration of an Italian banker based in London, named Roberto Ridolfi. The Ridolfi plot, as opposed to the earlier plan, which merely proposed marrying Norfolk to Mary, had distinctly dangerous objectives if its wildest aspects were taken seriously. Ridolfi himself was a man with an Italian love of intrigue but unfortunately with little of the Italian Renaissance skill at diplomacy; he understood little of the workings of the English mind, or indeed the workings of England itself. His aim was apparently to secure an invasion of England from the Netherlands, by Philip II's general there, the duke of Alva, which invasion was to be supplemented by a rising of native Catholics within England. This combination of invaders and internal rebels would free Mary and, having seized Elizabeth, place Mary on the throne of England, side by side with her consort Norfolk. These were rash and treasonable schemes indeed. There were many difficulties in the way of their being carried out—the principal one being, as Philip II was quick to notice, that there was no proof that there would be another Catholic rising within England. Yet Philip stipulated that there should be no Spanish invasion until the English themselves had risen. In the meantime Alva formed the lowest opinion of Ridolfi, whom he termed a *gran parlaquina* or chatterbox, and a lightweight; as late as September 1571 he wrote to Philip from the Netherlands with a sarcastic lack of respect for Ridolfi's ability to carry out any sort of practical scheme, that even if Philip and Elizabeth jointly agreed to the invasions it still would not be sure that Ridolfi would be able to carry it through! Alva also analysed with terrible correctness the danger, to both Norfolk and the queen of Scots, if such a scheme was discovered or miscarried: either or both might lose their lives.[29]

Mary's attitude to, and personal involvement in Ridolfi's schemes is open to question. She had not lost interest in Elizabeth's projects for her restoration to Scotland, which still dragged on. In October 1570, Cecil and Mildmay paid Mary a personal visit at Sheffield Castle, possibly spurred on by the king of France's representations to Elizabeth on the subject of Mary. They put before Mary a long list of articles proposing an alliance between herself and Elizabeth. Many of these articles reiterated the familiar English position since the abortive Treaty of Edinburgh: Mary was to give up her unlawful claims to the English throne. In addition Mary was to give up bargaining over her remarriage without Elizabeth's consent, and the question of James coming to England as a hostage if Mary was restored to Scotland was officially incorporated. In the course of their discussion, Cecil showed himself not immune to the famous charm of the queen of Scots: in a memoir of 1569 he had already referred to 'her cunning and sugared entertainment of all men' whereby she won many to her cause; now a personal experience of this sweetness led him to agree with Maitland: 'The Queen of Scots was of a clement and gentle nature, and was disposed to be governed by counsel of them in whom she reposed her trust.' Leslie, who reported this favourable verdict, even thought that Cecil had promised to bring Mary at last into Elizabeth's presence. Yet nothing concrete ever actually happened as a result of these articles, and by the spring of 1571 Mary was writing wearily to Sussex that she seemed to have been looking for a happy resolution to her affairs for so long 'which has been so many times delayed for every light matter that did occur, that we are for our own part in doubt if finally there shall be any good succeed unto us therein'.[30]

It is possible that under these circumstances of three years' onerous English captivity, Mary did allow herself to be persuaded to write the incriminating instructions and letters to Ridolfi quoted against her at Norfolk's trial. The originals of the credentials said to be given to Ridolfi by Mary and Norfolk have mysteriously disappeared.* In these instructions Mary wrote wildly concerning the miserable state of England, the cruelty of her own position, the persecutions of the Catholics, the fact that Huntingdon and Hertford (Catherine Grey's son) were threatening her rights to the English throne, the need for the Pope to press ahead with her nullity suit, and how she intended to send James to Spain to marry him to a Spanish princess. Norfolk was described as being the head of the enterprise, and a keen guardian of the rights of the Catholics. All practical details were to be left to him; furthermore Mary castigated the French who had, she said, done absolutely nothing to help her.[31] However, the evidence of Mary's other letters, written at the same time to Mothe de la Fénelon, the French ambassador, show that she was, to say the least of it, trying to keep all the options open. She had, for example, far from given up all hopes of French assistance and in October twice approached the ambassador begging him to continue to help her and to interest the king and queen of France in her cause 'because she had no means to help herself'.[32] Nor had Mary in any way despaired of Elizabeth's assistance: for at the same moment as her approaches to Mothe de la Fénelon, Mary was writing to the English queen, stating the full confidence she felt in Elizabeth, and her desire to have her (Mary's) succession rights discussed in the English Parliament.[33] Subsequently Mary did admit to having given some sort of financial commission to Ridolfi, but she al-

---

* See Francis Edwards, *Dangerous Queen*, London 1964, and *The Marvellous Chance*, London 1968, for a detailed consideration of the validity of the various documents in these intrigues.

ways denied that it had been anything so specific and dangerous to England as Cecil suggested.

The main architect of this unrealistic conspiracy, on Mary's side, other than the serpentine Ridolfi and the irresolute Norfolk, was Mary's envoy Leslie. Mary Stuart like most human beings was inclined to trust increasingly those whom she had trusted for a long time. Since the bishop of Ross first came to France in the spring of 1561 —when he incidentally propounded the foolish scheme for a northern Scottish invasion which Mary wisely rejected— Leslie had been an assiduous if not especially tactful servant of the queen; although he had managed to have good relations with both Darnley and Bothwell. As Mary's ambassador in England after her imprisonment, he was certainly in a position of enormous difficulty: the point has been well made that he was expected to act as the 'representative of a foreign ruler powerless to protect her servants but strong enough to attract discontented elements',[34] but Leslie was endowed with an unfortunate combination of energy and application—unfortunate in the sense that he lacked the essential *finesse* which would have enabled him to judge not only the right action to take on Mary's behalf but also the right time to do it. His anonymous publication in London in 1569 of the *Defence of the Honour of Queen Mary,* which asserted her old rights to the succession, was scarcely diplomatic when the favour of Elizabeth, so famously touchy on this particular subject, was all-important to Mary.

For all his erudition, which enabled him to write his long history of Scotland during this vital period of his stay in England, as Mary's ambassador, Leslie never quite appreciated the point which Alva quickly perceived: a plot in favour of Mary which miscarried could be far more dangerous than no plot at all. He was also, like his mistress in certain moods, a man of impulse with a quick rash temper. Yet Mary had perforce to put enormous faith in the bishop and his summing-up of situations, as well as in his capacity to amplify her own written communications by personal interviews. Many of Mary's letters at this period end by promising that the bishop of Ross will further enlighten the recipient. It was unfortunate under the circumstances that by March 1571 Leslie, Mary and Norfolk were all cut off from each other, with the dubious Ridolfi acting as a go-between. Mary deeply regretted the loss of Leslie's news bulletins, which she regarded as her window on the outside world: by the summer, the lack of 'the daily intelligence she was wont to receive from the bishop' was mentioned as being the thing which troubled her most.[35]

If the incriminating documents are genuine, it is possible that Mary gained such a falsely rosy picture of the situation that she allowed herself to be committed on paper to an extremely hazardous venture. Such a false picture would not necessarily have been painted on purpose by Leslie to confuse Mary: it is more than likely that Leslie himself was also bewildered and muddled in his intrigues. He was not after all able to confront Mary face to face to discuss the situation verbally; dependence had to be made on letters, and letters could all too easily be intercepted. Although Maitland's son later made harsh comments on Leslie's character, and accused him of aiming at his own glory, and the enrichment of his bastard offspring, the situation was wide open for Cecil if he wished to lure the intriguers to their downfall by misrepresenting what each had said to the other; with Mary in prison, cut off from her servant, Leslie showed himself at first to be impetuous and later cowardly; but these qualities did not necessarily make him a villain.

News of what was afoot began to trickle through to the English government in the late spring. Elizabeth received a private warning from the grand duke of Tuscany, who had learnt only too easily of Ridolfi's hazardous plans. Finally and most disastrously, a certain Charles Bailly was arrested at Dover with a whole packet of books and letters sent from Ridolfi to Leslie. The connection of Leslie and Ridolfi was a fatal one for Mary, because Leslie in turn led directly to the Scottish queen, whose official envoy he was. The next step was to uncover Norfolk's association with the whole plot, which proved easy enough when Norfolk was found to be sending money to Queen Mary's supporters in Scotland. On 7 September Norfolk was arrested once more and placed in the Tower. More harmful still was the arrest of Leslie himself: for he produced a series of most damaging confessions, under threat of torture, which mentioned not only the foreign troops which were going to be imported into England, but also the use of papal money in the affair, some of which had been sent to the Marians in Scotland.

On 3 November Leslie attributed the rising in the north to continuous communication between Mary and Norfolk, and between Norfolk and the northern earls—an injurious if inaccurate diagnosis. On 8 November his interrogator, Dr Wilson, the Master of Requests, described to Cecil how Leslie had said that Mary was not fit for any husband, for she had first poisoned Francis, then consented to the murder of Darnley, and thirdly matched with the murderer Bothwell, and after that she had brought Bothwell to Carberry Hill in the hopes that he would be killed in his turn; now she was pretending marriage with the duke of Norfolk, whom Leslie believed would not have survived long in the embraces of this female Bluebeard. Such confessions, however much promoted by physical fear, hardly pointed to Leslie as a stable and loyal servant. Even Wilson, shocked at this manifestation of what he took to be Scottish ingratitude, exclaimed: 'Lord what a people are these, what a Queen, what an Ambassador.'[36] But Leslie through all his tribulations did not lack self-confidence. On 8 November, the very day on which Leslie had outlined Queen Mary's marital career in such amazing terms, he wrote to her himself and said that he had been forced to confess everything since her letters had been produced in front of the Privy Council; nevertheless he could not help discerning the hand of providence in the discovery of the 'design', since Mary and her friends would be taught a sharp lesson against seeking relief by such means in the future![37] This egregious commentary on the outcome of the Ridolfi plot did not prevent Leslie from urging Mary to use all means in her power to get him released, and at the very least to help him financially.

In January 1572 the duke of Norfolk was tried for high treason. Shrewsbury was specially imported from the midlands to take part in the trial as one of the judges, leaving Sir Ralph Sadler temporarily in charge of Queen Mary. Norfolk was condemned, and finally executed in the following June. When Queen Mary heard of the execution of 'her Norfolk', she cried bitterly and kept to her room. Bess, finding her prisoner 'all bewept and mourning', asked her rather tactlessly what ailed her. Mary replied with some dignity that she was sure Bess knew what the cause of her grief was, and would sympathize with her in it; as for herself, she feared lest anything she herself had written to Norfolk might have brought him to such a pass. To these modest apprehensions, Bess replied ungraciously that nothing Mary had written could have done either good or harm, since Norfolk had been tried by a fair committee of his peers—including, of course, Shrewsbury.

Despite the snub administered by Bess, Mary had by her mere existence led Norfolk to conspiracy and death; in the same way Norfolk's trial and execution, and the revelations of the Ridolfi plot, were of acute relevance to Mary's position in England. It was not so much that she had lost a suitor—for there were many suitors in Europe of varying eligibility—as that her character in the eyes of the English nobility and the English Parliament now underwent a change. Popular opinion has a loud voice but a short memory. The circumstances of her arrival, now four years away, were quite forgotten in the tide of popular hatred which spread against her—this 'monstrous dragon' as one Member of Parliament termed her. Mary was now seen as a foreign-born Catholic spider, sitting in the centre of England spinning her webs in order to depose the English Protestant queen. The fact that she was an isolated prisoner with very little money was ignored in the light of the dangerous possibilities which the Ridolfi plot seemed to expose. It was at this point that Elizabeth herself seized her pen and wrote the famous lines on the subject of Mary, the 'daughter of debate', which ended:

No foreign banished wight shall anchor in this port;
Our realm it brooks no stranger's force, let them
    elsewhere resort
Our rusty sword, with rest, shall first his edge employ
To poll their tops that seek such change, and gape
    for joy.

But although Elizabeth's sword, rusty or otherwise, did eventually and reluctantly poll the top of Norfolk in June, despite the most ferocious baying for blood on the part of her faithful Commons, Elizabeth refused to consider the execution of Mary. In mid-June the English commissioners Shrewsbury, Delawarr and Sadler visited Mary at Sheffield and solemnly accused her of her heinous part in the Ridolfi plot as well as a list of other crimes: of having taken up arms against England, approving the papal bull of ex-communication of Elizabeth (*Regnans in Excelsis*), and actually claiming the crown of England. To all these charges Mary replied firmly that as a sovereign princess she could not recognize their jurisdiction over her; she requested to appear before the English Parliament to justify herself, and once more demanded to be taken into the presence of Elizabeth. In detailed answer to the charges, the queen freely admitted that she had written to the king of France, the king of Spain and the Pope and others asking for help, in order to be set at liberty and restored to her own country. She admitted the original offence of bearing the English title, when she had been a girl of seventeen, but denied ever bearing it since the death of Francis, over eleven years ago, which was correct. Over the Norfolk marriage, she reiterated her genuine belief that the match had been to the general liking of England. She admitted having given a commission to Ridolfi but said that it had been of a financial nature, and strongly denied any more compromising schemes with the Italian.[38]

Despite the Scottish queen's dignity, it was the will of Queen Elizabeth, not the answers of Queen Mary, which stayed the hand of the Commons against her in the summer of 1572. Elizabeth personally prevented the Commons from passing a bill of attainder on the Scottish queen; instead a bill was passed merely depriving Mary of her right to succeed to the English throne, and declaring her liable to a trial by peers (peers of the English realm, rather than her own peers, or equals, who would be sovereigns), should she be discovered plotting again. Most unfortunately the publication of the papal bull, *Regnans in Excelsis*, although not sought by Mary, and not even intended by Pius v to assist her personally, since he disapproved of her marriage to Bothwell, had begun the process of presenting her as a foreign traitor in their midst to English patriots. The massacre of the Huguenots on St Bartholomew's Day, 24 August 1572, at the hands of the French Catholics, led by the Guises, although once again hardly any fault of the prisoner of Sheffield Castle, only increased Mary's unpopularity in England. 'All men now cry out of [against] your prisoner,' wrote Cecil ominously to Shrewsbury. But Elizabeth would not allow this tide of xenophobia to sweep away her 'good sister and cousin', in spite of all the revelations of Ridolfi.

In the strange tortuous map of Mary's relations with Elizabeth, and Elizabeth's with Mary, Mary's feelings are much better charted than those of Elizabeth, since she gave many open declarations on the subject. But just as Elizabeth's incarceration of Mary on evidence she herself declared to be insufficient is greatly to her discredit, her preservation of Mary Stuart's life in 1572 by personal intervention must be allowed to be to her credit. Elizabeth, like Mary, had a constitutional dislike of spilling blood. Perhaps both of them were reacting against their blood-thirsty Tudor ancestors. Elizabeth was also conscious that Mary was by now by far her closest adult relation, since the sons of the dead Catherine Grey were still boys, and James was not only a mere child, but a child in control of the Scots; Elizabeth may have had some reluctance to abandon her kingdom to the care of young children (which had proved so fatal in the case of Scotland) if the assassin should find her as he had found Moray. Most of all, however, she was aware that Mary like herself was a sovereign princess: the death of one princess might strike at them all.

Too little is known of Elizabeth's inner feelings for Mary, since the English queen had learnt in childhood to hide all inner feelings, those dangerous traitors, within the breast. That closeness which two queens and near cousins should feel for each other, so often chanted by Mary, may have found more echoes in Elizabeth's heart than she ever admitted. In the meantime this merciful strain, this sneaking affection, could not fail to be noticed by Elizabeth's advisers: the point was taken that if ever the execution of Mary Stuart was to be secured, Elizabeth would have to be thoroughly convinced that her good sister had repaid her clemency with flagrant and harmful ingratitude.

'Tribulation has been to them as a furnace to fine gold—a means of proving their virtue, of opening their so-long-blinded eyes, and of teaching them to know themselves and their own failings.'

MARY QUEEN OF SCOTS *on the lives of rulers,* Essay on Adversity, 1580

By the summer of 1572 the public cause of Mary Stuart seemed lost indeed; she was left to discover for herself in the private life of captivity the uses of adversity, sweet or otherwise. This outward decline in her circumstances was due in great measure to the fact that the fickle wheel of fortune had rolled away from her direction in Scotland. Argyll, for example, had remained a Marian supporter after Langside, despite his failure at the scene of the battle. Mary harangued him with anxious letters from her prison, addressed at times to 'our Counsellor and Lieutenant', at times to 'our dearest cousin' and rising in a crescendo of supplication to 'Brother' (a relationship based on his marriage to her half-sister Jean Stewart) to whom she signed herself in a fevered personal postscript 'your right good sister and best friend forever'.[1] These frantic missives did not manage to dissuade Argyll from deserting Mary's side for that of Moray in April 1569; he leagued once more briefly with the pro-Marian Hamiltons after the regent's death in 1570 before, finding Mary's cause hopeless, he abandoned it once more. The attitude of Lord Boyd—the royal servant who had brought the fatal diamond from Norfolk—was typical of that of many of Mary's more stable former supporters: in the summer of 1571 he too began to despair of her cause. The death of the regent Lennox during a raid on Stirling in August 1571 led to the substitution of Morton as effective leader, under Mar as a nominal regent; Boyd agreed to Mar's election and was once more enrolled in the Privy Council. Mar's death in October 1572 confirmed Morton as regent in name as well as deed, and Morton was not only no friend to Mary at any time, but also an Anglophile, whom it suited Elizabeth to support. The final blow to Mary's prolonged hopes for restoration at English hands came in the following spring when the castle of Edinburgh, so long held by Kirkcaldy and Maitland on behalf of the Marians, and officially on behalf of Mary herself, was at last effectively besieged by heavy cannon brought north from England manned by English gunners under Drury. This lethal English intervention proved decisive: in May 1573 the castle fell.

The gallant Kirkcaldy was executed. Maitland either died naturally or, as Melville suggested, committed suicide 'after the old Roman fashion', before the executioner's axe could reach him. In any case his health had been deteriorating with a form of creeping paralysis: by March 1570 Randolph noted that his legs were 'clean gone', his body so weak that he could not walk, and even to sneeze caused him exquisite pain. Randolph commented spitefully: 'To this hath blessed joy of a young wife brought him.'[2] But Mary Fleming, for all Randolph's gibes, acted the part of a loyal wife after her husband's death. It was her moving personal plea to Cecil which saved Maitland's wasted corpse from the humiliating treatment accorded to Huntly's body after death in the shape of the traditional Scottish treason trial. In a firm letter to Morton, Queen Elizabeth pointed out that such barbarous habits were extremely distasteful to the English way of thinking: 'It is not our manner in this country to show cruelty upon the dead bodies so unconvicted, but to suffer them straight to be buried and put in the earth.' As God had shown His intentions towards Maitland by allowing him to die naturally and thus escape execution, so Maitland should be buried naturally and well and not 'pulled in pieces'.[3] Thus thanks to his wife, the foremost of the Maries, Maitland escaped the fate of Huntly.*

Mary kept her feelings to herself on the subject of Maitland's death: 'She makes little show of any grief,' reported Shrewsbury. 'And yet it nips her very near.' In

---

* Mary Fleming lived on for many years after her husband's death. She obtained the reversal of the forfeiture of his possessions in 1583. She seems to have brought up her children, including that son James Maitland who was to publish a defence of his father's honour, as Catholics.

the last years of his life since his quarrel with Moray, Maitland had energetically promoted Mary's interests; and he had died a loyal Marian. But he had not always lived as one. Queen Mary may well have reflected that if more years had been granted to him, he might have used them for further changes of allegiance. Nevertheless the death of Maitland brought to an end an era in Scotland; under Morton, a brutal man but one who showed himself to possess a certain administrative talent, the beleaguered country even enjoyed a period of comparative calm. Its quondam queen, Mary Stuart, also entered a phase of enforced tranquillity, in which the minor pains or pleasures of her prison routine became temporarily more important than European or Scottish politics.

The actual conditions of her captivity were not in themselves particularly rigorous during the 1570s by the standards of a state prisoner, except during moments of national crisis. In the first place Queen Mary was officially allowed a suite of thirty, which was enough to make her adequately comfortable if not a large number to one who had lived as queen her whole life. At the time of her first committal to Shrewsbury and Huntingdon in 1569 this thirty included Lord and Lady Livingston and their own attendants, Mary Seton, who had her own maid and groom, three other ladies of the bed-chambers, Jane Kennedy, Mary's favourite bed-chamber woman, John Beaton, her master of the household, her cupbearer and her physician; then there were her grooms of the chambers, one of them being that witty masque-maker Bastian Pages, Gilbert Curle, her secretary, Willy Douglas, now described as her usher, and her chair-bearer. There were four officers in the pantry, and three officers in the kitchen including a master cook and a pottager. Most of these were Mary's tried and loyal servants who made up the official thirty, but beyond this figure had crept in others, bringing the total up to forty-one. This proliferation, due not only to the infiltration of such further aides to the queen as Bastian's wife and some stable grooms, but also to the introduction of further attendants to look after the attendants, was tolerated by Shrewsbury out of kindness, as he himself admitted.[4]

But as the royal suite happily escalated through Shrewsbury's laxity, its increase in numbers inevitably reached the ears of the government in London, who took a much less generous view, especially when outside events seemed to threaten the safety of the queen of Scots. In times of danger there would be an outcry against this burgeoning suite—'too much enlarged at the present time' wrote Elizabeth angrily in September 1569, at the time of her discovery of the first Norfolk marriage negotiations. There would be demands from London that numbers should be cut; this would result in tears and protests from Mary, coupled with guilty denials from Shrewsbury to London that he had ever allowed the number to rise.

More servants, quite apart from the danger of official complaints from London, meant more mouths to feed. Here Shrewsbury was less indulgent. His allowance from the government for the feeding of the queen was the subject of agonizing solicitude on his part throughout all his long years as her guardian, and as late as 1584 he was still complaining about the number of dishes the attendants consumed—eight dishes at every meal for the queen's gentlemen, and five dishes for the ladies. When Queen Mary was first committed to Shrewsbury, he was allowed £52 a week to maintain her, but in 1575, without any reason being given, this allowance was cut to £30 a week. Shrewsbury squeaked with protest but all to no avail: it was an economy which the careful Elizabeth was determined to make. Shrewsbury's seventeenth-century biographer Johnston estimated that he was actually spending £30 *a day*, and was thus nearly £10,000 a year out of pocket; yet not only were his complaints disregarded, but he frequently had much difficulty in extracting the allowance which remained from the government.*[5] Eventually, on the advice of Walsingham, Shrewsbury applied to Queen Elizabeth for a fee farm to try and get back some of the expenses in a manner that would not hurt the royal pocket; even this request took a long time to be granted.

* It is difficult not to sympathize with the unfortunate Shrewsbury in his frequent moans of penury; he was certainly not justly treated by the Elizabethan government over the allowance. At the same time, it should be pointed out that it was at this same period that Shrewsbury felt himself able to embark on the major building-scheme of a new house—Worksop—although he was already amply endowed with residences. It does seem to argue that he was bankrupted more by his building-schemes than by the diet of the queen of Scots.

In the meantime Walsingham reflected that cutting Shrewsbury's allowance might turn out to be a false economy if it meant that the queen of Scots was allowed to escape through lack of guards—'I pray God the abatement of the charges towards the nobleman that hath custody of the bosom serpent, hath not lessened his care in keeping her'.[6]

In fact the care which Shrewsbury showed in keeping Queen Mary, like the numbers of her suite which he tolerated, varied very much with the attitude of the central government, and this in turn depended on the state of national security. Shrewsbury was not a cruel man and strictness generally had to be imposed from above. Even when the government resolved that the queen should be kept more 'straitly', its wishes were not always implemented very speedily; Derbyshire and Staffordshire were a long way from London, and travelling, especially in winter, from houses like Chatsworth set amidst the mountainous area of Derbyshire, represented considerable difficulties. This worked both ways. In the first place Shrewsbury, like all ambitious Elizabethans, constantly pined for the royal sunshine of the court, and bewailed the duties which kept him so long away from it: he felt he was being excluded from the glorious possibilities of the queen's favour, as well as an opportunity to make his case about his allowance. In 1582, in the autumn, deprived at the last minute of permission to make a longed-for visit to London, Shrewsbury commented sadly to Walsingham that neither the weather nor the time of the year would have prevented him arriving. Shrewsbury had to content himself with bombarding his friends at court with letters and gifts reminding them of his existence—such as some tasty 'red deer pies', made from his own deer, and posted off to London to win the favour of Cecil.*[7] But just as Shrewsbury was often tortured by the thought of the delights of London and the court, so the government who occupied this delightful city were themselves from time to time agonized at the idea that the Scottish queen in the far-off midlands was enjoying far too much liberty, seeing people, receiving visitors, holding a virtual court, riding about on horse-

---

* Cecil was created Lord Burghley in February 1571: but for the convenience of the present narrative, he will continue to be referred to by his original name.

back in conditions tantamount to liberty . . . such rumours, untrue as they were, spread by those recently arrived in London from the midlands, caused Elizabeth to choke with fury and fire off indignant reproaches to Shrewsbury for neglecting his duty.

Although Shrewsbury never failed to write in return protesting his extreme loyalty to Elizabeth and his eternal vigilance as a jailer, there was no doubt that the question of access to the Scottish queen was a delicate one, and whatever he swore to Elizabeth Shrewsbury did not always interpret the rules in the harshest possible light. In April 1574 he wrote down to London, in answer to some accusation that he was showing too much kindness to his captive: 'I know her to be a stranger, a Papist, my Enemy. What hopes can I have of good of her, either for me, or for my country?'[8] But of course there was a simple answer to Shrewsbury's question, as to what he—leaving out his country—could hope for from the queen of Scots, and Cecil and his fellows were well able to supply it for themselves: if Elizabeth died suddenly, who knew but that Mary's fortunes might not be dramatically reversed? If the captive were to be transformed overnight into the queen, and Mary were to ascend the throne of England, as would have been a possibility at least, had Elizabeth died while James was still a child, then Shrewsbury could expect much from his former charge if he had shown himself a sympathetic host to her in her times of distress. This consideration of Mary's potential as queen of England which died away in the 1580s after James grew to manhood, was very much present in the minds of the English statesmen in the 1570s; not only Shrewsbury but also Cecil and Leicester kept the possibility at the back of their minds in their dealings with the queen of Scots.

From Mary's own point of view she was of course anxious to be allowed to receive as many local people, and enjoy as much local life as possible. Such visits helped to while away the tedium of her imprisonment: the great families of Staffordshire and Derbyshire, the Manners and the Pagets, far from being Philistines, had the particular enjoyment of music and musical festivities which Mary shared.[9] These visits also provided an excellent cover for messengers and messages to slip by secretly. By the summer of 1569 irritating reports were reaching London that the Shrewsburys were allowing Mary some sort of social life at Wingfield. Lord Shrewsbury countered such complaints by detailing his extravagant precautions for Mary's safety—how, for example, when a child was born to his son and daughter-in-law, Gilbert and Mary Talbot, in March 1575 he deliberately christened the baby himself, to prevent unnecessary strangers entering the house. Nevertheless Shrewsbury was on some occasions accused of actually showing off his distinguished captive to his visitors —a charge of which one feels he was probably not completely innocent, since the presence of the famous queen of Scots in the midlands of England must have caused a sensation among the local gentry on her first arrival. Cecil told Shrewsbury that Elizabeth had heard in London of 'a gentleman of Lord B' who, on visiting Shrewsbury at his home, had been asked by him whether he had ever seen the queen of Scots. Cecil's indictment continued: 'Then, quoth your lordship, you shall see her anon.'[19] Such tales made Elizabeth's blood boil and Shrewsbury's run cold.

Mary's access to the baths at Buxton was the subject of a long drawn-out three-cornered skirmish between Elizabeth, Shrewsbury and Mary. Buxton, which lay comparatively close to Chatsworth, although cut off from it by rough countryside, was endowed with a well, the healing properties of whose waters had been known even to the Romans. In early Tudor times it had been known as the well of St Anne, and had become a centre of religious pilgrimage, where the people came to be cured as much by their faith as by the waters themselves; as at a modern centre of pilgrimage, Lourdes, the crutches and sticks of the cured were hung up in the little chapel over the springs where Mass used to be said on behalf of the afflicted. During the iron dominion of Thomas Cromwell these innocent pursuits were rudely interrupted; the crutches and sticks, and the offerings to the chapel were angrily swept away as manifestations of 'papist idolatry' by Cromwell's emissary; the baths themselves were locked up and sealed. However, by the time Queen Mary reached Derbyshire, the baths were once more unsealed, and were enjoying a considerable vogue even with the courtiers in far-away London, for their remedial powers which were thought to be particularly helpful in the case of gout. In 1572 a Dr Jones wrote a thesis on the benefits to be derived from the 'Ancient Baths at Buckstones' which described the commodious arrangements made there for the reception of the sufferers. Bess had apparently already turned her agile mind to the possible profit to be derived from these baths and their tepid, clear mineral waters: Dr Jones's narrative implies that she planned some sort of Buxton Bath Charity, in which it was intended to have a clear scale of charges according to the wealth of the patient—£3 10s. for a duke and 12d. for a yeoman.[11]

To visit these baths became the dearest object of Mary Queen of Scots; again and again she pleaded the near-breakdown of her health in an effort to secure the desired permission. Shrewsbury himself built a special house next to the famous baths, in which it would be possible to house the Scottish queen as she took her cure, without danger of escape. But every time Elizabeth appeared to be on the point of agreeing, she seemed to hear of some fresh plot to rescue the prisoner. These heart-searchings eventually culminated in permission being granted, albeit reluctantly. Mary paid her first visit to Buxton at the end of August 1573 and spent five weeks there. Thereafter it became the outing to which she most keenly looked forward, not only one may suppose for the remedial effects of the waters— considered efficacious also for female irregularities as well as gout—but for the unique opportunity which it gave her to mix with people. The presence of occasional court folk at Buxton was indeed a source of equal joy to both Mary and Shrewsbury. Thus Mary was able to meet Cecil, in 1575, and later Leicester, her former suitor, in 1578 and 1584. Cecil in his cautious way actually turned down a projected match of his daughter with Shrewsbury's son, on the grounds that it might confirm ugly reports that he had become too friendly with Mary while at Buxton. But Leicester went on after his cure at Buxton to be entertained by Shrewsbury at Chatsworth, where Mary was at that moment confined. Mary's keenest hope was of course that Elizabeth herself would succumb to the temptation to visit the baths, so that the longed-for meeting would be brought about. But although Elizabeth visited the town of Stafford and the nearby Essex house of Chartley in the course of a progress in August 1575—the moment in their lives at which the two queens were geographically nearest to each other—she did not journey on to Buxton.

Such visits gave Shrewsbury an opportunity of lavishing actual presents as well as showing kindness to prominent courtiers, or their wives and relations. Venison, fruit, fowl, meat, wine and ale flowed in a rich stream from the Shrewsbury domains to make the stay of these fashionable figures in distant Derbyshire more palatable. In August 1576 Sir Walter Mildmay, the Chancellor of the Exchequer, thanked Shrewsbury profusely for his kindness to his wife during the period of her cure, without which 'her being at Buxtons, in so could and raw a country, would be very odious to her'.[12] Happy Shrewsbury! The arrival at Buxton of Sir Thomas Cecil, Cecil's elder son, and his lady, my lady Essex, and the earl of Bedford's two daughters all with the clouds of court glory still freshly trailing about them, gave him a magnificent opportunity to load them with five hogsheads of beer and ale, further wine, sheep, rabbits, and further emoluments to supplement their diet, including 'a fat cow'.[13]

Yet so long as these visits of Mary to Buxton continued, they remained a source of apprehension on the part of Elizabeth. Dreadful rumours that Mary might be endearing herself to the common people there by small acts of charity began to reach London. In 1580 Shrewsbury was once more defending himself against the accusation that Mary was being allowed too much access to the world: he admitted that there had been one poor cripple who had spoken to the Scottish queen at the well, 'unknown to all my people that guarded the place', but he promised it would not happen again. In 1581 Cecil complained to Shrewsbury that Mary was known to have visited Buxton twice that summer, although she only had official leave for one visit. In 1584 Elizabeth apprehensively forbade an assembly of freeholders in the forest of the Peak, three miles from Buxton, on the grounds that the inhabitants were 'backward and for most part ill affected in religion', despite Shrewsbury's protests that these were good men who had been summoned in respect of Elizabeth's rights of vert and venison there, which had fallen into disuse for the lack of such courts.[14] Mary herself spoke the truest word on the subject of such terrors on the part of the Elizabethan government, that her charity might win her hearts. To Paulet, a subsequent jailer, who criticized her for giving a smock to a poor near-naked woman out of pity for her condition, she replied: 'You fear lest by giving alms I should win the favour of the people, but you ought rather to fear lest the restraining of my alms may animate the people against you.'[15]

Apart from these desirable visits to Buxton and the demands of safety in time of crisis, Mary's little household found the locality of their prison changing from time to time in any case, owing to the sanitary arrangements of the time: the contemporary method of cleansing large houses such as those inhabited by Shrewsbury was to empty them totally of their inhabitants, who would be transferred to another house, and then clean the dwelling thoroughly from top to bottom. Not all Mary's prisons were as uncomfortable and hateful to her as Tutbury—whose evil drainage system and notorious 'middens' stinking beneath her own windows became one of her chief sources of complaint during her later years there. Wingfield was a great Derbyshire manor house of considerable style and grandeur, and even Mary approvingly called it a palace. Sheffield Castle and Sheffield Manor lay close together, the castle in the valley and the newly built manor on the hill: one of the reasons why Shrewsbury was anxious to transfer Mary to Sheffield in the first place was that the propinquity of the two houses would make cleaning problems easier, since Mary could be shifted conveniently from one to the other. At Chatsworth Mary could enjoy the beauty of the wild country in which it was set—those moors from which Gerard hoped she could be plucked—or the park itself where Queen Mary's bower still commemorates today the little closed garden where she is said to have taken her exercise.

Within the pattern of these moves, the mimic court and household of the queen had its own tiny excitement and dramas. The queen was allowed to ride when governmental suspicions were not too keen, and even went hawking with Shrewsbury; at one point she had as many as ten horses in her stables, three grooms and a farrier, before this equestrian abundance was brought to an end by angry protests from London. She was allowed the pleasure of archery, which she had enjoyed in Scotland, exercising her long bow with 'her folks', to take her mind off her friends' losses in Scotland as Shrewsbury told Cecil.[16] She obtained a greyhound which she later tried to persuade Paulet to let her run at a deer. Then there were little pleasures of small dogs, caged birds (sent from France), other birds including barbary fowls and turtle doves, and much lute-playing as in Scottish days. Towards the end of her life Mary introduced a billiard table for the benefit of her house, although she herself does not seem to have used it. Nor did the queen lose all her interest in fashion and dress, being prepared to send off for patterns of dresses, such as were then worn at the London court, and cuttings of suitable gold and silver cloth.[17]

The romances of the chaste Mary Seton provided a positive drama within such a subdued setting. The only Marie to remain unmarried, and the only one therefore to follow her queen into captivity, Mary Seton had a naturally devout nature, and also a certain amount of pardonable family pride—the Setons being among the grandest of the Scottish court families, and her father and brother in turn playing a leading part as magnates, loyal to the crown. But these two aspects of Mary Seton's nature, admirable as they might be in theory, combined in practice to give her a certain spinsterish quality which was not a happy augury for marriage; nor was she herself as beautiful as Mary Fleming and Mary Beaton, or as vivacious as Mary Livingston. Yet in England this pious high-born Scottish lady did find her admirers: at Wingfield the younger son of Sir Richard Norton, Christopher Norton, was said to have fallen in love with her, although he was unfortunately executed at the time of the northern rising. She was no luckier with her next suitor, Andrew Beaton, who succeeded his brother John Beaton, Mary's master of the household, when he died in October 1572. Within the propinquity of the royal family circle, Andrew Beaton fell in love with Mary Seton. But the romance hung fire; there was some question that Mary Seton had sworn a vow of perpetual chastity, but the real trouble seems to have been that Andrew Beaton, although coming of an honourable Scottish family (the Beatons of Creich had given many loyal servants to the Scottish crown), was not quite on an equal social level with the daughter of Lord Seton.[18]

As Andrew Beaton struggled with the combined spiritual and material obstacles of a vow of chastity and family pride, he decided to resolve at least one of the difficulties; in August 1577 he went to France to obtain the nullification of Mary Seton's vow. On his homeward journey he was drowned. Mary Seton was left to mourn her last chance of married happiness, and as no one further attempted to dissuade her from the consolations of religion to which she had clung so long, she was able to die as she had lived under the name of Seton which she prized so much. From 1581 onwards her health declined, and began to interfere with the carrying out of her duties to her mistress, duties she had first incurred thirty-five years before when she had attended the child queen on her first journey to France. In 1583 Mary Seton was allowed to retire to France, and for the rest of her life lived at the convent of St Pierre at Rheims under the aegis of Mary's aunt, Mme Renée of Guise. Yet her devotion to her mistress was not diminished: in the same year a book and a box sent by Mary Seton in France to Mary Stuart via the French ambassador fell under suspicion; it was considered important that they should both be searched, for they would surely contain some secret messages for the Scottish queen.[19] Mary Seton's love of Scotland also remained; in 1586 she wrote sadly to M. de Courcelles, the new French ambassador on his way to Scotland: 'It is now nearly 20 years since I left Scotland and in that time it has pleased God to take the best part of my relations, friends and acquaintances; nevertheless I presume there remain still some who knew me, and I shall be obliged by your remembering me to them as occasion may serve.'*[20]

Another household event, less poignant than the blighted romance of Mary Seton, but of some significance for the future, was the death of Mary's secretary, Augustine Raullett, in August 1574. Shrewsbury took the opportunity of Raullett's demise to go through his papers where he found 'nothing of moment' as he reported to London. Mary's difficulty was indeed to replace him: for one problem which she had in common with her jailer, Shrewsbury, was

* The calm of the religious life led to longevity. Mary Seton survived her mistress by nearly thirty years, being last heard of in 1615. In 1602 an elaborate will provided for three High Masses to be said in the church of St Pierre for the repose of the soul of Mary Stuart, queen of Scotland. But her latter end was less glorious than her first beginning: in 1613 James Maitland reported that this once proud daughter of an ancient Scottish house was now 'decrepit and in want', and dependent on the charity of the nuns. Maitland begged James VI to help her, for his dead mother's sake.[21]

that her finances were causing her great concern. Her accounts were by now in chaos due either to the carelessness
or dishonesty of her treasurer, Dolin, a man who brought
his mistress no luck, since in 1577 her jewels were
actually stolen from his charge in Sheffield Park. The
queen's dowry from France was paid irregularly, and all
revenues from Scotland were apprehended by the current
regent. Mary was now anxious to have above all things
a new secretary with a good business brain; on the other
hand she could only offer little pay in return, as well as
the highly restrictive conditions of work.

Claude Nau, the candidate now submitted by her Guise
relations, was himself of a good Lorrainer family: one of
his brothers had been in Mary's service earlier and had
been with her at Bolton: Claude Nau had studied law and
practised it in Paris; he was clever and quick-witted, speaking and writing good Italian, accurate Latin and English
almost as fluent as his native French. Nau was a self-
centred man, fond of personal display as Riccio had
once been, and altogether a less engaging character than
Mary's other secretary, the melancholy but charming Gilbert Curle. But these faults seemed for the time being
outweighed by the fact that Nau was intelligent and
zealous: as Mendoza said later, Curle might be good, but
he was stupid. It was to Nau that Mary now related the
important memorials of her personal rule in Scotland, referred to in earlier chapters. Mary was also able to employ Nau's many gifts in her ceaseless foreign correspondence. His abilities impressed her sufficiently for her to
despatch him in 1579 on a mission to Edinburgh, the
principal object of which was to see and report on the
young James, now thirteen. Mary sent with Nau some
little golden guns of the sort to which young princes of
the period were so partial, designed to win the heart of
her son.[22] Perhaps she imagined James to be more martial,
more Guise-like, than the scholarly creature he had in fact
become. But the appeal of the little guns was never even
tested; for Nau was not allowed to have access to James.
After Mary's transference to Tixall at the time of the
Babington plot, one of these little guns was found
pathetically back at Chartley; she seems to have given
them to her surgeon as a memento just before her death,
and her groom of the chamber, Hannibal, received a little

golden bow and arrow which was probably originally intended for the same source.

It will be observed that with all these little activities, Mary's day-to-day life during the 1570s and early 1580s was not particularly arduous in itself: but there was one factor which made the whole era intolerably burdensome to her, and that was her own appalling health. This ill-health was grievously exacerbated by the mere fact that she was confined, and few springs, let alone winters, passed without her being subjected to some really severe bout of illness. Her severe illness in the summer of 1569, which she compared later to her near fatal attack at Jedburgh in October 1566, was followed in the autumn by a nagging pain in the side which prevented her sleeping; she was also constantly sick. Norfolk's death brought on a passion of sickness, and through the 1570s the eternal nagging pain in her side reduced her at times to real throes of agony. Apart from this pain, Mary also endured distressing pains in her right arm, which is often mentioned in her letters as preventing her either from writing herself, or from writing properly. A bad fall from her horse at Buxton in 1580 resulted in an unpleasant blow on her spine. In 1581 she had another dangerous illness, which began as gastric influenza, and in November 1582 the same symptoms led the royal physicians to believe that she was actually dying. Her legs were also extremely painful and by the date of her death she was almost permanently lame. Thereafter other different symptoms, thought at the time to be those of dropsy or nephritis (kidney disease), developed. Mary's health must be regarded as by far the heaviest physical burden which she had to bear in captivity: and by the late 1570s it was a sufficiently accepted phenomenon for all those who knew her to comment upon it, not only her friends but even such creatures of lesser sympathy as Bess writing to Walsingham. Babington in his confession mentioned that at the time of his first plotting in the early 1580s the queen of Scots was considered to be an old and sickly woman, who was not likely to live much longer.[23]

Yet apart from the weight of suffering itself, Mary had to endure two additional ordeals with regard to her health. In the first place her captors were extremely reluctant to believe that she was genuinely ill at all, suspecting that she merely invented her symptoms in order to secure further freedom or privileges such as visiting Buxton; such symptoms as they could not deny, they attempted to put down to hysteria. Shrewsbury himself admitted as much: 'I perceived her principal object was and is to have some liberty out of the gates,' he wrote in a covering letter to a report on her health, but added that, being finally convinced she was indeed ill, he had allowed her to walk at least upon the leads in the open air, in the dining-chamber, and also in the courtyard. In this report M. de Castellaune explained that he too had originally put down her illness to the 'painful, importunate and almost constant workings of her mind', but now the unmistakable evidence of constant vomitings, discharges from the brain and 'the greatest debility in the stomach' forced him to realize that her sufferings were all too genuine.[24] Secondly, quite apart from the difficulty of convincing her captors that she was ill at all, Mary was additionally unfortunate in that her whole being craved fresh air, the free physical exercise, the ability to ride regularly every day, which she passionately believed would alone cure her. All her life she had shown a desire for physical exercise, especially riding, bordering on a mania; as a queen it had been all too easy to gratify this wish. Now she found herself totally deprived of regular exercise, except when Shrewsbury's régime became lax enough to permit it, and at the same time her health rapidly deteriorated. Her very muscles seemed to seize up with lack of use. It was no wonder that her letters were permeated with agonizing pleas for more sympathetic regard to her physical needs in this respect, and that she herself attributed her increasing sickness to her deprivation of sufficient exercise and fresh air.

The exact medical causes of Mary's undoubted ill-health have been the subject of several modern investigations. It used to be suggested that her symptoms corresponded most nearly with those of a sufferer from a gastric ulcer.* But recently Drs Ida Macalpine and Richard Hunter, working on a group of diseases known as the porphyrias, have identified the recurrent illness of George III as belong-

---

* By Sir Arthur Salusbury MacNalty, *Mary Queen of Scots*, London 1960, Appendix I, where her symptoms are listed in detail and this conclusion is drawn.

ing to it.† An important aspect of this disorder is that it is hereditary, being transmitted as a Mendelian dominant character, showing itself in varying degrees of severity, from individual to individual. In the course of their investigations they have traced back similar symptoms to George III's ancestor and ancestress James VI and I and Mary Queen of Scots. There are of course difficulties in the way of any medical diagnosis made at the distance of four hundred years, if only because the medical language used then was inevitably angled towards the diseases of whose existence the doctors were aware. Sixteenth-century medicine was obsessed by the notion of the four 'cardinal humours' or chief fluids within the human body—blood, phlegm, choler and melancholy, or black choler; their relative proportions within individuals were thought to determine their physical and mental qualities as well as their total temperament. Since the various 'defluxions' or physical substances which proceeded from the unfortunate queen of Scots were always considered by her doctors in the context of this theory, contemporary commentators may well have overlooked clues vital to the modern diagnostician.

The symptoms of porphyria are severe attacks of abdominal 'colicky' pain with vomiting and extreme distress at the time, even transient mental breakdown, which may be interpreted by observers as hysterical. The attacks may be mild or severe and may occur frequently or at long intervals; another feature of the disorder is that often, despite the severity of the attack, the patient recovers quickly afterwards. It certainly seems far easier to relate these symptoms rather than those of a gastric ulcer to the case of Mary; in particular the episodic nature of her sufferings—bouts of severe illness followed by speedy physical recovery—fits better with the known pattern of the porphyria-sufferer than that of the ulcer subject. It is clear that Mary, like her descendant George III, underwent genuine rather than hysterical sufferings, which at

† See *Porphyria—a Royal Malady*, British Medical Association publication, 1968, including articles published in or commissioned by the *British Medical Journal* by Drs I. Macalpine, R. Hunter, Professor Rimington, on porphyria in the Royal Houses of Stuart, etc., and by Professor Goldberg on 'The Porphyrias' as a group of diseases.

times amounted to a complete breakdown, indistinguishable from madness.

The period when she definitely showed every sign of breakdown and hysteria to outsiders—after the birth of James until her incarceration at Lochleven—may even have been due to the exacerbating effects of her confinement upon the disease, such as have been traced by Drs Macalpine and Hunter, in the case of George III's granddaughter, Princess Charlotte. Mary's gastric symptoms, her 'colicky' pain, which James VI himself noted that he had inherited from his mother, fit with the known symptoms of acute and intermittent porphyria. Even the pains in her arms and legs to which she so often referred in her own letters, which she ascribed to rheumatism, correspond to the painful paresis of the extremities often experienced by the porphyria-sufferer. Her attacks of 'hysterical' distress certainly occurred at irregular intervals: and although they appeared to die away towards the end of her life, since her lifespan was cut short at forty-four it is impossible to tell how her medical history might have developed in later years. As to the hereditary nature of the disease, the mysterious 'hysterical' manner of the death of James V, which has so long puzzled historians, suggests that if Mary did suffer from porphyria, it was from her father that she inherited it.

But to Mary personally it was the intensity of her sufferings, not the origins of her disease, which was of importance; the fact that she was probably a victim of inherited porphyria was unknown to her as it was to her jailers, fascinating as the speculation is to both historians and doctors. For Mary at the time, the important fact was that the nineteen years of her captivity were darkened still further by the black clouds of genuine physical suffering, in which her captors often did not believe, when her horizon was already tragically obscured by lack of liberty.

Sick woman as Mary Stuart might be, she did not abandon hopes of release. Her own correspondence continued to buzz with schemes for assistance from abroad. The fact that she was generally regarded as marriageable meant that despite her captivity she never lost her place as a piece on the complicated chessboard of European politics in the 1570s. Her right on Catholic grounds of legitimacy actually to occupy—rather than succeed to—the English

throne was another factor which gave her prominence as
a chess piece; even if she herself was unable to organize
any move personally, there was always the possibility that
some foreign monarch would step in and help her to move
once more on these grounds alone. The excommunication
of Elizabeth by Pius v had brought this claim of Mary's
into fresh prominence; the new Pope Gregory XIII, who
succeeded Pius in 1575, believed strongly in Mary's claims
to the English throne, and consequently also interested
himself in the question of her future bridegroom. The most
likely foreign monarch to help Mary—because he was
the natural enemy of England—was of course Philip II.
Mary herself was so anxious to court Philip's approval
that in 1577 she made a will in which she actually made
over her rights to the English crown and elsewhere to
Philip, supposing that her immediate son and heir James
never returned to the true Catholic Church.[25] However,
such a will, made by a captive, had little reality, and was
intended rather to please Philip—who was apprised of its
sentiments—than to make any serious testamentary in-
novations.

Encouraged by the Pope, plans were now mooted by
which Mary should be married off to Philip's dashing illegitimate brother, the famous Don John of Austria. The
problem was of course not so much as how to bell the
cat, but how to rescue the cat from her captivity, before
the match could actually take place. The prelude to this
marriage was intended to be an invasion of England from
the Spanish Netherlands, organized by Philip II, with papal
approval and led by Don John, who would be rewarded,
as in a fairy story, by the hand of the captive princess;
together this romantic pair would then reign happily ever
after as Catholic king and queen of England. The idea of
a marriage between Mary and Don John, of whom even
Walsingham admiringly observed 'Surely I never saw a
gentleman for personage, speech, wit and entertainment
comparable to him. If pride do not overthrow him, he is
like to become a great personage', is a tantalizing one. Unfortunately the scheme, like so many involving the rescue
of the queen of Scots, was subject to all the complicated
pressure of politics in Europe at this period. The marriage
never actually left the realm of dreams to which it belonged, as Spain, England and France and their respective
sovereigns jockeyed among themselves to maintain their

position or increase it, and Elizabeth allowed her strange courtship by the duke of Anjou to hold out prospects of an Anglo-French alliance. In this situation the Spanish Netherlands, in a state of seething revolt against Spanish overlordship, acted as a perpetual apple of discord among these goddesses. From the point of view of English trade, Elizabeth was anxious to see the stabilization of the Netherlands; yet she was equally concerned that they should not be so stable that Spain should be able to use the provinces as a convenient jumping-off place for the invasion of England; at the same time unrest in the Netherlands at any moment might provide an excuse for France to intervene there, a prospect which horrified Elizabeth. In the meantime Philip continued to maintain his usual caution in considering any invasion schemes, which he was sensible enough to realize might result in the rapid execution of Mary long before her would-be rescuers ever reached her.

The curious fact was that although the Pope continued to take a great interest in the subject of Mary's fourth husband, she was still legally married to her third husband, Bothwell. Despite the report of the English ambassador in Paris, Norris, to that effect,[26] the nullification of Mary's marriage to Bothwell was not secured in the late summer of 1570. The validity of any marriage Mary might have contracted in the past had to be referred directly to Rome, the marriages of royal persons being reserved to the Pope himself as *causae majores*. In Mary's instructions to Ridolfi in February 1571, whether genuine or false, she bewailed the Pope's delay in giving the decree of nullity and asked him to speed matters on: about July 1571, Pius V seems to have authorized a commission to examine the case.[27] But it was not until 1575, when Leslie was freed from his English prison, that some serious action seems to have been taken on the subject. Notwithstanding his temporary betrayal of his mistress, under interrogation in the Tower, Leslie was re-adopted into Mary's service and his liberation was even celebrated by a short poem from her own pen, beginning:[28]

> *Puisque Dieu a, par sonbonte imence,*
> *Permis qu'ayez oblins tant de bon heur . . .* *

---

* *Since God, in His wondrous goodness*
  Hath given you so much joy . . .

Leslie subsequently went to Rome on Mary's behalf and in August 1576, a number of depositions were taken on behalf of the Bothwell marriage in Paris, at his instance, before a French judge ordinary.[29] The witnesses included John Cuthbert, Leslie's servant, James Curl, an elderly Scottish Catholic exile, Sebastian Davelourt, a Frenchman married to a Scotswoman who had abandoned Scotland for France on religious grounds, and Cuthbert Ramsay, brother of Lord Dalhousie, an expatriate Scot, as well as two Scottish priests living in Paris. Leslie's petition for nullity was based on the fact that the marriage of Bothwell and Jean Gordon had been a true marriage; that Bothwell had taken Mary by force; and that in any case Bothwell and Jean had not been properly divorced; he also added the fact—perfectly true—that Mary and Jean were kin. The depositions of the witnesses added little to what was already known about Bothwell's two marriages, but merely confirmed quite straightforwardly that Bothwell had lived with both Jean and Mary in turn as his lawful wedded wives.

Despite the establishment of this evidence, and despite the fact that Mary was obviously regarded as free to marry again by the Pope as by every other ecclesiastic, no decree of nullity was actually proclaimed.* The reason for this was the extreme danger which it felt threatened the queen of Scots if too much publicity was given to plans to free her: a declaration that she was no longer married to Bothwell carried the inevitable corollary that she intended to marry someone else. This would point a finger of suspicion at her. Not only might plots outside miscarry, but also her own head might be struck from its shoulders. A letter from the cardinal of Como in 1576 indicates the papal reasoning: 'As the Queen of Scotland is a prisoner, his Holiness sees not how it will be possible to treat with her as to providing her with a husband without running manifest risk of revealing what should be left secret.'[30] In April 1578 the death of Bothwell in his Danish prison freed Mary in any case from the bonds of matrimony, just six months before the death of Don John himself, probably of

* There is no record that such a decree was ever made and extensive recent researches in the Vatican Archives on the author's behalf by Dr C. Burns have failed to reveal it.

typhoid, in the Netherlands, put an end forever to Mary's hopes in this direction.

The conditions of Bothwell's last years were shockingly frightful: nothing he had done in life could justify the incarceration of this once active and vigorous man in a foreign prison for eleven years without trial. At first the Danish king had held him as a possible pawn against Elizabeth; now an Anglo–Danish alliance had put an end to his usefulness in that respect. In vain his Scottish enemies had repeatedly attempted to secure his extradition. Bothwell lingered on in prisons of increasing rigour, until the swift vengeance of his fellow-nobles might have seemed an infinitely preferable fate. It seems virtually certain that he was driven mad in his last years in the cruel fortress of Dragsholm, by the intolerable conditions in which he was held; James Maitland, who wintered in Copenhagen only twelve years after his death, heard this. There is a tradition—without definite proof—that he ended by being chained to a pillar half his height like an animal, so that he could never stand upright. The memoirs of Lord Herries wrote his epitaph thus: 'The King of Denmark caused him cast into a loathsome prison where none had access to him, but only those that carried him such scurvy meat and drink as was allowed, which was given in at a little window. Here he was kept ten years till being overgrown with hair and filth he died.'*[31]

If Mary would scarcely have recognized this demented and pitiful figure in the man to whom she had once looked above all for strength and support, perhaps Bothwell himself might not have easily discerned in the sad staid captive of Sheffield Castle the features of the young and beautiful queen whom he had first served and then married in the years of her personal rule in Scotland. The 'sweet face' which the good people of Edinburgh had blessed as their queen passed nearly twenty years ago on her first arrival in Scotland, had altered much as a result of ill-health and the privations and cares of close confinement. The largest and best known category of the portraits of Mary Stuart date from these later years of her life—being various versions of the picture sometimes termed the Sheffield portrait which shows her standing either full-length or three-

* The mummified corpse of Bothwell is still displayed in the crypt of Faarevejle church, near Dragsholm.

quarters, wearing a black velvet dress and the white peaked head-dress she immortalized.* The date is often painted in the corner of the picture. A number of versions of this picture were made and circulated about the Continent during Mary's lifetime, as she became increasingly a focus of Catholic respect and devotion. After her death, this Catholic devotion only increased, while after the accession of her son James to the throne of England, versions of this picture also found their way into the possession of grand English families, as part of the general rehabilitation of Mary's memory, as mother of the sovereign.

The origin of all these portraits seems to have been in miniatures, painted without the knowledge of the English government. Even a miniaturist was difficult enough to introduce into Mary's prison: in 1575 she had to ask her ambassador in Paris to have some little pictures of her made up abroad, in order to distribute them to faithful Catholics in England who were asking for them.[32] But by 1577 there was evidently some sort of miniaturist at work, at Sheffield, for Nau mentioned in a letter to Archbishop Beaton in Paris that 'he had thought to have accompanied this letter with a portrait of Her Majesty, but the painter has not been able to finish it in time'.[33] Two surviving miniatures in the Mauritshuis and in Blairs College, Aberdeen, are probably to be identified with the work of this unknown painter. The actual miniature from which the whole group of Sheffield portraits derives can, however, be identified: it is by Nicholas Hilliard.[34] It seems likely that Hilliard was one famous painter who did personally penetrate the queen's captivity: not only does the Hilliard miniature show signs of close observation from the life, but Bess of Hardwicke herself is known to have patronized Hilliard, and in 1591 there was some question of his painting a secret miniature of Arbella Stuart.[35] It would have been quite possible for Bess to have allowed Hilliard the privilege of painting her royal prisoner, in the same gambling spirit as she later considered the painting of Arbella, in order to forward Stuart claims. Although most of the later versions of this famous picture date from

* This 'Marie Stuart hood' consisted of a small white lawn headdress, dipping over the forehead and edged with lace; behind it flowed a lawn veil or head-rail, threaded with wire at the top to frame the head and shoulders in an arch.

after 1603, despite earlier dates painted in the corner, for the Hilliard miniature itself a date of 1578 is perfectly acceptable on costume grounds.*

The face in the Hilliard miniature and all versions of this portrait shows how much the queen's youthful beauty had been dimmed by the passage of time, even allowing for the woodenness of the treatment. Mary is now very far from being the laughing Goujon-like *belle* of the French court: this is a woman with a drawn face, a beaky prominent nose almost Roman in its shape but cut finely at the end, with a small rather pinched mouth; the smallness of the whole face is in contrast to the fulness of the body, which is now matronly in its proportions. It is well attested that by the date of her death nine years later Mary had fully lost that willowy slimness of figure which, combined with her elegant height, had been one of her chief attractions when she was young. It is evident from the Sheffield portrait, as also from the medallion portrait of her *en profil* which was the frontispiece of Leslie's history *De Origine Moribus et Rebus Gestis Scotorum* also published in 1578, that by then this process was at least well advanced. The profile, believed to have been done from a miniature in Italy, shows that the charming and clearly defined oval of Mary's face in youth had by now blurred into fulness round the chin. Health may have been responsible for Mary putting on weight: but the queen was by now presumably approaching the age of the menopause, and this too may have played its part in the process. One beauty remains in these portraits which time could not touch; although the once gay and slanting eyes are now sad and watchful and the mouth with its lips which once curved so prettily in a delicate arch above all other features shows the effect of pain and illness in the way the corners had newly tucked in, yet the hands of Mary Stuart are as beautiful as ever. Long and exquisite, the white fingers

* This Sheffield portrait used sometimes to be known as the Oudry portrait, after the words P. OUDRY PINXIT painted on the version of it at Hardwicke Hall. It was suggested that the unknown Oudry had been the original artist who painted Mary in captivity. But the Hardwicke Hall version is not listed in the 1601 inventory of the house; an entry in the accounts in 1613 probably relates to payments made for bringing the picture to the house. Since earlier versions of the picture do not have the words painted on them, the legend of Oudry the unknown artist is exploded.[36]

splay out against the black velvet gown, or drape themselves in some versions of the portrait on the red table, as romantically as they ever did in the days when Ronsard hymned their beauty.

The outward changes in the appearance of Mary Queen of Scots were paralleled by the inward changes in her character. In 1580 Mary wrote on her own initiative a long *Essay on Adversity* in which she explained that she of all people was most suited to write on this melancholy subject —in any case the mental exercise would save from indolence one who had once been accustomed to rule, and could no longer follow her destined calling. She concluded that the only remedy for the afflicted lay in turning to God.[37] Indeed those long white hands were now often clasped in prayer. It was no mere coincidence that in the portraits a great gold rosary is often shown hanging down from her belt. The woman who had once believed implicitly but unreflectively in the truths of the Catholic religion, and had allowed action not thought to rule her life, now found herself involuntarily forced back on the resources of meditation. It would be true to say that the quality of Mary's religious beliefs had never truly been tested up to the present. In France there had been nothing to try, much to encourage, them. In Scotland she had insisted on the practice of her own religion, but this minor concession had not been difficult to establish in view of the fact that she was the reigning queen, and was herself prepared to show total tolerance to the official Protestant religion of the country. In her early months in England she had seen no particular harm in allowing others to explain to her at their own invitation the truths of the Protestant religion as they saw them. But now to exercise her religion needed cunning and tenacity; she was living in a country where Catholics were not only not tolerated, but often persecuted, and persecuted with increasing severity after Pius v's bull of excommunication towards Elizabeth.

Sir John Morton, the secret priest, died and was succeeded by another secret chaplain, de Préau. For a short period in 1571, Ninian Winzet, the Scottish Catholic apologist, entered her service, nominally as her 'Scottish secretary' but in fact acting as her confessor, through the good offices of Beaton; he was subsequently sent away to

London to join Leslie in his house arrest.[38] In October 1575 Mary wrote to the Pope asking that her chaplain should have episcopal function, and the power to grant her absolution after hearing her confession. She named twenty-five Catholics whom she asked should be granted absolution for attending Protestant ceremonies in order to divert suspicion. Mary asked for a plenary indulgence as she prayed before the Holy Sacrament or bore in silence the insults of a heretic: with prescience for the future, she asked that in the moment of death, if she repeated the words *Jesu, Maria,* even if she only spoke them with 'her heart rather than her mouth', her sins might be forgiven her.[39] A Jesuit priest, Samerie, managed to visit the queen secretly on three occasions in the early 1580s, to act as her chaplain, disguised variously as a member of her household, including her valet and her physician.[40] Such manœuvres and the preservation in secret of the rites of the Mass by one means and another, demanded courage and the real will to take part in them. But to Mary, as to many others in whom the hectic and heedless blood of youth fades, giving place to a nobler and gentler temperament, her religion itself had come to mean much more to her.

It was not only that the Catholic powers abroad represented her best hope of escape from captivity; it was also that she herself had undergone a profound change of attitude to her faith, and indeed to life itself. It is the mark of greatness in a person to be able to develop freely from one phase into another as age demands it. Mary Stuart was capable of this development. Her whole character deepened. Having been above all things a woman of action, she now became under the influence of the imprisonment which she so much detested, a far more philosophical and contemplative personality. Two poems printed in Leslie's *Piae Afflicti Animi Consolationes* of 1574 speak of sad memories, of the world's inconstancy and of the need for sacrifice. Lines written in a Book of Hours in 1579 allude bitterly to false friends, and the need for solitary courage, in face of the fickle changes of fortune.

> *Bien plus utile est l'heure et non pas la fortune*
> *Puisqu'elle change autant qu'elle este opportune**

---

* *Time than fortune should be held more precious*
For fortune is as false as she is specious![41]

But in another poem, probably written in the early 1580s she showed more Christian resignation: . .

> *Donne seigneur, donne moi patience*
> *Et renforce ma trop debile foi*
> *Que ton esprit me conduise en ta loi*
> *Et me guarde de choir imprudence**

And at the end of her *Essay on Adversity*, after discussing a series of Biblical, Roman and medieval examples of rulers who had fallen into adversity, Mary quoted the parable of the talents to explain how much would be forgiven to those who had made the best of their lives: 'God, like the good father of a family, distributes His talents among His children, and whoever receives them and puts them out of profit is discharged and excused from eternal suffering.' She certainly put her own philosophy into practice to the extent that the talents she showed in her middle-age were very different from those she displayed in youth. The carefree buoyancy which Mary displayed then, so alluring in a young woman, would have been intolerable and even frivolous in the captive queen. Mary's utterances in her forties show on the one hand an infinitely nobler and deeper spirit, and on the other a serenity and internal repose quite out of keeping with her previous behaviour.

Mary Stuart achieved this serenity and this intelligence at the cost of much pain, heart-searching and suffering. She, who had never been known to exist without an adviser, and had never wished to do so, whether it was her grandmother, her Guise uncles, the lamentable Darnley, her half-brother Moray, Riccio or Bothwell, was compelled in the last years of her life to exist without any sort of reliable advice or support from outside. She was now the shoulder on whom her servants leant, and to whom her envoys, many of them of questionable loyalty, looked for direction. She might even secretly write to the outside world for advice, and receive it, but when it came to taking action, actually within the confines of the prison itself, there was Mary and only Mary to make decisions and inspire their implementation. The pretty

---

* *Give me, dear Lord, the true humility*
  And strengthen my too feeble halting faith;
  Let but Thy Spirit shed his light on me—
  Checking my fever with His purer breath.[42]

puppet-queen of France, the spirited but in some ways
heedless young ruler of Scotland, could never have
carried through the remarkable performance which Mary
Stuart was to display in her last years. The uses of adversity for Mary Stuart, bittersweet as they might have
been rather than sweet, were to teach her that self-control
and strength of character which was to enable her to
outwit Elizabeth at the last by the heroic quality of her
ending.

23 Mother and Son

'. . . nor let thy soul contrive
Against thy mother aught; leave her to heaven
And to those thorns that in her bosom lodge
To prick and sting her . . .'

*The advice of Hamlet's ghost-father on the subject of his
mother Gertrude (the relationship of Hamlet and Gertrude
is thought to have been founded by Shakespeare on the
story of Mary Queen of Scots and James VI)*

While Mary languished in captivity, the child whom she had
last seen as a ten-month-old baby at Stirling Castle in 1567
had grown to a precocious adulthood. Mary still pined for
James, or the idea of the infant she had lost. In return
she genuinely imagined that James also longed for her,
prompted by the dictates of natural affection which she
believed must always exist between a child and its mother.
No doubt she allowed herself to be buoyed up with the
falsely sanguine stories of his love for her related to her
by kindly courtiers. Such apocryphal tales were easily spun,
and greedily accepted by the maternal heart of the prisoner,
who had no means to check them, and every reason to hope
they were true. One such tale, from a Catholic source,
related how James as a boy had once been observed to
be in an especially happy mood at supper, and had smiled
all over his face; the reason for his genial temper proved
to be that he had secretly obtained a copy of Bothwell's
dubious *Testament of Confession,* read it and from this
had realized that his mother was in fact quite innocent
of the murder of his father. Similar stories must have
given Mary a very false impression of the way James's
mind was being bent. As late as 1584 Lady Margaret
Fleming wrote to Mary from Scotland and told her that
although Scottish court manners had sadly changed for
the worse, this was not James's fault, and he himself

would certainly always behave as 'a humble, obedient and most loving son' towards her.*[1]

The reality was to be very different: nor did James ever show himself in the light of a loving, let alone obedient, son to Mary. It was Mary's tragedy that she continued to believe that he would do so, and that she had from the first a totally false impression of the mother-and-son relationship. In the first vital years of infancy, James had been looked after by the countess of Mar, a 'Jezebel' of a woman as Knox called her, who hated Queen Mary. From four years onward his education was mainly in the hands of Mary's inveterate enemy and chief traducer George Buchanan. The man, once Mary's respectful admirer, who had allowed himself to concoct the disgusting stories of the *Detection* was scarcely likely to spare Mary's reputation when discussing his mother with the child. Later James imbibed a great deal of Calvinist theology from the one tutor, Peter Young, for whom he seems at least to have felt some affection. James's childhood was an unhappy compilation of long hours of learning—he later commented ruefully that he had been made to learn Latin before he could even speak Scots—with occasional dramatic and bloodthirsty interventions, as terrifying as any prenatal influence from Riccio's slaughter, as when at the age of five he witnessed the bleeding corpse of his grandfather Lennox being carried past him into Stirling Castle. Not only was he totally cut off from a mother's love in childhood, but he was also trained to regard his mother as the murderess of his father, an adulteress who had deserted him for her lover, and last of all, the protagonist of a wicked and heretical religion.

It was true that James subsequently turned on Buchanan for his libels on his mother; he called the Regent Moray that 'bastard who unnaturally rebelled and procured the ruin of his own sovereign and sister'; in 1584 he obtained the condemnation of Buchanan's writing in Parliament. Much later he counselled his own son against reading 'the infamous invectives' of Buchanan and Knox.[3] But the point remained that enough had been done in early child-

* One version of the Sheffield portrait which was definitely known to the engravers before 1603 is the large double portrait of Mary and James, now at Blair Castle, dated 1583. But although mother and son are shown tenderly side by side, such a meeting never actually took place outside the realm of the artist's imagination.[2]

hood to rob James of any natural feeling at all, let alone
for his mother. Intellectually he could replace Buchanan's
false picture of Mary with one he chose to believe was the
true one. But he could never replace in his heart the in-
born love of son for mother, since this flickering newly-
lighted flame had been extinguished shortly after his birth
by Mary's enemies.

James, like Mary herself, had been brought up to believe himself to be a ruling monarch, despite the fact
that his mother was still alive. In appearance he had grown
up to be a wizened creature with sad eyes, in stature very
unlike his tall and god-like parents. Fontenay, who visited
him at Mary's instigation in 1584, was impressed by
James's intelligence: he found him to have a retentive
memory, to be full of penetrating questions and able to
conduct a good argument; yet he had three faults which
Fontenay listed—over-confidence or an inability to estimate his own poverty and insignificance, and indiscreet
love of favourites, and a tendency to pursue pleasure
rather than politics which too easily allowed others to
seize the reins of the realm.[4] In 1580 Father Robert Aber-
cromby, a Jesuit on a mission to Scotland, gave his own
opinion on James: he found the king to be deep in
Calvinism, simply because he had known no other religion discussed since adolescence.[5] None of this added up
to much possibility of genuine sympathy with Mary; this
was not the tender charming boy of Mary's imagination
who would make every effort to release his mother from
the nightmare of her captivity. Like many people who have
had an unhappy and unaffectionate childhood, and withdrew into their own thoughts for security, James was already a practised deceiver by the time he reached his
teens. Elizabeth's comment when she heard of the execution of Morton in 1581 probably contained far more important guidance for Mary on the subject of James's
character than any of the more optimistic comments to
which Mary herself listened: 'That false Scotch urchin!'
exclaimed Elizabeth. 'What can be expected from the
double dealing of such an urchin as this!'[6]

Mary's picture of her son and of their relations was
very different: she had after all carried this child in her
womb through manifold dangers and difficulties, and he
was her only child—'One like the lioness' as the motto
proudly proclaimed which she had embroidered on her

hangings. She had few other objects on which to lavish her affections. The years in which James had grown up from unconscious babyhood to near adulthood had been spent by Mary cut off in captivity; her memories of her child kept green in her heart. Her will of 1577 in which she formally expressed the wish that her son should marry a Spanish princess and embrace the Catholic faith was only one example of how out of touch she had become with her son's true development. In 1561 when Mary returned to Scotland, one of her problems had been that having been brought up in France she had insufficient understanding of the working of the Scots mind: now from 1581 onwards, in the course of Mary's schemes for unity with James, her difficulty was not being able to follow the complexities of her son's mind after thirteen years of captivity.

Quite apart from this obstacle to their accord, Mary's position as queen of Scots threatened that of her son as king. Mary had revoked the abdication she made under duress at Lochleven, during her few days of liberty before Langside in May 1568. In her own mind, therefore, and those of her supporters, especially the Catholic powers abroad, she was still the true queen of the country: James despite his coronation at the age of thirteen months, and the government in his name which had existed ever since, was usurper. This was Mary's real hold over her son in 1580, rather than the natural ties of affection. There were advantages to James in having his *de facto* kingship recognized as *de jure:* not only would his position with France and Spain be improved, but also his position in the English succession might also be better secured. When James grew up, his letters to his mother struck an uneasy compromise: he addressed her as the queen of Scots, but signed himself James R. It was under these circumstances that, early in 1581, Mary outlined her own plan for 'Association'—or the joint rule of mother and son—through a Guise emissary: a scheme which naturally involved the restoration of Mary to Scotland.

The project naturally commended itself vividly to Mary, who had suggested it: once more she envisaged the prison gates opening and her own return to her throne. James himself was sufficiently attracted by the idea of the recognition of the Catholic powers at least to write a pleasant letter in return. The key to the whole project in James's mind was

of course the attitude of Elizabeth: English approval was
still in the reign of James, as it had been in the reign of
Mary, very much a factor of Scottish politics: the same
considerations of an English alliance, English subsidies, the
shared Protestant religion, and the involvement of the
Scottish monarchy in the English royal succession, still
obtained. In 1581 the emergence of James's first favourite,
his cousin Esmé Stuart whom he created duke of Lennox,
in alliance with the bold swashbuckling Captain James
Stewart,* led to the downfall of the pro-English regent,
Morton. Morton was tried and executed for the murder
of Darnley (who, like Banquo's ghost, seemed to play a
much more effective part in Scottish politics once he was
dead than when he was alive). Mary had never forgiven
Morton, and exulted over his death from her prison—'of
whose execution I am most glad', she wrote firmly.[7] The
new duke of Lennox did not long enjoy the power which
this denouement gave to him; in August 1582 a palace
revolution in the shape of the kidnapping of the king's
person by the Ruthven family, headed by the earl of
Gowrie, placed the government of Scotland once more in
pro-English hands. Esmé Stuart, duke of Lennox, retired
to France after the raid of Ruthven and there died. A
year later, however, James eluded his captors, and power
was once more in the hands of the apparently anti-English
Arran (James Stewart). James therefore professed himself
to the Guises ready to entertain the notion of the
Association, at the sacrifice of Elizabeth's favour. Arran's
position was further strengthened when an unsuccessful
attempt to unseat him on the part of pro-English lords including Mar and some Hamiltons, in the spring of 1584,
ended with their flight to England, as Moray had once
fled after the Chaseabout Raid in 1565; there was a further
parallel—these lords had expected English aid in the
project but had not received it.

James might be prepared to toy with the idea of the
Association—since it temporarily fitted with his plans—
but Mary herself was enthusiastic on the subject; into her
service in this cause she now enlisted Patrick, master of
Gray. Gray, a young man of Lucifer-like beauty, had also

---

* Now created earl of Arran by James despite the continued existence of the wretched, mad true incumbent of the title, Mary's former suitor.

all the mingled potentialities of talent and treachery of the
former archangel within his breast. In France Gray had
entered the service of Mary's ambassador, James Beaton,
archbishop of Glasgow, and on being received into the
inner circle of Mary's supporters in Paris, had become
extremely friendly with the Guises; the esteem in which
he was held in these circles may be judged by the fact
that he was presented with silver plate to the value of five
or six thousand crowns. Gray had paid one visit to Scotland, either with Esmé Stuart, or after the fall of Morton,
during which his ostensibly Catholic faith had wavered,
and he had promised to renounce it in favour of the reformed religion. His second visit occurred in November
1583, when he brought back Esmé Stuart's young son, at
James's request, to be brought up at the Scottish court.
Although entrusted by Mary to represent her counsels at
the Scottish court, and push forward the notion of the
association, Gray quickly appreciated that it would be
far more profitable personally to ally himself with the
son, a king on a throne, than the mother, a prisoner without a kingdom. He became the friend and confidant of
Arran, and from here reached the ear of James himself.
From the first, Gray was in possession of enough of
Mary's secrets, and those of her little clique of supporters
in France, to be able to betray both parties to James whenever he wished to convince him anew that, in a case of
mother versus son, it would always be the son whom he
would serve. Yet Mary, under the illusion that Gray was
her emissary, continued to trust him to work for her, as
she continued to believe in the affections of James.

It was now that the attitude of Elizabeth became so
vital to the future, if any, of this plan of the Association.
On mature reflection it was only too easy for James to see
that the return of a released Mary to Scotland would be
at least a serious nuisance to his own position; they were
of different religion, to say nothing of different generation;
how much better to secure the benefit of the association,
in the shape of Elizabeth's favour and foreign approval,
without the release of Mary. In an extreme case, it would
still benefit James more to have an alliance and subsidy
from Elizabeth, than the official recognition of France. Yet
such negotiations had to be conducted with enormous
delicacy, since Elizabeth's attitude could only be ascertained

by secret probing, and in the meantime Mary had to be
encouraged lest after all the Association might turn out to
be advantageous to James. In the summer of 1584 it was
Gray who was sent down to London to conduct these
negotiations on behalf of the king. In the meantime not
only was Mary specifically assured of James's welcoming attitude towards her proposals by a letter from James himself in July, but she was also further informed that Gray's
mission was merely to treat with Elizabeth over the subject
of the rebel lords who had fled to England.[8]

Mary had reluctantly to accept this story; from her
prison there was little else she could do. Her own emissary
Fontenay believed the season would never again be so
favourable—'jamais si belle'—to bring about the association since both James and the Scots were now inclined
towards Mary.[9] Nevertheless, in a series of letters written during October to Gray, and to Castelnau de Mauvissière, the French ambassador in London, she showed herself highly conscious of the dangers of her position should
James ever try to negotiate separately; Mary, with the
keen perception of the captive, saw that her only hope
of eluding her prison was if James made her release one
of his conditions of treating with Elizabeth. She emphasized
to Gray the importance of not letting Elizabeth think
that there were divisions between James and herself; furthermore Gray must demand Mary's liberty as one of the
conditions of an Anglo–Scottish rapprochement. Mary, still
believing herself to be employing Gray, gave him a series
of very explicit instructions as to how he was to negotiate
while in London, and although her eventual destination
after her release was left vague—either England or Scotland—the importance of the release was underlined.[10]
Yet from the first moment Gray arrived in London, it
was immediately realized by the English that he would
now serve the interests of James and Elizabeth rather than
those of James and Mary: indeed, in view of the excellent
knowledge Gray had acquired of Mary's organization and
her secrets while in her service, Elizabeth had acquired a
valuable potential ally and Mary a dangerous potential
traitor. In London Gray was given lodging by Sir Edward Hoby who had known him in France: Hoby, commenting to Cecil on Gray's keen personal ambition, the
desire for glory which 'burnt in his stomach', hinted that

Gray had much secret information about Mary which he was prepared to impart: 'he can speak and tell tales if he list . .'.[11]

In vain Mary underlined to Gray what those around her were in danger of overlooking but she herself would never forget, that her imprisonment was illegal from the first moment, since she had not even been captured in war. Mary begged Gray to make Elizabeth realize that by liberating Mary she would be meriting the approval of James.[12] But even as Mary wrote, it was being made clear to Elizabeth that in fact this was the very last thing that would merit James's approval. While Mary pleaded pathetically with Gray to pay her a personal visit in her prison, such contacts being most suitable to make mother and son better acquainted, Gray was busy in London betraying the cause of the mother at the instigation of the son. On 28 November Nau drew up twenty-eight heads of proposals on the subject of the Association at Mary's request:[13] Mary announced herself ready to stay in England if necessary, prepared to allow an amnesty to be declared over all the wrongs she had suffered at the hands of the English, renounce the Pope's bull of excommunication, and abandon forever her own pretensions to the English crown over those of Elizabeth. Although confident of French agreement to these proposals, she also offered to join an offensive league against France, so long as an English dowry was assured to her, equivalent to that she would have to abandon in France, in the event of the French not subscribing to the idea of the Association. In Scotland she was also prepared to allow an amnesty, to agree that there should be no upset in the present state of the religion of the country; the only condition she made was that James should marry with Elizabeth's knowledge and 'good counsel', and the only demand the immediate softening of her present harsh conditions of captivity. Such sweeping concessions on the part of Mary made it clear that, sixteen years after her first English imprisonment she had one aim in view, and one aim only, to which she was prepared to sacrifice all other considerations—her freedom, by any means at all.

On 8 December, her forty-second birthday, Mary wrote to Elizabeth still wistfully hoping for two hours' personal talk with her, the talk which she still felt after all these years would settle everything between them; and with her

birthday uppermost in her mind, she took the opportunity
to hope that Elizabeth would live to enjoy in the future
as many happy years as Mary had endured unhappy ones
in the past. On 14 December Mary reminded Gray by letter
that James was not the sole king of Scotland, and that
Gray must at all costs prevent mother and son being
driven apart by 'evil counsellors' since it was so important
to Mary's cause that James should show himself a 'natural
and obedient son'.[14] As late as January Mary was still
hoping that liberty for her on these new terms was just
round the corner, and desired the French king and queen
to write separately to James acknowledging the Association
in order to bring her son into accord with her.[15] Yet all
the while Gray had successfully concluded his mission in
London on James's behalf: he had indicated to Elizabeth
that the release of Mary was not necessary to win James's
friendship, and he had learnt from Elizabeth also that her
friendship could be won for James by a direct channel,
without taking into account the claims, rights and certainly not the desires of the imprisoned queen of Scots.
The Association was now doomed; it became stamped
merely as the unrealistic scheme of a tiresome middle-
aged woman in prison, to whom no further attention need
be paid in this context.

It was in March 1585 that the full horrifying truth
could no longer be kept from Mary: James in Scotland
assembled his whole Council as Gray gleefully wrote to
Elizabeth; at which point it was formally concluded that
the 'Association desired by his mother should neither be
granted nor spoken of hereafter'.[16] At first Mary, in her
pathetic desire to protect the image of her son in her own
mind, even tried to persuade herself that the betrayal
could be blamed on Gray. On being informed that James
could not negotiate with her while she was a prisoner, she
enquired miserably with child-like logic, why Elizabeth
could not then free her, so that she would at least be able
to negotiate with her son. A passionate postscript to
this letter, in her own hand, revealed the depth of her
agitation: 'I am so grievously offended at my heart,' she
scrawled, 'at the impiety and ingratitude that my child
has been constrained to commit against me, by this letter
which Gray made him write.' Wildly she threatened to
disinherit James and give the crown to the greatest enemy
he had, rather than allow this sort of treatment. In her let-

ter to Elizabeth the same day, Gray is *'ce petit broullon'* (troublemaker) and James this badly brought up child (*'mal gouverné enfant'*). In her next letter to Elizabeth she bewailed the mischief which had been made recently between herself and James by sinister counsels[17]—unaware of the grisly truth still more unbearable to a mother's heart, that it was not a few months' trouble-making by Gray but nearly twenty years of total separation which had led to the breach between mother and son. James's welcome of the Association in July 1584 had been apparently unrestrained: his repudiation of it the following March was total. He had betrayed Mary, and so had Gray. But in the delicate game of Anglo–Scottish relations, James had discovered that whereas he held some of the cards and Elizabeth held some of the others Mary held none at all. There was nothing Mary, still firmly within the four walls of her prison, could do except rage and weep alternately at the perfidy of her son, and the betrayal of her child.

In 1584, the year of Mary's repudiation by James, her own domestic circumstances underwent an unpleasant change. Mary had been able in the last years in prison to enjoy a pleasant quasi-maternal relationship with her own niece, little Arbella Stuart, the pretty pudgy dimpled child of Darnley's younger brother, Charles Stuart, and Bess of Hardwicke's own daughter, Elizabeth Cavendish. The marriage of Arbella's parents had been brought about under romantic circumstances within the orbit of Mary herself. In 1574 Charles's mother, countess of Lennox, now reconciled to Mary over the subject of James, had asked permission from Elizabeth to visit her ex-daughter-in-law at Chatsworth on her way to Scotland to see her grandson. To Elizabeth the possible combination of these two formidable matrons, Margaret Lennox and Bess of Hardwicke, seemed lethal; permission was refused. However, while the countess of Lennox was lodging at a neighbouring house on her way north, her son Charles fell ill; Bess of Hardwicke had already ridden over to visit the countess, bringing her daughter by the hand. As ten years before the timely illness of Darnley had led to his romance with Mary, so now once more the sick-room played its part in the fortunes of the Lennox Stuarts. Before the boy recovered, the young couple had fallen in love, and whether the circumstances of the romance were quite as fortuitous

as they seemed, certainly both the grand ladies involved
were pleased by it. Margaret Lennox was poor, but her
son stood in line to two kingdoms as his brother Darnley
had once done; furthermore she was the grandmother
of a little king of Scotland. Bess of Hardwicke, on the
other hand, was of low birth but had made herself rich
and powerful. Once more, as with Mary's marriage to
Darnley, Elizabeth flew into a violent rage at hearing of
this pretty romance which was supposed to have flared
up so innocently in the midlands. Both countesses were
summoned back to London, and both clapped into prison.

The terms of imprisonment were in both cases relatively
short. Out of this ill-starred marriage, some time during
the autumn of 1575 the little Arbella Stuart was born: her
sex must have been a sad disappointment to both grandmothers, but as with Mary Stuart herself, Arbella was not
destined to be replaced by the birth of a brother. Her
sickly young father died of consumption in the spring of
the next year; although her mother lived on till 1582, when
she too died in her early twenties, from then on the child
was brought up much of the time with her maternal grandmother Bess. In vain both grandmothers tried to secure
the earldom of Lennox for the little girl after her father's
death: the regent of Scotland admitted that the earldom
had originally been granted to Charles Stuart, instead of
to James, who as direct male heir and son of the elder son
Darnley should rightfully have inherited it from his grandfather, Matthew, earl of Lennox; but he stated that the
patent could be revoked as James had been a minor at the
time, especially as Charles's child was a female. In spite
of being known as the *comitessa* and having the formal
title grandly painted on her portrait as a two-year-old
child, little Arbella never did secure her earldom; and
when Esmé Stuart rose to favour in Scotland, it was this
earldom which James used to bestow honour upon him.

Only Mary Queen of Scots continued to acknowledge
the baby as the claimant: her will of February 1577 referred to 'Arbelle, *ma nièce*' as earl of Lennox and commanded James to respect Arbella's right if she, Mary,
died.[18] Mary also tried to get Queen Elizabeth to hand
over Margaret, countess of Lennox's jewels to Arbella after
the countess's death. She played with the idea of marrying
Arbella to her first cousin James. In addition to these
practical efforts on behalf of 'my precious jewel, Arbell'

as her grandmother Bess called her, Mary also enjoyed the innocent and touching companionship of the little girl, who with her royal blood and claims to two thrones, so incongruous with the simple routines of infancy, may have reminded Mary of the child she had once been. Mary had another favourite—Elisabeth Pierrepoint also one of Bess's grand-daughters—who was her own god-daughter, whom she loved to spoil and pet; she called her her 'mignonne', and 'little bedfellow' (since they sometimes shared a bed, according to the domestic custom of the time). Mary even took pains to make her little favourite a special black dress.[19] Marguerite de Valois in her memoirs condescendingly observed that it was natural for old people to love little children whereas those who were in their prime were apt to look down upon them and dislike 'their unfortunate simplicity'. In Mary's case, she had never looked down upon the unfortunate simplicity of children, showing fondness for the young such as her godson Francis Stewart even when she was barely twenty, not yet a mother herself and in the midst of the full excitement of reigning in Scotland; yet certainly once she was a prisoner, her maternal feelings increased, and the little Shrewsbury grandchildren who pattered about the many Shrewsbury palaces—or prisons —provided much solace for her affectionate nature, just as she in turn must have constituted a glamorous feature of their childhood.

Close contact between Arbella* and Mary was, however, put to an end by the reverberating row which now broke out between Mary and Bess of Hardwicke, an altercation in which Bess was entirely the aggressor since Mary was only involved as the innocent victim of the scandals surrounding the break-up of the Shrewsbury ménage. The Shrewsbury marriage troubles seem to have started some time after the death of Shrewsbury's son, Gilbert Talbot, in 1582; property was at the root of their quarrels. Now in her efforts to get the best of the dispute, Bess cast about her in her well-filled mental armoury and decided to accuse

---

* Despite her royal lineage, and the glorious plans laid for her future, Arbella Stuart never lived to enjoy the splendid destiny which might have been expected for one who combined the genes of the Stuarts with those of Bess of Hardwicke. At the age of thirty, no suitable bridegroom having been found for her, she eloped with William Seymour, grandson of Lady Catherine Grey. For this presumption, she was imprisoned in the Tower by her cousin, King James, where she died in 1615.

her husband of scandalous relations with his prisoner
Mary Queen of Scots. It was a sharp-edged weapon indeed; it was typical of Bess's clever but unscrupulous tac-
tics that she picked the accusation most likely to em-
barrass and wound her husband where it hurt—in his area
of public service. Such charges horrified Shrewsbury, for
they would surely confirm all the old rumours that he was
as a jailer too favourably disposed towards the queen of
Scots. Blown up by rumours, the scandal ballooned outwards. A certain John Palmer went on record as saying
at St James's Palace that the queen of Scots had borne
two bastard children to Lord Shrewsbury, and had to
make a public submission in consequence.[20] One Babs-
thorpe wrote a book full of lewd speeches on the subject,
and Shrewsbury was eventually allowed to sue him, although Elizabeth attempted to stop the case under the statute of *scandalum magnatum*.

Mary herself was indignant and furious. Her honour was
outraged and she persistently demanded that she should
be allowed to come to court to clear herself: it was like
the conference of Westminster all over again to her sensitive spirit—there was Bess at liberty in London spreading
malicious stories, and yet Mary was not even allowed the
opportunity to appear and contradict them. In a long letter
to Elizabeth in October 1584 she demanded that Bess and
her son Charles Cavendish should be publicly examined
and their servants examined also and then punished for
spreading such slanders; to Walsingham, Mary threatened
to make known the evil-doing of *'la bonne Comptesse'*, as
she sarcastically termed Bess, to all the princes of Chris-
tianity.[21] In the end Bess's calumnies proved too much for
Mary's self-control; in November she wrote a long and
burning letter to Elizabeth not only rebutting Bess's
charges against her, but, more to the point, detailing all
the many salacious stories which Bess had spread about
Elizabeth in the past. Mary described how Bess had been
wont to regale the household of Chatsworth and elsewhere
in days gone by with cruel stories of Elizabeth's vanity,
and shocking stories of her immorality. Elizabeth believed
herself to be so beautiful that she resembled a goddess of
the skies—how Bess and the countess of Lennox had
laughed at her behind her back! Mary had often heard
Elizabeth treated as *'une comédie'* even in the presence of
her own waiting-women. This ridiculous monster of vanity

had also been described as lying in bed with Leicester many times and, among other scandals, taking the wretched Christopher Hatton by force. Bess was supposed to have joined disloyalty to ridicule and scandal-making: Mary also retailed how delightful Bess had been when Elizabeth fell ill because this fulfilled an astrological prediction that Elizabeth would soon be dead and Mary reigning in her place, after which James and Arbella would succeed as king and queen.[22] It is easy to believe that most of this unsavoury scandal had indeed tripped off Bess's tongue in the course of those female conversations in Bess's chamber; private conversation of a gossiping nature never looks particularly pretty set down much later and Bess's tales were no exception. As for Mary's part in passing on all this stale and unprofitable abuse, it seems that even despite provocation she had second thoughts after she had written the letter. There is no evidence that Elizabeth, to whom it was addressed, ever read this bombshell: it was found later among the Cecil papers, and although it is possible that Cecil himself intercepted it before it reached the queen, the most likely explanation seems to be that Mary herself, like so many writers, reconsidered the letter after she had exhausted her venom with her pen, and kept it among her own papers without ever sending it. From here it would have been seized with the rest of her correspondence at Chartley in 1586.

There was certainly no grain of truth in all these rumours as Lady Shrewsbury and her daughter subsequently admitted to the English Council. Mary had by now a sufficient reputation as a *femme fatale* to be the natural target for such fabricated arrows. John Palmer's stories of bastard children by Shrewsbury may be seen as being the last of a long progression of such philoprogenitive rumours throughout Mary Stuart's life, which if all had been true would have made her instead of the lioness with her one whelp the mother of a sizeable family.* Shrewsbury was not immune to Mary's charm any more than had been Knollys, White or even Cecil himself; he had known her over a long period of time in circumstances of

* Even Elizabeth, the virgin queen, was not left free of this sort of imaginative calumny. In November 1575 the Venetian ambassador in Spain reported that Elizabeth had a natural daughter of thirteen in existence, who was about to marry Cecil's son, and thus cement their relations.[23]

great intimacy. One can understand that such propinquity, coupled with the kindness Shrewsbury generally showed to Mary, may have led to moments of gentleness between them, even tenderness, especially as the femininity of Mary must have contrasted forcibly with the masculinity of Bess, who was in any case the elder of the two by twenty years. But for Shrewsbury to seek to give this tenderness such as it was any sort of external expression beyond relaxation of the conditions of captivity, would have been quite out of keeping with his character. The queen of Scots might present a charming picture to him as she sat there plying her needle, but when it came to the prospect of physical relations with her she was terrifying to him as the Giant Hop O'Thumb's daughter in the fairy story, with the shadow of Elizabeth hanging over them in the role of the vengeful Giant. Mendoza was probably nearer summing up Shrewsbury's true feelings when he said that the earl was only too grateful to Elizabeth for delivering him from two demons—his wife and the queen of Scots.[24]

For reasons other than the seedy domestic wrangles of the Shrewsburys, Mary was being conducted remorselessly down the path which led to closer conditions of imprisonment. She herself at one point hesitated to complain too forcibly about the Shrewsbury scandal, lest she should be removed from his charge altogether and placed in the hands of a far more severe jailer. It was a valid fear. But even without the malice of Bess, Mary's days with Shrewsbury were numbered, due to external conditions in England over which she once more had no control. The effects of the papal bull of excommunication against Elizabeth, promulgated in 1570, only began to be properly felt towards the end of the decade when the reconversion of England was attempted once more from abroad; a trickle and then a faster flow of Jesuit missionaries, many of them Englishmen returning after training abroad, made this cause their own.* There were differences of temperament among the missionaries themselves, who ranged from men of incandescent faith and sanctity, such as Edmund Campion, to

* By 1582 the Jesuits had reached Staffordshire, close to where Mary lay; in the same year the Staffordshire county records show the first really large-scale prosecution of the recusants at the Easter sessions of the peace.[25]

the more diplomatic-minded missionaries, such as Robert Persons, who had contacts in every European capital. Both men arrived in England in 1580, although Persons subsequently went on to Spain from where, from knowledge gained during his visit, he suggested Catholicism should be restored in England by force rather than pure missionary fervour.

The appearance of these rekindlers of Catholic flames in English hearts had a two-fold effect: in the first place the English Catholics themselves became more sanguine and therefore more zealous; secondly the English government tightened up the laws against the recusants (those who refused to attend the official Protestant services once a week), increased the fines, which became heavy from 1577 onwards, and using the double-edge weapon of the papal excommunication, began to blur the distinction between recusant and rebel. The English Catholics themselves were divided by many gradations of feeling, apart from the Faith which united them. There were many English Catholics who, although they declined to abandon the faith of their fathers at the orders of Parliament, yet equally declined to forfeit their loyalty to their Queen Elizabeth at the instigation of the Pope. It was just these Catholics whom it was now possible for the English government to brand as rebels, using the papal bull as proof. As one of their number, the eloquent Jesuit missionary Father William Weston himself, wrote, these were now bitter days, filled with immeasurable suffering for the English Catholic community: 'Catholics now saw their own country, the country of their birth, turned into a ruthless and unloving land.'[26]

In view of the delicate situation of England, perpetually facing the prospect of a Spanish invasion, it was a natural act of public relations on the part of the government to seek to present the Catholics from 1580 onwards as dangerous aliens within the state. The Act of Persuasions, by which it was made high treason to reconcile or be reconciled to the Catholic faith, was passed in 1581. In 1585 it was further made high treason for a Jesuit to set foot in England. Just as the dangers to England from the Catholics were constantly emphasized, so too the personal danger of Queen Elizabeth was underlined in order to boost her popularity with her subjects, as a symbol of national solidarity. Both moves—early exercises in the subtle art of

propaganda—augured of course extremely ill for the future
of the queen of Scots, who was both a Catholic and a rival
queen to Elizabeth. To the forefront of this calculated
campaign was the leading secretary of state, Sir Francis
Walsingham. Walsingham was a prominent Puritan; but
he drew, as he said himself, a sharp and effective distinction between private and public morality, and had no intention of bringing the strict tenets of the Puritan faith into
the latter sphere. He was an experienced diplomatist, with
a useful knowledge of Europe, having been employed by
Elizabeth on missions to both the Low Countries and
France; and in 1583 he was sent on a mission to James in
Scotland. Walsingham also combined to a remarkable
degree the political abilities of an Italian Renaissance
statesman with a very modern conception of the uses of
a spy system within the state.*

Walsingham understood to perfection the art not only
of forgery but also of permeating his enemies' organiza-
tions with his own men—an art which often led to such
confusion of plotting at the time that the truth is impossible to disentangle at four hundred years' distance. Walsingham now managed to place at least one and probably more spies in the heart of Mary's councils in Paris.
In view of this fact, it was not surprising that Mary's
reputation became increasingly besmirched in the English
mind and in that of Elizabeth, as a result of each of the
three plots against her which were uncovered in the 1580s
before the final crisis of the Babington plot. The first of
these plots, the Throckmorton plot, was apparently Guise-
inspired, although right at the centre of it lay one of Walsingham's most successful agents, Charles Paget. Paget
came of a noble family, one of whose houses, Beaudesert,
was in Staffordshire. His elder brother Thomas, Lord
Paget, was a devout Catholic who refused to take the Oath
of Conformity, and was eventually obliged to flee to
France in 1583, although up till this time he had been

---

* Walsingham had already showed his enterprising attitude to the
production of compromising evidence at the time of the conference
of Westminster: he offered to Cecil 'that if for the discovery of the
Queen of Scots consent to the murder of her husband, there lack
sufficient proofs, he is able (if it shall please you to use him) to discover certain that should have been employed in the said murder'
in London.[27]

kindly treated by his friends at court who had attempted
to persuade him into wiser courses: indeed much of his
desire to leave England seems to have arisen not only
from his professed religion, but from his troubles with his
vociferous wife Nazareth, Lady Paget.[28] Charles Paget was,
on the other hand, an outright spy, who entered Walsingham's service secretly in 1581 when he reached Paris, at
roughly the same moment that he entered the little Marian embassy of Archbishop Beaton.

The Throckmorton plot, uncovered by Walsingham's
agents, led in November 1583 to the arrest of Francis
Throckmorton, a Catholic cousin of Sir Nicholas, on suspicion of carrying letters to and from Mary; the earl of
Northumberland was also placed in the Tower for being
implicated. The details of the Throckmorton plot involved
once more the invasion of England by Spain, and the release of Mary; Throckmorton, who had acted as messenger throughout, made a very full confession before his
execution in which he thoroughly implicated the queen.
She was said to have known every detail of the invasion
plans. Mary had certainly written encouraging letters to
the Spanish ambassador, who was banished for his part
in it all; but the true details of this invasion scheme are
still obscure, since it seems that Charles Paget in the
course of a short visit to England secretly poured cold
water on the scheme to Northumberland, having first of all
tried in vain to dissuade the duke of Guise from asking
for Spanish help.[29] In view of the troubles which Paget was
also brewing up in France, it is doubtful whether such a
scheme penetrated by a double-agent could ever have come
to very much; nevertheless, the discovery of the plot gave
Walsingham an excellent opportunity to excite a wave of
popular indignation against the Catholics, and their figure-
head, Mary.

Despite Throckmorton's revelations, and despite the fact
that Mary had clearly the details of the intended plot,
Mary herself was in fact at this point no longer in complete sympathy with her Guise relations or indeed with
her ambassador of so many years, James Beaton. One of
the cruellest aspects of Mary's last years from her own
point of view was that while Walsingham was engaged in
building up her image as this dangerous conspirator, the
spider at the centre of a network of plans with agents at
every foreign Catholic court, Mary herself was actually

becoming increasingly alienated from her own organization abroad. She was accused increasingly in the popular
imagination of crimes in which she was decreasingly involved. From 1583 onwards her relations with her ambassador Beaton were distinctly cool, and by the Autumn
of 1584 she actually accused him openly of mishandling
her finances, regretting that such an old servant should
choose this opportunity to treat her so shabbily.[30] She
believed that in France Beaton's wishes rather than hers
were being considered and that her other servants were
being mistreated.

Such complaints were not merely the querulous imaginings of a middle-aged woman who had been too long in
captivity. It was true that the handling of Mary's organization in France, and her finances in particular, left much
to be desired. Much of the muddle and maladministration
was due to the earlier actions of Mary's uncle, the cardinal
of Lorraine, who appears to have had little grasp of
finance. This dowry, so vital to Mary's existence, since it
represented her only income, was further impaired by the
actions of the king of France, who obliged her to exchange the profitable estates in Touraine, granted to her
under her marriage settlement, for others much less profitable, in favour of his brother, the duke of Anjou. The
income itself of 2,000 crowns which she took yearly for
personal expenses in England does not always seem to
have been paid regularly: at Mary's death the king of
France still owed her money. French officials battened
upon the estates, an easy enough action to perform without speedy retribution, since their owner was both abroad
and in prison. In 1580 the foolish or knavish Dolu was
replaced as Mary's treasurer by Chérelles's brother: but
even so by this time the French estates had a mortgage of
33,000 crowns upon them. Although it was believed that
if Mary put her dowry out to farm she would be able to
get 30,000 crowns yearly, the encumbrance of the mortgage was a fatal obstacle to this scheme. Mary was compelled to raise loans in London to pay for her necessities
in captivity: she borrowed money from de Mauvissière on
credit, and another loan was later arranged from Arundel,
which was only repaid after Mary's death by the king of
Spain, out of respect for her memory. Financial shortages,
the humiliation of not being able to pay for small luxuries
to be brought her from London as well as not being able

to grant *baillages* from her French estates to repay creditors freely, owing to the interference of the French court,
were naturally all exacerbating to Mary, who could do
little in prison except fire off anguished letters. But although she came to blame Beaton, he seems to have been
the least of the offenders in this respect. Furthermore, the
evidence points to the fact that there was a distinct campaign to create trouble between Mary and Beaton, a campaign once more all the more dangerous because it was
directed from within rather than without her organization.

Into Beaton's service had come in the late 1570s a certain Thomas Morgan, who had once been Shrewsbury's
secretary in the early days of Mary's imprisonment: he was
a friend of Walsingham's chief agent Phelippes and his
Catholicism was doubtful; most of the English Catholic
exiles seem to have regarded him as a spy and the fact
that it was he who introduced the arch spy Gilbert Gifford into Mary's service certainly tells against him.[31] Nevertheless, he managed to capitalize on the friendliness he
had once shown to Mary—perhaps he convinced her he
had been dismissed from Shrewsbury's service for helping her—to enlist her sympathy, and she regarded him as
'poor Morgan'. Although she did not recommend him to
Beaton personally, she endorsed his application and, at
different times, with her habitual sympathy for the financial plight of her servants, made him grants of money.
Morgan became Beaton's chief cipher clerk, a position of
enormous trust, since it put him in virtual control of the
French correspondence with Mary. But Morgan, although
trusted by Mary, was soon regarded as suspect in France.
According to the later testimony of Father Robert Persons, neither Morgan nor Paget was fully trusted with the
invasion plans of 1583, 'fearing lest they might hold secret
correspondence with some of the Council in England, although the said Queen trusted in them contrary to the
wish and opinion of the said Duke of [Guise] and Archbishop ambassadors'.*[32]

* At this point quite a separate dispute, originating at Rome in
1578, between English Jesuits and the English secular priests (called
the Welsh faction after their leader Dr Owen Lewis) was also spreading through the English Catholic community abroad and affecting
the trust of Jesuits and seculars. See Leo Hicks, *An Elizabethan
Problem*, for a detailed examination of the subject, in relation to
Morgan and Mary.

It was tragic that Mary's service should thus be permeated with spies and trouble-makers at this critical moment in her fortunes. From the tone of her own letters, certainly, her relations with Beaton seem to have been temporarily impaired, at the very moment when she had most need to be in complete accord with him. Such discord would have been only too easy for Morgan as cipher clerk to whip up. For example Mary's outspoken complaint that Beaton had not written to her for six months may easily have been due not to Beaton's neglect—which was unlike him—but to the suppression of his letters by his clerk. This trouble-making had two effects: as Samerie, the Jesuit chaplain who visited her secretly three times in prison and was devoted to her cause, warned Mary in October 1584, there were dangers in trusting such men as Morgan and Paget: 'You wish to have too many manners of proceeding,' he wrote, 'which clearly they know', and he advised her to abandon all private ways of dealing and treat of all her affairs through her ambassadors.[33] It was excellent advice, based on sound knowledge of Mary's predilection for intrigue. Unfortunately this advice did not stick. In March 1585 Ragazzini, the nuncio, told the cardinal of Como: 'This Morgan is considered by many here and particularly the Jesuits, to be a knave; yet the Queen of Scots relies upon him more than on her own ambassador [Beaton] as the ambassador himself has told me many times.'[34]

The second result of such dispute within Mary's organization was that her own feelings towards the Guises and Spain became permeated with distrust: she began to be convinced that the Guises were only intending to seize England in order to hand it over to Spain, and had no interest in her release. The prospect of losing touch with reality over the years is one which every long-term prisoner has to face. In Mary's case, at the exact moment when her struggles to free herself through the Association were crumbling about her, and the need to concentrate on the aid of Spain and the Guises grew more acute, she became the prey of false notions on the subject and grew to rely more on private schemes than on Beaton.

By January 1585, when the Association was virtually dead as a practical scheme, Mary was murmuring against Spain. She was indeed profoundly shocked by the new plot now uncovered in which a Dr Parry apparently intended to assassinate Elizabeth. Her horror was probably genuine; for she expressed it in a letter not only to Elizabeth herself, but also to her ally, the French ambassador in London.[35] When Parry proved to be implicated with her own agent in Paris, the wily Thomas Morgan, Mary could scarcely believe the news. Mary was quite right to be horrified by the news of the Parry plot, for it seems that Parry began his career as an *agent provocateur* for the Elizabethan government, and was only now sacrificed by his employers for propaganda reasons. Even without this inner knowledge, Mary was quite clever enough to see the dangers of such involvements: the plots of Parry against Elizabeth would always point indirectly at Mary, but the involvement of Parry with Morgan enabled the plot to be laid squarely at her door. In France, Morgan was put in prison for his part in the Parry plot. It was no wonder that Mary hastened to express her indignation. She was sympathetic towards the Jesuit Father Creighton who was captured aboard ship with a whole pile of incriminating letters and documents: she asked the French ambassador to see what could be done for the wretched man, to save him from destruction.[36] Parry on the other hand clearly brought her own neck into danger.

The point was all the more easy for Mary to appreciate since from June 1584 onwards there had been murmurings in Parliament for a new type of Association— not to be confused with Mary's Association with James— in this case a bond or pledge of allegiance. But this was a pledge with a difference. It was not enough for the signatories of this new bond to swear to bring about the death of all those who might plot against Elizabeth. In addition they also swore—and the inspiration was Walsingham's— to bring about the death of all those in whose favour such plots might be instigated, whether they had personally connived at them or not. In short, if it could be proved that a particular conspiracy had been aimed at the elimination of Elizabeth and the placing of Mary on the throne, Mary herself was as much eligible for execution as any of the plotters, even if she had been in complete ignorance of what was afoot. This bond was formally enacted into a statute by the English Parliament in the spring of 1585 when the murder of the prince of Orange brought home still further to the English the constant dangers of assassination to their own queen: in the meantime signatures

poured in from loyal subjects, and were presented to Elizabeth in an endless series of documents, from the autumn
onwards. Mary, ever conscious of the delicate path she
was treading, and the need for Elizabeth's favour, actually
offered to sign the bond herself.[37] But her pathetic offer
could not gloss over the fact that the enactment of the
bond into English law amounted to the drawing up of her
own death warrant: it was hardly likely that many years
would pass before some conspiracy or other in Mary's favour, to the detriment of Elizabeth, would be brought to
book by Walsingham: once such a charge should be
proved, it was now legal in England to try and execute
the Scottish queen. No one was more conscious of the
dangers of the bond to Mary than Elizabeth herself, and
the possibility of the trial of a crowned queen was one
Elizabeth preferred not to contemplate too closely in advance:[38] she therefore chose to regard the bond of Association as a spontaneous act of loyalty on the part of her
people in the first place, of whose genesis she had been
quite ignorant. In the parliamentary proceedings which
followed, she began by showing considerable reluctance
that the statute for her safety should be enacted at all and
went on to take care that James VI should be excepted
from the clause which debarred even the descendants of
the nameless beneficiary of her murder from the succession. Parliament itself, understandably less worried by the
problem of regicide, showed no such scruples. To them
the bond seemed only too natural, as well as essential. In
1572 when Mary's life had been in danger, the whys and
wherefores of her captivity, her original illegal detention,
had seemed already remote: but thirteen years later they
appeared positively prehistoric. The 'monstrous dragon'
was now considered to be part of the English policy—and
a singularly unpleasant part.

By the spring of 1585 there was very little that was encouraging to be discerned in the situation of the queen of
Scots. Her son had repudiated and betrayed her; her
French organization was in administrative chaos, and
penetrated by Walsingham's spies; the English Catholics
were quarrelling among themselves abroad and increasingly persecuted at home; Mary herself no longer felt
complete trust for her erstwhile allies abroad and at
times suspected the good faith of the Guises and Spain; in
the meantime her position in England may be compared

to that of someone tied down unwillingly over a powder
keg, which may at any moment be exploded by a match
held by an over-enthusiastic friend. To add to Mary's distress her prison was changed for the worse. In September
1584 she had been taken out of the custody of Shrewsbury
and handed into that of the upright and elderly Sir Ralph
Sadler. The real reason for the change was presumably to
free Mary from the imbroglio of the Shrewsbury scandals:
but according to Camden, in order not to offend Shrewsbury it was explained to him that Catholic plots now made
it essential for Mary to be put in charge of the Puritans.[39]
Sadler was a fair and considerate jailer. But in the autumn
of 1584 the edict went forth that Mary was to be taken
back to the hated Tutbury for greater security. She was
once more incarcerated in this loathsome if impregnable
fortress in early January 1585. Not only that but at the
same time the care of her person was handed over to a
new and infinitely more severe jailer, Sir Amyas Paulet,
who became in time as odious to her as the masonry of
Tutbury itself. Under these doleful circumstances, with
very little to cheer her as she surveyed her prospects for
the future, Mary Stuart entered on the last and most
burdensome phase of her captivity.

24 *The Babington Plot*

'The spring is past and yet it is not sprung;
The fruit is dead, and yet the leaves be green;
My youth is gone, and yet I am but young;
I saw the world and yet I was not seen;
My thread is cut, and yet it is not spun;
And now I live and now my life is done.'

CHIDIOCK TICHBORNE, *one of the Babington conspirators;
written while in the Tower of London, awaiting death*

The harsh character of Sir Amyas Paulet, Mary's new
jailer, was apparent from his very first action. This was
to take down from above her head and chair that royal
cloth of state by which she set such store, since it constituted a proof of her queenship. Paulet's reasoning was
that as the cloth of state had never been officially allowed,
it must be removed, however long it had been there. Mary
first wept and protested vigorously, then retired to her
chamber in a mood of great offence; finally she secured the
return of the dais. The incident was typical of the man,
who believed profoundly in the letter of the law: 'There
is no other way to do good to this people than to begin
roundly with them . . . whatsoever liberty or anything
else is once granted unto them cannot be drawn back
again without great exclamation', he wrote to London.[1]
Paulet came of a west country family, and his father had
been the governor of Jersey. He himself had been English
ambassador to the French court for three years, but had
otherwise not enjoyed a particularly distinguished career;
he was certainly not of the high rank of a Shrewsbury, or a
diplomat of great age and experience such as Sir Ralph
Sadler, whom he replaced. But he had been specially selected by Walsingham for the task in hand, because, as all
his contemporaries agreed, he was not only a prominent
Puritan but also a mortal enemy of the queen of Scots
and all she stood for. Walsingham understood his man;
Paulet was quite immune to the charms of the queen of
Scots and, unlike Knollys and even Cecil, found her irri-

tating and even tiresome as a character. Since honour and
loyalty were his gods, and these Mary Stuart seemed to
offend with every action, Paulet's Puritan conscience allowed him to hate her in advance. When they actually
met, Paulet was able to transform charms into wiles in his
own mind; like Knox so many years before, he disliked
his captive all the more for her possible attractions.

Paulet's instructions from London were clear: Mary's
imprisonment was to be transformed into the strictest possible confinement. She was not even to be allowed to take
the air, that terrible deprivation which she dreaded so
much, 'for that heretofore under colour of giving alms
and other extraordinary courses used by her, she hath won
the hearts of the people that habit about those places
where she hath heretofore lain . . .'.[2] In particular her
sources of untapped private letters and messages were to
be stopped once and for all; the only letters she was to be
allowed to receive were those from the French ambassador
in London—and these Paulet read in any case and stopped
at will, as he thought proper. At no point in her captivity
so far had Mary been cut off so completely. Her correspondence with Beaton, her ambassador in Paris, Morgan,
Paget and her other foreign agents, had depended on a
secret pipeline of letters, without which no foreign plotting could have taken place. During the whole of 1585,
under the orders of the Elizabethan government, this pipeline was shut off, and Mary was totally deprived of the
news she wanted so much.

Paulet achieved this isolation—which had a calculated
position in Walsingham's scheme for Mary Stuart's downfall—by the most rigorous supervision of the Scottish
queen's domestic arrangements. There were naturally to
be no more pleasant sojourns at Buxton; on her last visit
in the summer of 1584, still under the aegis of Shrewsbury, Mary had some premonition of this, for she wrote
with a diamond on a window-pane at the springs:

> *Buxtona, quae calida celebriris nomine Lymphae*
> *Forte mihi post hac non adeunda, Vale**

Mary complained furiously to Elizabeth of Paulet's de-

---

* *Buxton, whose warm waters have made thy name famous, per-*
chance I shall visit thee no more—Farewell.

meanour: she described him as being more fit to act as
the jailer of a common criminal than of a crowned queen.
But Elizabeth merely replied smoothly that Mary had
often professed herself ready to accept whatever served
Elizabeth best; in which case she would surely accept
Paulet.[3] In the meantime conditions under Paulet were
very different from the easy days under Shrewsbury. Not
only was Mary herself not allowed to ride abroad but
Mary's coachman Sharp was not allowed to ride out without permission, and then he had to be accompanied. He
was also deprived of the privilege of dining with Paulet's
servants, as he had done with Sadler's. Paulet also went
at great lengths into the difficult and, to him, vexatious
subject of the royal laundresses. These elusive maidens,
under the pretext of carrying out their work, had carried
on a merry trade of message-bearing; what was more,
two of them turned out to be the coachman Sharp's sister and sister-in-law. Paulet's Puritanical brow furrowed
over the subject of the laundresses, and at one point, de-
spairing of finding cooperation in their midst, thought of
importing some more malleable creatures from Somerset.
It was an easier matter to prohibit all Mary's servants
from walking on the thick walls of Tutbury (where they
could wave, it was thought, in an enlightening manner,
to passers-by). Another domestic change—of significance
for the future—was that the brewer of beer and ale
for the castle was installed at near-by Burton, with his
family.*

Mary's little private charities in which she had delighted, and by which she endeared herself to the local
people, were sternly quelled by Paulet. His crushing comment—more applicable perhaps to the modern welfare
state than to the Elizabethan polity—was that the laws of
the realm had provided so carefully for the relief of the
poor that no one could want for anything except through
their own 'lewdness' or the negligence of the officers of
several parishes. Mary said plaintively that she was ill in
body or in mind, that she depended on the prayers of the
poor to support her, and that it was barbarous to restrain

* The obtaining of beer for domestic consumption was an important item in Elizabethan housekeeping. It has been estimated that
a population of four millions consumed eighteen million barrels of
beer annually, three quarters of it brewed privately.[4]

her, but she did not get her way. Mary had a habit of presenting cloth to the poor on Maundy Thursday—in 1585 forty-two girls received 1¼ yards of woollen cloth and eighteen little boys, specified to be out of respect for her own son, were similarly endowed. Money was also given to the poor at Tutbury town. Paulet was furious to learn of such goings on and demanded that they should cease; he said that such unpleasant practices might not be new to Mary, but they were certainly new to him.

In June there was further trouble over the arrangements for feeding Mary's horses and Paulet grumbled that it was all due to the fact that the Cavendishes had all become far too friendly with the queen over the years. Paulet also tried to prevent Mary from making any personal payments to the Tutbury servants, since this would give her an opportunity of secretly bribing them. As a result, his own accounts underwent a financial crisis, augmented by the rocketing food prices in England at the time. 'This Queen's servants are always craving, and have no pity at all on English purses,' wrote Paulet angrily.[5] There was indeed apparently no end to the lack of consideration Mary's servants were prepared to show: when Bastian's wife Christina gave birth to a child, Paulet had to deal with the problem of a midwife, who might so easily try to slip secret messages in or out. Furthermore, the queen's waiting-woman, Barbara Mowbray,* who had married Gilbert Curle in October 1585 (Paulet suspected they had been married by a priest disguised as one of Mary's French 'readers') showed every sign of being about to produce a child herself.

Such domestic worries harried Paulet. But he stuck manfully to his duties, and executed them with as much if not more strictness than the government requested. How hopelessly optimistic then was Thomas Morgan's suggestion from the safety of Paris that Mary should try to bribe Paulet to accord her further liberty, by hinting that on her liberation he would be given virtual autonomy in Jersey where he was hereditary governor; this was not at all the stuff of which Paulet was made. This renewed so-

* Barbara Mowbray was one of the two daughters of the laird of Barnbogle who served Mary Queen of Scots. She had joined her service by the beginning of 1584. About the time of her marriage, her sister Gillis Mowbray applied to join her in the royal service and was duly given a passport.

journ at damp and draughty Tutbury thoroughly broke
down Queen Mary's system, and her pleas for a change of
air grew pitiful, as she wrote of the wind which whistled
through the thin wooden walls into every corner of her
chamber. Yet it is clear from Paulet's letter-books that
he felt no sympathy with her ill-health, and seems to have
regarded it as just retribution for her sins. In his attitude
to her religious beliefs, he showed, to put it at its kindest,
the total incomprehension of the bigot, who can see nothing fine or even sincere in the convictions of those with
whom they do not agree; and some of his actions or attempted actions on the subject even verged on the sadistic,
as when he tried to burn a packet sent to Mary from
Chérelles in London because it was full of 'abominable
trash'—including rosaries, pictures in silk marked with
the words *Agnus Dei* and other comparatively harmless
by-products of the Catholic religion. All in all, Paulet may
be said to have justified Mary's own description of him
as 'one of the strangest and most *farouche* men she had
ever known'.[6]

However, in the autumn of 1585 it was the protests
of the French court to Elizabeth, rather than the compassion of Paulet, which led to the search for a new
prison for Mary Stuart. Not only was Mary's health itself weakened, but the famous middens of Tutbury were
stinking to high heaven. Various Staffordshire residences
were proposed, including Tixall, the home of Sir Walter
Aston. But Sir Walter was a magistrate, and as it was by
no means considered an honour to have a house chosen as
a royal prison—rather the reverse—Paulet recommended
against it, on the grounds that Aston was one of the few
loyal men in 'this infected shire' and it would be a pity
to forfeit his affections.[7] Chillington, home of the Gifford
family, was well furnished but lacked brew-houses; on the
other hand Beaudesert, the Paget home, lacked furniture.
Burton was too near a river, and Sir Thomas Gerard's
house (which Mary favoured) too small. In the end the
lot fell upon Chartley Hall, an Elizabethan manor-house
belonging to the young earl of Essex, with a large moat
round it, which made it suitable for security reasons.
However, at this point the young Essex protested violently
against his mansion being used for this dishonourable
purpose. Chartley had certainly been the scene of more
chivalresque occasions: Queen Elizabeth herself had vis-

ited it during a round of summer visits with Leicester, and coming on from the famous festival of Kenilworth, had been entertained there by Lettice, Lady Essex. Chartley had romantic associations also: for it was there that Philip Sidney had first glimpsed Essex's sister, the thirteen-year-old Penelope Devereux, the inspiration of his muse, the Stella of his sonnets. Now Essex feared that all the trees on his estates would be cut down to warm the queen of Scots, and he also, more neurotically—if less plausibly —dreaded the damage she might do to the house deliberately, because she had hated his father (since the days when he had commanded the troops which guarded her at Tutbury), and was now said to have transferred this dislike to him.

Essex's protests managed to delay Mary's departure for Chartley throughout the autumn; but Paulet himself greatly approved of the change, especially as the amount of water round the house meant that the over-spirited laundresses would have less excuse for passing in and out of the gates as they went about their work. On Christmas Eve the journey was finally made. On arrival Mary found herself so reduced in health that she fell severely ill, and even Paulet found himself 'for charity's sake' bound to pass on her complaints about her bed which she said was 'stained and ill-flavoured'; he recommended the down bed which she herself requested.[8] On this occasion Mary was obliged to keep to her bed for more than four weeks, and it was towards the end of March, eight or nine weeks later, before she felt any real improvement, from the 'painful defluxions' which plagued her. It was scarcely to be wondered at that her own servants were gravely worried for her, and feared that the move from Tutbury might have come too late to save her.

While considerations of the queen's health appeared to engross the Chartley household, deep and very different currents were swirling beneath the surface of its domestic pattern. Walsingham took the opportunity of the move from Tutbury to Chartley to mount a new stage in his campaign to incriminate the queen of Scots. His aim was of course to provide England—and Elizabeth—with sufficient evidence to prove once and for all that it was too dangerous to keep Mary alive. Already the bond of Association passed through Parliament the previous year meant that a plot had only to be made in favour of the queen of Scots—rather than by her—and she would by English law merit the death penalty. Now Walsingham, through his many and devious agents, set about enmeshing Mary in two separate conspiracies against Elizabeth, which together made up the complicated and in part bogus machinations which are known as the Babington plot.

These machinations had two separate strands. In the first place there was the plot—whether genuine or not—to assassinate the English queen. Secondly, there was the plot to rescue the Scottish queen from captivity. In both cases, or in any combination of these two plans, foreign aid in the shape of a foreign invasion of England was absolutely essential for success: although Queen Elizabeth might fall a victim of the assassin's dagger, unless these assassins had sufficient resources to rescue Queen Mary immediately, they might find that by the time they reached her place of imprisonment, their candidate for the English throne had either been killed by her captors or else spirited away. In any case the English Catholics could not carry through such a revolution alone. This was a point which was thoroughly appreciated not only by all the level-headed conspirators, but also pre-eminently by Mary Queen of Scots herself, who never stopped stressing the danger to her personally of an amateur plan (as she had done many years before when Gerard and the Stanleys had thought of rescuing her). It was one of Walsingham's most subtle moves to make his agents at all points exaggerate the possibility of this foreign aid, generally supposed to be Spanish. In this way the English conspirators were led to believe that a Spanish invasion was certain, and so travelled even further along the road towards fruition of their plans. The Catholic parties abroad were on the other hand given the impression that the plans and numbers of possible English Catholic insurgents were far more stabilized and numerous than in fact they were. Although Mary, from her prison, emphasized in every letter that a Spanish invasion was a *sine qua non* of a successful rescue, these constant pleas in her letters were quite ineffective compared to the havoc wrought among the Catholic conspirators by the fact that so many of their numbers were actually renegades, secretly in the pay of the English government.

One false agent in a chain of correspondence can cast a

completely different slant on a whole subject: the pre-
liminaries of the Babington plot involved not only Charles
Paget and Thomas Morgan, but also a new Walsingham
double-agent—Gilbert Gifford—at their very heart. The
assassination plot against Elizabeth, which is at first sight
a dastardly conspiracy to kill the English queen, changes
character as it becomes clear that much of the plot consisted of mere provocation by which Walsingham hoped
to entangle Mary. The first stages of the intrigue which
ended in Mary's downfall did not in fact involve Babington and his associates at all, but merely the protagonists
of this earlier and dubious assassination plot. These were
Gilbert Gifford, his cousin George Gifford, a failed priest
of simple nature who was much under Gilbert's influence
named John Savage, and a more lively ordained priest,
Ballard, who was in close touch with Thomas Morgan,
and who had come to believe in his own political mission
to overthrow Elizabeth. The key figure in these early
plottings was Gilbert Gifford. He came from an ancient,
still Catholic family whose main seat was at Chillington in
Staffordshire; his cousin George came from a Hampshire
branch of the same family, but in neither case was the
possession of an honourable name any guarantee of in-
tegrity. Gilbert Gifford indeed seems to have had that
peculiar subtle turn of mind which actually enjoys spying
for spying's sake; he had gone abroad as a Catholic in
1577, had joined the English college at Rome to train as
a priest, been expelled, and then roamed Europe before
being innocently received back into the fold by Dr William
Allen, head of the English College at Rheims. With his
talents—not only was he highly intelligent but also an
excellent linguist—he knew how to make a strong impression on his friends so that he easily drew over the weaker
characters to his way of thinking, however tortuous. By
the time he landed in England in December 1585, he
had become thoroughly involved in the detailed matters of
Mary's correspondence abroad, and let into the secret of
all the new conspiracies to free her. On landing, however,
he was apprehended and taken before Walsingham: and
it was at this point that the details of their secret compact were arranged. It is not necessary to suppose that
Walsingham had planned the meeting in advance; as one
historian has put it, the probabilities seem to be that the
opportunity suggested the expedient.[9]

The first time it was known by Mary's supporters that some change in her isolated and news-deprived condition might be expected was when this same Gifford presented himself at the French embassy. The new ambassador who had replaced Castelnau de Mauvissière was Guillaume de l'Aubespine, baron de Châteauneuf; but Gifford was actually seen by Cordaillot, a secretary at the embassy. The secret letters from Morgan which could no longer be smuggled into the Scottish queen had been piling up at the embassy for the whole year. Now Gifford offered to get packets to Mary, saying that no one in Staffordshire was likely to recognize him, not even his father or his sister, since he had been abroad for so long; as he still looked strangely young, his real identity would remain unsuspected. This story hardly matched with his earlier offer to make a perfectly legitimate visit to Staffordshire on the excuse of seeing his father: and according to Châteauneuf's later statement,[10] the French embassy themselves never totally trusted Gifford, especially when he turned out to be lodging in London with Thomas Phelippes, one of Walsingham's chief agents, and an expert decipherer. Nevertheless, whatever Châteauneuf's inner suspicions, the die was cast. Thomas Morgan's letters were entrusted to Gifford. On 16 January 1586, to her unimaginable joy, Mary Stuart received the first secret communication she had had for over a year. Not only that, but she was informed that the same strange pipeline by which the packet had come—the local brewer—could be used to smuggle out her own notes.

The secret battle for the incrimination of the Scottish queen was now engaged. Mary was aware that Phelippes, Walsingham's arch agent had already paid a visit to Chartley to see Paulet, for she had passed some disparaging remarks on his character and his personal appearance; unfortunately she did not realize that the object of Phelippes' visit had been to set up the exact workings of the snare in which she was to be trapped. Mary was intoxicated by the pleasure of renewed communications. As she wrote her first outward messages, to be handed to the agreeable brewer as she had been directed, she little realized that the treacherous Gifford still lurked in near-by Burton. The method by which Mary believed she contacted the outside world, but in fact merely signalled her private thoughts and schemes directly to her jailer Paulet at Chart-

ley and her enemy Walsingham in London, was as follows:[11] Mary's secretary Nau first took down her letters,
according to the queen's directions and with the help of his
own notes made along the way, and then put them into
code. Next he would wrap the letters securely in a leather
packet and hand them privately to the Chartley brewer.
The packet was then slipped through a corked tube in the
bung of the cask. The merry brewer—'the honest fellow'
as Paulet sarcastically termed him—then drove away, back
to Burton. Here he handed the packet to Gifford, and the
same evening Gifford would bring the packet secretly
back to Chartley and Paulet. If Phelippes was still at
Chartley then the message was opened and deciphered
on the spot, and the decipher sent forward to Walsingham
in London; otherwise the original packet was sent by
express riders to London and the deciphering done by
Phelippes there. The code set up by the conspirators was
not an especially subtle one, involving the use of a mixture
of Greek letters, numbers and other symbols for the letters
of the alphabet and common words. But even if it had
been of a more complicated nature, the deciphering would
still not have been a very arduous task: at the opening of
her new communications, this particular code had been
specially set up for the future between Mary and her
correspondents, and passed on to them through the post;
Walsingham had thus merely to note it down, and any
of its variations, as and when they were established.

Once the deciphering was achieved, the packet was re-
sealed: this was the province of Arthur Gregory, an expert
in this individual art. Then Gilbert Gifford rode to London, taking the packet with him, and handed it over to
the French embassy, as had been the queen's original intention. From here it went to Paris, enjoying diplomatic
immunity at the ports, and was in Morgan's hands in
mid-March. The journey had thus taken two months: but
of course such delays were only too easy to explain, since
all parties agreed on the need for extreme secrecy. Nor
was the return journey any problem: the process was
merely reversed. Mary received her secret post via the
brewer as before, in a small packet containing a covering
note from Gifford, who had brought it down from London. By the time any message from France was received
by Mary, therefore it had been deciphered, scanned and
its contents well and truly noted by Walsingham.

In the spring of 1586 all those concerned in the conspiracy, from whatever angle, felt something like happiness. Mary, in blissful unconsciousness of being betrayed, revelled in the new sap flowing through her rescue schemes. Her secretary Nau even cast the 'honest fellow' in the role of Cupid: he had fallen in love with Mary's former bedfellow Bess Pierrepoint, Bess of Hardwicke's granddaughter by the marriage of her daughter Frances Cavendish to Sir Henry Pierrepoint. In this case propinquity had not led to love, or if it had, it was on Nau's side only. Nau's courtship of Bess led to an unfortunate coolness between Mary and her secretary at this critical moment. Mary's dearest '*mignonne*', so charming as a child, had grown up into a proud and rather unattractive young woman, who had inherited some of her grandmother's trouble-making nature. Despite the approval of Sir Henry, she was disdainful of the match with the voluble secretary, and enlisted Mary in her intrigues to get herself removed to court into Elizabeth's service.* Nau, however, used the secret pipeline to forward his marriage schemes.

Gifford enjoyed the luxurious god-like superiority of the spy, who can observe the whole battlefield from above. Paulet had the grim satisfaction of watching this woman he had never for a moment trusted reveal herself to be every bit as deceitful as he had suspected. As for the brewer, he was happy enough, since he was being paid twice over, once by Mary, and once by Paulet; furthermore, he thoroughly understood his own value, for what was Paulet's indignation when, despite the largesse inherent in the situation, the 'honest fellow' actually demanded a rise in his wages. Paulet's whole instinct was against employing so many people, especially people of such gross calibre—'I had learned not to trust two where it sufficed to trust one', he wrote.[12] But even Paulet had to admit that the harsh conditions to which Mary had previously been subjected had led her to leap joyously at any opportunity for correspondence: this, coupled with the need for secrecy which prevented Mary's side from making any effective double check on their arrange-

* In the end the arrogant Bess did not marry until she was thirty-five, and then to an Erskine, created Viscount Fenton and earl of Kellie, who had been loyal to James VI during the Gowrie conspiracy and had come to England with him.

ments, combined to make the operation virtually fool-
proof.*

It was at this point that the original and largely spurious
assassination plot of the Giffords, Ballard and Savage, was
joined by the quite different conspiracy of a number of
young English Catholic gentlemen, under the leadership of
Anthony Babington. These young men showed a very different attitude to the imprisoned queen of Scots from that of
the previous generation: indeed the Babington plot may
perhaps be regarded as the first manifestation of that romantic approach to the beleaguered Stuart dynasty which
was afterwards to play such a part in British history. After
all, Mary Stuart, although always a seductive figure to those
who knew her personally, had often been judged extremely harshly by those who did not know her. Her
domestic policy in Scotland in the 1560s could by no
stretch of the imagination be inscribed as pro-Catholic.
The previous Pope, Pius v, in particular, had gone out of
his way to show that he disapproved of her marriage to
Bothwell—a Protestant ceremony quite apart from its
scandalous genesis—and had made it clear that the
promulgation of the bull *Regnans in Excelsis* was intended
in origin to safeguard the spiritual welfare of English
Catholics, rather than advance the cause of Mary Queen
of Scots.

But by 1577 the attitude of the papacy had signally
changed: Pope Gregory XIII wrote in August of that year
rejoicing that calamity had taught Mary patience, approving of her new virtue, and believing that God would soon
requite it with eternal glory.[18] As Pope Gregory bid his
much-tried daughter to set great store by faith, hope and
charity, he struck a very different note from Pope Pius.
The attitude of Europe underwent an equal transformation;
increasingly in the Catholic literature on the Continent,
Mary came to symbolize the martyrdom of the Catholic
faith in England. Gone indeed were the days when she

---

* The story of 'Barnaby' shows how ready Mary's heart was to
be touched at this point. When Gifford needed to go to France, a
certain 'Barnaby' was introduced to Mary by letter as being her substitute carrier; Barnaby was in fact the pseudonym for Thomas
Barnes, a venal Catholic corrupted by Gifford. Mary developed such
a fondness for the helpful 'Barnaby' that he was preserved as her
nominal correspondent even after Gifford had in fact returned to
England.

had represented the spirit of religious compromise in
Scotland. Mary's Catholic apologists were already at work
long before her death. Adam Blackwood, whose dramatically pro-Marian account of her execution, *Martyre de
la Royne d'Ecosse*, was later to become a classic in this
field, published *De Regibus Apologia* in 1581; in this
work he defended Mary against the attacks of heretics,
who, he maintained, had no right to attack kings at all.
Towards the end of the 1570s, lives of Catholic martyrs,
brought out in answer to Foxe's Protestant martyrs, began
to include the name of Mary, now considered to be a
Catholic martyr in her English (Protestant) prison. Another Marian martyrologist, Nicholas Sanders, was also
at work in the 1570s, making such fanciful claims as that
Mary had deliberately refused the English throne for the
sake of the Catholic faith. The Act of Association in 1584
increased the spate. Mary, who had begun life as a beautiful young goddess of the French imagination, had progressed to become a controversial if exotic queen of Scotland, now became identified with the spirit of the Counter-
Reformation.[14]

English minds were not immune to the transformation.
By 1586 a whole generation had grown up in England
since those far-off days at Kirk o'Field and the shameful
hasty Bothwell marriage: to these young men Mary was
a Catholic princess held in an English Protestant tower.[15]
To them it was Elizabeth who was the monstrous dragon
who held Mary in thrall. These young men who dreamed
their dreams were headed by Sir Anthony Babington: the
quality of his romantic fancies can be seen in the high-
flown language of his letters to the queen of Scots. Babington was a Catholic squire from Dethick, in Derbyshire:
now twenty-five, he had been born about the time Mary
returned to Scotland; he formed part of that Catholic midlands society which included families like the Pagets (with
whom he was on familiar visiting terms).[16] As a boy he
had actually been a page to Shrewsbury, when the latter
was Queen Mary's jailer, so that he had had ample opportunity to conceive a quixotic admiration for her. In 1580
he went to France and here became involved with Thomas
Morgan, his schemes and his correspondence. Babington
was rich—his family had benefited from two marriages to
heiresses—and his income came to over £1,000 a year in
Elizabethan money; this put him in a position to entertain

and act the host to his friends in a way which could back up any ideas he wanted to inculcate into them. Perhaps this fact was partly responsible for the influence he exercised over his immediate circle: or else Babington was one of those unlucky people who attract others to them by force of personality without possessing the other sterner attributes of leadership. In any case Babington, while admired and looked up to by his cronies, Chidiock Tichborne, Tilney and the rest, also had a strong streak of the dreamer in his nature, which made him a dangerous plotter with whom to be involved. In addition, when his character came to be tested in the crucible of an Elizabethan interrogation he lacked the necessary strength to withstand the terrible trial of pain.

Yet Babington in early 1586 was above all attractive and gay: Father William Weston gave the contemporary estimate of him—how he had 'enchanting manners and wit', he was well-read, well-travelled, good-looking with a quick intelligence, apart from his considerable wealth. Weston also commented on the appeal he exercised over his contemporaries: 'When in London he drew to himself by the force of his exceptional charm and personality many young Catholic gentlemen of his own standing, gallant, adventurous and daring in defence of the Catholic faith in its day of stress; and ready for any arduous enterprise whatsoever that might advance the common Catholic cause.'[17] It was Babington at the head of these men who concocted a second plan to rescue the queen of Scots, to be distinguished from the foreign-based plots of Ballard, the Giffords and Savage. Mendoza, the former Spanish ambassador to London, now in Paris, gave lavish promises of foreign aid. Ballard returned to England, contacted Babington and told him further wild tales of foreign armies on their way. Babington and his companions decided to rescue Mary from her prison, topple Elizabeth from her throne and place Mary on it.

These two separate plots now became entangled with each other, although the two sets of conspirators did not meet until comparatively late in the summer. In the meantime Mary received a mass of old correspondence which had been piling up in the French embassy by the secret brewer's route, throughout March, April and May. The connection with Babington did not actually arise until Mary's former emissary, Fontenay, who was Nau's brother-in-law, wrote to Mary telling her that there was a despatch for her from Scotland which was now lodged at the house of Sir Anthony Babington in London. At the same moment Mary received from Morgan in Paris a letter which officially approved Babington as a contact.[18] Finding Babington independently approved from two sources, Mary now wrote off to Babington herself on 25 June, her first letter in this direction. It was short and to the point: 'I have understood that upon the ceasing of our intelligence, there were addressed unto you from France and Scotland some packets for me. I pray you, if any have come to your hands, and be yet in place to deliver unto the bearer thereof who will make them be safely conveyed to me.' This communication was duly put into the beer keg with the somewhat imprecise address of: 'Master Anthony Babington, dwelling most in Derbyshire at a house of his own within two miles of Wingfield, as I doubt not you know for that in this shire he hath many friends and kinsmen.'[19]

This brief and practical letter was duly read and noted by Walsingham and his agents. It finally reached Babington on 6 July. In reply, spurred on by Ballard and Gifford, he composed an extremely long letter which was neither brief nor practical, and under no circumstances could be considered discreet;* in short, as he himself put it, 'I writ unto her touching every particular of this plot'.[20] The main points of the conspiracy as outlined by Babington were as follows: first an invasion from abroad, of sufficient strength to ensure success; secondly, the invaders to be joined by 'a strong party at every place' of English Catholic sympathizers; thirdly, the deliverance of Mary; fourthly, 'the despatch of the usurping Competitor', as Babington put it, 'for the effectuating of all which it may please your Excellency [Mary] to rely upon my service'. He supplied Mary with details of each stage of the programme; the 'despatch of the usurping Competitor' (Queen Elizabeth) for example, was to be accomplished by six noble gentlemen among Babington's own friends. Mary was to be extracted from prison by Babington himself with ten of

---

* Another example of Babington's extraordinarily foolhardy nature was the fact that he had the whole group of conspirators sit for their portrait, with himself in the centre and the motto painted above them: *Hi mihi sunt comites, quos ipsa pericula dicunt.*

his other friends, at the head of a hundred followers. Babington concluded by hoping that he might assure his conspirators that in the event of the plot proving successful, they would be duly rewarded by Mary's generosity and bounty.

Mary received this communication on 14 July, by which time of course it had been thoroughly scrutinized by Walsingham, and every detail of the plot was as well-known to the Elizabethan government as to Mary herself. It was Mary's reaction which was crucial: for although she was already doomed by the terms of the Act of Association, it would have been far more difficult for Walsingham to work up Elizabeth's odium against her, if Mary had shown the Babingtons the cool reception she had displayed to other would-be rescuers in the past. While Mary pondered, she merely acknowledged receipt of Babington's plan. She asked for Nau's advice: Nau advised her to leave the letter unanswered as she had done before with similar offers. The English gloatingly attended her reply: 'We await her very heart in the next,' commented Phelippes. Finally on 17 July she wrote back to Babington an extremely long, full letter in principle approving his schemes.[21] Like the other letters of the secret correspondence, it was composed by Mary in French, the language which still came most naturally to her, but then drafted by Nau and Curle in English, before being translated into cipher and despatched into the brewer's pipeline.

Babington in his letter had talked of the killing of Queen Elizabeth. There can be no doubt but that Mary in her reply took this prospect briefly into consideration, weighed it against the prospect of her own liberty, and did not gainsay it. From first to last, in this letter, she quite understandably viewed the matter from her own point of view, but when she wrote: 'Orders must be given that when their design has been carried out I can be *quant et quant* got out of here,' it was clear to the recipients of her letters—as it was to Walsingham—that the design of which she wrote and thus tacitly accepted was that same design of which they too had written, the assassination of the English queen. Throughout her own letter, Mary put all her emphasis on the practical details involved: the conspirators must have horsemen always with them to let her, Mary, know immediately that the deed had been done; otherwise, as no definite date had yet been fixed,

Paulet might receive the news first and either transport her to another prison, or fortify the house successfully against her rescue; for the same reason, the conspirators must also take care to stop the progress of the ordinary posts.

Throughout the letter Mary took care to emphasize the terrible consequences to her personally should the plot explode prematurely and fail: the best that could happen to her would be that she would be buried in a dark prison for ever and ever. In this context Mary herself saw foreign help as being not so much desirable as absolutely essential. Not only did she reiterate to Babington that she would only be drawn forth from Chartley by 'a good army, or in some very good strength', but it was a point which she also tried to hammer home to Sir Francis Englefield in a letter written on 17 July, the same day as her fatal communication to Babington:[22] 'Before that they have sufficient promise and assurance, I have wished them plainly not to stir in any wise on this side, for fear they may ruin themselves in vain.' As she had told Beaton on 18 May, the action of the Spanish king must be regarded as crucial to any actions the English Catholics might take.[23]

There was no wonder that Phelippes drew a gallows mark on the outside of this letter when he passed it on to Walsingham. Mary had fallen plumb into the trap which had been laid for her. When Walsingham wrote to Leicester in the Netherlands on 9 July—a whole week incidentally, before Mary actually penned her reply—a highly confidential communication saying that the Scottish queen would shortly be caught out in practices which would condemn her, this was exactly the sort of letter which he had in mind.[24] The schemes of Gifford, combined with the restrictions of Paulet, had worked their effect in Mary's mind. Even so, Walsingham was not totally satisfied with Mary's reply: he added a forged postscript to the end of the letter also in cipher in which she was made to ask for the names of the six gentlemen who would perform the deed. It would, he felt, represent the climax of her guilt, as well as providing the English government with some additional useful information. This forged postscript provides the final ironic touch to the setting up of the Babington plot by Walsingham and his agents:[25] 'I would be glad to know the names and qualities of the six

gentlemen which are to accomplish the designment; for
that it may be I shall be able, upon knowledge of the
parties, to give you some further advice necessary to be
followed therein. . . . As also from time to time, particularly how you proceed: and as soon as you may, for
the same purpose, who be already, and how far every one,
privy hereunto.'

It is important to judge Mary's acceptance in principle
of the Babington conspiracy against the background of her
own mood in the course of the late summer of 1586 and
how it developed up till July. Her mental state was by now
very different from what it had once been; the old notion
of establishing her on the throne of England, however
much it appealed to her youthful champions, was not
uppermost in the mind of the middle-aged woman, by
now quite out of touch with Europe, let alone with England. Mary herself was beginning to feel weary of the
prolonged battle for some sort of decent existence, in
which she had now been involved for eighteen years, and
the constant strain of being ever on her guard, ever plotting, ever hoping, ever planning. The period in which she
was perforce cut off from her secret post contributed much
to this feeling of melancholy and lassitude. She began to
speak of liberty in terms of retirement rather than government. After James's betrayal of the Association, Mary told
Elizabeth that her own desire had been to 'retire out of this
island in some solitary and reposeful place, as much for
her soul as for her body'. She described herself poignantly
at the end of May 1586 as knowing not 'what line to sail,
nor how to lift anchor'. This feeling of isolation and not
understanding foreign matters any longer resounds through
all her letters to Morgan, once the post was resumed: 'My
dear friend,' she wrote to him on 20 May, 'I can found no
certain judgement nor know what course in the world
to take in my affairs I shall hear amply and more recently from every part.' On the same date, as if to prove
her lack of contact with reality Mary also wrote to
Mendoza in Paris confiding her rights to the crown of
England conditionally to his master Philip II, if James
had not become a Catholic by the date of her death. At
the end of June, Nau told how little Mary now felt she
understood concerning the mind and intentions of other
princes, thanks to her long solitude.[26]

In July this abandoned and exhausted frame of mind

received a terrible fillip from the news that James and Elizabeth had actually signed a treaty of alliance. The maternal heart-break Mary had suffered in the spring of 1585 was now spiked with fearful bitterness. It was one thing to repudiate the idea of the Association but at Berwick on 6 July, only eleven days before Mary's vital answer to Babington, a proper treaty was signed between the English and Scottish sovereigns, a treaty from which Mary and her interest were totally excluded. James was now to receive an actual agreed subsidy from Elizabeth. Mary's letter of 12 July to Beaton in Paris on the subject of James was written in a tone of the utmost despair.[27] There is no doubt that the publication of the treaty sent her temporarily off her balance, and robbed her of the sustained powers of calm reason which might have led her to act far more cautiously over the Babington plot. Even the fact that her health—for so long enfeebled— was now somewhat restored by the better conditions of Chartley contributed towards her downfall. On 3 June Paulet reported that the queen was now well enough to be carried down in her chair to the ponds near the house to watch the duck-hunting.[28] With renewed health came greater energy to escape, a prospect impossible to contemplate for an invalid endlessly confined to her chamber and her bed.

If to understand all is to forgive all, then it is certainly possible against this background to forgive Mary for tacitly acceding to—for her letter came to no more than that—a conspiracy involving the assassination of Elizabeth. Her own agreement was entirely in the context of a captive seeking to escape her guards, and may be compared to the actions of a prisoner who is prepared to escape by a certain route, even if it may involve the slaying of a jailer by another hand. If her own life in captivity could be considered to be in danger, then there was much theological doubt as to whether agreement to the slaying of Elizabeth was sinful at all. The immense theoretical problems which political assassination presented to the men of the sixteenth century caused Babington and his friends prolonged disquiet and heart-searching, but for Mary, illegally detained against her will, and not in any case concerned with the actual execution of the deed, or its instigation, the problem was considerably simpler: after so many years it was her rescue which mattered to her, not the safety of her jailer Elizabeth.* Even these same scruples of the Babington plotters do them credit in an age when many of the philosophers worked out good ethical reasons for the just death of a tyrant.

Yet in the sixteenth century the theory of resistance to one who had abused a ruler's sacred duties was given much prominence in the writings of both Jesuits, such as de Mariana, Suarez and Mola, and Calvinists, such as Hotman who wrote *Vindiciae contra Tyrannos*. The view of de Mariana in particular in *De Rege et Regis Institutione*, writing as he did in Catholic Spain, where there was religious unity, caused scandal in France and Germany where there was both religious and civil disorder: de Mariana's view that an individual might be justified in slaying a manifestly evil ruler, in accordance with the wishes of the people, was furiously condemned in countries where this imprudent advice might only too easily be put into effect.[29] Although many Jesuits rejected de Mariana openly, and later editions of his book contained modifications, the attitude of both Pius v and Gregory XIII to Elizabeth—first in the bull in 1570 and then in the ban of 1580—was still susceptible of the interpretation by their Catholic flock that it would be a holy deed to rid England of this heretic ruler—even if they were certainly not specifically exhorted to do so. From the other side of the fence, John Knox had proclaimed without further ado that it was not only lawful but positively necessary to kill a king who had betrayed his people.

It says much for the innate goodness of ordinary people at the time that, although political actions like the papal bull or the bond of Association, had truly wreaked havoc with the concept of public morality, nevertheless Babington and his friends were still bewildered about their moral position if they carried through Elizabeth's assassination. Babington wrote to Mary apropos 'the despatch of the usurper, from the obedience of whom we are by excom-

* Mary has been harshly judged for agreeing in principle to the assassination of Elizabeth, and this has been something held to justify Elizabeth's own execution of Mary. But this is to continue the propaganda of Walsingham successfully beyond the grave since there was, after all, little real danger to Elizabeth from a plot vetted throughout by Walsingham. The action of Elizabeth in suggesting that Mary, who was in her charge, should be secretly assassinated by Paulet was far more morally culpable.

munication of her made free', but revealed in his subsequent confession that he had been uncertain and worried
as to whether this excommunication was still in force.
Châteauneuf's memoir also revealed the genuine doubts
which all concerned felt on the subject.[30] In an apparently
violent age, when justification for the death of tyrants was
openly discussed, and princes—like William of Orange—
did meet their ends at the hands of the assassin, such
scruples showed that it was easier for decent people to listen to the arguments in favour of such a deed than actually stifle their consciences to perform it. But such arguments, vivid as they might be throughout the sixteenth
century, growing more intense after 1580, never really
concerned Mary Stuart; she was never indeed at liberty in
the society in which they were exploited; she continued to
view the subject from the more personal standpoint of her
own liberty.

The gallows letter was in Walsingham's hands by Tuesday 19 July. On 20 July Gilbert Gifford fled to the Continent; his work as an *agent provocateur* completed, he was
unwilling to be involved in the holocaust of arrests and
cross-examination which he was aware was about to break
in England.* On 29 July Babington himself received the
gallows letter and deciphered it the next day with the help
of Tichborne. On 3 August he wrote back to the Scottish
queen acknowledging the fatal letter.[31] By this date, however, as Mary's hopes of release began to rise, one of
Walsingham's agents, William Wade, had already secretly
visited Chartley to work out with Paulet the best manner
of securing her arrest. The gossamer plot began to fall
apart. On 4 August Ballard was arrested and at the news
Babington fled north through London to the leafy lanes of
St John's Wood; here he lay in safety for some time, until
on 14 August he too was seized, and brought in hideous
triumph to the Tower. William Weston, the Jesuit, lying
in his own dark captivity, heard the unusual and ominous
sound of the bells pealing at midnight: his guard told him

---

* Gifford got himself ordained priest in March 1587 in order to
continue his informer's trade; he was awarded an English pension
of £100 a year for his services. But the next year *hubris* was his un-
doing: he was arrested in a brothel, put in the archbishop's prison at
Rheims and died there in 1590. However, all efforts to bring a case
against him for his treachery to the Catholic cause in England failed,
as Thomas Morgan would not testify against him.

that the city was celebrating the capture of certain papists
—'traitors who had made a dastardly plot to assassinate
the sovereign and declare the Queen of Scots her rightful
heir'.[32] Finally on 18 August Babington made the first of
his confessions, in the course of which every detail of the
conspiracy was placed in the hands of Walsingham: the
queen of Scots, as well as all his fellow-conspirators, was
fatally incriminated. Although Babington had destroyed
Mary's letters to him, he now compliantly reconstructed
their text for Walsingham during his interrogations; and
should his memory fail, Walsingham could always call on
Phelippes, his decipherer, to help with the official recon-
struction document—after all, Phelippes and Walsingham,
through the medium of the secret pipeline, had read these
letters long before they ever reached Babington himself.[33]

In the meantime Mary herself, cut off at Chartley, had
absolutely no inkling of the dramatic turn which events
had taken. Her commitment to the plot had been limited
to letters; because of the time lag between the writing and
delivery of messages by the secret post she knew very
little of the various meetings which the conspirators had
held up and down the country. Her spirits were high at
the beginning of August: she felt she might even hope
again. On 11 August, when the dour Paulet suggested that
she might like to ride out of Chartley in the direction of
Tixall in order to enjoy a buck hunt, this seemed yet another favourable omen of future happiness, since such
manifestations of goodwill from her jailer were rare indeed. Mary took particular trouble with her costume under
the impression that she might be meeting some of the local
gentry at the hunt. The ebullient Nau was also smartly arrayed as usual. Also in the party were Curle, the queen's
other secretary, and Bourgoing, her personal physician (on
whose journal we depend for so many of the details of the
last months of Mary's life). It was a fine August day. The
queen's mood was so gay and so gentle that when she noticed Paulet lagging behind, she remembered that he had
recently been ill, and stopped her horse to let him catch
her up.[34]

As the little procession wound its way across the moors,
the queen suddenly spied some horsemen coming fast towards her. They were strangers. For one wild moment her
heart leapt up and she actually believed that these apoca-

lyptic horsemen were the Babington plotters, their plans
more advanced than she supposed, coming to rescue her.
The first words of their leader speedily undeceived her:
this was none other than Sir Thomas Gorges, Queen Elizabeth's emissary, dressed for this momentous occasion in
green serge, luxuriously embroidered. As Paulet introduced him Gorges dismounted from his horse and strode
over towards Mary. 'Madame,' said Gorges in a ringing
voice, 'the Queen my mistress, finds it very strange that
you, contrary to the pact and engagement made between
you, should have conspired against her and her State, a
thing which she could not have believed had she not seen
proofs of it with her own eyes and known it for certain.'
As Mary, taken off her guard and flustered, protested,
turned this way and that, explained that she had always
shown herself a good sister and friend to Elizabeth, Gorges
told her that her own servants were immediately to be
taken away from her, since it was known that they too
were guilty.

From Gorges's tone, Mary even imagined that she
might be now taken summarily to execution. She turned to
Nau and Curle and begged them not to allow her to be
snatched away without some defence. But there was little
the wretched secretaries could do: they were now dragged
from her side—in fact she never saw either of them again
—and taken up to prison in London. Mary herself, with
her physician, was conducted directly to Tixall, in the
pretty riding clothes she had donned to impress the 'pleasant company' she expected to find there. She was so utterly unprepared for her fate that she did not even have
the crucifix she habitually carried—when the inventory of
her belongings was made at Chartley during her absence,
it included the touching item: 'the gold cross Her Majesty
generally wore'.[35] Mary tried at first to resist: at one
point she actually sat on the ground and refused to proceed farther. Paulet then threatened to bring her own coach
and take her to Tixall by force if she would not ride on.
Under duress Mary then consented to proceed; but first of
all she knelt down underneath a tree and prayed out loud,
asking God to remember David whom he had once delivered from his enemies, and imploring his pity. In vain
Bourgoing tried to comfort her by saying that Elizabeth
was dead, and that these strange proceedings were intended
to ensure her safety. Mary cried out loud that she knew

well she was no longer of any use to anyone in this world, and she personally desired nothing left on earth 'neither goods, honours, power nor worldly sovereignty, but only the honour of His Holy Name and His Glory and the liberty of His Church and of the Christian people'.

Tixall, to which Mary was now taken without further protest on her part, was an Elizabethan house built about thirty years earlier; it included an imaginative novelty in the shape of an exquisite four-square gatehouse, the building of which had only been begun about 1580 and can therefore have only been very shortly completed—if completed it was—at the time of the Scottish queen's incarceration there. But the beauties, or its detail, like those of the house itself—including the near-by River Trent 'by lovely Tixall graced, of Aston the ancient seat' as the Warwickshire poet Michael Drayton wrote lovingly later—must have been fairly lost on the distraught and anguished woman who was now imprisoned there. Mary did not leave her chambers for the entire fortnight which she spent at Tixall. She begged to be allowed to write to Queen Elizabeth, but Paulet refused to bring her paper. Bourgoing was sent back by Paulet to Chartley the next day. But Paulet subsequently allowed two of Mary's ladies and Martin, an equerry, to join her, who presumably brought over at least some of her luggage, since the queen was otherwise without any clothes except that hopefully gay riding-habit.

Meanwhile Mary's apartments and belongings at Chartley were thoroughly searched: her letters and ciphers were taken away to London. Paulet also took the opportunity to draw up a complete list of her household, with suggestions as to how it could be cut down 'if this lady be restrained of her liberty'.[36] The household of thirty-eight, counting the servants' servants, could easily be reduced to nineteen in Paulet's opinion, if outdoor categories like the coachmen were eliminated. Curle's wife Barbara could be dispensed with, as could Christina Pages—which removal, Paulet hoped, would result also in the departure of her husband Bastian, who never seemed able to win the hearts of the English since that first merry masque at Holyrood. Paulet now called him 'cunning in his kind, full of sleights to corrupt young men'. The inventories of the queen's belongings showed how her prized possessions, once rich jewels like the Great Harry, now merely comprised miniatures or pictures: there were lists of these little portraits, one of her son James, one of Elizabeth, one of her first husband, one even of the dead countess of Lennox, and that other Catholic Queen Mary Tudor, as well as pictures of Henry II and many other members of the French royal family, and Mary's forbears the former kings of Scotland. It was as though she lived in the past, and sustained strength from the idea of the great many-branched family tree from which she had sprung.

After a fortnight at Tixall, in which anguish for the past mingled with apprehension for the future, Mary was conducted back to Chartley by Paulet. Outside Tixall's gatehouse a touching sight met her eyes: she found the beggars of Staffordshire had gathered to greet her, knowing the famous reputation of her charity. As the beggars cried out for alms, Mary replied sadly: 'Alas, good people, I have now nothing to give you. For I am as much a beggar as you are yourselves.' The whole incident was reported to London by Paulet in terms of the utmost indignation.[37] Back at Chartley, Mary found that her words to the beggars were only too true: her belongings had been rifled, her cupboards broken open, it was left for her to embrace her weeping servants 'as one who had returned home'. The only domestic incident which had taken place had also its sad aspects: Barbara Curle had given birth to her child in the absence both of her husband, now in prison in London, and of her mistress. Paulet had refused to baptize it, and as there was now no Catholic priest left even in disguise to perform the ceremony the queen did it herself. She named the baby 'Mary, in the name of the Father, the Son and the Holy Ghost'.*

The only thing which had not been taken from Mary was her actual money, on which she depended for paying her servants and for her own necessities; this she found still in the cupboard where she had left it. But later directives came from London that this too was to be seized; in order to effect the rapine, Paulet and Richard Bagot, a Staffordshire magistrate, forcibly entered the queen's apartments when she was lying ill in bed. Armed men were left in the ante-room and Paulet and Bagot went forward alone, sending Mary's servants out of the room, although Bour-

---

* Paulet professed himself to be scandalized by the procedure, but it was well within the regulations of the Catholic Church.

going managed to linger by the door, 'very sad and thoughtful'. At first Mary absolutely refused to surrender what was in fact undeniably her own property. When she saw that there was no gainsaying Paulet, she instructed Elizabeth Curle to open up the cabinet; even then, she forced herself to step out of bed, limped across the room on her crippled leg, barefoot without any slippers or shoes, and beseeched Paulet one last time to leave her the money. She had put the sum aside, she told him, as a last resort for her funeral expenses, and to enable her servants to return each to their own country after her death. But Paulet was unmoved by this pleading, and the money was taken away. Mary was now left with the two things which could never be taken from her—as she told Paulet proudly on her return to Chartley—her royal blood and her Catholic religion.[38]

In the meantime the revelations which Walsingham was able to make to Elizabeth concerning the abominable perfidy of her good friend and sister Mary were eminently satisfactory from his own point of view. Elizabeth was plunged into a panic of acute physical fear, unaware how much of the assassination plot had in fact been elaborated by Walsingham's own agents. The English queen's letter to Paulet on the subject of the discovery of the Babington plot was ecstatic with relief: 'Amyas, my most faithful and careful servant,' she wrote, 'God reward thee treble fold in three double for the most troublesome charge so well discharged.' Mary was now 'your wicked murderess' and any future fate, however rigorous, no more than 'her vile deserts'.[39] It was understandable that Elizabeth should feel a mixture of keen fear at the danger to her personal safety and righteous horror at Mary's ingratitude: the confessions of the Babington conspirators, arrested and examined in turn did nothing to reassure her. In mid-September they were tried and condemned, having pleaded guilty to the indictment of wanting to kill the queen; Mary Stuart's name was not introduced at any point into the trial, however, lest the assassination of Elizabeth would be further encouraged. The conspirators were then executed in two batches.

The manner of their ending was extremely savage, according to the general principle of the Elizabethan government that fierce penalties performed in public encouraged the people to believe the natural corollary that fierce crimes had been committed in private. As Camden put it: 'They were all cut down, their privities were cut off, bowelled alive and seeing, and quartered.' Babington murmured *'Parce mihi, domine Jesu';* Chidiock Tichborne, whose poem written in the Tower is one of the most moving of all Elizabethan apologia, made a noble final speech, which aroused the pity of the spectators. Savage actually broke the rope and fell before being disembowelled. Those privy councillors present felt impelled to point out to the queen that such blood-thirsty vengeance would do more harm than good. The next day Salisbury, Dunn, Jones, Charnock, Travers, Gate and Bellamy were dragged to the scaffold on hurdles as before, but were only cut down when they were actually dead. This act of mercy was attributed officially to Queen Elizabeth—although she was not at this point in a particularly merciful mood.

The next desiderata to be secured by Walsingham and Cecil, to complete their case against the queen of Scots, were the revelations of her secretaries, Nau and Curle. The all-important point was that they should testify to the authenticity of Mary's 'gallows' letter to Babington. At first the unhappy secretaries denied everything: Nau said afterwards that Walsingham shook his fist in his face, and had to be calmed down by Cecil. But the situation was a critical one, and neither of them was a man of steel. They were alone, helpless, and terrified out of their wits; they were quite cut off from any possible consultation with their mistress, and to Nau England was a dangerous foreign country. Not only that, but their antagonists were apparently able to produce in front of them the texts of all the secret letters they had written, in a way which must have seemed like some terrible witchcraft. As Curle himself said in his subsequent apologia:[40] 'They did show me the Majesty's letters to my lord Paget, Mr Charles Paget, Sir Francis Englefield and the Spanish Ambassador, all penned in my own hand which I could not deny. . . . Moreover they showed me the two very letters written by me in cipher and received by Babington. . . . Upon which so manifest and unrefusable evidence I could not deny.' In fact the documents which Nau and Curle were shown, which they finally attested, were not 'the two very letters' as Curle believed, since Babington had destroyed these. They were copies, in which the master-forger Phelippes probably had a hand, but in view of the exact reconstruc-

tion of the text, and the fact that Babington himself had
by now vouched for the letters, it is easy to understand
how the wretched secretaries fell victim to the deception.
As for Mary's long detailed letter to Babington on 17 July,
in which she ran through his plans at length, Nau and
Curle were only asked to attest to the body of the letter
itself; the forged postscript, added by Walsingham, in
which he asked for the names of the six men destined to
act as assassins, was deliberately left off the reconstructed
letters. Babington specifically mentioned this postscript in
his first confession; but when he was shown the reconstructed letter, he carelessly or compliantly passed it, without pointing out its absence. Had he insisted on its introduction, Nau and Curle would certainly have noticed
such an obvious interpolation. Nor was the critical passage
at the end of Babington's first confession, alluding to the
postscript, ever read out later in court—so that the forgery should not be uncovered.[41]

Mary afterwards both believed and said publicly that
she had been betrayed by Nau. Cecil also took a cynical
view of the secretaries' moral stamina, when he wrote to
Hatton on 4 September: 'Nau and Curle will yield somewhat to confirm their Mistress' crimes. But if they were
persuaded that they themselves might escape, and the blow
fall upon their Mistress betwixt her head and shoulders,
surely we should have the whole from them.'[42] But in retrospect, it is difficult to blame the secretaries too harshly
for attesting a text, whose validity they believed they
could hardly in honesty refute. In the critical and terrifying atmosphere of the interrogation, under circumstances
of fear and hopelessness, the impossibility of saving their
mistress in face of such evidence jostled with their very
human fears for their own safety. Nau's betrayal of his
mistress at the end does not necessarily mean that he was
engaged in a long-term policy of villainy. It was true that
Nau had fallen out with Mary over his use of the secret
pipeline to forward his matrimonial plans with Bess Pierrepoint. According to his enemies, Nau was bribed with
£7,000 to betray Mary; he was certainly housed with
Walsingham in London, and later sent back to his native
France in a boat of his own after a few months, whereas
the unfortunate Curle remained in close imprisonment for
a year.[43] Such signs of English favour, while they may
point to the fact that Nau exposed the truth about Mary's

intrigues to save his own skin, does not prove any further degree of treachery. Paulet always hated Nau in the old days at Tutbury and Chartley, and wished that he could get rid of him, and Paulet's dislike was an excellent indication of Nau's loyalty towards Mary. Nau also managed to straighten out Mary's finances to an admirable extent during the period in which he served her. Nau's surrender should be equated with the outburst of Leslie in the Tower over the Norfolk conspiracy: they were both the unfortunate but explicable lapses of servants who were enmeshed in webs which were altogether too strong for men of their calibre. In the event, the betrayal of Nau and Curle can hardly be said to have much historical significance; if they had persisted in their denials, it is not likely that Walsingham would have allowed such petty obstacles to stand in his way. He would have found other ways of getting the letters vouched for.*

By now, with the Babington conspirators dead or dying, Nau and Curle under lock and key and the Act of Association, by which she was already guilty, hanging over her head, there was little left for Mary to hope for. But there was one terrible thing left for her to dread: the secret death, the slow drip of poison, the assassin's knife, all the fates by which she would be deprived of the public martyrdom by which she now hoped to proclaim the Catholic faith at her death. During her fortnight at Tixall she seems to have thought coolly and courageously towards this end: from now on, she deliberately played every scene with this climax in view. Her hope was to triumph at the moment of her death, her fear was to be extinguished meaninglessly without an opportunity of bearing witness to the truths in which she believed. In September, while describing how wretchedly she was treated, she managed to write to this effect to her cousin the duke of Guise: 'For myself, I am resolute to die for my religion. . . . With God's help, I shall die in the Catholic faith and to maintain it constantly . . . without doing dishonour to the race of Lorraine, who are accustomed to die for the sustenance of the faith.'[44] Mary was by now so convinced that death was at hand, that she begged him to look after her poor ser-

---

* When Nau reached France, the Guises accepted his story that he had merely bowed to *force majeure*. In 1605 Nau went further and actually applied to James I and VI to have his good character established.

vants, and gave the most detailed instructions for the disposal of her body, which she wished to have buried at Rheims, with that of her mother. Her hand was now so stricken with pain that she could hardly hold the pen to write the letter, the terror of the unknown death haunted her, and yet Mary ended proudly: 'My heart does not fail me. . . . *Adieu, mon bon cousin.*' It was in this heroic frame of mind that Queen Mary allowed herself to be taken without protest out of Chartley on 21 September and set on her last journey towards Fotheringhay. It was Mary's triumph that by her deliberate behaviour in the last months of her existence, she managed to convert a life story which had hitherto shown all the elements of a Greek tragedy—disaster leading ineluctably to disaster—into something which ended instead in the classic Christian manner of martyrdom and triumph through death. This transfiguration in the last months of her life, which has the effect of altering the whole balance of her story, was no fortunate accident. The design was hers.

25 Trial

'As a sinner I am truly conscious of having often offended my Creator and I beg him to forgive me, but as a Queen and Sovereign, I am aware of no fault or offence for which I have to render account to anyone here below.'

MARY QUEEN OF SCOTS *to Sir Amyas Paulet, October 1586*

On 21 September Mary Queen of Scots was taken out of Chartley Hall and away to an unknown destination. It was a sinister and frightening scene. The men who came to fetch her, Gorges and Stallenge, arrived with pistols at their belts. Her own servants were locked in their rooms and their windows guarded, so that they should not witness her departure or signal their sympathy to her. The most that Paulet had imparted to Mary officially on the subject of her new prison was the mere fact that she was going to be moved. From hints gleaned secretly through the servants, Mary actually believed she was going to a royal castle about thirty miles from London.*[1] Under these doleful conditions Mary was conducted out of Chartley and Staffordshire by a body of Protestant gentlemen of the country, including Walter Aston and Richard Bagot. The first night was spent at Hill Hall, near Abbot's Bromley, where the queen's stay was commemorated by her name and the date scratched on a pane of glass by a Paget sympathizer at the end of the century: *Maria regina Scotia quondam transibat istam villam, 21 Septembris, 1586 usque Burton Fotheringhay.*† The next morning Gorges, on instructions from Elizabeth, attacked the queen on the dual subject of her culpability and her ingratitude, although Mary firmly and steadfastly refused to admit

---

* The Privy Council wanted to bring the Scottish queen to the Tower of London, but Elizabeth refused to hear of it.

† The signature is not actually that of Mary herself, lacking the characteristic level letters. The pane of glass is still to be seen in the William Salt Library, Stafford.

either guilt or guilty intentions. The next two nights were
spent at Leicester, in the house of the earl of Huntingdon
in Lord's Place: here the ordinary people showed signs of
favouring the prisoner rather than her jailer, Paulet, and
his coach had to be guarded against demonstrations. Finally, on 25 September, the queen reached the castle of
Fotheringhay in Northamptonshire, about twenty miles
south-west of Peterborough.

Mary Stuart first sighted its ancient towers from a path
called since the days of the Doomsday Book, Perryho
Lane—which according to tradition enabled her to make
a melancholy little play on the name as she exclaimed
aloud, 'Perio! I perish.' Quite apart from its heavy, brooding appearance, Fotheringhay had a stark history. Ironically Mary might have been able to claim it for her own,
since at one point it had been made the dowry of Maud
de Senlis, the English bride of King David of Scotland. It
had been built in the time of the Conqueror and rebuilt
in the reign of Edward III. It subsequently became a York-
ist castle and here in 1452, Richard III, that sad and twisted
king, had been born. It was now used entirely as a state
prison, but was considered of sufficiently bleak reputation
for the wretched Catherine of Aragon to refuse to go there
unless, as she said, she were to be bound with cart ropes
and dragged thither. The front of the castle and the enormous gateway faced north, the mighty keep rose to the
north-west; a large courtyard filled the interior of the
building, which included a chapel and a great hall; there
was a double moat system along three sides, and the
River Nene winding along the very edge of the castle
made up the fourth side of the defences. Around its grim
towers stretched the level Northamptonshire countryside;
this had more of the flatness of eastern England, and plains
stretching onwards to the Fens themselves, than the mountainous midland landscape which Mary had been accustomed to in Derbyshire and Staffordshire.

Despite the size of Fotheringhay, Mary found herself
incarcerated in comparatively mean apartments: this
brought back all her phobia of a secret killing, the sort
of barbarous death that stained the history of English
medieval castles. But when her servants reported that
many of the state rooms had been left empty, Mary drew
the correct conclusion that she was about to be tried, and

the rooms were awaiting the arrival of dignitaries from
London. At this evidence that she was about to undergo
the public martyrdom she sought, as Bourgoing reported:
'Her heart beat faster and she was more cheerful and she
was in better health than ever before.'[2] When Paulet came
to inform her on 1 October that her misdeeds were now to
be punished by the interrogation of certain lords, and advised her in her own interests to beg pardon and confess
her faults, before she would officially be declared culpable
by law, Mary was able to meet him in an extraordinarily
calm and even detached mood; she even made a little joke
saying Paulet was behaving like a grown-up with a small
child, asking her to own up to what she had done. Then
she went on more seriously: 'As a sinner, I am truly conscious of having often offended my Creator, and I beg Him
to forgive me, but as Queen and Sovereign, I am aware
of no fault or offence for which I have to render account
to anyone here below. . . .' And she concluded loftily: 'As
therefore I could not offend, I do not wish for pardon; I
do not seek, nor would I accept it from anyone living.'
Disgruntled, since he laid great emphasis on the fact that
this sinner should personally confess her misdeeds, Paulet
reported carefully back to London all that had happened.[3]
A few days later Mary was cheered by the arrival of her
steward Melville and his daughter, and Bastian Pages also
with his daughter Mary, who was the Queen's god-daughter. However, she rightly interpreted the dismissal of her
coachmen—Paulet had at last succeeded in effecting this
domestic economy—as an ominous sign that her days of
driving abroad were over.

In London the commissioners appointed to judge the
Scottish queen assembled at Westminster on 8 October.
They were read copies of the letters sent by Babington to
Mary, her answers and the evidence of Nau and Curle.
It was then agreed that Mary should be brought to trial
under the Act of Association enacted in 1585: this provided means whereby a commission of twenty-four peers
and privy councillors might be appointed to investigate
any conspiracy or attempt to hurt Elizabeth 'by any person or with the privity of any person that shall or may
pretend to the title to the Crown of this realm'.[4] The pun-
ishments for anyone found guilty under this act were to
be two-fold: firstly they were to be deprived of their title

to the English crown forever, and secondly they could be lawfully put to death under the provisions of the Act. It had been quite clear at the time that this Act had been especially framed in order to be able to try and execute the queen of Scots: now it was coming into its own. It was under this Act that the commissioners and peers were now summoned to meet in a few days' time at Fotheringhay—including Mary's former jailer, Shrewsbury. In vain he tried to duck this unpleasant task on grounds of health. Shrewsbury was smartly reminded by Cecil that his failure to appear might be interpreted by the malicious as confirmation of all those old rumours that he had been too lenient towards his prisoner: the Lord Chancellor Bromley also wrote meaningly to Shrewsbury: 'I would advise you not to be absent.'

The provisions of the Act of Association were so heavily weighted against Mary that she stood absolutely no chance of acquittal even if it had not been quite clear to all and sundry that her case had been pre-judged. Indeed Cecil mentioned calmly to Shrewsbury that if his health really did prevent him from attending, he ought to authorize Cecil in advance to deliver his (Shrewsbury's) opinion of Mary's guilt.[5] It was of no avail for Châteauneuf, the French ambassador, to plead with Elizabeth for Mary at least to have counsel to defend her on what was a capital charge: Elizabeth told him sharply that she did not need advice from strangers on how to manage her own business. At the forthcoming trial, therefore, Mary was to be allowed neither counsel nor witnesses in her defence; she was not even to be allowed a secretary or amanuensis to help her prepare her own case—her own secretaries being of course still in prison in London. She was to be left quite alone, a sick woman and a foreigner, who knew nothing of England, its laws, or customs, and had only begun to learn its language comparatively late in life, to conduct and manage her own defence against the best legal brains in the country. These eminent lawyers on the other hand were not even to be put to the simple task of bringing witnesses for the prosecution for none was to be called.

Yet, curiously enough, by the standards of the sixteenth century the innate injustice of the trial of Mary Queen of Scots lay not so much in its arrangements—the accused was never allowed counsel at an English treason trial at this date, and the barbarity of the Scottish treason trials

has been sufficiently commented upon*—as in the fact
that the trial took place at all. How, indeed, could it ever be
legal for Mary as sovereign, the queen of a foreign country, to be tried for treason, when she was in no sense one
of Elizabeth's subjects? In 1586 the sovereignty of a ruler
was taken extremely seriously with regard to his own subjects—how much more difficult then was it to try and execute one who was actually or had been the sovereign of
another country? Elizabeth herself was the first to perceive
the dangers for the future of pulling down any monarch
to the rank where he or she could be punished like any
other subject—let alone the monarch of another country.
If Mary had partaken in treasonable activities in England
where in any case she was a prisoner, held against her
will—the correct remedy (although of course it was never
considered) was surely to expel her from the country. The
mere judicial proceedings for trying a sovereign presented
enormous difficulties by English common law. In England
it was the foundation-stone of justice that every man had
a right to be tried by his peers; Mary being a queen had
no peers in England except Elizabeth herself. Neither
privy councillors nor earls nor barons gathered together in
no matter what profusion could be said to be the equals of
one who was an anointed queen.

As the English lawyers pondered these questions, it was
even suggested that the old claims of England to feudal
suzerainty over Scotland (last used by Henry VIII to justify
his depredations) might be brought out again, dusted over
and employed to prove that Mary was Elizabeth's subject
and as such capable of both treason against her, and of
trial by English law. In the end the line of proceedings taken
consisted of a long narration of circumstances ranging
down from ancient times—some of them very ancient indeed—when it had been considered suitable for one sovereign to try another for treason done within their state. The
most recent case cited was that of Conradin, last of the
Hohenstaufen, who, four centuries earlier, had been beheaded by the papal nominee for his father's thrones,
Charles, duke of Anjou, after being captured in battle and

---

* The practice of allowing no counsel to the defendant at a treason trial persisted: in 1746 at the trial in London of Simon, Lord
Lovat for his part in the '45, Horace Walpole described how pathetic
it was to see the old man (he was over eighty) struggling with his
defence without any counsel in what to him was a foreign country.

subjected to a form of treason trial. But the two cases were hardly comparable, as Mary had certainly not been captured in battle, and in any case was utterly ignorant of the laws of England, a country in which she had never been permitted to live at liberty.*[6]

In truth, the only possible justification for what was in fact unjustifiable was the Act of Association itself which, by defining the commission which was to try anyone found coming within the terms of the Act, disposed of such knotty problems as sovereignty and a queen's peers by merely cutting through them and all the laws, both national and international, of the time. In the case of the trial of Mary Queen of Scots the traditional blindfold across the eyes of Justice was ruthlessly torn aside by the English commissioners so that the desired verdict might be reached. In order to strengthen a weak case, Cecil took trouble to recall Parliament: it so happened that the English Parliament had been prorogued until November, and the existing Commons could not be brought back before then. Therefore the old Parliament was dissolved and writs of commission for the new one sent out on 14 September, in order that the Commons might be already sitting at the time of the trial. This would help to gloss over the illegality of the proceedings in France and elsewhere or, as Cecil put it: 'to make the burden better borne, and the world abroad better satisfied'. The hatred of the Commons for the queen of Scots had in no way abated over the years, but rather increased in violence: she was now regarded, in the words of one of its members, her former keeper, Sir Ralph Sadler, as 'this most wicked and filthy woman'; Cecil knew that he could rely on the faithful Commons to present this point of view forcibly after the trial to Elizabeth, herself more likely to be haunted by the spectacle of a crowned head rolled in the dust.

On Saturday 11 October, the commissioners began to arrive at Fotheringhay, the most important lodging in the castle, the others in the village and neighbouring farms.

* In his history, Froude attempted to justify the trial by pointing out that Mary had a place within the English succession which gave Elizabeth rights over her; this would be a more effective argument if Mary had not been persistently denied these rights by Elizabeth all her life despite her many attempts to secure their acknowledgement.

Mary was given a copy of the commission which had summoned them. The next day a deputation of lords waited on her—Sir Walter Mildmay, Stallenge, the usher of Parliament, Barker, Elizabeth's notary, and Paulet himself. The object of this mission was to get Mary to consent to appear in person at the trial and thus acknowledge its legality. They handed the Scottish queen an epistle from Elizabeth in which she announced to her that she had sent some peers and legal counsellors to examine Mary and judge her case since Mary persistently denied her participation in a plot against Elizabeth, despite the cogent proofs of her part in it which Elizabeth possessed. As for the legality of such proceedings—since Mary was in England, concluded Elizabeth boldly, she was subject to the laws of the country.

To this Mary replied in fine style, and without in any way conceding their right to try her: 'I am myself a Queen, the daughter of a King, a stranger, and the true kinswoman of the Queen of England. I came to England on my cousin's promise of assistance against my enemies and rebel subjects and was at once imprisoned.'* She stressed her oft expressed, never gratified, wish to speak to Elizabeth and ended: 'As an absolute Queen, I cannot submit to orders, nor can I submit to the laws of the land without injury to myself, the King my son .and all other sovereign princes. . . . For myself I do not recognize the laws of England nor do I know or understand them as I have often asserted. I am alone, without counsel, or anyone to speak on my behalf. My papers and notes have been taken from me, so that I am destitute of all aid, taken at a disadvantage.'⁸ On the subject of her actual guilt, whereas Mary admitted that she had thrown herself under the protection of Catholic kings and princes, she denied any knowledge of an actual attempt against Elizabeth. Mary's views were duly written down, to be communicated to the English queen.

The next morning Mary received another less courteous

---

* On the subject of Mary's conviction that Elizabeth had promised her assistance if she came to England, it may be recalled that Cecil in his memorandum of summer 1568 concerning the *pros* and *contras* of the imprisonment of the queen of Scots, cited as one argument *contra*, the fact that the queen of England had made Mary promises of assistance 'frequently expressed'.⁷

deputation, as she was sitting at her early dinner (ten o'clock in the morning). The Lord Chancellor Sir Thomas Bromley told her that whatever she might protest, she was subject to the laws of England, whether as a sovereign or as a captive, and that if she did not appear in person at her trial she would merely be condemned *in absentia*. Mary shed a few tears at such brusqueness and exclaimed that she was no subject, and she would rather die a thousand deaths than acknowledge herself one, since she would both betray the majesty of kings, and virtually admit that she was bound to submit to the laws of England even over religion. Once more, as she had done before, Mary offered to appear before a free Parliament and answer questions, rather than submit to the commissioners whom she suspected had already condemned her unheard. But even in her distress Mary managed to produce another dramatic watchword or rallying-cry for her supporters, if the news of it should ever leak out, as she cried: 'Look to your consciences and remember that the theatre of the world is wider than the realm of England.'[9]

Cecil now interrupted the conversation with considerable passion: his vehemence probably had a private cause, for there had been some embarrassing rumours that Cecil himself was favourably disposed towards Mary, based on the fact that his grandson William Cecil had visited Rome and had there been converted to the Catholic faith. Mary herself seems to have been under the illusion that the grandson had persuaded the grandfather into a more clement frame of mind.* Now Cecil was disposed to put an end publicly to such idle notions, and the process 'made him it is thought more earnest against her', for he now broke out quite rudely to the queen: 'Will you therefore hear us or not? If you refuse, the assembled Council will continue to act according to the Commission.'

The matter of Mary's personal appearance at the trial— by which she would acknowledge in some measure at least to the public eye their jurisdiction over her—was now the

* Throughout her captivity she seems to have been under the impression that Cecil was more generously inclined towards her than his private papers actually show him to have been. This suggests that Cecil, wise in his own generation, did not allow himself to forget altogether Mary's prominent position in the table of the English succession.

subject of prolonged discussion between Mary and her
would-be judges. Mary continually reiterated her sovereign status: it was not until 14 October that she finally
succumbed, and agreed to appear in order to answer the
single charge that she had plotted the assassination of Elizabeth. During the discussions, Mary received a letter from
Elizabeth in London, in which reproach and anger were
mixed: 'You have planned in divers ways and manners to
take my life and to ruin my kingdom by the shedding of
blood,' Elizabeth wrote. 'I never proceeded so harshly
against you; on the contrary, I have maintained you and
preserved your life with the same care which I use for
myself.' Now Elizabeth commanded Mary to reply to the
peers of her kingdom as if she herself were present. The
only possible note of friendliness was in the last phrase of
the letter: 'But answer fully, and you may receive greater
favour from us.'[10]

Did Mary detect in these ambiguous words some hint
that, if she appeared before the judges, she would in the
end receive pardon, whatever her crimes, and was this
then the motive that determined her to accede to their
pressing demands, thus jeopardizing her sovereign position? But by this stage in her life, and in the frame of
mind in which she had found herself since August, and
that grim meditative fortnight at Tixall, it does not seem
that Mary Stuart was animated by any hope of being
shown further mercy. The strange serenity which now possessed her, on which both Paulet and Bourgoing commented from different viewpoints, was the calm of a
woman who perfectly well realized that she was about to
die. The heroism of her sentiments was carefully and bril-
liantly angled towards the martyr's death, which would
bear witness to the cause of the Catholic Church: as Mary
herself had said, she was playing her last role towards the
theatre of the world, rather than the realm of England.

Mary has been criticized for rescinding her determination never to appear before this illegal court; but there can
be no doubt that her noble bearing at this trial, and the
magnificent speeches she made there, all directed towards
showing her in the light of the martyr queen, did much
to enhance this picture when they gradually became
known after her death. Furthermore the full publicity she
was able to give at it to her wrongs also distracted attention from points on which she might be held considerably

more vulnerable (although the court was still not competent to judge it) such as the letter she had written to Babington. Although on the one hand Mary sacrificed her
royal position by appearing before a tribunal which had
no right to try her, on the other she greatly improved her
position in the eye of history. The queen of Scots was
clever to see this when she agreed to appear before the
judges—intuition in this case being more potent than legal
knowledge. Even so, the stress of making this critical decision reduced Mary to faintness, and she had to be revived with wine before her resolve could be committed to
writing.

The trial of Mary Queen of Scots began on the next day,
Wednesday 15 October, in a room directly above the great
hall of Fotheringhay Castle. Even Bourgoing considered
this chamber spacious and convenient: it was nearly seventy feet long including the window, and twenty-one feet
wide. The most detailed plans were made for the trial, and
the position of every participant was carefully mapped
out in Cecil's chart. At the upper end of the room there
was a throne and a royal dais with the arms of England
over it; opposite the throne for the benefit of the prisoner
was placed one of Mary's own crimson velvet chairs, and
a crimson velvet cushion for her feet. The room was divided in two by a wooden barrier with a door through it.
Above the barrier two parallel benches were positioned on
each side of the room: on the right sat the Lord Chancellor Bromley, Cecil as Lord Treasurer, and the earls including Shrewsbury. In front of them sat the two premier
judges and the high Baron of the Exchequer. On the left
sat the barons and knights of the Privy Council including
Walsingham, Christopher Hatton and Sir Ralph Sadler,
with four other judges and two doctors of civil law in
front of them. A large table in front of the dais was for
the use of the crown representatives including the Attor-
ney-General and Solicitor-General and Barker, the notary, and on it were placed the documents to be used in
the case. Below the barrier, the remaining twenty-four feet
of the room was for the use of the spectators—the ordinary people of the village, and the servants of the commissioners.

Queen Mary entered the great hall at nine o'clock, with
an escort of soldiers. She wore her chosen garb of the sad

years of captivity—a dress and mantle of flowing black velvet, her traditional white head-dress with its widow's peak, and a long white gauzy veil. Her maid Renée de Beauregard bore her train, but Queen Mary was now so lame with rheumatism, and her muscles had lacked exercise for so long, that she could scarcely walk or even limp along, and had to be supported by Melville and Bourgoing. She was followed by her surgeon Jacques Gervais, her apothecary Pierre Gorion and three of her women, Jane Kennedy, Elizabeth Curle and Gillis Mowbray. The commissioners respectfully uncovered their heads as the queen passed, but there was still one delicate moment when the prisoner appeared to be about to jib at her treatment: this was when she realized that she was not to sit on the throne as she had imagined, but on the crimson velvet chair. Mary explained spontaneously: 'I am a Queen by right of birth and my place should be there under the dais!' But after this first instinctive reaction, she recovered her composure, as though she had in advance decided to go through with the ordeal, no matter what the humiliation, and this cry had merely been wrung from her by surprise. The queen sat down quietly in the chair allotted to her and merely observed to Melville as she scanned the faces of the English peers: 'Ah! here are many counsellors, but not one for me.'[11]

The trial was opened by a speech from the Lord Chancellor in which he explained the motives which had impelled Queen Elizabeth to institute these proceedings—how she had been informed that the queen of Scots had planned her downfall and was therefore bound to convoke a public assembly to examine the accusation—and ended by stating that Queen Mary would have every opportunity of declaring her own innocence. To all this Mary replied in terms very much as before, not only denying the jurisdiction of the court over a queen, but also laying great stress on the conditions under which she had first arrived in England: 'I came into this kingdom under promise of assistance, and aid, against my enemies and not as a subject, as I could prove to you had I my papers; instead of which I have been detained and imprisoned.' Queen Mary emphasized that the only reason she had condescended to appear before the commission was in order to show that she was not guilty of the particular crime of conspiring against Elizabeth's life. In answer the Lord Chancellor

utterly denied that Mary had arrived in England under
promise of assistance from Elizabeth, as also he declared
futile her protests against the jurisdiction of the court
itself over her. The commission to try the Scottish queen
was then read aloud in Latin: at which Mary now made
a further protest against the laws on which it was based,
which she said had been expressly framed to destroy her.

Gawdy, the royal sergeant, now rose in his blue robe,
with a red hood lying flatly on the shoulders. He detailed
the events leading up to the Scottish queen's arrest, including the seizure of Babington, and the listing of six men
who were intended to assassinate Elizabeth. To this Mary
replied that she had never met Babington, had never 'trafficked' with him and knew nothing of the six men. Letters said to have been dictated by Babington before his
death were then read aloud, and copies of the correspondence between Mary and Babington passed round, together
with the signed depositions of Curle and Nau, and the confessions of the other conspirators. Mary strongly protested
against this second-hand evidence and very sensibly continued to demand to see the originals of her so-called correspondence with Babington. She refused to admit anything
at all on such indirect proofs, and suggested that her own
ciphers could all too easily have been tampered with. Despite her lonely position without counsel, Mary never for
a moment lost her head: she continued to draw a sharp
distinction between the actions which she as a prisoner
had inevitably taken to try and secure her own rescue
('I do not deny that I have earnestly wished for liberty
and done my utmost to procure it for myself. In this I
acted from a very natural wish.') and actual connivance at
the death of Elizabeth, which she strongly denied. As for
the letters, once more she rejected them *in toto*. 'Can I be
responsible,' she demanded passionately, 'for the criminal
projects of a few desperate men, which they planned without my knowledge or participation?'

The depositions and letters of Babington were now read
aloud. The mention of the name Arundel and his brothers,
who had been involved in conspiracies in her favour, drew
from Mary the exclamation: 'Alas, why should this noble
house of Howard have suffered so much for me. . . .' After
the midday meal further letters were read aloud including
the depositions and confessions of Nau and Curle.
Throughout the trial, the speeches were addressed to the

lords rather than to Mary, so that in order to make a point about a passage in a letter she had to interrupt them; she also complained that the evidence was produced in no particular order, on purpose to confuse her in her answers for she had after all no previous warning of what was going to be produced against her, no opportunity to study the letters privately, and of course no counsel to assist her in making her case. The strain of keeping sufficiently mentally alert was considerable. Nevertheless Mary continued calmly to emphasize the wrongfulness of her imprisonment and call to witness her own ill-health—'I cannot walk without assistance nor use my arms, and I spend most of my time confined to bed by sickness'. She also said that much of her memory had faded with age, captivity and ill-health, and she hardly knew any longer how to act the queen, since it had been so long—nearly twenty years—since she had actually reigned. Although Mary vehemently contradicted the ludicrous notion that the English might have the right to try her because they had in ancient times claimed suzerainty over Scotland, which she claimed would dishonour the memory of her own ancestors, yet she freely admitted that she no longer wished to rule: 'My advancing age and bodily weakness both prevent me from wishing to resume the reins of government. I have perhaps only two or three years to live in this world, and I do not aspire to any public position, especially when I consider the pain and desperance which meet those who wish to do right, and act with justice and dignity in the midst of so perverse a generation, and when a whole world is full of crimes and troubles'—this was indeed the cry of sad disillusioned middle-age.[12]

At this Cecil, either determined to make an impressive showing of his disapproval of the queen of Scots, or with his memory of those far-off days of the abortive Treaty of Edinburgh nearly thirty years before, in which he had been much involved, still burning in his mind, reproached Queen Mary with having assumed the English royal arms at the time of her French marriage and having thus attempted to usurp Elizabeth's throne. Mary gave in reply her stock answer to this accusation: that being then very young, she had merely acted in obedience to the commands of her father-in-law, Henry II. To this Cecil retorted that she had later aggravated the offence by refusing to ratify the Treaty of Edinburgh in which her pretensions to the English throne were formally abandoned, and the argument then proceeded as often before on well-worn lines, except that Mary took care to reiterate at every turn the significance of her status as a queen, which meant that she could never be expected to cede her rights without receiving any concessions about the succession in return. Cecil now accused her of having personally coveted Elizabeth's throne, and Mary responded with a long and closely argued speech on the subject of the English royal succession, which she had evidently prepared carefully in advance, and may be regarded as incorporating her ultimate views on the subject. She made two main points: firstly, she had never at any time wished to usurp the English throne while Elizabeth lived; secondly, and in no way contradicting her previous point, she had 'no scruple of conscience in desiring the second rank as being the legitimate and nearest heir'. It was the right to inherit at the proper time rather than the right to reign immediately, which Mary was not prepared to surrender.

The queen now went on to declare that although she knew that her enemies wished to compass her death by unlawful means, yet with God's help she would still manage to meet her end publicly, as a witness to the faith in which she believed. In a moving passage, which marked her out as far more tolerant than the age in which she lived, and contrasted with the sly venom of Cecil and the cold vindictiveness of Paulet, Mary gave her own philosophy of life, in which there was no place for revenge: 'I do not desire vengeance. I leave it to Him who is the just Avenger of the innocent and of those who suffer for His Name under whose power I will take shelter. I would rather pray with Esther than take the sword with Judith.' And she reminded the judges once more that she had come to England seeking Elizabeth's protection. Mary now attempted valiantly to combat the charges based on the cipher letters. She accused Walsingham of inventing the ciphers and manufacturing the whole plot, and said that she had been warned long before from France to be on her guard against Ballard since he had 'great intelligence' with Walsingham. She repudiated her own letter to Babington in its entirety. She battled with Cecil in a game of wits in which Cecil denied that any Catholic had been put to death in England for religion merely, but only for treason against the queen. Walsingham, stung by Queen Mary's charges, made his own apologia, as vivid as Mary's own on the subject of vengeance, in which he drew a sharp distinction between public and private morality. 'God is my witness,' he declared, 'that as a private person I have done nothing unworthy of an honest man, and as a Secretary of State, nothing unbefitted of my duty.' Another topic discussed in this first day of the trial was that of Thomas Morgan, Mary's agent in France, now in prison there for his involvement in the Parry plot to assassinate Elizabeth. Cecil tried to make out that the fact that Morgan was her pensioner contaminated Mary with his guilt. Mary answered with some asperity that Morgan was not her pensioner, but merely someone to whom she had given money from time to time, much as England had subsidized the master of Gray, and many other Scots, including the king, James himself. It was a pertinent point.

The evidence of Nau and Curle was now examined in much detail: in vain the queen enquired angrily why the two secretaries themselves were not produced in court as witnesses, since their absence cast a sinister light on the truth of their depositions. Mary pointed out that as it was admitted that Nau had actually written the text of the letters in cipher, it would have been easy enough for him to have incorporated some extra matter without her knowledge, more especially since over the past year he had taken to doing the correspondence apart in his own little cabinet, giving the excuse that it was thus easier to compose and concentrate. 'Nau had many peculiarities, likings and intentions that I cannot mention in public,' added Mary darkly.[13] Despite this outburst, at heart Mary realized the truth about her secretaries, and even in this extremity was prepared to show the human understanding for which she was rightly famous; for she went on: 'For my part, I do not wish to accuse my secretaries, but I see plainly that what they have said is from fear of torture and death. Under promise of their lives and in order to save themselves, they have excused themselves at my expense, fancying that I could thereby more easily save myself, at the same time, not knowing where I was, and not suspecting the manner in which I am treated.' She also distinguished the betrayal of Nau from that of Curle, knowing the characters of both men, saying that if Curle had done anything wrong, he must have been forced into it by Nau. Mary and Cecil now argued about who had employed

Nau—whether the fact that he was paid by the king of France might explain his disloyalty to Mary. Having made this point, however, Mary returned to her main thesis on the subject of the secretaries, that they themselves in person rather than their evidence should have been produced against her: 'If they were in my presence now they would clear me on the spot of all blame and would have put me out of case. . . .' Mary was right in the importance she attached to the secretaries' evidence: Walsingham smugly reported to Leicester the next day that the fact that her own secretaries had testified against Mary was proof of her guilt, in the minds of even her friends on the commission.[14]

According to the physician Bourgoing's account, the whole trial now broke down into a bedlam of accusations on the part of Mary's judges: these *chicaneurs* (as he persistently termed them—pettifogging lawyers) attacked her like furies, sometimes one by one, sometimes all together, all shouting that she was guilty. When Mary returned to her own apartments, she was so exhausted that she told her own servants, without wishing to carry the comparison too far, that the whole scene had reminded her of the Passion of Christ: for the judges had treated her as the Jews treated Jesus, shouting at him *'Tolle, Tolle, Crucifige'*. And so ended the first day of the trial. The queen passed an anxious and sleepless night, and began the next day early praying in her private oratory.

As she entered the great hall on the second morning of her ordeal, it was noticed that the queen was extremely pale. But her first action was to make it known that she wished to address the assembly personally. Curiosity to hear her was enormous: for over the years the legend of the imprisoned Scottish queen, whether a dragon or a captive princess, had grown quite sufficiently to arouse the keen interest of the spectators. Mary's first point was to protest strongly and movingly against the manner in which she had been treated on the previous day, being attacked on every issue, although she had only consented to answer accusations specifically related to the assassination plot against Elizabeth. Weak and ill as she was, she was alone among them, a sick woman, with no paper, no notes and no secretary, taken by surprise by a commission which had long been preparing such charges against her: under such circumstances she concluded 'there is not one, I think, among you, let him be the cleverest man you will, but would be incapable of resisting or defending himself were he in my place.'[15]

Strangely enough this speech met with a moderate reply from Cecil, in contrast to the roughness of the previous day. Bourgoing noted that the whole behaviour of the judges was now more courteous and that Cecil on several occasions gave them hints on how to proceed. Not only that, but Mary's servants, with the quick observation of those long imprisoned, noticed that many of the nobles had come to the assembly in riding-dress and boots, from which they deduced that the proceedings were already designed, willy-nilly, to end that day. The morning was spent in going over most of the main points again—the pretended overthrow of Elizabeth, Mary's correspondence with foreign princes and her attempts to be delivered from prison. Cecil took particular care to try and persuade Mary that she was being well treated, and that although she was only being examined on the subject of the assassination, all the other evidence had to be taken into account. Cecil concluded by saying that Mary had behaved particularly badly in seeking to escape at the exact moment when the last treaty for her freedom had been about to be concluded (he was referring to the Association with James) and sending Parry to kill Elizabeth. At this corruption of the truth, Mary burst out 'Ah! You are indeed my adversary!' 'I am the adversary to the adversaries of Queen Elizabeth,' replied Cecil smoothly.[16]

The second stage of the trial concerned Mary's transference of the inheritance rights of the Scottish crown to Philip II. In a tone not unlike that of her cousin Elizabeth when her Commons grew too presumptuous, Mary sharply repudiated the right of the court even to consider this matter. It was true that as an English prisoner she hardly had much of a crown to offer, but in any case 'It is not your affair to speak of matters concerning princes, and to inquire whether they have secret intelligences with each other'. When Cecil questioned her as to how she would have acted if the Spanish army had arrived, Mary stuck to the answer that she was not answerable for the Spanish, and again and again declared: 'I desired nothing but my own deliverance'. Accusations were now piled on her head from the intended murder of the queen, to the prayers said at Rome for Mary as the true queen of En-

gland. Throughout all these speeches, Mary adhered steadfastly to the statement that she had neither planned nor
known of any lethal enterprise. She appealed to her own
reputation for mercy and, how in Scotland she had always
been blamed for being so tolerant to the Protestants: 'It
has been the cause of my ruin,' she reflected sadly, 'for
my subjects became sad and haughty and abused my clemency; indeed they now complain that they were never so
well off as under my government.'[17]

In short Mary took her stand on the two things which
she had always desired, and freely admitted to having
done so—her own deliverance and the support of the
Catholic cause in England. Beyond these aims, she no
longer wished for anything, neither honours nor kingdoms; and in defence of this last aim she was prepared to
die. If the Pope in Rome had chosen to give her the title
of queen of England, it was not for her to correct him.
As for the famous bull, she herself had offered to prevent
its execution. Yet she felt herself more than ever as one
with the whole Catholic community in England, whose
prayers were sustaining her, and against whose cruel persecution she once more vigorously protested. The queen's
last demand was to be granted a full hearing in front of
Parliament; instead of being limited to this unjust trial,
and to be permitted to confer personally with Queen Elizabeth. Mary then rose. As she proceeded from her chair,
she regarded the whole assembly, and most regally declared that she pardoned them for what they had done.
Mary then had a few private words with Walsingham,
which seemed to displease him, for she once more turned
and addressed the assembly as a whole: 'My lords and
gentlemen, I place my cause in the hands of God'. As the
queen passed the table full of lawyers she permitted herself a last little pleasantry: she called on God to pardon
them for the way they had treated her—'somewhat rudely'
—as she put it, and she added with a smile: 'May God
keep me from having to do with you all again'. At this the
lawyers also exchanged smiles.[18]

In answer to the express wish of Elizabeth who wanted
no sentence pronounced before she herself had considered
the proceedings, the court was now prorogued, to meet in
ten days' time at the Star Chamber at Westminster. The
noblemen, booted and spurred in advance, rode away
from Fotheringhay. Mary was left to go back once more

to the little round of captivity. Her tranquillity was not
in the slightest disturbed by the harrowing ordeal through
which she had just passed. It was as though she had predicted long ago in her own mind the course which events
were likely to take and had even found in the working out
of her prophecies, melancholy as they were, a source of
strength. Just as the populace had been curious to see the
baleful queen of Scots, Mary herself had derived some
minor enjoyment from this brief glimpse of English society—the only true sight of it she ever had. Throughout
the trial she questioned Paulet concerning the faces of
various English gentlemen among the judges, many of
whose names had been long familiar to her. After so many
years of virtual solitude the crowded court scene brought
at least the compensation of satisfying her curiosity about
England.

Paulet of course found her conduct at the trial utterly
distasteful: to his way of thinking, the queen of Scots was
never more odious than when displaying the full counterfeit charm of her character. He wrote to London that her
intention had been by 'long and artificial speeches' to excite the pity of the judges, and throw all the blame on
Elizabeth, or rather upon her Council. Whereas Mary told
her servants she had discerned expressions of compassion
among the crowd, Paulet cheered himself with the reflection that they had all been 'of one consent and mind to
hear her cause with indifference'.[19] But to those less prejudiced than the queen's jailer, and to those who would
come after him and attempt to pass the judgement of history upon the Scottish queen, Mary would elicit not so
much pity as profound admiration for the cool and clever
manner in which she had single-handedly conducted her
defence against all the odds. In her essay on Adversity
she had referred to the 'disagreeable and ugly slough of
pusillanimity', the one pitfall into which those called by
God to wield the sceptre should never fall.[20] It was not a
trap into which Mary had fallen herself. Throughout her
trial she had shown herself unwaveringly regal, and not
all the petty spite of Paulet could take this triumph from
her.

The next few weeks represented a strangely serene inter-
lude in Mary's life, the Indian summer of her captivity,
when she was able to add to the self-discipline of the

THE CATACLYSM

long-held prisoner, the peace of mind of one who knew
her confinement was rapidly moving towards its finish.
Mary now read much concerning English history, a habit
she had already begun to develop at Chartley, since the
inventory of her belongings in June 1586 mentions a number of books on the subject as well as a map. She embroidered. She made arrangements in her own mind for the
final journey she was now convinced lay ahead. Bourgoing
found her so far from being troubled by what had passed
that 'I had not seen her so joyous, nor so constantly at her
ease for the last seven years. She spoke only on pleasant
subjects, and often in particular, gave her opinion on some
points of the history of England, in the study of which she
passed a good portion of the day, afterwards discoursing
on the subject of her reading with her household, quite
familiarly and joyously, showing no signs of sadness, but
with even a more cheerful countenance than previous to
her troubles'.[21] It was clear that Mary's words at her trial
were no hypocrisy—she truly did not fear to die in a good
cause: Mary, like many other philosopher-prisoners, took
comfort in the perusal of the past, from whose study one
lesson can always be learnt: that the single action of a
human being, be it a heroic life or a noble death, can have
incalculable effects upon the course of history.

On 25 October the commissioners met again in the Star
Chamber in London. On this occasion Nau and Curle
were actually produced, raising once more the question
why in all decency they could not have appeared at
Fotheringhay. Both reaffirmed their evidence on oath
and stated that they had given it 'frankly and voluntarily'.
The commission accordingly found Mary guilty of 'com-
passing and imagining since June 1st matters tending to
the death and destruction of the Queen of England.' Only
Lord Zouch, a youngish peer, who had lived through a
somewhat wild youth in which he spent his patrimony, had
the courage to express himself not altogether satisfied. The
commission took particular trouble to except King James
from his mother's guilt since, by the terms of the Act of
Association, her disablement from the succession would
have applied also to her son. The two Houses of Parliament now presented an address to Queen Elizabeth in
which they prayed fervently for the execution of the Scottish Queen for the sake of Elizabeth's own safety which
would be in peril 'so long as the said Scottish Queen shall

be suffered to continue and shall not receive that due punishment, which by justice and the laws of this your realm
she hath so often and for so many ways for her most detestable and wicked offences deserved'. Elizabeth replied
in a long and ambivalent speech, in which she showed how
much she personally was aware, even if her Commons
were not, that 'we princes are set as it were upon stages,
in the sight and view of all the world' and that the execution of Mary was one thing for the Commons to
demand, quite another for Elizabeth, a fellow-queen, to
confirm.[22] Twelve days later, Elizabeth, having indicated
that it would be highly desirable in any case to secure a
full confession from the queen of Scots, asked her two
Houses with further ambiguity whether they could not
devise some better remedy whereby the queen of Scots'
life might be spared and her own security provided for.

Mary herself was not immediately informed that the sentence of death had been passed against her in London. In
the meantime Paulet endeavoured to carry out his instructions from London and secure that full confession, that
humiliating pleading for pardon from the Scottish queen,
for which the English queen so passionately wished. On
1 November, the Feast of All Saints, which Mary spent
in prayer and reading the lives of the saints since she was
still deprived of her chaplain, de Préau, she received a visit
from Paulet after dinner. Paulet showed unexpected courtesy in actually waiting until her prayers were over. They
argued a little on the subject of history. Mary observed
how blood never ceased to flow in the course of English
history, and Paulet commented that this was the same in
many countries, especially in time of national peril. Mary
then enquired after one or two people at her trial whom
she had imagined to be sympathetic to her, and asked
their names that she might remember them. 'Not one of
them was favourable to your cause', said Paulet crossly.
'And everyone else is astonished to see you so calm under
the circumstances in which you find yourself. No living
person has ever been accused of crimes so frightful and
odious as yours'. But Mary was not disposed to admit in
any way to these frightful and odious crimes. Instead she
reiterated her claim that she stood witness for the truths
of the Catholic religion, and argued with Paulet about
whether or not Elizabeth claimed to be supreme head of
the Church. Paulet maintained that Elizabeth was on the

contrary 'head and governor under God of things ecclesiastical and temporal in England', but Mary dismissed the difference between the two titles in an expressive French phrase: *'C'était manteau blanc ou blanc manteau'*, she remarked. Paulet was obliged to report back to London his disappointment: 'I see no change in her, from her former quietness and serenity, certified in my letters,' he wrote. In the meantime Paulet greatly disliked these battles of wits, in which he could scarcely hold himself to be the winner. He told Walsingham: 'I pray you let me hear from you whether it is expected that I should see my charge often, which as I do not desire to do, so I do not see that any good can come of it'.[23]

On the evening of 19 November, Lord Buckhurst, who had arrived at Fotheringhay with Beale, the clerk of the Council, delivered his message to Mary. Buckhurst now warned Mary that it was considered impossible that both she and Elizabeth should continue to live. Although Elizabeth had not given her consent to the execution, Buckhurst solemnly called on Mary to repent; to that end he offered her the services of a Protestant clergyman, the bishop or dean of Peterborough. Mary described the whole interview in her letter to Beaton in Paris at the end of November. 'I thanked God and them,' she wrote proudly, 'for the honour they did me in considering me to be such a necessary instrument for the re-establishing of religion in this island. . . . In confirmation of all this as I had before protested, I offered willingly to shed my blood in the quarrel of the Catholic Church'. This was of course the very last answer which Paulet and Buckhurst were prepared to receive: they told Mary roughly that as she was to die for the intended murder of Elizabeth, she would certainly not be regarded as either a saint or a martyr. But Mary was quite intelligent enough to see that despite Paulet's protests matters were going in the direction she hoped. It was no wonder Camden heard that her face was now illumined with extraordinary joy at the thought that God had thus chosen her to be a martyr. It was left to Paulet to castigate her speeches angrily in his report to London as 'superfluous and idle', and tell Walsingham that he had no doubt Buckhurst too had found the queen of Scots' endless speech-making extremely tedious.[24]

Such pieces of oratory might be superfluous and idle to Paulet but to Mary they were essential planks in the

platform from which she intended to undergo her martyrdom for the Catholic faith: Paulet's opinion was a matter
of indifference to her, so long as her words would one
day echo forth in the theatre of the world. But Paulet's
next action—the removal of the royal cloth of state over
Mary's chair, by which she set such store—offended her
in the vital matter of her queenship. The reasons which
Paulet gave hardly added to the grace of the occasion:
'You are now only a dead woman,' he said, 'without the
dignity or honours of a Queen'. Mary responded with a
spirited defence of her station, in which her studies in
English history prompted her to compare herself to King
Richard II in the hands of his enemies. Her own attendants
refused to obey Paulet's command to remove the dais, so
that it had to be thrown down by his own men. Paulet now
added insult to injury by sitting in the queen's presence
with his head covered, and furthermore ordering the removal of the royal billiard table, on the grounds that it
was now no time for the queen to be indulging in amusement. However, it would seem from Paulet's own account
of the scene that he had exceeded his instructions to a
certain extent; the removal of the dais was due to his own
excess of zeal, prompted rather by a rumour from London
that Elizabeth disliked the idea of the dais, than by the
specific instructions of the English queen. The next day
Paulet went to Mary and offered to write to London for
official leave to restore the dais, saying it had been removed on the Council's orders. This merely gave Mary
opportunity to point sublimely to the symbol which she
had already hung in the place of the vanished cloth of
state—a crucifix. In her own words to Henry of Guise, 'I
showed them the Cross of my Saviour in the place where
my dais had been'.[25]

It was now the end of November. Mary imagined that
her days were truly numbered. She spent two days writing
her farewell letters, with a hand crippled by rheumatism.*
She wrote to the Pope at length, professing the truth of the
Catholic faith by which she had always lived, and towards
which she had ever done her duty in the past, so far as
the dour conditions of captivity and illness had enabled

---

* These letters, which Mary handed to her servants to deliver, did
not reach their destinations until the following autumn, owing to the
long imprisonment of these servants after their mistress's death.

her. Now, however, she was to be granted a supreme opportunity, as the one remaining Catholic member of the
royal house of England and Scotland, to testify on behalf
of her religion by her death 'for my sins and those of this
unfortunate island'.[26] Religious rather than dynastic interests were now paramount in her mind, and it was the
Catholic faith, rather than maternal feelings, which now
swayed Mary in the dispositions she laid down for the
English throne after her death: she begged the Pope to let
the Catholic king of Spain secure her rights to the crown
of England, in place of James, if he remained obstinately
outside the Catholic Church.

Another letter went to Mendoza, that companion of
her intrigues, now in Paris, assuring him that she had
all the courage necessary to receive her sentence for the
honour of God.[27] To Mendoza, Mary repeated solemnly
her bestowal of the rights of the English throne upon the
Spanish king if James did not embrace the Catholic religion. She recommended to him her poor destitute servants, including Leslie, the bishop of Ross, whom she had
heard was in dire straits, and bequeathed to Mendoza,
who had cared so prolongedly and so passionately for the
cause of her deliverance, the diamond which Norfolk had
given her so long ago. Lastly Mary wrote to her cousin,
Henry of Guise, whom she now held to be her closest
blood relation since the betrayal of James and addressing
him as 'you whom I hold as dearest to me in the world'.
To him once more she stressed the nobility of the end
which awaited her: 'Although no executioner has ever
before dipped his hand in our [Guise] blood, be not
ashamed of it, my dear friend, for the condemnation of
heretics and enemies of the Church (and who have no
jurisdiction over me, a free Queen) is profitable before
God for the children of His Church'. As for the Faith: 'I
esteem myself born, both on the paternal and the maternal
side to offer my blood for it. . . .'[28] Yet lest the full details
of her martyrdom should be concealed by the English,
and because not everything could be trusted to letters,
Mary begged Henry of Guise and Mendoza to listen carefully to the eye-witness accounts of her own servants after
her death, when they should manage to deliver them.

As she wrote, Queen Mary could hear the banging of
the workmen in the great hall of the Council. She imagined quite genuinely that she was listening to the sound

of her own scaffold being erected. She mentioned the subject to Mendoza as she wrote: 'I think they are making a scaffold to make me play the last scene of the Tragedy. . . .' In fact it was to be over two months before this final scene was actually played. The reason of course was that Elizabeth obstinately hesitated to confirm the sentence. The most the Parliament could secure from her was the public proclamation of the sentence of death on 4 December, on the understanding of which Parliament was prorogued till the spring. The English people might rejoice and ring their bells at the news, but their queen was still very far from resolving her own dilemma. Quite apart from the fact that Mary was an anointed queen and her own cousin, there were the problems of foreign relations to consider. How would France, where Mary had once been queen, react to the news of her death—and still more Scotland, where Mary had once actually reigned, and her own son now ruled. As the prospect of war with Spain loomed nearer, the goodwill of France and the continuance of the alliance with Scotland became more important than mere diplomatic friendship. Were such vital benevolences really worth sacrificing for the death of one old and sick woman, who had been a prisoner for nearly twenty years? It was Mary the prisoner at Fotheringhay who was calm and tranquil, who wrote her letters, considered how she could best dispose her affairs for her servants, contemplated her crucifix, and showed herself more joyous than she had been for years. It was Elizabeth the jailer, in London, muttering to herself *Aut fer aut feri, ne feriare, feri*—suffer or strike, strike or be struck—who suffered the torments of indecision.

26 *The Dolorous Stroke*

'Rue not my death, rejoice at my repose
It was no death to me but to my woe;
The bud was opened to let out the rose,
The chain was loosed to let the captive go.'

From Decease, release, *ode by* ROBERT SOUTHWELL, S.J.,
on the death of Mary Queen of Scots

When King James first heard the news of his mother's arrest at Chartley, he contented himself with observing that
she should 'drink the ale she had brewed' and in future
be allowed to meddle with nothing except prayer and the
service of God.[1] Not only did he ostentatiously ignore the
possibility that his mother might now be in danger of her
life, but he also chose this moment to sound out Elizabeth on the question of a marriage between them, through
the medium of Archibald Douglas. Elizabeth was now over
fifty, thirty years senior to James, and, although James
was evidently prepared to pardon the disparity in their
ages most magnanimously if he could thus strengthen his
claim to the English throne, Elizabeth herself showed no
inclination towards this bizarre union.[2] Nevertheless
throughout the autumn James continued to maintain in
public that he had no objections to his mother being imprisoned in the most rigorous manner in the world—let
her be put in the Tower or some other 'firm Manse'—so
long as her actual life was not forfeited. It was not until
after the trial and death sentence that it was made clear
to James by Archibald Douglas from London that he
might shortly have to choose between his mother's life,
and the continuation of the newly formed Anglo-Scottish
alliance, which in turn involved his hopes of inheriting the
English throne.

James's dilemma in Scotland did not cause him the
human anguish which Elizabeth in her reluctance to confirm the death sentence was undergoing in England. She
told the French ambassador at the beginning of December
that she had never shed so many tears over anything, not

even at the deaths of her father, her brother Edward or her sister Mary, as at what she termed this 'unfortunate affair', and whether her grief was at her own indecision or at the prospect of shedding Mary's blood, there is no reason to doubt the genuineness of her emotion.[3] James, on the other hand, felt considerable perplexity as to what course to take, but no purely personal feelings; the chief concern of the Scottish mission to Elizabeth in November was to ensure that nothing would be done against Mary 'to the prejudice of any title of the King's'. In the meantime it was widely rumoured in Scotland that James feared to request any sort of favour from Elizabeth as regards Mary, lest he should lose the goodwill of the English queen, although Scottish public opinion was reacting most strongly to the idea that their former sovereign should be executed by a foreign country. As Gray wrote to Douglas on 23 November: James would find it hard to keep the peace if her life were touched. 'I never saw all the people so willing to concur in anything as in this. They that hated most her prosperity regret her adversity.' James himself pointed out his invidious position to Elizabeth, in language which made clear that it was fear of a national outcry which animated him, rather than some more personal emotion: 'Guess ye in what strait my honour will be, this disaster being perfected,' he wrote, 'since before God I already scarce dare go abroad, for crying out of the whole people'.[4]

Despite these fears, the one sanction which James had it in his power to invoke to save his mother's life—and which in the opinion of at least one historian would have effectively preserved her from execution at English hands[5] —was never made. James hovered over the subject of the death sentence with a series of dire but meaningless threats. At no point did he say that he would break the Anglo-Scottish league if his mother's death was brought about by England, although Elizabeth anxiously enquired of his ambassadors whether that was in fact his intention. His fulminations and his embassy were both intended to save his face in Scotland: they were not intended to save his mother's life in England. Nor did all his emissaries agree with Gray in expressing their disgust at the idea of the execution: Sir Alexander Stewart expressed the damaging view that James would somehow manage to digest his

mother's death.* Once it became apparent to the English
that despite all James's protests the league was to be considered inviolable whatever action they took against Mary,
the date of the Scottish queen's death drew appreciably
nearer.

The protests made by the French were more authenti-
cally passionate, but proved in the end equally ineffective:
a special ambassador, de Bellievre, was sent by King Henry
III to plead with Elizabeth who was answered, in Cecil's
words 'that if the French King understood her Majesty's
peril, if he loveth her as he pretendeth, he would not press
her Majesty to hazard her life'. The resident French ambassador, Châteauneuf, continued to make valiant efforts
to save Mary, but in January his attempts were sharply
curtailed by the fortunate discovery by Walsingham of yet
another plot against Elizabeth's life. This providential coincidence led to Châteauneuf's house arrest, and rendered
him impotent to help Mary further during the crucial
weeks in the new year; it also aroused a wave of anti-
French feeling in England—although the plot itself was
highly dubious in origins, and seems to have been largely
concocted by Walsingham to produce these precise effects.[7]
In December Cecil had drawn up in his own hand-writing
a list of reasons against the execution of the queen of
Scots. Among the reasons cited was the cogent argument
Sanguis sanguinem procreat—blood breeds blood—the
supposition that Mary's health was in any case so afflicted
that she might die naturally at any moment, and the fact
that the king of France had promised to go surety in the
future for the end of the attempts on Elizabeth's life.[8] By
January, it appeared that as Mary's foreign champions
had either retired or were being swept from the lists, the
fact that blood might breed blood was no longer so important.

There was certainly to be no question of the captive
eluding her fate: at Paulet's request the garrison at Fotheringhay was strengthened to seventy foot-soldiers and
fifty bowmen. In November Paulet had been joined in his
charge by Sir Drue Drury. In mid-December Mary sent

* Dr D. H. Willson, in his biography of James I, thinks it not impossible that Stewart had secret instructions over Gray's head, on
the subject; in spite of James's publicly expressed anger at Stewart's
statements, Stewart was allowed to return to Scotland with impunity.[6]

for both her custodians, and asked them to despatch on
her behalf a farewell letter to Elizabeth. Dramatically,
Mary wiped her cheeks with both sheets, in order to show
that the leaves were not poisoned. She then sealed the
letter with Spanish wax and closed it with white silk.[9]
Mary's main points to Elizabeth concerned firstly the disposal of her body after death—she was anxious that her
servants should be allowed to convey it to France, rather
than Scotland, where the Protestant burial rites would constitute a profanation by her standards; secondly she expressed her fears of the 'secret tyrannies' of those whom
Elizabeth had placed around her, which she dreaded
would result in her secret assassination; thirdly Mary asked
to be allowed to send a jewel and last farewell to her son
James; finally Mary raised once more the vexed question
of the royal dais. She concluded on a magisterial note of
warning to Elizabeth: 'Do not accuse me of presumption if, on the eve of leaving this world and preparing
myself for a better one, I remind you that one day you
will have to answer for your charge, as well as those that
are sent before. . . .' Mary signed the letter: 'Your sister
and cousin, wrongfully imprisoned'.[10]

Despite the innocuous character of Mary's last requests,
Paulet and Drury did not immediately despatch this missive, not so much out of fear of Elizabeth's anger, as out
of dread that its mildness might move the English queen
to clemency, and further delay the execution of justice.
Paulet confided to Davison, the secretary of the Council,
that as they were strongly hoping the sentence would be
carried out before Christmas, it was planned that the letter should arrive a few days afterwards, when the queen of
Scots would be already dead and it would be too late for
Elizabeth to exercise mercy. In Paulet's opinion, there
were many pressing reasons why the sentence should be
carried out as fast as possible, not the least among them
being the return of Mary's priest (or almoner as she always termed him) de Préau.[11]

On de Préau's arrival, Paulet took the precaution of
searching his papers, and was rewarded by finding two
leaves of paper in the form of a diary inserted among his
philosophical exercises; luckily he decided de Préau was of
no particular account—being 'of weak and slender judgement'. All the same, for what he chose to describe as
Christian reasons, Paulet wished that de Préau had been re-

stricted to a single visit to the queen on the eve of her death: the spiritual perils of his continual association with his mistress seemed yet another reason for bringing Mary's life to a speedy close. After all, expostulated Paulet, Mary showed no signs of repentance, no signs even of wishing to live, and an ignorant papist priest would surely only confirm her in such reprobate tendencies. The return of the little store of money which had been seized from Mary at Chartley, although performed by Paulet with some reluctance, seemed a minor evil compared to this quite unnecessary display of tolerance on behalf of the central government.

Around Christmas Paulet either fell ill or pleaded a diplomatic illness to avoid those argumentative interviews with Mary which he so greatly disliked. Paulet's withdrawal affected Mary herself depressively: Paulet might dread the interviews, but to Mary they were her solitary contact with the outside world, and represented her only source of stimulus, to rehearse her arguments, and in arguing to keep up her spirits. The weeks now passed slowly and heavily: without Paulet to joust with verbally, for the first time Mary began to feel the suspense of her situation. By 8 January Mary was begging Paulet to pay her another visit, for although both were within the confines of the same castle, she had not seen him since before Christmas, and as to his illness she had heard he had been out of doors the previous day. Part of Mary's anxiety arose through having heard nothing from Elizabeth in answer to her farewell requests. On 12 January she wrote another long letter, in which she pleaded with Elizabeth to end the miserable uncertainty of the situation, not so much for herself as for her poor servants, on whom the strain was telling. In her last paragraph she even tried to tempt Elizabeth's curiosity once more by enquiring to whom she might confide her death-bed's secrets; it was as though the notion of the unfulfilled meeting still haunted her after all these years, and she had some wild hope that Elizabeth might still pay her a personal visit at the end. The bait, however, was never extended where Elizabeth might see it: for Paulet refused to despatch this second letter at all, on the grounds that he was lying in bed with his arms bandaged, and that Mary must content herself with awaiting the answer to her first missive. Later he explained that

he would not send the letter at all, because he had no orders to do so.[12]

Slowly the winter days passed by. It was now over three
months since those booted and spurred judges had galloped
away from Fotheringhay and there was still no news from
London that the end was even near. It was inevitable that
the hopes of those faithful partisans and observers, Mary's
servants, should begin to rise. Although Mary had no doubts
herself that sooner or later she would die, when Christmas
had passed, the long delay encouraged her retainers to
begin to hope on her behalf. On 20 January Melville interpreted a remark of Paulet's on the subject of the royal
servants' wages as meaning that the period of their service
to Mary was likely to be extended indefinitely into the
future. This made the blow which fell upon them the next
day all the more painful to bear: brusquely Paulet informed
Melville and the chaplain de Préau that although they were
to continue in residence at Fotheringhay, henceforth they
were to be parted from their mistress. Only the physician
Bourgoing was to be allowed to continue in attendance.
The removal of these loyal servants lowered Mary's spirits
further: her old fears of a secret death were revivified. But
when Mary expressed these anxieties to Paulet through the
medium of Bourgoing, she succeeded in causing him considerable offence: he fell into a rage at her taunts, and told
Bourgoing that 'he was a man of honour and a gentleman,
and he would not wish so to dishonour himself as to wish
to exercise such cruelty or to conduct himself like a
Turk'.[13] Man of honour as he professed himself—and time
was to prove the truth of his claim—Paulet had no objections to imposing a series of further petty humiliations on
his prisoner. On the following Monday Mary's butler was
forbidden to carry the rod before her meat dishes, a service
he was performing in the absence of the steward Melville.
Once again Mary jumped to the conclusion that this regal
dignity was being stripped from her in order to kill her
secretly. In answer to her protest she received the chilling
reply from Paulet that her priest, her steward, her dais and
her rod had all been taken from her for the same reason:
because she was no longer a queen but 'an attained, convicted and condemned woman'. It was left for Mary to derive what consolation she could from the reflection that
King Richard II also had been treated in this opprobrious
manner.

Attained, convicted, and condemned Mary might be, yet there was still no official word concerning her execution. But it was said afterwards that on the Sunday 29 January, between midnight and one o'clock in the morning, the heavens gave their own portent that the end was not far off: for a great flame of fire illuminated the windows of the queen's room three times. The light was bright enough to read by, and blinded the guards stationed beneath her chamber, already made nervous and apprehensive by the phenomenon, which was seen nowhere else in the castle.[14] This supernatural warning,* if warning it was, was certainly borne out by events. Three days later, at her court at Greenwich, Queen Elizabeth at last sent for Davison to bring the warrant for the execution, which for so long had lacked her own signature. Davison discreetly placed the warrant in the middle of a pile of other papers which the queen was due to sign. The ruse—for Elizabeth had made it increasingly clear to her anxious ministers that she must be the subject of a ruse—was successful. It was thus, in the midst of an innocuous conversation on the subject of the weather, that Elizabeth finally signed the warrant, with all her other papers, and having done so, threw them idly down on the table. But the queen could not quite bear to let this vexatious yet momentous subject, on which she had expended so much emotion, pass so easily. She asked Davison teasingly if he felt distressed to see her give the famous signature after so long. Davison replied tactfully that he preferred to see the death of a guilty person to that of an innocent one. Elizabeth now instructed Davison to get the Great Seal of England attached to the warrant by the Lord Chancellor and then take it to Walsingham. Her vein of humour was not exhausted: 'I fear the grief thereof will go near to kill him outright,' said Elizabeth happily. She then concluded the subject with a practical direction— the execution was under no circumstances to be held in public, but in the great hall of the castle. Elizabeth then

---

* A more rational explanation might be that the mysterious fire was produced by a comet. In Elizabethan England, comets were traditionally associated with the deaths of famous people, or as Shakespeare put it in *Julius Caesar*: '*When beggars die, there are no comets seen; the heavens themselves blaze forth the deaths of princes.*'[15]

laid it down that she personally was to be told no more on the subject until the execution was successfully completed.[16]

Despite this Pilate-like observation, Elizabeth still did not totally wash her hands of the matter. Mary's fears of a secret death were not altogether groundless. Even before Elizabeth had affixed her signature to the warrant, she had been heard muttering in the hearing of her ministers that the provisions of the Act of Association might make it a positive duty for a loyal subject to kill the queen of Scots . . . thus ridding the English queen of the responsibility. Her ministers, understanding her intentions only too well, pretended not to grasp her meaning. On 1 February, however, Elizabeth was more explicit. Having signed the warrant she murmured wistfully to Davison that if a loyal subject were to save her from embarrassment by dealing the blow, the resentment of France and Scotland might be disarmed. The obvious loyal subjects to assume this helpful role were Paulet and Drury at Fotheringhay. Davison's first reaction was to fear yet another excuse for delaying the execution itself. But against his advice, the queen insisted on the point being made to Paulet: a letter was duly sent to the custodians regretting that they had not 'found out some way to shorten the life of that Queen [Mary] considering the great peril she [Elizabeth] is subject unto hourly, so long as the said Queen shall live'.[17]

Now the issue which Mary had so long dreaded was squarely placed before her jailer: and it is one of the ironies of history that Paulet, the man whom Mary had for so long both disliked and feared, hesitated for an instant, but seized his pen and wrote back to his royal mistress in the most trenchant language refusing the odious commission: 'I am so unhappy to have lived to see this unhappy day,' he replied, 'in which I am required by direction from my most gracious sovereign to do an act which God and the law forbiddeth. . . . God forbid that I should make so foul a shipwreck of my conscience, or leave so great a blot on my poor posterity, to shed blood without law or warrant'.[18] Paradoxically Mary was saved from the private extinction which she dreaded by the action of the Puritan who had done so much to make her last months uncomfortable and humiliating. Elizabeth, on the other hand, by a course of action which did neither her courage, her char-

acter nor her reputation any credit, gave Paulet a chance
to redeem himself at the bar of history—unimaginative,
bigoted, petty tyrant he might be, he was still no assassin.
It was left to Elizabeth when his answer was conveyed to
her to exclaim furiously over his 'daintiness', the 'niceness'
of 'those precise fellows' such as Paulet, who professed
great zeal for her safety, but would perform nothing.[19]

Elizabeth's Council, experienced in the ways of their
mistress, did not wait for Paulet's answer before acting.
With the warrant in their possession, it was unanimously
decided to set proceedings in hand immediately. Elizabeth's
ability to continue to toy with the subject despite her signature was confirmed on 5 February when she told Davison
roguishly that she had dreamt the night before she was
running him through with a sword for causing the death of
Mary. Her interest in assassination was also not exhausted:
she appeared to play with the idea of having Mary smoth-
ered by Robert Wingfield, pretending that this had been
the advice of Archibald Douglas. The Council did not wait
to see through the full comedy of such behaviour before
acting. The warrant was handed to Beale, the clerk of the
Council, who was instructed to set forth immediately for
Fotheringhay, accompanied by Shrewsbury and the earl of
Kent, with a covering commission to go into Hertfordshire
and Bedfordshire to hear 'hues and cries', in order to cloak
his mission in the utmost secrecy.* The greatest thought
was given to the details of the execution in Walsingham's
memorial on the subject—down to the speeches which the
two earls were to make at the ceremony. Cecil added his
own comment on the subject in the margin of the memorial: the speeches should be used 'To express her many
attempts both for destruction of the Queen's person, and
the invasion of this realm'.[20]

More practical aspects of the affair were not neglected.
Walsingham made himself responsible for contacting the
actual executioner. In the greatest secrecy, his servant
Anthony Hall acquired the services of one Bull, £10 being
the agreed fee for 'his labour'. Another of Walsingham's

* Afterward Beale believed that this mission had fatally blighted
his career: in 1599 he attributed his failure to find advancement 'for
that my name was made odious to the whole world for conveying
down the Commission for the execution of the Scottish Queen'.

servants, Digby, conducted Bull down to Fotheringhay, disguised as a serving-man with 'his instrument'—the axe—hidden in a trunk. Such efficiency resulted in the smooth working of all the preliminary arrangements, except that Sir Walter Mildmay, whether out of fear of public opinion, apprehension regarding Elizabeth's reactions, or genuine fastidiousness, refused to house the executioner at his own house of Apethorpe, so that he had to be lodged secretly in an inn at Fotheringhay. On arrival, in order to give every appearance of legality to the proceedings, Beale took care to inform the local justices of the peace and officials, both of Northamptonshire and Huntingdon, including the sheriff of Northampton who was to be responsible for providing the surgeons for the occasion.[21]

Still the sadly depleted royal household at Fotheringhay had no inkling of what was afoot. On the Saturday 4 February, Bourgoing went to Paulet and asked if he could go visit the neighbouring villages and search for certain herbal remedies which might help the queen against her rheumatism for the rest of the winter season. Paulet was evasive, and said he could take no decision until the Monday. On Sunday, however, Mary learnt that Beale had arrived at Fotheringhay and, interpreting the significance of his arrival correctly, told Bourgoing he might cease searching for a cure since she would now have no need of it. But no authoritative intimation was given to the queen concerning her fate, which left her servants free to continue to hope for the next few days. It was not until the Tuesday 7 February, that the arrival of several more people at the castle, including Shrewsbury and Kent who had been lodging at Orton near-by 'threw the household into a terrible state of apprehension, 'Having for the last three months imagined many coming evils for Her Majesty,' as Bourgoing put it,[22] there could now be no doubt that the blow so long anticipated was about to fall.

The official time given to the queen to prepare for death was of the minimum. It was not until after dinner that the two custodians and the two earls asked to see Mary. She had retired to bed, but on being told that the matter was urgent, asked for a little time in which to dress, and then received them in her room, seated in a chair at the foot of her bed. Of the deputation, including Beale, it was Shrews-

bury who told Mary that she had been found guilty and
condemned to death. Beale now read aloud from the warrant, from which the yellow wax Great Seal of England
dangled, in order to emphasize once more that Mary's
judges were acting legally, in accordance with the Act of
Association. Mary received the news with absolute calm.
When Beale had done, she replied with great dignity and
no show of emotion: 'I thank you for such welcome news.
You will do me great good in withdrawing me from this
world out of which I am very glad to go.' She touched on
her queenly position and royal blood, adding that in spite
of this 'all my life I have had only sorrow', and saying
that she was now overjoyed to have the opportunity at the
end to shed her blood for the Catholic Church. Mary then
placed her hand on the New Testament and solemnly protested herself to be innocent of all the crimes imputed to
her. When Kent objected that it was a Catholic version of
the Bible, Mary answered: 'If I swear on the book which
I believe to be the true version, will your lordship not believe my oath more than if I were to swear on a translation in which I do not believe?'

But Mary's captors were not prepared to concede either
the sincerity of her religious convictions or the need to
display a certain tolerance towards a woman *in extremis*.
They now offered her the services of the Protestant dean
of Peterborough to help her make ready for her end, and
eliminate from her mind at the last 'the follies and
abominations of popery'. Mary crossed herself, and utterly refused even to consider the suggestion, saying that
when she had first arrived in England she had listened to
both sides of the question, but now all that was past,
and the hour of her death was the very moment to show
constancy. The result of this interchange, in which as
Paulet reported afterwards 'we prevailed nothing', was that
when Mary proceeded to ask for her own chaplain to be
readmitted to her presence, in order to make ready her
soul, in Paulet's words 'we utterly denied that unto her'.
This was a serious blow to Mary, who had not anticipated
this final inhumanity. However, when Kent exclaimed:
'Your life would be the death of our religion, your death
would be its life,' her face lit up.[23] At least his words revealed that already in the opinion of the world her death
was linked with the survival of the Catholic Church in
England.

When the queen asked at what hour she was to die, Shrewsbury replied in a faltering voice: 'Tomorrow morning at eight o'clock.'* Mary remarked that the time was very short since it was already late. She then made a series of requests, all of which were denied to her: she applied for her papers and account books, which were refused on the grounds that they were still in London in the hands of Wade; once more she begged vainly for her chaplain; thirdly she asked that her body might be interred in France at either St Denis or Rheims, only to be told that Elizabeth had ruled against it. Her last questions were on the subject of Nau and Curle, and whether they were already dead; on hearing that Curle was in prison, and that Nau had gone to France, Mary exclaimed sadly that she was about to die for him who had borne false witness against her. Mary's servants, in a state of hysteria, tried to get some sort of reprieve or at least a stay of execution, weeping and crying and protesting that the time was too short. Bourgoing pleaded with Shrewsbury, recalling not only how he had cured him of his illness, but also all the mercies which Shrewsbury himself had shown to Mary in the past. Shrewsbury either was not or dared not be moved. He said there was to be no delay.[24]

The queen of Scots was left alone to spend the last evening of her life with her servants, some of whom like Jane Kennedy had spent a whole generation in her service. She tried to rally them. 'Well, Jane Kennedy,' said the queen. 'Did I not tell you this would happen? . . . I knew they would never allow me to live, I was too great an obstacle to their religion.' Mary then asked for her supper to be served as speedily as possible, in order that she might have time to put her affairs in order. It was a heart-breaking meal, the servants outdoing themselves in the assiduousness of their service, as though there was some comfort to be had in making each little gesture as perfect as possible: Bourgoing, acting as steward in Melville's absence, presented the dishes to his mistress and, as he did so, he could not control the tears from pouring down his cheeks. The queen herself ate little. She sat in a sort of dream, from time to time referring to Kent's outburst on the subject of

* In fact, so far as can be made out from divergent accounts, the queen did not die at 8 A.M., but later.

her death and her religion: 'Oh how happy these words make me,' she murmured. 'Here at last is the truth.' When the meal was over, the queen asked her servants to drink to her, and as they did so, kneeling before her, their tears mingled with the wine.

Mary now seated herself and went through the contents of her wardrobe in detail. Her remaining money she sorted personally into little portions, and placed in packets, on which she wrote in her own hand the name of the servant for whom they were destined. From belongings she divided off certain mementoes for royalties and her relations abroad, such as the king and queen of France, Queen Catherine, and the Guises; from the rest she bestowed numerous little personal objects on all her servants;* Bourgoing received rings, silver boxes, her music book bound in velvet to remind him of the many musical evenings of the captivity, as well as the red hangings of Mary's bed; Elizabeth Curle received miniatures set in gold and enamelled tablets of Mary, Francis II and James. Melville received a little tablet of gold set with another portrait of James. Having thus disposed of those actual physical possessions which remained within her sphere, the queen drew up an elaborate testament[25] of which Henry, Duke of Guise, Beaton, the bishop of Ross, and du Ruisseau, her chancellor in France, were to be executors. She asked for Requiem Masses to be held in France, and made elaborate financial arrangements for the benefit of her servants, whether of her household or superior rank such as Beaton in France; Curle for example was to receive the marriage portion which had been promised him but never paid, and even the graceless Nau was to be allowed his pension, if he should manage to prove his innocence. Beyond that, there were charitable bequests for the poor children and friars of Rheims, and instructions that her coach was to be used to convey her women to London, when the horses were

---

* These objects did not appear in the later inventories as Paulet reported: 'They have nothing to show for these things from their mistress in writing . . . all the smaller things were delivered by her own hands.' It seems, from the subsequent history of some of these mementoes, that in certain instances they were entrusted to servants still in attendance at Fotheringhay to be handed on to others who had left, or been debarred from the queen's service, at the end.

tó be sold to defray their expenses, and her furniture likewise, that they might be able to afford to return to their
countries of origin.*

Having completed these detailed dispositions for the
welfare of those she would leave behind, Mary considered
her own spiritual welfare in the shape of a farewell letter
to be handed to the chaplain de Préau. Deprived of his
physical presence, she used the medium of the letter as a
general confession of her sins, in which she asked him to
spend the night in prayer for her.[26] Mary's last letter of all
was to her brother-in-law, King Henry of France; she related the abrupt circumstances in which her sentence had
been broken to her, and her conviction that it was her
religion, coupled with her place in the English succession,
which was the true cause of her death, as it had been with
Francis of Guise; she begged him to listen to the personal
testimony concerning her execution which her physician
should give to him so soon as he could reach France, and
not trust to her letter alone; her last thoughts were the
faithful servants who had served her for so long—she asked
that their pensions and wages might be paid throughout
their lives, and in particular that de Préau her chaplain
might be awarded some little benefice in France from which
he could spend the rest of his days in prayer for his dead
mistress.[27] When these elaborate dispositions were finally
completed, it was already two o'clock in the morning.
Mary's letter to the king of France was thus dated Wednesday 8 February 1587, the day of her execution.

The traveller was now ready for her last journey on earth.
The queen lay down on her bed without undressing. She
did not try to sleep. Her women gathered round her already wearing their black garments of mourning, and
Mary asked Jane Kennedy to read aloud the life of some
great sinner. The life of the good thief was chosen, and
as the story reached its climax on the cross, Mary observed
aloud: 'In truth he was a great sinner, but not so great as I
have been'. She then closed her eyes, and said nothing
further. Throughout the night the sound of hammering

---

* It is notable that in his extremely detailed account of the queen's
last hours, Bourgoing does not mention that she paused to compose
or extemporize the Latin prayer *O Domine Deus! speravi in te* traditionally attributed to her, on the eve of her execution.

came from the great hall where the scaffold was being
erected. The boots of the soldiers could be heard ceaselessly tramping up and down outside the queen's room, for
Paulet had ordered them to watch with special vigilance
in these final hours, lest their victim escape her captors at
the last. The queen lay on her bed without sleeping, eyes
closed and a half smile on her face.

So the short night passed. At six o'clock, long before
light, the queen rose, handed over the will, distributed her
purses, and gave her women a farewell embrace. Her men
servants were given her hand to kiss. Then she went into
her little oratory and prayed alone. She was extremely pale
but quite composed. Bourgoing handed her a little bread
and wine to sustain her. The day now dawned fine and
sunny: it was one of those unexpected early February
days when it suddenly seems possible that the spring will
come. It was between eight and nine when a loud knocking
was heard at the door, and a messenger shouted through
it that the lords were waiting for the queen. Mary asked
for a moment to finish her prayers, at which the lords outside in a moment of panic feared some sort of last-minute
resistance might be planned; unable to believe in the
courage of their captive, they had given credit to reports
that the queen of Scots had said she would not come to
the block on her own accord, but would have to be dragged
thither. But when the sheriff of Northampton, Thomas
Andrews, entered, he found Mary kneeling quietly in
prayer in front of the crucifix which hung above her altar.

It was this crucifix which her groom Hannibal Stuart now
bore before her as she was escorted towards the great
hall. The queen was totally calm, and showed no signs
of fear or distress. Her bearing was regal, and some of
the contemporary observers afterwards even described her
as cheerful and smiling.[28] The last moment of agony came
in the entry chamber to the hall, when her servants were
held back from following her and the queen was told that
she was to die quite alone, by the orders of Elizabeth.
Melville, distracted at this unlooked-for blow, fell on his
knees in tears and exclaimed: 'Oh Madam, it will be the
sorrowfullest message that I ever carried when I shall report that my Queen and dear mistress is dead'. The queen
dashed away her own tears and said gently: 'You ought to
rejoice and not to weep for that the end of Mary Stuart's

troubles is now done. Thou knowest, Melville, that all this
world is but vanity and full of troubles and sorrows.
Carry this message from me and tell my friends that I
died a true woman to my religion, and like a true Scottish
woman and a true French woman. . . .' And commending
Melville to go to her son, and tell him that her dearest
wish had always been to see England and Scotland united,
that she had never done anything to prejudice the welfare
of the kingdom of Scotland, she embraced Melville and
bade him farewell.

Mary now turned to Paulet and the lords and pleaded
with them to allow at least her own servants to be with
her at the death, so that they could later report the manner
of her death in other countries. Kent replied that her
wish could not well be granted, for before the execution
her servants were sure to cry out and upset the queen
herself, as well as disquieting the company, while afterwards they might easily attempt to dip their napkins in
her blood for relics which, said Kent grimly, 'were not
convenient'. 'My Lord,' replied Mary, 'I will give my word
and promise for them that they shall not do any such
thing as your Lordship hath named. Alas poor souls, it
would do them good to bid me farewell'. As for her
women she refused to believe that these were the instructions of Queen Elizabeth herself, for surely Elizabeth, herself a maiden queen, would not condemn a fellow-woman
to die without any ladies about her to attend her, besides
which, added Mary, 'You know that I am cousin to your
Queen and descended from the blood of Henry VII, a married Queen of France, and the anointed Queen of Scotland'.
She then appealed to history where she had read in
chronicles that other gentlewomen had had their ladies
with them at their execution. After a hurried whispered
consultation, the lords decided that Mary might have after
all the choice of six of her servants to accompany her.
Thus Melville, Bourgoing, Gervais, and the old man
Didier who had been for many years Mary's porter, were
allowed to go forward, together with the two dearest of
Mary's women, who shared her bed, Jane Kennedy and
Elizabeth Curle. Mary then went to follow the sheriff,
having first bestowed a small gift (probably a seal) on
Sir William Fitzwilliam, the castellan of Fotheringhay: he,
unlike Sir Amyas Paulet, had shown especial courtesy
to her in the carrying-out of his office.

The queen now entered the great hall in silence.* The spectators gathered there—about 300 of them by one account—gazed with awe and apprehension at this legendary figure whose dramatic career was about to be ended before their eyes. They saw a tall and gracious woman, whom at first sight seemed to be dressed entirely in black, save for the long white lace-edged veil which flowed down her back to the ground like a bride's, and the white stiffened and peaked head-dress, that too was edged with lace, below which gleamed her auburn hair. Her satin dress was all in black, embroidered with black velvet, and set with black acorn buttons of jet trimmed with pearl; but through the slashed sleeves could be seen inner sleeves of purple, and although her shoes of Spanish leather were black, her stockings were clocked and edged with silver, her garters were of green silk, and her petticoat was of crimson velvet. She held a crucifix and a prayer book in her hand, and two rosaries hung down from her waist; round her neck was a pomander chain and an *Agnus Dei*. Despite the fact that Mary's shoulders were now bowed and stooping with illness, and her figure grown full with the years, she walked with immense dignity. Time and suffering had long ago rubbed away the delicate youthful charm of her face, but to many of the spectators her extraordinary composure and serenity had its own beauty. Above all, her courage was matchless, and this alone in many people's minds, whatever honours and dignities had been stripped from her by Paulet, still gave her the right to be called a queen.

In the centre of the great hall, which lay on the ground floor of the castle, directly below the room in which Mary had been tried, was set a wooden stage, all hung with black about twelve feet square, and two feet high off the ground. Within the precincts of the stage were two stools for Shrewsbury and Kent. Beside them was placed, about two

---

* An adagio piece of music marked as having been played at the execution of Mary Queen of Scots was reproduced by George Robert Gleig in his *Family History of England* (1836); he related that 'a fortunate accident' had thrown a copy of it in his way. But as the contemporary sketch of the scene within the great hall itself does not illustrate musicians, and none of the contemporary accounts mentions the fact that there was music, the piece, if authentic, must presumably have been played before the queen's appearance.[29]

feet high, also draped in black, the block, and a little
cushioned stool on which it was intended that the queen
should sit while she was disrobed. The great axe was already lying there—'like those with which they cut wood'
said Bourgoing later. Outside the stage were two other
seats for Paulet and Drury, and a rank of soldiers en-
closing it; behind them gathered the ordinary people who
had been given the privilege of watching the execution, as
well as some local dignitaries including Shrewsbury's eldest
son Lord Talbot, Sir Edward Montagu, and his son and
brother, Sir Richard Knightly, and Mr Thomas Brudenell.
A huge blaze had been lit in the fireplace against the cold
of the great hall.

Once led up the three steps to the stage, the queen listened patiently while the commission for her execution was
read aloud. Her expression never changed. Cecil's own
official observer, Robert Wise, commented later that from
her detached regard, she might even have been listening to
a pardon, rather than the warrant for her own death.
The first sign of emotion was wrung from her, when Dr
Fletcher, the Protestant dean of Peterborough—he who
afterwards described the fine weather as a sign that Heaven
looked with favour on the execution—stepped forward,
and proposed to harangue the queen according to the
rites of the Protestant religion. 'Mr Dean,' said the queen
firmly, 'I am settled in the ancient Catholic Roman religion, and mind to spend my blood in defence of it'.
Shrewsbury and Kent both exhorted her to listen to him,
and even offered to pray with the queen, but all these proposals Mary resolutely rejected. 'If you will pray with
me, my lords,' she said to the two earls, 'I will thank you,
but to join in prayer I will not, for that you and I are not
of one religion'. And when the dean, in answer to the
earls' direction, finally knelt down on the scaffold steps and
started to pray out loud and at length, in a prolonged
and rhetorical style as though determined to force his way
into the pages of history, Mary still paid no attention but
turned away, and started to pray aloud out of her own
book in Latin, in the midst of these prayers sliding off her
stool on to her knees. When the dean was at last finished,
the queen changed her prayers, and began to pray out
loud in English, for the afflicted English Catholic Church,
for her son, and for Elizabeth, that she might serve God
in the years to come. Kent remonstrated with her: 'Madam,

settle Christ Jesus in your heart and leave those trumperies'. But the queen prayed on, asking God to avert his wrath from England, and calling on the Saints to intercede for her; and so she kissed the crucifix she held, and crossing herself, ended: 'Even as thy arms, O Jesus, were spread here upon the cross, so receive me into Thy arms of mercy, and forgive me all my sins'.

When the queen's prayers were finished, the executioners asked her as was customary, to forgive them in advance for bringing about her death. Mary answered immediately: 'I forgive you with all my heart, for now I hope you shall make an end of all my troubles'. Then the executioners, helped by Jane Kennedy and Elizabeth Curle, assisted the Queen to undress—Robert Wise noticed that she undressed so quickly that it seemed as if she was in haste to be gone out of the world. Stripped of her black, she stood in her red petticoat and it was seen that above it she wore a red satin bodice, trimmed with lace, the neckline cut low at the back; one of the women handed her a pair of red sleeves, and it was thus wearing all red, the colour of blood, and the liturgical colour of martyrdom in the Catholic Church, that the queen of Scots died.* According to their usual practice, the executioners stretched forth their hands for the queen's ornaments which were their perquisites. When they touched the long golden rosary, Jane Kennedy protested, and the queen herself intervened and said that Bull would be compensated with money in its place, and the same promise had to be made regarding the *Agnus Dei*.† Yet all the time her belongings were being stripped from her, it was notable that the queen neither wept nor changed her calm and almost happy expression of what one observer called 'smiling cheer'; she even retained her composure sufficiently to remark wryly of the executioners that she had never before had such grooms of the chamber to make her ready. It was the queen's women who could not contain their lamentations as they wept and crossed themselves and muttered snatches of Latin prayers. Finally

---

* But it was a dark red, a sort of crimson-brown, not scarlet as is sometimes suggested.[30]

† This gold rosary was intended for Mary's friend Anne Dacres, wife of Philip, earl of Arundel, to whom it was subsequently delivered by Jane Kennedy; it is now in the possession of the earl of Arundel's descendant, the 16th duke of Norfolk.

Mary had to turn to them and, mindful of her promise to Shrewsbury that they would not weep aloud if they were admitted to the hall, she admonished them softly in French: *'Ne crie point pour moi. J'ai promis pour vous . . .'* Once more she bade them not mourn but rejoice, for they were soon to see the end of all her troubles; turning to her menservants, standing on a bench close by the scaffold, who also had tears pouring down their faces and were calling out prayers in French and Scots and Latin, and crossing themselves again and again, she told them to be comforted, with a smile on her lips to reassure them. She asked the men too to pray for her unto the last hour.

The time had come for Jane Kennedy to bind the queen's eyes with the white cloth embroidered in gold which Mary had herself chosen for the purpose the night before. Jane Kennedy first kissed the cloth and then wrapped it gently round her mistress's eyes, and over her head so that her hair was covered as by a white turban and only the neck left completely bare. The two women then withdrew from the stage. The queen without even now the faintest sign of fear, knelt down once more on the cushion in front of the block. She recited aloud in Latin the Psalm *In te Domino confido, non confundar in aeternum*—In you Lord is my trust, let me never be confounded—and then feeling for the block, she laid her head down upon it, placing her chin carefully with both her hands, so that if one of the executioners had not moved them back they too would have lain in the direct line of the axe. The queen stretched out her arms and legs and cried: *'In manus tuas, Domine, confide spiritum meum'*—'Into your hands O Lord I commend my spirit'—three or four times. When the queen was lying there quite motionless, Bull's assistant put his hand on her body to steady it for the blow. Even so, the first blow, as it fell, missed the neck and cut into the back of the head. The queen's lips moved, and her servants thought they heard the whispered words: 'Sweet Jesus.' The second blow severed the neck, all but the smallest sinew and this was severed by using the axe as a saw. It was about ten o'clock in the morning of Wednesday 8 February, the queen of Scots being then aged forty-four years old, and in the nineteenth year of her English captivity.

In the great hall of Fotheringhay, before the wondering eyes of the crowd, the executioner now held aloft the dead woman's head, crying out as he did so: 'God Save the

Queen.' The lips still moved and continued to do so for a quarter of an hour after the death. But at this moment, weird and moving spectacle, the auburn tresses in his hand came apart from the skull and the head itself fell to the ground. It was seen that Mary Stuart's own hair had in fact been quite grey, and very short at the time of her death: for her execution she had chosen to wear a wig. The spectators were stunned by the unexpected sight and remained silent. It was left to the dean of Peterborough to call out strongly: 'So perish all the Queen's enemies', and for Kent, standing over the corpse to echo: 'Such be the end of all the Queen's, and all the Gospel's enemies'. But Shrewsbury could not speak, and his face was wet with tears.

It was now the time for the executioners to strip the body of its remaining adornments before handing it over to the embalmers. But at this point a strange and pathetic memorial to that devotion which Mary Stuart had always aroused in those who knew her intimately was discovered: her little lap dog, a Skye terrier, who had managed to accompany her into the hall under her long skirts, where her servants had been turned away, had now crept out from beneath her petticoat, and in its distress had stationed itself piteously beneath the severed head and the shoulders of the body. Nor would it be coaxed away, but steadfastly and uncomprehendingly clung to the solitary thing it could find in the hall which still reminded it of its dead mistress. To all others save this poor animal, the sad corpse lying now so still on the floor of the stage, in its red clothes against which the blood stains scarcely showed, with its face now sunken to that of an old woman in the harsh disguise of death, bore little resemblance to her whom they had known only a short while before as Mary Queen of Scots. The spirit had fled the body. The chain was loosed to let the captive go.

At Fotheringhay now it was as if a murder had taken place. The weeping women in the hall were pushed away and locked in their rooms. The castle gates were locked, so that no one could leave and break the news to the outside world. The body was lain unceremoniously in the presence chamber, and even, so Brantôme heard from Mary's distraught women who had peeped through a crack in the door, wrapped in the coarse woollen covering of

her own billiard table. The blood-stained block was burnt.
Every other particle of clothing or object of devotion
which might be associated with the queen of Scots was
burnt, scoured or washed, so that not a trace of her blood
might remain to create a holy relic to inspire devotion in
years to come. The little dog was washed and washed
again, although he subsequently refused to eat, and so
pined away. The remaining rosary which Jane Kennedy had
not managed to rescue and which the queen had worn was
burnt. Even the executioners were not allowed to enjoy
the benefits of the perquisites for which they had fought,
since the custodians confiscated them, and replaced them
with money.* At about four o'clock in the afternoon the
body was further stripped and the organs including the
heart were removed and handed to the sheriff, who with
the fear of creating relics ever in his mind, had them
buried secretly deep within the castle of Fotheringhay. The
exact spot was never revealed. The physician from Stam-
ford examined the body before he embalmed it with the
help of two surgeons: he found the heart sound, and the
health of the body itself, and the other organs apart from
a slight quantity of water, not so much impaired as to
justify Cecil's prognosis that the queen would have died
anyway. The body was then wrapped in a wax winding-
sheet and incarcerated in a heavy lead coffin, on Walsingham's explicit orders.

Only Shrewsbury's eldest son, Lord Talbot, was allowed
to gallop forth from the castle about one o'clock, hard
towards London, to break the news of what had taken
place that morning to Elizabeth. He reached the capital
next morning at nine. The queen was at Greenwich and
had been out riding early; on her return she held a conversation with the king of Portugal. When she was told
the news, according to Camden, she received it at first
with great indignation, and then with terrible distress:
'her countenance changed, her words faltered, and with
excessive sorrow she was in a manner astonished, insomuch
as she gave herself over to grief, putting herself into mourning weeds and shedding abundance of tears.'³¹ In the

---

* These rigorous precautions on the part of the English government, carried out savagely, cast a doubtful light on the many so-
called relics of Mary Stuart which are said to date from her execution.

meantime, before grief could overcome her altogether, she turned like an angry snake on the secretary Davison and had him thrown into prison for daring to use the warrant for the execution which she herself had signed. Elizabeth now maintained that she had only signed the warrant 'for safety's sake' and had merely given it to Davison to keep, not to use. Her Council were cross-examined as though they were criminals, and Davison impeached before the Star Chamber. Further ostentatious manifestations of her displeasure might have followed, had not Cecil himself felt obliged to remonstrate with Elizabeth. He pointed out that such theatricals even if they salved her own conscience would cut little ice with the outside world, when it was known that Davison had both her Commission and her seal, at his disposal. On the other hand, the papists and the queen's enemies might all too easily be encouraged, if it was suggested that the queen of Scots had been killed unlawfully. In the end Davison, the scapegoat, underwent a token period of imprisonment and had a fine of £10,000 imposed on him; the other members of the Council went free. Unlike its queen London itself suffered from no such doubts: the bells were rung, fires were lighted in the streets and there was much merry-making and banqueting to celebrate the death of her whom they had been trained to regard as a public enemy. Some bold spirits even asked the French ambassador to give them some wood for their bonfires and when he indignantly refused, lit an enormous blaze in the street in front of his house.

But at Fotheringhay itself nothing was changed. It was as though the castle, cut off from the rest of the world, had fallen asleep for a thousand years under an enchantment, as a result of the dolorous stroke which had there slain Mary Queen of Scots. The queen's servants were permitted to have one Requiem Mass said by de Préau the morning after her death; but otherwise everything went on as before. Her attendants were still kept in prison within the castle, in conditions which were harsher than ever; nor were any of them allowed to return to their native lands of France and Scotland as Mary had so urgently stipulated at the last. Sir Amyas Paulet, made a knight of the Garter in April for his pains, was still in charge of arrangements at Fotheringhay, and continued to complain over the excessive expenses of his prisoners' diet.[32]

The queen's farewell letters to the Pope remained unposted and undelivered, lingering in the hands of her household. Spring turned to summer. The snowdrops which had scattered the green meadows round the River Nene on the day of her death gave place to purple thistles, sometimes romantically called Queen Mary's tears. Still the body of the dead queen, embalmed and wrapped in its heavy lead coffin, was given no burial, but remained walled up within the precincts of the castle where she had died.

27 Epilogue: The Theatre of the World

'Remember that the theatre of the world is wider than the realm of England.'

MARY QUEEN OF SCOTS *before her judges, October 1586*

As the gates of Fotheringhay were locked, so were the English ports closed immediately after the death of the queen of Scots. It was three weeks before the French ambassador Châteauneuf could write back to his master in Paris with tidings of the calamity. The news of the death of Mary Stuart, their own queen dowager, was received in France with national and solemn mourning. On 12 March a Requiem Mass was held in the black-draped cathedral of Notre Dame; the whole court was present including King Henry III, the Queen Mother Catherine, others who had known Mary well such as her uncle René of Elboeuf, and the younger generation of Guises. The preacher was Renaud de Beaune, archbishop of Bourges, a man old enough to recall in poignant language that day nearly forty years before, when Mary had been married in that self-same cathedral to the dauphin of France:* 'Many of us saw in the place where we are now assembled to deplore her, this Queen on the day of her bridal, arrayed in her regal trappings, so covered in jewels that the sun himself shone not more brightly, so beautiful, so charming withal as never woman was. These walls were then hung with cloth of gold and precious tapestry; every space was filled with thrones and seats, crowded with princes and princesses, who came from all parts to share in the rejoicing. The palace was overflowing with magnificence, splendid fêtes and masques; the streets with jousts and tourneys. In short it seemed as if our age had succeeded that day in surpassing the pomp of all past centuries combined. A

* To be compared in eloquence with the famous passage of Edmund Burke on Marie-Antoinette as dauphiness, written over 200 years later.

little time has flowed on and it is all vanished like a cloud. Who would have believed that such a change could have befallen her who appeared then so triumphant, and that we should have seen her a prisoner who had restored prisoners to liberty; in poverty who was accustomed to give so liberally to o'hers; treated with contumely by those on whom she had conferred honours; and finally, the axe of a base executioner mangling the form of her who was doubly a Queen; that form which honoured the nuptial bed of a sovereign of France, falling dishonoured on a scaffold, and that beauty which had been one of the wonders of the world, faded in a dreary prison, and at last effaced by a piteous death. This place, where she was surrounded with splendour, is now hung with black for her. Instead of nuptial torches we have funereal tapers; in the place of songs of joy, we have sighs and groans; for clarions and hautboys, the tolling of the sad and dismal bell. Oh God, what a change! Oh vanity of human greatness, shall we never be convinced of your deceitfulness. . . .'[1]

Despite the vivid sorrow of the French nation and in spite of Mary's own desire to be buried in France, either at St Denis or Rheims, her wishes in this respect were never met. Elizabeth could scarcely plead ignorance of her request, since it had been expressed most passionately in Mary's letter of 15 December, the letter which Paulet had finally forwarded. However, in other respects, Mary's last wishes were being met. By 7 March Mendoza, who was in Paris, was able to spread the tale of her heroic death to Spain for, despite all the English precautions, news of her bravery during the last hours had leaked out. Not only her courage but even her sanctity was discussed. Pierre l'Estoile recorded in his Journal that Paris was the scene of mass demonstrations, as well as sermons that virtually canonized Mary as a saint who had died in the cause of the Catholic faith.[2] Among those who hailed her death as a form of martyrdom in the cause of the faith, was the youthful Maffeo Barberini, the future Pope Urban VIII, who wrote a lyrical elegy on the subject referring to her 'darkened sorrows turned to glorious joy'. The woman who deliberately chose the story of the good thief to be read aloud to her on the eve of her death because she considered herself in all humility to be a great sinner would have viewed this popular canonization with detachment; on the other hand Mary would undoubtedly

have been pleased at the way the Catholic League and
Philip II were galvanized by her death as by a Catholic
rallying-cry; even the French king, who generally viewed
the Guise-inspired Catholic League with suspicion, gave
vent to some newly bellicose sentiments towards the
Protestants, on receiving the news of Mary's death.

The grief of the French court was genuine enough in
its personal aspects. That of the Scottish court was more
difficult to estimate, and contemporary accounts differ
radically in their reports of how James received the news
of his mother's execution. According to one story, he
shammed sorrow in public, but observed to his courtiers
gleefully in secret: 'Now I am sole King.'³ Archibald
Douglas on the other hand was told that the 'King moved
never his countenance at the rehearsal [telling] of his
mother's execution, nor leaves not his pastimes more than
of before'.⁴ Still other reports spoke of his evident grief,
how he became very sad and pensive when the intelligence
reached him, and went to bed without eating. Whatever
James's outward show of lamentation, it is difficult to
believe that the news of his mother's death aroused at long
last the filial passion of which he had shown so little
evidence during her life. His conduct subsequently showed
that so long as the English crown still dangled within his
reach, he was prepared to swallow the insult to his family
and his nation. The Scottish people as a whole showed more
spirit than their king: and seemed to evince both humiliation and anger at the killing of one who had once sat on
the throne of Scotland. When James ordered the Scottish
court into mourning as a formal gesture, according to one
tradition⁵ the earl of Sinclair appeared before him dressed
in steel armour in place of black. When James asked him
whether he had not seen the general order for mourning,
Sinclair replied sternly: 'This *is* the proper mourning for
the Queen of Scotland'. Prayers were said for the defunct
queen in a form specially prescribed by the Council. Some
of Mary's former subjects discussed plans for reprisals.
One of Cecil's spies heard that the Hamiltons had proposed
to burn Newcastle with a levy of 5,000 men, if only James
would match their force with an equivalent army. Walsingham was also advised that there were posters in the streets
against England and James, and a general clamour for
war. To indicate the prevailing atmosphere, his agent in
Scotland sent him a piece of hemp tied like a halter and

the accompanying jingle, aimed by a patriot at Elizabeth:

> To Jezebel that English whore
> Receive this Scottish chain
> A presage of her great malheur
> For murdering our Queen.

James did make the gesture of breaking off formal communications with England. Sir Robert Carey was sent north by Elizabeth with the unenviable mission of explaining that his mistress had not authorized the execution personally and had been dumbfounded and grief-stricken when it was carried out. James refused at first to receive him. But by the end of February Gray was writing to Douglas in London, indicating that James would now be susceptible to further arguments from Elizabeth and that old Latin tag—necesse est unum mori pro populo—it is necessary for one person to die for the sake of the people—might perhaps be brought into play.[6] Finally James consented to listen to Carey's arguments, and accepted Elizabeth's explanation of her own 'unspotted' part in the execution. By mid-March the English were confident that James would not fight to avenge his mother's death. The Anglo-Scottish alliance remained unsevered by the axe of Fotheringhay.

It was, however, in deference to James's feelings, or the sort of appropriate feelings he might be supposed to cherish for his mother, that the subject of the burial of the queen of Scots was raised again in the summer after her death. Walsingham had specified in his instructions that the coffin should be bestowed 'by night' on an upper shelf of the local Fotheringhay church—and Cecil afterwards underlined the word upper in his own hand.[7] But in fact the coffin had not been accorded even this obscure resting-place, but remained quite unburied, like the corpse of Achilles, within Fotheringhay itself. Now it was planned to give the coffin an honourable burial at Peterborough Cathedral. So far as anything explained this curious ceremony the line adopted seemed to be that Mary had been a revered dowager queen of Scotland who happened to die in England of natural causes. Under the auspices of Garter King of Arms, heralds, nobles and mourners were imported from London to give the occasion the right degree of solemnity due to the mother of the king of Scotland.[8] But no Scots were present: and although the cathedral was hung with black

paid for by the master of the wardrobe, and the heraldic
details of the decoration worked out with care—there
were the royal arms of Scotland, for example, as well as
those of Mary's first two husbands Francis II and Darnley
[James's father]—neither in the escutcheons nor in the
service was there any reference to her third husband Bothwell, to the events leading to her imprisonment in England,
let alone the manner of her death.

Although the red lion of Scotland blazed forth in the
nave of Peterborough Cathedral, and Elizabeth's personal
friend, the countess of Bedford, acted the role of chief
mourner with due gravity, while the procession was headed
with 100 poor widows also dressed for the occasion in
black at the government's expense, the dichotomy at the
heart of this strange apologetic ceremony was revealed by
the fact that the coffin was actually transported from
Fotheringhay to Peterborough at dead of night for fear of
demonstrations. On Sunday 30 July, Queen Mary's body
left the castle for the last time by the light of torches, in
a coach draped in black velvet from which little pennons
fluttered—'a chariot' the state accounts called it later.[9] The
accompanying heralds rode with bared heads. They reached
Peterborough at two o'clock in the morning, being met
by a distinguished convoy of ecclesiastics including the
bishop and the egregious Dean Fletcher. The coffin was
then lodged temporarily in the Bishop's Palace.

The whole ceremony was of course Protestant and thus
sung in English. But the late queen's servants, who had
been allowed out of their seclusion at Fotheringhay to attend the service, were all pious Catholics with the exception of Andrew Melville and Barbara Mowbray. They therefore withdrew from the body of the church once the procession was over. Even so, the fact that the chaplain de
Préau walked with a heavy gold crucifix on his breast during the procession called forth angry Protestant criticism.
At the head of the procession, just behind the bailiff of
Peterborough with his black staves of mourning, was
borne the royal standard of Scotland with the motto:
In my defence God me defend. Among the distinguished
English mourners were Cecil's elder son, and Shrewsbury's
daughter and daughter-in-law, Lady Mary Savill and
Lady Talbot. The ladies of Mary's former household
walked just ahead of the attendants of the English peeresses,
in black taffeta head-dresses, with veils of white lawn

hanging down behind; their names recalled those last melancholy months at Fotheringhay, for they included Barbara Mowbray and her sister Gillis, Elizabeth Curle, Jane Kennedy, Christina Pages and her daughter Mary.

In one respect the ceremony deviated from the common practice at state funerals: it was not found possible to process the coffin round the cathedral owing to the great quantity of lead used on Walsingham's instructions, estimated at over nine hundredweight. Not only was the weight inordinate, but it was feared by the prudent that the casing might even rip and 'being very hot weather, might be found some annoyance'. The coffin was therefore placed immediately in its vault in the south aisle of the cathedral. Otherwise the arrangements were as was customary in such interments: a 'representation' or effigy of the queen of Scots was carried in the procession beneath a canopy supported by four knights.*[10] The five pursuivants from London, Portcullis, Rouge Dragon Clarenceaux, the Somerset and the York herald bore the emblems of state, the sword, target, crown, the crest, the helmet and the like which were later hung formally over the grave. Even the sermon given by William Chaderton, bishop of Lincoln, represented a clumsy attempt to gloss over the very different circumstances in which the

---

* It is thought that this effigy was modelled from a death mask taken shortly after the execution by the surgeons at Fotheringhay. The death mask from which this effigy was taken cannot, however, be identified with the Lennoxlove death mask, discovered at Holyrood Palace in the last century. This, although beautiful, is clearly the mask of a much smaller woman. It measures seven inches long and 4¾ inches across, to be compared with the Westminster Abbey monument which is nine inches by seven inches across. (Queen Elizabeth's monument, also taken from a death mask, measures 8 inches by 8 inches and portraits confirm that she had a much broader face than Mary.) Nor can the Lennoxlove measurements be explained by wax shrinkage: Mr Wismark of Madame Tussauds' told the author that a two-inch shrinkage would destroy portraiture altogether, ¼ inch being the maximum for which allowance could be made. In any case the Lennoxlove mask bears only a superficial resemblance to the queen of Scots: the mouth and setting of the eyes are quite different; the nose is blunt at the end in profile, lacking any sort of aquiline finish, and in front view looks almost *retroussé*; the width of the jaw is remarkable in a small face, and quite unlike the bone structure shown in all Mary's known portraits. The Lennoxlove face is also thin, lacking the fulness upon which every observer at Mary's execution commented, and which is present, for example, in the face on the Westminster monument.

woman whom they were now burying with such honour
had actually died. He called on God to bless the happy
dissolution of the late Scottish queen, adding 'Of whose
life and departure, whatsoever shall be expected, I have
nothing to say, for that I was unacquainted with the one,
and not present at the other'. By citing what he termed a
charitable saying of Martin Luther: 'Many one liveth a
Papist and dieth a Protestant', he even suggested that the
queen of Scots might have undergone a last-minute conversion to the reformed faith, before adding that at any
rate he had heard she took her death patiently, recommending herself at the last to Jesus Christ.

The service completed, the procession filed out of the
cathedral once more, and as they passed the mourning
women who had once served Queen Mary, standing at the
side, in order to take no part in the Protestant service,
some of the grand English ladies, many of whom like
Shrewsbury's family had known them well in happier days,
embraced and kissed them sympathetically. The courtiers
and the ecclesiastics now adjourned to the Bishop's Palace
for a funeral banquet of considerable festivity: but Mary's
former servitors were not so easily transferred from tears
into laughter; what to the worshipful company from London was only a ritual proceeding to round off a distasteful incident in English history, was to them the last obsequies of their beloved mistress. There, while the English caroused, Mary's servants gathered in another room
and wept bitter tears.

The most passionate desire left to these poor people
was that they should now be released from their melancholy prison and allowed to go their several ways. Despite the completion of the interment, there was a further
delay of two months before they were allowed to depart,
possibly because some report of their obstinate heretical
behaviour at the burial service and their unseemly grief at
the banquet had come to Elizabeth's ears and displeased
her. Shortly after the service, Adam Blackwood, one of
Mary's most loyal partisans, who was already at work on
the task of presenting her to the world as a royal heroine
and a Catholic martyr, came secretly to Peterborough and
put up on the wall above her tomb a long epitaph in
Latin protesting against the crime of regicide which had
taken place at Fotheringhay: 'A strange and unusual
monument this is, wherein the living are included with the

dead: for, with the Sacred Ashes of this blessed Mary, know, that the Majesty of all kings, and princes, lieth here, violated and prostrate. And because regal secrecy doth enough and more admonish Kings of their duty— traveller, I say no more.' But this loyal monument was pulled down. Nor did 'regal secrecy' admonish any kings of their duty, beyond the £321 which Queen Elizabeth spent on this funeral to placate King James, of which pantry and buttery charges accounted for one third.[11]

At last in October the ordeal of the little royal household was at an end. Bourgoing went to King Henry III, as he had been instructed, and told his tale of the uplifting last months and hours of the late queen of Scots. Gorion went to Mendoza, handed him the diamond ring which Mendoza subsequently passed to Philip II, and he too related the story of his mistress's martyrdom. The farewell letters written nearly a year before reached their destinations at last, and King Philip, moved by this reminder from beyond the grave of the woman who had once been his sister-in-law, and long his Catholic confederate, out of natural chivalry honoured Mary's last requests for the payment of her servants' wages, and her debts in France. He also pursued in correspondence with Mendoza the subject of what he believed to be Mary's last gift to him in her will—the reversion of the English crown. In the interests of his own foreign policy, Philip conveniently allowed himself to credit the story that Mary had finally disinherited James altogether on the eve of her execution, and had consequently ceded to Philip directly her own claims to the English throne.* It was now late in 1587. It was in the next year, 1588, that King Philip took the momentous decision to pursue his supposed English inheritance with the great force of the Spanish Armada. Ironically enough, therefore, the mighty Spanish fleet of rescue for which

---

* But Philip was allowing himself to be deluded. Although Mary had twice confided England conditionally to Philip, if James failed to become a Catholic—in her will of 1577 and in her letter to Mendoza of May 1586—no such clause existed in the last testament which Mary made on the eve of her death at Fotheringhay, and no other will has ever been found, supporting his claims.[12] In any case, it is clear from the contemporary accounts, that Mary went to her death serenely, rather than in the bitter mood which might have led to a last minute official disinheritance of her son.

Mary had waited so long and so hopefully, only sailed towards England after, and as a direct result of, her death.

Mendoza was left in France to deal with the problems of these old servants: Philip had authorized a pension of 300 crowns a year for Jane, and forty crowns a month for Gilbert Curle, and Mendoza acted with kindness and charity in the course of his administration, receiving in the course of it such tremulous confidences as the fact that it had been Jane Kennedy not Elizabeth Curle who had tied the blindfold around the queen's eyes at the end: 'because I was of better family'.[13] Having delivered a diamond ring which Mary bequeathed to Thomas Morgan for faithful service—many of her supporters would willingly have denied it to him for his supposed treachery—Jane Kennedy returned to Scotland, where she had the melancholy privilege of describing the scene of his mother's death personally to King James. She subsequently married Mary's steward, Andrew Melville; despite the differences in their religion they were drawn to each other by memories of the past and long years together in the royal service. But Jane did not live long enough to enjoy a peaceful old age with her husband: in 1589 King James commissioned her to go to Denmark to fetch back his bride Princess Anne, as a reward for her faithful service to his mother, and she was drowned in a storm at the outset of her journey. Gillis Mowbray also went back to Scotland, where she married Sir John Smith of Barnton: her relics of her royal mistress, which she bequeathed to her granddaughter, now form the heart of the Penicuik Bequest in the National Museum of Antiquities at Edinburgh.

Elizabeth Curle, and her sister-in-law Barbara Curle, born Mowbray, ended their lives together at Antwerp. Gilbert Curle, the sad but good-hearted secretary, died in 1609; but Barbara lived to 1616, and Elizabeth to 1620, over thirty years after the death of Mary. Before her death, Elizabeth Curle had an interesting memorial to the queen carried out in the shape of a full-scale portrait of her mistress at the time of her execution, the figure presumably modelled on the miniature which Mary confided to Jane on the eve of her death. The portrait was bequeathed by Elizabeth to her nephew Hippolytus Curle, a Jesuit, and from him it was handed on to the Scots College at Douai. On either side of the standing figure of the queen are shown two vignettes of the execution scene at

Fotheringhay: on the left, the queen kneels at the block, and on the right are shown Elizabeth Curle and Jane Kennedy standing together, wearing the black religious habits these good ladies appear to have adopted for the rest of their lives in perpetual and devout mourning for their mistress. At Douai the portrait even survived the depredations of the French revolutionaries, rolled up and built into a chimney; it has now come to rest at the Blairs College, Aberdeen. The pious legend that Elizabeth Curle somehow managed to carry the head of Mary Queen of Scots abroad and have it buried with her in her tomb may be dismissed in view of the extraordinary and zealous precautions which were taken at the time to prevent even a drop of the dead woman's blood being taken as a martyr's relic; the head itself was certainly replaced on the body by the surgeons, wrapped securely in the heavy lead coffin that very afternoon. But the joint memorial to Elizabeth and Barbara in St Andrew's Church, Antwerp, flanked with their respective patron saints, is today still crowned with a portrait of Mary Stuart, the woman whom Elizabeth believed to have been a martyred queen, and to whose life she dedicated her service; the Latin inscription on the memorial still proclaims proudly that it was she, Elizabeth Curle, who received the last kiss of Mary Queen of Scots.

With the departure at last of the sorrowing servants, the castle of Fotheringhay was released from its spell; soon its very masonry began to decay. Although Camden loyally but inaccurately reported that it was King James who had the stones beaten to the ground in a rage, to avenge the deed of shame which had taken place there,[14] in fact its demolition was a gradual process, increased as local builders and landowners helped themselves to its materials. The antiquarian Sir Robert Cotton, conscious of his royal Bruce ancestry, actually acquired the great hall in which the execution had taken place, and incorporated it in his own near-by manor of Connington in Huntingdonshire (although that too was pulled down in the eighteenth century). Today not even the ruins of Fotheringhay survive. The interested wayfarer finds the site of the castle, which is not in public hands, but belongs to the owners of the near-by farm, at the end of a cart-track. All that can be seen of the once mighty castle of Fotheringhay is a grassy mound indicating the position of the keep, and a

huge Ozymandias-like hump of masonry, encased in railings, recalling Shelley's line on the trunkless stone in the
desert, *'Look on my works ye mighty and despair'*. The
river meanders by. Sheep peacefully graze on the meadows
opposite. There is no national memorial or official com-
memoration of the stirring events, so much part of British
history, which once took place at Fotheringhay.*

Even now with the burial at Peterborough, the earthly
peregrinations of the queen of Scots were not at an end.
When James ascended the throne of England in the spring
of 1603, he marked his respect for his mother's tomb the
following August by despatching a rich pall of velvet to
Peterborough, with instructions to the bishop to hang it
over her grave. By the time, however, that James had
erected a large and handsome monument to Queen Elizabeth in Westminster Abbey, it was generally felt that something still further ought to be done for his mother's memory.
Considerable influence in this respect was exerted by
James's favourite Henry Howard, earl of Northampton,
brother of Mary's Norfolk, who had strongly Catholic
sympathies all his life and died an outright member of
the Church. In 1606 Cornelius Cure, master mason of
works, was instructed to commence the carving of an imposing monument, which was later continued and finished
by his son William. By September 1612 the work was
sufficiently completed for the order of exhumation to be
given to the clergy at Peterborough: the corpse of James's
'dearest mother' was to be taken up in 'as decent and respectful manner as is fitting'. James did not, however,
lose his head over the splendour of his gesture—for although the monument in Westminster Abbey was costly
and sumptuous, the sculptors alone receiving £825, and
an overall sum of £2,000 being mentioned, James had not

---

* In 1964 two small notices were placed privately on the railings
surrounding the block of masonry; one, at the instance of the Richard III Society recorded his birth in the castle in 1452; the other,
affixed by the Stuart History Society, commemorated Mary Queen
of Scots' death in 1587. More colourful were the visits of an eccentric Jacobite sympathizer, at the turn of the present century, who
used to make an annual pilgrimage from Edinburgh to Northamptonshire on the anniversary of the queen's death to lay a wreath at
Fotheringhay. Unfortunately, in his enthusiasm for the cause of
Mary Stuart, he used such violent language about the existing British royal family that his visits had to be discouraged by the then
owners of the site.

forgotten that rich pall he had sent down to Peterborough nine years earlier. This was to be employed again, and if the chapter happened to think it belonged to them, it was to be redeemed for a reasonable fee. Today the site of the original vault is covered by a marble pavement. The heraldic symbols over the grave were pulled down at the time of the Civil War, when the tomb of Queen Catherine of Aragon was also destroyed. The twenty-five-year-long sojourn of the queen of Scots' body in Peterborough Cathedral is marked by a stone tablet on an adjoining pillar, and two Scottish banners hang facing the site, placed there in 1920 by the Peterborough Caledonian Society.

In Westminster Abbey at last, the queen of Scots' body found its final resting-place. The tomb is magnificent, a monument to James's taste if not to his filial piety. By the white marble of which it is composed, Mary Stuart becomes once more 'la reine blanche' of her first widowhood. It shows her lying full-length beneath a great ornamental canopy, her face serene and noble, her eyes closed, her long fingers stretched out in an attitude of prayer; she wears the simple peaked head-dress in which she died, but a royal cloak edged with ermine stretches round her body; at her feet rests the lion of Scotland. The face is extremely realistic and was evidently modelled on either the death mask or the effigy taken from it at Peterborough, since it shows all the features which observers noticed at the time of her death, and bears also a strong resemblance to the later portraits. The chin is full and soft although still pointed, the oval shape of the face is characteristic as is the setting of the eyes with its pronounced gap before the hairline. The nose has a Roman bridge to it, and the aquiline tendency of later years, consonant with the Sheffield-type portraits, which was probably exaggerated by the conditions of the death mask. The mouth shows the delicate almost sensual curve of the portraits, but is set in a more tranquil expression than the sad martyr of the Sheffield-type pictures. Altogether the whole impression of this awe-inspiring catafalque is of beauty—beauty which is made up of both majesty and repose.

A long Latin epitaph was composed by the earl of Northampton and is now to be seen on the tomb: it extols Queen Mary's virtues, and deplores her misfortunes and her wrongful English imprisonment, without going into the controversial events which led to this imprisonment.

The Cotton MSS show that Northampton had composed
other still more eulogistic versions, in which it was suggested that, as Mary had stated herself, she had been executed solely for her religious faith, and lured into England
by the false promises of Elizabeth. These, however,
James discarded in favour of an uncontroversial panegyric
—which, however, Northampton still signed 'H.N. Gemens'
—Henry Northampton, mourning.[15]

So the queen of Scots found peace at last. There can
be little doubt that Mary who cared so much and so prolongedly for the English succession would have been satisfied at the last with her burial place in Westminster Abbey
among the kings and queens of England. Her rights as a
queen, to which she attached such importance to the end,
had thus been respected. Viewing that splendid edifice in
marble, white in the darkness of the Henry VII Chapel, the
last of the royal monuments and the most imposing of
them all, she would surely have felt that the cruelty of
Elizabeth in denying her the French burial she craved had
been atoned for in an unlooked-for and glorious manner.
Nor was the significance of her tomb entirely royal: a
few years after this new interment, pious Catholics were
spreading the news that holy benefits could be gained from
a visit to the tomb as to a shrine; Demster in Bologna
wrote in his history of the Scottish Church, published in
1627: 'I hear that her bones, lately translated to the burial place of the Kings of England at Westminster, are resplendent with miracles.'[16] As Mary's literary supporters
developed the theme of the martyr queen, the white tomb
itself became a place of pilgrimage for the faithful.

Once more, however, the repose of the Queen of Scots
was destined to be disturbed. In 1867 a search was instituted by Dean Stanley within the royal tombs of Westminster Abbey for the body of James I, whose position was
unrecorded. It was eventually discovered in the tomb of
Henry VII, the first Tudor and the first Stuart monarch of
England lying appropriately together with Elizabeth of
York, the woman who had made the foundation of both
dynasties possible. But in the course of the search, among
the places it was thought he might have appropriately
chosen for his own sepulchre was the tomb of his mother.
An entry was made below the monument to Mary, and at
the foot of an ample flight of steps marked WAY was
found a large vault of brick, twelve feet long, six feet high

and seven feet wide. A startling and harrowing sight greeted the gaze of the Victorian searchers: the queen of Scots was far from lying alone in her tomb. A vast pile of lead coffins rose upwards from the floor, some of them obviously of children, some so small as to be of mere babies, all heaped together in confusion, amid urns of many different shapes, which were scattered all through the vault.

It was discovered that Mary shared her catacomb with numbers of her descendants, including her grandson Henry, prince of Wales, who died before his prime, her grand-daughter Elizabeth of Bohemia, the Winter Queen, and her great-grandson Prince Rupert of the Rhine, among the most romantic of all the offshoots of the Stuart dynasty. Most poignant of all were the endless tiny coffins of the royal children who had died in infancy: here were found the first ten children of James II, and one James Darnley, described as his natural son, as well as the eighteen pathetic babies born dead to Queen Anne, and her sole child to survive infancy, the young duke of Gloucester.

Finally the coffin of the queen of Scots herself was found, against the north wall of the vault, lying below that of Arbella Stuart, that ill-fated scion of the royal house who had been the child-companion of Mary's captivity. The coffin itself was of remarkable size, and it was easy to see why it had been too heavy to carry in procession at Peterborough Cathedral at the first burial. But so securely had the royal body been wrapped in lead at the orders of the English government on the afternoon of the execution, that the casing had not given way in the slightest, even after nearly 300 years. The searchers felt profoundly moved even by this inanimate spectacle. No attempt was made to open it now. 'The presence of the fatal coffin which had received the headless corpse at Fotheringhay,' wrote Dean Stanley, 'was sufficiently affecting without endeavouring to penetrate further into its mournful contents.'[17] The vault was thus reverently tidied, the urns rearranged, and a list made of the contents. But the queen's own coffin was left untouched, and the little children who surrounded her were not removed.

Meanwhile in the opposite chapel, underneath the monument to Queen Elizabeth I also raised by James, were found together in one grave the two daughters of Henry VIII, Mary Tudor and Elizabeth. Barren in life, they had been left to lie alone together in death. Mary, however, lies amid her Stuart posterity, her face locked in the marble of repose on the monument above, and her hands clasped in prayer, her body in the vault below which harbours so many of her descendants. She who never reigned in England, who was born a queen of Scotland, and who died at the orders of an English queen, lies now in Westminster Abbey where every sovereign of Britain since her death has been crowned; from her every sovereign of Britain since her death has been directly descended, down to the present queen, who is in the thirteenth generation. As Mary herself embroidered so long ago at Sheffield on the royal dais of state which was destined to hang over the head of a captive queen: *In my end is my Beginning.*

Appendix

The English and Scottish Versions of the Long Casket Letter

1. The contemporary English copy of the long (second) casket letter was made by the clerk at the Westminster Conference, December 1568. Calendar of Scottish Papers, Vol. 2, Appendix 2, pp. 722ff. (An ellipsis of four dots represents a gap left in the original; an ellipsis of three dots represents words torn off or worn from the original.)

Being gon from the place where I had left my harte, it may be easily judged what my countenance was, consydering what the body may, without hart, which was cause that till dynner I had used lyttle talke, neyther wold any body advance him selfe therunto, thinking that it was not good so to doo. Fowre myles from thence a gentleman of the Erle of Lennox cam to made [*sic*] his commendacions and excuses unto me, that he cam not to meete me, because he durst not enterprise so to doo, consydering the sharp wordes that I had spoken to Conyngham, and that he desyred that I wold com to the inquisition of the facte which I did suspecte him of. This last was of his own head without commission, and I tolde him that he had no receipte against feare, and that he had no feare, if he did not feele him selfe faulty, and that I had also sharply aunsweared to the doubtes that he made in his lettres, as though ther had bene a meaning to poursue him. To be short: I have made him hold his peace; for the rest, it weare to long to tell you. Sir James Hamilton cam to meete me, who told me that at another tyme he went his waye when he hard of my comming; and that he sent unto him Houstoun, to tell him that he wold not have thought that he wold have followed and accompany him

selfe with the Hamiltons. He aunsweared that he was not
come but to see me, and that he wolde not follow Stuard
nor Hamilton, but by my commandement. He prayed him
to go speake to him: he refused it. The Lard Lus, Houston, and the sonne of Caldwell, and about xl hors came
to meete me, and he told me that he was sent to one day
a lau from the father, which shuld be this daye, against
the signing of his own hand which he hathe; and that
knowing of my comming he hath delayed it, and hath
prayed to go see him; which he hatt refused, and swearith
that he will suffer nothing at his handes. Not one of the
towne, is come to speake with me, which makith me to
think that they be his, and then he speakith well of them,
at leaste his sonne. The King sent for Joachim, and asked
him why I did not lodge nighe to him? and that he wold
ryse sooner, and why I cam, whither it wear for any good
appoynment that he cam, and whither I had not take
Paris and Guilbert to write, and that I sent Joseph. I
wonder who hath told him so muche, evin of the mariage
of Bastian. This bearer shall tell you more upon that. I
asked him of his lettres, and where he did complayne of
the crueltye of som of them, he saide that he did dreme,
and that he was so glad to see me that he thought he
shuld dye. Indeede that he had found faulte with me . . . .
I went my waye to supper, this berer shall tell you of
my arryv . . . praied me to com agayne, which I did, and
he told me his grefe and that he would make no testament
but leave all unto me, and that I was cause of his sicknes
for the sorrow he had that I was so strange unto him,
'And' (said he) 'you asked me what I ment in my lettre
to speake of cruelty: it was of your cruelty who will not
accepte my offres and repentance: I avowe that I have don
amisse, but not that I have always disavowed: and so have
many other of your subjectes don, and you have well perdonid them, I am yong. You will saye that you have also
perdonid me many tymes, but that I returne to my faultes.
Many not a man of my age for want of counsell, fayle
twise or thrise, and mysse of promes, and at the last repent and rebuke him selfe by his experience? Yf I may
obtayn this perdon, I protest I will never make faulte
agayne, and I aske nothing but that we may be at bed
and at table together as husband and wife. And if you will
not, I will never rise from this bed. I pray you tell me
your resolution heerof; God knowith that I am punished

to have made my God of you, and had no other mynd but of you: and when I offende you som tyme, you are cause thereof. for if I thought whan any body doth any wrong to [me] that I might for my refuge make my mone therof unto you, I wold open it to no other. But whan I heare any thing, being not familiar with you, I must keepe it in my mynde, and that troublith my wittes for anger.' I did still answear him, but that shall be to long. In the end I asked him why he wold go in the English shipp? He doth disavow it and swearith so, but confessith to have spoken to the men. Afterward I asked him of the inquisition of Hiegate? He denyed it till I tolde him the very woordes, and then he said that Minto sent him word that it was said that som of the counsayle had brought me a lettre to signe to putt him in prison, and to kill him if he did resiste, and that he asked this of Minto him selfe, who said unto him that he thought it was true. I will talke with him tomorrowe upon that poynte: the rest as Wille Hiegate hath confessed, but it was the next daye that he cam hither. In the end he desyred much that I shuld lodge in his lodging; I have refused it. I have told him that he must be pourged, and that could not be don heere. He said unto me, 'I have hard saye that you have brought the lytter, but I would rather have gon with your selfe.' I told him that so I wolde myselfe bring him to Cragmillar, that the phisicians and I also might cure him without being farre from my sonne. He said that he was ready when I wolde, so as I wolde assure him of his requeste. He hath no desyre to be seene, and waxeth angry whan I speake to him of Wallcar, and sayth that he will pluck his eares from his head, and that he lyeth: for I asked before of that and what cause he had to complayne of . . . the Lordes, and to threaten them? He denyeth it and sayth that he had already prayed them to think no such matter of him. As for myself: he wold rather lose his lyfe than doo me the leaste displeasour. And then used so many kindes of flatteryes so coldly and so wysely as you wold marvayle at. I had forgotten that he sayde that he could not mistrust me for Hiegates wordes, for he could not beleve that his own flesh (which was my selfe) wold doo him any hurte (and in deede it was sayde that I refused to have him lett blud) but for the others he wold at leaste sell his lyfe deere ynoughe: but that he did suspecte no body, nor wolde, but wolde love all that I did love. He wolde not lett me go, but wold have me to watche with him. I made as though I thought all to be true, and that I would think upon it. And have excused my selfe from sytting up with him this night, for he sayth that he sleepith not. You never hard one speake better nor more humbly, and if I had not proofe of his hart to be as waxe and that myne weare not as a dyamant, no stroke but comming from your hand, could make me but to have pitie of him. But feare not, for the place shall contynue till death. Remembre also in recompense therof not to suffer yours to won by that fals race that wold doo no lesse to your selfe. I think they have bene at schoole togither, he hath allwais the teare in the eye. He saluteth every man evin to the meanest, and makith much of them, that they may take pitie of him. His father hath bled this daye at the nose and at the mouth: gesse what token that is! I have not seene him, he is in his chambre. The King is so desyrous that I shuld give him meate with my own handes, but trust you no more there where you are than I doo here. This is my first journay, I will end tomorrow. I write all, how little consequence so ever it be of, to the end that you may take of the wholle that that shall be best for *you to judge.** I doo here a work that I hate muche, but I had begon it this morning. Had you not lyst to laughe, to see me so trymly make a lye, at the leaste, dissemble? and to mingle truthe therwith? He hath almost told me all on the bisshops behalfe and of Suderland, without touching any word unto him of that which you had told me, but only by muche flattering him and pr[essing?] him to assure selfe of me, and by my complayning of the r . . . en the wormes out of his nose.†

You have hard the rest. We have tyed to with two false races, the goodyeere untye us from them. God forgive me, and God knytt us togither for ever, for the most faythfull couple that ever he did knytt together. This is my fayth, I will dye in it. Excuse it, yf I write yll, you must gesse the one halfe, I can not doo with all, for I am yll at ease, and glad to write unto you when other folkes be asleepe, seeing that I cannot doo as they doo, according to my desyre, that is betwene your armes, my deere lyfe, whom I besech God to preserve from all yll, and send you good

* On margin 'your purpose'.

† Follows here on margin, 'I have disclosed all, I have known what I wold'.

rest as I go to seeke myne till tomorrow in the morning, that I will end my bible. But it greevith me that it shuld lett me from wryting unto you of newes of myselfe, so much I have to write. Send me word what you have determinid heerupon, that we may know the one the others mynde for marryng of any thing. I am weary and am asleepe, and yet I cannot forbeare scribling, as long as ther is any paper. Cursed be this pocky fellow that troublith me thus muche, for I had a pleasanter matter to discourse unto you, but for him. He is not muche the worse, but he is yll arayde. I thought I shuld have bene kylled with his breth, for it is worse than your uncles breth, and yet I was sett no neerer to him than in a chayre by his bolster, and he lyeth at the furder syd of the bed.

The message of the father by the waye:—

The talke of Sir James Hamilton of the ambassade—

That that the Lard a Luss hathe tolde me of the delaye.

The questions that he asked of Jochim of my state, of my companye, and of the cause of my coming, and of Joseph.

The talke that he and I have had, and of his desyre to please me, of his repentance, and of th'interpretation of his lettre of Will Hiegates doinges and of his departure, and of the L. of Levinston.

I had forgotten of the L. of Levinston, that at supper he sayd softly to the Lady Rivees [Rires] that he dronk to the persons that I knew [if] I wold pledge them. And after supper he said softly . . . I was leaning upon him and warming myselfe—'You may well go and see sick folkes, yet can you not be so wellcom unto them, as you have this daye left som body in payne, who shall never be meary till he have seene you agayne.' I asked him who it was? he tooke me about the body, and said 'One of his folkes that hath left you this daye.' Gesse you the rest.

This daye I have wrought till two of the clock upon this bracelet to putt the keye in the clyfte of it, which is tyed with two laces. I have had so lyttle tyme that it is very yll, but I will make a fayrer, and in the meane tyme take heed that none of those that he heere doo see it, for all the world wold know it, for I have made it in haste in theyr presence. I go to my tedious talke; you make me dissemble so muche, that I am afrayde thereof with horrour, and you make me almost to playe the parte of a traytour. Remembre that if it weare not for obeyeng you, I had rather be

dead; my hart bleedith for yt. To be shorte: he will not
com but with condition that I shall promise to be with
him as heeretofore at bed and borde, and that I shall for-
sake him no more, and upon my worde he will doo whatsoever I will, and will com, but he hath prayed me to
tarry till after tomorrow. He hath spoken at the fyrst more
stoutly, as this bearer shall tell you, upon the mater of
his Englishmen, and of his departure; but in the end he
commith to his gentlenes agayne. He hath told me among
other tak, that he knew well that my brother had told me
at Sterling that which he had said there, whereof he denyed
the halfe, and specially that he was in his chambre. But
now to make him trust me, I must fayne somthing unto
him: and therfore when he desyred me to promise that
when he shuld be wholle, we shuld make but one bed, I
told him (fayning to beleve his faire promesses . . . did
not change his mynde betwene this tyme and that, I was
contented, so as he wold saye nothing therof: for (to tell
it betwene us two) the Lordis wisshed no yll to him, but
did feare, leste (consydering the threateninges which he
made in case we did agree togither) he wolde make them
feele the small accompte they have maid of him, and that
he wold persuade me to poursue som of them; and for
this respecte shuld be in jelousy if *at one instant** without
their knowledge, I did breake a game made to the contrary in their presence. And he said unto me very pleasant
and meary, 'Think you that they doo the more esteeme you
therfore? but I am glad that you talke to me of the lordis.
I here that you desyre now that we shall lyve a happy
lyfe, for if it weare otherwise, it could not be but greater
inconvenience shuld happen to us both than you think:
but I will doo now whatsoever you will have me doo, and
will love all those that you shall love, so as you make
them to love me allso. For so as they seeke not my lyfe, I
love them all egally.' Therupon I have willed this bearer
to tell you many prety thinges, for I have to muche to
write, and it is late, and I trust him upon your worde. To
be short, he will goe any where upon my worde; alas! and
I never deceavid any body, but I remitt myself wholly to
your will: and send me word what I shall doe, and whatever happen to me, I will obey you. Think also yf you will

---

* 'By and by' written above.

not fynde som invention more secret by phisick, for he is
to take phisick at Cragmillar, and the bathes also, and shall
not com fourth of long tyme. To be short, for that that I
may learne, he hath greate suspicion, and yet nevertheles
trustith upon my worde, but not to tell me as yet anything.
Howbeit if you will that I shall *avowe* him, I will know
all of him, but I shall never be willing to beguile one that
puttith his trust in me. Nevertheles you may doo all, and
doo not estyme me the lesse therfore, for you are the
caus ther of; for, for my own revenge, I wold not doo it.
He givith me certain charges (and those strong) of that
that I feare evin to saye, that his faultes be published, but
there be that committ some secret faultes and feare not
to have them spoken of so lowdely, and that ther is
speeche of greate and small. And evin touching the Lady
Rires, he saide, 'God graunte that she serve you to your
honour,' and that men may not think nor he neyther,
that myne owne powre was not in my selfe, seeing I did
refuse his offres. To conclude, for a suerety he mistrustith
us of that that you know, and for his lyfe. But in the end,
after I had spoken two or three good wordes to him, he was
very meary and glad. I have not seene him this night, for
ending your bracelet, but I can fynde no claspes for yt: it
is ready therunto, and yet I feare least it shuld bring you
yll happ, or that it shuld be knowen if you were hurte.
Send me worde whither you will have it, and more mon-
ney, and whan I shall returne, and how farre I may speake.
Now as farre as I perceave, *I may do much with you:** gesse
you whither I shall not be suspected. As for the rest: he
is wood when he hearith of Ledinton, and of you and of
your brother he sayth nothing, but of the Erle of Arguile
he doth. I am afraide of him to heare him talke, at the
leaste he assurith him selfe that he hath no yll opinion of
him. He speakith nothing of those abrode, neither good nor
yll, but avoydith speaking of them. His father keepith his
chamber; I have not seene him. All the Hamiltons be
heere, who accompany me very honestly. All the frendes
of the other doo com allwais when I goe to visitt him. He
hath sent to me and prayeth me to see him ryse to morrow
in the morning early. To be short, this bearer shall declare unto you the rest, and if I shall learne any thing, I
will make every night a memoriall therof. He shall tell you

* On margin, 'Jay bien la vogue avec vois'.

the cause of my stay. Burne this lettre, for it is to dangerous, neyther is ther anything well said in it, for I think
upon nothing but upon greefe if you be at Edinboroughe.
Now if to please you my deere lyfe, I spare nether honour, conscience, nor hazard, nor greatnes, take it in good
parte, and not according to the interpretacion of your false
brother in lawe, to whom I pray you give no credit, against
the most faythfull lover that ever you had or shall have.
See not also her whose faynid teares you ought not more
to regarde than the true travails which I endure to deserve
her place, for obtayning of which against my own nature,
I doo betraye those that could lett me. God forgive me,
and give you my only friend the good luck and prosperitie
that your humble and faythfull lover doth wisshe unto
you; who hopith shortly to be an other thing unto you, for
the reward of my paynes. I have not made one worde,
and it is very late, althoughe I shuld never be weary in
wryting to you, yet will I end, after kyssing of your
handes. Excuse my evill wryting, and reade it over twise—
excuse also that . . . for I had yesternight no paper, wher
I tooke the paper of a [memoriall] . . . Remembre your
frende and wryte unto her and often. Love me all [wais] . . .

2. The Scottish translation of the long (second) casket
letter was first published in George Buchanan's *Detection*,
1571. The text here is taken from Andrew Lang's *The
Mystery of Mary Stuart*, London, 1901.

Being departit from the place quhair I left my hart, it
is esie to be judgeit quhat was my countenance, seeing
that I was evin als mekle as ane body without ane hart;
quhilk was the Occasioun that quhile Denner tyme I held
purpois to na body; nor zit durst ony present thameselfis
unto me, judging yat it was not gude sa to do. Four myle
or I came to the towne, ane gentilman of the Erle of Lennox come and maid his commendatiounis unto me; and
excusit him that he came not to meit me, be ressoun he
durst not interpryse the same, becaus of the rude wordis
that I had spokin to Cuninghame: And he desyrit that
he suld come to the inquisitioun of ye matter yat I suspectit him of. This last speiking was of his awin heid,
without ony commissioun. I answerit to him that thair was

na recept culd serve againis feir; and that he wold not be affrayit, in cace he wer not culpabill; and that I answerit bot rudely to the doutis yat wer in his letteris. Summa, I maid him hald his toung. The rest wer lang to wryte. Schir James Hammiltoun met me, quha schawit that the uther tyme quhen he hard of my cumming he departit away, and send Howstoun, to schaw him, that he wald never have belevit that he wald have persewit him, nor zit accompanyit him with the Hammiltounis. Heanswerit, that he was only cum bot to see me, and yat he wald nouther accompany Stewart nor Hammiltoun, bot be my commandement. He desyrit that he wald cum and speik with him: He refusit it. The Laird of Lusse, Howstoun, and Caldwellis sone, with xl. hors or thairabout, come and met me. The Laird of Lusse said, he was chargeit to ane Day of Law be the Kingis father, quhilk suld be this day, aganis his awin hand-writ, quhilk he hes: and zit notwithstanding, knawing of my cumming, it is delayit. He was inquyrit to cum to him, quhilk he refusit, and sweiris that he will indure nathing of him. Never ane of that towne came to speik to me, quhilk causis me think that thay ar his; and neuertheles he speikis gude, at the leist his sone. I se na uther Gentilman bot they of my company. The King send for Joachim zisternicht, and askit at him, quhy I ludgeit not besyde him? And that he wald ryse the soner gif that wer; and quhairfoir I come, gif it was for gude appointment? and gif I had maid my estait, gif I had takin Paris [this berer will tell you sumwhat upon this], and Gilbert to wryte to me? And yat I wald send Joseph away. I am abaschit quha hes schawin him sa far; zea he spak evin of ye mariage of Bastiane. I inquyrit him of his letteris, quhairintill he plenzeit of the crueltie of sum: answerit, that he was astonischit, and that he was sa glaid to se me, that he belevit to die for glaidnes. He fand greit fault that I was pensive. I departit to supper. Yis beirer wil tell yow of my arryuing. He prayit me to returne: the quhilk I did. He declarit unto me his seiknes, and that he wald mak na testament, bot only leif all thing to me; and that I was the caus of his maladie, becaus of the regrait that he had that I was sa strange unto him. And thus he said: Ze ask me quhat I mene be the crueltie contenit in my letter? it is of zow alone that will not accept my offeris and repentance. I confess that I haue failit, bot not into that quhilk I ever denyit; and siclyke hes failit to sindrie of zour subjectis, quhilk ze haue forgeuin. I am zoung. Ze wil say, that ze have forgevin me oft tymes, and zit yat I returne to my faultis. May not ane man of my age, for lacke of counsell, fall twyse or thryse, or inlacke of his promeis and at last repent himself, and be chastisit be experience? Gif I may obtene pardoun, I protest I sall never mak fault agane. And I crafit na uther thing, bot yat we may be at bed and buird togidder as husband and wyfe; and gif ze wil not consent heirunto, I sall never ryse out of yis bed. I pray zow, tell me your resolutioun. God knawis how I am punischit for making my God of zow, and for hauing na uther thocht but on zow; and gif at ony tyme I offend zow, ze ar the caus, becaus quhen ony offendis me, gif, for my refuge, I micht playne unto zow, I wald speik it unto na uther body; bot quhen I heir ony thing, not being familiar with zow, necessitie constranis me to keip it in my breist; and yat causes me to tyne my wit for verray anger . . . . I answerit ay unto him, but that wald be ovir lang to wryte at lenth. I askit quhy he wald pas away in ye *Inglis* schip. He denyis it, and sweiris thairunto; bot he grantis that he spak with the men. Efter this I inquyrit him of the inquisitioun of Heigairt. He denyit the same, quhill I schew him the verray wordis was spokin. At quhilk tyme he said that Mynto had advertisit him, that it was said, that sum of the counsell had brocht an letter to me to be subscrivit to put him in Presoun, and to slay him gif he maid resistance. And he askit the at same Mynto himself; quha answerit, that he belevit ye same to be trew. The morne I wil speik to him upon this Point. As to the rest of Willie Hiegait's, he confessit it, bot it was the morne efter my cumming or he did it. He wald verray fane that I suld ludge in his ludgeing. I refusit it, and said to him, that he behovit to be purgeir, and that culd not be done heir. He said to me, I heir say ze have brocht ane lytter with zow; but I had rather have passit with zow. I trow he belevit that I wald have send him away Presoner. I answerit, that I wald tak him with me to Craigmillar, quhair the mediciner and I micht help him, and not be far from my sone. He answerit, that he was reddy quhen I pleisit, sa I wald assure him of his requeist. He desyris na body to se him. He is angrie quhen I speik of Walcar, and sayis, that he sal pluk the eiris out of his heid and that he leis. For I in-

quyrit him upon that, and yat he was angrie with sum of
the Lordis, and wald threittin thame. He denyis that, and
sayis he luifis thame all, and prayis me to give traist to
nathing againis him. As to me, he wald rather give his
lyfe or he did only displesure to me. And efter yis he
schew me of sa money lytil flattereis, sa cauldly and sa
wysely that ze will abasche thairat. I had almaist forzet
that he said, he could not dout of me in yis purpois of
Hiegaite's; for he wald never beleif yat I, quha was his
proper flesche, wald do him ony evill; alsweill it was
schawin that I refusit to subscrive the same; But as to
ony utheris that wald persew him, at leist he suld sell his
lyfe deir aneuch; but he suspectit na body, nor zit wald
not; but wald lufe all yat I lufit. He wald not let me depart
from him, bot desyrit yat I suld walk with him. I mak it
seme that I beleive that all is trew, and takis heid thairto,
and excusit my self for this nicht that I culd not walk. He
sayis, that he sleipis not weil. Ze saw him never better,
nor speik nair humbler. And gif I had not ane prufe of
his hart of waxe, and yat myne wer not of ane dyamont,
quhairintill na schot can make brek, but that quhilk cum-
mis forth of zour hand, I wald have almaist had pietie
of him. But feir not, the place sall hald unto the deith.
Remember, in recompence thairof, that ye suffer not zouris
to be wyn be that fals race that will travell na les with
zow for the same. I beleve thay have bene at schuillis
togidder. He hes ever the teir in his eye; he salutis every
body, zea, unto the leist, and makis pieteous caressing unto
thame, to make thame have pietie on him. This day his
father bled at the mouth and nose; ges quhat presage that
is. I have not zit sene him, he keipis his chalmer. The
king desyris that I suld give him meit with my awin
handis; bot gif na mair traist quhair ze ar, then I sall do
heir. This is my first journay. I sall end ye same ye morne.
I wryte all thingis, howbeit thay be of lytill wecht, to the
end that ze may tak the best of all to judge upon. I am
in doing of ane work heir that I hait greitly. Have ze not
desyre to lauch to se me lie sa weill, at ye leist to dis-
sembill sa weill, and to tell him treuth betwix handis? He
schawit me almaist all yat is in the name of the Bischop
and Sudderland, and zit I have never twichit ane word of
that ze schawit me; but allanerly be force, flattering, and
to pray him to assure himself of me. And be pleinzeing
on the Bischop, I have drawin it all out of him. Ye have

hard the rest . . . . We ar couplit with twa fals races; the
devil sinder us, and God knit us togidder for ever, for the
maist faithful coupill that ever be unitit. This is my faith,
I will die in it. Excuse I wryte evill, ye may ges ye half of
it; bot I cannot mend it, because I am not weil at eis; and
zit verray glaid to wryte unto zow quhen the rest are
sleipand, sen I cannot sleip as thay do, and as I wald
desyre, that is in zour armes, my deir lufe, quhome I pray
God to preserve from all evill, and send zow repois: I am
gangand to seik myne till ye morne, quhen I sall end my
Bybill; but I am faschit that it stoppis me to wryte newis
of myself unto zow, because it is sa lang . . . . Advertise
me quhat ze have deliberat to do in the mater ze knaw
upon this point, to ye end that we may understand utheris
weill, that nathing thairthrow be spilt. I am irkit, and
ganging to sleip, and zit I ceis not to scrible all this paper
in sa mekle as restis thairof. Waryit mot this pokische man
be that causes me haif sa mekle pane, for without him I
suld have an far plesander subject to discourse upon. He
is not over mekle deformit, zit he hes ressavit verray mekle.
He hes almaist slane me with his braith; it is worse than
zour uncle's; and zit I cum na neirer unto him, bot in
ane chyre at the bed-seit, and he being at the uther end
thairof. The message of the father in the gait. The purpois
of Schir James Hamilton. Of that the Laird of Lusse
schawit me of the delay. Of the demandis that he askit at
Joachim. Of my estait. Of my company. Of the occasion
of my cumming: And of Joseph. *Item,* The purpois that
he and I had togidder. Of the desyre that he hes to pleis
me, and of his repentance. Of the interpretatioun of his
letter. Of William Hiegaite's mater of his departing. Of
Monsiure de Levingstoun. I had almaist forzet, that Monsiure de Levingstoun said in the Lady Reres eir at supper,
that he wald drink to ye folk yat I wist of, gif I wald
pledge thame. And efter supper he said to me, quhen I
was lenand upon him warming me at the fyre, Ze have
fair going to se seik folk, zit ze cannot be sa welcum to
thame as ze left sum body this day in regrait, that will
never be blyth quhill he se zow agane. I askit at him quha
that was. With that he thristit my body, and said, that
sum of his folkis had sene zow in fascherie; ze may ges at
the rest. I wrocht this day quhill it was twa houris upon
this bracelet, for to put ye key of it within the lock thairof,
quhilk is couplit underneth with twa courdounis. I have

had sa lytill tyme that it is evill maid; bot I sall mak ane fairer in the mean tyme. Tak heid that nane that is heir se it, for all the warld will knaw it, becaus for haist it was maid in yair presence. I am now passand to my fascheous purpois. Ze gar me dissemble sa far, that I haif horring thairat; and ye caus me do almaist the office of a traitores. Remember how gif it wer not to obey zow, I had rather be deid or I did it; my hart bleidis at it. Summa, he will not cum with me, except upon conditioun that I will promeis to him, that I sall be at bed and buird with him as of befoir, and that I sall leif him na ofter: and doing this upon my word, he will do all thingis that I pleis, and cum with me. Bot he hes prayit me to remaine upon him quhil uther morne. He spak verray braifly at ye beginning, as yis beirer will schaw zow, upon the purpois of the Inglismen, and of his departing: Bot in ye end he returnit agane to his humilitie. He schawit, amangis uther purposis, yat he knew weill aneuch that my brother had schawin me yat thing, quhilk he had spoken in Striviling, of the quhilk he denyis ye ane half, and abone all, yat ever he came in his chalmer. For to make him traist me, it behovit me to fenze in sum thingis with him: Thairfoir, quen he requeistit me to promeis unto him, that quhen he was haill we suld have baith ane bed: I said to him fenzeingly, and making me to beleve his promisis, that gif he changeit not purpois betwix yis and that tyme, I wald be content thairwith; bot in the meane tyme I had him heid that he leit na body wit thairof, becaus, to speik amangis our selfis, the Lordis culd not be offendit nor will evill thairfoir: Bot thay wald feir in respect of the boisting he maid of thame, that gif ever we aggreit togidder, he suld make thame knaw the lytill compt thay take of him; and that he counsallit me not to purchas sum of thame by him. Thay for this caus wald be in jelosy, gif at anis, without thair knawledge, I suld brek the play set up in the contrair in thair presence. He said verray joyfully, And think zow thay will esteme zow the mair of that? Bot I am verray glaid that ze speik to me of the Lordis; for I beleve at this tyme ze desyre that we suld leif togidder in quyetnes: For gif it wer utherwyse, greiter inconvenience micht come to us baith than we are war of: bot now I will do quhatever ze will do, and will lufe all that ze lufe; and desyris zow to make thame lufe in lyke manner: For sen thay seik not my lyfe, I lufe thame all equallie. Upon yis point this

beirer will schaw zow mony small thingis. Becaus I have
over mekle to wryte, and it is lait: I give traist unto him
upon zour word. Summa, he will ga upon my word to all
places . . . . Allace! I never dissavit ony body: Bot I remit
me altogidder to zour will. Send me advertisement quhat
I sall do, and quhatsaever thing sall cum thairof, I sall
obey zow. Advise to with zourself, gif ze can find out ony
mair secretit invention be medicine; for he suld take medicine and the bath at Craigmillar. He may not cum furth of
the hous this lang tyme. Summa, be all that I can leirne,
he is in greit suspicioun, and zit notwithstanding, he gevis
credit to my word; bot zit not sa far that he will schaw ony
thing to me: bot nevertheles I sall draw it out of him, gif
ze will that I avow all unto him. Bot I will never rejoyce
to deceive ony body that traistis in me: Zit notwithstanding ze may command me in all thingis. Have na evill
opinioun of me for that caus, be ressoun ze are the
occasion of it zourself; becaus, for my awin particular revenge, I wald not do it to him. He gevis me sum chekis
of yat quhilk I feir, zea, evin in the quick. He sayis this
far, yat his faultis wer publeist: bot yair is that committis
faultis, that belevis thay will never be spokin of; and zit
thay will speik of greit and small. As towart the Lady
Reres, he said, I pray God that scho may serve zow for
your honour: and said, it is thocht, and he belevis it to
be trew, that I have not the power of myself into myself,
and that becaus of the refuse I maid of his offeris. Summa,
for certainetie he suspectis of the thing ze knaw, and of
his lyfe. Bot as to the last, how sone yat I spak twa or
thre gude wordis unto him, he rejoysis, and is our of
dout. I saw him not this evening for to end your bracelet,
to the quhilk I can get na lokkis. It is reddy to thame: and
zit I feir that it will bring sum malhure, and may be sene
gif ze chance to be hurt. Advertise me gif ze will have it,
and gif ze will have mair silver, and quhen I sall returne,
and how far I may speik. He inragis when he heiris of
Lethingtoun, or of zow, or of my brother. Of your brother
he speikis nathing. He speikis of the Erle of Argyle. I am
in feir quhen I heir him speik; for he assuris himself yat
he hes not an evill opinioun of him. He speikis nathing
of thame that is out, nouther gude nor evill, bot fleis that
point. His father keipis his chalmer, I have not sene him.
All the Hammiltounis ar heir, that accompanyis me verray
honorabilly. All the freindis of the uther convoyis me

quhen I gang to see him. He desyris me to come and se him ryse the morne betyme. For to mak schort, this beirer will tell zow the rest. And gif I leirne ony thing heir, I will mak zow memoriall at evin. He wil tel zow the occasioun of my remaning. Burne this letter, for it is ovir dangerous, and nathing weill said in it: for I am thinkand upon nathing bot fascherie. Gif ze be in Edinburgh at the ressait of it, send me word sone. Be not offendit, for I gif not ovir greit credite. Now seing to obey zow, my deir lufe, I spair nouther honour, conscience, hasarde, nor greitnes quhat sumevir tak it, I pray zow, in gude part, and not efter the interpretatioun of zour fals gude-brother, to quhome, I pray zou, gif na credite agains the maist faithful luifer that ever ze had, or ever sall have. Se not hir, quhais fenzeit teiris suld not be sa mekle praisit nor estemit, as the trew and faithful travellis quhilk I sustene for to merite hir place. For obtening of the quhilk aganis my naturall, I betrayis thame that may impesche me. God forgive me, and God give zow, my only lufe, the hap and prosperitie quhilk your humble and faithful lufe desyris unto zow, quha hopis to be schortly ane uther thing to zow, for the reward of my irksum travellis. It is lait: I desyre never to ceis fra wryting unto zou; zit now, efter the kissing of zour handis, I will end my letter. Excuse my evill wryting, and reid it twyse over. Excuse that thing that is scriblit, for I had na paper zisterday quhen I wrait that of ye memoriall. Remember upon zour lufe, and wryte unto hir, and that verray oft. Lufe me as I sall do zow. Remember zow of the purpois of the Lady Reres. Of the Inglismen. Of his mother. Of the Erle of Argyle. Of the Erle Bothwell. Of the ludgeing in Edinburgh.

REFERENCE NOTES

Reference Notes

The following abbreviations have been commonly used:

C.S.P. Foreign: Calendar of State Papers, Foreign Series, Elizabeth

C.S.P. Roman: Calendar of State Papers relating to English affairs (Rome)

C.S.P. Scot.: Calendar of State Papers relating to Scotland

C.S.P. Spanish: Calendar of State Papers relating to Spain, Elizabeth

C.S.P. Venetian: Calendar of State Papers, Venetian

D.N.B.: Dictionary of National Biography

Hamilton: Hamilton Papers

Hat. Cal.: Calendar of manuscripts at Hatfield House

Keith: R. Keith, *History of the Affairs of Church and State in Scotland*

Knox: John Knox, *History of the Reformation*, translated and edited by W. C. Dickinson

Labanoff: *Lettres de Marie Stuart*, edited by Prince Labanoff

R.P.C.: Register of the Privy Council of Scotland

For further details of these and other books cited (which have been described below in the shortest convenient form) the reader is referred to the bibliography.

PART ONE

1. ALL MEN LAMENTED

1 Leslie, *Historie*, II, p. 260
2 Knox, I, p. 28
3 *Letters of James V*, p. 172
4 See entry under *Lineage* for Moray in *Burke's Peerage*, etc., 1963
5 Michel, *Les Français en Ecosse*, p. 420
6 Pitscottie, *Chronicles*, I, p. 377 et seq.
7 Diurnal of Occurrents, p. 22
8 Hamilton, I, p. 329
9 *Balcarres Papers*, I, *passim*
10 *Ibid.*, I, p. 81 et seq.
11 *Ibid.*, I, p. 83
12 *Ibid.*, I, p. 149
13 Pitscottie, *op. cit.*, I, p. 394
14 *Balcarres Papers*, I, p. 61
15 Knox, I, p. 29
16 Hamilton, I, p. 328
17 *Balcarres Papers*, I, p. 228
18 Knox, I, p. 37

19 Hamilton, I, p. 307
20 Knox, I, p. 38
21 Pitscottie, *op. cit.*, I, p. 406
22 *Letters of James V*, p. 417
23 Hamilton, I, p. 348
24 Knox, I, p. 39; Leslie, *op. cit.*, II, p. 259
25 Labanoff, VI, p. 68
26 Hamilton, I, p. 328; p. 340; p. 342; C.S.P. Spanish, VI (II), p. 189
27 Knox, I, p. 40
28 Leslie, *op. cit.*, I, p. 24; Hume Brown, *Early Travellers*, p. 236
29 Leslie, *ibid.*, II, p. 260; Hamilton, I, p. 342
30 Sadler State Papers, I, p. 115
31 Mathew, *Scotland under Charles I*, p. 152
32 Hay Fleming, *Mary Queen of Scots*, p. 180
33 Knox, I, p. 11-12; p. 40
34 Hamilton, I, p. 342
35 Sadler State Papers, I, p. 88
36 Knox, I, p. 45
37 Pitscottie, *op. cit.*, II, p. 8
38 Hume Brown, *op. cit.*, p. 118
39 Hamilton, I, p. 633
40 Knox, I, p. 50
41 Hamilton, II, p. 33

2. ENGLAND'S ROUGH WOOING

1 Leslie, *History*, II, p. 310
2 Hamilton, II, p. 326
3 Dalyell, *Scottish Fragments: The Late Expedition in Scotland*, sent to Lord Russell, Lord Privy Seal, by a friend of his, 1544
4 Archivo di Stati di Napoli, Carte Famesiane, tascio 709
5 Pollen, *Papal Negotiations*, p. 528; Donaldson, *Accounts of the Collector of the Thirds of Benefices*, Introduction, p. xv
6 Knox, I, p. 19; Knox, II, Appendix V, p. 255; Donaldson, *Scottish Reformation*, p. 12; p. 33
7 Pitscottie, *Chronicles*, II, p. 84
8 *Ibid.*, II, p. 85; Knox, I, p. 95
9 R.P.C., I, pp. 77 *et seq.*
10 Fergusson, *The White Hind*, p. 19; Dalyell, *Scottish Fragments;* William Patten, *Diary of Somerset's Campaign*, 1547
11 R.P.C., I, p. 11
12 Leslie, *op. cit.*, p. 310; Fraser, *Red Book of Menteith*, I, p. 503; Hay Fleming, *Mary Queen of Scots*, p. 192
13 Brantôme, *Oeuvres Complètes*, II, p. 460
14 De Beaugué, *Histoire de la Guerre en Ecosse*, p. 12
15 Teulet, *Papiers d'Etat*, I, p. 662; C.S.P. Scot., I, p. 99
16 C.S.P. Scot., I, p. 157
17 Leslie, *op. cit.*, II, p. 311; Jamieson, *Etymological Dictionary of the Scottish Language*, Vol. 3
18 Hamilton, II, p. 618
19 Printed in full, Stoddart, *Girlhood of Mary Queen of Scots*, Appendix
20 W. M. Bryce, *Voyage of Mary Queen of Scots in 1548*
21 *Ibid.*
22 Knox, I, p. 103

3. THE MOST PERFECT CHILD

1 De Ruble, *La première jeunesse de Marie Stuart*, p. 19
2 Albert le Grand, *Les Saints de la Bretagne Armorique*, Part II, p. 279
3 Stoddart, *Girlhood of Mary Queen of Scots*, Appendix, p. 416
4 Bouillé, *Ducs de Guise*, I, p. 225
5 *Balcarres Papers*, II, p. 6; p. 32
6 *Lettres de Catherine de Medicis*, I, p. 66
7 De Ruble, *op. cit.*, p. 17
8 *Lettres de Catherine de Medicis*, I, p. 6
9 Guiffrey, *Lettres inédites de Dianne de Poytiers*, Introduction, p. xxxiii
10 *Ibid.*, p. 35; p. 42
11 De Ruble, *op. cit.*, p. 30
12 Brantôme, *Oeuvres Complètes*, V, p. 85
13 De Ruble, *op. cit.*, p. 31; Labanoff, I, p. 10
14 *Balcarres Papers*, II, p. 135
15 De Ruble, *op. cit.*, p. 63
16 Guiffrey, *op. cit.*, p. 91
17 De Ruble, *op. cit.*, p. 69
18 *Shorter Oxford Dictionary*, Vol. 1
19 *Tresorier des Enfants de France. Fonds français.* 11207f., pp. 128 *et seq.* Printed De Ruble, pp. 281 *et seq.*
20 De Ruble, *op. cit.*, p. 51
21 Brantôme, *op. cit.*, V, p. 83; Montaiglon, *Latin Themes of Mary Queen of Scots*
22 Brantôme, *op. cit.*, V, p. 86
23 Labanoff, I, p. 4
24 De Ruble, *op. cit.*, p. 300
25 Register House, Edinburgh: GD/97/3/ no. 7
26 Labanoff, VII, 2nd supplement, p. 277
27 *Balcarres Papers*, II, Introduction, p. xxvi
28 Cameron, *Scottish Correspondence of Mary of Lorraine*, p. 149
29 C.S.P. Foreign (Edward VI), p. 103
30 *Ibid.*, p. 97
31 *Ibid.*, p. 109
32 Pollen, *Papal Negotiations*, p. 414
33 Brantôme, *op. cit.*, IX, p. 490
34 Pimodan, *La Mère des Guises*, p. 380

4. BETROTHAL

1 Labanoff, I, p. 10
2 Bouillé, *Ducs de Guise*, II, p. 27
3 *Balcarres Papers*, II, p. 110
4 Labanoff, I, p. 45
5 Claude de l'Aubespine, *Histoire Particulière de la Court de Henry II*
6 Labanoff, I, p. 14
7 Neale, *Catherine de Medici*, p. 12; C.S.P. Venetian, VII, p. 187
8 Bouillé, *op. cit.*, I, p. 229
9 Stoddart, *Girlhood of Mary Queen of Scots*, Appendix B, p. 450; Labanoff, I, p. 29
10 *Balcarres Papers*, II, p. 253; p. 271
11 *Ibid.*, II, p. 237; Introduction, p. li

12 Labanoff, I, p. 29
13 *Ibid.*, p. 41
14 *Ibid.*, p. 34
15 *Ibid.*, p. 21
16 Stoddart, *op. cit.*, Appendix B, p. 448
17 C.S.P. Venetian, VI, pt 3, p. 1365
18 *Ibid.*, pt 1, p. 532
19 Stoddart, *op. cit.*, p. 143
20 Baschet, *La Diplomatic Vénitienne*, p. 486
21 Regnier de La Planche, *Estat de France sous François*, II, p. 75
22 De Ruble, *La première jeunesse de Marie Stuart*, p. 35
23 Phillips, *Images of a Queen*, p. 14
24 Hume Brown, *Early Travellers*, p. 75

5. QUEEN-DAUPHINESS

1 *Discours du Grand et Magnifique Triomphe Faict du Mariage de François et Marie Stuart;* Hamer, *Marriage of the Queen of Scots to the Dauphin*
2 De Ruble, *La première jeunesse de Marie Stuart*, p. 149
3 C.S.P. Venetian, VI, pt 3, p. 1486
4 Hay Fleming, *Mary Queen of Scots*, Appendix, p. 491
5 Knox, II, p. 78; Ronsard, *Poésies choisies*, p. 353
6 Brantôme, *Oeuvres Complètes*, V, p. 83; Knox, II, p. 78; Hat. Cal., I, p. 400
7 Brantôme, *op. cit.*, V, p. 94

8 C.S.P. Venetian, VII, p. 383
9 Printed Maxwell-Stuart, *Tragedy of Fotheringhay*, Appendix; Melville, *Memoirs*, p. 96
10 C.S.P. Foreign, III, p. 251; *Tudor and Jacobean Portraits* (P.P.G.), p. 219
11 C.S.P. Venetian, VI, pt 2, p. 1058
12 Brantôme, *op. cit.*, V, p. 86
13 See Arbuthnot, *Queen Mary's Book*
14 Blanchemain, *Ronsard*, VIII, p. 28
15 Arbuthnot, *op. cit.*, p. 131; Castelnau, *Memoirs*, I, p. 528
16 Hay Fleming, *op. cit.*, p. 29; p. 213 note
17 C.S.P. Foreign, II, p. 14
18 MacNalty, *Mary Queen of Scots*, Appendix I, p. 214
19 Labanoff, I, p. 57
20 Leslie, *History*, II, p. 385
21 C.S.P. Venetian, VI, pt 3, p. 1571
22 Phillips, *Images of a Queen*, p. 12 *et seq.;* p. 237
23 C.S.P. Foreign, II, p. 145; C.S.P. Venetian, VII, p. 29
24 Melville, *op. cit.*, p. 49
25 C.S.P. Foreign, II, p. 382; p. 406; p. 434; p. 466
26 C.S.P. Venetian, VII, p. 167
27 *Ibid.*, p. 75
28 C.S.P. Foreign, I, p. 256
29 *Ibid.*, p. 347
30 Bouillé, *Ducs de Guise*, I, p. 526
31 De Ruble, *op. cit.*, p. 173
32 Bouillé, *op. cit.*, I, p. 529

6. THE WHITE LILY OF FRANCE

1 C.S.P. Foreign, I, p. 561
2 C.S.P. Venetian, VII, p. 113
3 De Ruble, *La première jeunesse de Marie Stuart*, p. 181
4 C.S.P. Venetian, VII, p. 138, 178
5 Baldwin Smith, *Elizabethan Epic*, p. 120; Belleval, *Les fils de Henri II*, p. 42
6 Bouillé, *Ducs de Guise*, II, p. 29
7 Stoddart, *Girlhood of Mary Queen of Scots*, p. 258
8 De Ruble, *op. cit.*, pp. 187–8; C.S.P. Foreign, II, p. 171
9 C.S.P. Venetian, VI, pt 3, p. 1486; De Ruble, *op. cit.*, p. 188
10 C.S.P. Foreign, II, p. 111
11 Labanoff, I, p. 70
12 Hamer, *Marriage of Mary Queen of Scots*
13 Knox, I, p. 319; p. 116
14 Teulet, *Papiers d'Etat*, I, p. 721; Regnier de La Planche, *Estat de France sous François*, II, p. 279
15 Melville, *Memoirs*, p. 51; C.S.P. Foreign, II, p. 511; III, p. 73
16 C.S.P. Venetian, VII, p. 227; p. 234
17 C.S.P. Foreign, III, p. 394
18 *Ibid.*, p. 394; C.S.P. Foreign, II, p. 410
19 Forneron, *Ducs de Guise*, p. 290
20 C.S.P. Foreign, II, p. 186; Hay Fleming, *Mary Queen of Scots*, p. 220
21 Regnier de La Planche, *op. cit.*, p. 203
22 De Ruble, *op. cit.*, p. 202
23 See Dr Potiquet, *La Maladie et La Mort de François II;* Armstrong-Davison, *The Casket Letters*, Appendix A
24 C.S.P. Venetian, VII, p. 275
25 *Ibid.*, p. 269; Hardwicke State Papers, I, p. 156
26 *Ibid.*, p. 275
27 Forneron, *op. cit.*, p. 327
28 Stoddart, *op. cit.*, p. 316; C.S.P. Venetian, VII, p. 278

7. MARY THE WIDOW

1 Froude, *History*, VI, p. 443
2 C.S.P. Foreign, III, p. 472
3 C.S.P. Foreign, IV, p. 201
4 C.S.P. Foreign, III, p. 472
5 Conyers Read, *Cecil*, p. 285
6 C.S.P. Foreign, III, p. 472; Wright, *Queen Elizabeth*, I, p. 58
7 Labanoff, I, p. 80
8 C.S.P. Venetian, VII, p. 290
9 C.S.P. Foreign, III, p. 423
10 *Lettres de Catherine de Médicis*, I, p. 158; p. 576; Chéruel, *Marie Stuart et Catherine de Médicis*, pp. 17–28
11 Hat. Cal., I, p. 258
12 Strong, *Portraits of Queen Elizabeth*, I, p. 24
13 C.S.P. Foreign, III, p. 565
14 Melville, *Memoirs*, p. 62
15 Leslie, *History*, II, p. 453
16 Knox, I, p. 354

17 C.S.P. Foreign, IV, p. 84
18 Camden, *Annales*, p. 53
19 Melville, *op. cit.*, p. 62
20 C.S.P. Foreign, IV, p. 154
21 Keith, *History*, II, p. 268
22 Leslie, *op. cit.*, II, p. 256
23 C.S.P. Foreign, IV, p. 154
24 *Ibid.*, p. 200
25 Keith, *op. cit.*, III, p. 211; *Despatches of Suriano and Barbaro*, p. 33
26 Hay Fleming, *Mary Queen of Scots*, p. 246
27 *Ibid.*, p. 246
28 Leslie, ed. Bannatyne Club, p. 297
29 C.S.P. Foreign, IV, p. 243
30 *Les Affaires du Conte de Boduel*, p. 7
31 C.S.P. Foreign, III, p. 409
32 Gore-Browne, *Lord Bothwell*, p. 128
33 Brantôme, *Oeuvres complètes*, V, p. 93
34 C.S.P. Foreign, IV, p. 263

PART TWO

8. THE STATE OF THE REALM

1 *Lettres de Catherine de Médicis*, I, p. 605
2 Brantôme, *Oeuvres complètes*, V, p. 92
3 Hardwicke State Papers, I, p. 176
4 C.S.P. Foreign, IV, p. 260; p. 261
5 Knox, II, p. 7
6 Herries, *Memoirs*, p. 56; Knox, II, p. 8
7 C.S.P. Foreign, III, p. 224; Pollen, *Papal Negotiations*, p. 132
8 Robertson, *Inventaires*, p. cxviii; Hume Brown, *Early Travellers*, p. 73; Cameron, *Scottish Correspondence of Mary of Lorraine*, p. xix
9 Hume Brown, *op. cit.*, p. 83
10 *Painted Ceilings of Scotland*, p. 9
11 Hay Fleming, *Mary Queen of Scots*, p. 255
12 Knox, II, p. 8
13 Leslie, *History*, II, p. 281 footnote
14 Macqueen, *Alexander Scott and the Scottish Court Poetry*
15 Leslie, *op. cit.*, I, p. 116
16 C.S.P. Scot., I, p. 205
17 Michel, *Les Français en Ecosse*, pp. 9–10
18 Castelnau, *Memoirs*, I, p. 186
19 Hume Brown, *Scotland in the Time of Queen Mary*, pp. 7 *et seq.*
20 Leslie, *op. cit.*, I, p. 5
21 Hume Brown, *op. cit.*, p. 77
22 Hume Brown, *op. cit.*, p. 52; Levassieur, *La Population Française*
23 C.S.P. Scot., I, p. 649
24 Leslie, *op. cit.*, I, p. 95; Hume Brown, *Early Travellers*, p. 39
25 Pitscottie, *Chronicles*, p. 275
26 *Chronicles of the Families of Atholl and Tullibardine*, I, p. 32
27 Robertson, *Inventaires*, p. 49
28 G. Seton, *History of Seton Family;* Leslie, *op. cit.*, I, p. 93
29 Cameron, *Scottish Correspondence of Mary of Lorraine*, p. xx; Hume Brown, *Early Travellers*, p. 47

30 Hat. Cal., II, p. 285
31 Fergusson, *Lowland Lairds*, p. 14
32 C.S.P. Spanish, I, p. 381
33 Macqueen, *op. cit.*; C. S. Lewis, *English Literature in the 16th Century*, p. 94
34 Child, *Ballads*, VI, p. 411
35 Hat. Cal., III, p. 47
36 C.S.P. Scot., I, p. 206

9. CONCILIATION AND RECONCILIATION

1 Knox, II, p. 8; C.S.P. Foreign, IV, p. 278
2 Laing, *Knox*, IV, p. 439
3 Eustace Percy, *Knox*, p. 59
4 Laing, *Knox*, IV, p. 373
5 Knox, II, p. 13 *et seq.*
6 C.S.P. Scot., I, p. 551; Knox, II, p. 20; Laing, *Knox*, VI, p. 132
7 Diurnal of Occurrents, p. 67; Knox, II, p. 21
8 C.S.P. Scot., I, p. 555
9 Diurnal of Occurrents, p. 69
10 Donaldson, *Scottish Reformation*, p. 45
11 Knox, II, p. 21
12 C.S.P. Scot., I, p. 566
13 R.P.C., I, Introduction, p. xl
14 Melville, *Memoirs*, p. 102; Castelnau, *Memoirs*, I, p. 179
15 Pollen, *Papal Negotiations*, p. 75
16 Skelton, *Maitland*, I, p. 305
17 *Ibid.*, II, p. 395
18 Levine, *Early Elizabethan Succession Questions*, p. 7
19 *Kervyn de Letterhoven*, II, pp. 24–5
20 Neale, *Queen Elizabeth*, p. 114

21 C.S.P. Foreign, III, p. 573
22 Labanoff, I, p. 110
23 *Ibid.*, p. 123
24 C.S.P. Foreign, IV, p. 523; Hay Fleming, *Mary Queen of Scots*, p. 295
25 Conyers Read, *Cecil*, p. 235
26 Wright's *Elizabeth*, I, p. 84; p. 58
27 Philippson, *Marie Stuart*, III, p. 457
28 Robertson, *Inventaires*, p. lxxx
29 Conyers Read, *op. cit.*, p. 237

10. GOVERNOR GOOD AND GRACIOUS

1 C.S.P. Scot., I, p. 582
2 Knox, II, p. 33
3 C.S.P. Scot., I, p. 609
4 *Ibid.*, p. 613
5 *Ibid.*, p. 563; Mackinnon, *Constitutional History*, p. 276
6 Exchequer Rolls, Vol. 19, Introduction, p. lxxi
7 Donaldson, *Scotland: James V–James VI*, p. 133
8 Neale, *Queen Elizabeth*, p. 215
9 Donaldson, *op. cit.*, p. 169
10 Robertson, *Inventaires*, p. xii
11 C.S.P. Scot., I, p. 206; Hume Brown, *Early Travellers*, p. 43
12 Lythe, *Economy of Scotland*, p. 57
13 Hume Brown, *op. cit.*, p. 122
14 Chronicles of Atholl, p. 36
15 C.S.P. Scot., I, p. 621

16 Robertson, *op. cit., passim*
17 *Libraries of Mary Queen of Scots;* Robertson, *Inventaires*, p. cxliii
18 Melville, *Memoirs*, p. 96
19 *Ibid.*, p. 96
20 C.S.P. Scot., p. 675
21 C.S.P. Scot., II, p. 148
22 Knox, II, p. 43
23 Robertson, *op. cit.*, p. 125
24 *Ibid.*, p. 60
25 *Ibid.*, p. 75
26 Macgeorge, *Miscellaneous Papers*, p. 12; C.S.P. Scot., II, p. 448
27 Hume Brown, *op. cit.*, p. 121; Hesketh, *Tartan*
28 Brantôme, *Gallant Ladies*, II, p. 215
29 C.S.P. Scot., II, p. 148
30 C.S.P. Scot., I, p. 579
31 Robertson, *op. cit., passim*
32 Knox, II, p. 32
33 C.S.P. Scot., II, p. 8
34 Knox, II, p. 102
35 Child, *Ballads*, VI, p. 379
36 Robertson, *op. cit.*, p. xlix, note 3
37 Hay Fleming, *Mary Queen of Scots*, Additional notes, p. 490
38 Neale, *op. cit.*, p. 65
39 Gatherer, *Buchanan*, p. 53

11. THE FALL OF HUNTLY

1 Gatherer, *Buchanan*, p. 79
2 C.S.P. Scot., I, p. 513
3 Robertson, *Inventaires*, p. 49
4 Knox, II, p. 63; C.S.P. Scot., I, p. 665
5 R.P.C., I, p. 219
6 C.S.P. Scot., I, p. 651
7 *Accounts of the Lord High Treasurer*, II, p. 197;
James Fraser, *True Geneologie of the Frasers*, 1666
8 C.S.P. Scot., I, p. 651
9 Batten, *Charters of the Priory of Beauly*
10 C.S.P. Scot., I, p. 665; Knox, II, p. 54
11 Knox, II, p. 59
12 Diurnal of Occurrents, p. 74
13 *Accounts of the Lord High Treasurer*, II, p. 205; p. 226
14 Dickinson, *Scottish Parliament*
15 Pollen, *Papal Negotiations*, p. 162; Labanoff, I, p. 175
16 Keith, II, p. 182
17 Labanoff, I, p. 112
18 C.S.P. Scot., I, p. 684
19 Knox, II, p. 69
20 Hay Fleming, *Mary Queen of Scots*, p. 315; Pollen, *op. cit.*, p. 251
21 C.S.P. Foreign, VI, p. 211
22 *Ibid.*, p. 260

12. A HUSBAND FOR A GIRL

1 Gatherer, *Buchanan*, p. 85
2 Hamilton, I, p. 358
3 C.S.P. Spanish, I, p. 312
4 C.S.P. Scot., II, p. 19
5 Keith, II, p. 213
6 Pollen, *Papal Negotiations*, p. 130
7 Knox, II, p. 73
8 *Ibid.*, pp. 82 et seq.
9 *Ibid.*, p. 85, note 6
10 C.S.P. Scot., II, p. 54
11 *Ibid.*, p. 28
12 Melville, *Memoirs*, p. 92
13 C.S.P. Foreign, VII, p. 264
14 *Ibid.*, p. 268
15 Strong, *Eworth*
16 Melville, *Memoirs*, p. 82
17 C.S.P. Foreign, VII, p. 299

18 Melville, *op. cit.*, p. 101; Read, *Cecil*, p. 315
19 Melville, *op. cit.*, p. 92
20 Hay Fleming, *Mary Queen of Scots*, p. 238; Knox, II, p. 203; Teulet, *Papiers d'Etat*, II, p. 112
21 Bannatyne MSS, II, p. 227
22 C.S.P. Scot., II, p. 126
23 Teulet, *op. cit.*, II, p. 42
24 Melville, *op. cit.*, p. 107
25 C.S.P. Scot., II, p. 126
26 *Ibid.*, p. 75
27 *Ibid.*, p. 129
28 Teulet, *op. cit.*, II, p. 32

23 *Ibid.*, p. 296
24 C.S.P. Scot., II, p. 234; p. 236
25 Knox, II, p. 174
26 Gatherer, *op. cit.*, p. 92
27 Labanoff, I, p. 342
28 C.S.P. Scot., II, p. 231; p. 241; p. 243; p. 327
29 Leslie, *Defence*, printed Anderson, *Collections*, I, p. 11
30 C.S.P. Foreign, VII, pp. 539, 541; Stewart, *Scottish Coinage*, p. 89
31 Herries, *Memoirs*, p. 73

13. THE CARNAL MARRIAGE

1 Bannatyne MSS, *Oxford Book of Scottish Verse*, p. 176
2 C.S.P. Scot., II, p. 166
3 *Papiers de Granville*, XIV, p. 33
4 C.S.P. Scot., II, p. 168
5 *Ibid.*, p. 171
6 Bannatyne MSS, II, p. 227
7 Register House, Edinburgh, S.P., 70 A
8 Pollen, *Papal Negotiations*, p. lxxv; p. xcv
9 Hay Fleming, *Mary Queen of Scots*, p. 348
10 Wright, *Queen Elizabeth*, I, p. 202
11 Knox, II, p. 158
12 Robertson, *Inventaires*, p. lxxxiv
13 Hat. Cal., I, p. 33
14 Knox, II, p. 162
15 C.S.P. Scot., II, p. 201
16 *Ibid.*, p. 139
17 *Ibid.*, p. 213
18 Gatherer, *Buchanan*, p. 93
19 Melville, *Memoirs*, p. 102
20 C.S.P. Scot., II, p. 232
21 Melville, *op. cit.*, p. 104
22 Labanoff, I, p. 300

14. OUR MOST SPECIAL SERVANT

1 Pollen, *Papal Negotiations*, p. 232
2 C.S.P. Scot., II, p. 254
3 C.S.P. Foreign, VIII, p. 13
4 Knox, II, p. 178
5 Keith, II, p. 404
6 C.S.P. Scot., II, p. 255
7 Tytler, *History*, V, p. 334
8 Keith, III, p. 265
9 C.S.P. Scot., II, p. 258
10 Gordon, *Genealogical History of the Earldom of Sutherland*
11 Froude, *History*, VII, p. 44
12 Melville, *Memoirs*, p. 113
13 Wright, *Queen Elizabeth*, I, p. 234
14 Labanoff, I, p. 342; Keith, III, p. 260
15 Chambers, *Life of James I*, p. 21
16 Birrel, *Diary*, p. 5 footnote
17 Herries, *Memoirs*, p. 79
18 *Ibid.*, p. 77
19 Nau, *Memorials*, p. 4
20 *Ibid.*, p. 15
21 *Ibid.*, p. 16

22 Lennox Narrative: printed Mahon, *Mary Queen of
   Scots*, Appendix A, p. 129
23 Nau, *op. cit.*, p. 17
24 Labanoff, I, p. 351

15. BREAKDOWN

1 Diurnal of Occurrents, p.
   7; Hay Fleming, *Mary
   Queen of Scots*, p. 400
2 Nau, *Memorials*, p. 7;
   C.S.P. Scot., II, p. 282
3 Nau, *op. cit.*, p. 28
4 Labanoff, VII, p. 297
5 Donaldson, *Scotland:
   James V–James VI*, p.
   130
6 C.S.P. Scot., II, p. 254
7 Gore-Browne, *Lord Bothwell*, p. 351; Herries,
   Memoirs, p. 80
8 Pitcairn, *Criminal Trials*,
   I, pt 1, p. 502
9 Nau, *op. cit.*, p. 41
10 Hat. Cal., XIII, p. 82
11 Robertson, *Inventaires*, p.
   xxvi
12 *Ibid.*, p. 93
13 Register House, Edin-
   burgh: Clerk of Penicuik
   MSS GD 18/1305
14 *Accounts of the Lord High
   Treasurer*, II, p. 512; p.
   499; p. 501
15 R. Bannatyne's *Memorials*,
   p. 238; C.S.P. Scot., II,
   p. 289
16 Woodgate, *Reminiscences
   of an Old Sportsman*
17 Gent, 'The Edinburgh Castle Mystery', *Chambers
   Journal*, September and
   October 1944
18 Melville, *Memoirs*, p. 131
19 Hat. Cal., I, no. 1116; Levine, *Early Elizabethan
   Succession Question*, p.
   188

20 Herries, *Memoirs*, p. 79
21 C.S.P. Domestic (James
   I), I, no. 102
22 Gatherer, *Buchanan*, p.
   168
23 C.S.P. Foreign, VIII, p.
   114; Keith, III, p. 349
24 C.S.P. Foreign, VIII, p.
   118; Hay Fleming, *op. cit.*,
   p. 411
25 Nau, *op. cit.*, p. 30
26 Hay Fleming, *op. cit.*, Appendix, p. 500
27 Keith, II, p. 447; p. 450
28 Labanoff, I, p. 374
29 R.P.C., I, p. 494
30 Pollen, *Papal Negotiations*,
   pp. 282 *et seq.*
31 Tytler, *History*, new enlarged edition, II, p. 400
32 Nau, *op. cit.*, p. 31; Knox,
   II, p. 191
33 Nau, *op. cit.*, p. 32
34 Gatherer, *Buchanan*, p.
   169
35 Stevenson's Introduction
   to Nau, *Memorials*, p. cxlii
36 Diurnal of Occurrents, p.
   103
37 Keith, I, p. xcvi
38 Keith, III, p. 290
39 Hosack, *Mary Queen of
   Scots*, I, p. 532
40 Lee, *Moray*, p. 184; Donaldson, *op. cit.*, p. 124
41 Diurnal of Occurrents, p.
   103
42 Robertson, *op. cit.*, p. 61;
   p. 63; p. 69
43 Melville, *op. cit.*, p. 143
44 Keith, I, p. xcvii

16. THE MURDER OF
DARNLEY

1 *Les Affaires du Conte de
   Boduel*, p. 12; Diurnal of
   Occurrents, p. 105; Pitscot-

tie, *Chronicles*, II, p. 91

2 Pearson, 'Skull and Portraits of Lord Darnley'

3 Armstrong-Davison, *Casket Letters*, p. 312

4 Mahon, *Tragedy of Kirk o'Field*, p. 248

5 Keith, II, p. 460

6 C.S.P. Spanish, I, p. 597

7 Labanoff, I, p. 395

8 Keith, I, p. ciii

9 Gore-Browne, *Lord Bothwell*, p. 293

10 *Les Affaires du Conte de Boduel*, p. 12

11 Nau, *Memorials*, p. 31

12 Henderson, *Mary Queen of Scots*, II, Appendix C, p. 664

13 Pitcairn, *Criminal Trials*, I, pt 1, p. 501

14 Nau, *op. cit.*, p. 33; Forbes-Leith, *Narratives*, p. 117

15 Gatherer, *Buchanan*, p. 111; Mahon, *Mary Queen of Scots*, Appendix A, p. 127

16 Robertson, *Inventaires*, p. ci.

17 Gatherer, *op. cit.*, p. 115; Pitcairn, *op. cit.*, I, pt 1, p. 501; Robertson, *op. cit.*, p. 177

18 Nau, *op. cit.*, p. 34; Mahon, *op. cit.*, p. 115

19 Hosack, *Mary Queen of Scots*, I, p. 535

20 Pitcairn, *op. cit.*, I, pt 1, p. 496

21 *Ibid.*, pt 1, p. 498

22 *Ibid.*, pt 1, p. 502

23 Labanoff, II, p. 3

24 Mahon, *Mary Queen of Scots*, Appendix A, p. 127; C.S.P. Venetian, VII, p. 389

25 Nau, *op. cit.*, p. 34

26 Pitcairn, *op. cit.*, I, pt 1, p. 493

27 Mahon, *Tragedy of Kirk o'Field*, p. 57

28 Nau, *op. cit.*, p. 44

29 Knox, II, p. 201

30 C.S.P. Foreign, VIII, p. 182

31 Pitcairn, *op. cit.*, I, pt 1, p. 495

32 *Ibid.*, pt 2, p. 149

33 Mahon, *Mary Queen of Scots*, Appendix A, p. 128

34 Pitcairn, *op. cit.*, I, pt 1, p. 502; Herries, *Memoirs*, p. 84

35 Gatherer, *op. cit.*, p. 116

36 C.S.P. Roman, II, p. 223

37 Labanoff, VII, p. 108

17. THE MERMAID AND THE HARE

1 *Les Affaires du Conte de Boduel*, p. 13

2 C.S.P. Venetian, VII, p. 388

3 Labanoff, II, p. 3

4 *Les Affaires du Conte de Boduel*, p. 13

5 Knox, II, p. 202

6 Robertson, *Inventaires*, p. lviii

7 Keith, I, p. xcviii

8 Anderson, *Collections*, I, p. 24

9 C.S.P. Venetian, VII, p. 389

10 C.S.P. Foreign, VIII, p. 211

11 *Ibid.*, p. 182

12 C.S.P. Scot., II, p. 318

13 Tytler, *History*, VII, p. 372

14 C.S.P. Foreign, VIII, p. 185

15 R.P.C., I, p. 500

16 Robertson, *op. cit.*, p. 53;

C.S.P. Foreign, VIII, p. 198; Gore-Browne, *Lord Bothwell,* p. 374

17 Keith, II, p. 532; C.S.P. Foreign, VIII, p. 198

18 Diurnal of Occurrents, p. 108

19 Keith, II, p. 562

20 Nau, *Memorials,* p. 37

21 Labanoff, II, p. 20

22 Pollen, *Papal Negotiations,* p. 386

23 C.S.P. Scot., II, p. 322

24 Pitcairn, *Criminal Trials,* I, pt 1, p. 502

25 Melville, *Memoirs,* p. 149

26 Labanoff, II, p. 31

27 C.S.P. Foreign, VIII, p. 217

28 Phillips, *Images of a Queen,* p. 44

29 Lang, *Mystery of Mary Stuart,* p. 210

30 Stuart, *A Lost Chapter in the History of Mary Queen of Scots, passim*

31 *Les Affaires du Conte de Boduel,* Appendix XIV

32 Hat. Cal., XIII, p. 82

33 Diurnal of Occurrents, p. 110

34 Hay Fleming, *Mary Queen of Scots,* p. 454

35 Mahon, *Tragedy of Kirk o'Field,* p. 182

36 Diurnal of Occurrents, p. 111

37 Robertson, *op. cit.,* p. 175

38 Anderson, *op. cit.,* I, p. 27; Keith, II, p. 588

39 Melville, *op. cit.,* p. 154

40 Teulet, *Papiers d'Etat,* II, p. 170

41 C.S.P. Foreign, VIII, p. 229; Teulet, *op. cit.,* II, p. 170

42 Mahon, *op. cit.,* p. 184

43 Labanoff, II, p. 31

44 *Ibid.,* p. 55

45 Tytler, *History,* new edition, III, p. 3; Teulet, *op. cit.,* II, p. 156

46 Nau, *op. cit.,* p. 40

47 C.S.P. Scot., II, p. 336

48 Macgeorge, *Miscellaneous Papers*

49 C.S.P. Foreign, VIII, p. 246

50 Teulet, *op. cit.,* II, p. 171 *et seq.;* Keith, II, p. 628; Herries, *Memoirs,* p. 93

51 Labanoff, II, p. 23

52 Nau, *op. cit.,* p. 47

53 *Ibid.,* p. 48

54 *Ibid.,* p. 51

55 Melville, *op. cit.,* p. 156

18. LOCHLEVEN

1 Melville, *Memoirs,* p. 156

2 Nau, *Memorials,* p. 52

3 Macgeorge, *Miscellaneous Papers,* pp. 12 *et seq.*

4 C.S.P. Scot., II, p. 730

5 Pitcairn, *Criminal Trials,* I, pt 1, p. 495

6 C.S.P. Foreign, VIII, p. 269; p. 287

7 Nau, *op. cit.,* p. 59

8 C.S.P. Scot., II, p. 356

9 *Ibid.,* p. 373

10 *Ibid.,* p. 372

11 *Ibid.,* p. 354

12 *Ibid.,* p. 355

13 Nau, *op. cit.,* p. 62

14 C.S.P. Foreign, VIII, p. 252; C.S.P. Spanish, I, p. 649

15 C.S.P. Scot., II, p. 231

16 Donaldson, *Scotland: James V–James VI,* p. 125, footnote 43

17 C.S.P. Scot., II, p. 376

18 Castelnau, *Memoirs,* I, p. 648; Labanoff, II, p. 63, footnote 2

19 Nau, *op. cit.,* p. 62

20 *Ibid.*, p. 64
21 Keith, II, p. 736
22 C.S.P. Scot., II, p. 390
23 Nau, *op. cit.*, p. 69
24 Keith, II, p. 738; Nau, *op. cit.*, p. 69; C.S.P. Scot., II, p. 845
25 Labanoff, II, p. 61
26 C.S.P. Foreign, VIII, p. 345
27 Macgeorge, *op. cit.*, pp. 12 *et seq.*
28 C.S.P. Foreign, VIII, p. 363
29 *Ibid.*, p. 333
30 *Ibid.*, p. 356
31 Henderson, *The Casket Letters*, Appendix D, p. 177
32 *Acts of the Parliament of Scotland*, III, 27
33 Nau, *op. cit.*, p. 71
34 *Ibid.*, p. 59
35 Pitcairn, *op. cit.*, I, pt 1, p. 491; Diurnal of Occurrents, p. 128
36 Wright, *Queen Elizabeth*, I, p. 206
37 Labanoff, II, p. 69
38 *Ibid.*, p. 65
39 Hat. Cal., I, no. 1172; Cecil Papers folio no. 147/26; Labanoff, II, p. 67
40 Melville, *op. cit.*, p. 168
41 Keith, II, p. 790
42 Nau, *op. cit.*, pp. 84 *et seq.*
43 Labanoff, III, p. 15
44 C.S.P. Venetian, VII, p. 414
45 Hay Fleming, *Mary Queen of Scots* (unpublished documents), p. 511

PART THREE

19. IN FOREIGN BANDS

1 Diurnal of Occurrents, p. 129
2 Henderson, *Mary Queen of Scots*, II, p. 494
3 Labanoff, II, p. 76
4 Argyll Papers
5 Brantôme, *Oeuvres complètes*, V, p. 99
6 Labanoff, II, p. 117
7 *Ibid.*, VI, p. 472
8 Nau, *Memorials*, p. 95.
9 Labanoff, II, p. 71
10 Strickland, *Queens of Scotland*, VI, p. 103
11 C.S.P. Scot., II, p. 410
12 H.M.C., Vol. V, Appendix to 5th Report, p. 615; Ailsa Muniments folio 17
13 C.S.P. Venetian, VII, p. 416
14 C.S.P. Scot., II, p. 409
15 *Ibid.*, p. 428
16 *Ibid.*, p. 416
17 *Ibid.*, p. 420
18 *Ibid.*, p. 448
19 *Ibid.*, p. 453; Macgeorge, *Miscellaneous Papers*, p. 17
20 Arbuthnot, *Queen Mary's Book*, p. 100
21 C.S.P. Scot., II, p. 452
22 Labanoff, II, p. 91
23 C.S.P. Scot., II, p. 433
24 Conyers Read, *Cecil*, p. 402
25 Mahon, *Indictment*, p. 3
26 C.S.P. Scot., II, p. 442
27 Conyers Read, *op. cit.*, p. 401
28 C.S.P. Scot., II, p. 435
29 *Ibid.*, p. 457
30 *Ibid.*, p. 443
31 *Ibid.*, p. 509; p. 510
32 Goodall, *Casket Letters*, II, p. 360
33 C.S.P. Scot., II, p. 494
34 *Ibid.*, p. 510
35 *Ibid.*, p. 495
36 Labanoff, II, p. 182
37 *Ibid.*, p. 237

38 C.S.P. Scot., II, p. 516
39 Ibid., p. 541
40 Labanoff, II, p. 181

20. HER PRIVY LETTERS

1 R.P.C., I, p. 641
2 C.S.P. Scot., II, p. 526
3 Hat. Cal., I, p. 369
4 Ailsa Muniments, folio 31;
   Labanoff, II, p. 225
5 Labanoff, II, p. 420
6 Hosack, Mary Queen of
   Scots, I, p. 549
7 Goodall, Casket Letters,
   II, p. 261
8 Labanoff, II, p. 254
9 Ibid., p. 257
10 Goodall, op. cit., p. 305
11 Macgeorge, Miscellaneous
   Papers, p. 13
12 Lady Baillie-Hamilton, 'A
   Historical Relic'. Quoted
   Lang, Mystery of Mary
   Stuart, p. 368
13 Public Record Office, London, SP/52/2; Cecil Papers 252/1–4; Cotton
   MSS: Caligula, 1, folio
   271
14 C.S.P. Scot., II, Appendix
   II, p. 722; Mahon, Mary
   Queen of Scots, p. 111
15 Ibid., Appendix II, p. 722
16 Ibid., Appendix II, p. 728
17 Hat. Cal., I, p. 376
18 Gatherer, Buchanan, p.
   173
19 C.S.P. Scot., II, Appendix
   II, p. 722
20 Hat. Cal., I, p. 379
21 Henderson, Casket Letters,
   pp. 171, 172; Armstrong-
   Davison, Casket Letters, p.
   195
22 Hosack, op. cit., I, Appendix F, p. 562
23 Cotton MSS: Caligula I,
   folio 271; Goodall, op.

cit., II, p. 54
24 Hosack, op. cit., I, p. 549
25 Goodall, op. cit., II, p. 54
26 Ibid., II, p. 256
27 Labanoff, II, p. 203

21. MY NORFOLK

1 C.S.P. Scot., II, p. 907
2 Morris, Letter-books of Sir
   Amias Paulet, p. 108
3 Plot, History of Staffordshire; Somerville, Guide to
   Tutbury Castle
4 Labanoff, VI, p. 176
5 C.S.P. Scot., II, p. 616
6 Lodge, Illustrations of
   British History, p. xvii
7 Bagot Letters, Microfilm
   no. II, nos. 820–821
8 C.S.P. Scot., II, p. 632
9 Girouard, Robert Smyth-
   son and Elizabethan Architecture, p. 58
10 Hat. Cal., I, p. 400
11 C.S.P. Scot., II, p. 632
12 Ibid., p. 649
13 Hat. Cal., I, p. 400
14 Edwards, Dangerous
   Queen, p. 30
15 Neale, Elizabethan House
   of Commons, p. 186
16 Labanoff, II, p. 369
17 Ibid., III, p. 5
18 Camden, Annales, p. 129
19 Labanoff, III, p. 19
20 Maidment, Miscellany of
   Abbotsford Club, I, p. 23
21 Lee, Moray, p. 261
22 Harris, Unpublished documents relating to Town
   Life in Coventry, p. 98
23 Labanoff, III, p. 6
24 C.S.P. Scot., II, p. 574
25 Labanoff, III, p. 387
26 Hat. Cal., I, p. 505
27 Ibid., p. 510
28 Ibid., p. 512

29 Black, *Reign of Elizabeth*, p. 150
30 Labanoff, III, p. 188
31 *Ibid.*, p. 221; C.S.P. Roman, I, p. 401
32 Labanoff, III, p. 110; p. 117
33 *Ibid.*, p. 115
34 Lockie, *Political Career of the Bishop of Ross*
35 Edwards, *Marvellous Chance*, p. 107
36 Hat. Cal., I, p. 564
37 *Ibid.*, p. 563
38 Labanoff, IV, p. 48

22. THE USES OF ADVERSITY

1 Argyll Papers
2 Melville, *Memoirs*, p. 224 C.S.P. Scot., III, p. 92
3 C.S.P. Scot., IV, p. 590; p. 600
4 Shrewsbury Papers (Lambeth Palace Library), MS 698, folio I
5 Johnston, *Shrewsbury*
6 Hat. Cal., II, p. 428
7 Johnston, *op. cit.*, 19 September 1582
8 *Ibid.*, 15 April 1574; Lodge, *Illustrations*, *op. cit.*, p. 117
9 Paget Papers, Staffordshire County Record Office, D(W) 1734/3/3/280
10 Johnston, *op. cit.*, 5 September 1571
11 Heape, *Buxton under the Dukes of Devonshire*, p. 15
12 Johnston, *op. cit.*, 4 August, 1576
13 *Ibid.*, 9 July, 1580
14 *Ibid.*, 10 July, 1584
15 Morris, *Letter-books of Sir Amias Paulet*, p. 40

16 Johnston, *Shrewsbury*, 11 May 1570
17 Labanoff, IV, p. 183; p. 10; VI, p. 187
18 Seton, *History of the Family of Seton*
19 Shrewsbury Papers, MS 705 folio 33
20 C.S.P. Scot., II, p. 1014
21 C.S.P. Domestic (James I) 17 July 1613
22 Lang, *Portraits and Jewels of Mary Queen of Scots*, p. 58; Labanoff, V, p. 89
23 Pollen, *Babington Plot*, p. 56
24 MacNalty, *Mary Queen of Scots*, p. 235
25 Labanoff, IV, p. 251
26 C.S.P. Foreign, IX, p. 346; p. 372
27 Vatican Archives, Fondo Borghese 1.824, folios 49v; 50v; Labanoff, III, p. 231
28 Arbuthnot, *Queen Mary's Book*, p. 112
29 C.S.P. Roman, II, pp. 215 et seq.
30 *Ibid.*, p. 250
31 Gore-Browne, *Lord Bothwell*, p. 456; Herries, *Memoirs*, p. 96
32 Labanoff, IV, p. 256
33 *Ibid.*, p. 390
34 Cust, *Authentic Portraits of Mary Queen of Scots*, p. 78
35 C.S.P. Domestic 1591–4, p. 99
36 *Tudor and Jacobean Portraits* (N.P.G.), p. 221
37 Arbuthnot, *op. cit.*, p. 116
38 Burns, 'Catholicism in Defeat'
39 Labanoff, V, p. 280
40 Pollen, 'Mary Stuart's Jesuit Chaplain'

41 Arbuthnot, *op. cit.*, p. 106
42 Arbuthnot, *op. cit.*, p. 129

23. MOTHER AND SON

1 Calderwood, *History*, III, p. 207; Hat. Cal., III, p. 26
2 *Tudor and Jacobean Portraits* (N.P.G.), p. 221
3 Willson, *King James VI and I*, p. 39
4 Hat. Cal., III, p. 47
5 Register House, Edinburgh: Blairs College Correspondence, R.H. 2/7/9
6 C.S.P. Scot., III, p. 35
7 Labanoff, V, p. 264
8 Hat. Cal., III, pp. 46 *et seq.*
9 *Ibid.*, p. 47
10 Labanoff, VI, pp. 14 *et seq.*
11 Hat. Cal., III, p. 71
12 Labanoff, VI, p. 30
13 *Ibid.*, p. 58
14 *Ibid.*, p. 65; p. 70
15 *Ibid.*, p. 77
16 Hat. Cal., III, p. 95
17 Labanoff, VI, p. 125; p. 129
18 *Ibid.*, IV, p. 356
19 *Ibid.*, V, p. 370
20 Shrewsbury Papers, MS 698 folio 39v
21 Labanoff, VI, p. 33; p. 42
22 *Ibid.*, p. 50
23 C.S.P. Roman, II, p. 238
24 D.N.B., XIX, p. 315
25 Caraman, *William Weston*, p. 31
26 *Staffordshire Historical Collections*, Introduction, p. xxxii and pp. 35–62
27 C.S.P. Scot., II, p. 551
28 Paget Papers, VI, *passim*
29 Hicks, *Elizabethan Problem*, p. 21

30 *Ibid.*, p. 119; Labanoff, VI, p. 14
31 Hicks, *op. cit.*, pp. 80 *et seq.*
32 Persons, *Notes concerning the English mission*, quoted Hicks, *op. cit.*, p. 7
33 Hicks, *op. cit.*, p. 123
34 Knox, *Allen*, p. 434
35 Labanoff, VI, p. 130; p. 132
36 *Ibid.*, p. 45
37 *Ibid.*, p. 76
38 Williams, *Elizabeth*, p. 277
39 Camden, *Annales*, p. 41

24. THE BABINGTON PLOT

1 Morris, *Letter-books of Sir Amias Paulet*, p. 15
2 *Ibid.*, p. 6
3 *Ibid.*, p. 6
4 Monckton, 'Beer and Ale in Shakespeare's Time'
5 Morris, *op. cit.*, p. 122
6 Labanoff, VI, p. 368
7 Morris, *op. cit.*, p. 98
8 *Ibid.*, p. 139
9 Pollen, *Babington Plot*, p. l; Read, *Walsingham*, III, p. 9
10 Labanoff, VI, p. 281
11 Pollen, *op. cit.*, p. lvi
12 Morris, *op. cit.*, p. 152
13 C.S.P. Roman 1572–8, p. 330
14 Phillips, *Images of a Queen*, p. 108
15 Mathew, *Celtic Peoples of Europe*, p. 49
16 Paget Papers, Staffordshire County Record Office D(W) 173/3/3/280
17 Caraman, *William Weston*, p. 99

18 Hat. Cal., III, p. 140
19 Labanoff, VI, p. 345; Pollen, *op. cit.*, p. 15
20 Pollen, *op. cit.*, p. 18
21 *Ibid.*, *op. cit.*, p. 38
22 Labanoff, VI, p. 404
23 *Ibid.*, p. 294
24 Black, *Reign of Elizabeth*, p. 381
25 Pollen, *op. cit.*, p. 32; p. 45; Conyers Read, *op. cit.*, III, p. 43
26 Labanoff, VI, p. 330; p. 325, p. 309; p. 351
27 *Ibid.*, p. 362
28 Morris, *op. cit.*, p. 201
29 *Dictionnaire de Théologie Catholique* (*Tyrannicide*)
30 Pollen, *op. cit.*, p. 53; Labanoff, VI, p. 288
31 Pollen, *op. cit.*, p. 46
32 Caraman, *William Weston*, p. 81
33 Pollen, *op. cit.*, p. 49 *et seq.*
34 Chantelauze, *Bourgoing's Journal*, p. 467 *et seq.*
35 Labanoff, VII, p. 242
36 *Ibid.*, VII, p. 250
37 Morris, *op. cit.*, p. 275
38 *Ibid.*, p. 276
39 *Ibid.*, p. 267
40 Pollen, *op. cit.*, p. cxc
41 *Ibid.*, p. clxxxii
42 *Ibid.*, p. clxxxix
43 Stevenson's Introduction to Nau, *Memorials*, p. xxiv
44 Labanoff, VI, p. 438

25. TRIAL

1 Chantelauze, *Bourgoing's Journal*, p. 490 *et seq.*
2 *Ibid.*, p. 490
3 Morris, *Letter-books of Sir Amias Paulet*, p. 297
4 27 Elizabeth C.I.
5 Johnston, *Shrewsbury*, 22 October 1586
6 Stuart, *Trial of Mary Queen of Scots*, p. 86 *et seq.;* Hardwicke State Papers, I, p. 224
7 Labanoff, VII, p. 36; Maxwell-Stuart; *Tragedy of Fotheringhay*, p. 31
8 Read, *Cecil*, p. 402
9 Maxwell-Stuart, *op. cit.*, p. 35
10 Strickland, *Queens of Scotland*, VII, p. 428
11 Chantelauze, *op. cit.*, p. 513 *et seq.;* Maxwell-Stuart, *op. cit.*, p. 51 *et seq.*
12 Chantelauze, *op. cit.*, p. 520
13 *Ibid.*, p. 522
14 Chantelauze, *op. cit.*, p. 527
15 Pollen, *Babington Plot*, p. cxcii
16 Stuart, *op. cit.*, p. 41
17 Chantelauze, *op. cit.*, p. 532
18 *Ibid.*, p. 539
19 Morris, *op. cit.*, p. 301
20 Arbuthnot, *Queen Mary's Book*, p. 127
21 Chantelauze, *op. cit.*, p. 539
22 D'Ewes, *Journals*, pp. 375 *et seq.*
23 Chantelauze, *op. cit.*, p. 544; Morris, *op. cit.*, pp. 299, 300
24 Labanoff, VI, p. 467; Morris, *op. cit.*, p. 311
25 Labanoff, VI, p. 461
26 *Ibid.*, p. 447
27 *Ibid.*, p. 456
28 *Ibid.*, p. 461

26. THE DOLOROUS STROKE

1 Willson, *King James VI and I*, p. 73
2 Hat. Cal. XIII, p. 300
3 C.S.P. Scot., IX, p. 417
4 Rait and Cameron, *King James' Secret*, pp. 55 et seq.
5 *Ibid.*, Preface, p. viii; pp. 158–72; pp. 176–82
6 Willson, *op. cit.*, p. 78
7 Read, *Walsingham*, III, p. 60
8 Hat. Cal., III, p. 206
9 Chantelauze, *Bourgoing's Journal*, p. 552
10 Labanoff, VI, p. 474
11 Morris, *Letter-books of Sir Amias Paulet*, p. 328
12 Chantelauze, *op. cit.*, p. 560; p. 579
13 *Ibid.*, p. 566
14 Teulet, *Relations Politiques*, IV, p. 163
15 Nicolas, *Life of Davison*, p. 83
16 Black, *Reign of Elizabeth*, p. 308
17 Nicolas, *op. cit.*, p. 86
18 Morris, *op. cit.*, p. 361
19 Nicolas, *op. cit.*, p. 103
20 Hat. Cal., III, p. 216
21 Maxwell-Stuart, *Tragedy of Fotheringhay*, p. 168
22 Chantelauze, *op. cit.*, p. 571
23 Camden, *Annales*, p. 108
24 Chantelauze, *op. cit.*, pp. 575 et seq.; Jebb *De Vita et Rebus Gestis*, II, pp. 175 et seq.; II, pp. 611 et seq.; Camden, *op. cit.*, pp. 109 et seq.
25 Labanoff, VI, p. 491
26 *Ibid.*, p. 484
27 *Ibid.*, p. 483
28 See Maxwell-Stuart, *op. cit.*, Appendix for three contemporary accounts of execution
29 G. R. Gleig, *Family History of England*, II, iii; W. Chappell, *Popular Music of the Olden Time*, p. 519; Strickland, *Queens of Scotland*, VII, p. 487
30 Morris, *op. cit.*, p. 369
31 Camden, *Annales*, p. 115
32 Morris, *op. cit.*, p. 364

27. THE THEATRE OF THE WORLD

1 Jebb, *De Vita et Rebus Gestis*, II, p. 671, Translated Strickland, *Queens of Scotland*, VII, p. 499
2 Phillips, *Images of a Queen*, p. 163; Teulet, *Lettres de Marie Stuart*, p. 375
3 Calderwood, *History*, IV, p. 611
4 Hat. Cal., XIII, p. 334
5 Strickland, *op. cit.*, VII, p. 498
6 Hat. Cal., XIII, p. 230
7 *Ibid.*, III, p. 216
8 Pitcairn, *Collections relative to the Funereals of Mary Queen of Scots*
9 Public Record Office A.O. 1/2119/3
10 Pitcairn, *op. cit.*, p. 22
11 Public Record Office A.O. 1/2119/3
12 Teulet, *op. cit.*, p. 391; J. D. Mackie, *The Will of Mary Stuart*
13 *Ibid.*, p. 397
14 Camden, *Britannia*, II, p. 181

15 Cotton MSS, Titus C. VI,
ff. 207–209b

16 Demster, *Historia*, II, p. 464

17 Dean Stanley, *Memorials of Westminster Abbey*, Appendix, p. 507

BIBLIOGRAPHY

Bibliography

The bibliography of Mary Queen of Scots is potentially enormous: the following list contains only those works mentioned in the references and works which have been of actual assistance in the writing of this book. The place of publication is London, unless otherwise specified, and in the case of a series, published over a number of years, only the earliest publication date is given.

Accounts of the Lord High Treasurer of Scotland. Ed. T. Dickson and J. Balfour Paul. Edinburgh. 1877.

Accounts of the Masters of Works. Vol. I. 1529–1615. Ed. H. M. Paton. H.M.S.O. Edinburgh. 1957.

Acts of the Parliament of Scotland. Ed. T. Thomson. 1814.

Acts and Proceedings of the General Assemblies of the Kirk of Scotland. Ed. T. Thomson. 1839.

C. Ainsworth Mitchell, *The Evidence of the Casket Letters.* Historical Association Pamphlets. 1927.

Inventory of Ailsa Muniments. Historical Manuscripts Commission. Vol. III. Supplement. 1431–1599.

J. W. Allen, *History of Political Thought in the 16th century.* 1941.

James Anderson, *Collections relating to the history of Mary Queen of Scotland.* 4 vols. 1727.

Mrs P. Stewart-Mackenzie Arbuthnot, *Queen Mary's Book.* 1907.

Argyll Papers, Inveraray Castle.

M. H. Armstrong-Davison, *The Casket Letters.* 1965.

Chronicles of the families of Atholl and Tullibardine. Ed. 7th Duke of Atholl. Edinburgh. 1908.

Claude de l'Aubespine, *Histoire Particulière de la Court de Henry II.* Archives curieuses de l'histoire de France. 1ère Serie. Vol. 3. Paris. 1834.

Bagot Papers. Folger Shakespeare Library, Washington, D.C. Microfilm in Staffordshire County Record Office.

Lady Baillie-Hamilton, 'A Historical Relic'. *Macmillan's Magazine.* Vol. LXXX.

Balcarres Papers: *Foreign correspondence with Marie de Lorraine Queen of Scotland,* from Balcarres Papers. Vol. I, 1537–48, Vol. II, 1548–57. Ed. Marguerite Wood. Scot. Hist.

Soc. 3rd Series. IV. Edinburgh. 1923 and 1925.

Lacey Baldwin Smith, *The Elizabethan Epic*. 1966.

R. Bannatyne, *Memorials of Transactions in Scotland*. Ed. R. Pitcairn. Bannatyne Club. Edinburgh. 1836.

Bannatyne Manuscript Ed. and introduced by W. Tod Ritchie. Vols. I to IV. Scottish Text Society. 1934.

E. Bapst, *Les mariages de Jacques V*. Paris. 1889.

A. Baschet, *La Diplomatie Venitiènne*. Paris. 1862.

E. Chisholm Batten, *Charters of the Priory of Beauly*. Grampian Club. 1877.

Jean de Beaugué, *Histoire de la Guerre en Ecosse*. Foreword by Comte de Montalembert. Maitland Club. 1862.

R. de Belleval, *Les Fils de Henri II*. Paris. 1898.

Robert Birrel, *Diary*. 1532–1605. Included in *Fragments of Scottish History*. Ed. J. G. Dalyell (q.v.).

J. B. Black, *Andrew Lang and the Casket Letter Controversy*. Edinburgh. 1951.

J. B. Black, *The Reign of Elizabeth*. 1959.

Prosper Blanchemain, ed. *The Works of Ronsard*. Paris. 1857.

Collection Blis, *Manuscrits, Livres, Estampes et Objets d'Arts relatys à Marie Stuart*. Bibliothèque Nationale. Paris.

Anthony Blunt, *Art and Architecture in France. 1500–1700*. 1953.

James Hepburn, Earl of Bothwell, *Les Affaires du Conte de Boduel*. Ed. H. Cockburn and T. Maitland. Bannatyne Club. Edinburgh. 1829.

René de Bouillé, *Histoire des Ducs de Guise*. Paris. 1850.

Pierre Brantôme, *Oeuvres complètes*. Paris. 1823.

Pierre Brantôme, *The Lives of Gallant Ladies*. Trans. by H.M. 2 vols. 1924.

J. Bruce, *Letters of Queen Elizabeth and James VI of Scotland*. Camden Society. 1849.

W. M. Bryce, 'The voyage of Mary Queen of Scots in 1548'. *English Historical Review*. Vol. XXII. 1907.

George Buchanan, *The Tyrannous Region of Mary Stewart*. See W. A. Gatherer.

Burke's Peerage, etc. 1963 edition.

E. Burns, *Scotish Coins*. 1887.

J. H. Burns, 'Catholicism in Defeat'. *History Today*. November 1966.

D. Calderwood, *History of the Kirk of Scotland*. Ed. T. Thomson, Edinburgh. 1842.

Calendar of State Papers, Domestic. Edward VI, Mary and Elizabeth. Ed. R. Lemor. 1856.

Calendar of State Papers, Domestic. James I. Vol. I. Ed. Mary Anne Everett Green. 1857.

Calendar of State Papers, Foreign. Edward VI. Ed. W. Turnbull. 1861.

Calendar of State Papers, Foreign. Mary. Ed. W. Turnbull. 1861.

Calendar of State Papers, Foreign. Elizabeth. Ed. J. Stevenson. 1863.

Calendar of State Papers relating to English affairs (Rome). Ed. J. M. Rigg. 1916.

Calendar of State Papers relating to Scottish affairs. Ed. J. Bain. 1898.

Calendar of State Papers, Spanish. Elizabeth. Ed. M. A. S. Hume. London. 1892.

Calendar of State Papers, Venetian. Ed. R. Brown and G. C. Bentinck. 1890.

William Camden, *Annales Rerum Anglicarum et Hibernicarum Regnante Elizabetha.* Trans. R. Norton, 1635 and T. Hearne, 1717.

William Camden, *Britannia.* Trans. Gough. 1789.

Annie Cameron, ed. *Scottish Correspondence of Mary of Lorraine.* Scot. Hist. Soc. 1927.

Annie Cameron and R. S. Rait, ed., *Warrender Papers.* Scot. Hist. Soc. 3rd series. Vol. 17. Edinburgh. 1931.

Michel de Castelnau, Seigneur de Mauvissière, *Memoirs.* Ed. Le Laboureur. Paris. 1731.

Lettres de Catherine de Médicis. Ed. H. de la Ferrière-Percy. Paris. 1880.

Philip Caraman, S.J., *John Gerard, the Autobiography of an Elizabethan.* 1951.

Philip Caraman S.J., *William Weston, the Autobiography of an Elizabethan.* 1955.

Cecil Papers, Hatfield House.

G. Chalmers, *Life of Mary Queen of Scots.* 1818.

R. Chambers, *Life of James I.* Edinburgh. 1830.

W. Chappell, *Popular Music of the Olden Time.* 1855.

M. R. Chantelauze, *Marie Stuart, son procès et son exécution.* 1874. (Containing the Journal of Bourgoing.)

R. Chauviré, *Le Secret de Marie Stuart.* Paris. 1937.

A. Chéruel, *Marie Stuart et Catherine de Médicis.* Paris. 1858.

F. J. Child, *English and Scottish Ballads.* 1882.

Cobbett's Complete Collection of State trials. Vol. I. 1809.

Cooper, ed., *Correspondence of M. de la Mothe Fénelon.* 1838.

Cotton MS, British Museum.

Crossby and Bruce, ed., *Accounts and papers relating to Mary Queen of Scots.* Camden Society. 1867.

C. W. and P. Cunnington, *Handbook of English Costume in the Sixteenth Century.* 1959.

Lionel Cust, *Authentic Portraits of Mary Queen of Scots.* 1903.

Sir John Dalyell, ed., *Fragments of Scottish History*. 1798.

Demster, *Historia*. Bannatyne Club. Edinburgh. 1829.

Dépenses de la Maison Royale. Register House. Edinburgh.

Sir Simonds D'Ewes, *Journals of the Parliaments during Elizabeth's Reign*. 1693.

G. Dickinson, *Two Missions of Jacques de la Brosse*. Scot. Hist. Soc. 3rd series. Vol. 36. Edinburgh. 1942.

W. Croft Dickinson, *History of Scotland*. Vol. I. 1961.

W. Croft Dickinson, *Scottish Parliament and the Trial of Treason*. Seton Memorial Lecture. University College, London. March 1956.

Dictionary of National Biography. 1909 edition.

Discours du Grand et Magnifique Triomphe Faict du Mariage de François et Marie Stuart. Ed. William Bentham. Roxburghe Club. 1818.

Diurnal of Occurrents. Ed. T. Thomson. Bannatyne Club. Edinburgh. 1833.

Gordon Donaldson, ed., *Accounts of the Collectors of the Thirds of Benefices*. Scot. Hist. Soc. 3rd series. Vol. XIII. Edinburgh. 1949.

Gordon Donaldson, *Scotland: James V–James VI*. Edinburgh. 1965.

Gordon Donaldson, *The Scottish Reformation*. 1960.

T. Duncan, 'Mary Stuart and the House of Huntly'. *Scot. Hist. Review*. IV. 1906.

T. Duncan, 'Relations of the Earl of Murray with Mary Stuart'. *Scot. Hist. Review*. VI. 1909.

T. Duncan, 'The Queen's Maries'. *Scot. Hist. Review*. II. 1905.

Francis Edwards, S.J., *The Dangerous Queen*. 1964.

Francis Edwards, S.J., *The Marvellous Chance*. 1968.

Exchequer Rolls. Vol. 19. Ed. G. P. McNeill. Edinburgh. 1898.

Sir James Fergusson, *Lowland Lairds*. 1949.

Sir James Fergusson, *The White Hind*. 1963.

Fonds français, Bibliothèque Nationale, Paris.

W. Forbes-Leith, ed., *Narratives of Scottish Catholics under Mary Stuart and James VI*. Edinburgh. 1885.

H. Forneron, *Les Ducs de Guise et leur Epoque*. Paris. 1877.

James Fraser of Wardlaw, *True Genealogie of the Frasers*. 1666.

Sir William Fraser, *The Book of Douglas*. 4 vols. 1885.

Sir William Fraser, *The Lennox*. 2 vols. 1874.

Sir William Fraser, *The Red Book of Menteith*. 2 vols. 1880.

J. A. Froude, *History of England from the Fall of Wolsey to the Defeat of the Spanish Armada*. 1862.

W. A. Gatherer, trans. and ed., *The Tyrannous Reign of Mary Stewart by George Buchanan.* Edinburgh. 1958.

Jules Gauthier, *Histoire de Marie Stuart.* Paris. 1875.

Frank Gent, 'The Edinburgh Castle Mystery'. *Chambers Journal.* September and October 1944.

Mark Girouard, *Robert Smythson and the Architecture of the Elizabethan Era.* 1966.

G. R. Gleig, *Family History of England.* 1836.

John Glen, *Early Scottish Melodies.* Edinburgh. 1900.

W. Goodall, *Examination of the (Casket) Letters said to be written by Mary Queen of Scots to James, Earl of Bothwell.* 1754.

W. Goodall, *Introduction to the History of the Antiquities of Scotland.* 1860.

Sir R. Gordon, *Genealogical History of the Earldom of Sutherland.* Edinburgh. 1813.

R. Gore-Browne, *Lord Bothwell.* 1935.

Albert le Grand, *Les Saints de la Bretagne Armorique.* Quimper. 1901.

I. F. Grant, *Social and economic development of Scotland before 1603.* 1930.

Papiers d'Etat du Cardinal de Granvelle. Paris. 1841.

Letters and papers of Patrick Master of Gray. Bannatyne Club. Edinburgh. 1835.

G. Guiffrey, *Lettres inédites de Dianne de Poytiers.* Paris. 1866.

P. Guillaume, 'La Mort de François II'. *Bulletin du Société Archéologique d'Orléans.* Vol. I. No. 7. 1960.

Douglas Hamer, ed., *Marriage of the Queen of Scots to the Dauphin.* Scottish Printed Fragments. 1932.

Douglas Hamer, ed., *Works of Sir David Lyndsay of the Mount.* Scot. Text Society. 3rd series. 1931.

Hamilton Papers. Ed J. Bain. Edinburgh. 1890.

R. K. Hannay, 'The Earl of Arran and Queen Mary'. *Scot. Hist. Review.* XVIII. 1920.

P. M. Handover, *Arbella Stuart.* 1957.

Hardwicke State Papers. Vol. I. 1778.

Calendar of the Manuscripts of the Marquess of Salisbury at Hatfield House. Historical Manuscripts Commission. 1883.

M. Dormer Harris, *Unpublished documents relating to Town Life in Coventry.* Trans. Roy. Hist. Soc. 4th series. Vol. III. 1920.

D. Hay Fleming, *Mary Queen of Scots from her birth till her flight into England.* 1897.

R. G. Heape, *Buxton under the Dukes of Devonshire.* 1948.

T. F. Henderson, *Mary Queen of Scots.* 2 vols. 1905.

T. F. Henderson, *The Casket Letters.* 1890.

John Maxwell, Baron Herries, *Historical Memoirs of the reign of Mary Queen of Scots*. Abbotsford Club. Ed. R. Pitcairn. Edinburgh. 1836.

Christian Hesketh, *Tartan*. 1963.

Leo Hicks, S.J., *An Elizabethan Problem*. 1964.

J. Hosack, *Mary Queen of Scots and her Accusers*. Edinburgh. 1969.

P. Hume Brown, *Early Travellers in Scotland*. 1891.

P. Hume Brown, *Scotland in the Time of Queen Mary*. 1904.

Letters of James V. Ed. Denys Hay, calendared by R. K. Hannay. Edinburgh. 1954.

Jamieson, *Etymological Dictionary of the Scottish Language*.

S. Jebb, *De Vita et Rebus Gestis Sereuissima Principis Marie Scotorum Reginae, Franciae Dotariae*. 2 vols. 1725.

Nathaniel Johnston, M.D., *Life of George Earl of Shrewsbury and Appendix to Life of Francis Earl of Shrewsbury—Matters omitted from Life of George Earl of Shrewsbury pertaining to the Execution of Mary Queen of Scots*. 1710.

M. S. Jourdain, *English Secular Embroideries*. 1910.

R. Keith, *History of the Affairs of Church and State in Scotland down to 1567*. Ed. J. P. Lawson. 3 vols. and Appendix. Spottiswoode Society. 1844.

Kervyn de Letterhoven, *Relations Politiques des Pays-Bas et de l'Angleterre, 1555–1579*. Belgium. 1882.

Works of John Knox. Ed. D. Laing. Edinburgh. 1895.

John Knox, *History of the Reformation in Scotland*. Trans. and ed. by W. Croft Dickinson. 1949.

T. F. Knox, ed., *Letters and memorials of William Allen*. 1882.

Prince Labanoff (A. I. Lobanov-Rostovsky), *Lettres et Mémoires de Marie, Reine d'Ecosse*. 7 vols. 1844.

H. H. Lamb, *Trees and Climatic History in Scotland*. 1964.

Andrew Lang, *The Mystery of Mary Stuart*. 1901.

Andrew Lang, *Portraits and Jewels of Mary Queen of Scots*. 1906.

Regnier de La Planche, *Estat de France sous François II*. Ed. Henneschet. 1836.

J. D. Leader, *Mary Queen of Scots in Captivity*. 1880.

Maurice Lee, *James Stewart, Earl of Moray*. Columbia University Press. 1953.

Le Plessis, *Les Triomphes à Chenonceau*. Paris. 1557.

John Leslie, Bishop of Ross, *The Historie of Scotland*. Trans. into Scottish by Fr. James Dalrymple. Scottish Text Society. 1895. Ed. Fr. E. G. Gody and William Murison. Vols. I and II (to which references are given). Also Bannatyne Club edition. Vol. 39. Ed. T. Thomson. Edinburgh. 1830.

E. Levassieur, *La Population Française*. Histoire de la population française avant 1789. Paris. 1889.

Mortimer Levine, *Early Elizabethan Succession Question, 1558–68,* California. 1966.

C. S. Lewis, *English Literature in the 16th century.* 1954.

D. M. Lockie, 'The Political Career of the Bishop of Ross. 1568–90.' *University of Birmingham Historical Journal.* 1953.

E. Lodge, *Illustrations of British History.* Vol. I. 1791.

S.G.E. Lythe, *Economy of Scotland. 1550–1625.* Edinburgh. 1960.

I. Macalpine and R. Hunter, *Porphyria: A Royal Malady.* B.M.A. Publication. 1968.

A. Macgeorge, ed., *Miscellaneous papers principally illustrative of events in the Reigns of Queen Mary and James VI.* Maitland Club. Glasgow. 1834.

D. Macgibbon and T. Ross, *The castellated and domestic architecture of Scotland.* 5 vols. Edinburgh. 1887.

Dan McKenzie, 'The Obstetrical History of Mary Queen of Scots'. *Caledonian Medical Journal.* Vol. XV. 1921.

J. D. Mackie, *The Earlier Tudors.* 1966 edition.

J. D. Mackie, 'The Will of Mary Stuart'. *Scot. Hist. Review.* No. 11.

J. Mackinnon, *Constitutional History of Scotland from Early Times to the Reformation.* 1924.

Sir Arthur Salusbury MacNalty, *Mary Queen of Scots: the daughter of debate.* 1960.

John MacQueen, *Alexander Scott and the Scottish Court Poetry of the Middle Sixteenth Century.* Proceedings of the British Academy. Vol. LIV. 1968.

John MacQueen and Tom Scott, ed., *Oxford Book of Scottish Verse.* 1967.

R. H. Mahon, *Indictment of Mary Queen of Scots.* 1923.

R. H. Mahon, *Mary Queen of Scots: a study of the Lennox Narrative.* 1924.

R. H. Mahon, *The Tragedy of Kirk o'Field.* 1930.

J. Maidment, ed., *Miscellany of the Abbotsford Club.* Vol. I. 1837.

Marlowe Society Collections. Vol. I. 1900.

Inventaires of the jewels of Mary Queen of Scots. 1556–69. Bannatyne Club. 1863.

Libraries of Mary Queen of Scots and James VI. Maitland Club Miscellany. 1834.

Catalogue of the Tercentenary Exhibition of Mary Queen of Scots, at Peterborough. 1887.

David Mathew, *The Celtic Peoples of Europe in the Age of the Renaissance.* 1932.

David Mathew, *Scotland under Charles I.* 1955.

Hon. Mrs. Maxwell-Scott, *The Tragedy of Fotheringhay, founded on the Journal of Bourgoing and unpublished MS documents.* 1905.

Sir James Melville of Halhill, *Memoirs.* Ed. Francis Steuart. 1929 (to which references are given). Also ed. T. Thomson. Bannatyne Club. Edinburgh. 1827.

F. Michel, *Les Français en Ecosse, les Ecossiers en France.* 1862.

H. A. Monckton, 'Beer and Ale in Shakespeare's Time'. *History Today.* December, 1967.

A. Montaiglon, *Latin Themes of Mary Queen of Scots.* Wharton Club. 1855.

J. Morris, *Letter-books of Sir Amias Paulet.* 1874.

Claude Nau, *Memorials of Mary Stewart.* Ed. J. Stevenson. Edinburgh. 1883.

J. E. Neale, *The Age of Catherine de Medici.* 1943.

J. E. Neale, *The Elizabethan House of Commons.* 1949.

J. E. Neale, *Queen Elizabeth I.* 1934. Also paperback edition, 1960, to which references are given.

J. E. Neale, *Queen Elizabeth I and her Parliaments.* 1953.

Sir Henry Nicolas, *Life of Davison.* 1823.

Sir Charles Oman, *History of the Art of War in the 16th century.* 1937.

Painted Ceilings of Scotland. M. R. Apted. H.M.S.O. Edinburgh. 1966.

Paget Papers. Staffordshire County Record Office.

Karl Pearson, 'Skull and Portraits of Lord Darnley'. *Biometriks* XX.

Lord Eustace Percy, *John Knox.* 1937.

J. E. Phillips, *Images of a Queen: Mary Stuart in 16th century literature.* California. 1964.

M. Philippson, *Histoire du Règne de Marie Stuart.* Paris. 1891.

Le Marquis de Pimodan, *La Mère des Guises.* Paris. 1900.

R. Pitcairn, ed., *Collections relative to the Funereals of Mary Queen of Scots.* Edinburgh. 1822.

R. Pitcairn, ed., *Ancient Criminal Trials in Scotland.* Vol. I. Bannatyne Club. Edinburgh. 1833.

Robert Lindsay of Pitscottie, *History and Chronicles of Scotland.* 2 vols. Scottish Text Society. Ed. A. J. G. Mackay. 1899. 1911.

William Plot, *History of Staffordshire.* 1686.

J. H. Pollen, S.J., *Letters from Mary Queen of Scots to the Duke of Guise.* Scottish History Society. 1st series. 1904.

J. H. Pollen, S.J., *Mary Queen of Scots and the Babington Plot.* Scottish History Society. 3rd series. 1922.

J. H. Pollen, S.J., 'Mary Stuart's Jesuit Chaplain'. *The Month.* January and February 1911.

J. H. Pollen, S.J., *Papal Negotiations with Mary Queen of Scots.* Scottish History Society. 1st series. Edinburgh. 1901.

John Pope Hennessy, *A lecture on Nicholas Hilliard.* 1949.

Dr. Potiquet, *La Maladie et la Mort de François II.* Paris. 1893.

Quarterly Journal of the Royal Meteorological Society, Vol. 90.

R. S. Rait, *The Parliaments of Scotland.* 1924.

R. S. Rait and Annie Cameron, *King James' Secret: Negotiations between Elizabeth and James VI relating to the execution of Mary Queen of Scots.* 1927.

Conyers Read, *Bibliography of British History.* Tudor period. 1485–1603.

Conyers Read, *Mr. Secretary Cecil and Queen Elizabeth.* 1955.

Conyers Read, *Mr. Secretary Walsingham and the policy of Queen Elizabeth.* 1925.

Register of the Privy Council of Scotland. Ed. J. Hill Burton. Vols. I and II. Edinburgh. 1877.

Registrum Magni Sigilli Regum Scotorum. Ed. J. Balfour Paul and J. M. Thompson. Edinburgh. 1883.

G. Reynolds, *Nicholas Hilliard and Isaac Oliver.* Victoria and Albert Museum Exhibition Catalogue. 1947.

J. Robertson, ed. *Inventaires de la Royne d'Ecosse, Douairière de France.* Bannatyne Club. Edinburgh. 1883.

Ronsard, *Poésies choisies.* Ed. Pierre de Nolhac. Paris. 1954.

A. L. Rowse, *The England of Elizabeth.* 1950.

Alphonse de Ruble, *La première jeunesse de Marie Stuart.* 1891.

State Papers and Letters of Sir Ralph Sadler. Ed. A. Clifford. Edinburgh. 1809.

Scots Peerage. Ed. J. Balfour Paul. 9 vols. 1904.

J. D. Scott, *Bibliography of works relating to Mary Queen of Scots.* (until 1700). Edinburgh. 1890.

G. Seton, *History of the family of Seton.* 1896.

Shrewsbury and Talbot Papers. Vol. I: Shrewsbury Papers. Calendared by C. Jamison; ed. E. G. W. Bill. Lambeth Palace Library. H.M.S.O. 1966.

Sir John Skelton, *Maitland of Lethington and the Scotland of Mary Queen of Scots.* Edinburgh. 1894.

Sir Robert Somerville, *Guide to Tutbury Castle* (published by the Chancellor of the Duchy of Lancaster).

J. Spottiswoode, *History of the Church of Scotland.* 1668.

Staffordshire Historical Collections. Quarter Session I. 1929.

Dean Stanley, *Memorials of Westminster Abbey.* 1867.

I. M. Stewart, *Scottish coinage.* 1955.

J. Stevenson, *Selections from unpublished manuscripts in the college of Arms and the British Museum illustrating the Reign of Mary Queen of Scotland.* Maitland Club. Glasgow. 1837.

Jane T. Stoddart, *The Girlhood of Mary Queen of Scots.* 1908.

Agnes Strickland, *Lives of the Queens of Scotland.* 1854.

Roy Strong, *Eworth.* Catalogue of the National Portrait Gallery Exhibition. 1966. (See also *Tudor & Jacobean Portraits,* below.)

Roy Strong, *Portraits of Queen Elizabeth I.* 1964.

John Stuart, *A lost chapter in the history of Mary Queen of Scots recovered.* Edinburgh. 1874.

Despatches of Suriano and Barbaro. Huguenot Society Publication. Vol. IV.

G. H. Tait, 'Tudor Historiated Jewellery'. *Antiquaries Journal.* Vol. XLII. 1962.

S. and M. Tannenbaum, *Marie Stuart. Bibliography.* 3 vols. New York. 1944.

A. Teulet, *Papiers d'Etat relatifs à l'Histoire de l'Ecosse au 16e siècle.* Bannatyne Club. Edinburgh. 1852.

A. Teulet, *Relations politiques de la France et de l'Espagne avec l'Ecosse au 16e siècle.* Paris. 1862.

A. Teulet, *Lettres inédites de Marie Stuart.* Paris. 1859.

Marcel Thomas, *Le procès de Marie Stuart. Documents originaux présentes par Marcel Thomas.* Paris. 1956.

George Malcolm Thomson, *The Crime of Mary Stuart.* 1967.

T. Thomson, ed., *Historie and Life of King James the Sext.* Bannatyne Club. Edinburgh. 1825.

Tudor & Jacobean Portraits. National Portrait Gallery Catalogue, Roy Strong. 1969.

P. F. Tytler, *History of Scotland.* Edinburgh. 1841. Vols. V, VI, and VII. Also new and enlarged edition. 1870.

Neville Williams, *Elizabeth Queen of England.* 1967.

D. H. Willson, *King James VI and I.* Bedford Historical Series. 1959.

W. Woodgate, *Reminiscences of an Old Sportsman.* 1909.

T. Wright, *Queen Elizabeth and her Times.* 1838.

Francis de Zulueta, *Embroideries by Mary Stuart and Elizabeth Talbot at Oxburgh Hall.* 1923.

❧ INDEX

Index

The triumphant bestseller

The story of
the love that ended an empire

NICHOLAS AND ALEXANDRA

Here, for the first time, is the intimate account
of the last Tsar of Russia, his lovely, tormented
wife, his four enchanting daughters, and his
only son, a victim of hemophilia, the hereditary
flaw that placed him, and ultimately the fate of
the empire, in the hands of a Siberian mystic.

A DELL BOOK
with 16 pages of rare photographs
$1.25

If you cannot obtain copies of this title from your local
bookseller, just send the price (plus 15c per copy for
handling and postage) to Dell Books, Post Office Box 1000,
Pinebrook, N. J. 07058. No postage or handling charge is
required on any order of five or more books.

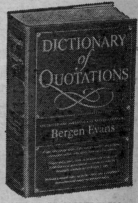

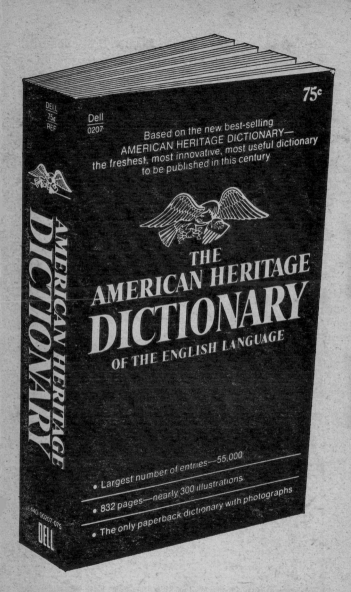

DELIVERANCE

by James Dickey

This novel, by one of America's finest poets, is a tale of violent adventure and inner discovery. Four men embark on a canoe trip down a wild section of a river in the heartland of today's South. When two of the group are attacked viciously and perversely by mountaineers, a mildly adventurous canoe trip explodes into a gruesome nightmare of horror and murder.

Soon to be a major movie.

A DELL BOOK　$1.25